Contemporary Issues in Business Ethics

Third Edition

JOSEPH R. DesJARDINS
College of St. Benedict

JOHN J. McCALL
St. Joseph's University

Wadsworth Publishing Company
I⊤P® An International Thomson Publishing Company

Belmont • Albany • Bonn • Boston • Cincinnati • Detroit • London • Madrid
Melbourne • Mexico City • New York • Paris • San Francisco • Singapore
Tokyo • Toronto • Washington

Philosophy Editor: Peter Adams
Editorial Assistant: Heide Chavez
Production Editor: Jennie Redwitz
Managing Designer: Stephen Rapley
Print Buyer: Barbara Britton
Permissions Editor: Bob Kauser
Copy Editor: Denise Cook-Clampert
Compositor: Wadsworth Digital Productions
Cover: Janet Wood/Lexikos Design
Cover Photo: *Untitled 1990.* © 1995, Jan Groover.
Courtesy Robert Miller Gallery, New York.
Printer: Malloy Lithographing, Inc.

Printed in the United States of America
1 2 3 4 5 6 7 8 9 10

For more information, contact Wadsworth Publishing Company.

Wadsworth Publishing Company
10 Davis Drive
Belmont, California 94002
USA

International Thomson Editores
Campos Eliseos 385, Piso 7
Col. Polanco
11560 México D.F. México

International Thomson Publishing Europe
Berkshire House 168-173
High Holborn
London, WC1V 7AA
England

International Thomson
Publishing GmbH
Königswinterer Strasse 418
53227 Bonn
Germany

Thomas Nelson Australia
102 Dodds Street
South Melbourne 3205
Victoria, Australia

International Thomson Publishing Asia
221 Henderson Road
#05-10 Henderson Building
Singapore 0315

Nelson Canada
1120 Birchmount Road
Scarborough, Ontario
Canada M1K 5G4

International Thomson Publishing Japan
Hirakawacho Kyowa Building, 3F
2-2-1 Hirakawacho
Chiyoda-ku, Tokyo 102, Japan

Library of Congress Cataloging-in-Publication Data

DesJardins, Joseph R.
    Contemporary issues in business ethics / Joseph R. DesJardins, John J. McCall. — 3rd ed.
        p. cm.
    Includes bibliographical references and index.
    ISBN 0-534-25542-6 (pbk.)
    1. Business ethics. I. McCall, John J. II. Title.
HF5387.D39 1996   95-40086
174'.4—dc20

Brief Contents

Contents

Preface

We began the First Edition of this text over a decade ago with four major concerns. We wanted to approach business ethics from more of a social and political perspective than was common in other textbooks at the time. Business is one of the most powerful social institutions in history and thus philosophers need to evaluate business practices from a social as well as an individual moral perspective. Second, we sought to balance philosophical rigor with accessibility to a wide range of student interests and abilities. We sought to create a textbook that would stimulate student interest both at first glance and after sustained study. Third, we wanted to bring special attention to the rights and responsibilities of employees. In our judgment, too many other textbooks focused almost exclusively on the perspective of the business manager. Finally, we sought to counter a philosophical tendency toward armchair analysis by including many empirically based sources. We furthered this goal in the Second Edition by greatly increasing the number of case studies.

We remain committed to these goals in the Third Edition. Throughout this text, readers will be asked to consider the proper role of business within a democratic political framework. Often, this issue will arise as tension between strategies that rely on market mechanisms and strategies aimed at protecting individual rights. When and where does reliance on market forces result in furthering the overall good of a society? When does it not? When will the rights of individuals legitimately trump the economic goals of business? We think that these important questions are often overlooked in texts that emphasize the managerial perspective.

We have been happy to see that this text is used in courses as diverse as an "intro-level" undergraduate lecture course and an MBA-level seminar. This suggests that we have maintained a reasonable balance between rigor and accessibility. In this edition we continue to strive for this balance. Most noticeably, we have expanded the chapter introductions in this edition to include more of the conceptual work previously left to individual essays. Thus we try to do the work of philosophical ethics in the introductions, leaving more room in the readings for normative and applied ethics. We think that this accomplishes two goals: it allows us to present more difficult philosophical topics in a less abstract format and it allows for a greater diversity in the normative positions considered in the readings.

While many students who use this text will eventually hold management positions, with few exceptions they will all first and always be employees. Thus we continue to devote a large section (all of Part II) to employee issues. We have expanded this section with new readings on lay-offs, due process, participation, genetic screening, fetal protection policies, and AIDS testing. In addition, besides four chapters on employee rights, we include a thoroughly revised chapter on employee responsibilities concerning honesty, loyalty, whistleblowing, and conflicts of interests. Readings in later sections examine the employee-related issues of sexual harassment and the rights of disabled workers.

Finally, we continued to seek out readings and cases that are well-grounded in the "real world" of contemporary business. We include over a dozen new cases and decision scenarios, as well as keeping many from previous editions that have been proven in the classroom. It is commonplace to say that contemporary business exists in a global economy, and we include a thoroughly revised chapter on international business responsibilities in an effort to address this changing reality. In addition, we have emphasized comparative international issues in a number of other chapters, especially those in Part II.

Overall, readers of the first two editions will recognize a familiar logical structure to this text. Students enter the conversation with the classic essay by Milton Friedman, "The Social Responsibility of Business Is to Increase Its Profits." Over the first four chapters, this essay and the social, economic, and ethical views it presupposes, are used to introduce students to the basics of philosophical ethics: utilitarianism, rights, responsibilities, relativism, egoism, law and ethics, etc. The conclusion from these chapters is that business has responsibilities beyond the narrow ones described by Friedman. To discover the range and content of these responsibilities, the following three sections focus on the various constituencies with which business interacts: employees (Part II), consumers (Part III), and society (Part IV).

Acknowledgments

Joe DesJardins would like to acknowledge support from the Faculty Development Funds at the College of Saint Benedict. He also expresses his gratitude for the work of his student assistants, Peg Arola and Jenny Greunes. John McCall would like to acknowledge sabbatical support from Saint Joseph's University. John also thanks his colleague, Rich George, for the understanding of marketing and advertising gained through years of team teaching in exec ed seminars.

We both acknowledge the helpful suggestions from our reviewers: David Adams, California State Polytechnic University—Pomona; Douglas Birsch, Villanova University; William Davis, Mount Union College; James Spalding, Bellarmine College; Ann Waters, Albuquerque Vocational Technical College; and Kenneth Weare, University of Dayton. Once again, the staff at Wadsworth has been wonderful. We especially want to acknowledge the patience and support of Tammy Goldfeld, Kelly Zavislak, Heide Chavez, and Jennie Redwitz.

Finally, we would be remiss if we failed to mention our families. Linda, Michael, and Matthew in Minnesota and Kate and Alexa in Philadelphia made the schedule adjustments and lifestyle changes necessary for us to see this Third Edition to completion. Thanks.

PART I

Business and Philosophy

1

Philosophy, Ethics, and Business

Business is among the most powerful and influential social institutions in human history. The decisions made in business affect nearly every aspect of contemporary life. Almost half of our waking hours are spent in the workplace (at least for those of us fortunate enough to have full-time employment; for those who lack full-time work, *that* fact also is highly influenced by business decisions). What we eat, where we live, if and how we work, how we are governed, how we spend our leisure time, as well as access to or availability of education and health care are all strongly influenced by what happens in business.

It is crucial, therefore, that we think carefully about the ethical status of business. Businesses are not natural objects that humans have discovered; they are human institutions that humans have created. Therefore, we are responsible for the existence and structure of business institutions and must acknowledge that responsibility by monitoring the ethical dimensions of business activities.

What is the appropriate role of business in a society? How should business institutions be structured to ensure that they are consistent with the fundamental values of a society? What responsibilities do businesses have to the society in which they operate? to their employees? to the consumers of their goods and services? Conversely, what responsibilities does a society have to business owners and managers? These questions make it is easy to see why business ethics should be relevant to every individual—as citizen, as employee, as consumer, as responsible business manager.

Nevertheless, discussions about business ethics are often met with skepticism. "Business ethics," so the joke goes, is a lot like "jumbo shrimp" and "military intelligence." It is an oxymoron, a contradiction in terms. Given the social and ethical importance of business, it will be helpful to begin our text by responding to this skepticism.

There are three skeptical reactions to business ethics. Some people believe that business activities are inherently unscrupulous or corrupt, that "ethics" and "business" are contradictory. Others believe that business ethics is a well-intentioned but naive approach to the real world. The tough and competitive world of business is no place for innocent moralizing. Still others believe that "ethics" itself is defective and will only interfere with the important operation of business. Ethical concerns, after all, are a matter only of personal feelings and can serve only to confuse the rational and objective decision-making required in business.

We believe that ethical thinking is unavoidable in business and that doubts about the relevance of ethics are unfounded. As this text will show, a large majority of the issues faced in business—ranging from what goods to produce to the grounds for hiring and firing and from marketing practices to the disposal of wastes—are ethical issues. The choice we face is whether to think about these ethical issues explicitly or leave them unexamined. As a first step in addressing these issues let us consider the nature of ethics itself.

WHAT IS "ETHICS"?

It is common to distinguish three different forms of ethics: descriptive, normative, and philosophical. "Descriptive ethics" refers to the general beliefs, values, attitudes, and standards that, as a matter of fact, guide behavior. The word *ethics* was derived from the Greek word *ethos*, meaning "custom." Thus, descriptive ethics examines the typical beliefs or values that determine what is customarily done.

As a form of descriptive ethics, "business ethics" refers to the actual customs, attitudes, values, and mores that operate within business. For example, in practice many businesses believe that drug testing employees is appropriate and legitimate. We might say that the ethics of American business supports drug testing. In this sense, business ethics *describes* the actual and customary practice found in business. A helpful starting point for doing business ethics is to learn what, in fact, is accepted as ethical or customary in business. Business ethics in this descriptive sense is most at home in fields such as sociology and management, which describe for us what goes on in business.

From the earliest days of Greek philosophy, however, philosophers have not been satisfied with simply accepting what is customary as being right. Ethics as a branch of philosophy seeks a reasoned examination of what custom tells us about how we ought to live. Indeed, it is fair to say that Western philosophy was born in Socrates' lifelong critical examination of the customary norms of Greek society. Philosophy asks us to step back and abstract ourselves from the actual practices of society to examine and evaluate these practices. Socrates described philosophy as the gadfly that buzzes around a noble but sluggish horse. The role of the gadfly (philosophy) is to prod the horse (society) out of complacency and keep it moving forward.

As the initial stepping back from the customary and actual practices, "normative ethics" evaluates these practices by appealing to some standards or norms that are independent of custom. Rather than describing the actual beliefs, values, and attitudes, normative ethics *prescribes* what we *should* believe or value. The difference between descriptive and normative ethics, therefore, is the difference between what *is* and what *ought to be*.

Business ethics done as a form of normative ethics evaluates the practices and customs of business. For example, a normative analysis might claim that drug testing violates principles of justice or rights of privacy. Most of the readings in this text are examples of normative ethics (sometimes called "applied ethics"). The authors of these readings, like Socrates, suggest you step back from what is normal or customary in business and ask questions about what *ought* to or *should* be done, even if in actual practice, it is not.

But what about the standards or norms that are used in evaluating what ought to be? How do we know that they provide a reasonable basis for making normative judgments? Might these normative evaluations be little more than social customs? Are the "oughts" and "shoulds" that are applied in normative ethics legitimate? What is the difference between *ethical* norms and, say, economic or financial norms? To answer these types of questions, philosophy again asks us to step back from the evaluations of normative ethics and think about the legitimacy of the standards and norms themselves, to seek a rational justification for our ethical principles.

This level of stepping back to analyze normative judgments is the domain of ethical theory, or "philosophical ethics." In this sense, "ethics" refers to a branch of philosophy that systematically examines more abstract questions about how humans ought to live. Philosophical ethics provides analyses, justifications, and theoretical accounts of the basic concepts and categories of ethics. Thus, business ethics will also involve examination of more abstract theories and concepts. In examining the drug testing example, philosophical ethics might offer various theories of justice with which to examine the issue, or it might contribute an analysis of such concepts as responsibility, rights, and privacy.

This textbook, and most courses in business ethics, operates at all three levels. We need to do descriptive ethics to understand the actual rules and practices operating in business. We also will do normative ethics, stepping back from these practices to articulate and defend specific conclusions about controversial issues in business. Finally, we will do philosophical ethics when we reason about the fundamental norms and values that guide how we ought to live.

Thus, the skepticism that we spoke about is unfounded. To suggest that business activities are unscrupulous is already to be engaged in normative ethics. To say that ethics is unsuitable in the real world of business assumes conclusions about descriptive, normative, and philosophical ethics. Finally, to suggest that ethics can only confuse the rational and objective decision-making of business is to assume a philosophical theory (called "ethical relativism") about ethics. In each case, this skepticism is more a call to business ethics than a denial of its importance.

In summary, ethics is concerned with answering questions about how we ought to live, both as individuals and as members of a community. Business ethics applies philosophical concepts and reasoning to the world of business so that we

Ethical Relativism: Who's to Say What's Right or Wrong?

Perhaps the most serious challenge to any textbook or class in business ethics is a position called "ethical relativism." Ethical relativists hold that all ethical beliefs and values are relative to one's own culture, feelings, or religion. Said another way, ethical relativism denies that ethical judgments can ever be objectively or universally valid. The most common expression of relativism is found in the rhetorical question often asked in the middle of a debate on some moral matter: "Who's to say what's right or wrong?"

Relativism poses a serious challenge because if it is true that there is no way for rationally deciding what is right or wrong, then business ethics is a waste of time. Why bother thinking about what ought or ought not be done if, ultimately, it's all relative anyway?

Several considerations count strongly against the validity of ethical relativism. First, we should be careful to distinguish what people *believe* is right or wrong from what *is* right or wrong. This, after all, is the distinction between *descriptive* ethics and *normative* ethics introduced earlier in this chapter. Certainly beliefs about what is right or wrong may vary widely across and within cultures. Some cultures believe that women are inferior beings deserving treatment comparable to that given to animals or slaves. But believing this is right does not make it right. By the same token, some cultures have believed that the earth is flat or at the center of the universe. But no matter how many people believe the earth is flat, it still remains round. We must recognize that mere disagreement alone is not evidence that objective agreement is impossible. If ethical relativism is to be defended, it must rely on something other than the fact that people and cultures disagree.

Second, we should be careful not to confuse a tolerance and respect for diversity with ethical relativism. Many of us believe that we should respect diverse cultures and tolerate a wide diversity within our own culture. But this doesn't commit us to relativism. The very values we cite in defending these conclusions—respect and tolerance—must be assumed to be valid and ethically required. When one says that diversity *ought* to be respected, one is making an ethical judgment that, if we want to be taken seriously, we must assume can be rationally defensible. Either respect and tolerance are rationally defensible, in which case we are justified in making the judgment that diversity ought to be respected and tolerated; or respect and tolerance are themselves relative to one's own culture, in which case others have no reason to accept our prescriptions.

This raises a third consideration. We need to be careful to distinguish disagreement about ethical principles from disagreement about par-

might determine the proper place of business in our society and our own roles within business institutions. Such questions are unavoidable for any thoughtful and responsible person.

BUSINESS ETHICS:
THE "FREE MARKET" THEORY

Rather than continuing a discussion of business ethics in the abstract, perhaps we should jump in and practice doing ethics. In response to certain skeptical doubts about business ethics, we suggested that ethical questions are unavoidable in business. Business institutions are too influential in determining how we live not to raise ethical questions.

ticular judgments based on those principles. There may be wide disagreement on particular ethical judgments—for example, on such issues as abortion, affirmative action, and the death penalty. But this might be more the result of a disagreement over the application of basic principles (for example, equality, the right to life) than a disagreement about the basic principles themselves. Again, disagreement alone does not prove the ethical relativist conclusion. In fact, disagreement about the application of ethical principles calls for more, not less, ethical reasoning and discussion.

A fourth consideration reminds us not to ask too much of ethics. It is tempting to think that if ethical judgments cannot be proven beyond a doubt, then they are relative and unreasonable. But surely few if any of our rational beliefs can be proven beyond a doubt. The alternatives are not certainty or "anything goes" relativism. Ethics, like most other fields of inquiry, relies on a standard better understood as "rational justification" than as "certain proof." If we give reasons to support our ethical views, if they can withstand criticism, if they are consistent with the facts, if they are coherent with other deeply held values, if they are revised in light of contrary evidence, then we can be said to be rationally justified in holding them. If we hold ethics to a standard of absolute proof—attainable in mathe

matics, perhaps, but in few other fields—then we will be unlikely to ever prove anything in ethics. However, if we use standards of rational justification—standards common in such diverse fields as medicine, history, and law—then we can be as justified in our ethical judgments as we are in medical, historical, and legal judgments.

Finally, we must recognize the costs involved in being a consistent ethical relativist. The relativist must claim that there is no reasonable and objective basis for establishing that freedom is better than slavery, representative democracy is better than totalitarianism, heroism is better than murder, and friendship is better than hatred. The ethical relativist must claim that there is no objective and rational moral difference between a parent who loves and nurtures her child and one who abuses or kills her child. These examples should throw a very different light upon relativistic claims like, to choose an example from Milton Friedman, "One man's good is another's evil."

Of course, one of the best ways to assess the objectivity of ethical reasoning is to participate in ethical reasoning. This chapter's assessment of Friedman's essay is an example of that process. We encourage you to pursue each controversy in business ethics with intellectual care and rigor and then return to the question of objectivity and relativism.

In much of Europe and North America, but especially in the United States, there is a specific theory of business ethics that is implicit in the thinking of many people. What we will be calling the "free enterprise" or "free market" theory provides a systematic view of the proper role of business in society. For many people, especially for many business owners and managers as well as many economists, this theory functions as the "official" ethics of business. Like the moral customs and norms that Socrates discovered when he questioned the Athenian leaders, this theory can serve as our own starting point for philosophical analysis.

In general, the free market theory tells us that business managers have one overriding responsibility: to maximize the profits of business owners. This responsibility is constrained only by the responsibility to avoid fraud and coercion, and the obligation to obey the law. This theory also holds that government's responsibility is to protect the workings of the free market and otherwise remain out of economic matters. Markets should be "free" in the sense that individuals should be allowed to make choices free from outside interferences, both from other individuals and from government regulation.

Fortunately, free market ethics has many articulate defenders. One such defender is the economist Milton Friedman, who sketches this view in the now classic article that follows. As you read through this article, begin your practice of philosophical ethics by asking the types of questions described in this introduction. Why is Friedman's view an ethical position? What values and norms does he appeal to? What, exactly, does he see as the proper role of business in society? What responsibilities do business managers have? What is the proper relationship between business and government? What reasons are offered to support this view? Are the reasons convincing?

THE SOCIAL RESPONSIBILITY OF
BUSINESS IS TO INCREASE ITS PROFITS
Milton Friedman

When I hear businessmen speak eloquently about the "social responsibilities of business in a free-enterprise system," I am reminded of the wonderful line about the Frenchman who discovered at the age of 70 that he had been speaking prose all his life. The businessmen believe that they are defending free enterprise when they declaim that business is not concerned "merely" with profit but also with promoting desirable "social" ends; that business has a "social conscience" and takes seriously its responsibilities for providing employment, eliminating discrimination, avoiding pollution and whatever else may be the catchwords of the contemporary crop of reformers. In fact they are—or would be if they or anyone else took them seriously—preaching pure and unadulterated socialism. Businessmen who talk this way are unwitting puppets of the intellectual forces that have been undermining the basis of a free society these past decades.

The discussions of the "social responsibilities of business" are notable for their analytical looseness and lack of vigor. What does it mean to say that "business" has responsibilities? Only people can have responsibilities. A corporation is an artificial person and in this sense may have artificial responsibilities, but "business" as a whole cannot be said to have responsibilities, even in this vague sense. The first step toward clarity in examining the doctrine of the social responsibility of business is to ask precisely what it implies for whom.

Presumably, the individuals who are to be responsible are businessmen, which means individual proprietors or corporate executives. Most of the discussion of social responsibility is directed at corporations, so in what follows I shall mostly neglect the individual proprietor and speak of corporate executives.

In a free-enterprise, private-property system a corporate executive is an employee of the owners of the business. He has direct responsibility to his employers. That responsibility is to conduct the business in accordance with their desires, which generally will be to make as much money as possible while conforming to the basic rules of the society, both those embodied in law and those embodied in ethical custom. Of course, in some cases his employers may have a different objective. A group of persons might establish a corporation for an eleemosynary purpose—for example, a hospital or a school. The manager of such a corporation will not have money profit as his objective but the rendering of certain services.

In either case, the key point is that, in his capacity as a corporate executive, the manager is the agent of the individuals who own the corporation or establish the eleemosynary institution, and his primary responsibility is to them.

Needless to say, this does not mean that it is easy to judge how well he is performing his task. But at least the criterion of performance is straightforward, and the persons among whom a voluntary contractual arrangement exists are clearly defined.

Of course, the corporate executive is also a person in his own right. As a person, he may have many other responsibilities that he recognizes or assumes voluntarily—to his family, his conscience, his feelings of charity, his church, his clubs, his city, his country. He may feel impelled by these responsibilities to devote part of his income to causes he regards as worthy, to refuse to work for particular corporations, and even to leave his job, for example, to join his country's armed forces. If we wish, we may refer to some of these responsibilities as "social responsibilities." But in these respects he is acting as a principal, not an agent; he is spending his own money or time or energy, not the money of his employers or the time or energy he has contracted to devote to their purposes. If these are "social responsibilities," they are the social responsibilities of individuals, not of business.

What does it mean to say that the corporate executive has a "social responsibility" in his capacity as businessman? If this statement is not pure rhetoric, it must mean that he is to act in some way that is not in the interest of his employers. For example, that he is to refrain from increasing the price of the product in order to contribute to the social objective of preventing inflation, even though a price increase would be in the best interests of the corporation. Or that he is to make expenditures on reducing pollution beyond the amount that is in the best interests of the corporation or that is required by law in order to contribute to the social objective of improving the environment. Or that, at the expense of corporate profits, he is to hire "hardcore" unemployed instead of better-qualified available workmen to contribute to the social objective of reducing poverty.

In each of these cases, the corporate executive would be spending someone else's money for a general social interest. Insofar as his actions in accord with his "social responsibility" reduce returns to stockholders, he is spending their money. Insofar as his actions raise the price to customers, he is spending the customers' money. Insofar as his actions lower the wages of some employees, he is spending their money.

The stockholders or the customers or the employees could separately spend their own money on the particular action if they wished to do so. The executive is exercising a distinct "social re-

sponsibility," rather than serving as an agent of the stockholders or the customers or the employees, only if he spends the money in a different way than they would have spent it.

But if he does this, he is in effect imposing taxes, on the one hand, and deciding how the tax proceeds shall be spent, on the other.

This process raises political questions on two levels: principle and consequences. On the level of political principle, the imposition of taxes and the expenditure of tax proceeds are governmental functions. We have established elaborate constitutional, parliamentary and judicial provisions to control these functions, to assure that taxes are imposed so far as possible in accordance with the preferences and desires of the public—after all, "taxation without representation" was one of the battle cries of the American Revolution. We have a system of checks and balances to separate the legislative function of imposing taxes and enacting expenditures from the executive function of collecting taxes and administering expenditure programs and from the judicial function of mediating disputes and interpreting the law.

Here the businessman—self-selected or appointed directly or indirectly by stockholders—is to be simultaneously legislator, executive and jurist. He is to decide whom to tax by how much and for what purpose, and he is to spend the proceeds—all this guided only by general exhortations from on high to restrain inflation, improve the environment, fight poverty and so on and on.

The whole justification for permitting the corporate executive to be selected by the stockholders is that the executive is an agent serving the interests of his principal. This justification disappears when the corporate executive imposes taxes and spends the proceeds for "social" purposes. He becomes in effect a public employee, a civil servant, even though he remains in name an employee of a private enterprise. On grounds of political principle, it is intolerable that such civil servants—insofar as their actions in the name of social responsibility are real and not just window-dressing—should be selected as they are now. If they are to be civil servants, then they must be selected through a political process. If they are to impose taxes and make expenditures to foster "social" objectives, then political machinery must be set up to guide the assessment of taxes and to determine through a political process the objectives to be served.

This is the basic reason why the doctrine of "social responsibility" involves the acceptance of the socialist view that political mechanisms, not market mechanisms, are the appropriate way to determine the allocation of scarce resources to alternative uses.

On the grounds of consequences, can the corporate executive in fact discharge his alleged "social responsibilities"? On the one hand, suppose he could get away with spending the stockholders' or customers' or employees' money. How is he to know how to spend it? He is told that he must contribute to fighting inflation. How is he to know what action of his will contribute to that end? He is presumably an expert in running his company—in producing a product or selling it or financing it. But nothing about his selection makes him an expert on inflation. Will his holding down the price of his product reduce inflationary pressure? Or, by leaving more spending power in the hands of his customers, simply divert it elsewhere? Or, by forcing him to produce less because of the lower price, will it simply contribute to shortages? Even if he could answer these questions, how much cost is he justified in imposing on his stockholders, customers and employees for this social purpose? What is his appropriate share and the share of others?

And, whether he wants to or not, can he get away with spending his stockholders', customers' or employees' money? Will not the stockholders fire him? (Either the present ones or those who take over when his actions in the name of social responsibility have reduced the corporation's profits and the price of its stock.) His customers and his employees can desert him for other producers and employers less scrupulous in exercising their social responsibilities.

This facet of "social responsibility" doctrine is brought into sharp relief when the doctrine is used to justify wage restraint by trade unions. The conflict of interest is naked and clear when union officials are asked to subordinate the interest of their members to some more general social purpose. If the union officials try to enforce wage restraint, the consequence is likely to be wildcat strikes, rank-and-file revolts and the emergence of strong competitors for their jobs. We thus have the ironic phenomenon that union leaders—at least in the U.S.—have objected to Government interfer-

ence with the market far more consistently and courageously than have business leaders.

The difficulty of exercising "social responsibility" illustrates, of course, the great virtue of private competitive enterprise—it forces people to be responsible for their own actions and makes it difficult for them to "exploit" other people for either selfish or unselfish purposes. They can do good—but only at their own expense.

Many a reader who has followed the argument this far may be tempted to remonstrate that it is all well and good to speak of government's having the responsibility to impose taxes and determine expenditures for such "social" purposes as controlling pollution or training the hardcore unemployed, but that the problems are too urgent to wait on the slow course of political processes, that the exercise of social responsibility by businessmen is a quicker and surer way to solve pressing current problems.

Aside from the question of fact—I share Adam Smith's skepticism about the benefits that can be expected from "those who affected to trade for the public good"—this argument must be rejected on grounds of principle. What it amounts to is an assertion that those who favor the taxes and expenditures in question have failed to persuade a majority of their fellow citizens to be of like mind and that they are seeking to attain by undemocratic procedures what they cannot attain by democratic procedures. In a free society, it is hard for "good" people to do "good," but that is a small price to pay for making it hard for "evil" people to do "evil," especially since one man's good is another's evil.

I have, for simplicity, concentrated on the special case of the corporate executive, except only for the brief digression on trade unions. But precisely the same argument applies to the newer phenomenon of calling upon stockholders to require corporations to exercise social responsibility (the recent G.M. crusade, for example). In most of these cases, what is in effect involved is some stockholders trying to get other stockholders (or customers or employees) to contribute against their will to "social" causes favored by the activists. Insofar as they succeed, they are again imposing taxes and spending the proceeds.

The situation of the individual proprietor is somewhat different. If he acts to reduce the returns of his enterprise in order to exercise his "social responsibility," he is spending his own money, not someone else's. If he wishes to spend his money on such purposes, that is his right, and I cannot see that there is any objection to his doing so. In the process, he, too, may impose costs on employees and customers. However, because he is far less likely than a large corporation or union to have monopolistic power, any such side effects will tend to be minor.

Of course, in practice the doctrine of social responsibility is frequently a cloak for actions that are justified on other grounds rather than a reason for those actions.

To illustrate, it may well be in the long-run interest of a corporation that is a major employer in a small community to devote resources to providing amenities to that community or to improving its government. That may make it easier to attract desirable employees, it may reduce the wage bill or lessen losses from pilferage and sabotage or have other worthwhile effects. Or it may be that, given the laws about the deductibility of corporate charitable contributions, the stockholders can contribute more to charities they favor by having the corporation make the gift than by doing it themselves, since they can in that way contribute an amount that would otherwise have been paid as corporate taxes.

In each of these—and many similar—cases, there is a strong temptation to rationalize these actions as an exercise of "social responsibility." In the present climate of opinion, with its widespread aversion to "capitalism," "profits," the "soulless corporation" and so on, this is one way for a corporation to generate goodwill as a by-product of expenditures that are entirely justified in its own self-interest.

It would be inconsistent of me to call on corporate executives to refrain from this hypocritical window-dressing because it harms the foundations of a free society. That would be to call on them to exercise a "social responsibility"! If our institutions, and the attitudes of the public make it in their self-interest to cloak their actions in this way, I cannot summon much indignation to denounce them. At the same time, I can express admiration for those individual proprietors or owners of closely held corporations or stockholders of more broadly held corporations who disdain such tactics as approaching fraud.

Whether blameworthy or not, the use of the cloak of social responsibility, and the nonsense

spoken in its name by influential and prestigious businessmen, does clearly harm the foundations of a free society. I have been impressed time and again by the schizophrenic character of many businessmen. They are capable of being extremely farsighted and clear-headed in matters that are internal to their businesses. They are incredibly shortsighted and muddle-headed in matters that are outside their businesses but affect the possible survival of business in general. This short-sightedness is strikingly exemplified in the calls from many businessmen for wage and price guidelines or controls or income policies. There is nothing that could do more in a brief period to destroy a market system and replace it by a centrally controlled system than effective governmental control of prices and wages.

The short-sightedness is also exemplified in speeches by businessmen on social responsibility. This may gain them kudos in the short run. But it helps to strengthen the already too prevalent view that the pursuit of profits is wicked and immoral and must be curbed and controlled by external forces. Once this view is adopted, the external forces that curb the market will not be the social consciences, however highly developed, of the pontificating executives; it will be the iron fist of Government bureaucrats. Here, as with price and wage controls, businessmen seem to me to reveal a suicidal impulse.

The political principle that underlies the market mechanism is unanimity. In an ideal free market resting on private property, no individual can coerce any other, all cooperation is voluntary, all parties to such cooperation benefit or they need not participate. There are no "social" values, no "social" responsibilities in any sense other than the shared values and responsibilities of individuals. Society is a collection of individuals and of the various groups they voluntarily form.

The political principle that underlies the political mechanism is conformity. The individual must serve a more general social interest—whether that be determined by a church or a dictator or a majority. The individual may have a vote and a say in what is to be done, but if he is overruled, he must conform. It is appropriate for some to require others to contribute to a general social purpose whether they wish to or not.

Unfortunately, unanimity is not always feasible. There are some respects in which conformity appears unavoidable, so I do not see how one can avoid the use of the political mechanism altogether.

But the doctrine of "social responsibility" taken seriously would extend the scope of the political mechanism to every human activity. It does not differ in philosophy from the most explicitly collectivist doctrine. It differs only by professing to believe that collectivist ends can be attained without collectivist means. That is why, in my book

Capitalism and Freedom, I have called it a "fundamentally subversive doctrine" in a free society, and have said that in such a society, "there is one and only one social responsibility of business—to use its resources and engage in activities designed to increase its profits so long as it stays within the rules of the game, which is to say, engages in open and free competition without deception or fraud."

DOING BUSINESS ETHICS:
AN ANALYSIS OF FRIEDMAN

Let us begin our practice of doing philosophical ethics by developing a clear understanding of Friedman's ethical views. Following common usage, we will refer to the views expressed in this essay as the "classical model of corporate social responsibility." This view is classical in two senses: First, as previously mentioned, it is a view that has been presupposed by many people in Western culture; second, it is a view of business and industry that is derived from classical, free market economics.

The classical model offers recommendations about the responsibilities of business managers. These responsibilities follow from the role of business in a free market economic system. This economic system itself is justified by appeal to certain ethical values. To understand these claims we now turn to a closer examination of Friedman's essay.

First, we should be clear that Friedman is advocating a position that is an *ethical* position. When he recommends that business managers seek only to "increase profits" and "make as much money as possible," he is not suggesting that managers ignore ethical responsibilities and simply pursue their own greed and self-interest. Rather, he suggests that in pursuing maximum profits a business manager is fulfilling her responsibility to society and doing what is ethically correct.

Friedman also is doing more than descriptive ethics; he does much more than describe what, in fact, occurs in business. If Friedman's recommendations were followed, we would be required to change our social and political institutions dramatically.

Finally, Friedman is not merely offering his *opinion* about what one should do in business. He presents numerous *reasons* to support these recommendations and, in this way, he is involved in doing *normative ethics*. Friedman does not simply accept what is customary in business practice. He steps back from what is actually occurring within business (the widespread assumption that business has a "social responsibility" to "promote desirable 'social' ends") and offers a reasoned critique of these practices. In his view, the doctrine of social responsibility violates important social norms and is therefore ethically irresponsible. Let us look more closely at these normative ethical claims.

Friedman presents reasons that criticize the doctrine of corporate social responsibility, and he presents reasons that support his own alternative theory. In arguing against the social responsibility thesis, Friedman suggests that to sacrifice profits for the sake of some "social objective" like "providing employment, eliminating discrimination, [and] avoiding pollution" is potentially to become "unwitting puppets of the intellectual forces that have been undermining the basis of a free society." This doctrine of social responsibility is called a "fundamentally subversive doctrine in a free society." Thus, Friedman rejects the business practice of pursuing social objectives because doing so violates certain fundamental norms of a free society.

In arguing to support his own alternative, Friedman appeals to the values of a "free-enterprise, private-property system" and concludes that in such a system a business manager's "primary" and "direct" responsibility is to act in accord with the desires and interests of the business owners. In all but the exceptional case, this means that the business manager's responsibility "will be to make as much money as possible while conforming to the basic rules of society, both those embodied in law and those embodied in ethical custom." To do otherwise, according to Friedman, is to usurp the role of duly elected government officials by imposing taxes on other individuals and by deciding how those taxes are to be spent.

Thus, we can see that the classical model of corporate social responsibility advances numerous normative ethical claims. It makes recommendations about how we as individuals *ought* to act within business ("act always so as to maximize profits") and about how we as citizens *ought* to arrange our social institutions ("business ought to be free from government interference in its pursuit of profits").

FRIEDMAN'S RADICAL POSITION

Described in this way, we can begin to see a wide gap between the actual society that we live in and the society envisioned by Friedman's normative ethics. In terms of requiring changes in customarily accepted behavior, Friedman's recommendations are quite radical. He offers a normative principle that will, on every occasion, determine our ethical responsibilities. He tells us that an ethical individual in business must always make the decision that will increase profits and that any government intervention in the market is ethically wrong. In other words, business managers need only look to their accountants and economists to determine their ethical responsibilities.

Consider the example of drug testing mentioned in the opening section of this chapter. An individual manager who is considering drug tests for employees should, in Friedman's view, ask only one question: "Of all the alternatives, which policy will tend to increase profits?" The manager need not, and should not, be concerned with such issues as fairness, privacy, health and safety, or his responsibilities to employees. Managers need only calculate costs and benefits and adopt whatever policy will maximize profits. So, too, with any other moral or public policy issue. Business managers can and should ignore all other ethical considerations for the sake of one overriding principle: Maximize profits.

Ethics and Law: Is Obedience to the Law Enough?

A common view among many people in business, and one that we can find in Friedman's essay, is that obedience to the law is all that is ethically required of business. One version of this view suggests that people should be free to do pretty much as they choose as long as they don't harm anyone. Furthermore, the only harms serious enough to justify denying someone freedom are those prohibited by law. But is obeying the law all that it takes to be a moral person? There are good reasons for thinking not.

First, holding that obedience to the law is enough to be ethically responsible begs the question of whether or not the law itself is ethical. Certainly there are many examples throughout history of unethical and unjust laws. Nazi Germany, apartheid South Africa, and slaveholding America are just some examples in which ethical responsibility runs counter to obeying the law. You do not forgo your ethical responsibility by blind obedience to the law.

Second, societies that value individual freedom will be reluctant to legally require more than just a moral minimum. Liberal societies typically will seek legally to prohibit the most serious ethical harms, but they do not legally require acts of charity, decency, or integrity. The law can be an efficient mechanism for preventing harms, but it is not very efficient at promoting goods. Even if it were, the cost in human freedom would be too high. Imagine a society that tried to enforce legally the ethical responsibility to love one's child.

Finally, on a more practical level, telling the business community that their ethical responsibilities end with obedience to the law is just inviting more and more legal regulation of business. For example, many corporations have fine records of making generous contributions to the arts, education, and other charities. No doubt much of this is motivated by the simple belief that as citizens we all owe something back to our communities. But imagine if corporate managers followed Friedman's advice and rediverted all of this money back into dividends for stockholders. We would thus have a situation in which corporate profits are up and charities are suffering. At this point we should not at all be surprised to find the public demanding that government fill the void and, in turn, legislators increasing corporate taxes to pay for it. Similar points could be made for decisions concerning product safety, deceptive advertising, employee health, environmental pollution, and workplace discrimination and harassment. If business restricts its ethical responsibilities to obedience to the law, it should not be surprised to find a new wave of governmental regulations that require formerly voluntary actions.

This perspective is quite radical for a number of reasons. First, it conflicts with our ordinary understanding of ethical responsibilities. Ordinarily, it seems that our ethical responsibilities, on occasion at least, will require us to restrict our own behavior out of consideration for the well-being of others. Friedman tells us that, at least in our role as business managers, we can best fulfill our responsibilities to others by ignoring their interests and pursuing our own self-interest.[*]

This perspective is also radical in its political implications. Imagine a society in which government does not interfere with the economy except to prevent or rectify the harms done by fraud and coercion. Some government regulation of

---

[*]Friedman's view is reminiscent of the conclusion of Adam Smith (1723–1790). In *The Wealth of Nations*, the earliest exposition of market economics, Smith claimed that widespread pursuit of individual self-interest within the structure of a free market would result, as if led by "an invisible hand," in the attainment of the greater overall good.

the market could be accepted. The Securities and Exchange Commission, for example, might be justified as protection against security fraud or insider trading. Public utilities commissions might be required on more local levels to set prices in ways that mimic the market in cases where natural monopolies exist. But there would be little if any role for such regulatory agencies as the Occupational Safety and Health Administration, the Environmental Protection Agency, the Consumer Products Safety Commission, the Food and Drug Administration, the Nuclear Regulatory Agency, or the Federal Deposit Insurance Commission. More dramatically, any taxation for reasons other than for policing the free market would be an unethical interference with the market. (Imagine the effect that this recommendation would have on the legal and accounting professions!) Such governmental departments and programs as education, Health and Human Services, unemployment compensation, Social Security, or Medicare would all be unethical interferences with a free society. Finally, even government activities that seek to promote economic growth would be unethical. Aid to interstate commerce in such forms as highway, railroad, and airport subsidies; aid to specific industries like farming, oil, steel, automobiles; and government regulation of international trade through import quotas and tariffs would also be rejected if we adopt Friedman's normative ethics.

We have characterized Friedman's position as radical not because we disagree with him on the issues. Rather, we believe that each of these issues should be examined in turn on its merits. This is, after all, the only intellectually responsible approach, and it is the approach that a textbook especially needs to adopt. But part of the intellectual responsibility requires us to examine clearly the normative views of others. In doing ethics, we need to understand not only the specific claims of normative positions, but also the logical implications of these positions. The classical model of corporate social responsibility, as represented by Friedman's essay, asks us to change dramatically many of our standard ways of thinking and living.

Upon further examination, it might turn out that in any particular case Friedman's conclusion will be the reasonable one. It might turn out, for example, that regulating consumer product safety is best left to the workings of the market. In challenging Friedman's views, we do not want to defend the equally radical position that in every case one must forsake profit in the pursuit of other moral responsibilities. Despite offering a critical evaluation of the classical model in this chapter, we will return to give a fair hearing to this perspective on many specific issues throughout the remainder of this text.

FREE SOCIETY

Let us now examine the ethical reasoning that Friedman uses to defend his normative conclusions. He claims that a doctrine of social responsibility requiring business managers to sacrifice profits for other social objectives subverts our free society. The assumption here seems to be that a "free society" is identical to the type of society envisioned in Friedman's essay—that is, a society with totally free markets in which government's role is restricted to the prevention of coercion and fraud and where business is free to operate on a principle of self-interested pursuit of profit. Is this assumption valid?

The term *free society* has tremendous emotional appeal and positive connotation. We need to be careful not to let such appeals to emotion cloud our thinking or end the discussion. Presumably "free society" refers to *democratic* political structures where the ultimate authority for making political decisions rests in the hands of the voting population. It would be difficult to defend a society as free if it denied political participation to its citizens and gave authority only to some political elite.

But political thinkers for centuries have recognized that democratic structures alone don't guarantee freedom. Majorities can be just as tyrannical as minorities. For this reason, free societies also extend to their citizens a wide range of individual social and civil liberties. Among these liberties are freedom of speech, freedom of religion, freedom of the press, and the right to own and control private and productive property. As is the case in the United States and most contemporary democracies, these liberties are protected by constitutional restrictions on the freedom of the majority. The Bill of Rights to the U.S. Constitution, for example, limits the freedom of the majority when the First Amendment begins with "Congress shall make no laws which…." Thus, we can see in the notion of a constitutional democracy that the concept of a free society is complex, typically involving trade-offs between many different freedoms.

Historically, the economic liberties and rights of individuals found expression in essentially *capitalist* or *free market* economic systems. In general, economic systems involve the social practices that determine how economic goods and services are *produced* and how they are *distributed*. Capitalism is an economic system in which the means of production are privately owned and in which economic distribution occurs through the workings of a free market.

Thus, capitalism is an *economic* system distinct from the *political* system of democracy. We could easily envision a society with widespread political freedoms without capitalist economic structures (the democratic socialist societies of many European countries, for example). We can also envision societies with capitalist economic structures (private individuals owning the means of production and unregulated markets to distribute these products) and few democratic and civil liberties. Historically, many dictatorships throughout Central and South America fit this model.

While these issues will be examined in more detail in Chapter Three, we can draw some lessons here. The crucial thing to note is that freedom is not an either/or concept—either you have freedom, or you do not. Rather, there are many different freedoms, and a free society inevitably will involve trade-offs among these freedoms. Sometimes the freedom of the majority is limited by the freedom of the minority as when, for example, mandatory prayer is prohibited in public schools even when the majority of citizens would want it. Sometimes economic freedoms are restricted by civil liberties, as when private business owners are prohibited from discriminating on the basis of race or sex.

Furthermore, because democracy and capitalism are different concepts, it does not follow that a free society is threatened or subverted by restrictions upon the sort of capitalist economy that Friedman defends. Most of us would consider the United States a free society even though it falls far short of the laissez-faire capitalist society that Friedman envisions. When a business manager sacrifices profits for some social objective, she may well be restricting the freedom of stockholders to direct their property, but she may be doing it to increase the freedom of others to enjoy unpolluted air or a nondiscriminatory workplace. Friedman is simply wrong then when he claims that sacrificing profits for social objectives like "providing employment, eliminating discrimination, [and] avoiding pollution" undermines the basis of a free society.

THE "TAX ARGUMENT"

Friedman's only other explicit argument is what we might call the "tax argument." Here he claims that business managers who act against the economic interests of the firm to achieve some social objective such as lowering unemployment are, in effect, imposing taxes on the owners, consumers, and/or employees in order to benefit society. Friedman tells us that imposing such taxes is wrong on two levels: principle and consequences. It is wrong in principle because it violates the political principle that taxes should not be imposed by private individuals. It is wrong at the level of consequences because business managers lack the expertise to solve social problems.

Before we begin a careful assessment of this argument, we should again take care when using emotionally charged language. Friedman speaks of "taxes" here, and many of us will have an automatic negative reaction to taxes. But we need to be careful that we not prejudge the question and accept Friedman's conclusion simply because he has chosen a rhetorically persuasive term. To avoid this temptation, we should translate Friedman's tax language into a more neutral discussion of costs. This should be unobjectionable since the manager's decision doesn't really impose taxes in the traditional sense of government levies, but does add costs that otherwise would not exist. So hereafter we will speak of a manager's expenditures on social objectives that reduce profits as the imposition of costs on shareholders, employees, and consumers.

Now, why is it wrong for managers to impose costs on shareholders, employees, and consumers in the pursuit of some social objective? Friedman tells us that on the level of political principle such objectives and costs should be the product of joint decisions by the citizens; unilateral imposition of such costs is contrary to accepted and ethically justified democratic political principles. Additionally, even if such unilateral actions were not wrong on principle, the likely consequences of these private decisions would be harmful to society. Thus, Friedman has offered two moral reasons to support this normative claim.

Let us deal with the consequentialist branch of the argument first. Friedman claims that management lacks the expertise for making judgments about what acts would produce the greatest net benefit to society. His example is that of a manager who tries to reduce inflation. Ordinary managers have no procedure for making a careful estimate about the consequences of their pricing policy on inflationary trends in a society.

Perhaps this is an accurate description of management expertise on the complex economic problem of inflation. But Friedman has provided no reason for thinking that there cannot be other situations where a manager does have the expertise needed to address social problems. Suppose a manufacturing firm was discharging the by-products of its production process into a nearby river. Management of this firm should have exactly the expertise needed to determine if this by-product was harmful to local residents. (Indeed, if it was harmful and management claimed ignorance of that fact, the law would likely hold them negligent for not knowing!) Suppose that, knowing this, management could eliminate this toxic discharge with expenditures that would reduce profitability but not threaten the economic viability of the firm. Again, accomplishing corporate goals in an economically efficient manner is exactly the kind of expertise that is ordinarily required of management. Now, would voluntarily stopping the discharge, an action that Friedman would prohibit unless required by law, produce negative social consequences? Presumably it would not, especially if the discharge was harmful to the health of many people and the costs were relatively minor.

Thus, whether management assumption of responsibilities beyond the narrow range defined by Friedman would have unacceptable consequences appears to depend on the particular responsibility at issue. So we cannot assume that management lacks the expertise and ability for reasonable action on the basis of any social responsibility simply because it lacks the expertise or ability in one case. In some cases, management may have exactly the expertise necessary. Friedman's consequentialist argument commits the fallacy of overgeneralizing from a small set of examples to a universal claim about all cases. This argument must be rejected as unconvincing.

Friedman's defense of his conclusion must rest with his argument from political principle. That argument demands that the imposition of costs in pursuit of social objectives must be the result of proper political decisions. The imposition of costs by private individuals is intolerable in principle, according to Friedman.

A word about costs can help begin our analysis of this argument. As any student of introductory economics who is familiar with the concept of opportunity costs will attest, a cost is a relative thing. The full cost of any purchase, policy, or decision can be measured only in relation to the alternatives that one thereby forgoes. Thus, since resources are finite, to spend money on defense spending, for example, has a cost not only in terms of dollars but more specifically in the inability to use those dollars for health care or education. Similarly, when a business executive spends money for new pollution control equipment, that spending represents a cost to shareholders in that it precludes using those same dollars for greater dividends. Note that this expenditure is a cost to employees and consumers as well because it also precludes spending those dollars for higher salaries or lower product prices.

This reveals a characteristic mark of costs: What is a cost to one person or group is usually a benefit to another. Providing expensive workplace safety equipment is a benefit to employees but a cost to shareholders and consumers if it means lower profits or higher prices. Costs and benefits can also be exchanged for a single individual. Increased wages can be an employee benefit won at the cost of decreased corporate pension contributions or of fewer health care benefits. The economic point is clear. Since costs are always relative to alternatives forgone, every managerial decision will involve the imposition of costs. Friedman's economic system is no exception. In that system, when a manager acts to increase profits within the rules of the game, that action carries an implicit cost for others affected by corporate policy: consumers, employees, and society at large.

As an economist, Friedman of course recognizes that the imposition of costs is unavoidable. Therefore, his point cannot be that it is wrong in principle to impose costs on others without their consent. Thus, to be fair to his view we need to look for another interpretation of his principle. But what might that be?

Perhaps Friedman is suggesting that it is wrong in principle for managers to impose costs on the basis of their own personal moral decisions. At this point in his essay he does say that "one man's good is another's evil," and this suggests that he is skeptical about the legitimacy of any individual's moral opinions. Unfortunately, if this is his view, Friedman cannot sustain an in-principle rejection of the social responsibility thesis while remaining consistent with his own conclusions.

Remember that Friedman himself describes the only direct responsibility of managers as involving conformity to "the basic rules of society, both those embodied in law and those embodied in ethical custom." Surely there will be cases where conforming to these rules, both legal and ethical, will impose costs on shareholders. And just as surely, there will be times when what is required by these rules is unclear and the manager will need to exercise some discretion (and why else have managers except to make just these sorts of judgments?). Thus, on Friedman's own view, there can be times when a manager will, on the basis of his own personal judgment, impose costs on shareholders for the sake of some ethical objective.

For example, suppose that a manager is considering a proposed advertising campaign for a sweepstakes contest that plays on the vulnerability of elderly people. The sweepstakes has been carefully crafted to ensure that it violates no law. Experience shows that they can be profitable. Yet the manager believes that it is so deceptive that it really amounts to fraud. It would seem that on Friedman's view, the manager should exercise her personal judgment and avoid the fraudulent advertising, even at the risk of imposing significant costs upon stockholders.

We can consider one final interpretation of Friedman's in-principle objection to the social responsibility thesis. Perhaps the key to understanding this view rests with the claim that "a corporate executive is an employee of the owners of the business." This suggests that what is wrong is imposing costs on *owners* in the pursuit of social objectives. But what would the political principle violated by such actions be? Supposedly it is that private owners have the right to control their property and when managers disregard the owner's desire to make as much money as possible, they violate this right.

Two serious challenges can be raised to this view. The first focuses on the nature of political and moral rights, and the second focuses on the nature of corporate ownership and control. We will examine these issues in more detail in Chapters Three and Four, but for now we can make a few brief observations.

First, even if imposing costs in the pursuit of social objectives does restrict the rights of private property owners, Friedman would need to say more to show that it is always in-principle wrong to do this. As we saw earlier, free societies often require trade-offs among various and competing freedoms. This suggests a distinction between overriding rights (restricting freedom with a legitimate justification) and violating rights (restricting freedom without justification). The existence of zoning laws, for example, attests to society's willingness to override the rights of private property owners in pursuit of such social objectives as the aesthetic integrity of a historical neighborhood, or for the sake of public safety. A zoning law restricting a certain neighborhood to single-family homes imposes significant costs on a property owner who seeks to build an apartment complex for college students. Yet few of us believe that such laws are "fundamentally subversive" to a free society. They may override the property owner's rights, but we don't say that they *violate* her rights.

Second, this interpretation really misrepresents the nature of corporate ownership and control. At least for large firms with publicly traded stocks, it is better to think of stockholders as "investors" than as "owners." While the right of ownership of personal property (your car, for example) implies a right to do with it what you want (within limits of course), the same cannot be said for owners of corporate stock. Here, ownership does not imply the right to control. That right is vested in corporate management. Ownership of stock, which rests more often with institutional investors like mutual funds, pension plans, and financial institutions than with private individuals, does imply certain rights. Investors can profit from this stock, sell it (usually), deed it to their children, give it away, and so on. But they cannot try to "micromanage" the daily operations of the firm. That responsibility rests with the management, who owes them only a competitive rate of return on their investment. If investors disagree with the decisions of management, they retain the freedom to sell their stock and seek a higher rate of return elsewhere.

IN SUMMARY

Normative ethics involves stepping back from what is customarily accepted as proper behavior and asking questions about what *ought* to be proper. The views of Milton Friedman, identified as the classical model of corporate social responsibility, are an example of normative business ethics. Friedman offers numerous prescriptions for how one ought to behave in business and how business ought to be structured. He defends these prescriptions by appeal to certain ethical norms and values.

Our analysis of Friedman's practice of normative ethics must conclude that his supporting reasons are unconvincing. He relies on emotional appeals in several instances, he overgeneralizes from the evidence, he misunderstands or misrepresents the nature of a free society, and he even appears to be inconsistent with his own views.

But we should be careful not to make a logical mistake ourselves. Even if we conclude that Friedman's reasons are invalid, we are not justified in rejecting his overall conclusions and prescriptions. The classical model of corporate social responsibility is an important and influential normative theory. Just because one particular defense of it proves unconvincing doesn't mean that we are justified in rejecting the entire theory. After all, Friedman's essay was written for the popular press and perhaps was not intended to be a philosophically careful defense of this position. (Perhaps there is a lesson in here as well about how to read journalistic accounts of complex ethical issues!)

The views represented by Friedman's essay—the classical model of corporate social responsibility and the free market theory of economics on which it is based—continue to be influential positions throughout contemporary society. They have also received defenses that are much more philosophically sophisticated. In the next two chapters we will examine two of these philosophical defenses, each based in a major ethical theory. We will use our examination of these defenses to introduce the next level of ethics—philosophical ethics—and the two leading approaches to ethical theory—utilitarianism and individual rights.

In conclusion, we should step back from the content of this chapter to reflect on what we did, on the *activity* of ethical analysis. In one way, this chapter is an example of the kind of reasoning that philosophical ethics asks of us, and it provides an answer to the relativist and skeptic who thinks that ethics is all a matter of personal opinion. We did reason; we did make rational progress. We may not have proven anything absolutely, but we have advanced the debate. We encourage you to continue this activity throughout this text. We invite you to continue doing philosophy.

STUDY QUESTIONS

1. What are the three skeptical reactions to business ethics mentioned at the beginning of this chapter? Construct counterarguments to these skeptical claims.

2. What is the classical model of corporate social responsibility, and how, exactly, does it follow from the free market view of economics?

3. Milton Friedman claims that business as a whole cannot have responsibilities and that "only people have responsibilities." Do you agree? Why or why not?

4. What is ethical relativism? What reasons can be given for rejecting relativism? Can you construct rational counterarguments to these reasons?

2

Ethical Theory

Utilitarianism and the Free Market

In Chapter One we introduced three different types of ethical thinking: descriptive, normative, and philosophical. Descriptive ethics, as the name suggests, seeks to describe the actual norms and customs that guide behavior. Normative ethics steps back from customary behavior to evaluate and prescribe behavior. Normative ethics focuses on how people *ought* to or *should* behave, rather than how people *do* behave. In this chapter we move to the third level of ethical thinking: philosophical ethics or, as it is sometimes called, ethical theory. Philosophical ethics refers to a branch of philosophy that examines more abstract questions of ethics, seeking a general and systematic answer to how we ought to live. An ethical "theory" is simply any systematic and coherent approach to ethical questions. In Chapters Two and Three we examine two theories, each very influential in the modern world and each with direct implications for business ethics. We will call these two theories "utilitarianism" and a "rights-based approach to ethics." As we will see, versions of each theory have been used to defend free market economics and the classical model of corporate social responsibility that follows from it.

As we begin our discussion of ethical theory, it will be useful first to say a little more about the nature of ethics. In examining Friedman's essay we spoke of norms as the "oughts" and "shoulds" that guide behavior. We also pointed out that there are various norms that we use in guiding behavior: ethical, economic, financial, religious, political, even the norms of etiquette. How, then, do we distinguish between ethical norms and other types of norms?

Consider economic or financial norms. Perhaps the most fundamental prescription in finance is "buy low and sell high." If we were to ask *why* buy low and sell high, the answer would be something like "because that will maximize your return on investment." Thus, the complete form of the financial prescription is "*if* you want a maximum return on your investment, *then* you ought to buy low and sell high." In logical terms, this is a hypothetical, or "if...then," statement. Likewise, other norms fit this hypothetical model. If you want to attain eternal salvation, then you ought to obey the teaching of your church. If you want to be considered polite, then you ought to follow the norms of etiquette. If you want to get reelected, then you ought to provide good constituent service.

Hypothetical norms depend upon other considerations for their force or legitimacy. The "if" in the hypothetical statement shows that I can be exempt from the norm by rejecting the hypothesis. The norms apply to me only if I care about or have an interest in maximizing return, eternal salvation, a reputation for politeness, or reelection.

Ethical norms, on the other hand, are seen as applying to all rational people regardless of their personal wants or interests. Ethical norms tell us how we, as rational human beings, ought to live our lives. Philosophers traditionally identified ethical norms as "universal," meaning that they apply to all people. (The great German philosopher, Immanuel Kant, called such ethical norms "categorical imperatives" to distinguish them from the hypothetical imperatives just mentioned.) An ethical theory attempts to provide a rational basis for making such universal judgments. Of course, an ethical relativist (as described in Chapter One) *denies* that such judgments are possible. Thus, ethical theories must also provide an answer to the relativist challenge that no norm can be applied to all people.

Besides this universal character, ethical norms are said to be impartial or fair. A norm that gives special privilege to my own interests is not an ethical norm; a norm that denies equal standing for the interests of others is not an ethical norm. Impartiality requires that the interests of all people involved be given equal consideration and equal weight. Ethics requires that everyone counts equally, and no one counts for more.

We can say that an ethical theory attempts to systematically account for certain fundamental norms that apply to all people and that do so in an impartial, or fair, manner. An ethical theory explains and defends universal principles that prescribe, in an impartial manner, how we ought to live. Normative ethics, in turn, uses these fundamental norms and universal principles to prescribe more specific behavior. One influential ethical theory is utilitarianism.

UTILITARIANISM

How ought we to live? How can we decide what we should do? One general answer tells us to look to the consequences of our acts. Utilitarianism directs us to the consequences of our acts to determine right from wrong. Utilitarianism begins with the intuitively reasonable observation that, given a choice between two alternative actions, we *ought* to do the one that will bring about the best results.

Utilitarianism is an ethical theory that, roughly speaking, directs us to seek the "greatest good for the greatest number" or to "maximize the overall good." Thus, utilitarianism involves two components: an account of what is "good" and a norm for judging whether acts are right or wrong. An act is ethically right if it leads to a net increase in the overall good; an act is ethically wrong if it leads to a net decrease in the overall good.

From this description, we can see that utilitarians distinguish two types of value: *intrinsic value* and *instrumental value*. The "good," that against which all other things are measured, must be something that is valued for its own sake: it can be said to have *intrinsic value*. All other things are judged to have value, not in themselves, but only insofar as they produce good consequences. Thus, utilitarians evaluate the *instrumental value*, or "utility," of acts or policies by judging the degree to which they produce that which is valued for its own sake.

Consider the example of truth-telling. Utilitarians will value telling the truth because it will generally produce good consequences; for example, it engenders trust, it allows for accurate communication and understanding, and it earns one a good reputation. That is, truth-telling is not good in itself, but it is valued instrumentally as a means to an end. It is useful. Again, if we ask, "Why value trust, or accurate communication, or a good reputation?" the utilitarian will answer "Because it will produce beneficial consequences." For the utilitarian, no act is ever good in itself, at all times, in all situations. Right or wrong always depends on the consequences.

Ultimately this means–ends reasoning must stop somewhere. If the value of everything depends upon something else, then we would be involved in an infinite regress (value A because of B, value B because of C, value C because of D,…) and ultimately value nothing. If all utilitarian reasoning was of this instrumental and consequentialist form, utilitarian ethics would always remain hypothetical and contingent. To stop this regress, utilitarians must defend some good that is valued for its own sake, not solely for its utility in producing other goods. The utilitarian answer to relativism ("Who's to say what's right or wrong?") is to defend an account of the good that is universally and objectively valid for all rational persons. If there is some good that is objectively valuable, and if some act produces more of this good than alternative acts, then you objectively ought to do that act. In this way, utilitarianism satisfies the universal and impartial nature of ethical norms. The "good" is universally valid, the good of each person is treated as equally deserving, and attaining the optimal amount of this good is a fair and impartial goal. No one could object to maximizing the overall good except by claiming that an increase in his or her own good is more important than a greater increase in the goods of others.

VERSIONS OF UTILITARIANISM

The classical statements of the utilitarian tradition are found in the writings of Jeremy Bentham (1748–1832) and John Stuart Mill (1806–1873). Through the writings of Adam Smith (1723–1790), utilitarian reasoning has been especially influential in economics, and provides one important ethical justification of free market economics and the classical model of corporate social responsibility that flows from it.

The major challenge for utilitarians is to defend an account of the good that is rationally defensible and that can therefore serve as the basis for making objective moral judgments. Utilitarians have differed over what is thought to be the good and, as a result, a variety of utilitarian theories have been defended by philosophers. Several of these versions will be helpful in examining utilitarianism, the free market, and the classical model of corporate social responsibility.

Early utilitarians like Jeremy Bentham argued that only pleasure, or at least the absence of pain, is universally valued for its own sake. Bentham believed that it was a fact of human psychology that pleasure and pain were the ultimate human motivations. Pleasure is good, and pain is bad. This version of utilitarianism, usually called "hedonistic utilitarianism," directs us to maximize pleasure and minimize pain.

John Stuart Mill proposed that happiness rather than pleasure was the ultimate human good. According to Mill, happiness adds a qualitative dimension to human well-being that is missing in mere pleasure and the absence of pain. For Mill, fulfilling important human interests is a higher level of good than attaining pleasure alone. In a famous passage, Mill tells us that it is better to be a human being dissatisfied (that is, without pleasure) than a pig satisfied (that is, feeling great pleasure). Thus, Mill's version of utilitarianism directs us to maximize the overall happiness.

It is worth noting that in the late eighteenth and nineteenth centuries, utilitarianism was a radical and very progressive social philosophy. Utilitarians were promoting an approach to ethics that took seriously the good of all people. Utilitarians sought to maximize the *overall* good or promote the greatest happiness for the *greatest number*, not to maximize the good of the king or promote the greatest good for the aristocracy. Thus, utilitarianism was part of the eighteenth and nineteenth centuries' great social movement towards democracy.

Utilitarianism also provided a defense of individual freedom of choice. While pleasure or happiness were thought to be universally good, the particular things that give one pleasure or happiness were left to be determined by the individual. You may find pleasure in a life of public service; I may find it in a life of material comfort. Either way, we can still objectively agree that a world in which you get what gives you pleasure and I get what gives me pleasure is ethically better than a world in which we are denied our pleasures. Mill's classic essay, *On Liberty,* defended the view that individuals should be free from any interference as long as they were not harming any other person. Thus, utilitarianism played an important role in the tradition of liberal democratic societies.

Contemporary Versions

"Preference utilitarianism," a more contemporary version, defines human good in terms of satisfying one's wants or desires. In this view, the only thing that is valued for its own sake is getting what one wants. (Does anyone not want what one wants?) This version argues that in general it is better for us to have our wants satisfied than having them frustrated. If satisfying wants is good, satisfying more is better and satisfying as many as possible is best. In this view, the ethically ideal world is one in which as many people as possible get as much of what they want as possible.

Recognizing that scarcity and competition among our own wants (I want both a new car and a new computer system, but have money for only one) prevent us from getting all that we want, defenders of this view typically leave it to the individual to determine the want with the highest value. Rank-ordering your own wants like this is to establish preferences, giving this version its name.

Another contemporary version of utilitarianism, "interest utilitarianism," criticizes preference utilitarianism by distinguishing between *wants* and *interests*. We often will distinguish what a person wants from what is in that person's interests. For example, although a child may not want to eat vegetables, we would say nonetheless that eating vegetables is in the child's interests. Or we might acknowledge that it is not in our best interest to drink and drive, yet desire to have one more drink before leaving a party. The difference here seems to be one between what we might believe is good for us and what actually is good for us. Our desires are those things that, as a matter of fact, we just happen to want at any given time. Our interests are those things that will actually benefit us. Of course, wants and interests can be identical. My desire for an excellent education coincides with the fact that it is in my best interest to have such an education.

Interest utilitarianism points out that a world in which as many people get as much of what is in their interests as possible is ethically preferable to a world in which people get as much of what they want as possible. The satisfaction of interests, not wants, should be our ethical goal. This debate between preference utilitarianism and interest utilitarianism parallels the debate between Bentham and Mill. We could simply identify pleasure as getting what one wants and happiness as getting what is in one's interests. These debates give rise to a number of important issues. For example, interest utilitarians charge that preference utilitarianism can lead to the kind of ethical relativism discussed in Chapter One. Wants and desires seem to be very subjective things, with no way open for rationally criticizing another's wants. In response, preference utilitarians claim that their view is very democratic, and they fear the potential tyranny that may follow from a willingness to disregard what people in fact want in favor of what is judged (by others?) to be in their best interests.

One important compromise between these views suggests that the best way to bring wants into line with interests is to rely on the informed judgment of the individuals themselves. If a person pursues something he wants and it turns out not to be in his best interests, he can learn from this mistake and change his wants. People learn that a diet without vegetables is unhealthy and that drinking and driving is dangerous. As people reflect on their wants and study the consequences of their actions, they can learn for themselves what is in their best interests. In this way, many utilitarians continue to argue that we should leave people alone to make their own choices and protect individual liberty as a highly valued means to ethical ends.

UTILITARIANISM AND THE FREE MARKET

Given this overview of utilitarianism, we can now turn to the utilitarian defense of the free market economic system and the classical model of corporate social responsibility that follows from it. We remember that the free market system was used to justify specific ethical recommendations. Individual business managers should seek to maximize profits because this is required of them by the free market economic system. For utilitarians in the classical economic tradition of Adam Smith, the free market system itself is ethically justified because it will maximize the overall good of society. Let us examine how this would work.

Consider a simple example. Alexa wants to sell her car, and two people, Michael and Matthew, want to buy it. This means that Alexa has decided that she would be better off with money than she presently is with the car. Michael and Matthew each have decided that they would be happier with a car than with the money they now have. What happens if we leave these people alone to pursue their own individual self-interest? Presumably these people would engage in the kind of bargaining that occurs in markets. Alexa offers her car for sale, and Michael and Matthew make bids for it. Initially, Michael offers $1000 and Matthew offers $1100. Alexa, looking to become as happy as possible, asks for more. Michael and Matthew continue bidding, pushing the price higher and higher and therefore making Alexa happier and happier. Finally, one of the bidders drops out when he decides, completely on his own according to his preferences, that he would rather keep his money than exchange it for the car. The other bidder, say it is Michael, offers $2000 and gets the car. Again, this choice was freely made, so we must conclude that Michael is happier with the car than with his money (otherwise, why would he agree to the sale?). Assuming that Alexa also agrees to the sale, she, too, is as happy as she can be in that she has received what she most wants. Finally, assuming a competitive market (that is, assuming that there are other sellers competing with Alexa), Matthew will eventually get what he most wants, a car for under $2000.

By allowing rational, self-interested individuals to bargain for themselves, by giving them the freedom to decide what they most want and what they are willing to pay for, we have reached a point where we have optimally satisfied the wants of all parties. There is no way to improve the overall situation in the sense of increasing overall happiness. If any exchange would benefit two parties, rational and self-interested people would have agreed to it. Anything we now do to increase Alexa's happiness—for example, by increasing the price she is paid—would decrease Michael's happiness, by requiring him to give up more for the car. Thus, we have reached a point of optimal happiness: No one's happiness can be increased without a loss of other happiness. We have, in short, maximized the overall happiness.

According to utilitarians and economists who follow Adam Smith, if we expand this example over an entire society we can see that open and competitive markets produce the optimal outcome. With just a few structural requirements (that is, there is open and free competition, coercion and fraud are not allowed, individuals are rational and are pursuing their own self-interests), the workings of the market will guarantee maximizing the overall good. If we provide the appropriate social structure (that is, a laissez-faire economy), the individual pursuit of self-interest will result—as if led by "an invisible hand," according to Smith—to the greatest overall good.

The ethical imperative for business managers follows from this as well. Managers ought to seek profit maximization because profits testify to the successful functioning of the market. When Alexa pursued maximum profits, she was ensuring that the person who most valued the car, that is, the person who was willing to pay most for it, would in fact get it. Michael was willing to pay more for the car than Matthew; therefore, pursuit of profits guarantees that goods get to those people who most want, or prefer, them. Alexa, of course, is happiest with maximized profits because now she will be able to satisfy other wants that she has (for example, she can now afford her vacation to Mexico). If a manager could have increased profits and did not, that manager has prevented products from reaching people who more value them, in other words, preventing exchanges that would have benefitted everyone involved.

Accordingly, we have two major claims being made by the utilitarian defense of the free market. The first claim is that a competitive, free, and open market is the best means to achieve the utilitarian goal of maximizing the overall good, or end. The second claim is that the end achieved by a free market—maximum satisfaction of preferences—is the ethically best end. Thus, we can think of this defense in terms of means and ends: The free market is the best means to attaining the best end. Now let us examine each of these claims in turn.

AN ANALYSIS OF THE
UTILITARIAN DEFENSE

The Free Market Is the Best Means

There are two general ways in which the free market could be an appropriate means to the utilitarian end of overall good. On one hand, the market could be *necessary* to that end. That is, unless we adopt the market as our means, we will not be able to attain this end. On the other hand, the free market could be a *sufficient* means to that end. In this sense, the market might not be necessary (we could get there in some other way), but it does guarantee that we will get there. Thus, we can evaluate the claim that the market is the best means by evaluating whether the market is either necessary or sufficient for that end.

Before starting this evaluation, it is necessary to briefly address the utilitarian goal of overall good (in the next section we will look in more detail at this issue). We need to know something about where we are going before deciding if a particular means is either necessary or sufficient to get us there.

Our simple example suggests that the utilitarian defense of the market is a version of preference utilitarianism. On this view, the human good is understood in terms of the satisfaction of those desires, or preferences, that individuals express in

Psychological Egoism: Are Humans Naturally Selfish?

Ethical norms have been described as impartial and universal norms that seek to promote human well-being. To be impartial is to give the interests of each person equal and fair consideration. In practice, impartiality will sometimes require that our own personal interests be subordinated to the interests of others. This seems to fit our ordinary understanding of ethics: There can arise occasions in which we could cheat to further our own advantage, but our ethical responsibility prohibits cheating. In other words, ethics would seem to require that we sometimes act unselfishly.

However, there is a common view of human beings as incapable of acting unselfishly. "Psychological egoism" views human beings as naturally self-interested, acting always and only out of their own self-interest. Insofar as ethics requires us to act unselfishly, it conflicts with the facts of psychological egoism. If psychological egoism is true, then we would have to do some major revisions to our understanding of ethics. Before evaluating this theory, it will be helpful to first consider what might follow if this theory is true.

One reaction to psychological egoism might be simply to give up on ethics. Since ethics requires us to subordinate our own interests to the interests of others, and since, according to psychological egoism, that is impossible, we can ignore ethics because it requires us to do the impossible. This strategy is similar to the relativist theory described in Chapter One: "Since people

are all selfish anyway, why bother about ethics?"

Another strategy would try to reformulate the requirements of ethics to fit the facts of psychological egoism. What is often called "ethical egoism" is the normative position that people *ought* to act out of their own self-interest. We can see one version of this in some utilitarian defenders of the free market. Given the facts of psychological egoism (a descriptive theory), we should arrange social structures in such a way that egoistic acts lead to ethically beneficial results (a normative theory). Following Adam Smith's speculation about the workings of an "invisible hand," some defenders of laissez-faire economics see the free market as exactly this type of social arrangement. Of course, as we see in this chapter, there seems to be no guarantee that egoistic acts will lead to ethical results.

But is psychological egoism true? Are humans naturally selfish? As a first step, we should note that if psychological egoism is merely a claim about human tendencies—that people generally tend to act selfishly—then it provides little reason to give up on ethics or to reshape social institutions to take advantage of selfishness. If people tend to act selfishly but are capable of acting otherwise, then this seems more rather than less of a reason to support the aims of ethics. And if people are capable of acting unselfishly, then it might be better to support social institutions that discourage rather than encourage selfishness.

market transactions. In our example, Alexa, Michael, and Matthew all aimed to satisfy their desires, and they were allowed to rank-order their own desires as personal preferences. In fact, economists understand consumer demand in just this way. Thus, the goal of the free market is the optimal satisfaction of consumer demand or, in perhaps more common terms, a high standard of living.

Is the Market Necessary? Now, is a free market *necessary* for attaining such an end? On the surface, we know that some of the highest standards of living exist in Scandinavia, North America, Japan, and Western Europe. Measured in such terms as per capita income, life expectancy, education and literacy levels, infant mortality rates, health care, and civil liberties, countries in these regions boast of very high standards of living. Yet no country in these regions could be classified as having a laissez-faire, free market economy. Within these regions, there is widespread government regulation of the market and centralized economic planning; it is very common to find business managers actively pursuing social objectives beyond

So psychological egoism is a challenge to the ethical requirement that we should act unselfishly only if it makes the stronger claim that people always and only act selfishly. But stated so clearly, this seems obviously false. As any parent or friend will testify, there are many occasions when people sacrifice their own interests for the well-being of others. From the commonplace examples of people volunteering for charities to the more dramatic case of heroes risking their lives to save others, the world seems full of counterexamples to psychological egoism.

Psychological egoists know this, of course. Two answers to these common examples are typically offered by the egoist, but neither will rescue this theory. It is sometimes answered that in cases of apparently unselfish acts, people really are just doing what they want. A doctor may volunteer at a neighborhood clinic, but that's just because she wants to help others. Consequently, psychological egoism is still correct: People always and only do what they want. A second answer claims that even when people help others, they still take pleasure out of it and this fact shows that they are, after all, egoists.

However, the first answer is not a threat to ethics. To say that people always do what they want is either an empirical claim, in which case it, too, seems obviously false (I don't want to go to the dentist, but I will anyway). Or it is an attempt to define wants as *whatever* people aim for, in which case it is still open for ethics to require people to want (aim for) the well-being of others, a possibility already admitted to occur in the example.

The second answer fares no better. We need to distinguish the reason for someone's act from the feelings that follow from the act. I am not selfish if my reason in acting is to help another person, even if I derive pleasure in doing so. On the other hand, if I give to charity in order to feel good about myself, then maybe I am being selfish, even if I have done something to benefit others. It makes no sense to say that a parent who stays awake all night to nurse a sick child is selfish because the parent derives pleasure from seeing a healthy child in the morning; this would be true in only the most bizarre case.

At bottom, psychological egoism rests on a serious confusion about facts and definitions. If psychological egoism is put forward as an empirical, factual claim, then it is false. People do unselfish acts all the time. If it is put forward as a matter of definition (*whatever* people do is, by definition, in their self-interest), then the door is still open for the ethicists to distinguish those self-interested acts that benefit others from those self-interested acts that benefit only the self. Ethics asks only that we not always give our own personal, selfish interests priority over the interests of others.

profit maximization; and, in some cases, the entire economy is better characterized as socialist (that is, social ownership and control of the means of production) than as free market capitalist. It would appear, at least at first glance, that a free market economy is not necessary for attaining a high standard of living.

Of course, defenders of the market can claim that in all of these cases the standards of living would only improve by doing away with government regulation. But we need to be careful here. To say that the market is necessary is to make an in-principle claim: In all cases a freer economy would increase the overall good. But it is difficult to believe that this is true, especially in light of historical evidence. Critics of the market would argue that the overall quality of life in these regions increased only after these societies recognized failures within free markets and began regulating the economy.

Committed utilitarians always look to the consequences of actions to determine right from wrong action. The consequences of our acts seem to depend on a wide variety of occurrences "out there" in the world. Utilitarians must take a "let's see what happens" attitude; holding that a free market is always, in principle, necessary to attain certain consequences seems too strong a position for a utilitarian, unless (and here's the potential trouble) *whatever* results from the workings of a free market is *defined* as ethically good. But if this is the view, then we have no independent ethical justification of the market, which is, after all, what we started out in search for. (If the consequences of the free market are *defined* as good, then to justify the market because it attains the good is to justify the market because it attains what it attains!)

Consider the following example. In the United States the Federal Reserve Board sets monetary policy by establishing the interest rates at which banks are loaned money. The people who serve on this board are respected economists who, we can presume, share the utilitarian goal of maximizing the overall good. One very plausible way to interpret the workings of the Federal Reserve Board is to see it in utilitarian terms. If the economy is in a recession, then we are not maximizing consumer satisfaction. Thus, interest rates should be lowered to stimulate economic activity. The board then watches the consequences of its action: Too little growth, then perhaps rates should be lowered further; too much growth and a potential for inflation, then rates should be increased. Utilitarians look at economic policy the way the Federal Reserve Board looks at monetary policy. It has only instrumental value: Sometimes less government regulation increases the good; sometimes further regulation is needed. Since the right answer depends on the consequences and since the consequences will depend upon the specifics of each particular set of circumstances, seldom would utilitarians claim that any particular social or economic policy is necessary.

Is the Market Sufficient? Nonetheless, perhaps a free market is *sufficient* for attaining this end. Perhaps a free market will get us there, even if other types of economic arrangements could do this as well. Is there any guarantee that a free market will maximize the overall good? A variety of phenomena that economists identify as *market failures* suggest that there are no such guarantees. Economists call these market "failures" precisely because they are instances in which the market fails to maximize the satisfaction of wants.

Let us return to the simple example that started this discussion to see how the market is thought to guarantee maximizing the good. The mechanism of the marketplace, the force that makes it work, is the pursuit of rational self-interest. The market promises the optimal satisfaction of preferences as long as all participants are allowed to, and in fact do, pursue their own rational self-interest. Individuals should calculate the expected benefits of alternative action and then act in the way that will produce the highest net benefit. As Adam Smith suggested, when individuals "intend only their own gain," they will "be led by an invisible hand" to promote the good of society as a whole. But is it true that the whole of society benefits when each individual pursues only his or her own self-interest?

While a great deal of attention has been given to this question by philosophers and economists alike, no clear consensus has been reached. To understand certain problems associated with this claim, consider the well-known traffic phenomenon called "rubbernecking."

Imagine yourself driving to work during morning rush hour. There has been a traffic accident across the roadway in the lanes coming out of the city. Being the rational, self-interested individual that classical economics takes you to be, you calculate the costs and benefits involved in slowing down for a look. On one hand, you don't want to be late for work, and slowing down will cost you a few seconds of time. On the other hand, you would gain something by learning about the accident; you would be satisfying your curiosity at the cost of only a few seconds. Calculating the net benefits, you ease off the accelerator and look across the road to take a look. Of course, every other rationally self-interested driver makes a similar calculation. This seems the reasonable choice for each individual. Unfortunately, the result of each individual pursuing their own self-interest and easing off the accelerator is a bumper-to-bumper traffic jam. The final overall result is that everyone is significantly late for work, much later than the mere seconds calculated by each individual.

Further, if any individual decides on her own to forgo a look and not slow down, she will still be caught in a traffic jam but without the benefits that would have come from looking. Further still, if everyone agreed not to slow down, then it would be in my interest to slow down to look, thereby getting the benefits without the loss. In all possible scenarios, it seems to be in my own interest to slow down and look. But again, the same is true for every individual. The result is that it seems that the group is worse off, not better off, by the widespread pursuit of individual self-interest. The group would have been better off had everyone followed a strategy of cooperation and sacrificed the pursuit of individual self-interest.

Defenders of the free market will rightly point out that this single example does not capture the essence of a large-scale, free, and competitive market exchange. Nevertheless, rubbernecking and other so-called "prisoner dilemmas" do give us some reason for thinking that, at certain levels in the day-to-day life of individuals at least, the pursuit of individual self-interest will not guarantee that the group as a whole will be best off. There seems reason to doubt Smith's "invisible hand."

Another reason to doubt the claim that a free market will attain the maximum overall good has to do with what economists call "externalities." Economists have long recognized that the price established in a market can fail to account for all of the costs involved. Certain costs may fall on someone other than the buyer or seller, with the result being an efficient exchange (both buyer and seller are made better off), but one that is not good for the entire society. Since the person who bears the cost is not a party to the exchange (the person is "external" to the transaction), he cannot influence the exchange and therefore the price does not accurately reflect the full costs.

Environmental pollution is often given as an example where such externalities occur. The cost (or "disutility") of a production process might include contaminating ground water with toxic discharges. Without government regulation to prevent this (which is the recommendation of free market defenders like Milton Friedman), the cost of this pollution is paid by neither the industry nor its customers. As a result, while both parties to the exchange are better off (through production costs that do not reflect the costs of pollution), society as a whole is harmed by the uncompensated loss of clean water.

Likewise with the use of nonrenewable resources. The price of oil and gas for present generation users does not reflect the opportunities for use of these resources that are forgone by future generation users. (Remember from Chapter One that costs are defined in terms of "opportunities forgone.") There are significant costs to our present production of oil and gas that are not reflected in the present price. The parties to this exchange (the oil companies and all of us consumers) benefit, while those who are external to this transaction (future generations) must suffer the uncompensated loss of resources. Thus, whenever externalities exist, there can be no guarantee that free market exchanges work to the greatest good for the greatest number.

The final challenge to the claim that the free market is the best means points out that the market is unlikely to lead to the maximization of happiness because not everyone's interests will get represented in the market. Specifically, in practice individuals with less money will have less of an opportunity to participate in the market. With less opportunity, there is less likelihood that their interests will be satisfied. Hence, so critics claim, unless markets are somehow adjusted to offset the advantages of wealth, there can be no guarantee that markets will maximize overall happiness. This point, of course, not only raises problems concerning the effectiveness of the market as a means but also raises serious problems about the fundamental fairness of the ends of the market as well.

The Free Market Achieves the Best Ends

Even if we assume that a free market could achieve its goal of maximally satisfying preferences, we need to consider if this end is a legitimate ethical goal. Many critics, both those who defend other versions of utilitarianism and those who reject all utilitarian theories, charge that it is not. There are three general problems with the utilitarian claim that the free market attains the ethically best end: measurement, character, and ends and means problems.

Measurement Problems Because utilitarianism necessarily involves a process of measurement and comparison, it requires that the good be the kind of thing that can be measured and quantified. How else can one determine if the good has been maximized unless there is a way of measuring more or less? Unfortunately, while a great deal of clever work has been done by defenders of this theory, this may be an insurmountable problem.

First, there is the problem of quantifying some goods. What we often call "quality" of life issues—precisely to distinguish them from "quantifiable" goods—can be overlooked by the market version of utilitarianism. Can we measure happiness? Can we compare the happiness of two different people? How do we measure pleasure? Are all desires equal, so that my desire for friendship is equivalent to your desire for a new CD player? As difficult as these questions are, utilitarianism must provide answers to them if it is to have any practical content at all.

Defenders have developed answers, of course. Bentham, for example, presented what he called a "hedonistic calculus" for quantifying pleasures: We can measure pleasure in terms of intensity, duration, likelihood of producing other pleasures, and so forth. Likewise, defenders of the market will claim that "willingness to pay" (as measured by an object's *price*) is an appropriate way of comparing desires. My willingness to pay more for a college education than for a stereo shows that I value education more than I value listening to music. The fact that I am willing to pay more for a piece of property than my neighbors shows that I value it more and hence that happiness will be increased more by my getting it than by my neighbors getting it.

Nevertheless, critics charge that such measurement misses important quality of life desires. The old adage that "you can't put a price on happiness" rings true, not only about happiness, but also about such things as health, life, love, friendship, and nurturing children. Just as the value of a college education cannot be measured by such things as a grade point average, so, too, such things as respect for life cannot be measured by such things as infant mortality rates or average life spans. Nor can health be measured by doctors per capita, or per capita spending on health care. Perhaps the ultimate utilitarian tendency in this regard is to treat an entire society's happiness in terms of gross national product or per capita income.

Second, there is the problem of determining the consequences of our acts for *everyone* who is affected by them. This is necessary because utilitarianism is concerned with the *overall* consequences of actions. Yet surely this is an impractical if not impossible requirement. Can we ever know everyone who will be affected by our acts? Or how they might be affected? Should we consider how our decisions might affect the happiness of our grandchildren? Should the pleasure and pain of animals count in our calculation?

Again, defenders have answers to these challenges, but they seem unconvincing. For example, it is common for economists to refer to "expected utility" when evaluating the consequences of some economic policy. Since we can never know the actual consequences before an action is taken, we can make judgments only in terms of something's "expected" utility. But this seems more a confession of the failure of utilitarianism than anything else. Since we can't know what is right (in terms of actual consequences), we must do the best we can and recognize that sometimes we'll do what is wrong (that is, when what is expected does not happen).

Another common strategy by utilitarian defenders is to limit the *range* of people who are factored into the utilitarian calculation. Critics charge that in practice utilitarians will artificially and arbitrarily limit the range of the calculation to, say, present-generation Americans, as when gross national product is used as the measure of some policy's effectiveness. But a consistent utilitarian calculation of the overall good should include all people affected, including future generations and people living outside of present political boundaries. Since such calculations are difficult at best, utilitarians have a tendency to restrict their theory to consequences that can easily be measured. This, critics charge, is a serious flaw of the utilitarian goal in practice, if not in theory.

Virtue Ethics: Good Acts and Good People

When we think about ethics, especially within the context of a field like business ethics, it is easy for us to concentrate on questions like "What should I do?" "How should I act?" After all, normative ethics is concerned with the norms of ethical behavior. In doing normative ethics, we often look for a rule or principle that will answer these questions and guide our actions. Thus, utilitarianism answers by telling us to "act so as to maximize the overall good." Kantian ethics (to be considered in Chapter Three) tells us to "treat people as ends, never as means only."

But there is an older tradition in ethics that deemphasizes the place of rules or principles for guiding behavior and, instead, looks to the *character* of the person. "Virtue ethics," associated primarily with the ancient Greek philosopher Aristotle, asks not "What should I do?" but rather "What kind of person should I be?" In this way the challenge of ethics is not to defend rules, but to describe the characteristics of the ethically good (or bad) person. "Virtues" are those traits of character that promote human well-being; the "vices" are those character traits that thwart human well-being.

The language of virtues and vices might seem foreign or old-fashioned to many of us, but with just a little thought we see that we experience a wide range of virtue-talk everyday. We commonly speak of honest, courageous, loyal, trustworthy people. Likewise, we are all familiar with arrogant, selfish, self-righteous, envious people. In the Aristotlean tradition, the virtues were understood as an appropriate mean between two extremes: The virtue of courage was a mean between the vices of cowardice and foolhardiness; the virtue of compassion was a mean between a cold-hearted disregard and a patronizing pity for others. This tradition speaks of other virtues such as wisdom, moderation, justice, loyalty, and self-respect. The Christian tradition speaks of the virtues of faith, hope, and charity. Even the Boy Scouts have their list of virtues: A scout is trustworthy, loyal, helpful, friendly, kind, courteous, obedient, thrifty, brave, clean, and reverent.

Do we need the virtues for business ethics? Some commentators believe that virtue ethics adds nothing that cannot be accomplished through the use of rules. For example, to promote the virtue of honesty is, in this view, simply to follow the rule that one ought to tell the truth. However, there are some good reasons for us not to ignore the virtues in our discussion of business ethics.

First, it is worthwhile never to forget the primary question of virtue ethics: "What kind of person should I be?" Self-examination of our own character traits and habits is always an important aspect of living an ethical life. This can be particularly important when we find ourselves in institutions and roles, as we often do in the

Character Problems A second group of problems for the utilitarian goal of maximizing happiness considers the effects that this goal will have on the character of the people who adopt it. When judging an ethical theory, we should ask not only what the theory does *for* human beings (for example, provides us with a more pleasurable or happy life), but what it does *to* human beings. If we guide our decisions and social policy by a particular ethical theory, we should recognize that our own attitudes, beliefs, and values will in turn be shaped by the society created by that theory. What kinds of people are produced, encouraged, created, shaped, molded by the society? What does utilitarianism, particularly the version that justifies free market economics, do to people affected by it?

Consider an individual who sought to be a consistent utilitarian. Would a consistent utilitarian be a good person? In general, a consistent utilitarian would always be calculating the effects of her actions and adjusting her acts in light of those effects. Now consider what effects such calculation would have on some of the most important commitments and projects of our lives. A utilitarian's com-

workplace, where our behavior is governed by the rules and expectations of others.

Second, thinking of ethics solely in terms of rules can encourage us to understand ethics as some external force commanding our obedience. The rules seem "out there," distinct and separate from our own personal motivations and interests. (For example, a common view among social scientists is that moral development is simply the "internalization of external norms.") Like the law, ethical rules function to restrict us and prevent us from doing what we otherwise would want to do. But this kind of thinking creates serious difficulties. We face the challenge of motivating people to accept these rules. If we start with the assumption that ethical behavior is something that people are not already predisposed to do (since they need rules and laws to guide them), then we may be left with an unbridgeable gap between what the rules command and what people are inclined to do. By focusing on a person's character, virtue ethics addresses the very source of human motivation. The virtuous person does the ethically right thing because that's the kind of person she is. On this view, moral development is not a process of adopting or internalizing some external norms, but is a matter of teaching the right kinds of habits and dispositions.

Third, the virtues provide a very different perspective on ethical dilemmas and moral quan-

daries. When we begin with rules, it is tempting to assume that there is one correct and unambiguous answer to every moral dilemma. Faced with a difficult ethical choice, one simply takes the appropriate rule, applies it to the situation, and deduces the right answer. This very mechanical approach to ethics is common in many areas of applied ethics. This thinking no doubt is behind the development of "codes of ethics" within many corporations and professional associations. But of course life is seldom as simple as this model suggests, and ethical problems are unlike problem-solving in science and technology. A person who relies exclusively on rules (or a corporation that relies exclusively on a code of ethics) may despair when faced with a new ethical problem or with conflicting rules. A virtuous person, however, always has the strength of character—ingrained habits like compassion, courage, humility, honesty—to rely on in the face of difficult decisions.

It would seem wise to remember the role of virtues in ethics. On many occasions in this text, it will be insightful to step back from an issue and ask "What kind of person would act this way?" "What would an honest, or compassionate, or fair person do in this situation?" "What kind of person am I becoming?"

mitment to friends, family, spouse, community, or career would always be contingent upon good consequences. A person who says "I will be your friend as long as our friendship contributes to the overall good" is no friend. Imagine parents whose love for their children is contingent upon that love contributing to the overall happiness of society. We would say that such a person lacked integrity and was not a very good person at all.

Utilitarian defenders of the market might claim that they use utilitarian reasoning to justify only social practices like the free market and corporate responsibility, not as a general guide for every individual act. But remember that the classical model of corporate social responsibility also directs business managers to guide their decisions by one overriding principle: Maximize profits. All other social considerations are said to be secondary to this primary responsibility.

We are all familiar with examples of people who adopt such a single-minded devotion to profits. Remembering the so-called "yuppie" phenomenon of the 1980s and early 1990s, we should be conscious of the type of person we could become given an overriding commitment to the pursuit of profit. Alienation from family and friends, "burnout," and self-indulgence with drugs and alcohol are extreme examples of the failure to keep the pursuit of profits in perspective.

Of course, not all people who seek to maximize profits are as selfish or unhappy as this. Nevertheless, the free market version of utilitarianism can encourage us to think of our own good in terms of material well-being alone. After all, more is better. Furthermore, business managers directed to maximize profits will often face conflicting ethical and social commitments to family and community. Critics suggest that institutions that ask us to divorce ourselves from our own personal values and commitments are ethically suspect at best. Do we want to create social institutions that tell people that they can satisfy their social responsibilities by the single-minded pursuit of profit?

Ends and Means Problems A final problem strikes at the very heart of utilitarian thinking. Utilitarianism, remember, is concerned with maximizing the *overall* good. So, when a utilitarian decides how he should act, the only things that count in his calculation are the predicted consequences of the action. Whether a particular act is justified depends entirely on the expected results. Clearly, this purely consequentialist approach to moral decision-making reduces to accepting that the end justifies the means. Many people find this aspect of utilitarianism troubling.

Another way to explain this point is to recognize that we sometimes describe good people as acting out of a duty or on principle. There seem to be many cases in which we have a duty or an obligation to do something *even if* doing otherwise produces better results in terms of collective happiness. (Philosophers sometimes refer to this approach to ethics as "deontological," derived from the Greek word for "duty," to distinguish it from consequentialist theories like utilitarianism.) Truth-telling, keeping one's promises, treating other people with respect, honoring friendships, maintaining loyalty to one's family or country are some simple examples of acting out of a duty or acting on principle. In contrast, utilitarians always calculate the effects of their acts before deciding what to do— seemingly just the opposite of acting from a duty or according to principle. Utilitarians will always reserve their final evaluation of such duties, as they will of such central human interests as respect, freedom, and life, until all resultant consequences have been calculated.

Perhaps the most troubling aspect of this ends/means problem arises when we recognize that utilitarianism is concerned not just with consequences, but with consequences for *aggregate* or *collective* welfare. That overriding concern for collective happiness runs counter to the moral sensibilities of many people. Most of us are committed to the belief that some individual interests should be protected from actions aimed at improving the common good, that the good of the many is not always sufficient justification for sacrificing the interests of the few. In other words, the dominant contemporary picture of morality holds that individuals have *rights* that should not be sacrificed merely for marginal increases in the collective welfare (or simply to satisfy the preferences of a majority). This alternative, rights-based picture of morality regards at least some aspects of individuals as off-limits to utilitarian maximizing calculations.

An admittedly extreme example can highlight this point. In theory, nothing prevents the utilitarian from endorsing slavery of a minority if it can be shown that this would result in a net increase in the overall good. If a small minority were enslaved, it might increase the aggregate happiness, perhaps because it would be the most efficient means to ensure completion of undesirable but socially necessary work. Most of us, of course, would reject such a policy as unfair or unjust. We believe instead that each person possesses a dignity that prohibits him or her from being used solely as a means to the ends of others. It would be unjust to enslave people even if doing so would make the rest of society happier.

This rights problem arises especially for free market utilitarianism. Some utilitarians defend the free market because they believe that markets maximize the satisfaction of individual preferences. On this view, each preference equally deserves to be satisfied (at least insofar as they produce equal happiness). But critics will charge that not all preferences are morally equal. Sometimes what people prefer is silly or trivial; more importantly, sometimes it is unethical and unjust. Given this, it would seem unreasonable to hold that we should simply strive to maximize the satisfaction of preferences without first determining what they are preferences *for*. Certain preferences do not deserve satisfaction while others, such as desires for freedom, life, and family, deserve special protection because they are so closely tied to the inherent value of the individual. The mere fact that a free market could maximize aggregate preference satisfaction, then, would not be enough to prove that a free market policy is morally appropriate. One must also investigate the distributional impact of the market on the basic interests of individuals. Critics reject free market utilitarianism for the same reason they reject basic utilitarian cost/benefit calculation—because it focuses only on the overall good and ignores the rights of individuals.

Of course, utilitarians are aware of this challenge and have developed responses to the charge that they allow the ends to justify the means and that they fail to recognize individual rights. Some utilitarians suggest that the focus of utilitarian evaluation be shifted from assessing the consequences of individual actions (the traditional version of utilitarianism, known as "act utilitarianism"). Instead, they suggest that utilitarians should assess the overall consequences of social *practices* or *rules* (a version known as "rule utilitarianism"). Rule utilitarians claim that if we choose practices and rules that maximize overall happiness and judge individual acts according to their conformity to the approved practice or rule, then utilitarianism will be able to accommodate both the rights and the duties referred to earlier.

Consider, they argue, that if we defend the practice of promise-keeping because of its social utility (and the disutility of not being able to depend on the promises of others), we can condemn individual actions that break promises and uphold a general obligation to abide by our commitments. Hence, it seems that rule utilitarianism can account for a class of duties that act utilitarianism cannot.

They also suggest imagining that we assess the social consequences of a rule requiring respect for property. Surely, rule utilitarians argue, that rule would produce better consequences for collective happiness than would an alternative that made people constantly worry about the security of their possessions. Of course, such a property-respecting rule is the practical equivalent of a *right* to property.

The essence of the rule utilitarian argument, then, is that a concern for maximizing collective welfare requires that we encourage respect for individuals' rights. In this view, rights are valued not as ends in themselves, but as important or necessary means to ethical ends. Thus, rule utilitarians claim that their new version of utilitarianism can avoid the ends/means and rights criticisms leveled against more traditional versions of utilitarianism.

In spite of this clever utilitarian response, however, we believe that the ends/means and rights problems remain, even for rule utilitarianism. First, the general duties and obligations recognized by rule utilitarianism must allow for exceptions. To be consistent, rule utilitarians must determine what counts as an exception by determining whether, say, keeping or breaking a particular promise would maximize happiness. If happiness is marginally improved by allowing the exception to the rule in a particular case, then we would have no obligation to keep the promise in that case. However, since any given promise could conceivably be an exception, rule utilitarians will be forced to assess the consequences for each promise in order to determine if it is an exception to the general rule. The same will be true for other types of duties besides promise-keeping. So it appears that rule utilitarianism is no different than act utilitarianism because it too must assess the consequences of individual actions in order to determine what ought to be done.

Second, in any case, we need to question whether the purpose of a system of rights would adequately be captured under the rule utilitarian account. It is very odd, in fact, paradoxical, to believe that we want to protect some interests of persons from being sacrificed for the common good merely because by doing so we are maximizing the very same common good. An alternative account of why we believe in individual rights would stress them as necessary for expressing a commitment to persons as having inherent value and dignity. Such an individual-centered, respect-based account of rights seems more natural than arguing that rights are a means of achieving the greatest collective welfare. In the end, then, our judgment remains that the rule utilitarian response to the ends/means and rights problem is unconvincing.

IN SUMMARY

The ethical theory of utilitarianism advises us to calculate the consequences of our decisions and act in such a way that we maximize the overall welfare. Some versions of utilitarianism also maintain that a free market is the best economic and social arrangement for attaining this goal. However, significant challenges can be raised against this claim, both from within the utilitarian tradition and from alternative ethical perspectives.

Many utilitarians believe that a free market is neither a necessary nor sufficient means for attaining the maximum overall good. In more economic terms, many people now believe that a mixed economy, one that features both market mechanisms and government regulation and support, is more likely to produce a high standard of living. One important lesson from this is that utilitarians are committed neither to endorsing nor to rejecting market solutions for every issue. The question about what decision is most appropriate in a given case will depend on the specific consequences of that decision. What we have seen is that, even on utilitarian grounds, one cannot argue that market solutions are always the preferable alternative.

Challenges have also been raised against the ends of the market version of utilitarianism. Some utilitarians argue that preference satisfaction as it occurs within markets is not an appropriate ethical goal at all. Further difficulties arise for any attempt to measure the likely consequences of our actions. Finally, many people reject the utilitarian approach to ethics entirely. According to one alternative view, utilitarianism ignores important questions of ethical character and virtue. According to another alternative view, important human interests such as respect, freedom, and life (as well as our duty to honor these interests) should not be subject to utilitarian calculations. This approach to ethics holds that some human interests ought to receive special protection as individual rights. Even if free markets attained the maximum overall good, they would still be ethically flawed if they did not protect individual rights. In the next chapter, we examine this alternative, rights-based conception of ethics and critically examine how some versions of this approach have also been used to defend the workings of free markets.

STUDY QUESTIONS

1. What are the ethical and philosophical assumptions of utilitarians who support a free market economic system? What do they take as inherently valuable, and why do they believe that a free market will maximize this value?

2. What are the challenges to the view that free markets are the best means for attaining the overall good? Are you persuaded by these challenges? Why or why not?

3. Should the welfare of children be included in utilitarian calculations? How could these interests be represented in economic markets? Can, and should, markets take into account the welfare of future generations? of animals?

4. Consider the following roles and imagine how a consistent utilitarian would act in them: a judge in a criminal trial; a parent; a CIA agent; a lawyer; a minister.

3

Rights and the Market

The previous chapter considered utilitarian ethical theory and, in particular, the application of that theory in defense of a Friedman-like extreme free market view. We argued that utilitarianism provides insufficient justification for that free market view of management responsibility and government authority. The utilitarian defense failed because there were serious questions about whether an extreme "laissez-faire" approach would achieve maximal happiness. It also failed because that very goal of maximal happiness prevents us from giving adequate consideration to individual rights.

This chapter will present an alternative to utilitarianism by sketching an ethical theory that gives individual rights a place of primacy. In parallel with Chapter Two, this chapter will also consider attempts to use individual rights—in particular, the rights to liberty and property—to defend the extreme free market view. And, again paralleling the preceding chapter, this one will argue that rights-based defenses of that laissez-faire theory also fail.

We should reiterate here a caution about our argument. The phrase "free market" can mean many things. In criticizing arguments for the free market, we certainly do not intend to disparage the economic value of markets as mechanisms for allocating and pricing goods. We are critiquing only an extreme interpretation of the free market that holds that management should, aside from obligations to avoid fraud and coercion, be free from moral and legal constraints in its pursuit of profit. Instead, we will urge a view that allows the legitimacy of more limits on the pursuit of profit. Later chapters will provide opportunity for debate about just what those additional limits might be. Now, though, we turn to a discussion of rights and the market.

RIGHTS THEORY

Rights and Respect

As we saw in the last chapter, talk of rights arises as we attempt to express a belief about the inherent value of individuals. Most of us strongly hold that persons ought to be treated with dignity and respect. However, adopting a utilitarian, interest-maximizing perspective prevents us from giving that belief practical significance. Utilitarianism requires that we be willing to sacrifice any interest of any person, even the most basic, on the altar of collective welfare. At its heart, utilitarianism requires us to see persons merely as tools for achieving aggregate interest satisfaction. Individual persons under utilitarianism seem to have little inherent value. Their significance is mainly as loci for the interests that are to be satisfied or frustrated in pursuit of the greatest common good.

In the eighteenth century, Immanuel Kant suggested that the problem with aggregating, consequentialist theories was that they treated persons merely as means and not as ends in themselves. More recently, John Rawls has argued that utilitarianism fails to take seriously the distinction between persons. Perhaps this anti-aggregate perspective is most forcefully maintained by traditional religious moralities that hold each person to be created in the image of God and, for that reason, to have intrinsic worth.[*]

We cannot, then, claim to respect individuals if we are willing to do anything to them—for example, kill them, debase them, or enslave them—for the sake of some desired social goal. We can only give practical significance to the belief that persons deserve respect if we place some aspects of the person off limits. This is a primary function of rights: to protect some areas of a person's life from utilitarian or majority rule deliberations, or merely from the harmful acts of other individuals. A right to life aims to protect the person's life from others; a right to free speech aims to protect a person's ability to express an opinion even if others disagree with it.[†]

---

[*]Utilitarianism's failure to distinguish between persons also exists for political views that adopt a pure majority rule principle. That principle would allow a majority to adopt any policy, no matter how harmful to the interests of a few individuals.

[†]Some resist the idea that rights are protected interests because they find that exercising some rights would not be in the person's interests. Philosopher Virginia Held uses the example that I have a right to make a bet that I know I will lose. (Another philosopher friend describes life insurance as a bet you hope you lose!) We admit that not every exercise of particular rights will be in the individual's interests. Nevertheless, we also think there are still good reasons for linking rights and interests. First, what possibly could be the value of rights unless they were somehow tied to human interests? Second, examples such as the one above show merely that not every concrete instance of exercising a right is in the person's interests. That does not establish, however, that possessing the right is in general not in the interest of persons who hold it. Having the freedom to make bets could be in my interest even if a particular bet is not. Similarly, while some particular person may not have an interest in a particular right, this is of little significance since, as part of a broad social institution, rights must be linked to what are generally interests of persons.

In protecting interests from society or from other individuals, rights can be seen as entitlements or justified claims that impose obligations on others. In fact, there is a standard thesis about rights known as the "correlativity thesis." It maintains that all rights create obligations for some other party or parties. If I have a constitutional right to freedom from self-incrimination (as under U.S. law), I am entitled to refuse to testify at my own trial and the state is under an obligation not to punish me merely for that refusal. If I have a moral right to some property, my claim to possess and use it places other individuals under an obligation not to deprive me of that property. (In talking about rights it is usually important to identify specifically what claims or entitlements that right justifies and which other person or persons are placed under an obligation by the right.)

So we start with an intuition that persons deserve to be treated with dignity and respect, and we use rights to give that intuition some real, practical significance. This, however, only scratches the surface of a theory of rights. A more developed theory must also address a number of other questions in detail: What is the basis of this belief in the dignity of persons? If rights are to be seen as protecting interests, what interests of the person should be elevated to this protected status? For any given right, what is its limit or scope? For example, what specific entitlements are included in the right to property? What procedures, if any, are available when the rights of different persons conflict, as they inevitably will?

Here we will only outline answers to these questions. We cannot hope to provide a detailed and complete account in the few pages available. And, in any case, the answers we provide will be controversial. Philosophers disagree widely about how to understand rights. Nonetheless, we believe that the picture of rights that follows best accounts for our deep commitment to rights and best explains how rights actually function in our shared moral experience. We will leave it to the reader to evaluate whether our confidence in the account is warranted or misplaced.

Dignity and Autonomy

What gives rise to the intuition that persons deserve respect? Two answers present themselves. The first is that the intuition is just a basic tenet of our morality, a commitment that depends on nothing and is explained by nothing further. This answer, though possible, is not terribly satisfying. Usually we prefer to be able to explain our central beliefs, although, of course, explanation cannot go on to infinity. Moreover, if the belief in the dignity of persons is itself basic, we will not be able to integrate that belief into an account of what particular interests ought to be protected as rights, of what behavior the dignity of others requires from us.

In fact, a second answer is given by a historically important tradition running from the ancient Greeks to the medievals to contemporary moral theorists. That tradition finds the dignity of persons grounded in a peculiarly human attribute that philosophers have sometimes characterized as rationality, sometimes as free will. To unify these characterizations, we will identify this attribute as "autonomy." We define autonomy as the capacity to make reasoned, deliberative choices about how to act. This definition includes the human capacities of both reason and free will. It is interesting to note that explaining dignity by reference to autonomy parallels not only a long philosophical tradition but also many Western religious traditions that regard humans as created in the image of God. What could that mean other than having free will guided by reason?

If autonomy explains the belief in the dignity of persons, we have to ask what, in practical terms, it would mean to respect that autonomy. Certainly, it cannot mean allowing individuals complete control over their lives, absolute ability to act in any way they choose. That would be anarchy. More importantly, it would be impossible because allowing me to act as I want would inevitably prevent some others from doing what they wanted. This then is too strong an understanding of what is required by respect for autonomy.

Just as certainly, respect for a person's autonomy cannot mean merely allowing a person to have some formal choice available. This is too weak an understanding. It would mean that the behavior of a thief who sticks the barrel of a pistol in my ribs and says "Your money or your life" is behavior that is compatible with respect for my autonomy. (He gave me a choice, didn't he?) What is needed is some understanding of respect for persons that steers between anarchy and the meaningless and merely formal existence of choice.

What Rights?

Since it is unreasonable to allow unlimited latitude of action and insufficient merely to provide formal choices, we have to articulate what constitutes respect for a person and her autonomy in some other way. A promising alternative is to sketch a zone of autonomy that would allow a person to exercise a real opportunity to control her life. We could sketch such a zone if we protected a set of important interests (life, for one instance). With these interests not in jeopardy from society or from others, a person could have a secure space within which she could deliberate and act. Of course, threats to these interests cannot be completely removed. But if threats from other persons or from humanly alterable conditions (such as disease or abject poverty) can be minimized, capacities for choice would be substantially increased. This is true even if other persons occasionally violate the protection society tries to provide. Therefore, we can steer between anarchy and meaningless choice if we can identify a set of basic rights.

The crucial question then becomes, What interests ought to be protected? The interests must be important, not trivial. We could say that basic rights should be drawn from those interests whose enjoyment constitutes an adequate human life. To get any more specific than this will require some vision about the specific elements that constitute a decent human existence. Any attempt to completely describe "the human good" will be controversial, of course. But there are many elements of "the good" on which most will agree. Life is an undeniable element of human existence; protecting it would be a "no-brainer" selection. We might also say that a reasonable human life would require the minimal conditions of biological survival (food, clothing, shelter), or at the very least, the real opportunity to acquire them. In a less material vein, some will argue that other specific things are essential for a truly human life: freedom from threats of severe bodily harm by others; freedom to express one's opinions; the ability to collectively determine the conditions of a shared social system; freedom to associate with others of one's choosing; and freedom to exercise religious commitments. A number of these items are found in the U.S. Bill of Rights and/or the UN Declaration of Human Rights.

If interests such as these are protected—in other words, recognized as rights—persons would gain substantial control over their lives and, hence, be able to exercise their autonomy meaningfully. With no threat to my shelter or my physical security, I can more freely choose what to do. Alternatively, if I constantly must worry about my shelter or security, the courses of action open to me will be much more limited.

There is no denying that some of the items just identified as candidates for rights may be disputed, and the list is certainly incomplete. The point, here, is not to provide an exhaustive, uncontroversial catalog of basic rights. It is rather to indicate how one could argue for a right as basic by tying it to central human interests. Each of these interests is arguably constitutive of a decent human life, and violation of these interests cuts at the core of what it means to be a person. Consider the right to freedom of speech. If we regard persons as autonomous, as capable of deliberative choice about how to live their lives, we must regard the consideration of ideas as central to human life. Deliberation requires that we form opinions, consider criticisms of those opinions, and offer suggestions to others. This process demands that people be able to *express* their ideas, opinions, and criticisms to each other. Hence, some level of free speech is required if we are to properly respect persons as capable of directing their own lives.

We leave you to articulate more carefully how the other items mentioned might be core human goods and how interference with those might involve disrespect for an individual as a person. We also leave it to you to add (or subtract) from the list. We do that with a caution, however. The idea is to articulate how dignity, autonomy, and respect might be integrated into a picture of morality that reserves a central place for individual rights. This notion of respect is not the same as respect for an individual because of his or her position (your "elders") or power (on some streets you can "dis" someone merely by making eye contact). Respect in this account is respect for a person's humanity.

You should note, too, that this account of rights thus far only addresses core or basic rights. We need to recognize that there are other, lower-level rights as well. Relationships between rights of different levels is addressed in a later section, "Basic and Derivative Rights: Resolving Conflicts."

Scope of Rights

Identifying a list of core rights will raise further questions. Two are especially important, and the first is the topic of this section: What is the scope of each right? The second is the topic of the next section: What do we do when rights conflict?

When we speak of the scope of a right, we mean a specific list of the protections that are included. Since these protections by definition impose obligations on others, defining the scope of a right will also require us to specify just which other persons are obligated because someone else holds a particular right. So "scope" refers to both the specific protections and the specific audience the protections are addressed to.

Since this is what the scope of a right involves, no general, easy answer applies to the question, What is the scope of each right? The particular protections and audiences will depend on the right at issue. Take my right to life. Presumably it creates some obligation for *all* other people not to kill me. It also might obligate some smaller set of people to provide me positive assistance if my life is in danger (if, for example, I am in an accident, need CPR, and there is an emergency medical technician present at the scene). Also, the presumptive obligation not to kill might fail to exist for you if I am threatening your life while committing a crime against your person or property. Hence the scope of even a right to life will be difficult to identify in general terms. Additionally, the scope of a right will depend crucially on what other rights are in conflict and on how that conflict is to be adjudicated.

So we give no general answer to the question of the scope of rights. We caution, however, that the difficulty of detailing the scope of rights means neither that rights are empty of all content (as some critics have suggested) nor that any interpretation of the content of a right is as acceptable as any other. There will be clear cases where rights prohibit specific acts by others (your murdering me in retaliation for having to read this text) and clear cases where one's action falls outside of what one's rights entitle (falsely yelling fire in the proverbial crowded theater). Even in less immediately clear cases, there is the possibility that careful argument can provide a reasonable basis for concluding that something is either included or excluded from the scope of a particular right. In fact, later in this chapter we will present such arguments for the rights to liberty and property. Following chapters present arguments concerning the scope of other rights, such as the right to privacy for employees.

Finally, before leaving the issue of scope, we must address a common distinction relevant to deciding the scope of rights. Sometimes rights are said to impose merely obligations to refrain from harming the interests of others. Rights of this sort are called "negative rights." Other times rights are said to impose affirmative obligations to help secure another's interests. These rights are called "positive rights." One theory—too commonly held, from our perspective—suggests that all rights are negative, that is, that rights never require others to give positive assistance to the right holder. (This view is typically held by libertarians; it also has some affinity with Friedman's ideas about the limits of management responsibility.)

We believe that this limiting of all rights to negative rights is mistaken. First, as many have pointed out, the line between negative and positive rights is far from sharp. Henry Shue, for instance, shows that even classic negative interpretations of rights, such as the right not to be killed by others, require enforcement, which in turn requires a significant institutional apparatus.[*] For us to enforce the right not to be killed requires that we all make positive contributions to support institutions such as the courts and police. Thus, it is hard to believe that the rights of others merely oblige us not to harm them.

---

[*]Henry Shue, *Basic Rights: Subsistence, Affluence and U.S. Foreign Policy* (Princeton: Princeton University Press, 1980).

Second, if rights, at least core rights, are justified by the need to respect others, and if that respect requires that persons have a real opportunity to exercise their autonomy, then surely it seems contrary to the point of rights to allow an individual near us to starve when we have abundant food. If respect is defined in terms of conditions necessary for a decent human existence, then it is unlikely that rights are always negative, unlikely that rights never impose on us positive obligations to ensure that people have those conditions of a decent existence. Another's right to life may not require us to put our own life at risk, but surely it sometimes requires us to render positive assistance when we have the ability and the proximity, and are under no great risk ourselves.

The thesis that all rights are negative is unduly restrictive. We ought to reject it. We turn next to the second question regarding core rights: What do we do when rights conflict?

Basic and Derivative Rights: Resolving Conflicts

The rights people claim often conflict. For instance, the claim by an employer to a right to select the best possible worker from a list of job applicants, perhaps by using undisclosed background checks, may conflict with a potential employee's claimed right to privacy.

Resolving such conflicts requires that we have some procedure for ranking rights by importance because if all rights have exactly the same moral status, there is little hope of adjudicating conflicts. Conflicts will merely be cases of brute and irresolvable opposition. In that case, appeal to rights will be of little practical assistance in determining what we should do. Given the centrality of rights in modern moral discourse, moral debate will degenerate into the assertion of a list of proliferating rights to whatever people simply desire. (Some commentators believe that this is an accurate description of the state of morality in the late twentieth century: selfishness masking itself as moral discourse.)

The first step, then, is to construct some schema that allows us to place right claims into a hierarchy and that provides a rational process for settling conflicts. Once again, we do not suggest that the analysis we provide is without controversy or that it will easily and mechanically resolve all conflict. We do, however, believe that something like it is the best available procedure.

Until now, our focus has been on rights as the necessary antidote to the aggregating tendencies of utilitarianism and as a way of treating individuals with dignity and respect. A moment's reflection reveals that not all right claims familiar in our culture are tied to respect for the person, however. Intuitively, the legal right to drive a car does not have the same status as the constitutional right to free speech. So, as a start in understanding how moral rights might be rank-ordered, let's consider the relationships between legal rights.[*]

---

[*]This analysis of rights depends on that provided by philosophers Ronald Dworkin and Jeffrie Murphy. See: Ronald Dworkin, *Taking Rights Seriously* (Cambridge: Harvard University Press, 1977); and *A Matter of Principle* (Cambridge: Harvard University Press, 1985); and Jeffrie Murphy and Jules Coleman, *Philosophy of Law: An Introduction* (Boulder, Colo.: Westview Press, 1990).

Moral and Legal Rights

When we talk about rights, we need to keep in mind that rights can be legal or moral. As rights, both legal and moral rights share the same function—to protect individual interests by entitling the right holder to act in a certain way (for example, a right to freedom of religion) or possess something (for example, a right to property). The sets of legal and moral rights also often have overlapping membership; in a decent society, we would expect the overlap to be considerable. In spite of these similarities, legal and moral rights differ.

The most significant difference between the two sets of rights lies in the differing conditions for membership in the respective sets. Legal rights are those protections and entitlements that derive from the principles and rules of the legal system. (Some suggest that legal rights are those rights that are enforced by the law. That is mistaken, however, since it makes sense to say that a citizen has a right to free speech in a given case where the government does not enforce it, and may even violate it.) Legal rights can be entitlements created by acts of legislatures (the right to apply for a driver's license at age 16), by contractual agreements between parties (my right to be paid by my employer), or by a constitution (the right to freedom from unwarranted search and seizure). A new legal right can also be created (or recognized?) by the courts when they interpret the Constitution or a particular statute (the right to privacy). In this last category we might say that the newly acknowledged right was always implied by the principles or rules of the law but has only recently been recognized and enforced by the courts.

Many believe that legal rights are easier to identify than moral rights since they are the products of clear legal rules. While this may be true of some legal rights created by statute (my right to deduct the interest paid on a home mortgage from my taxes), other legal rights require significant interpretation and reference to background legal history or political theory before they can be identified. Arguments for the existence of those legal rights can often be as

Consider the following three legal rights: the right to free speech, the right to privacy, and the right to deduct from my taxable income the interest paid on my home mortgage. Each of these is an existing legal right, and each is recognized for different reasons. The differences in their underlying justifications will give the three rights different status or importance. We have already seen that the right to free speech can be directly tied to respect for the person since speech and the exchange of ideas is an integral part of what we take a person to be. In a political context, free speech also has great instrumental value in that civil liberties and democratic institutions are more secure when people have a right to express their grievances against the government. A right to speech free from government censorship, as enshrined in the First Amendment of the U.S. Constitution, has extremely strong foundations.

The right to a mortgage deduction, created by statute of the Congress, has much less significant foundations. That right was created to encourage home ownership and to stimulate the critical housing industry. Its primary purpose is to create economic benefits such as greater employment that can be shared throughout the society. While the benefits are real, the justification for the legal right is that it is one among a number of instruments for promoting the collective welfare. This right, then, is not tied to respect for the person but rather to a utilitarian calculation that it is beneficial policy.

obscure as any argument for moral rights.

Moral rights are those protections or entitlements that derive from the principles and the rules of a moral system. When enforced, it is often through subtler sanctions than those found in the criminal law. For example, violators of moral rights can be subject to rebuke and social disapproval that range from mild expressions of disdain to being shunned (as in the Amish practice of refusing all social interaction) or being treated as a social pariah.

Moral rights can come in a variety of forms as well. They can be special rights created by the actions of others (the right of a spouse to fidelity by his or her partner); they can be rights inherent in a particular role that one occupies (the right of parents to choose how to educate their child); or they can be rights possessed by all persons equally (the right to life).

Clarifying exactly which category of rights we have in mind can help us avoid some confusions. Some apparent disagreements between parties about the existence of a right might be easily resolved if the parties understood that one is asserting a legal right while the other denies that there is a moral right. Clarity about whether rights are legal or moral may also help us understand some cases where we say, "You have a right to do that but you shouldn't." I have a legal right to drive at twenty miles an hour on a two-lane highway with a posted speed limit of 55 mph, but perhaps I shouldn't morally if doing so needlessly delays scores of other drivers.

Of course, we can also say that a moral right should not be exercised if there are weighty moral reasons against exercising it. Maybe I shouldn't tell my boss what I think of him if that jeopardizes my ability to provide for my child. That is, having a moral (or legal) right to do something does not automatically make your doing it right—in other words, make it correct or appropriate behavior. Rights are important in morality, but they are not always the only or the last word on a topic, especially when they are lower-order rights.

The right to privacy also has instrumental value but of a different sort. It promotes individual autonomy by reducing chances that a person can be controlled by blackmail or manipulation. It provides a sense of security by helping people consider particular relationships as more intimate than others because they can control what personal information is shared with others. Privacy thus has instrumental value, to be sure, but what it promotes is of greater moment than an incremental increase in collective welfare. We might reasonably see privacy as falling between the other two rights in its importance.

These examples show that legal rights can be hierarchically ordered according to their underlying justifications. Some rights are based directly on the need for respect, some are based only on their instrumental value, and some, such as free speech, are based on both of these foundations.

A similar analysis can be given for moral rights. In fact, the justifying reasons for speech and privacy rights are weighty enough from a moral perspective for those to be moral rights as well. In any case, the import of the preceding account of legal rights is that it suggests a method for ordering rights whether they be legal or moral. We can categorize rights by looking to the values underlying them. The different types of justifying reasons (respect, utility, and so on) provide us with a rough schema that allows us to distinguish between what we will call "basic rights" and other nonbasic or "derivative rights." Basic rights are ones whose recognition is essential for individuals to be treated with dignity and respect. (Obviously, as was noted earlier, determining which rights are basic will require some vision of the elements that constitute an adequate human life.) Derivative rights usually depend for their importance on an instrumental contribution towards achieving some other good. Although derivative rights are not tied essentially to respect, they could nonetheless be very important in that the goods they help to secure may be of great significance. The right to privacy, as previously analyzed, is one example. Freedom of the press would be another derivative right of great importance since it is instrumental in protecting other, more basic rights. However, at least some derivative rights are clearly less important because they are granted merely to promote some desired social goal or policy.

Some derivative rights have their origins in the particular positions or relationships of an individual. For instance, presidents have the legal right to veto legislation. Parents have morally recognized rights to discipline their children. I have a moral right that my friend fulfill his promise to me.

This proposed method for categorizing rights by their foundational justifications provides a clue about how to resolve conflicts between right claims. If, after analyzing the relative justifications of two competing rights, we find that the rights are of different levels (basic vs. derivative; derivative but crucial vs. derivative and less compelling), the presumptive conclusion would be that the higher-level right takes precedence. This is, however, only a presumptive conclusion since questions about the scope of the rights might complicate matters. For instance, in the abstract, a right to free speech takes precedence over matters of mere convenience. But extending the right to free speech to cover a particular case might not promote the underlying values and could cause great inconvenience. Consider if a right to free speech included a right to express political opinions by parading down the center lane of an urban expressway at rush hour. Obviously, restrictions on the time, place, and manner of speech might be justified in the name of convenience, especially when other effective avenues of expression are available. Thus, with conflicts between higher-order rights and lower-order rights, final conclusions about which right takes precedence must await more careful analysis of individual cases.

The need for such careful analysis is even more crucial when conflicting rights are of the same level or have the same foundations. When two claimed rights rest on the same moral grounds, a defense for the priority of one over the other must show that, in the given case, the justifying values are more centrally at stake in the one taking priority. To put this point another way, when two such rights conflict, we must decide which right to restrict by asking which restriction would least damage the values that underlie the rights.

Consider a business-related case. Owners of corporate property claim a right to control that property, including a right to control who has access to it. Employees claim a right not to be fired unjustly or arbitrarily. Both right claims can be supported by appeals to fairness, utility, and autonomy. (Detailed discussion of these justifications will come later in this chapter and in Chapter Five.) If employers' rights to control access include the right to hire and fire anyone for any reason (as had been the case in the United States until recently), then their rights would conflict with the rights claimed by employees. We have to decide this conflict by asking which does greater damage to the values of fairness, autonomy, and utility: (1) allowing owners the right to fire at will and not allowing workers the right to be free from arbitrary dismissal or (2) restraining the ability to fire at will by granting the employees a right to be fired only for just cause. We leave the answer to that question open. (It is one major theme of Chapter Five.) What we emphasize is that resolving conflicts between rights of the same level requires us to look to the underlying foundations of the rights and to determine which right to limit by asking which limit least harms those values.

So while there are compelling reasons for introducing talk of rights into our moral discussions, introducing them into the debate does not make moral analysis any easier. Identifying which right claims are legitimate ones, defining the scope of particular rights, and resolving conflicts between rights are not simple tasks. Each requires that you carefully analyze the reasons justifying a right claim. In fact, if there is any single lesson that is most important in our discussion of rights, it is that we always need to clarify the foundations of right claims before there is any hope of progress in contemporary moral debate. Clarity about foundations will help us sort out those right claims that are frivolous and help us evaluate conflicts between those that are not.

A major note must be made about the procedure of ethical analysis we have proposed. The procedure is not algorithmic. Steps in the analysis will be open to debate and will involve value judgments in the assessments of the relative importance of rights. What the process of analysis provides is a framework for reasonable debate between opposing points of view. Without such a framework, those most pessimistic about our ethics are probably right: Ethical debate reduces merely to a conflict of wills. Under those circumstances, debate about issues in business ethics will not be reasonable deliberation but mere assertion of opinion. Careful analysis of moral concepts along the lines of our suggestions will help avoid that result. Now that we have the necessary analytical tools, we can turn to a discussion of rights-based defenses of the free market view.

RIGHTS ARGUMENTS
FOR THE FREE MARKET

It has been more than a few pages since we last addressed the free market view of business responsibility. It might be helpful at this point to review what that position involved. What we are dubbing the "free market view" is an extreme position that claims two things: (1) management is responsible only for maximizing profits without using fraud or coercion, and (2) government regulation of business is acceptable only when necessary to prevent fraud or coercion. We will not reiterate the reasons for calling this view extreme. We will, however, remind students that along a spectrum of positions about the degree to which markets may be properly constrained, the free market view as defined here is at one extreme. It accepts very few constraints, whether legal or moral, on the behavior of persons in the market-place. We should also reiterate that to challenge the free market view is not to re-ject the value of markets. Rather, it is to suggest that markets best serve the purposes of human societies when they are subject to some limitations.

For the remainder of this chapter we will consider two common rights-based arguments for the free market approach to corporate responsibility. The first ar-gues that the free market is required in order to respect individuals' rights to lib-erty. The second argues that the free market view is the only view compatible with a recognition of a right to private property.

These two respective rights play a major role in contemporary Western moral-ity, and they deserve careful attention. In the following pages we consider both of these arguments for the free market by applying some of the analytical tools de-veloped earlier. We suggest that both arguments fail because both inadequately understand the rights they appeal to. The presumptive conclusion we draw is that there are strong reasons for thinking that any morally defensible view of business responsibility must accept many more responsibilities than the free market posi-tion does. Just what those responsibilities are will be left for the issue-oriented debates of Chapters Five through Fourteen.

The Right to Liberty and the Market

One straightforward argument for the laissez-faire view starts with a right that is familiar in the rhetoric of our culture—a right to liberty. Traditionally, the right to liberty is understood to be a right to be free from human interference in one's pursuits. If we acknowledge such a right, it is easy to generate an argument for the free market: If individuals have a right to an absence of interference in their affairs, then they should be free to engage in any voluntary (in other words, non-coercive, nondeceptive) economic transactions they wish to enter. Similarly, gov-ernment should respect liberty by regulating only to ensure that transactions are free and nondeceptive. According to this argument, a just society would be one where management was free to pursue profits and the government's role was lim-ited to maintaining free and open competition.

Whether this argument succeeds will depend on whether we accept the gen-eral right to liberty with which it starts. Certainly, in our society there is a great attraction to the idea of a general right to noninterference. The free and indepen-dent individual is a character who plays a major role in our national mythology. But equally certain, any legitimate understanding of a right to liberty must admit that liberty cannot be absolute and unrestrained. This is for at least two reasons. First, an absolute right to liberty would result in social chaos. The conditions of any social life demand that sometimes people must be prevented from doing what they want.

Second, the concept of an absolute right to liberty is a practical impossibility. If I have an absolute right to be free in my pursuits and one of my pursuits is to steal your car, then you cannot have an absolute right to noninterference in your continued possession of the car.

In fact, interferences are an unavoidable and sometimes unobjectionable ele-ment of economic transactions. (I would always rather pay less for a product and, hence, I am often prevented from getting what I want.) Since interferences are unavoidable and sometimes unobjectionable, what we need is some approach to picking out those interferences that should be prohibited.

One traditional approach is to say that each of us ought to be able to do what we wish so long as we do not interfere with the liberty of others. This sounds nice but ultimately is of no help in specifically defining the limits of liberty because defining what my right to liberty includes will require that we already have an independent idea of what your right to liberty includes. The problem here is similar to the classic problem of using a word in the definition of that same word. So to say that my right to liberty allows me to do anything that does not violate the liberty of others is to say nothing in particular about what I am and am not allowed to do. We still need a principle that can tell us which interferences to prohibit and which to permit.

Another commonly used approach is to say that we will prohibit the greatest interferences. This will not help if "greatest" is understood in its usual quantitative sense. Quantitative judgments demand some unit of measurement. What is a unit of interference or of liberty? If we propose to measure liberty by the number of times a person is interfered with, we are likely to get counterintuitive results about which among a group of interferences is most objectionable. Which ban would cause the greatest number of interferences: a ban on Monday night football, Sunday beer sales, or Thursday religious services?

Any comparative evaluation of two interferences must look not to the quantity but to the quality of the interference. Making such a qualitative judgment requires that we look at the specific content of the interference and decide about the importance of what is being interfered with.*

Consider a number of examples to illustrate this point: Should we allow individual suburban homeowners the liberty of erecting ten-foot fences around their front lawns, or should we allow neighbors the liberty to set zoning ordinances requiring open vistas along streets? Should we allow private college fraternities and sororities the liberty to exclude minorities from membership, or should we allow every person, regardless of race and ethnicity, the liberty to apply for membership in any campus organization? Should we allow contemporary consumers the liberty of driving large and inefficient private autos, or should we allow future generations the liberty of access to more plentiful fossil fuels?

Obviously, any answer to these questions will result in a limit on someone's liberty. Limits on liberty are the unavoidable consequence of living with others. Also, no matter what side of these debates you come down on, it should be clear that the solution to the debate does not involve "measuring" liberty. Rather, our opinions on these issues are driven by beliefs about the qualitative importance of liberty in certain areas of life. Decisions about what interferences are legitimate, then, are decisions specifying areas of human conduct that ought to remain open to individual choice. In deciding to protect ourselves from interference in these areas, we will be forced to define what interests are most basic and central to human life. As a consequence, it makes little sense to speak of a "general right to

---

*See Dworkin's *Taking Rights Seriously,* Chapter 12, "What Rights Do We Have?"

Capitalism and Democracy

Issues in business ethics invariably involve questions about social and political structures. In fact, the root idea of this textbook is that an adequate understanding of business's responsibility can be achieved only with careful attention to social and political theory. Unfortunately, our culture often shows a damaging lack of precision about core social and political concepts. That lack of precision is perhaps most damaging when it affects the very definition of the basic political and economic institutions: capitalism and democracy.

Capitalism is an economic system characterized by private ownership of the "means and resources of production"—productive property such as businesses and raw materials. Typically, capitalist economic systems make generous use of markets as instruments for distributing and pricing goods, allocating resources, and setting wage rates. Capitalist systems can range from laissez-faire approaches to ones that involve significantly more state regulation of the economy. Our economic system in the United States is a state-regulated variant of capitalism.

The dominant alternative to capitalism is socialism. It is characterized by public ownership of productive property. Usually, socialist economies execute the idea of public ownership through state control over production. There are, however, variations of socialism just as there are

for capitalism. Some socialist economies are like the old Soviet system, with centralized state planning of all major productive enterprises from agriculture to heavy industry. A decentralized (or worker-controlled) form of socialism would, however, have the state merely set broad monetary and fiscal policies and be the nominal owner of businesses. Those who work in the business, though, are given collective authority to determine such things as production levels, pricing strategy, and product diversification.

It is also important to note that both capitalism and socialism are compatible with the existence of markets to help allocate resources and set prices. Under either approach, what factories produce still must be sold and products that do not sell will influence what is later produced. This is particularly true of decentralized socialism. The defining difference between the systems, then, is a matter of ownership patterns and not a matter of the existence of markets. (A different definition of socialism is operative when people refer to socialist economies as those that are more or less egalitarian in the distribution of income, perhaps through progressive taxation and generous funding of what Americans call welfare benefits. Sweden might be a prime example. We need to be cautious not to confuse these two definitions since welfare socialism is certainly

liberty." We must reject a view of liberty as one undifferentiated right and instead recognize that liberty is really a set of rights to specific liberties. (The Founding Fathers were more sophisticated than many contemporary Americans in that they recognized this point and, in the Bill of Rights, enumerated specific liberties that are crucial.)

Accordingly, the argument for the laissez-faire theory of business responsibility that depends on a general right to liberty must be rejected as unsound. It rests on an untenable understanding of liberty. It is only when we see liberty as many separate rights that we can profitably discuss how and when freedom of choice can legitimately be limited. Any cogent liberty defense of the free market must depend, then, on the value of the specific economic liberties that the laissez-faire view proposes.

How central to human life is the good of unhindered, laissez-faire economic activity? Some have argued that production (economic activity) is a characteristic human activity and that it, therefore, ought to be protected. From this we might derive a universal right to employment (as does the UN Charter of Human

possible even with private ownership of capital.)

Capitalism and socialism are economic systems. Democracy, in contrast, is a political system. It is defined as a system that grants the citizens sovereign political power. Typically it operates on a principle of majority rule. Democracy can be direct, as in ancient Greece, or representative, as in modern large states. Democracy can also be limited democracy in that the power of the majority to affect policy is limited by constitutionally guaranteed liberties given to citizens. For example, the First Amendment of the U.S. Constitution says that Congress (the legislative arm of the majority) "may make no law...prohibiting the free exercise" of religion. Alternatives to democratic political structures include monarchy, dictatorship, oligarchy, and the like.

What are the relationships between capitalism and democracy? Conceptually, there is no relationship. That is, nothing in the definition of democracy requires that it be associated with capitalist, private ownership economic systems. The same is true in reverse; nothing about the definition of capitalism requires that it be linked to democracy.

Historically, however, there has been a significant factual relationship between the two. Most modern democracies have capitalist economies. Most socialist economies have had decidedly undemocratic political systems. (Note, however, that many capitalist countries are not democratic. Consider recent Latin American capitalist nations: Nicaragua under Somoza; Chile under Pinochet; Cuba before Castro.)

The implications of this historical correlation are unclear. It seems true that the emerging economic power of independent artisans helped create the conditions in which modern Western democracies arose from monarchies. Some take this to show that private spheres of economic power are practically essential for maintaining democratic political freedoms. They fear that public ownership by the state would remove forces that help keep modern bureaucratic democracies from turning into all-powerful Leviathans.

Others, notably democratic socialists, argue that the real contemporary threat to healthy democracy comes from the power of concentrated capital to shape the political process to its own ends. Democratic socialists fear that it is the fact that the top 1 percent of the population owns 42 percent of the wealth in the United States that constitutes the true threat to democratic rule. They argue instead that public ownership would promote democracy, especially in nations where democracy and civil liberties have become deeply ingrained in the political culture.

Rights). Nevertheless, a laissez-faire right to be free from government regulation or broader management responsibilities does not seem to be required even if productive activity is central to human life. We could, of course, engage in productive activity without having an extensive laissez-faire economic liberty.

Moreover, allowing a right to such economic liberty would place other goods at the mercy of market bargaining power and, therefore, would effectively undermine the attempt to protect them from threat. Without coercing or defrauding, an ethnically biased WASP management might refuse to promote a Jew into a position of authority. A politically conservative management might dismiss an employee who spoke in favor of liberal causes. (In our current non-laissez-faire climate, the first action would be illegal under the Civil Rights Act. Interestingly, however, the second would not be a violation of the First Amendment right to freedom of speech. Courts have almost unanimously held that, since the constitutional prohibition pertains to acts by the government, private employers' retaliation for disfavored political speech is not unconstitutional.)

There is reason to believe, then, that threats to the effective enjoyment of important civil liberties can arise not just from government action. The laissez-faire system itself could threaten the effective exercise of these civil liberties since an extreme economic liberty makes it impossible to protect other liberties. (This point can be generalized to show that extreme liberty in one area can always make protecting liberty in other areas more difficult.)

Protecting basic liberties requires us to achieve a balance between free economic activity and legal or moral limits on corporate behavior. Thus, a real guarantee of important liberties demands broader government authority and management responsibility than the free market view is willing to accept. The free market view is supported neither by an appeal to a general right to liberty nor by an argument that a specific laissez-faire economic liberty ought to be recognized as on a par with basic liberty rights. A rights-based defense of the free market must look to other rights for support, then.

Private Property Rights and the Market

There is another argument in the arsenal of laissez-faire theorists, even if the liberty arguments fail to convince. Proponents of the extreme free market view of business responsibility and government regulation often claim that theirs is the only view compatible with a right to private property. The argument runs as follows: Property rights, if they mean anything, mean that the owner of property should be free to control that property. Ethical constraints and government regulation interfere with that control and are thus inconsistent with a belief in private property.

Stated so boldly, this argument is unlikely to convince anyone. We all, even laissez-faire theorists, recognize the need to limit the ability of property owners to determine what they will do with their property. (Laissez-faire theorists, by definition, will disapprove of any uses of property that are coercive or fraudulent.) The issue before us is what are the proper limits on the power of owners to control property? A particular instance is the emerging debate over federal environmental regulations such as the "wetlands" rules. Some claim that these regulations are illegitimate government "takings" of property because the rules limit the owner's ability to develop the property and because they reduce the market value of the land. Others find that the regulations are within the proper authority of government to protect the health and safety of citizens by ensuring clean water supplies.

Since the failings of the previous liberty arguments arose from an inviable understanding of the right to liberty, perhaps we ought to begin this analysis with some attention to the nature and justification of private property rights.

Traditionally, a "right to private property" has been understood as a shorthand expression for a set of more specific rights, all having to do with control over goods. Under this umbrella, a right to private property means a right to possess something, use it, benefit from it, exclude others from using or benefitting from it, dispose/sell it, and so forth. Having a private property right to something means that an individual is entitled to exercise control over it in the ways specified and that others have obligations not to interfere with that control.

Most contemporary political theorists, even those of a socialist stripe, are willing to accept the legitimacy of some private property rights. Disagreements arise over what kinds of things can be privately owned (socialists reject private ownership of *productive* resources; some religions reject private ownership of species and patents for genetically engineered "stock") and over the scope of each of the rights in the bundle. The issue between proponents and critics of laissez-faire is the scope of the rights to possess, use, exclude, dispose, and so on. Free market theorists understand private property rights as an entitlement to do anything with one's property except coerce or defraud. To see whether this is a viable understanding of property rights we need to follow our suggested method of analysis and identify the reasons offered to justify private property rights.

We obviously cannot catalog every possible justification of private property that might be offered. We will, however, briefly discuss what are probably the three most historically significant arguments for property. In fact, variations of these arguments can be found in Adam Smith and John Locke, the respective intellectual sources of our economic and political systems. The three arguments are based on utility, autonomy, and fairness.

1. *Utility.* This defense of property asserts that allowing people to privately own goods expands the economic product of the society and increases collective welfare. If we allow people to acquire goods through work or investment, that will provide the incentive needed for increasing levels of productivity and output. Alternatively, if we do not allow people to accumulate property, they will have little reason for working hard. (A major complaint about centralized socialist economies was that there was little economic incentive for workers or management to produce since rewards were not tied to levels of output.) Hence, a private property system will generate more jobs, more goods, and more wealth for the society to enjoy. Recognizing private property rights is a wise utilitarian policy.

2. *Autonomy.* Ever since the days of John Locke, private property has been seen as a way of preserving autonomy. On one hand, if the material conditions of our lives depend on the largesse of others, as the feudal serfs' lives depended on their lords, we are less able to exercise our autonomy. (Compare the job situation of most American workers!) On the other hand, if individuals have the security provided by a base of material goods (land, money, housing), then they can be much more independent. In fact, the economic independence of the nobility and the emerging artisan class is seen as one major factor in the decline of monarchy and the development of democracy in Europe. Privately held goods are thus instrumental in promoting the ability of persons to speak and act independently.

3. *Fairness.* Locke also provided the germ of a fairness argument for private property. Locke explained that private rights to possess goods were created when an individual "mixed his labor with nature." He suggested that if I clear an unowned plot of land, till it, plant it, tend and harvest the crops, then it is only fair that I be given rights to the harvest I reap. (At least. One might also suggest that I also gain rights to the land since my labor made it into productive property.) We can imagine any number of contemporary variations of

Locke's labor theory of property, but the main point is constant: Private property rights are the fair return for one's productive labor.

The Laissez–Faire Conception of Property Given these historically powerful justifications of private property, we seem to be on firm ground in accepting the legitimacy of private property. Such rights are clearly in our derivative category inasmuch as they depend on their instrumental contributions to other values. Accepting private property as legitimate, however, still leaves plenty of questions about the scope of those rights. One of those questions is ours about the range of control that property rights confer on owners. Should the rights to use, exclude, and so on be so strong as to allow owners to do anything but coerce or defraud?

That question, we believe, is answered by the preceding justifications of property. And it is answered in the negative. The exercise of a right needs to be compatible with the underlying justifications of that right. If, for instance, we accept a right because it promotes fairness, that very rationale will place limits on how the right may be exercised. The right holder ought not to be allowed to act unfairly under the guise of the right since that action would undermine the very foundation of the right. We find that laissez-faire conceptions of property are not compatible with the three traditional rationales.

The best way to show this is to consider instances of the more specific rights that make up the right to property. Under the laissez-faire picture of property, owners should be able to dispose of their property so long as they do not coerce or defraud. Is it possible that this extensive disposal right could be net harmful to society (incompatible with utility)? Suppose I dispose of toxic materials, say old lead containing batteries, on my farm. Suppose I revealed this fact to my neighbors and compensated them as they requested for any risk posed. Suppose also that I disclose the fact to buyers and lower my asking price when I sell the farm. I have not deceived nor coerced anyone, yet I have acted in a way that is arguably net harmful to overall social utility of current and future generations. If property rights are grounded on considerations of utility, the laissez-faire conception of property is potentially incompatible with that justification.

The laissez-faire conception also has probable conflicts with the value of fairness in the scope that it admits for the right to exclude. A laissez-faire conception of corporate property would give owners and management a right to exclude employees from the workplace—in other words, fire them for any reason. If I, the employer, dismiss an employee, I am merely revoking the right of access that I temporarily granted to the employee. Since I can do this for any reason, I can do it for arbitrary and unfair reasons as well. Hence the laissez-faire conception runs counter to the fairness justification of property rights in that it permits those rights to be exercised unfairly.

Another example can illustrate the point further. The laissez-faire view allows employers to pay the smallest wage that the market will bear. No minimum wage would be morally or legally required. However, we think it obvious that some wages that the market allows are not fair return for one's labors. Pennies a day paid to Pakistani child weavers for long hours and hard work is not a fair wage.

Thus, the free market understanding of property has serious potential for under-mining another foundational value of the right to private property.

Finally, the laissez-faire view also has strong potential for conflict with the last remaining justifying value—autonomy. We have already seen in the previous section how an extreme economic liberty can jeopardize the effective enjoyment of core civil liberties that are crucial to personal autonomy. Additionally, the laissez-faire conception would permit concentrated accumulations of wealth that might allow a moneyed elite inordinate influence over the political process, thus threatening the autonomy that comes with real political democracy. (The usual response to this concern is that competitive markets will prevent monopolistic or oligopolistic developments. We do not find this comforting both on historical grounds and because competitive games tend to reward those with the largest initial stake.)

We conclude that the laissez-faire conception of property is inadequate because it has too great a potential for undermining the very values that make private property legitimate. Limiting owners' responsibility and government authority merely to prohibitions on fraud and coercion fails to ensure that private property systems achieve the goals of utility, autonomy, and fairness. Paying attention to these rationales for property rights reveals that acceptable approaches to property must recognize greater management responsibility and government authority.

The Alternative to Laissez-Faire   Before we close this discussion, we feel some responsibility to more clearly outline the alternative to laissez-faire that is implied in the preceding chapters. This alternative theory cannot be applied easily or mechanically. In fact, what our alternative advises about practical moral problems of public policy or individual choice will often be open to debate. We consider that a virtue, since the problems of the Friedman view or of a belief in a general right to liberty derive from their very simple and mechanical resolutions of complex moral problems.

Our alternative begins with a commitment to human dignity expressed in a belief that individuals have rights that should not be sacrificed merely for increases in the general happiness. Those rights are best understood as socially sanctioned protections for basic or important human interests. The interests that are worthy of protection include but are not limited to the interest in liberty. Other interests such as life, health, and privacy are also important, since liberty is of little significance when these others are jeopardized. Thus, the social and governmental institutions ought to be designed in ways that balance the importance of these interests and that treat the respective interests of each person fairly.

Achieving such a balance is not an easy task. It requires careful attention to the relationships between various rights. It requires us to determine the rationale for commonly claimed rights, such as property. It requires us to decide, when interests and rights conflict, which is based on the more central value and which should take precedence.

No simple answers can be given to these questions in advance. But any acceptable answers must admit that liberty and its underlying value of autonomy

How (and How Not) to Make Moral Decisions

Ethics has a poor reputation for the "wooliness" of its discussions, especially among people who imagine their own professional decisions are guided by clear, unambiguous procedures. We admit that moral decision-making is not algorithmic or mathematical; we also suspect that those business decisions that are deemed "objective" depend more on "wooly" value assumptions than their less reflective practitioners realize. In any case, the fact that moral judgments are not the determinate conclusions of mathematically certain deductions should not be taken to indicate that there is no process of moral analysis that can lead us to more reliable conclusions. We offer the following process as a start for those who want to make their moral decisions more systematic.

WHAT TO DO, PART I
1. *Get clear on the facts*. Morality is largely about the effect of actions on the interests of others. To make a moral assessment, you must understand the current situation and what effects will be created by the alternative avenues of action before you. Who will be harmed and who benefitted by each possible action? What effect will your action have not just on discrete individuals but on the social systems and institutions those individuals are members of and depend on (such as families and neighborhoods)? What contribution will your action make to the ethos of the communities it affects—the workplaces, industries, marketplaces, and political institutions?

Identifying these probable consequences for your actions will not always be easy. Sometimes, reasonable people disagree about what the likely result of an action will be. But the possibility of such disagreement and uncertainty is not an excuse for failing to make careful investigation. The same uncertainty and disagreement, after all, is present in every aspect of decision-making. Would investors forgive financial managers who failed to investigate stock and bond purchases because the outcome of the purchases was uncertain?
2. *Exercise your imagination*. Moral decision-making requires that you be imaginative. You need to imagine the possible outcomes of action, what others will feel, and how they will respond to the circumstances created by your actions. Most important, you need to imagine other circumstances to which your principles of deci-

sion-making might have application. For instance, if you conclude that "I was following orders" was not an acceptable excuse for a Nazi death camp guard, you must also admit, other things being equal, that it is not an acceptable excuse for corporate officers who break laws or who violate moral rules. If you believe that it is unfair to discriminate on grounds of ethnicity because that is something over which individuals have no control, then you might have to admit that discriminating between applicants on the basis of test scores (such as IQ or SAT scores) is also unfair if the evidence is that those test measure skills that are primarily native rather than acquired. Consistency requires that you accept the results of your reasons and principles wherever they apply instead of picking and choosing when to apply them. Moral imagination is important in seeing cases where your principles might have further application.
3. *Identify your intentions, both ends and means*. When you act, you have some end you intend to achieve. That intention would be hard to overlook. But you also need to be aware of how you intend to achieve that objective. Intentions are important morally not just in terms of the ends you seek but also in terms of the means you employ. Often people conveniently neglect to analyze their means–intentions. One example would be the marketer who says, "I only intended to make the product appear more attractive to the consumer" when defending an ad for children's action figures that depicts them as larger than they are and against a background that is "not available" or, maybe worse, "sold separately."

WHAT NOT TO DO
The three previous steps are important ingredients in any careful moral deliberation. In themselves, however, they are not enough to generate conclusions about how to act. For that, you need more than formal processes. You need substantive moral principles that identify proper and improper courses of action. Unfortunately, many of the commonly suggested principles have serious problems. It's instructive to look at these principles in order to avoid the difficulties they create. Here are a few problem principles:

Do no harm. This commonly suggested principle is both too strong and too weak. It is too strong because it requires the impossible. Social life is fraught with conflicts of interest. It is inevitable that the interests of some will be frustrated if the interests of others are satisfied. This is especially true for competitive situations that are zero sum games where one party is made worse off as an outcome of the competition. In fact, a main purpose of morality is to identify just what harms are to be avoided when interests collide. This principle is also too weak because it neglects the occasional responsibility to prevent harm. Sometimes we are obligated to come to another's assistance even though we are not the cause of that other person's distress. (See the box in Chapter Four, "Positive and Negative Duties.") "Do no harm" thus does not say enough about what morality requires.

Do no net harm. This principle is better than the former one because it recognizes the inevitability of some party being made worse off. But while moral evaluation does involve comparing the respective harms and benefits caused by an action, this principle is unacceptable in that it reduces to the utilitarianism we criticized in Chapter Two. In addition, this principle is too strong in that it imposes too great an obligation—there is almost no case where we could not imagine an act that might cause more benefit than the one we are considering. For example, should I buy a case of beer or contribute the money to a reputable charity? The "net benefit" principle seems to require that we always choose the happiness maximizing alternative and, therefore, that we never have a chance to relax and enjoy.

The golden rule: Do unto others as you would have them do unto you. (Not the "business golden rule": Do to others before they do to you.) This principle is a long-standing bit of moral advice that urges us to be fair and to empathically imagine ourselves in the place of others. If we all followed its advice more often, the world would undoubtedly be a kinder, gentler place. Despite its strengths and long tradition, the golden rule does have some shortcomings. First, it can privilege the beliefs and desires of the decision-maker. (Do what *you* would want done to *you.*) It is possible that those beliefs are inappropriate for a society like ours. A committed fundamentalist might decide that he would want to compel attendance at religious services or that

he might want censorship of literature he believes is scandalous. Thus, while noble, the golden rule still lacks a mechanism for determining what beliefs and desires are appropriate. Second, the application of the rule to the competitive situation of business is unclear. Should we never exploit a competitive advantage? That is too strong a demand. Should we always exploit an advantage? That is too weak because it ignores the real limits on economic competition that the first three chapters have been stressing. The golden rule needs additional criteria to help identify morally acceptable behavior.

Act only in ways that you can comfortably defend in public. Again, this is a bit of advice that might make the world a better place if it were followed. But it presupposes (a) that the values the person is comfortable defending in public are appropriate and (b) that the *de facto* moral norms of the culture are in need of no critique. Under this rule, a faulty or corrupt but widely shared system of values would permit acts that are still wrong. Imagine how a person or society so committed to the values of competition, individuality, and progress through survival of the fittest could comfortably abandon society's weakest members to the vagaries of the marketplace. Is the absence of mercy and charity in this value system acceptable? If not, the proposed rule must be missing something.

WHAT TO DO, PART II

It would be nice if moral evaluation were a simple and easy matter. Unfortunately, serious moral analysis is as complicated and difficult as serious analysis in any other field. So we do not propose that moral decisions follow any simple rules such as the preceding. Rather, we suggest that moral decision-makers follow a series of analytical steps. These steps are not mechanical, nor will they always produce clear, determinate, single answers to our moral quandaries. They will, however, provide some guidance and will make the decision process more systematic.

1. Follow steps 1, 2, and 3 described in Part I.
2. Know the law. This is not to identify how much you can get away with. In a generally just society, there is a presumptive obligation to obey the law. This obligation ought to include respect for the spirit of the law as well. The law should not

How (and How Not) to Make Moral Decisions (continued)

be treated as a game where you can see how much you can "bend" the regulations without breaking them.

3. Survey the field for any rights that might be claimed by the parties affected.

4. For each right that may be claimed, clarify whether it is claimed as a legal or moral right. For legal right claims, check with your lawyer. For moral right claims, ask what justification that right might have. On the basis of your answer to that question, determine whether the claim is a legitimate right or merely the expression of what some party wants. (Not all wants are rights.) Consulting others, with this and other questions, will help you in forming your answers. Be able to explain your evaluation in public.

5. For each legitimate moral right claim, determine whether the proper scope of the right covers the case at hand and, if it does, whether it obliges the company or its representatives. Help in determining the scope can come from looking to the justifications offered for the rights. Ask whether the underlying values that the right promotes in general are furthered by recognizing the right in this particular case. For example, I

have a right to life. Does it require that absolutely everything be done to sustain my life even when I am in a permanent and persistent vegetative state? I also have a right to free speech. Does it grant me the right to harangue my neighbors through a bullhorn at 3:00 a.m.—a practice used by a radical group in one Philadelphia neighborhood?

Even if the right covers a particular case, does it place obligations only on the company or on the company together with some other institution? The drug AZT appears to help delay the onset of symptoms in those who are HIV infected, but should a company take a loss in order to make it more affordable and readily available? Would a company be obligated to sell the drug at cost, or might some other institutions also be obliged to defray the costs of such drugs?

6. When rights claims conflict, be sure there is a conflict, that both rights are legitimate, and that both apply to the case at hand. Categorize the rights by their justifications as basic or derivative. Is the right essential for treating persons with respect? Or is it a right that derives its value from a contribution to some other goal? Is it

are values that apply in limited albeit important realms of life. Controlling our lives cannot mean that we control *everything* about our lives.

As a consequence, we must recognize that there will be legitimate limits on business activity. This, however, is not to suggest the propriety of arbitrary interference with economic activity when more central goods are not at stake. It's still important to have autonomy in areas beyond the autonomy that would be guaranteed when basic interests are protected from threat. This more general absence of interference, however, must have a secondary moral importance that does not jeopardize the protections of more fundamental interests.

If we assume a moral perspective on social institutions, we should commit ourselves to institutions that by law or moral convention respect equally the fundamental and common interests of each person, guaranteeing against other interference as much as is compatible with a similar guarantee for all. As an example, the social institution of business should operate so that the interferences that jeopardize life and health are prohibited before interferences that threaten only the ability to enter specific economic transactions. What the other responsibilities of business are is up to you to decide.

instrumental for sustaining important institu-tions? Is it the result of a contractual agreement, promise, or institutional role? We sometimes may be presented with tragic moral dilemmas, but reason suggests that we choose which of two real and competing rights will override by choosing the one that has the most compelling foundation. (Compare the analysis of rights in the section "Basic and Derivative Rights: Resolv-ing Conflicts," found earlier in this chapter.)

7. If there are no rights involved, determine if there are any other obligations present. Such obligations could be obligations of charity (where there is probable great harm, where you can probably prevent it with no great risk to yourself, and where no one else seems likely to give the necessary help). They could also be obligations to protect, or at least not dismantle, institutions that provide important benefits to society. For instance, some companies, excluding the major pharmaceutical companies, have re-cently lobbied Congress not just to limit but rather to abolish the Federal Drug Administra-tion. Reform of FDA procedures is one thing; abolition is another. Would lobbying for aboli-tion in order to reap greater financial gains count

as a violation of a corporate duty to support important social institutions?

8. If there are no rights or other obligations present, are there actions the corporation should take to benefit others at its own expense? Merck, the pharmaceutical company, discovered a drug called Invermectin, which could protect against a water-borne African parasite that caused blind-ness in millions. Merck decided to make the drug available free of charge. Its decision, aided by a profitable business position, could have been the result of a (nonobligatory) charitable concern. It might also have been driven by its corporate credo, which stated that a primary value of the company was preserving and improving human life. Consistency with the credo is the cost of promoting integrity and commitment among the employees. As in the Merck case, some acts may not be required by rights or obligations but are still acts that one can feel a strong moral reason for performing.

Following these eight steps will help you clarify and analyze the complicated issues that arise in business ethics, and thus help you make moral decisions more systematically. More than that we cannot promise.

IN SUMMARY

Retracing our steps a bit, we began in Chapter One with the free market view that business has no responsibility to society, consumers, or employees beyond the responsibility to avoid coercion and deception. That view also held that govern-ment's only proper role is to maintain free and open competition. Friedman's ar-ticle provided arguments for that view. We saw, however, that his arguments were not cogent.

Consideration of other arguments for the free market view led us to two ap-proaches to ethics that dominate the Western tradition: utilitarianism, in Chapter Two, and rights-based approaches in this chapter. Each of these is sometimes used to defend the laissez-faire view. After analysis, we found the utilitarian defense of the free market wanting for two reasons. First, its empirical claim that laissez-faire policies will maximize happiness was suspect. Second, the utilitarian theory on which the defense was based is itself flawed because it is unable to accommodate a commitment to individual rights.

We also found the two rights-based defenses of the free market were faulty. Both the liberty and property rights arguments depend on untenable conceptions of the rights at issue. Our presumptive conclusion is that the laissez-faire view of corporate responsibility must be abandoned and that a more adequate conception of property and liberty rights allows for more frequent management responsibility.

We hope that the introductory moral theory provided in the preceding chapters will provide some of the tools necessary for you to carefully determine the obligations of business. We also hope that the specific discussions of utilitarianism, liberty, and property will alert you to how that theory is used in some of the issue-oriented debates of the later chapters. In the next chapter, we examine the nature of the corporation. There we sketch a view of the corporation as an essentially social institution, discuss the content of corporate responsibilities, and review some of the mechanisms available for controlling corporate action.

STUDY QUESTIONS

1. Define the difference between basic rights and derivative rights. Try to apply that distinction to rights that you believe you possess.

2. What is the procedure suggested for settling conflicts between rights of the same level?

3. What arguments are presented in the text against the idea of a general right to liberty? How do these arguments accord with your own understanding of liberty rights?

4. How are property rights analyzed in the text? What are the consequences of this analysis for the responsibilities of those owning and/or managing corporate property?

4

The Corporation as
a Social Institution

Chapters One through Three explored some basic issues in social and political theory in order to defeat an extreme view of the corporation's social responsibility. This chapter develops a contrary view that identifies the corporation as an essentially social institution. It focuses on the structure of the corporation, on possible categories of corporate obligation, and on how the perceived obligations of corporations have changed over the last century. Since we assume throughout that the corporation, in some sense, does have responsibilities, we must also address recent debates about whether the corporation is the type of entity that can possess obligations. Finally, this chapter describes approaches to corporate control—external, through government regulation, and internal, through alternative governance structures.

Any adequate understanding of the corporation must view it as an essentially social institution. Corporations exist only because individuals come together to carry out jointly the business of producing goods and services. The particular form of that joint activity in any society is determined by social norms. For instance, in contemporary American society, corporations are enterprises with explicit state charters, and they must function according to the positive laws of the society. At a deeper level, the particular form of the contemporary American corporation is the product of socially evolved conceptions of property rights. The powers those property rights confer and the limits on the exercise of those powers are defined by norms that develop over time through the pull and tug of forces within the society. Corporations exist in a particular historical form only because their society sanctions institutions with that form.

Corporations are also social institutions in another sense. The form they take helps determine the social relations and patterns of behavior for individuals. A given corporate structure will naturally lead to specifically defined duties and responsibilities for the persons who inhabit that institution. The norms that define these duties, when internalized by corporate employees, will help shape the values and behavior of those employees. Given all this, we reach the inescapable conclusion that the corporation is social by its very nature.

THE NATURE OF THE CORPORATION

The "American corporation" is an abstraction (corporations have evolved many different organizational forms). However, we can understand the nature of the corporation better if we think about some generalities concerning the role, structure, and status of corporations.

The Role of the Corporation The role of the corporation varies according to the perspective from which one views it. From the point of view of the investor, a corporation is a vehicle for potentially increased wealth. For an employee, the corporation is a place to exchange labor for an income with which to support oneself and one's family. Consumers see the corporation as a mechanism from which to acquire needed goods and services. From the perspective of society, however, the corporation is an institution that enables both human and material resources to be organized for the (one hopes) efficient production of the things the people of the society need to maintain a way of life.

The Structure of the Corporation In our society, corporations are structured typically as follows. Institutions are created to attract investment from outside owners. These owners invest their funds to receive a profit, but they delegate the control of the operations to a team of managers who act as legal agents for them. This professional class of managers is expected to run the corporation efficiently and to produce a return for the investors. Successfully achieving that management task requires the cooperation of a third group—the workers. Employees are hired on a fee-for-service basis to carry out the directions of management in the activities necessary for producing goods and services, which are in turn offered for sale to consumers in a market. Consumer purchases provide the funds necessary for satisfying the ongoing labor and material costs of production.

Most contemporary American corporations are operated by a group of managers headed by a board of directors. These managers must direct the corporation in a way that responds adequately to the respective demands of investors, workers, and consumers. Management must provide investors sufficient return so that the corporation can hold investors and attract new infusions of capital. But management must also adopt policies that guarantee a supply of productive workers and an adequate demand for the products or services produced. Corporate structure, then, reflects a complex web of interrelated activities and constituencies.

The Legal Status of the Corporation In our society the corporation has a peculiar legal status. It is legally chartered and recognized as a person in the eyes of the law. That recognition, in part, allows the corporation standing to sue or to be sued in the courts. Also, as already noted, corporations differ from most property in that they are not directly controlled by their owners. Perhaps the most interesting feature of the corporation has to do with the liability of the shareholder-owners. The law, perhaps originally as a means of encouraging investment and production, limits the risk for investors. Ordinarily, if you cause a compensable harm to someone with your property, you can be held liable for the full extent of the harm caused. This means that you are responsible for the costs to the victim even if those costs exceed the value of the property causing the harm. Thus, if my old VW (worth $200) accidentally rolls out of my driveway and damages my neighbor's Mercedes, I am liable for the thousands of dollars in repairs my car has made necessary. However, incorporated property has a much more limited liability. Shareholders in a corporation have a legal liability limited to the value of their investment, regardless of the amount of harm caused by their property. With this background about the peculiar institution that is the American corporation, we can move on to a brief discussion of issues surrounding the notion of "corporate responsibility."

CORPORATE SOCIAL RESPONSIBILITY

From the material in Chapters Two and Three we can see that the responsibilities of the corporation must extend beyond mere responsibility to shareholders. Even Milton Friedman acknowledges this. Moreover, any realistic view of the contemporary corporation will see that, at least politically, the management of a corporation must take account of interests in addition to those of its shareholder constituency. This recognition has led to an understanding of the corporation that is growing in popularity among management theorists. This "Stakeholder Theory" distinguishes between a narrow concern for shareholder interests and a broader concern for all those who have a stake in corporate policy. While not specifying management responsibility precisely, this theory encourages management to expand corporate responsibility to include a concern for consumers, employees, and members of the community at large.

Stakeholder Theory

Critics of Stakeholder Theory claim that it cannot be operationalized in a way that would allow managers to apply it in concrete circumstances. How can management weigh the interest of its various constituencies (consumers, employees, shareholders, and so on) in reaching a decision about how to act? Critics suggest that it is impossible to answer that question adequately and that Stakeholder Theory will end up a hopeless morass. Better, they contend, to stick to a well-understood and well-governed approach that merely asks management to maximize shareholder wealth.

Positive and Negative Duties

Philosophers have traditionally distinguished between two broad classes of responsibility: positive duties and negative duties. Negative duties are duties to avoid causing (unjustifiable) harms. Positive duties, on the other hand, are duties to provide needed assistance to others. Ordinarily, positive duties are understood to exist even when the need for assistance was not caused by the individual who has the duty. Another way of understanding positive duties is to see them as responsibilities to engage in acts of charity. Thus, the traditional distinction between types of duties implies that while some acts of charity are morally discretionary, others are morally obligatory. Contributing to the United Way might be an example of a discretionary act of charity; pulling your unconscious grandmother from the full bathtub after she fell and hit her

head would be an example of an obligatory act of charity. The existence of some instances of both types of duties is generally admitted even if positive duties are given somewhat less weight.

If we apply these categories of responsibility to the context of business, however, we often find resistance. Even those of a liberal political persuasion often find that business has only duties of the negative sort. Many commentators take this view because they find the existence of positive duties for business inconsistent with business's goal of profit.

To deny, in principle, the existence of positive duties for business seems hasty, however. If we analyze the conditions under which positive duties normally obtain, we must admit that it is at least possible for a business to find itself in those conditions. If this is true, it would be pre-

Proponents of Stakeholder Theory respond by noting that uncertainty and disagreement about the precise responsibility of management are not unique to their theory. Once any moral responsibility is recognized, people will disagree about its content. Proponents argue that unless we are willing to abandon completely the idea that management has moral responsibilities to constituencies other than shareholders, it will always be difficult to operationalize those responsibilities in a mechanical way. Moreover, proponents say that the simple demand that management maximize profits will be subject to disagreement over how that is best achieved. Even that demand cannot be fully "operationalized."

Finally, proponents of Stakeholder Theory have some support from the Total Quality Management (TQM) movement. TQM emphasizes that the way to ensure a profitable business is, paradoxically, to concentrate attention on the consumer. Management should see its objective as providing goods and services that best satisfy the customer. Ironically, an overemphasis on shareholder wealth might produce less profit because it leads management to undervalue the customer. If this is correct, TQM provides additional support for the idea that management ought to focus on the interests of groups other than just shareholders. (Although the thrust of Stakeholder Theory is normative—that management has a moral responsibility to other stakeholders—TQM may make the focus on the customer merely instrumental.)

Chapters Five through Fourteen present discussions of proposed specific responsibilities that corporations might have. At this point, however, we can only begin to investigate the ways in which corporations might come to possess obligations.

sumptively unreasonable to deny that business has such duties.

Acts of charity are normally held to be obligatory when, among other things: (a) the act does not place the agent in danger of suffering a great loss; (b) the agent has the real power to prevent substantial harm to others; and (c) no other agent seems likely to provide the needed assistance. It is perfectly possible for business to find itself in these conditions. Consider the major earthquake that devastated Mexico City a few years ago. Some of the city's hospitals were destroyed by the earthquake. If, by hypothesis, the only remaining hospitals were private, for-profit institutions, most of us would still believe that those remaining hospitals had a duty to provide care to the injured.

It would appear that we could say, then, that corporate responsibilities can fall into either of the two classic types. What the specific duties in each type are, of course, will be open to debate. For instance, the federal government recently discontinued certain subsidies for the controversial and expensive AIDS drug AZT. Consequently, we can argue whether private drug companies have a responsibility to subsidize the drug themselves. This case, and the case of "orphan drugs" generally, is vexing because we are unsure about how to allocate responsibilities among the various institutions involved. But the controversial nature of this potential positive duty does not distinguish it from many proposed negative duties. Hence the controversy cannot be a reason for denying that the entire category of positive duties applies to business.

The Social Contract Theory

Once we recognize how controversial proposed corporate responsibilities are, and once we notice how our expectations of corporations have changed over the years, we have to ask how corporate obligations are determined. The answer will depend in part on what human interests the society believes are important enough to protect as rights. In part, the answer will also depend on what the society believes about the factual consequences of certain corporate and institutional arrangements. Both of these beliefs are open to change and debate.

One instructive way of understanding this process is through Social Contract Theory. The notion of a social contract originated with political philosophers who hypothesized an implicit contract between the members of a society. Initially, this implicit contract was a device used to explain both the legitimacy of particular forms of government and the respective obligations of rulers and citizens. Recent applications of this theory to business can help explain how the perceived social obligations of business are determined and how they change over time. Consider how the social contract between American society and its corporations developed.

In the United States the rise of the modern industrial corporation can be dated to the late 1800s. When those corporations were chartered, social expectations of them were centered on the expansion of production. As experience gradually accumulated regarding the social, economic, and political effect of the developing corporations, society perceived a need to alter the norms for corporate behavior: Corporate behavior that was once viewed as good for the society came to be viewed as having undesirable consequences as well. Since all contracts supposedly operate for the mutual benefit of the parties, changed perceptions of the consequences of corporate activity led to a change in the obligations of the implicit contract between the corporation and society. If we view the obligations of corporations as deriving from such an implicit contract, we can understand how those obligations are determined in the ongoing flux of social life.

Some of us might wonder about the fairness of this view of corporate responsibility. Ordinarily, unilaterally changing the terms of an agreed-upon contract to suit the interests of one of the parties is considered unacceptable. We should caution against too easy a charge of unfairness, however. The concept of fairness is, as we saw in Chapter Three, open to different interpretations. For instance, allowing one generation to bind another to harmful contract provisions would seem to violate a principle of fairness that holds that individuals should have a say in the policies that affect their lives.

Of course, Social Contract Theory does not imply that the particular contractual understanding at any given time is a fully adequate one. Nor does it suggest that those understandings cannot be cynically manipulated by persons with special interests in the "contract." The model is meant only as a heuristic device for helping us understand how conceptions of corporate responsibility evolve in a given society.

The Corporation as a Morally Responsible Agent

All along we have been assuming that corporations are the sorts of things that can possess responsibilities. That proposition has been challenged recently. Some commentators have held that corporations fail to satisfy ordinary, commonsense conditions necessary for having responsibilities.

The challenge to the idea of corporate responsibility comes from those who look to the paradigm case of an entity that can have moral responsibilities and can be held accountable: the human moral agent. Some of these theorists find that the characteristics that allow ascribing responsibility and accountability to human beings are not possessed by the corporation.

When we see a human being as responsible, we do so because we implicitly believe that he or she is capable of autonomous, rational decision-making. Part of what is involved in such decision-making is that the agent must understand the situation, intend to act on that understanding, and, finally, act. Those who question ascribing responsibility and accountability to corporations find that it is only in an obscuringly metaphorical or anthropomorphic sense that we can speak of corporations in this way. For example, often corporate "acts" are the result of the combined actions of separate individuals within the corporation. It need not be the case that any single individual's intentional act brought about that corporate "act." Conversely, consider that corporate actions are not equivalent to the specific actions of individuals within the firm. As Manuel Velasquez points out, individuals do not merge with corporations; only other corporations can do that.[*]

---

[*]Manuel G. Velasquez, "Why Corporations Are Not Morally Responsible for Anything They Do," *Business and Professional Ethics Journal* 2 (Spring 1983): 8.

Opposing theorists contend that corporations can have responsibilities and be held accountable because there are senses in which corporations act rationally and with intention. For example, an expansion of production to meet increased consumer demand, though it may not be solely the product of one human individual's intentional decision, is surely a considered and rational action on the part of the business.

The position one takes in this somewhat metaphysical debate about conditions for responsibility can have potentially far-reaching practical consequences. For instance, if corporations cannot properly be held responsible, then who should bear the liability for harm caused by corporations? If corporations cannot act in a morally relevant way and if the policies of the corporation are not equivalent to the acts of individual members of the corporation, must corporately caused harm go unpunished and uncompensated? Or should we penalize each individual who had a part in the creation of the corporate "act"? Should the file clerk who simply stuffed an envelope be penalized for his part in a case of mail fraud? If corporations *are* morally responsible, is it just that we punish the corporation (through fines, perhaps) when doing so hurts ordinary shareholders or employees who had no part in the creation or execution of the harmful policies? (Interestingly, some of these same issues arise in considering the Nuremberg war crimes trials.)

Perhaps we can find a way around the problems posed by this debate if we hold that the notion of responsibility as applied to corporations differs from the application of that notion to human moral agents. For instance, as we will see in the discussion of product liability in Chapter Ten, there are defensible ways of talking about corporate liability that differ from our ordinary understanding of our personal liability for harm we cause. For instance, there are public policy reasons for holding corporations liable for injuries caused by their products even when the corporation could not have prevented those injuries. These same public policy considerations do not apply with equal force in the case of accidents caused by private individuals. Thus, we might be able to translate this talk of corporate responsibility and accountability into a language that allows us to speak about shaping the way our social institutions function. Public policy sanctions on corporations might be seen simply as the attempt to fashion a system of interrelated incentives for encouraging the desired institutional behavior. In creating a system of incentives (such as fines or exposure to economic liability) we would still need to be sensitive to the consequences of our incentives for the human individuals involved. For example, if corporate exposure to extreme degrees of liability for harms caused by products created shortages of necessary goods or unacceptably high levels of unemployment, we might abandon that as a mechanism for ensuring product safety. In addition, levying corporate fines that affect shareholders does not necessarily have to be seen as assigning to those investors moral blame for corporate policies. (Of course, identifiably criminal acts of individuals within the corporation can still be considered personally blameworthy.)

If we understand corporate responsibility in these terms, we might be able to discuss public policy toward corporations without committing ourselves to either a moral equating of corporations and human beings or an abandoning of all reference to a corporation's responsibility for its policies.

CORPORATE GOVERNANCE AND CONTROL

If we do adopt the concept of corporate responsibility as just outlined, then the norms created as policy incentives are of crucial importance in governing the actions of corporations. Accordingly, in this final section of Chapter Four we consider some approaches to controlling the corporation. We describe the external approach to corporate governance—government regulation—by exploring its history and discussing some recent debates about that regulation. Finally, we briefly address two separate models for internal governance of the corporation.

The History of Government Regulation

Though governmental regulation is the primary external mechanism for controlling corporate policy, it has a rather short history. In the United States, the initial forays into government control of industry began in the late nineteenth and early twentieth centuries. However, that regulation was far different from the protective legislation we know today. The primary purpose of this early regulation was to protect businesses from the anticompetitive practices of other businesses. The early federal agencies created to regulate commerce, such as the Interstate Commerce Commission, were patently aimed at maintaining open, nonmonopolistic competition. This form of regulation supposedly provided indirect benefits to consumers, but the direct and principal beneficiary was the business community itself.

Much of the contemporary regulation that intends to promote the welfare of consumers, employees, or members of the society at large is a product of the last three decades. For instance, the Environmental Protection Agency (EPA) and the Occupational Safety and Health Administration (OSHA) were both created in 1970; the Consumer Product Safety Commission was created in 1972. This explosion of new regulatory bodies was a response to increased awareness of the external costs of business being shouldered by the public. These costs to health, safety, and the environment were the subject of ever more effective political complaint through the 1960s and 1970s. There are, then, two broad periods in the history of government's attempt to guarantee that business operates as the society wishes.

The Debate on the New Government Regulation

Not surprisingly, the business community has little fondness for many of the actions of the new regulatory agencies of government. In the past decade business has joined a debate about the acceptability of much government regulation. While defenders claim that the regulation generally serves to protect the public effectively, critics have levelled a series of blasts at government involvement in corporate activity. Among the criticisms are the following: Regulatory agencies do not coordinate their directives and hence often work at cross purposes; many regulations are not effective at protecting the public (a charge often used against OSHA, as we will see in Chapter Nine); the cost of complying with regulations outweighs the benefits the regulations provide; and regulation causes product shortages and unemployment. We invite you in the chapters that follow to consider these challenges to specific public policies involving government intervention in the marketplace.

Models of Internal Corporate Governance

Internal mechanisms for controlling corporate behavior are numerous. They range from the use of corporate social audits (by which management explicitly evaluates the social consequences of its policies), to the enforcement of professional codes of ethics, to the creation of a corporate ombudsman who manages issues of social responsibility. Quite a bit of literature in the field of business ethics concerns the effectiveness of these different mechanisms. We leave that debate about mechanisms of control for you to pursue on your own. Instead, we will concentrate on two models of corporate governance. The issue here is not so much how corporate policy should be controlled internally as it is who should exercise that control.

Somewhat artificially and simplistically, we will divide models of corporate governance into two types: the traditional hierarchical model and the less common democratic or participatory model. (Of course, these models represent only ideal types. In actuality, the differences between governance structures are often more a matter of different degrees of authority sharing.)

A spatial representation of these two models of governance would describe them, respectively, as vertical or horizontal methods of distributing authority throughout the workplace. The hierarchical model locates primary authority in top management: Derivative authority flows vertically from the delegation of responsibility by those managers. The participatory model locates primary decision-making authority horizontally among the ordinary employees. The degree to which real governance control is exercised by employees differs according to the specific versions of participatory governance. At one extreme would be a pure worker-cooperative enterprise in which workers have direct or indirect control of all aspects of the organization. At the other extreme within the participatory model are recent experiments with the Japanese concept of quality circles in which workers' advice about production concerns is regularly sought.

The traditional model of corporate governance derives from two basic sources. First, it derives from a belief that management, as the legal agent of shareholders, has the sole right to make decisions and set policy (in the absence of express shareholders' wishes). The connection between ownership and control, as we saw in Chapter Three, is not only deeply embedded in our ideology but also seems entailed by any coherent understanding of the concept of ownership. The second source for the traditional model of corporate governance is a belief that efficient decision-making requires that authority be allocated to a small number of individuals. (This is the corporate version of "Too many cooks spoil the broth.")

The participatory model of governance derives from wholly different beliefs. Some proponents of greater employee participation in decision-making base their preference on productivity studies. There is evidence, for example, that employees who have a sense of participating in decision-making feel higher levels of satisfaction with their work lives and hence are more productive. Others argue that (a) property ownership cannot mean an absolute right to control and (b) the need to respect the autonomy of workers is sufficient for justifying limits on management–ownership authority.

Development of the Stakeholder Theory has also provided some impetus for extending control to those affected by corporate policy. Such proposed extensions are defended on the ground that individuals can best judge their own interests and therefore ought to be allowed a voice of their own in corporate policies that might affect those interests. Similar arguments are found in recent political debates about plant closings; some argue that not only workers but also local communities should be allowed a say in such decisions. Throughout the remaining chapters you will find frequent instances of these debates about who should exercise control over the corporation.

IN SUMMARY

Corporations as social institutions are chartered by society and owe responsibilities to society. Two current theories for helping to understand those responsibilities are Stakeholder Theory and Social Contract Theory. Stakeholder Theory suggests that when management acts, it needs to consider the interests of all constituencies—owners, employees, customers, and society at large. (See the Evan and Freeman article at the end of this chapter for a classic statement of Stakeholder Theory.) Social Contract Theory attempts to explain why management must consider all those interests.

There is a recurrent philosophical debate about the locus of corporate responsibility: Can corporations themselves be considered morally responsible agents, or is this possible only for the human beings in them? (See the Goodpaster and Matthews article at the end of the chapter for more on this debate.) Whatever answer to that question you decide on, the need to control corporate action is obvious. Government regulatory actions have evolved as a mechanism for corporate control.

This chapter has outlined some general views on these topics of responsibility and regulation. In the chapters that follow, you will be repeatedly asked to become more specific about just what responsibilities business has and just when government intervention in the marketplace is appropriate.

STUDY QUESTIONS

1. How can proponents of Stakeholder Theory respond to the charge that they make the content of management responsibility hopelessly unclear?

2. What is the difference between positive and negative duties? Can you describe a circumstance in which you believe a corporation has a positive duty to others?

3. What practical significance is there to how one answers the philosophical question about whether corporations can be considered moral agents?

4. What advantages and disadvantages do you see for the two respective models of internal corporate governance?

A STAKEHOLDER THEORY OF THE MODERN CORPORATION: KANTIAN CAPITALISM

William M. Evan and R. Edward Freeman

INTRODUCTION

Corporations have ceased to be merely legal devices through which the private business transactions of individuals may be carried on. Though still much used for this purpose, the corporate form has acquired a larger significance. The corporation has, in fact, become both a method of property tenure and a means of organizing economic life. Grown to tremendous proportions, there may be said to have evolved a "corporate system"—which has attracted to itself a combination of attributes and powers, and has attained a degree of prominence entitling it to be dealt with as a major social institution.[1]

Despite these prophetic words of Berle and Means (1932), scholars and managers alike continue to hold sacred the view that managers bear a special relationship to the stockholders in the firm. Since stockholders own shares in the firm, they have certain rights and privileges, which must be granted to them by management, as well as by others.... Sanctions, in the form of "the law of corporations," and other protective mechanisms in the form of social custom, accepted management practice, myth, and ritual, are thought to reinforce the assumption of the primacy of the stockholder.

The purpose of this paper is to pose several challenges to this assumption, from within the framework of managerial capitalism, and to suggest the bare bones of an alternative theory, *a stakeholder theory of the modern corporation*. We do not seek the demise of the modern corporation, either intellectu-

ally or in fact. Rather, we seek its transformation. In the words of Neurath, we shall attempt to "rebuild the ship, plank by plank, while it remains afloat."[2]

Our thesis is that we can revitalize the concept of managerial capitalism by replacing the notion that managers have a duty to stockholders with the concept that managers bear a fiduciary relationship to stakeholders. Stakeholders are those groups who have a stake in or claim on the firm. Specifically we include suppliers, customers, employees, stockholders, and the local community, as well as management in its role as agent for these groups. We argue that the legal, economic, political, and moral challenges to the currently received theory of the firm, as a nexus of contracts among the owners of the factors of production and customers, require us to revise this concept along essentially Kantian lines. That is, each of these stakeholder groups has a right not to be treated as a means to some end, and therefore must participate in determining the future direction of the firm in which they have a stake....[3]

The crux of our argument is that we must reconceptualize the firm around the following question: For whose benefit and at whose expense should the firm be managed? We shall set forth such a reconceptualization in the form of a *stakeholder theory of the firm*. We shall then critically examine the stakeholder view and its implications for the future of the capitalist system.

THE ATTACK ON MANAGERIAL CAPITALISM

The Legal Argument
The basic idea of managerial capitalism is that in return for controlling the firm, management vigorously pursues the interests of stockholders. Central to

the managerial view of the firm is the idea that management can pursue market transactions with suppliers and customers in an unconstrained manner.[4]

The law of corporations gives a less clearcut answer to the question: In whose interest and for whose benefit should the modern corporation be governed? While it says that the corporations should be run primarily in the interests of the stockholders in the firm, it says further that the corporation exists "in contemplation of the law" and has personality as a "legal person," limited liability for its actions, and immortality, since its existence transcends that of its members.[5] Therefore, directors and other officers of the firm have a fiduciary obligation to stockholders in the sense that the "affairs of the corporation" must be conducted in the interest of the stockholders. And stockholders can theoretically bring suit against those directors and managers for doing otherwise. But since the corporation is a legal person, existing in contemplation of the law, managers of the corporation are constrained by law.

Until recently, this was no constraint at all. In this century, however,...the law has evolved to effectively constrain the pursuit of stockholder interests at the expense of other claimants on the firm. It has, in effect, required that the claims of customers, suppliers, local communities, and employees be taken into consideration, though in general they are subordinated to the claims of stockholders....

For instance, the doctrine of "privity of contract," as articulated in *Winterbottom v. Wright* in 1842, has been eroded by recent developments in products liability law. Indeed, *Greenman v. Yuba Power* gives the manufacturer strict liability for damage caused by its products, even though the seller has exercised all possible care in the preparation and sale of the product and the consumer has not bought the product from nor entered into any contractual arrangement with the manufacturer. Caveat emptor has been replaced, in large part, with caveat venditor.[6] The Consumer Product Safety Commission has the power to enact product recalls, and in 1980 one U.S. automobile company recalled more cars than it built....Some industries are required to provide information to customers about a product's ingredients, whether or not the customers want and are willing to pay for this information.[7]

In short, the supplier-firm-customer chain is far from that visualized by managerial capitalism. In their roles as customers and suppliers, firms have benefitted from these constraints, but they have been harmed to the degree to which the constraints have meant loss of profit....

The same argument is applicable to management's dealings with employees. The National Labor Relations Act gave employees the right to unionize and to bargain in good faith. It set up the National Labor Relations Board to enforce these rights with management. The Equal Pay Act of 1963 and Title VII of the Civil Rights Act of 1964 constrain management from discrimination in hiring practices; these have been followed with the Age Discrimination in Employment Act of 1967.[8] The emergence of a body of administrative case law arising from labor-management disputes and the historic settling of discrimination claims with large employers such as AT&T have caused the emergence of a body of practice in the corporation that is consistent with the legal guarantee of the rights of the employees....The law has protected the due process rights of those employees who enter into collective bargaining agreements with management. As of the present, however, only 30 percent of the labor force are participating in such agreements; this has prompted one labor law scholar to propose a statutory law prohibiting dismissals of the 70 percent of the work force not protected....[9]

The law has also protected the interests of local communities. The Clean Air Act and Clean Water Act have constrained management from "spoiling the commons." In an historic case, *Marsh v. Alabama,* the Supreme Court ruled that a company-owned town was subject to the provisions of the U.S. Constitution, thereby guaranteeing the rights of local citizens and negating the "property rights" of the firm. Some states and municipalities have gone further and passed laws preventing firms from moving plants or limiting when and how plants can be closed. In sum, there is much current legal activity in this area to constrain management's pursuit of stockholders' interests at the expense of the local communities in which the firm operates....

We have argued that the result of such changes in the legal system can be viewed as giving some rights to those groups that have a claim on the firm, for example, customers, suppliers, employees, local communities, stockholders, and management. It raises the question, at the core of a theory of the firm: In whose interest and for whose benefit should the firm be managed? The answer proposed by managerial capitalism is clearly "the stockholders," but we have argued that the law has been progressively circumscribing this answer.

The Economic Argument

In its pure ideological form managerial capitalism seeks to maximize the interests of stockholders. In its perennial criticism of government regulation, management espouses the "invisible hand" doctrine. It contends that it creates the greatest good for the greatest number, and therefore government need not intervene. However, we know that externalities, moral hazards, and monopoly power exist in fact, whether or not they exist in theory. Further, some of the legal apparatus mentioned above has evolved to deal with just these issues.

The problem of the "tragedy of the commons" or the free-rider problem pervades the concept of public goods such as water and air. No one has an incentive to incur the cost of clean-up or the cost of nonpollution, since the marginal gain of one firm's action is small. Every firm reasons this way, and the result is pollution of water and air. Since the industrial revolution, firms have sought to internalize the benefits and externalize the costs of their actions. The cost must be borne by all, through taxation and regulation; hence we have the emergence of the environmental regulations of the 1970s.

Similarly, moral hazards arise when the purchaser of a good or service can pass along the cost of that good. There is no incentive to economize, on the part of either the producer or the consumer, and there is excessive use of the resources involved. The institutionalized practice of third-party payment in health care is a prime example.

Finally, we see the avoidance of competitive behavior on the part of firms, each seeking to monopolize a small portion of the market and not compete with one another. In a number of industries, oligopolies have emerged, and while there is questionable evidence that oligopolies are not the most efficient corporate form in some industries, suffice it to say that the potential for abuse of market power has again led to regulation of managerial

activity. In the classic case, AT&T, arguably one of the great technological and managerial achievements of the century, was broken up into eight separate companies to prevent its abuse of monopoly power.

Externalities, moral hazards, and monopoly power have led to more external control on managerial capitalism. There are de facto constraints, due to these economic facts of life, on the ability of management to act in the interests of stockholders....

A STAKEHOLDER THEORY OF THE FIRM

Foundations of a Theory

Two themes are present throughout our argument. The first is concerned with the rights and duties of the owners (and their agents) of private property, and the effects of this property on the rights of others. The second theme is concerned with the consequences of managerial capitalism and the effects of the modern corporation on the welfare of others. These themes represent two branches of modern moral theory, Kantianism and consequentialism, and they are pitted together as the main tension in most existing moral theories. Our purpose here is to argue that the stockholder theory of the firm seems to give precedence to one or the other interpretation, but that both are important in grounding a theory of the modern corporation. In other words, we need a theory that balances the rights of the claimants on the corporation with the consequences of the corporate form.

Those who question the legitimacy of the modern corporation altogether because of the evils of excessive corporate power usually believe that the corporation should have no right to decide how things are going to be for its constituents. While we believe that each person has the right to be treated not as a means to some corporate end but as an end in itself, we would not go so far as to say that the corporation has no rights whatsoever. Our more moderate stance is that if the modern corporation requires treating others as means to an end, then these others must agree on, and hence participate (or choose not to participate) in, the decisions to be used as such. Thus, property rights are legitimate but not absolute, particularly when they conflict with important rights of others. And any theory that is to be consistent with our considered judgment about rights must take such a balanced view. The right to property does not yield the right to treat others as means to an end, which is to say that property rights are not a license to ignore Kant's principle of respect for persons.

Those who question the legitimacy of the modern corporation altogether because of the resulting possibility of externalities or harm usually do not see that the corporation can be held accountable for its actions. We maintain that persons (even legal persons) are responsible for the consequences of their actions, regardless of how those actions are mediated, and must be able and willing to accept responsibility for them. Therefore, any theory that seeks to justify the corporate form must be based at least partially on the idea that the corporation and its managers as moral agents can be the cause of and can be held accountable for their actions.

In line with these two themes of rights and effects,…we suggest two principles that will serve as working rules, not absolutes, to guide us in addressing some of the foundational issues. We will not settle the thorny issues that these principles raise, but merely argue that any theory, including the stakeholder theory, must be consistent with these principles.

Principle of Corporate Rights (PCR) The corporation and its managers may not violate the legitimate rights of others to determine their own future.

Principle of Corporate Effects (PCE) The corporation and its managers are responsible for the effects of their actions on others.

The Stakeholder Concept
Corporations have stakeholders, that is, groups and individuals who benefit from or are harmed by, and whose rights are violated or respected by, corporate actions. The notion of stakeholder is built around the Principle of Corporate Rights (PCR) and the Principle of Corporate Effects (PCE)….The concept of stakeholders is a generalization of the notion of stockholders, who themselves have some special claim on the firm. Just as stockholders have a right to demand certain actions by management, so do other stakeholders have a right to make claims. The exact nature of these

claims is a difficult question that we shall address, but the logic is identical to that of the stockholder theory. Stakes require action of a certain sort, and conflicting stakes require methods of resolution….

Freeman and Reed (1983)[10] distinguish two senses of *stakeholder*. The "narrow definition" includes those groups who are vital to the survival and success of the corporation. The "wide-definition" includes any group or individual who can affect or is affected by the corporation. While the wide definition is more in keeping with PCE and PCR, it raises too many difficult issues. We shall begin with a more modest aim: to articulate a stakeholder theory using the narrow definition.

Stakeholders in the Modern Corporation
Figure 1 depicts the stakeholders in a typical large corporation. The stakes of each are reciprocal, since each can affect the other in terms of harms and benefits as well as rights and duties. The stakes of each are not univocal and would vary by particular corporation. We merely set forth some general notions that seem to be common to many large firms.

Owners have financial stake in the corporation in the form of stocks, bonds, and so on, and they expect some kind of financial return from them. Either they have given money directly to the firm, or they have some historical claim made through a series of morally justified exchanges. The firm affects their livelihood or, if a substantial portion of their retirement income is in stocks or bonds, their ability to care for themselves when they can no longer work. Of course, the stakes of owners will differ by type of owner, preferences for money, moral preferences, and so on, as well as by type of firm. The owners of AT&T are quite different from the owners of Ford Motor Company, with stock of the former company being widely dispersed among 3 million stockholders and that of the latter being held by a small family group as well as by a large group of public stockholders.

Employees have their jobs and usually their livelihood at stake; they often have specialized skills for which there is usually no perfectly elastic market. In return for their labor, they expect security, wages, benefits, and meaningful work. In return for their loyalty, the corporation is expected to provide for them and carry them through difficult times. Employees are expected to follow the instructions

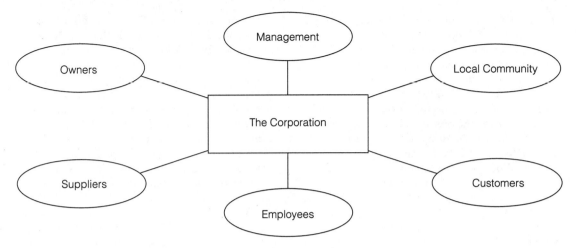

FIGURE 1 A Stakeholder Model of the Corporation

of management most of the time, to speak favorably about the company, and to be responsible citizens in the local communities in which the company operates. Where they are used as means to an end, they must participate in decisions affecting such use. The evidence that such policies and values as described here lead to productive company-employee relationships is compelling. It is equally compelling to realize that the opportunities for "bad faith" on the part of both management and employees are enormous. "Mock participation" in quality circles, singing the company song, and wearing the company uniform solely to please management all lead to distrust and unproductive work.

Suppliers, interpreted in a stakeholder sense, are vital to the success of the firm, for raw materials will determine the final product's quality and price. In turn the firm is a customer of the supplier and is therefore vital to the success and survival of the supplier. When the firm treats the supplier as a valued member of the stakeholder network, rather than simply as a source of materials, the supplier will respond when the firm is in need. Chrysler traditionally had very close ties to its suppliers, even to the extent that led some to suspect the transfer of illegal payments. And when Chrysler was on the brink of disaster, the suppliers responded with price cuts, accepting late payments, financing, and so on. Supplier and company can rise and fall together. Of course, again, the particular supplier relationships will depend on a number of variables such as the

number of suppliers and whether the supplies are finished goods or raw materials.

Customers exchange resources for the products of the firm and in return receive the benefits of the products. Customers provide the lifeblood of the firm in the form of revenue. Given the level of reinvestment of earnings in large corporations, customers indirectly pay for the development of new products and services. Peters and Waterman (1982)[11] have argued that being close to the customer leads to success with other stakeholders and that a distinguishing characteristic of some companies that have performed well is their emphasis on the customer. By paying attention to customers' needs, management automatically addresses the needs of suppliers and owners. Moreover, it seems that the ethic of customer service carries over to the community. Almost without fail the "excellent companies" in Peters and Waterman's study have good reputations in the community. We would argue that Peters and Waterman have found multiple applications of Kant's dictum, "Treat persons as ends unto themselves," and it should come as no surprise that persons respond to such respectful treatment, be they customers, suppliers, owners, employees, or members of the local community. The real surprise is the novelty of the application of Kant's rule in a theory of good management practice.

The local community grants the firm the right to build facilities and, in turn, it benefits from the tax base and economic and social contributions of the firm. In return for the provision of local services, the firm is expected to be a good citizen, as is any person, either "natural or artificial." The firm cannot expose the community to unreasonable hazards in the form of pollution, toxic waste, and so on. If for some reason the firm must leave a community, it is expected to work with local leaders to make the transition as smoothly as possible. Of course, the firm does not have perfect knowledge, but when it discovers some danger or runs afoul of new competition, it is expected to inform the local community and to work with the community to overcome any problem. When the firm mismanages its relationship with the local community, it is in the same position as a citizen who commits a crime. It has violated the implicit social contract with the community and should expect to be distrusted and ostracized. It should not be surprised when punitive measures are invoked.

We have not included "competitors" as stakeholders in the narrow sense, since strictly speaking they are not necessary for the survival and success of the firm; the stakeholder theory works equally well in monopoly contexts. However, competitors and government would be the first to be included in an extension of this basic theory. It is simply not true that the interests of competitors in an industry are always in conflict. There is no reason why trade associations and other multiorganizational groups cannot band together to solve common problems that have little to do with how to restrain trade. Implementation of stakeholder management principles, in the long run, mitigates the need for industrial policy and an increasing role for government intervention and regulation.

The Role of Management

Management plays a special role, for it too has a stake in the modern corporation. On the one hand, management's stake is like that of employees, with some kind of explicit or implicit employment contract. But, on the other hand, management has a duty of safeguarding the welfare of the abstract entity that is the corporation. In short, management, especially top management, must look after the health of the corporation, and this involves balancing the multiple claims of conflicting stakeholders. Owners want higher financial returns, while customers want more money spent on re-

search and development. Employees want higher wages and better benefits, while the local community wants better parks and day-care facilities.

The task of management in today's corporation is akin to that of King Solomon. The stakeholder theory does not give primacy to one stakeholder group over another, though there will surely be times when one group will benefit at the expense of others. In general, however, management must keep the relationships among stakeholders in balance. When these relationships become imbalanced, the survival of the firm is in jeopardy.

When wages are too high and product quality is too low, customers leave, suppliers suffer, and owners sell their stocks and bonds, depressing the stock price and making it difficult to raise new capital at favorable rates. Note, however, that the reason for paying returns to owners is not that they "own" the firm, but that their support is necessary for the survival of the firm, and that they have a legitimate claim on the firm. Similar reasoning applies in turn to each stakeholder group.

A stakeholder theory of the firm must redefine the purpose of the firm. The stockholder theory claims that the purpose of the firm is to maximize the welfare of the stockholders, perhaps subject to some moral or social constraints, either because such maximization leads to the greatest good or because of property rights. The purpose of the firm is quite different in our view. If a stakeholder theory is to be consistent with the principles of corporate effects and rights, then its purpose must take into account Kant's dictum of respect for persons. The very purpose of the firm is, in our view, to serve as a vehicle for coordinating stakeholder interests. It is through the firm that each stakeholder group makes itself better off through voluntary exchanges. The corporation serves at the pleasure of its stakeholders, and none may be used as a means to the ends of another without full rights of participation in that decision. We can crystallize the particular applications of PCR and PCE to the stakeholder theory in two further principles. These stakeholder management principles will serve as a foundation for articulating the theory. They are guiding ideals for the immortal corporation as it endures through generations of particular mortal stakeholders.

Stakeholder Management Principles

P1: The corporation should be managed for the benefit of its stakeholders: its customers, suppliers, owners, employees, and local communities. The rights of these groups must be ensured, and, further, the groups must participate, in some sense, in decisions that substantially affect their welfare.

P2: Management bears a fiduciary relationship to stakeholders and to the corporation as an abstract entity. It must act in the interests of the stakeholders as their agent, and it must act in the interests of the corporation to ensure the survival of the firm, safeguarding the long-term stakes of each group.

P1, which we might call The Principle of Corporate Legitimacy, redefines the purpose of the firm to be in line with the principles of corporate effects and rights. It implies the legitimacy of stakeholder claims on the firm. Any social contract that justifies the existence of the corporate form includes the notion that stakeholders are a party to that contract. Further, stakeholders have some inalienable rights to participate in decisions that substantially affect their welfare or involve their being used as a means to another's ends. We bring to bear our arguments for the incoherence of the stockholder view as justification for P1. If in fact there is no good reason for the stockholder theory, and if in fact there are harms, benefits, and rights of stakeholders involved in running the modern corporation, then we know of no other starting point for a theory of the corporation than P1.

P2, which we might call The Stakeholder Fiduciary Principle, explicitly defines the duty of management to recognize these claims. It will not always be possible to meet all claims of all stakeholders all the time, since some of these claims will conflict. Here P2 recognizes the duty of management to act in the long-term best interests of the corporation, conceived as a forum of stakeholder interaction, when the interests of the group outweigh the interests of the individual parties to the collective contract. The duty described in P2 is a fiduciary duty, yet it does not suffer from the difficulties surrounding the fiduciary duty to stockholders, for the conflicts involved there are precisely those that P2 makes it mandatory for management to resolve. Of course, P2 gives no instructions for a magical resolution of the conflicts that arise from prima facie obligations to multiple parties. An analysis of such rules for decision making is a subject to be addressed on another occasion, but P2 does give these conflicts a legitimacy that they do not enjoy in the stockholder theory. It gives management a clear and distinct directive to pay attention to stakeholder claims.

P1 and P2 recognize the eventual need for changes in the law of corporations and other governance mechanisms if the stakeholder theory is to be put into practice. P1 and P2, if implemented as a major innovation in the structure of the corporation, will make manifest the eventual legal institutionalization of sanctions....

Structural Mechanisms

We propose several structural mechanisms to make a stakeholder management conception practicable. We shall offer a sketch of these here and say little by way of argument for them.

1. *The Stakeholder Board of Directors.* We propose that every corporation of a certain size yet to be determined, but surely all those that are publicly traded or are of the size of those publicly traded, form a Board of Directors comprised of representatives of five stakeholder groups, including employees, customers, suppliers, stockholders, and members of the local community, as well as a representative of the corporation, whom we might call a "metaphysical director" since he or she would be responsible for the metaphysical entity that is "the corporation." Whether or not each representative has an equal voting right is a matter that can be decided by experimentation; issues of governance lend themselves naturally to both laboratory and organizational experiments.

These directors will be vested with the duty of care to manage the affairs of the corporation in concert with the interests of its stakeholders. Such a Board would ensure that the rights of each group would have a forum, and by involving a director for the corporation, would ensure that the corporation itself would not be unduly harmed for the benefit of a particular group. In addition, by vesting each director with the duty of care for all stakeholders, we ensure that positive resolutions of conflicts would occur....The task of the metaphysical director, to be elected unanimously by the stakeholder representatives, is especially important. The fact that the director has no direct constituency would appear to enhance management control. However, nothing could be further from the truth. To represent the abstract entity that is the corporation would be a most demanding job. Our metaphysical director would be responsible for convincing both stakeholders and management that a certain course of action was in the interests of the long-term health of the corporation, especially when that action implies the sacrifice of the interests of all. The metaphysical director would be a key link between the stakeholder representatives and management, and would spearhead the drive to protect the norms of the interests of all stakeholders....

2. *Corporate Law*. The law of corporations needs to be redefined to recognize the legitimate purpose of the corporation as stated in P1. This has in fact developed in some areas of the law, such as products liability, where the claims of customers to safe products have emerged, and labor law, where the claims of employees have been safeguarded. Indeed, in such pioneering cases as *Marsh v. Alabama* the courts have come close to a stakeholder perspective. We envision that a body of case law will emerge to give meaning to "the proper claims of stakeholders," and in effect that the "wisdom of Solomon" necessary to make the stakeholder theory work will emerge naturally through the joint action of the courts, stakeholders, and management.

While much of the above may seem utopian, there are some very practical transitional steps that could occur. Each large corporation could form a stakeholder advisory board, which would prepare a charter detailing how the organization is to treat the claims of each stakeholder. Initially this stakeholder advisory board would serve as an advisor to the current board of directors, and eventually it would replace that board. Simultaneously, a group of legal scholars and practitioners, such as the American Law Institute, could initiate discussion of the legal proposals and methods to change corporate charters, while business groups such as the

Business Roundtable could examine the practical consequences of our proposals. Given the emergence of some consensus, we believe that a workable transition can be found....

NOTES

1. Cf. A. Berle and G. Means, *The Modern Corporation and Private Property* (New York: Commerce Clearing House, 1932), 1. For a reassessment of Berle and Means' argument after 50 years, see *Journal of Law and Economics* 26 (June 1983), especially G. Stigler and C. Friedland, "The Literature of Economics: The Case of Berle and Means," 237–68; D. North, "Comment on Stigler and Friedland," 269–72; and G. Means, "Corporate Power in the Marketplace," 467–85.

2. The metaphor of rebuilding the ship while afloat is attributed to Neurath by W. Quine, *Word and Object* (Cambridge: Harvard University Press, 1960), and W. Quine and J. Ullian, *The Web of Belief* (New York: Random House, 1978). The point is that to keep the ship afloat during repairs we must replace a plank with one that will do a better job. Our argument is that Kantian capitalism can so replace the current version of managerial capitalism.

3. Kant's notion of respect for persons (i.e., that each person has a right not to be treated as a means to an end) can be found in (1) Kant, *Critique of Practical Reason* (1838 edition). See J. Rawls, *A Theory of Justice* (Cambridge: Harvard University Press, 1971) for an eloquent modern interpretation.

4. For an introduction to the law of corporations, see A. Conard, *Corporations in Perspective* (Mineola, NY: The Foundation Press, 1976), especially section 19; and R. Hamilton, *Corporations* (St. Paul: West Publishing, 1981), Chapter 8.

5. For a modern statement of managerial capitalism, see the literature in managerial economics, for example R. Coase, "The Nature of the Firm," *Economica* 4 (1937): 386–405; M. Jensen and W. Meckling, "Theory of the Firm: Managerial Behavior, Agency Costs and Ownership Structure," *Journal of Financial Economics* 3 (1976): 305–60; and O. Williamson, *The Economics of Discretionary Behavior* (London: Kershaw Publishing, 1965).

6. See R. Charan and E. Freeman, "Planning for the Business Environment of the 1980s," *The Journal of Business Strategy* 1 (1980): 9–19, especially p. 15 for a brief account of the major developments in products liability law.

7. See S. Breyer, *Regulation and Its Reform* (Cambridge: Harvard University Press, 1983), 133, for an analysis of food additives.

8. See I. Millstein and S. Katsh, *The Limits of Corporate Power* (New York: Macmillan, 1981), Chapter 4.

9. Cf. C. Summers, "Protecting All Employees Against Unjust Dismissal," *Harvard Business Review* 58 (1980): 136, for a careful statement of the argument.

10. See E. Freeman and D. Reed, "Stockholders and Stakeholders: A New Perspective on Corporate Governance," in

C. Huizinga, ed., *Corporate Governance: A Definitive Exploration of the Issues* (Los Angeles: UCLA Extension Press, 1983).

11. See T. Peters and R. Waterman, *In Search of Excellence* (New York: Harper and Row, 1982).

CAN A CORPORATION HAVE A CONSCIENCE?
Kenneth E. Goodpaster and John B. Matthews, Jr.

During the severe racial tensions of the 1960s, Southern Steel Company (actual case, disguised name) faced considerable pressure from government and the press to explain and modify its policies regarding discrimination both within its plants and in the major city where it was located. SSC was the largest employer in the area (it had nearly 15,000 workers, one-third of whom were black) and had made great strides toward removing barriers to equal job opportunity in its several plants. In addition, its top executives (especially its chief executive officer, James Weston) had distinguished themselves as private citizens for years in community programs for black housing, education, and small business as well as in attempts at desegregating all-white police and local government organizations.

SSC drew the line, however, at using its substantial economic influence in the local area to advance the cause of the civil rights movement by pressuring banks, suppliers, and the local government:

> "As individuals we can exercise what influence we may have as citizens," James Weston said, "but for a corporation to attempt to exert any kind of economic compulsion to achieve a particular end in a social area seems to me to be quite beyond what a corporation should do and quite beyond what a corporation can do. I believe that while government may seek to compel social reforms, any attempt by a private organization like SSC to impose its views, its beliefs, and its will upon the community would

be repugnant to our American constitutional concepts and that appropriate steps to correct this abuse of corporate power would be universally demanded by public opinion."

Weston could have been speaking in the early 1980s on any issue that corporations around the United States now face. Instead of social justice, his theme might be environmental protection, product safety, marketing practice, or international bribery. His statement for SSC raises the important issue of corporate responsibility. Can a corporation have a conscience?

Weston apparently felt comfortable saying it need not. The responsibilities of ordinary persons and of "artificial persons" like corporations are, in his view, separate. Persons' responsibilities go beyond those of corporations. Persons, he seems to have believed, ought to care not only about themselves but also about the dignity and well-being of those around them—ought not only to care but also to act. Organizations, he evidently thought, are creatures of, and to a degree prisoners of, the systems of economic incentive and political sanction that give them reality and therefore should not be expected to display the same moral attributes that we expect of persons.

Others inside business as well as outside share Weston's perception. One influential philosopher—John Ladd—carries Weston's view a step further:

> "It is improper to expect organizational conduct to conform to the ordinary principles of morality," he says. "We cannot and must not expect formal organizations, or their representatives acting in their official capacities, to be honest, courageous, considerate, sympathetic, or to have

any kind of moral integrity. Such concepts are not in the vocabulary, so to speak, of the organizational language game."[1]

In our opinion, this line of thought represents a tremendous barrier to the development of business ethics both as a field of inquiry and as a practical force in managerial decision making. This is a matter about which executives must be philosophical and philosophers must be practical. A corporation can and should have a conscience. The language of ethics does have a place in the vocabulary of an organization. There need not be and there should not be a disjunction of the sort attributed to SSC's James Weston. Organizational agents such as corporations should be no more and no less morally responsible (rational, self-interested, altruistic) than ordinary persons.

We take this position because we think an analogy holds between the individual and the corporation. If we analyze the concept of moral responsibility as it applies to persons, we find that projecting it to corporations as agents in society is possible.

DEFINING THE RESPONSIBILITY OF PERSONS

When we speak of the responsibility of individuals, philosophers say that we mean three things: someone is to blame, something has to be done, or some kind of trustworthiness can be expected.

We apply the first meaning, what we shall call the *causal* sense, primarily to legal and moral contexts where what is at issue is praise or blame for a past action. We say of a person that he or she was responsible for what happened, is to blame for it, should be held accountable. In this sense of the word, *responsibility* has to do with tracing the causes of actions and events, of finding out who is answerable in a given situation. Our aim is to determine someone's intention, free will, degree of participation, and appropriate reward or punishment.

We apply the second meaning of *responsibility* to rule following, to contexts where individuals are subject to externally imposed norms often associated with some social role that people play. We speak of the responsibilities of parents to children, of doctors to patients, of lawyers to clients, of citizens to the law. What is socially expected and what the party involved is to answer for are at issue here.

We use the third meaning of *responsibility* for decision making. With this meaning of the term, we say that individuals are responsible if they are trustworthy and reliable, if they allow appropriate factors to affect their judgment; we refer primarily to a person's independent thought processes and decision making, processes that justify an attitude of trust from those who interact with him or her as a responsible individual.

The distinguishing characteristic of moral responsibility, it seems to us, lies in this third sense of the term. Here the focus is on the intellectual and emotional processes in the individual's moral reasoning. Philosophers call this "taking a moral point of view" and contrast it with such other processes as being financially prudent and attending to legal obligations.

To be sure, characterizing a person as "morally responsible" may seem rather vague. But vagueness is a contextual notion. Everything depends on how we fill in the blank in "vague for _____ purposes."

In some contexts the term "six o'clockish" is vague, while in others it is useful and informative. As a response to a space-shuttle pilot who wants to know when to fire the reentry rockets, it will not do, but it might do in response to a spouse who wants to know when one will arrive home at the end of the workday.

We maintain that the processes underlying moral responsibility can be defined and are not themselves vague, even though gaining consensus on specific moral norms and decisions is not always easy.

What, then, characterizes the processes underlying the judgment of a person we call morally responsible? Philosopher William K. Frankena offers the following answer:

> A morality is a normative system in which judgments are made, more or less consciously, [out of a] consideration of the effects of actions…on the lives of persons…including the lives of others besides the person acting… David Hume took a similar position when he argued that what speaks in a moral judgment is a kind of sympathy…A little later,…Kant put the matter somewhat better by characterizing morality as the business of respecting persons as ends and not as means or as things…[2]

Frankena is pointing to two traits, both rooted in a long and diverse philosophical tradition:

1. *Rationality*. Taking a moral point of view includes the features we usually attribute to rational decision making, that is, lack of impulsiveness, care in mapping out alternatives and consequences, clarity about goals and purposes, attention to details of implementation.

2. *Respect*. The moral point of view also includes a special awareness of and concern for the effects of one's decisions and policies on others, special in the sense that it goes beyond the kind of awareness and concern that would ordinarily be part of rationality, that is, beyond seeing others merely as instrumental to accomplishing one's own purposes. This is respect for the lives of others and involves taking their needs and interests seriously, not simply as resources in one's own decision making but as limiting conditions which change the very definition of one's habitat from a self-centered to a shared environment. It is what philosopher Immanuel Kant meant by the "categorical imperative" to treat others as valuable in and for themselves.

It is this feature that permits us to trust the morally responsible person. We know that such a person takes our point of view into account not merely as a useful precaution (as in "honesty is the best policy") but as important in its own right.

These components of moral responsibility are not too vague to be useful. Rationality and respect affect the manner in which a person approaches practical decision making: they affect the way in which the individual processes information and makes choices. A rational but not respectful Bill Jones will not lie to his friends *unless* he is reasonable sure he will not be found out. A rational but not respectful Mary Smith will defend an unjustly treated party *unless* she thinks it may be too costly to herself. A rational *and* respectful decision maker, however, notices—and cares—whether the consequences of his or her conduct lead to injuries or indignities to others.

Two individuals who take "the moral point of view" will not of course always agree on ethical matters, but they do at least have a basis for dialogue.

PROJECTING RESPONSIBILITY TO CORPORATIONS

Now that we have removed some of the vagueness from the notion of moral responsibility as it applies to persons, we can search for a frame of reference in which, by analogy with Bill Jones and Mary Smith, we can meaningfully and appropriately say that corporations are morally responsible. This is the issue reflected in the SSC case.

To deal with it, we must ask two questions: Is it meaningful to apply moral concepts to actors who are not persons but who are instead made up of persons? And even if meaningful, is it advisable to do so?

If a group can act like a person in some ways, then we can expect it to behave like a person in other ways. For one thing, we know that people organized into a group can act as a unit. As business people well know, legally a corporation is considered a unit. To approach unity, a group usually has some sort of internal decision structure, a system of rules that spell out authority relationships and specify the conditions under which certain individuals' actions become official actions of the group.[3]

If we can say that persons act responsibly only if they gather information about the impact of their actions on others and use it in making decisions, we can reasonably do the same for organizations. Our proposed frame of reference for thinking about and implementing corporate responsibility aims at spelling out the processes associated with the moral responsibility of individuals and projecting them to the level of organizations. This is similar to, though an inversion of, Plato's famous method in the *Republic*, in which justice in the community is used as a model for justice in the individual.

Hence, corporations that monitor their employment practices and the effects of their production processes and products on the environment and human health show the same kind of rationality and respect that morally responsible individuals do. Thus, attributing actions, strategies, decisions, and moral responsibilities to corporations as entities distinguishable from those who hold offices in them poses no problem.

And when we look about us, we can readily see differences in moral responsibility among corporations in much the same way that we see differences among persons. Some corporations have built features into their management incentive systems, board structures, internal control systems, and research agendas that in a person we would call self-control, integrity, and conscientiousness. Some have institutionalized awareness and concern for consumers, employees, and the rest of the public in ways that others clearly have not.

As a matter of course, some corporations attend to the human impact of their operations and policies and reject operations and policies that are questionable. Whether the issue be the health effects of sugared cereal or cigarettes, the safety of tires or tampons, civil liberties in the corporation or the community, an organization reveals its character as surely as a person does.

Indeed, the parallel may be even more dramatic. For just as the moral responsibility displayed by an individual develops over time from infancy to adulthood,[4] so too we may expect to find stages of development in organizational character that show significant patterns.

EVALUATING THE IDEA
OF MORAL PROJECTION

Concepts like moral responsibility not only make sense when applied to organizations but also provide touchstones for designing more effective models than we have for guiding corporate policy.

Now we can understand what it means to invite SSC as a corporation to be morally responsible both in-house and in its community, but *should* we issue the invitation? Here we turn to the question of advisability. Should we require the organizational agents in our society to have the same moral attributes we require of ourselves?

Our proposal to spell out the processes associated with moral responsibility for individuals and then to project them to their organizational counterparts takes on added meaning when we examine alternative frames of reference for corporate responsibility.

Two frames of reference that compete for the allegiance of people who ponder the question of corporate responsibility are emphatically opposed to this principle of moral projection—what we

might refer to as the "invisible hand" view and the "hand of government" view.

The Invisible Hand

The most eloquent spokesman of the first view is Milton Friedman (echoing many philosophers and economists since Adam Smith). According to this pattern of thought, the true and only social responsibilities of business organizations are to make profits and obey the laws. The workings of the free and competitive marketplace will "moralize" corporate behavior quite independently of any attempts to expand or transform decision making via moral projection.

A deliberate amorality in the executive suite is encouraged in the name of systemic morality: the common good is best served when each of us and our economic institutions pursue not the common good or moral purpose, advocates say, but competitive advantage. Morality, responsibility, and conscience reside in the invisible hand of the free market system, not in the hands of the organizations within the system, much less the managers within the organizations.

To be sure, people of this opinion admit, there is a sense in which social or ethical issues can and should enter the corporate mind, but the filtering of such issues is thorough: they go through the screens of custom, public opinion, public relations, and the law. And, in any case, self-interest maintains primacy as an objective and a guiding star.

The reaction from this frame of reference to the suggestion that moral judgment be integrated with corporate strategy is clearly negative. Such an integration is seen as inefficient and arrogant, and in the end both an illegitimate use of corporate power and an abuse of the manager's fiduciary role. With respect to our SSC case, advocates of the invisible hand model would vigorously resist efforts, beyond legal requirements, to make SSC right the wrongs of racial injustice. SSC's responsibility would be to make steel of high quality at least cost, to deliver it on time, and to satisfy its customers and stockholders. Justice would not be part of SSC's corporate mandate.

The Hand of Government

Advocates of the second dissenting frame of reference abound, but John Kenneth Galbraith's work has counterpointed Milton Friedman's with insight and style. Under this view of corporate responsibility, corporations are to pursue objectives that are rational and purely economic. The regulatory hands of the law and the political process rather than the invisible hand of the marketplace turns these objectives to the common good.

Again, in this view, it is a system that provides the moral direction for corporate decision making—a system, though, that is guided by political managers, the custodians of the public purpose. In the case of SSC, proponents of this view would look to the state for moral direction and responsible management, both within SSC and in the community. The corporation would have no moral responsibility beyond political and legal obedience.

What is striking is not so much the radical difference between the economic and social philosophies that underlie these two views of the source of corporate responsibility but the conceptual similarities. Both views locate morality, ethics, responsibility, and conscience in the systems of rules and incentives in which the modern corporation finds itself embedded. Both views reject the exercise of independent moral judgment by corporations as actors in society.

Neither view trusts corporate leaders with stewardship over what are often called noneconomic values. Both require corporate responsibility to march to the beat of drums outside. In the jargon of moral philosophy, both views press for a rule-centered or a system-centered ethics instead of an agent-centered ethics. These frames of reference countenance corporate rule-following responsibility for corporations but not corporate decision-making responsibility.

The Hand of Management

To be sure, the two views under discussion differ in that one looks to an invisible moral force in the market while the other looks to a visible moral force in government. But both would advise against a principle of moral projection that permits or encourages corporations to exercise independent, noneconomic judgment over matters that face them in their short- and long-term plans and operations.

Accordingly, both would reject a third view of corporate responsibility that seeks to affect the thought processes of the organization itself—a sort of "hand of management" view—since neither

seems willing or able to see the engines of profit regulate themselves to the degree that would be implied by taking the principle of moral projection seriously. Cries of inefficiency and moral imperialism from the right would be matched by cries of insensitivity and illegitimacy from the left, all in the name of preserving us from corporations and managers run morally amok.

Better, critics would say, that moral philosophy be left to philosophers, philanthropists, and politicians than to business leaders. Better that corporate morality be kept to glossy annual reports, where it is safely insulated from policy and performance.

The two conventional frames of reference locate moral restraint in forces external to the person and the corporation. They deny moral reasoning and intent to the corporation in the name of either market competition or society's system of explicit legal constraints and presume that these have a better moral effect than that of rationality and respect.

Although the principle of moral projection, which underwrites the idea of a corporate conscience and patterns it on the thought and feeling processes of the person, is in our view compelling, we must acknowledge that it is neither part of the received wisdom, nor is its advisability beyond question or objection. Indeed, attributing the role of conscience to the corporation seems to carry with it new and disturbing implications for our usual ways of thinking about ethics and business.

Perhaps the best way to clarify and defend this frame of reference is to address the objections to the principle found in the last pages of this article. There we see a summary of the criticisms and counterarguments we have heard during hours of discussion with business executives and business school students. We believe that the replies to the objections about a corporation having a conscience are convincing.

LEAVING THE DOUBLE STANDARD BEHIND

We have come some distance from our opening reflection on Southern Steel Company and its role in its community. Our proposal—clarified, we hope, through these objections and replies—suggests that it is not sufficient to draw a sharp line between individuals' private ideas and efforts and a corporation's institutional efforts but that the latter can and should be built upon the former.

Does this frame of reference give us an unequivocal prescription for the behavior of SSC in its circumstances? No, it does not. Persuasive arguments might be made now and might have been made then that SSC should not have used its considerable economic clout to threaten the community into desegregation. A careful analysis of the realities of the environment might have disclosed that such a course would have been counterproductive, leading to more injustice than it would have alleviated.

The point is that some of the arguments and some of the analyses are or would have been moral arguments, and thereby the ultimate decision that of an ethically responsible organization. The significance of this point can hardly be overstated, for it represents the adoption of a new perspective on corporate policy and a new way of thinking about business ethics. We agree with one authority, who writes that "the business firm, as an organic entity intricately affected by and affecting its environment, is as appropriately adaptive...to demands for responsible behavior as for economic service."[5]

The frame of reference here developed does not offer a decision procedure for corporate managers. That has not been our purpose. It does, however, shed light on the conceptual foundations of business ethics by training attention on the corporation as a moral agent in society. Legal systems of rules and incentives are insufficient, even though they may be necessary, as frameworks for corporate responsibility. Taking conceptual cues from the features of moral responsibility normally expected of the person in our opinion deserves practicing managers' serious consideration.

The lack of congruence that James Weston saw between individual and corporate moral responsibility can be, and we think should be, overcome. In the process, what a number of writers have characterized as a double standard—a discrepancy between our personal lives and our lives in organizational settings—might be dampened. The principle of moral projection not only helps us to conceptualize the kinds of demands that we might make of corporations and other organizations but also offers the prospect of harmonizing those demands with the demands that we make of ourselves.

IS A CORPORATION A MORALLY RESPONSIBLE "PERSON"?

Objection 1 to the Analogy

Corporations are not persons. They are artificial legal constructions, machines for mobilizing economic investments toward the efficient production of goods and services. We cannot hold a corporation responsible. We can only hold individuals responsible.

Reply

Our frame of reference does not imply that corporations are persons in a literal sense. It simply means that in certain respects concepts and functions normally attributed to persons can also be attributed to organizations made up of persons. Goals, economic values, strategies, and other such personal attributes are often usefully projected to the corporate level by managers and researchers. Why should we not project the functions of conscience in the same way? As for holding corporations responsible, recent criminal prosecutions such as the case of Ford Motor Company and its Pinto gas tanks suggest that society finds the idea both intelligible and useful.

Objection 2

A corporation cannot be held responsible at the sacrifice of profit. Profitability and financial health have always been and should continue to be the "categorical imperatives" of a business operation.

Reply

We must of course acknowledge the imperatives of survival, stability, and growth when we discuss corporations, as indeed we must acknowledge them when we discuss the life of an individual. Self-sacrifice has been identified with moral responsibility in only the most extreme cases. The pursuit of profit and self-interest need not be pitted against the demands of moral responsibility. Moral demands are best viewed as containments—not replacements—for self-interest.

This is not to say that profit maximization never conflicts with morality. But profit maximization conflicts with other managerial values as well. The point is to coordinate imperatives, not deny their validity.

Objection 3

Corporate executives are not elected representatives of the people, nor are they anointed or appointed as social guardians. They therefore lack the social mandate that a democratic society rightly demands of those who would pursue ethically or socially motivated policies. By keeping corporate policies confined to economic motivations, we keep the power of corporate executives in its proper place.

Reply

The objection betrays an oversimplified view of the relationship between the public and the private sector. Neither private individuals nor private corporations that guide their conduct by ethical or social values beyond the demands of law should be constrained merely because they are not elected to do so. The demands of moral responsibility are independent of the demands of political legitimacy and are in fact presupposed by them.

To be sure, the state and the political process will and must remain the primary mechanisms for protecting the public interest, but one might be forgiven the hope that the political process will not substitute for the moral judgment of the citizenry or other components of society such as corporations.

Objection 4

Our system of law carefully defines the role of agent or fiduciary and makes corporate managers accountable to shareholders and investors for the use of their assets. Management cannot, in the name of corporate moral responsibility, arrogate to itself the right to manage those assets by partially noneconomic criteria.

Reply

First, it is not so clear that investors insist on purely economic criteria in the management of their assets, especially if some of the shareholders' resolutions and board reforms of the last decade are any indication. For instance, companies doing business in South Africa have had stockholders question their activities, other companies have instituted audit committees for their boards before such auditing was mandated, and mutual funds for which "socially responsible behavior" is a major investment criterion now exist.

Second, the categories of "shareholder" and "investor" connote wider time spans than do immediate or short-term returns. As a practical matter, considerations of stability and long-term return on investment enlarge the class of principals to which managers bear a fiduciary relationship.

Third, the trust that managers hold does not and never has extended to "any means available" to advance the interests of the principals. Both legal and moral constraints must be understood to qualify that trust—even, perhaps, in the name of a larger trust and a more basic fiduciary relationship to the members of society at large.

Objection 5

The power, size, and scale of the modern corporation—domestic as well as international—are awesome. To unleash, even partially, such power from the discipline of the marketplace and the narrow or possible nonexistent moral purpose implicit in that discipline would be socially dangerous. Had SSC acted in the community to further racial justice, its purposes might have been admirable, but those purposes could have led to a kind of moral imperialism or worse. Suppose SSC had thrown its power behind the Ku Klux Klan.

Reply

This is a very real and important objection. What seems to be appreciated is the fact that power affects when it is used as well as when it is not used. A decision by SSC not to exercise its economic influence according to "noneconomic" criteria is inevitably a moral decision and just as inevitably affects the community. The issue in the end is not whether corporations (and other organizations) should be "unleashed" to exert moral force in our society but rather how critically and self-consciously they should choose to do so.

The degree of influence enjoyed by an agent, whether a person or an organization, is not so much a factor recommending moral disengagement as a factor demanding a high level of moral awareness. Imperialism is more to be feared when moral reasoning is absent than when it is present. Nor do we suggest that the "discipline of the marketplace" be diluted; rather, we call for it to be supplemented with the discipline of moral reflection.

Objection 6

The idea of moral projection is a useful device for structuring corporate responsibility only if our understanding of moral responsibility at the level of the person is in some sense richer than our understanding of moral responsibility on the level of the organization as a whole. If we are not clear about individual responsibility, the projection is fruitless.

Reply

The objection is well taken. The challenge offered by the idea of moral projection lies in our capacity to articulate criteria or frameworks of reasoning for the morally responsible person. And though such a challenge is formidable, it is not clear that it cannot be met, at least with sufficient consensus to be useful.

For centuries, the study and criticism of frameworks have gone on, carried forward by many disciplines, including psychology, the social sciences, and philosophy. And though it would be a mistake to suggest that any single framework (much less a decision mechanism) has emerged as the right one, it is true that recurrent patterns are discernible and well enough defined to structure moral discussion.

In the body of the article, we spoke of rationality and respect as components of individual responsibility. Further analysis of these components would translate them into social costs and benefits, justice in the distribution of goods and services, basic rights and duties, and fidelity to contracts. The view that pluralism in our society has undercut all possibility of moral agreement is anything but self-evident. Sincere moral disagreement is, of course, inevitable and not clearly lamentable. But a process and a vocabulary for articulating such values as we share is no small step forward when compared with the alternatives. Perhaps in our exploration of the moral projection we might make some surprising and even reassuring discoveries about ourselves.

Objection 7

Why is it necessary to project moral responsibility to the level of the organization? Isn't the task of defining corporate responsibility and business ethics sufficiently discharged if we clarify the responsibilities of men and women in business as individuals? Doesn't ethics finally rest on the honesty and integrity of the individual in the business world?

Reply

Yes and no. Yes, in the sense that the control of large organizations does finally rest in the hands of

managers, of men and women. No, in the sense that what is being controlled is a cooperative system for a cooperative purpose. The projection of responsibility to the organization is simply an acknowledgment of the fact that the whole is more than the sum of its parts. Many intelligent people do not an intelligent organization make. Intelligence needs to be structured, organized, divided, and recombined in complex processes for complex purposes.

Studies of management have long shown that the attributes, successes, and failures of organizations are phenomena that emerge from the coordination of persons' attributes and that explanations of such phenomena require categories of analysis and description beyond the level of the individual. Moral responsibility is an attribute that can manifest itself in organizations as surely as competence or efficiency.

Objection 8

Is the frame of reference here proposed intended to replace or undercut the relevance of the "invisible hand" and the "government hand" views, which depend on external controls?

Reply

No. Just as regulation and economic competition are not substitutes for corporate responsibility, so corporate responsibility is not a substitute for law and the market. The imperatives of ethics cannot be relied on—nor have they ever been relied on—without a context of external sanctions. And this is true as much for individuals as for organizations.

This frame of reference takes us beneath, but not beyond, the realm of external systems of rules and incentives and into the thought processes that interpret and respond to the corporation's environment. Morality is more than merely part of that environment. It aims at the projection of conscience, not the enthronement of it in either the state or the competitive process.

The rise of the modern large corporation and the concomitant rise of the professional manager demand a conceptual framework in which these phenomena can be accommodated to moral thought. The principle of moral projection furthers such accommodation by recognizing a new level of agency in society and thus a new level of responsibility.

Objection 9

Corporations have always taken the interests of those outside the corporation into account in the sense that customer relations and public relations generally are an integral part of rational economic decision making. Market signals and social signals that filter through the market mechanism inevitably represent the interests of parties affected by the behavior of the company. What, then, is the point of adding respect to rationality?

Reply

Representing the affected parties solely as economic variables in the environment of the company is treating them as means or resources and not as ends in themselves. It implies that the only voice which affected parties should have in organizational decision making is that of potential buyers, sellers, regulators, or boycotters. Besides, many affected parties may not occupy such roles, and those who do may not be able to signal the organization with messages that effectively represent their stakes in its actions.

To be sure, classical economic theory would have us believe that perfect competition in free markets (with modest adjustments from the state) will result in all relevant signals being "heard," but the abstractions from reality implicit in such theory make it insufficient as a frame of reference for moral responsibility. In a world in which strict self-interest was congruent with the common good, moral responsibility might be unnecessary. We do not, alas, live in such a world.

The element of respect in our analysis of responsibility plays an essential role in ensuring the recognition of unrepresented or underrepresented voices in the decision making of organizations as agents. Showing respect for persons as ends and not mere means to organizational purposes is central to the concept of corporate moral responsibility.

NOTES

1. See John Ladd, "Morality and the Ideal of Rationality in Formal Organizations," *The Monist* (October 1970): 499.

2. See William K. Frankena, *Thinking About Morality* (Ann Arbor: University of Michigan Press, 1980), 26.

3. See Peter French, "The Corporation as a Moral Person," *American Philosophical Quarterly* (July 1979): 207.

4. A process that psychological researchers from Jean Piaget to Lawrence Kohlberg have examined carefully; see Jean Piaget, *The Moral Judgement of the Child* (New York: Free Press, 1965) and Lawrence Kohlberg, *The Philosophy of Moral Development* (New York: Harper & Row, 1981).

5. See Kenneth R. Andrews, *The Concept of Corporate Strategy*, rev. ed. (Homewood, Ill.: Dow Jones–Irwin, 1980), 99.

PART II

Business and Employees

5

Job Security

Dismissals and Layoffs

Job security, perhaps even more than wages and economic benefits, has become a primary concern of today's workers. For example, in these days of corporate downsizing, unions are often placing greater emphasis on keeping jobs than on increasing members' wages. However, the employer's right to terminate employment through either a mass "layoff" or the "dismissal" of an individual is an almost unquestioned assumption in the United States. So the increased concerns about job security run into conflict with traditional conceptions of employer rights. This chapter will examine that conflict. We will consider whether any limits should be placed on the employer's ability to discharge workers, and in turn, whether new (that is, new for the United States) employee rights that constrain management authority should be recognized. Since job security issues involve questions of both mass layoffs and individual dismissals, it is best if we analyze those topics separately.

INDIVIDUAL DISMISSALS

An understanding of the history of dismissal law in the United States will help us identify today's available options for dismissing individuals. Historically, employment law in the United States was governed by a doctrine known as "employment at will." This doctrine held that when an explicit agreement of contractually binding terms of employment is absent, the employment relationship exists only so long as both parties will it to continue. That is, either party is free to end the relationship at his or her will. Moreover, the relationship may be terminated at any time and for any reason. One court even said that employment may be ended "for good cause, for no cause, or even for cause morally wrong." The doctrine of employment at will (EAW) thus gives the employer absolute discretion to hire and fire.*

Over time, this EAW doctrine has been challenged as providing insufficient protection to workers. Although it is true that employers and employees have equal formal rights under EAW (either may exit the relationship at any time), many commentators believe that employers have the greater power since most employees need their job more than the employer needs them. (Employers can find replacement workers more easily than employees can find replacement jobs under normal rates of unemployment.) In addition, some reasons for dismissing employees, for example, race, were found morally intolerable. As a result, the doctrine of EAW has been incrementally modified over recent decades so that employers' discretionary authority has been limited.

Modifications to EAW

The modifications to EAW have come primarily from two sources: legislative actions and precedents set by court decisions. Federal and state legislatures have enumerated exceptions to the employer's authority by prohibiting firings for, among other things: race or sex (the Civil Rights Act); requesting a safety inspection of the workplace (the Occupational Safety and Health Act); supporting unionization (the Wagner Act); and physical disability that is not related to reasonable job requirements (the Americans with Disabilities Act).

Courts have also carved out new legal exceptions to the employer's power to fire workers. Three exceptions are most significant. First, there is the "public policy exception" to EAW. Courts have sometimes found that the dismissal of an at-will employee, while not a violation of any explicit statute, nonetheless undermines the state's ability to pursue legitimate public policies and for that reason will not be accepted. An early case of this sort involved a food business employee who noticed that cans of food were regularly underweighted. Cans that should have contained twelve ounces were often fractionally less than that weight. The employee noted this in a complaint to his employer and was dismissed. (Apparently the underweighting was an intentional corporate policy.) Since he was an at-will employee, he could be dismissed for any or no reason; the firing was not technically illegal. However, the court held that permitting a dismissal in this case

---

*While the doctrine of EAW was the dominant legal rule, there were always employees who were not subject to it. Workers with explicit contracts, such as union members, typically have contractually guaranteed grievance procedures that specify how and when an employer may fire an individual worker. Additionally, government workers are not subject to EAW since the government is bound by constitutional constraints of due process and the like. These are significant exceptions, but they still constitute a distinct minority of American employees. At least 80 percent of the private sector labor force is currently governed by the modified EAW doctrine described in this chapter.

would undercut the state's ability to enforce its truth in labelling legislation and, hence, the firing was an unacceptable violation of public policy.

The second judicial exception to EAW is found in cases where courts have found implicit contracts on the basis of representations that were made to employees either in their employee handbooks or through statements made in the hiring process. (Decision Scenario 3, "Unwritten Employment Contracts," at the end of this chapter identifies some examples of this "implied contract exception.")

The third exception to EAW is the "implied covenant of good faith exception." Courts have fashioned this exception to EAW to prevent, for example, the discharge of employees days before they are due to receive annual bonuses for yearly sales performances.

The modified EAW that has evolved in the United States is perceived by many to have a number of serious problems. It is uncertain for both employers and employees. To be protected in their jobs, especially by the judicial exceptions to EAW, employees must file suit against their employers. Whether their particular jurisdiction will find an exception to EAW in their specific case is highly uncertain. The exceptions are defined rather vaguely. Similarly, employers suffer uncertainty in that they are never sure whether a discharge will be found to fall under some new exception. The employer's uncertainty is compounded when multimillion-dollar damages are possible if a discharge is found unacceptable. (As an ironic result of this uncertainty, employers are becoming extremely cautious about dismissals. To block suits based on the implied contract exception, they are beginning to require signed disclaimers that specify employment is at will when they distribute employee manuals. They even sometimes fail to discharge unproductive workers for fear of large damage awards if the fired employee sues.)

Just Cause Policies

Because they believe current legal policy fails to protect workers adequately or because they believe business is hamstrung by the threat of lawsuits, some commentators have begun to call for a different approach to employment law in the United States. They urge that the United States adopt a "just cause policy" modelled on those of most other industrialized nations. Just cause policies essentially require that any individual firing be done only for reasons judged to be legitimate. So, instead of identifying those reasons that are unacceptable and letting employers fire for any other reason (as the U.S. approach does), just cause policies further limit the power of employers by establishing a finite list of reasons that will justify a dismissal.

Typical just cause policies define acceptable reasons for dismissal loosely and let further definition come through decisions of arbitrators or labor courts. While acceptable reasons are not precisely defined by statute, common law develops a rather clear list of acceptable and unacceptable reasons for discharge of employees. Acceptable reasons will include theft, excessive absenteeism, intoxication on the job, substandard performance, and business downturns. Unacceptable reasons include political opinion, religion, race, personal bias of managers, and ethnicity.

(It should be noted that the U.S. Constitution's guarantees of free speech and religion are currently constraints only on government employers. Courts have consistently held that private employers are not bound by constitutional rights such as these, which citizens hold against their government.)

Just cause policies also usually include the following: specified minimum performance standards; a probationary period before employees are covered by just cause requirements; a requirement that employees be given notice of and reasons for intent to dismiss; a pretermination hearing to minimize the chance of unfair dismissal; an opportunity to appeal the employer's decision to an independent arbitrator; and some clearly defined remedy if the arbitrator finds the dismissal unjust. Remedies are usually limited to some multiple of wages plus back pay. Sometimes, though rarely, remedies will include reinstatement for dismissed employees.

One advantage of just cause policies for employers is that these remedies are known in advance and employers are not thrown into a litigation lottery where they might lose millions. It was a consideration like this that led some Montana businesses to support the only just cause policy in the United States. (See Decision Scenario 6, "Montana's Just Cause Legislation," at the end of this chapter.)

Opponents of just cause argue that it is likely to be economically inefficient. Many believe that with increased job security comes decreased worker output. When workers have no fear of losing their employment, they will be less motivated and less productive. Anecdotal evidence for this claim is often offered by reference to a caricature of government employees or tenured faculty who are unproductive and who have high job security. Opponents of just cause also point to the inefficiency created when management's time is so taken up with the need to document performance problems and to appear at hearings. Finally, opponents claim that formal just cause policies are unnecessary because an employer who fires productive workers without cause will be penalized by the marketplace. Workers, then, need no protections beyond what the market provides.

Proponents of just cause respond to these efficiency concerns in a number of ways. They challenge the notion that fear is an effective motivation. They claim, instead, that workers who fear arbitrary actions from management may make sure they comply with performance mandates, but they will be alienated, resentful, and unwilling to take risks. Workers with job security, proponents contend, will be more committed to the company and more likely to see their interests as tied to the long-term interests of the firm. (This particular debate mirrors management theory debates about worker motivation between followers of Frederick Taylor's "scientific management" and followers of Douglas McGregor's "Theory Y.") Moreover, they note that just cause is not equivalent to absolute job security. Workers may still be dismissed if their work is subpar.

Those defending just cause policies respond to the complaints about government employees by questioning whether, if the characterization is accurate, the poor performance is a consequence of job security alone or a conjunction of job security with work that is either alienating or that offers few incentives. They offer evidence of their own from studies showing union plants are more productive than nonunion plants and from facts about the productivity of European workers with just cause protections. From this evidence, they argue that cases of lazy workers with job security need to be explained by something other than the job security alone. Perhaps the perceived lack of worker output is due, instead, to a failure of management to enforce productivity standards (possibly out of fear of lawsuits).

Those in favor of just cause also challenge the claims that it is a waste of management time and unnecessary for protecting workers. They argue that documenting employee performance can create a climate that leads to procedures for improving the productivity of current employees. Also, they point out, if the market selected against unfair dismissals, we would not expect neutral parties (arbitrators and courts) to judge as without cause half (over two hundred thousand a year) of all contested firings.

Just Cause vs. EAW

The articles by Werhane and Maitland engage the debate over just cause and EAW, or the modified U.S. version of EAW. They give a clear picture of how different interpretations of efficiency and rights produce different conclusions in this debate (note the parallels with the utilitarian and rights-based theories of Chapters Two and Three). Typically, those in favor of EAW argue that it is the approach most consistent with the rights to property and liberty. Maitland, for example, explicitly argues that mandatory due process rights will conflict with the rights of employees to freely contract for their preferred conditions of employment (an application of a liberty right). Others argue that owners, having the rights to control who gains access to their property and to exclusive benefit from their property, ought to be free to terminate any individual's employment at will. This is merely a corporate instance of the right homeowners have to permit or deny entry to any individual.

Werhane argues to the contrary that due process rights are required by autonomy and fairness. She contends that employees are autonomous agents and not mere "human resources" (a common phrase that implicitly compares persons with material resources of the productive process). Moreover, in contemporary times, the security of one's income functions to promote a person's autonomy in the way that ownership of land would have in an agrarian economy.

Werhane also argues that employees deserve a guarantee of fairness in dismissal proceedings as a matter of right. She contends that due process should be required of any institution that has the power to do serious and unfair damage to the welfare of individuals. As a result, she urges that we abandon the notion that civil rights bind only public institutions and not private corporations.

It should be noted that while the two authors present the debate as one about process, pure process is obviously not all that is at issue here. Requiring merely a formal procedure before dismissal would be little hindrance to an employer who wanted to dismiss a worker and little protection for the worker. If there were no limits on the reasons that can justify a dismissal, procedures would mean nothing. Real due process rights require as a corollary the existence of substantive standards identifying acceptable and unacceptable grounds for termination. So, while the articles employ the terminology of due process, the debate is really about whether dismissals should be governed by a just cause policy.

In assessing this debate, we suggest that you recall the comments on rights in Chapter Three. The debate here presents a conflict between property and liberty rights on one hand and fairness and autonomy for employees on the other hand. From Chapter Three we know that property rights are derivative rights whose underlying values are fairness, autonomy, and utility. We also know that we need to justify liberty in specific areas (such as freedom of contract) by articulating why liberty in that area is important. These points would suggest that the conflict of claimed rights in this case is a conflict between rights that have the same status and the same foundational values. You need, then, to determine in which of the two competing rights are those underlying values most at stake in this issue of employment termination. Your evaluation will tell help you determine whether you prefer an EAW or just cause approach.

MASS LAYOFFS

The other major job security topic—layoffs—has received quite a bit of notice lately as a result of the waves of corporate "downsizing" that the United States has experienced in the past decade. Just as the issue of individual dismissal involved questions of reasons (when to fire) and questions of process (how to fire), the issue of layoffs raises when and how questions as well. Morally, we need to ask what economic circumstances would justify terminating the employment of a group of workers and, when a termination is justified, what process ought to be followed. For instance, we need to ask whether a temporary downturn in demand for a company's product justify a layoff in the same way that a permanent, structural change in demand does.

Answers to these questions range as widely as answers to the questions about firing individuals. In fact, in the United States the traditional EAW doctrine now applies more to layoffs than it does to firing because, as the case study for this chapter shows, American employers have had relatively unlimited layoff powers. American employers are subject only to one legal requirement in layoffs, the very recent demand that companies with more than one hundred employees provide advance notice when layoffs involve either five hundred workers or one third of a company's work force.

Elsewhere, employers must comply with stricter notice requirements and must often provide severance payments to dismissed workers. (It should be noted that a number of U.S. corporations voluntarily give extended notice and severance packages during layoffs. Sunoco, for example, recently offered laid off workers something on the order of two weeks' severance for every year of service, provided employees would sign a promise not to sue.) Moreover, as the case study also discusses, government and corporate policies in other nations often tend to discourage the use of temporary layoffs in favor of other alternatives.

The debate over layoff policies once again forces us to consider arguments about both efficiency/utility and rights. Concerns about the efficiency of imposing layoff responsibilities on corporations often center on what Ian Maitland calls "Eurosclerosis," or what Ronald Reagan called "Euro-malaise" when he commented on the 1988 bill requiring advance notice of layoffs. The concern is that such responsibilities raise the cost of hiring an employee and, as a result, reduce the overall levels of employment in the nation. Europe, with its strong job security, has, of course, experienced decades of high unemployment.

Those more sympathetic to layoff responsibilities, however, note that job security provisions are only one variable affecting European economies and it is dangerous to attribute unemployment effects to that single variable. In fact, one of the few empirical studies of the topic suggests that the effects are small. Another comparative study suggested that economies that rely on layoffs in periods of economic downturns are likely to have longer and deeper recessions, presumably because layoffs reduce the willingness of consumers to spend the economy out of recession.

In addition, some will argue that strong commitment to job security can produce changes in employee attitudes that, in turn, increase productivity. They argue that frequent layoffs (65 percent of firms that downsize do so repeatedly) severely damage morale and lower productivity, especially when the same amount of work is spread among fewer employees. Other discussions of the efficiency of job security provisions can be found in the readings by Maitland, Phillips, and Singer.

At its deepest level, however, this debate about layoff responsibilities reflects disagreements about corporate property rights and the rights of employees. On one hand, opponents of employee job security provisions often argue that the benefits of corporate property to shareholders should not be reduced to provide benefits for nonshareholders, namely, employees or local communities. On the other hand, proponents of job security argue that corporate property ought to be treated differently from personal property. They argue that the specific rights associated with corporate property ought to be limited because of the major social impacts of mass layoffs and because of the contribution society has made to the value of shareholders' investments (for example, through support for necessary infrastructures such as highways, transportation systems, and public education).

For a more pragmatic perspective on these points, consider that while the long-term data on productivity and profitability is unclear, stock prices generally increase significantly once a company announces a downsizing. Layoffs, then, can be seen as one way of allocating costs and benefits among the various constituencies of a corporation. The question is what allocation best accords with the rights of the parties involved. Determining whether there ought to be ethical limits on when and how employees are laid off will require you to identify the foundations of these claimed employee rights: continued employment in temporary economic downturns, notice before dismissal, and severance pay. Then, as before, you will need to compare those rights and their foundations against the traditional rights to property and freedom of contract that support broad management rights to downsize. The readings by Singer and Maitland provide a resource for that comparison.

CASE STUDY   Layoffs: American and European Style

Layoffs have dominated the economic news in the United States recently. It seems that every week a major corporation announces a new round of "downsizing." The emphasis on job loss is somewhat surprising given that unemployment rates are at historical lows. The composition of the unemployed, however, has changed dramatically over the last decade. Now, white-collar employees constitute a higher percentage of the unemployed than do blue-collar workers. In addition, the current round of layoffs appear not to be temporary responses to the business cycle but rather permanent and structural decreases in corporate employment levels. These new features of contemporary downsizing help explain the increased media attention. Corporate shedding of payroll is now threatening middle-class suburbia.

The economic conditions that lead to corporate downsizing are affecting most of the first-world industrial nations. Not all nations, however, approach the problems in the same way. In the United States, management has broad legal discretion to determine when and how employees will be laid off. Management may terminate employment for groups of employees for almost any reason. In the past, layoffs were often management's preferred response to temporary fluctuations in demand. Recent permanent layoffs have been done to achieve "international competitiveness" and to please the marketplace. They have, in fact, usually improved investors' share values, at least in the short term (which is what large institutional investors are concerned about).

While management in the United States has a free hand in deciding *when* to downsize, one limit was placed on *how* American management may downsize by the Worker Adjustment and Retraining Act of 1988. It demands that plants with more than one hundred workers provide sixty days' notice of impending layoffs if those layoffs will involve either five hundred workers or more than one third of the plant's work force. These requirements were imposed by the federal congress in an attempt to cushion the impact of mass layoffs on both individual employees and local communities. For example, while laid-off workers are eligible for unemployment, the time it takes them to find new, permanent work is substantially shortened when they are given advance notice. The drain on state unemployment insurance coffers is thereby reduced as well.

A study of the effectiveness of the WARN Act by the nonpartisan Government Accounting Office has raised doubts about how well the act has achieved its purposes, however. The GAO study noted that the one-hundred-employee threshold effectively exempts 98 percent of American workplaces from the act. Moreover, the study found that two thirds of the employers covered by the act failed to provide the required advance notice, most by failing to provide any notice at all. Workers whose employers violate the act may sue for lost wages, but the study also found that only 1 percent of the violations have been enforced in that way.

Layoff policies in other industrial nations are more limiting than those in the United States. This is particularly true of Europe. In Europe, both government and corporate policies have discouraged the use of layoffs as a short-term response to fluctuations in demand. Some European nations give public authorities the power to delay a layoff. France had a law, repealed in the 1980s, that required the approval of public authority for any mass layoff. Corporations themselves take steps to minimize layoffs caused by the business cycle. They often reduce the hours worked for each employee rather than terminate the employment of a few. Those employees experiencing such "short-time" work are eligible for pro-rated unemployment benefits, and they retain their fringe benefits. (Governments subsidize the cost of these benefits for employees.)

When permanent reductions of employment levels become unavoidable due to structural changes in the economy, reductions are first attempted through early retirement incentives and worker buyouts. When involuntary layoffs are needed, advance notice is required and severance pay is the norm. A study of layoffs in Germany between 1980 and 1985 found that median severance wages were the equivalent of seventeen weeks' pay. In the privatizing of the British Steel Corporation by Margaret Thatcher's government, laid-off steel workers were given severance of six

---

This case was prepared from the following sources: K. G. Abraham and S. N. Houseman, *Job Security in America* (Washington, D.C.: Brookings Institution, 1993); S. N. Houseman, *Industrial Restructuring with Job Security* (Cambridge, MA: Harvard, 1991); 140 Congressional record S.3796.

months' wages in many cases, and they were also eligible for a fifty-two-week retraining program with 100 percent of previous pay and benefits.

Of course, it is the case that many companies in the United States provide generous notice and severance for their laid-off employees. Yet there are major differences between the typical patterns for layoffs in the United States and Western Europe. Those differences are a function of legally mandated employment policies, government fiscal choices, and corporate responses to government incentives. The differences affect both how readily layoffs are instituted and how they are accomplished. The differences also reflect radically different social understandings of how the pain of economic change, whether cyclical or structural,

should be allocated. Clearly the European model means that there will be more delay before a corporation can shift work to newer, more technologically advanced and efficient plants. It also means that investors, remaining workers, and citizens in general will experience a larger share of the costs of economic downturns. That cost shifting has been an accepted part of the implicit social compact between European workers, companies, and governments. In an age of increasing global competition for investment monies, it remains to be seen whether Europe moves away from its historical compact. It also remains to be seen whether the increasing anxiety about layoffs moves the United States closer to the European model or further in the direction of at-will downsizing policies.

THE RIGHT TO DUE PROCESS
Patricia H. Werhane

EMPLOYMENT AT WILL

The principle of Employment at Will, referred to in this essay's introduction, is an unwritten common-law idea that employers as owners have the absolute right to hire, promote, demote, and fire whom and when they please. The principle, hereafter abbreviated as EAW, was stated explicitly in 1887 in a document by H. G. Wood entitled *Master and Servant*. Wood said, "A general or indefinite hiring is prima facie a hiring at will."[1] But the principle behind EAW dates at least to the seventeenth century and perhaps was used as early as the Middle Ages. EAW has commonly been interpreted as the rule that all employers "may dismiss their employees at will...for good cause, for no cause, *or even for causes morally wrong,* without being thereby guilty of legal wrong."[2]

The principle of EAW is not self-evident and stands in need of defense. The most promising lines of defense involve appeals to the right to freedom, to the common notion that property is defined as private ownership (for example, of land, material

possessions, or capital), to the supposed moral right to dispose freely of one's own property as one sees fit, or to the utilitarian benefits of freely operating productive organizations. Let us briefly characterize the main elements of each defense.

The first justification for EAW in the workplace, at least in the private sector of the economy, involves both appeals to the right to freedom and considerations about the nature of places of employment in a free society. Places of employment are privately owned, voluntary organizations of all sizes, from small entrepreneurships to large corporations. As such, it is claimed, they are not subject to the same restrictions governing public and political institutions. And, as they are voluntary organizations, employees join freely and may quit at any time. Political procedures, needed to safeguard citizens against arbitrary exercise of power in society at large, do not apply to voluntary private institutions. Any restriction on the principle of EAW, those who argue in this way conclude, interferes with the rights of persons *and* organizations not to be coerced into activities that either are not of their own choosing or limit their freedom to contract.

The principle of EAW is also sometimes defended purely on the basis of property rights. The

From Patricia H. Werhane, "Individual Rights in Business," in *Just Business: New Introductory Essays in Business Ethics*, ed. Tom Regan (New York: Random House, 1984), pp. 107–113, 124–126. Reprinted by permission of McGraw Hill, Inc.

rights to freedom and to private ownership, we are assuming, are equally valid claims, and the latter right entitles owners, it is argued, to use and improve what they own, including all aspects of their businesses, as they wish. According to this view, when an employee is working for another, this activity affects, positively or negatively, the employer's property and production. Because employers have property rights, and because these rights entitle them to control what happens to what they own, the employer has the right to dispose of the labor of employees whose work changes production. In dismissing or demoting employees, the employer is not denying *persons* political rights; rather, the employer is simply excluding their *labor* from the organization.

Finally, EAW is often defended on practical grounds. Viewed from a utilitarian perspective, hiring and firing "at will" is necessary in productive organizations if they are to achieve their goal of maximum efficiency and productivity. To interfere with this process, it is claimed, would defeat the purpose of free enterprise organizations. We shall consider each of these arguments more fully in the following section.

THE RIGHT TO DUE PROCESS IN THE WORKPLACE

Due process is a procedure by which one can appeal a decision or action in order to get a rational explanation of the decision and a disinterested, objective review of its propriety. In the workplace due process is, or should be, the right to grievance, arbitration, or some other fair procedure to evaluate hiring, firing, promotion, or demotion. For example, Geary and Alomar were fired without a hearing. Should they have been given some warning, a hearing by peers, a chance to appeal? The call to recognize the right to due process in the workplace extends the widely accepted view that every accused person, guilty or innocent, has a right to a fair hearing and an objective evaluation of his or her guilt or innocence. Those who deny due process in the workplace could argue (a) that this right does not extend to every sector of society, or (b) that rights of employers sometimes override those of employees and do so in this case. However we decide the merits of these arguments, the ab-

sence of due process in the workplace is not merely an oversight, as witness the principle of Employment at Will discussed in the last section. An employer, according to this principle, need not explain or defend its employee treatment in regard to dismissal nor give a hearing to the employee before he or she is dismissed.

In order to support the validity of the claim to the right to due process in the workplace, we must examine the defenses of the principle of EAW given in the previous section. First, EAW was defended on the ground that every person has the right to own and accumulate private property and, relatedly, every person, and analogously every corporation, has the right to dispose of what they own as they see fit. To say that employers have the right to dispose of their property "at will" is a legitimate claim, which follows from the right to ownership. To say that employers have this same right to "dispose of," that is, to fire for *any* reason, their employees is quite another sort of claim. The right to private ownership gives one the right to dispose of *material possessions* as one pleases, but it in no sense implies that one has the right to dispose of *persons* as one pleases. Employees, although they work on, and labor to improve, the business of their employers, are not themselves property. They are autonomous persons. Their employers do not own them, just as the employers do not own members of their own families. So the right of an employer to hire or demote "at will' cannot be defended simply by appealing to employer ownership rights, because employees are not the property of employers.

A second attempted justification of EAW, we saw earlier, appeals to an employer's right to freedom. Voluntary private organizations in a free society rightly argue that they should be as free as possible from coercive and restrictive procedures. Due process might be thought of as such a procedure, since it requires checks for arbitrariness on the part of employers. However, one needs to evaluate the role of the employer and the coercive nature of "at will" employment in voluntary organizations more carefully before accepting a negative view of due process in the workplace.

Though private businesses are voluntary organizations which employees are free to leave at any time, employers are in a position of power relative to individual employees. This by itself is not a sufficient reason to restrict employer activities. But the possible abuse of this power *is* what is at issue when we question the principle of EAW. By means of his or her position, an employer can arbitrarily hire or fire an employee. The employee can, of course, quit arbitrarily too. But an "at will" employee is seldom in a position within the law to inflict harm on an employer. Legally sanctioned "at will" treatment by employers of employees, on the other hand, frequently harms employees, as the following observations confirm.

When one is demoted or fired, the reduction or loss of the job is only part of an employee's disadvantage. When one is demoted or fired, it is commonly taken for granted that one *deserved* this treatment, whether or not this is the case. Without an objective appraisal of their treatment, employees are virtually powerless to demonstrate that they were fired, demoted, and so forth, for no good reason. Moreover, fired or demoted employees generally have much more difficulty than other persons in getting new jobs or rising within the ranks of their own company. The absence of due process in the workplace places arbitrarily dismissed or demoted employees at an *undeserved* disadvantage among persons competing for a given job. Viewed in this light, the absence of due process is unfair because workers who do not deserve to be fired are treated the same as those who do, with the result that the opportunities for future employment for both are, other things being equal, equally diminished.

To put the point differently, a fired employee is harmed, at least prima facie. And this raises the question, Do employers exceed their right when they fire or demote someone arbitrarily? For it is not true that one has the right to do just anything, when one's activities harm those who have not done anything to deserve it. In order to justify the harm one does to another as a result of the exercise of one's freedom, one must be able to give good reasons. And good reasons are precisely what are lacking in cases where employers, by firing those in their employ, prima facie harm these people for "no cause, or even for causes morally wrong." It is difficult to see how a defense of EAW can elicit our rational assent, if it is based exclusively on an appeal to an employer's liberty rights, because the unrestrained exercise of such rights may cause undeserved harm to those employees who are the victims of its arbitrary use.

Worse, "at will" practices violate the very right the principle of EAW is based on. Part of the appeal of the principle of EAW is that it protects the employer's right not to be coerced. According to the libertarian thinker Eric Mack, a coercive act is one that renders individual or institutional behavior involuntary.[3] Due process might be thought of as a coercive procedure because it *forces* employers to justify publicly their employment practices. But some of the employment practices sanctioned by EAW also are, or can be, coercive, according to Mack's definition. Persons who are fired without good reason *are involuntarily* placed in disadvantageous, undeserved positions by their employer. It is, therefore, difficult to defend "at will" employment practices on the basis of avoidance of coercion, since these practices themselves can be, and often are, coercive.

Defenders of EAW might make the following objection. EAW, they might claim, balances employee and employer rights because, just as the employer has the right to dispose of its business and production, so the employee has the right to accept or not to accept a job, or to quit or remain in a job once hired for it. Due process creates an imbalance of rights, this defense continues, because it restricts the freedom of the employer without restricting the freedom of the employee.

This objection lacks credibility. It supposes that the rights of employees and employers are equal when EAW prevails, but this is not the case. The principle of EAW works to the clear advantage of the owner or employer and to the clear disadvantage of the employee, because the employee's opportunity to change jobs is, other things being equal, significantly impaired when the employee is fired or demoted, while the employer's opportunity to hire is not similarly lessened. The employee's decreased opportunity to dispose of his or her labor, in other words, normally is *not* equal to the employer's decreased ability to carry on his business activities. So the operation of EAW, judged in terms of the comparative losses normally caused to employers and employees, does not treat the two, or their rights, equally.

"At will" treatment of employees is also advocated on the basis of maximizing efficiency. Unproductive or disruptive employees interfere with the business of the employer and hamper productivity. Employers must have the liberty to employ whom and when they wish. But without due process procedures in the workplace, what is to prevent an employer from making room for a grossly unqualified son-in-law by firing a good employee, for example, an action which is itself damaging to efficiency? And how inefficient *is* due process in the workplace really? Due process does not alter the employee-employer hierarchical arrangement in an organization. Due process does *not* infringe on an employer's prima facie right to dispose of its business or what happens in that business. The right to due process merely restricts the employer's alleged right to treat employees arbitrarily. Moreover, would not knowledge that employees are protected against arbitrary treatment go some way toward boosting employee morale? And will anyone seriously suggest that employee morale and employee efficiency are unrelated? In spite of the fears of some employers, due process does not require that employees never be dismissed on grounds of their inefficiency. Due process merely requires that employees have a hearing and an objective evaluation before being dismissed or demoted.

Finally, proponents of EAW will argue as follows. Ours is a free-market economy, they will say, and government should keep out of the economy. To heed the call for legally mandated due process in the workplace, which is what most critics of EAW seek, is to interfere with the free enterprise system. The government and the courts should leave employees and employers to work out matters on their own. Employees have the freedom to quit their jobs "at will." Therefore, the freedom of the employer to fire "at will" should be protected.

This is a peculiar defense. The plain fact is that employers, at least when they have the status of corporations, have not been reluctant to involve the government and the courts in the name of protecting *their* interests. The courts have recognized the right of corporations to due process while by and large upholding the principle of EAW for employees in the workplace. This at least appears to contravene the requirement of universality.... For if corporations have a moral right to be treated fairly, and this moral right grounds legal rights to due process for them, then one would naturally expect that employees would also have this moral right, and that the law should protect employees by requiring fair grievance procedures in the workplace, including, in particular, legal protection against

arbitrary dismissals or demotions. Yet the situation is not as expected. *Employers* have a legally protected right to due process. Employees hired "at will" do *not*. The universality we expect and require in the case of moral rights is missing here.

The difference in the status of employers and employees under the law is defended by the courts by the claim that corporations, all of which have state charters, are "public entities" whose activities are "in the public interest." Employees, on the other hand, are not public entities, and, at least in private places of employment, the work they perform is, so the courts imply, *not* in the public interest. Now there are celebrated problems about conceiving of corporations as public entities, and one might want to contest this defense of EAW by challenging the obscurity of the difference on which it is based. The challenge we should press in this essay, however, is not that the distinction between what is and what is not a public entity is too obscure. It is that the distinction is not relevant. The *moral* importance of due process—of being guaranteed honest attempts at fair, impartial treatment—has nothing to do with who is or is not a public entity. Fundamentally, it has to do with the rights of the private citizen. The right to due process is the right to a fair hearing when the acts or accusations of others hold the promise of serious harm being done to a person who does not deserve it. To deny due process of employees in the workplace, given the prima facie harm that is caused by dismissal or demotion, and given that those who are harmed in these ways may not deserve it, is tantamount to claiming that *only some* persons have this right. Such a conclusion conflicts with the view, widely held in our society, that due process is a *moral* right, one that is possessed by *everyone* in *all* circumstances.

To make what is an obvious point, due process is an essential political right in any society that respects just treatment of every person. When people who do not deserve it are put at risk of being significantly harmed by the arbitrary decisions of others, the persons put at risk ought to be protected. Indeed, if those who make decisions are powerful, and those who are the recipients of these decisions are, by comparison, both weak and in danger of significant harm, then we must insist *all the more* on measures to protect the weak against the strong. Paradoxically, therefore, precisely in those cases where workers are individually weak—

precisely, that is, in those areas where EAW prevails—is where it should not. Thus, the democratic political ideal of fairness is threatened if the principle of EAW is allowed.

There is, then, for the reasons given, a very strong presumptive case to be made against EAW and in favor of the right of employees to impartial grievance procedures in the workplace, independently of the presence of a contractual guarantee of such procedures. Let us give a summary statement of the right.

> Every person has a right to a public hearing, peer evaluation, outside arbitration or some other mutually agreed upon grievance procedure before being demoted, unwillingly transferred or fired.

The arguments given in favor of recognizing the right of employees to due process in the workplace were characterized as being strong presumptive arguments. It was not contended that the reasoning given "proves" this right conclusively. Rather, the arguments collectively provide a set of reasons that make it logical to recognize this right, while allowing that objections might be raised that show that there are better reasons against recognizing the right to due process in the workplace.

According to strong advocates of employee rights, the right to due process does not go far enough. It does not give an employee much in the way of *rights.* It simply precludes dismissal without a formal hearing. However, the worker's right to due process would, if appropriately institutionalized, make progress in the area of employee rights. This is because due process helps to prevent arbitrary treatment of persons in the workplace by making the cause and reason for the employee treatment public and by guaranteeing the opportunity to appeal. Respect for the rights of employees as persons will not be satisfied with anything less, even if it is true, as some contend, that genuine respect requires much more.

CONCLUSION: GUARANTEEING RIGHTS IN EMPLOYMENT

The widespread and persistent nonrecognition of employee rights in this country is inconsistent with the primary importance our nation places on the rights of the individual. This non-recognition remains one of the most questionable elements in the political and economic structure of our society. If the arguments in this essay are sound, standardly accepted individual rights need to be recognized and honored in the workplace. The rights to due process…are moral rights honored politically in public life. To deny them a place in the workplace is to assume that employer rights or economic interests always take precedence over the rights of employees. Neither assumption is tenable.

How does one institutionalize the recognition of rights in employment? In many European countries employee rights are recognized by law and enforced by the government. In West Germany, for example, after a trial period, employees acquire a right to their jobs. Persons may be dismissed for job-related negligence, absences, or disruptive and criminal activities, but the grounds for dismissal must be documented and hearings must be conducted before an employee can be fired. The United States is the only major industrial nation that offers little legal protection of the rights of workers to their jobs. It has been suggested that what is needed in this country is statutory protection for employees against unjust firing, an idea that embodies some of the principles of the German model. It has been further suggested that this statutory protection should include rights to expenses incurred in finding a new job, and rights to back pay for those unjustly dismissed.[4]

A second fruitful way to institutionalize recognition of employee rights is through written contracts between employers and employees, contracts that state the exchange agreement, the rights of each party, and the means for enforcing these rights (for example, arbitration, peer review, or outside negotiators). If properly done, such contracts could be relied upon to help give meaning to the sometimes loose talk about the moral rights of each party and would help settle, without the intervention of the courts, many disagreements about employee *and* employer rights.

A third, most propitious and less coercive way to institutionalize recognition of employee rights is simply for employers to do this voluntarily. This suggestion is not as preposterous as it may seem. Increasingly, employees are demanding rights in the workplace. Correspondingly, employers are beginning to recognize the expediency and, sometimes, the fairness of such employee demands. And the courts are beginning to take interest in employee rights. There is an obvious way for employers to avoid "coercive intervention" by government and the courts. This is for employers *voluntarily* to institute programs that respect and protect employee rights on their own.

There are many employee rights that remain to be considered in another essay. The rights to work safety, information, and participation in management decision-making, for example, are essential for employee autonomy and job development. And the question of meaningful work cannot be dismissed if employees are to be considered as autonomous individuals.... The continuation of a private free enterprise economy set within a democratic free community where individual rights are viewed as fundamental requires that employee rights be fully and fairly recognized *and* protected in the workplace.

NOTES*

1. H. G. Wood, *A Treatise on the Law of Master and Servant* (Albany, N.Y.: John D. Parsons, Jr., 1877), p. 134.

2. Lawrence E. Blades, "Employment at Will versus Individual Freedom: On Limiting the Abusive Exercise of Employer Power," *Columbia Law Review* 67 (1967), p. 1405, quoted from *Payne* v. *Western*, 81 Tenn. 507 (1884), *Hutton* v. *Watters*, 132 Tenn. 527, S. W. 134 (1915).

3. Eric Mack, "Natural and Contractual Rights," *Ethics* 87 (1977), pp. 153–59.

4. Clyde W. Summers, "Individual Protection Against Unfair Dismissal: Time for a Statute, " *Virginia Law Review* 62 (1976), pp. 481–532.

---

*Some notes have been deleted and the remaining ones renumbered.

RIGHTS IN THE WORKPLACE: A NOZICKIAN ARGUMENT
Ian Maitland

ABSTRACT. There is a growing literature that attempts to define the substantive rights of employees in the workplace, a.k.a. the duties of employers toward their employees. Following Nozick, this article argues that—so long as there is a competitive labor market—to set up a class of moral rights in the workplace invades workers' rights to freely choose the terms and conditions of employment they judge best.

There is a growing literature that attempts to define the substantive rights of workers in the workplace, a.k.a. the duties of employers toward their workers. Thus it has been proposed that employers have (at least *prima facie*) duties to provide workers with meaningful/fulfilling/self-actualizing work, some degree of control over work conditions, advance notice of plant closures or layoffs, due process before dismissal, etc. (See, for example, Goldman, 1980; Schwartz, 1984; Donaldson, 1982; Werhane, 1985).

The argument of this paper is that in a competitive labor market these standards are superfluous and, indeed, may interfere with workers' rights to freely choose their terms of employment. Furthermore, these supposed moral rights in the workplace may come at the expense of non-consenting third parties—like other workers or consumers.

NOZICK ON MEANINGFUL WORK

Since my argument basically extends Nozick's (1974, pp. 246 ff) discussion of meaningful work, let us start with that. Assuming that workers wish to have meaningful work, how does and could capitalism respond? Nozick notes that if the productivity of workers *rises* when the work tasks are segmented so as to be more meaningful, then individual employers pursuing profits will reorganize the production process in such a way out of simple self-interest. Even if productivity were to remain the same, competition for labor will induce employers to reorganize work so as to make it more meaningful.

From *Journal of Business Ethics* 8 (1989): 951–954. © 1989 Kluwer Academic Publishers. Reprinted by permission of Kluwer Academic Publishers.

Accordingly, Nozick says, the only interesting case to consider is the one where meaningful work leads to reduced efficiency. Who will bear the cost of this lessened efficiency? One possibility is the employer. But the individual employer who unilaterally assumes this cost places himself at a competitive disadvantage and eventually—other things equal—will go out of business. On the other hand, if *all* employers recognize their workers' right to meaningful work (and if none cheats), then consumers will bear the cost of the industry's reduced efficiency. (Presumably, too, we would have to erect trade barriers to exclude the products of foreign producers who do not provide their workers with meaningful work, otherwise they would drive the domestic industry out of business.)

What about the workers? If they want meaningful work, they will presumably be willing to give up something (some wages) to work at meaningfully segmented jobs:

> They work for lower wages, but they view their total work package (lower wages plus the satisfactions of meaningful work) as more desirable than less meaningful work at higher wages. They make a trade-off....

Nozick observes that many persons make just such trade-offs. Not everyone, he says, wants the same things or wants them as strongly. They choose their employment on the basis of the overall package of benefits it gives them.

THE MARKET FOR MEANINGFUL WORK

Provided that the firm's lessened efficiency is compensated for by lower wages, then the employer should be indifferent between the two packages (meaningful work at lower wages or less meaningful work at higher wages). Indeed, if workers prize meaningful work highly, then they might be prepared to accept *lower* wages than are necessary simply to offset the firm's lower productivity. In that case, entrepreneurial employers seeking higher profits should be expected to offer more meaningful work: they will, by definition, reduce labor costs by an amount greater than the output lost because of less efficient (but more meaningful) production methods. In the process, they will earn higher profits than other firms (Frank, 1985, pp. 164–5).

In other words, there is a market for meaningful work. The employer who can find the combination of pay and meaningful work that matches workers' desires most closely will obtain a competitive advantage. Thus Goldman (1980, p. 274) is wrong when he claims that "profit maximization may...call...for reducing work to a series of simple menial tasks." On the contrary, profit maximization creates pressures on employers to offer workers meaningful work up to the point where workers would prefer higher pay to further increments of meaningfulness. Goldman's claim holds only if we assume that workers place no value at all on the intrinsic rewards of their work.

To "legislate" moral rights in the workplace to a certain level of meaningfulness, then, would interfere with workers' rights to determine what package of benefits they want.

EXTENDING THE LOGIC (1): EMPLOYMENT AT WILL

In her discussion of employment at will (EAW), Werhane (1985, p. 91) says "[i]t is hard to imagine that rational people would agree in advance to being fired arbitrarily in an employment contract." According to her estimate, only 36% of the workforce is covered by laws or contracts which guarantee due process procedures with which to appeal dismissal. Werhane regards EAW as a denial of moral rights of employees in the workplace.

But, is it inconceivable that a rational worker would voluntarily accept employment under such conditions? Presumably, if the price is right, some workers will be willing to accept the greater insecurity of EAW. This may be particularly true, for example, of younger, footloose and fancy-free workers with marketable skills. It is also likely to be truer in a metropolitan area (with ample alternative employment opportunities) than a small town and when the economic outlook is good.

Likewise, some employers may value more highly the unrestricted freedom to hire and fire (smaller businesses, for example) and may be willing to pay higher wages for that flexibility. There may be other employers—larger ones in a position to absorb the administrative costs or ones with more stable businesses—who will find it advantageous to offer guarantees of due process in return for lower wages. Such guarantees are also more likely to be found where employees acquire firm-specific skills and so where continuity of employment is more important (Williamson, 1975).

According to this logic, wage rates should vary inversely with the extent of these guarantees, other things equal. In other words, workers purchase their greater security in the form of reduced wages. Or, put another way, some firms pay workers a premium to induce them to do without the guarantees.

If employers were generally to heed business ethicists and to institute workplace due process in cases of dismissals—and to take the increased costs or reduced efficiency out of workers' paychecks—then they would expose themselves to the pirating of their workers by other (less scrupulous?) employers who would give workers what they wanted instead of respecting their rights.

If, on the other hand, many of the workers not currently protected against unfair dismissal would in fact prefer guarantees of workplace due process—*and* would be willing to pay for it—then such guarantees would be an effective recruiting tool for an entrepreneurial employer. That is, employers are driven by their own self-interest to offer a package of benefits and rights that will attract and retain employees. If an employer earns a reputation for treating workers in a high-handed or inconsiderate way, then he (or she) will find it more difficult (or more expensive) to get new hires and will experience defections of workers to other employers.

In short, there is good reason for concluding that the prevalence of EAW does accurately reflect workers' preferences for wages over contractually guaranteed protections against unfair dismissal. (Of course, these preferences may derive, in part, from most workers' perception that their employers rarely abuse EAW anyway; if abuses were widespread, then you would expect the demand for contractual guarantees to increase.)

EXTENDING THE LOGIC (2): PLANT CLOSURE/LAYOFF NOTIFICATION

Another putative workplace right is notice of impending layoffs or plant closures. The basis for such a right is obvious and does not need to be rehearsed here. In 1988 Congress passed plant-closing notification provisions that mandate 60-days notice.

Earlier drafts of the legislation had provided for 6 months' advance notification.

But the issue of interest here is employers' moral responsibilities in this matter. The basic argument is by now familiar: if employers have not universally provided guarantees of advance notice of layoffs, that reflects employers' and workers' choices. Some workers are willing to trade off job security for higher wages; some employers (e.g., in volatile businesses) prefer to pay higher wages in return for the flexibility to cut costs quickly. If employers have generally underestimated the latent demand of workers for greater security (say, as a result of the graying of the baby boomers), then that presents a profit opportunity for alert employers. At the same (or lower) cost to themselves, they should be able to put together an employment package that will attract new workers.

A morally binding workplace "right" to X days' notice of a layoff would preempt workers' and employers' freedom to arrive at an agreement that takes into account their own particular circumstances and preferences. In Nozick's aphorism, the "right" to advance notice may prohibit a capitalist act between consenting adults

It would mean, for example, that workers and managers would be (morally) barred from agreeing to arrangements that might protect workers' jobs by enhancing a firm's chances of survival. This might be the case if, say, the confidence of creditors or investors would be strengthened by knowing that the firm would be free to close down its operations promptly if necessary.

Likewise, the increased expenses associated with a possible closure might deter firms from opening new plants in the first place—especially in marginal areas where jobs are most needed. In that case workers won't enjoy the rights due them in the workplace because there won't be any workplace. As McKenzie (1981, p. 122) has pointed out, "[r]estrictions on plant closings are restrictions on plant openings."

The effects of rights to notice of layoffs are not limited to the workers. If resources are diverted from viable segments of a (multiplant) firm in order to prolong the life of the plant beyond its useful economic life, then the solvency of the rest of the firm may be jeopardized (and so too the jobs of other workers).

If the obstacles to plant shutdowns are serious enough and if firms are prevented from moving to locations where costs are lower, then (as McKenzie, p. 120, points out) "Workers generally must pay higher prices for the goods they buy. Further, they will not then have the opportunity of having paying plants moving into their areas...." And if such restrictions reduce the efficiency of the economy as a whole (by deterring investment, locking up resources in low-productivity, low-wage sectors of the economy), then all workers and consumers will be losers. Birch (1981, p. 7) has found that job creation is positively associated with plant closures: "The reality is that our most successful areas [at job creation] are those with the highest rates of innovation and failure, not the lowest." Europe has extensive laws and union agreements that make it prohibitively expensive to close plants, order layoffs or even fire malingerers and, not coincidentally, it has barely added a single job in the aggregate in the 1980's (as of 1987). Europe's persistent high unemployment is usually attributed to such "rigidities" in its labor market—what the London *Economist* picturesquely terms "Eurosclerosis."

It may be objected by some that workers' "rights claims cannot be overridden for the sake of economic or general welfare" (Werhane, 1985, p. 80; see also Goldman, p. 274). This is probably not the place to debate rights vs. utilities, but this discussion raises the question of whether workplace rights may sometimes violate the rights of third parties (other workers, consumers).

RESPECTING WORKERS' CHOICES

The argument of this paper has been that to set up a class of moral rights in the workplace may invade a worker's right to freely choose the terms and conditions that he (or she) judges are the best for him. The worker is stuck with these rights no matter whether he values them or not; they are inalienable in the sense that he may not trade them off for, say, higher wages. *We* might not be willing to make such a trade, but if we are to respect the

worker's autonomy, then *his* preferences must be decisive.

Along the way the paper has tried to indicate how competition between employers in the labor market preserves the worker's freedom to choose the terms and conditions of his employment within constraints set by the economy. This competition means that employers' attempts to exploit workers (say, by denying them due process in the workplace without paying them the "market rate" for forgoing such protections) will be self-defeating because other would-be employers will find it profitable to bid workers away from them by offering more attractive terms. This point bears repeating because many of the accounts of rights in the workplace seem to assume pervasive market failure which leaves employers free to do pretty much what they want. Any persuasive account of such rights has to take into account the fact that employers' discretion to unilaterally determine terms and conditions of employment is drastically limited by the market.

REFERENCES

Birch, David: 1981, 'Who creates jobs?', *Public Interest* (vol. 65), fall.

Donaldson, Thomas: 1982, *Corporations and Morality* (Prentice Hall, Englewood Cliffs, N.J.).

Frank, Robert: 1985, *Choosing the Right Pond* (Oxford University Press, New York).

Goldman, Alan: 1980, 'Business ethics: profits, utilities, and moral rights', *Philosophy and Public Affairs* 9, no. 3.

McKenzie, Robert: 1981, 'The case for plant closures', *Policy Review* 15, winter.

Nozick, Robert: 1974, *Anarchy, State and Utopia* (Basic Books, New York).

Schwartz, Adina: 1984, 'Autonomy in the workplace', in Tom Regan, ed., *Just Business* (Random House, N.Y.).

Werhane, Patricia H.: 1985, *Persons, Rights and Corporations* (Prentice Hall, N.Y.).

Williamson, Oliver E.: 1975, *Markets and Hierarchies* (Free Press, N.Y.).

THE RELIANCE INTEREST IN PROPERTY
Joseph William Singer

The world has never had a good definition of the word liberty. And the American people just now are much in want of one. We all declare for liberty; but in using the same *word* we do not mean the same *thing*. With some, the word liberty may mean for each man to do as he pleases with himself and the product of his labor; while with others the same word may mean for some men to do as they please with other men, and the product of other men's labor. Here are two, not only different, but incompatible things, called by the same name, liberty. And it follows that each of the things is by the respective parties called by two different and incompatible names, liberty and tyranny.
——Abraham Lincoln

Dependence is the expression of the permanent reciprocity that, because of their needs, exists between most of the members of a group: dependence of the weak on the strong, but also of the strong on the weak; dependence on providers by those who have nothing, and the opposite.
——Albert Memmi

THE PLANT CLOSING PROBLEM

The Setting
On April 28, 1982, the United States Steel Company demolished two steel plants at Youngstown, Ohio. The next day, a dramatic photograph in the New York Times showed four huge blast furnaces crumbling to the ground after being blown up by explosive charges. One plant, the Ohio Works, had been in operation since 1901; the second, the McDonald Works, since 1918. Together, the two plants employed 3,500 workers. After so many years of operation, the plants had become technologically obsolete. The management of the corporation faced a decision whether to modernize the plants

or to abandon them and discharge the workers. On November 27, 1979, in a meeting in New York City, the board of directors of U.S. Steel decided to close both plants, along with a dozen other smaller facilities. The effects of that decision would be momentous. As noted by the Court of Appeals for the Sixth Circuit:

> For all of the years United States Steel has been operating in Youngstown, it has been a dominant factor in the lives of its thousands of employees and their families, and in the life of the city itself. The contemplated abrupt departure of United States Steel from Youngstown will, of course, have direct impact on 3,500 workers and their families. It will doubtless mean a devastating blow to them, to the business community and to the City of Youngstown itself. While we cannot read the future of Youngstown from this record, what the record does indicate clearly is that we deal with an economic tragedy of major proportion to Youngstown and Ohio's Mahoning Valley.

In the face of this crisis, the local union representing the workers at the two plants took a series of actions to prevent the plants from closing and to protect the interests of the workers and the community. These actions included community organizing, picketing, sit-ins at corporate headquarters, contact with public officials in state and local government, attempts to bargain with the company, and finally, legal action. The initial theory of the lawsuit was that the local managers had explicitly promised the workers that the plants would not be closed as long as they were profitable and that the workers had relied on those promises to their detriment by agreeing to changed work practices to increase the plants' profitability and by foregoing opportunities elsewhere. After the lawsuit was filed, the union considered the possibility of buying the plants from the company and even began negotiations with company representatives. On January 31, 1980, however, David Roderick, Chair of the Board of Directors of U.S. Steel, announced to the press that the company would refuse to sell the

From *Stanford Law Review*, vol. 40, no. 611 (February 1988): 614–733. © 1987 by Joseph William Singer. Reprinted by permission of the author.

plants to the union because such a purchase would be subsidized by government loans and would arguably result in unfair competition for U.S. Steel. The company's refusal to consider selling the plant to the union formed the basis of a second set of legal claims against the company in the litigation.

After an initial demonstration of sympathy to the union, the federal district judge, Judge Thomas Lambros, decided that U.S. Steel had no legal obligation to sell the plants to the union and could do whatever it wanted with the property. The Sixth Circuit affirmed this ruling on July 25, 1980. Roughly two years later, the company destroyed the plants.

The property issue addressed by both the district court and the court of appeals was expressed as a choice between the union's right to purchase the plant and the company's freedom to control it. The employees claimed that they had a legal right to buy the plant from the company while the company claimed that it had the legal right to do anything it wanted with the plant, including destroy it, without regard to the workers' or the community's interests. To recast the dispute in Hohfeldian terminology: (1) The union claimed both (a) a power to purchase the plant with a correlative liability in the company to have the plant transferred against its will to the union for its fair market price and (b) a right to have the plant not be destroyed with a correlative duty on the company not to destroy the plant if the union sought to exercise its power to purchase. (2) The company claimed both (a) an immunity from having the plant taken away from it involuntarily even with compensation (with a correlative disability in the union to force the company to sell the plant to the union) and (b) a privilege in the company to destroy the plant with the union having no right to legal relief on that account.

Can Relationships Create Property Rights?

During the pretrial hearings in the *United Steel Workers* case, Judge Lambros listened to statements of the attorneys representing the union and the company. In the middle of one of those hearings, Judge Lambros delivered a statement charged with emotion.

> We are not talking now about a local bakery shop, grocery store, tool and die shop or a body shop in Youngstown that is planning to close and move out....

It's not just a steel company making steel.... [S]teel has become an institution in the Mahoning Valley....

Everything that has happened in the Mahoning Valley has been happening for many years because of steel. Schools have been built, roads have been built. Expansion that has taken place is because of steel. And to accommodate that industry, lives and destinies of the inhabitants of that community were based and planned on the basis of that institution: Steel.

....

We are talking about an institution, a large corporate institution that is virtually the reason for the existence of that segment of this nation [Youngstown]. Without it, that segment of this nation perhaps suffers, instantly and severely. Whether it becomes a ghost town or not, I don't know. I am not aware of its capability for adapting.

....

But what has happened over the years between U.S. Steel, Youngstown and the inhabitants? Hasn't something come out of that relationship, something that out of which—not reaching for a case on property law or a series of cases but looking at the law as a whole, the Constitution, the whole body of law, not only contract law, but tort, corporations, agency, negotiable instruments—taking a look at the whole body of American law and then sitting back and reflecting on what it seeks to do, and that is to adjust human relationships in keeping with the whole spirit and foundation of the American system of law, to preserve property rights....

The judicial process cannot survive by adhering to the attitudes of the 1800's. My daily function cannot be regulated by those persons that reach into the dungeons of the past and attempt to stranglehold our present day thinking by 1800 [sic] concepts.

Were the framers of our Constitution or the judges of previous decades able to perceive the conditions that we find in America today and the reliance of a whole community and segment of our society on an institution such as the steel industry?

Well, the easy solution is: "Well, we haven't dealt with it in the past. There is no precedent.

You have no case. The case is dismissed. Bailiff, call the next case."

Well, the law has to be more than mere mechanical acts. There has to be more than just form. There has to be substance.

It would seem to me that when we take a look at the whole body of American law and the principles we attempt to come out with—and although a legislature has not pronounced any laws with respect to such a property right, that is not to suggest that there will not be a need for such a law in the future dealing with similar situations—*it seems to me that a property right has arisen from this lengthy, long-established relationship between United States Steel, the steel industry as an institution, the community in Youngstown, the people in Mahoning County and the Mahoning Valley in having given and devoted their lives to this industry.* Perhaps not a property right to the extent that can be remedied by compelling U.S. Steel to remain in Youngstown. *But I think the law can recognize the property right to the extent that U.S. Steel cannot leave that Mahoning Valley and the Youngstown area in a state of waste, that it cannot completely abandon its obligation to that community, because certain vested rights have arisen out of this long relationship and institution.*

After this demonstration of concern by the judge, the steelworkers amended their complaint to include a claim based on property law along the lines suggested by Judge Lambros. The amended claim read:

52. A property right has arisen from the long-established relation between the community of the 19th Congressional District and Plaintiffs, on the one hand, and Defendant, on the other hand, which this Court can enforce.

53. This right, in the nature of an easement, requires that Defendant:

a. Assist in the preservation of the institution of steel in that community;

b. Figure into its cost of withdrawing and closing the Ohio and McDonald Works the cost of rehabilitating the community and the workers;

c. Be restrained from leaving the Mahoning Valley in a state of waste and from abandoning its obligation to that community.

Despite his tentative conclusion that the company should have a continuing legal obligation to the community, Judge Lambros decided that no precedent for such a property right existed and that he lacked the power to create one. He reached this conclusion even though he had earlier defended the power of judges to recognize or create a new property right when social conditions and values had changed to warrant it. He saw the issue as a divergence of the company's moral and legal obligations. This disjunction existed because the federal court lacked the legal authority to change state property law to conform to the dictates of morality:

> United States Steel should not be permitted to leave the Youngstown area devastated after drawing from the lifeblood of the community for so many years.
>
> Unfortunately, the mechanism to reach this ideal settlement, to recognize this new property right, is not now in existence in the code of laws of our nation.

The Sixth Circuit also voiced "great sympathy for the community interest" reflected in the union's amended complaint. However, like Judge Lambros, the court concluded that such a property right did not exist, either in legislation or in the common law, and that the court lacked the authority to create it.

I argue that the *United Steel Workers* case was wrongly decided. Judge Lambros' initial intuition about the correct legal result was better than his ultimate disposition. The courts should have recognized the workers' property rights arising out of their relationship with the company. Such a new legally protected interest would place obligations on the company toward the workers and the community to alleviate the social costs of its decision to close the plant. Protection of this reliance interest could take a variety of forms: It could grant the workers the right to buy the plant from the company for its fair market value; it could require the company to review possible modernization proposals to determine the feasibility and profitability of updating the plant; it could give workers access to information held by the company regarding operation of the facility; it could impose obligations on the company to make severance payments to workers and tax payments to the municipality to protect them until new businesses could be established in the community; it could require the company to assist in finding a purchaser for the plant; it could mean other things as well. The goal should be to identify flexible remedies that are appropriate to protect the workers' reliance interests.

Moreover, contrary to the conclusions of the judges in this case, precedent for the creation of property rights of the kind asserted by the union does exist. I do not want to be so disingenuous as to claim that recognition of such entitlements would not constitute a substantial change in the law, but I do want to assert that the legal system contains a variety of doctrines—in torts, property, contracts, family law and in legislative modifications of those common law doctrines—that recognize the sharing or shifting of various property interests in situations that should be viewed as analogous to plant closings. If I am right, the courts had access to enforceable legal rules based on principles that could have been seen as applicable precedent for extension of existing law by creation of this new set of entitlements.

I argue that the judges in the *United Steel Workers* case failed to find these precedents and principles in the rules in force because they asked the wrong questions. They wrongly defined the issue as a search for the "owner" of the property. They then assumed that, in the absence of specific doctrinal exceptions to the contrary, owners are allowed to do whatever they want with their property. This approach is seriously misleading: Property rights are more often shared than unitary, and rights to use and dispose of property are never absolute. Moreover, this approach takes our attention away from the relations of mutual dependence that develop within industrial enterprises and between those enterprises and the communities in which they are situated. Legitimate reliance on such relationships constitutes a central aspect of our social and economic life—so central that numerous rules in force protect reliance on those relationships. Although both the district court and the court of appeals sympathetically noted the legitimate interests of the workers and the community, and the long term relationships that had developed between U.S. Steel, the workers and the community, the courts deemed those interests irrelevant in

defining property entitlements. Consideration of competing interests in access to resources and past reliance on relationships granting such access should be a central component of any legal determination of how to allocate lawful power over those resources.

A wide variety of current legal rules can be justified in terms of an underlying moral principle that I call "the reliance interest in property." They include, for example, the rules about adverse possession, prescriptive easements, public rights of access to private property, tenants' rights, equitable division of property on divorce, welfare rights. These currently enforceable doctrines encompass the full range of social relationships, from relations among strangers, between neighbors, among long-term contractual partners in the marketplace, among family members and others in intimate relationships, and finally, between citizens and the government. At crucial points in the development of these relationships—often, but not always, when they break up—the legal system requires a sharing or shifting of property interests from the "owner" to the "non-owner" to protect the more vulnerable party to the relationship. The legal system requires this shift, not because of reliance on specific promises, but because the parties have relied on each other generally and on the continuation of their relationship. Moreover, the more vulnerable party may need access to resources controlled by the more powerful party, and the relationship is such that we consider it fair to place this burden on the more powerful party by redistributing entitlements.

SOCIAL VISION: RELIANCE ON RELATIONSHIPS

Independence? That's middle class blasphemy. We are all dependent on one another, every soul of us on earth.
—George Bernard Shaw

In this State, we do not set people adrift because they are the victims of misfortune. We take care of each other.
—New Jersey Supreme Court Justice
Morris Pashman

The Free Market Model

The *United Steel Workers* case posed two legal questions related to property rights: (1) did the workers have any power to control the use or disposition of the factories? (2) upon closing the plants, did the corporation have any obligations to the workers beyond those agreed to in the collective bargaining agreement? The judges addressed these issues by asking a particular set of questions that set the terms of the debate. These questions presupposed a particular vision of social relationships. The assumptions underlying the questions fundamentally shaped the courts' understanding of existing law; they caused the judges to make specific presumptions about the legal distribution of power in the marketplace. If the judges had asked a different series of questions and had a different model of social relations, they would have found precedents that they missed or marginalized. In this section I develop the court's implicit model of society and legal rules about the marketplace, which I will call the "free market model." I then explain what is wrong with this paradigm, and propose a different way to conceptualize market relations. This alternative model—the "social relations approach"—highlights aspects of social life and legal doctrine that are suppressed in the free market model and which I think should be brought to center stage.

The judges asked two central questions: (1) who owns the plant? and (2) what promises did the corporation make? These questions reveal a great deal about the social vision implicit in the judges' conceptualization of the problem because the questions create presumptions. The judges presumed that in the absence of specific doctrinal exceptions, owners can do what they like with their property unless they have made promises to the contrary. The judges further presumed that people have no obligations to act affirmatively to help others unless they have promised to do so or unless they fall within a narrow set of special relationships creating affirmative duties.

This construction of the problem rests on a social vision and a form of legal consciousness that reinforce each other. The social vision divides the world into the public sphere of the state and the private sphere of society, with society subdivided into the spheres of the market and the family. The social problem of plant closings and industrial relations fits into the private sphere of the market. The imagery behind this categorization has a core and a periphery. It places the market at the center of the picture and marginalizes both the state and the family. Both the public sphere of state regulation and the sphere of the family are treated as peripheral and supplementary. In this picture, the market is an area of freedom and autonomy, while both the state and the family appear as areas of regulation or altruistic obligation. This social vision correlates with a form of legal consciousness: Within the market realm, legal obligations are generally negative duties not to harm others; positive obligations to help others ordinarily arise only as the result of voluntary promises. State regulation enforces the negative obligations (through tort law or legislation) and the voluntary agreements. In this model, the family is the only area of social life in which affirmative obligations arise out of relationships.

The market itself contains a core of possessive individualism with a periphery of altruistic obligation. The core of possessive individualism is based on a particular model of private property and freedom of contract. This model contains several features. First, as Gregory Alexander explains, it "exhibits a strong preference for a consolidated form of property interests." Alexander means that the legal rules seek "to concentrate in a single legal entity, usually an individual person, the relevant rights, privileges, and powers for possessing, using, and transferring discrete assets." In other words, the presumption is that the legal rules identify a single owner of all valued resources and that that owner has the legal power to control those resources to the exclusion of others. Second, there is a general presumption in favor of free use of property. Owners are generally allowed to do what they like with their property—including destroy it if they wish—even if their use interferes with the interests of others. Limits to freedom of action are narrowly defined and exceptional. This presumption promotes a policy of autonomy and self-reliance. Third, the free market model "promotes individual freedom of disposition as the basic mechanism for allocation." Property owners are generally free to decide when and to whom to convey their property. This means that property owners have the legal power to transfer or share their property on terms chosen by them and that they are immune from having their property interests transferred to others against their will. This presumption furthers the policy of free alienability of property in competitive markets. Fourth, people are free to make agreements regarding access to property or exchange of entitlements, and those agreements will be enforced in accordance with their terms. This presumption furthers a particular vision of freedom of contract that emphasizes self-determination and facilitation of private arrangements without regulation of the agreements for fairness or equality of bargaining power.

The Myth of the Free Market

The myth of consent Plant closings create enormous human suffering, and the people who are victimized by plant closings complain bitterly about their predicament. The evidence, moreover, seems to indicate that this suffering is almost entirely unnecessary and avoidable; indeed, it serves no useful social purpose. Why is nothing done about it? People who oppose plant closing regulation generally give two types of answers to this question. The first answer is a consequentialist argument; the second is a normative argument about economic liberty. The consequentialist argument maintains that any regulation of plant closings will simply make things worse rather than better; it will hurt the very people the regulators are trying to help. The problem we are trying to address involves creating jobs for people and organizing the economy in a way that will satisfy human needs. The free market operates efficiently to do this; and plant closings are part of the process of allocating investment efficiently and maximizing social wealth. Interfering with plant closings prevents the market from working its magic. Therefore, plant closings are part of the solution rather than part of the problem. It is true that plant closings create hardships for workers, but they are perfectly able to protect themselves by bargaining for protection in contract negotiations. Any further regulation of the terms of employment contracts will interfere with the workers' freedom to make the necessary trade-offs in whatever manner they prefer. Thus, there is no need for special government policies to help workers. I will not answer this argument here, but will address it in my later discussion of the political economy of plant closings.

The second argument gives a normative spin to the social vision of the free market. Plants are owned by someone, and owners have the right to determine what they will do with their property. If workers want to interfere with managerial discretion—if they want to control someone else's property—let them bargain for such rights in contract negotiations. In the absence of such voluntarily assumed obligations, owners should be free to do as they please with their property. Any interference with freedom of contract and free property use or transfer is an infringement on economic liberty. The work of Richard McKenzie, the most vocal academic critic of plant closing regulation, epitomizes this view of the world:

> The right of entrepreneurs to use their capital assets is part and parcel of a truly free society; the centralization of authority to determine where and under what circumstances firms should invest leads to the concentration of economic power in the hands of the people who run government. Private rights to move, to invest, to buy, to sell are social devices for the dispersion of economic power.

Plant closing regulation therefore decreases the economic liberty of both workers and entrepreneurs (managers and investors) by transferring decision-making power away from them to government officials.

Many political liberals similarly rely on the free market model as the core of their social vision. Whether based on rights theories (Dworkin) or economic theories (Calabresi and Ackerman), liberals often preserve the free market system as the core image and justify governmental regulation of the market by reference to the concept of "market failure" or to cases where "unequal bargaining power" vitiates consent. Thus their core images relate to the free market even though they support extensive government regulation of the market.

What these arguments share is the attempt to legitimate the mass of our social, economic, and institutional practices by reference to the myth of the free market. The ultimate effect of this project is to make the great bulk of market transactions appear to be the result of free consent.

Ideologies are powerful and persistent. Perhaps the most tenacious ideology in the American legal culture is the myth of the free market. Undermined by the rise of giant corporations, shaken by the Great Depression, regulated by the New Deal, civil rights, environmental, and labor laws, thoroughly trashed by the legal realists throughout the twentieth century, the myth persists and flourishes. The myth extols the rightness, the simplicity, and the liberty embodied in a system of private property and freedom of contract.

According to the free market model, people are free to enter the marketplace and structure their own activities free from governmental control and private coercion. In this picture of the world, the government is not fundamentally implicated in the processes and outcomes of the marketplace or social life. Instead, the government merely facilitates private transactions entered into freely. Society is composed of individuals, busily pursuing happiness. Sometimes those individuals voluntarily join forces to maximize their welfare by aggregating their wealth or efforts. Since everyone has the right to participate in these organized efforts, it is impossible for any organization to achieve power permanently over the lives of other citizens. Every person is free to leave an organization and join another or compete on her own. Every powerful organization is met by countervailing powers. No individual or organization can dominate such a world. Competition insures that individuals always have choices and that power is met by power. No one and no group can permanently get the upper hand. The market is an arena of freedom, not coercion.

The market is also a world where hard work is rewarded and no one has a fixed social status; a world where wealth abounds because the incentives to produce it are unlimited and assured; a world where people get what they want if they are willing to work for it. If people are unhappy, they have only themselves to blame: Wealth and power are there for the taking. Once they have acquired property through honest labor or genius, they are secure in the knowledge that others cannot take their property or damage it (even slightly) against their will and that they can use their property as they see fit. They can develop it, they can preserve it from development; they can keep it, they can sell it; they can give it away, they can leave it to their children; they can even destroy it. It is *theirs* to control; no one else can touch it without their consent.

The free market model describes the market as an area of social life immune from both governmental control and private coercion. This vision relies on a fundamental distinction between the public sphere of state control and the private sphere of individual freedom. It identifies maximization of private freedom (and minimization of government control) as the paradigm of a free society.

Economic liberty What is wrong with this story of the free market? To begin with, this paradigm fails to address the difficult question of what we mean by economic liberty. Liberty means freedom to act, as long as one's actions are compatible with a like freedom for others. Liberty means freedom from having the government tell us what to do (public coercion) and freedom from having our neighbors harm us or take our property or services against our wishes (private coercion). Traditional social contract theory is premised on the notion that one purpose of government is to protect people from the domination by others that could happen in the state of nature. The free market is not the state of nature; by definition, it requires collective coercion to protect property rights and personal security and to enforce agreements. The image of a private sphere of free market activity with minimal government regulation still requires a certain amount of regulation. This compels us to define limits on freedom of action necessary to make us secure from harm; those limits are constituted by property and contract rights. The project of achieving economic liberty thus requires us to define those rights. And this is not an easy thing to do.

Property and contracts rights are not self-defining. In allocating them, we must often choose between competing principles: between title and possession, between contract and reliance, between freedom and security, between voluntariness and duress. There is simply no way to derive logically the inherent meaning either of contract or of property because each contains within it an accommodation between the contradictory claims of freedom and security. Every entitlement implies a correlative vulnerability of others. This is the Hohfeldian lesson: For every benefit there is a cost; for every entitlement, there is a correlative exposure. To the extent I have a liberty to act, you are exposed to potential harm; to the extent I have a right to security, your liberty to act is limited. The image of absolute freedom and absolute security underlying the myth of the free market is a false description of social reality and of the rules in force. It ultimately proves incoherent and self-refuting as an ethical goal.

Because all legal rights protect some interests at the expense of other competing interests, we must choose whom to protect and whom to leave vulnerable. Property and contract rights do not define themselves for us. We cannot define them without reference to controversial political and moral commitments.

Indeterminacy of freedom of contract In a freedom of contract system, people are free to make whatever agreements they wish. They are also free not to agree; other people cannot force them to agree against their will. Freedom of contract therefore requires us to enforce voluntary agreements in accordance with their terms, and to refuse to enforce agreements that are the result of coercion by one party over the other. We must make judgments about which agreements are sufficiently voluntary to enforce and which are illegitimate impositions of power by one party over the other. We could define duress narrowly to include only physical duress (arm twisting) or physical threats (gun to the head); or we could define it more broadly to include economic duress caused by unequal bargaining power. There is no purely logical answer to this question.

Suppose that you have fallen into a deep pit filled with poisonous snakes. I come along and observe you in the pit. I am not responsible for your predicament and have no legal duty to help you. I offer to sell you a ladder in exchange for half your future earnings. You agree to buy; I agree to sell. It is a Pareto superior exchange; you are happier with your life and half your future earnings than the alternative; I am happier as well with this outcome. Is the contract voluntary? There is no simple answer to this question. You obviously felt forced to agree; you paid an awful lot for the ladder. But you also benefited substantially by the deal. Is the contract fair? The terms are onerous for you, but so was the alternative. We could, consistent with a regime of freedom of contract, enforce this contract (because it was the result of voluntary choice and was mutually beneficial) or not enforce it (because it was the result of coerced choice and its terms are unconscionable).

A free market system also encompasses goals other than freedom of contract, and we may need

to limit freedom of contract to achieve these goals. For example, we sometimes refuse to enforce anti-competitive covenants to achieve the goal of preserving economic competition. We refuse to enforce racially discriminatory covenants to promote equal access to real property. We refuse to enforce certain future interests to promote the goal of increasing the alienability of property in the marketplace. The goals of competition, alienability, and equal access to property are part of our conception of what a free market system means. Yet all of them require limits to freedom of contract. Again, there is no easy way to determine what the goals of a free market system should be, or how we should resolve conflicts between the principle of freedom of contract and competing principles.

Circularity of defining property by reference to bargains The opponents of plant closing regulation argue that if the workers wanted a right to buy the plant upon closing, they should have bargained for this right in their contract; in the absence of such an agreement, the workers cannot have this right. This argument is flawed for two reasons. First, the argument is unconvincing until we have answered the question of whether the circumstances of the agreement accord with our ideals of freedom of contract: Was the bargaining power between the parties sufficiently equal to be enforced as a voluntary agreement or was it sufficiently unequal to constitute an illegitimate imposition of terms by the company on the workers?

Second, it is circular to define properly rights by reference to bargains. Whatever bargain is agreed to by the parties will be a function of their relative bargaining power. Their bargaining power, in turn, is a function of their relative property rights. The assignment of the property entitlements determines the relative bargaining power of the parties which then determines what they agree to in the contract. What people agree to in their contracts is part of what determines what property rights they have. We cannot define property rights purely by reference to bargains because bargains are a function of property rights. Bargains determine property rights, but property rights also determine what bargains are made. There is no purely logical starting point to the analysis. We need some independent criterion of justice (other than freedom of contract) to determine what the initial distribution of property rights should be.

Property as delegation of sovereign power I have argued that property and contract rights are not self-defining. But the problem is even worse than this. It is impossible to describe accurately a free market system by reference to the idea of minimizing government intrusion on private freedom in the marketplace. Even in a laissez-faire system, the government is fundamentally implicated in the most minute details of every market transaction. The legal realists taught us that both property and contract rights can be understood as delegations of sovereign power. The definition and enforcement of entitlements necessarily entails application of public power. When the state enforces contracts, it coerces individuals to comply with their commitments rather than leaving them free to make new arrangements that are more beneficial to them. When the state refuses to enforce contracts, it prevents powerful individuals from binding vulnerable persons. When the state enforces property rights, it enables the owner to exclude others from access to her property. When the state refuses to enforce property rights, it delegates to non-owners the power to take what they need from owners.

Property and contract rights are powers delegated by the state; they assign decision-making power. These rights determine the relative bargaining power of the parties to voluntary transactions. There is therefore no such thing as a private sphere removed from state regulation. In the midst of every transaction sits the state, determining the balance of power between the parties, and hence the result of the bargain. There is no question then of deference to a private bargain; no bargains are purely private. There is no core to our social or legal system that can be fruitfully conceptualized as an unregulated sphere of free property use and free exchange. Every individual action is inherently social; every act is both free and coerced. As Hale tried to teach us, every transaction takes place against a background of property rights. And the definition, allocation, and enforcement of those entitlements represent social decisions about the distribution of power and welfare. No transaction is undertaken outside this sphere of publicly delegated power; the public sphere defines and allocates the entitlements that are exchanged in the private

sphere. At the core of any private action is an allocation of power determined by the state.

It is not the case that everyone in our society has equal access to wealth and power or that opportunities in the marketplace are even roughly equal. It is also not the case that these inequalities primarily result from differences in individual talent or efforts. To a large extent, the inequalities present in the economic system are the result of the legal allocation of entitlements. The question, then, is not whether or not to regulate. The question is what kind of regulation we are going to have: What distribution of power we want to establish in the market; what interests we want the market to protect; what consequences we want the market to foster. The free market model is indeterminate. There is no such thing as a single "free market"; we must choose among alternative possible market structures.

New Questions About Plant Closings
In 1937, Leon Green wrote an article for the *New Republic* about the sit-down strikes. His analysis tracked his theory that the modern market system should be understood in terms of the need to protect various relational interests. These are "the interests a person may have in his *relations with other persons*." He wrote:

> The industrial relation in its initial or formative state is the result of a contractual nexus between the two parental organisms of industry—those who supply its property-capital on the one hand and those who supply its service-capital on the other. But as in the case of family, corporate, partnership, carrier, and all other important relations, the slender tie of the initial contract is overgrown by a network of tissue, nerves and tendons, as it were, which gives the relation its significance. The respective rights, duties, privileges and immunities of the parties to the industrial relation are too numerous to recite here, but they are well known.
>
> Both participating groups have contributed heavily to the joint enterprise of industry. The contributions of those who make up the corporate organization on the one hand are visualized in plant, machinery, raw materials and the like. They can be seen, recorded and valued in dollars. We call them property. On the

other side are hundreds of personalities who have spent years training their hands and senses to specialized skills; who have set up habitations conveniently located to their work; who have become obligated to families and for the facilities necessary for maintaining them; who have ordered their lives and developed disciplines; all to the end that the properties essential to industry may be operated for the profit of the owner group and for their own livelihoods. Their outlays are not so visible, nor so easily measured in dollars, but in gross they may equal or even exceed the contributions of the other group. Both groups are joint adventurers, as it were, in industrial enterprise. Both have and necessarily must have a voice in the matters of common concern. Both must have protection adequate to their interests as against the world at large as well as against the undue demands of each other.

Green argued that the company should be understood as a common enterprise. He further argued that the law should recognize and protect the ongoing relation between management and labor. This relation is not fully articulated by the agreement between the parties. Expectations develop during the relationship that are legitimate. Because these expectations have developed, the relation must be regulated to prevent the more powerful party—the corporation—from using its superior bargaining power in ways that illegitimately threaten the interests of workers relying on continuation of the relationship.

> The right to fire is an incident of the simplest form of contract, that of employment at the will of both parties; it has no place in a relation which is based upon infinitely more than mere contract. A wife cannot fire her husband, a parent his child, a corporate stockholder other stockholders, one partner another member of the firm, an insurer the insured, a carrier its passengers, with impunity. Neither can an employer fire his employees *en masse*. These other relations are at best only analogous, but they give point. All institutions built upon relational interests of the groups concerned must submit to the obligations which have grown up around the particular relation, and if it is to be destroyed it must be done subject to such obligations.

The relational approach shifts our attention from asking "Who is the owner?" to the question "What relationships have been established?" The shift is partly a shift from focusing on the relation between the owner and the resources owned to the relation between the owner and non-owners who have benefited from the resources. But more important, the shift is from a perspective that focuses on the owner as an isolated individual whose presumptive control of the resource is absolute within her sphere of power to a perspective that understands individuals to be in a continuing relation to each other as part of a common enterprise. Rights are not limited to the initial allocation of property entitlements or the agreement of the parties, but emerge and change over the course of the relationship.

The relational idea forces us to turn our attention to facts that would otherwise be obscured. It allows us to take seriously Judge Lambros's intuition that property rights should be recognized from the long-standing relation between U.S. Steel, its workers, and the town. Rather than seeing the corporation and the workers in isolation, and assuming that the corporation has absolute freedom to dispose of "its" property as it sees fit, in the absence of a clear contractual obligation to the contrary, we can see the corporation and the workers as together having established and relied on long-standing relations with each other in creating a common enterprise. The rights of the members of the common enterprise cannot be fully articulated by reference to ownership rights defined *a priori* or by the explicit terms of written contracts. If workers are considered to be part of the corporation, rather than factors of production or hired hands, our analysis of property rights changes. As Clyde Summers explains:

> [T]he corporation is more than the shareholders and includes the employees. If the corporation is conceived in relatively narrow terms as an operating institution combining all factors of production to conduct an on-going business, then the employees who provide the labor are as much members of that enterprise as the shareholders who provide the capital. Indeed, the employees may have made a much greater investment in the enterprise by their years of service, may have much less ability to withdraw,

and may have a greater stake in the future of the enterprise than many of the stockholders.

This image allows us to consider the moral character of that relationship and the obligations that should be imposed on the more powerful party to protect the interests of the more vulnerable party. It allows us to address as a legal matter the question that Lambros ultimately treated as non-legal, as a matter of morality. The relational idea does not tell us what to do, but it helps us define the issue of the case in a way that does not exclude consideration of the legitimate obligations of powerful parties to their partners in common enterprises.

Legal obligations are imposed on parties to relationships even though the parties did not agree to such obligations and even though such obligations were not clearly defined by the state at the start of the relationship. These obligations are imposed for a wide variety of reasons. As Unger has written:

> The circumstances suitable for [the] application [of an intermediate standard between total devotion to community and complete self-centeredness] might be selected on the basis of features that would include expressed intent, induced or even unwarranted trust in fact, disparity of power manifest in one party's greater vulnerability to harm, and the continuing character of the contractual relationship.

As Peter Linzer explains:

> I believe that the traditional approaches to tort, contract and property are wrong, and that private law is a relatively seamless area in which the society, speaking primarily through the courts, assigns rights and duties based on relationships among people and firms, in light of many factors, among them the particular community needs, the needs of the parties themselves, their relative power, fairness among them *and* their assent.

Thus, we should ask a series of questions about the ongoing relations among the parties to the common enterprise. What relations have been established? What expectations have been generated on both sides by continuation of the relationship? To what extent should those expectations be pro-

tected? What was the explicit agreement between the parties? What is the distribution of power in that relationship? What alternatives do the parties have open to them? How have the parties relied on continuation of the relationship? How have the parties contributed to the joint enterprise? What are the consequences of giving complete control of the property to the putative owner or limiting the corporation's obligations to those agreed to in the contract? What are the consequences of imposing greater obligations on the corporation toward the workers? What moral obligations should the more powerful party have in this context to protect the more vulnerable party?

THE POLITICAL ECONOMY OF PLANT CLOSINGS

> Bargaining power would be different were it not that the law endows some with rights that are more advantageous than those with which it endows others. It is with these unequal rights that men bargain and exert pressure on one another. These rights give birth to the unequal fruits of bargaining.…With different rules as to the assignment of properly rights…we could have just as strict a protection of each person's property rights, and just as little government interference with freedom of contract, but a very different pattern of economic relationships. Moreover, by judicious legal limitation on the bargaining power of the economically and legally stronger, it is conceivable the economically weak would acquire greater freedom of contract than they now have—freedom to resist more effectively the bargaining power of the strong, and to obtain better terms.
> —Robert Hale

Traditional notions of contract and property greatly favor the economically dominant party, even though a strong case can be made that all contributors to an enterprise deserve some security and some share of the enterprise itself. The focus [should be] on the relationship as a firm with the members' rights depending on communal notions of fairness.…[P]eople who contribute to a relationship are owed something beyond a salary or other compensation that can terminate at the will of the owner.

—Peter Linzer

The Politics in Economics

When should the legal system protect the reliance interest in property in the context of plant closings? How should it be protected? I have already argued that we should have a normative commitment to recognizing social obligations of property ownership to protect fundamental needs of the community. The most wealthy and powerful owners—the large corporations that control economic life in a community—should have the greatest obligations. I have also argued that the legal system should protect the more vulnerable party to a long-lasting relationship when that person has relied on the relationship. This moral obligation is especially powerful when the relationship itself was premised partly on the parties' satisfying each other's needs.

Protecting the reliance interest in property in the context of plant closings would require us to regulate the industrial relation between managers and workers. This poses several additional questions. What types of regulation should be imposed? What consequences will that regulation have? Will it interfere in the ability of workers and managers to come to arrangements that are mutually beneficial, and thereby make them both worse off rather than better off? What will be the social consequences of this regulation? Who will it hurt and who will it benefit? How do we measure the costs and benefits of different types of regulation and how do we compare them to the costs and benefits of not regulating plant closings? Will regulation increase or decrease the general welfare? What moral obligations should corporations have toward their employees regardless of the effects of those obligations on allocative efficiency?

The free market model relied on by the judges in the *United Steel Workers* case is based on an economic theory as well as a social vision. This theory is a version of utilitarianism; the central question is "how can we maximize the sum total of individual satisfaction?"

I want to offer a competing view. Because the social relations approach sees people as situated in relationships rather than as autonomous individuals, the central economic question is "what kind of society do we want to create and what kinds of relationships should we foster?" This question broadens our view; it asks us to pay attention not only to maximization of individual satisfaction, but to the market and social structures within which individual freedom is situated. It asks us to consider how we want to structure the contours of those relationships.

Individual satisfaction is important; indeed, it is central. But we cannot decide what arrangements maximize individual satisfaction simply by asking what agreements people would make in the absence of transaction costs. This is because whatever agreements they would make would differ depending on their relative bargaining power. Bargaining power is a function of the legal definition and allocation of property and contract rights. Those rights represent decisions about the distribution of wealth and power. We therefore cannot judge which market structures best satisfy human needs without simultaneously making normative judgments about the types of human relationships that we want to foster.

It is impossible to separate economic analysis from politics. Economic analysis must include political choices about how to measure costs and benefits, and choices about how to structure the institutions within which human beings will engage in their activities and develop their conceptions of their interests. To make economic analysis a useful way to develop policy recommendations, we must consider these questions in conjunction with a normative commitment to a form of social life. In developing this social vision, we must allow people to have freedom to develop various kinds of relationships without intrusion by the state; at the same time, we must make judgments both about the kinds of relationships we want to foster and the kinds of relationships that require regulation to prevent oppression. Cost/benefit analysis only makes sense in conjunction with judgments of this sort. This insight can, perhaps, shed some light on the current debates about economic analysis of law.

Everyone acknowledges that markets can fail. There is a standard debate in the legal academic community about externalities. This is my understanding of it. First, the conservatives argue that the free market generally maximizes the general welfare through the market's invisible hand. Profits and the price mechanism generally allocate resources efficiently. In response, the liberals argue that when private and social costs diverge, the market may allocate resources inefficiently. Thus, the legal system could further the goal of allocating resources efficiently by creating liability rules that force companies to internalize their external costs.

The conservatives answer by invoking the Coase Theorem: There is no way to determine, in an unproblematic way, what is a cost of what. Joint costs arise because competing market activities may clash; the homeowner who wants clean air is externalizing the costs of homeowning on the polluting factory, just as surely as the polluting factory is externalizing its costs on the homeowner. Moreover, in the absence of transaction costs, liability rules will not affect allocative efficiency, since affected parties will simply bargain with each other to redistribute entitlements to achieve efficient results. Conservatives who seek to decrease regulation of market activity limit the situations in which transaction costs are thought to be serious. The liberals respond by seeing transaction costs everywhere. They focus on imperfect information, moralisms, and other kinds of third-party effects, as well as bargaining impediments such as holdout, agency, and freeloader problems. The conservatives then reply by developing models of how to increase efficiency in the face of uncertainty about how all these arguments play out. Who is in the best position to make the cost-benefit determination? The conservatives also point to the idea of administrative costs. They argue that the costs of litigation, and of second-guessing business decisions may outweigh any social benefits of regulation.

Finally, conservatives argue that any attempts to alleviate negative externalities by judicial redefinition of common law rules is bound to fail. A company would simply pass along the cost of the regulation to its consumers or its workers or shareholders. So the very people liberals are trying to help will be the ones hurt by the decision. The uncertainty and costs caused by substantial regulation of business decisions may decrease incentives and hence investment so substantially that regulation does more harm than good. The liberals respond to this set of arguments by acknowledging that reforms may have unintended, counterproductive consequences. But they argue that this is not always the case, and we can distinguish situations

when this is the case from those in which it is not the case. They argue, furthermore, that the question of who is the best decisionmaker in the presence of uncertainty fails to acknowledge that determinations of efficiency are always relative to background entitlements. Thus, the question of efficiency cannot be divorced from fundamental questions about the distribution of wealth and power that determine who is in the best position—courts versus corporate managers—to make the relevant cost-benefit calculus. Efficiency is relative to power and power is determined by the legal rules defining property, contract and tort obligations. Analysis of what transactions would occur in the absence of impediments to those transactions gets mixed up with fundamental questions of how to distribute decision-making power before the efficiency analysis even gets off the ground.

The crux of the liberal/conservative debate seems to be a difference of opinion about how strong the presumption should be, in the face of uncertainty, that property owners (or their representatives—corporate managers) are the best judges of what will maximize the general welfare. On this issue, I contend that the liberals are right and the conservatives are wrong. In situations like plant closings, where the number of people affected by the corporate action is substantial and the social effects are enormous, there is simply no good reason to presume that what is good for the corporation is good for the community. The divergence between private costs and social costs in this kind of situation is enormous, and there is no reason to believe that transactions will occur that remedy the situation. Determinations of efficiency, moreover, are always relative to background entitlements that must be justified on other grounds. We have good reasons of equality, democracy, community, as well as efficiency, to redefine property rights to redistribute power from corporate managers to workers and their communities.

The difference of opinion between liberals and conservatives should be explained as a disagreement about facts. After all, the language of economic analysis asks us to make only one relatively uncontroversial value judgment—that satisfying human wants is a good thing. The analysis then proceeds to ask what set of rules will maximize satisfaction of human wants. Conservatives tend to ask: "What would people agree to in the absence of transaction costs?" Liberals ask: "What would people agree to if they had relatively equal bargaining power?" The goal in either case appears to be giving people what they want.

It is impossible to answer either of these questions without making moral and political judgments. To answer the conservative question adequately, we must decide what rules to hold constant while we do the analysis. If we allow too many rules to be considered at once, efficiency analysis becomes indeterminate; it becomes a matter of bargaining about the fundamental terms of social life. And yet, if we hold everything constant but the one rule in question, we have biased the analysis in favor of the status quo. To answer the liberal question, we must make moral and political judgments about the meaning of power, and the relation between process and outcome. We must determine what outcomes are sufficiently inequitable for us to conclude that the parties were not sufficiently equal in power to defer to the terms of their bargain. Judgments about the legitimacy of the bargaining process therefore become bound up with judgments about the fairness of the outcome.

It is obvious, in addition, that liberals and conservatives disagree about more than what people want. They fundamentally disagree about what people *should* want. More precisely, they disagree about the kind of society we should create. They disagree about how to distribute power and wealth between governments and citizens, between corporations and consumers, between owners and non-owners, between managers and workers. Economic analysis takes place in the context of political judgments of this sort. It is with this factor in mind that I canvas the economic arguments about regulating plant closings.

The Economic Argument Against Protecting the Reliance Interest in Property

The free market argument To focus the economic discussion, I will address two issues. First, in the absence of contractual obligations, should the company have an obligation to sell the plant to the workers rather than destroy it? Second, should the company have an obligation to make severance payments to employees upon closing the plant? I argue, first, that the standard economic arguments supporting deregulation of property are based on empirical assertions about the effects of different regulatory regimes. Those assertions are either tautological (and therefore non-falsifiable) or they are contestable. My purpose is to convince readers that there is no good reason to presume that free alienability and use of property will maximize the general welfare. Instead, economic analysis supports a mixture of regulation and deregulation; that is a major reason why current legal rules about property use and ownership substantially limit the power of owners to control absolutely the resources allocated to them by the legal system.

Second, economic analysis cannot be done without simultaneously making a series of value judgments about the proper and just distribution of power and wealth in the market system. I will identify the implicit value choices in the free market economic analysis and argue that they define "wealth maximization" in a way that is wrongly biased toward concentration of economic power in the hands of corporate managers. Moreover, these value choices fail to adequately protect social interests in equality, community, democracy and reliance on continuing relationships.

The chief tenet of the free market argument is that the goal of the legal system should be to maximize the general welfare. Rules creating property and contract entitlements establish the framework within which individuals can engage in productive activity in the marketplace with the assurance that their efforts will benefit them personally. Those rules give individuals freedom to do what they want to do and security from having their efforts undermined by others.

In the absence of countervailing considerations, or when the facts are uncertain or hard to determine, it is reasonable to presume that the general welfare (or social wealth) will be maximized if we establish the following rights: (1) *Individual rights to exclude:* All resources should be owned by someone and ownership should be concentrated in the hands of individual persons who have the right to determine the conditions under which others will have access to the property; (2) *Liberty to use the property:* Owners should be allowed to do whatever they want with their property free from governmental control and should not have to account to others about their decisions about what they do with the property; (3) *Power to transfer the property and immunity from loss of the property*: Owners alone should have the power to determine whether, and to whom, they will sell their property; and (4) *Freedom of contract:* contracts should be enforced in accordance with their terms. These four criteria will generally ensure that property is allocated to its most productive use which in turn will maximize social wealth. This argument can be conveniently divided into a series of arguments about property and a series of arguments about contracts.

The Property Argument

Maximizing social wealth Social wealth will be maximized if property is controlled by the persons who value it most highly. Value is determined by willingness and ability to pay for property. Thus property should be controlled by the person who would pay the most to purchase it. In the absence of significant transaction costs, we can assume that whoever owns property values it the most; if they did not value it the most, then whoever did would buy it from them.

Free use of property Individuals seek to maximize their satisfaction. Individuals, moreover, are the best judges of what will do this. If property owners are free to decide what to do with resources under their legal control, they will be able to maximize their satisfaction. If the legal rules interfere with their ability to decide what to do with their property, those rules will decrease individual satisfaction and therefore the general welfare. We will therefore maximize social wealth if we let property owners use their property as they see fit. It is true that this freedom of action must be limited to protect the legitimate security interests of non-owners or neighbors; regulation of property use should be enforced to prevent harm (through nuisance law or building codes or the like). But affirmative obligations to use property in a way that benefits others should be limited to those contractual obligations voluntarily accepted by the property owner. Destruction of the plant by the company does not directly harm anyone else. Thus, the company should be able to deal with its property as it sees fit. The company has no affirmative obligation not to destroy the plant unless it has voluntarily given up its right to destroy it.

Free transfer and immunity from losing the property involuntarily The Board of Directors of U.S. Steel wants to maximize the satisfaction of the shareholders by maximizing company profits. The Board must have done a cost/benefit analysis to determine the relative advantages and disadvantages of destroying the plants and selling them to the workers. If U.S. Steel wants to destroy the plants rather than sell them to the workers, it is presumably because the company (and its shareholders) are better off in dollar terms when the property is destroyed than when it is transferred. If the workers really valued the plants more than the company, they would offer the company enough money to induce it to sell. It is probable that at some price, the company would be better off selling the plants than destroying them. Since the workers have not offered the company more than the company would ask to sell the plants, the company values the property more than they do. A forced transfer would therefore decrease social wealth because it would transfer the property to a user who valued it less. It is therefore inefficient to prohibit the company from destroying the plants.

Investment incentives Forcing a sale of the plant to the workers will channel investment in a way that is inefficient. First, the plant has been closed either because it is unprofitable or because other investments are more profitable. For the legal rules to encourage continued investment in an industry that is relatively less profitable than alternative investments is to prevent the competitive marketplace from working to allocate resources efficiently. If the court prevents the company from selling the property to another buyer, or from using the property for another purpose itself, it will be preventing the most efficient result from emerging by requiring a forced transfer.

Second, when the company closes the plant, it is either going to open a new plant somewhere else or channel its investment in some different way. Any regulation that would prevent the movement of capital might help one city but would hurt another. Since operation in the other city or investment of capital there would be more profitable than continued investment in the city where the plant is closing, the end result is a decrease in social wealth (or, at any rate, an impediment to wealth maximization).

Third, requiring the company to sell the plant or transfer it to the workers will increase the company's costs of operations. We want to encourage capital mobility; we want investment to travel to its most profitable and, therefore, productive use. Imposing obligations on the company to protect the workers' reliance interests will discourage investment. Thus, the strategy will ultimately be self-defeating.

Fourth, in a federal system, if one state places higher obligations on companies than other states, those other states will win out in the marketplace for capital investment. Thus the economy of the state that is trying to help the workers will only end up by destroying incentives for investment and make everyone in the state worse off.

Redistribution of wealth to workers cannot be achieved by protecting the reliance interest in property If the reliance interest is recognized, companies will simply respond as they would to a tax. Recognition of this new right in the workers represents a loss of property rights for the company. It will compensate for the loss by decreasing wages or benefits or raising prices of its products or otherwise passing the cost along to workers and consumers. Thus, the people intended to be benefited will be hurt. The only way to prevent this is to introduce national planning or price controls, but this kind of planning will distort incentives and prevent the market from efficiently allocating investment. The end result will be stagnation and general lack of investment. The effort at redistributing property rights will simply decrease total social wealth and make everyone worse off.

The Free Contract Argument

Freedom of contract The court should enforce contracts in accordance with their terms. To imply a term into the collective bargaining agreement can only reduce efficiency. Voluntary agreements are Pareto efficient since they make both parties better off without hurting anyone else. If the terms of contracts are regulated, people are prevented from making exchanges that benefit both sides. Compulsory contract terms therefore reduce social wealth.

Externalities are law and we are better off if people take care of themselves While it is true that adverse economic circumstances may follow in a community that is the victim of a plant closing, the external effects are likely to be low. Workers get new jobs either in the same community or elsewhere. Legal protection of the reliance interest would interfere with this process of economic adjustment. Because workers take care of themselves by re-entering the marketplace, the external effects of the plant closing are temporary and are corrected by normal market functioning. To the extent that workers need money to tide them over, unemployment insurance and bargained-for severance payments are already available.

Ex ante compensation To the extent that workers are vulnerable to plant closings, they will have exacted a premium from the company to compensate them for the risks involved in job termination. There is no need for the court to impose obligations on the company to provide unbargained for severance payments or to require a forced sale. To imply either of these terms into the labor contract gives the workers something they did not bargain for. If it had been worth it to the workers to have severance payments or a right to purchase the plant at the time they entered the collective bargaining agreement, then they would have bargained for these terms by giving up something in exchange. To force a transfer of the plant when the workers did not bargain for a right to purchase gives the workers something for nothing; by taking away the company's property right (to control use and disposition of the plant) the court creates a forced exchange that harms the company. The exchange is therefore not Pareto superior to enforcing the contract as written. Moreover, it is not even potentially Pareto superior. If the workers had more to gain than the company had to lose by a right to purchase the plant, then the workers would have offered the company enough in the way of concessions to induce the company to grant the right to the workers. Since this did not happen, the company would lose more from recognition of the entitlement than the workers would gain. Since the winners from the entitlement could not compensate the losers for what they lose, the term is therefore inefficient and reduces social wealth.

Ex post efficiency distorts incentives It might be plausible to protect the reliance interest if it turned out that the parties had miscalculated the chances of the plant closing and the social costs of closure. In that case, the social costs of allowing the company to destroy the plants might be out-weighed by the social benefits of transferring the plant to the workers or the community. Even if this were the case, however, we would ordinarily expect the market to take care of it; the workers would offer the company enough money to induce the company to sell. Since that has not happened, the benefits of the transfer to the workers must be less than the benefits to the company of destroying the plants. Moreover, this kind of ex post determination will distort incentives by changing the risks of entering the marketplace. The workers and the company will have to guess not only the chances of the plant closing, and the value to them of the right to purchase versus the right to destroy in ex ante negotiations, but the chances of their being wrong and having a court step in and force an exchange. The uncertainties of the marketplace are magnified by having a standard that allows creation of a new entitlement in uncertain circumstances. This uncertainty will distort incentives and result in decreased investment and less social wealth. A rigid rule that allows companies to do what they want with their property, unless they have agreed otherwise, maximizes social wealth in the long run, even if it has adverse consequences in some specific cases. Case-by-case adjudication will simply make investment too uncertain.

The Economic Argument for Protecting the Reliance Interest in Property

Why profitable plants close As an initial matter, it is unclear why a court should even consider forcing a sale of the plant to the workers. Companies normally close only unprofitable plants, and if the plant cannot be operated profitably, what good would it be to the workers? It is important to recognize that companies sometimes close plants that can be operated profitably. This may happen for several reasons.

First, the plant may be owned by a conglomerate that includes different kinds of industries as subsidiaries. The company may be able to maximize its profits by using the earnings of one of its subsidiaries to subsidize operations of the others. This is in fact what happened with the Youngstown Sheet and Tube Company in Youngstown, Ohio, which was taken over by the Lykes Corporation. Lykes used the company's profits to finance capital investment in other subsidiaries. It did this rather than re-invest the profits in the steel industry for modernization of obsolete plants. In another example, the Sheller-Globe Corporation bought in 1974 the Colonial Press in Clinton, Massachusetts. Until the plant was closed in 1977, the Press was charged an average of $900,000 yearly in corporate over-head costs with little justification. Companies like Youngstown Sheet and Tube and Colonial Press are referred to as "cash cows," said to be "milked" for benefit of the conglomerate's other operations. Once the company has been milked for a long enough time, it may become unprofitable because its plant has been run down and because it has not been modernized in ways needed to compete with other producers in the industry. Thus, these plants are closed not because they are inherently unprofitable; they are unprofitable because the parent company has decided to *make* them unprofitable by milking them or by failing to modernize them.

Second, a plant may also be closed not because it is unprofitable but because it is not profitable *enough*. The company decides that whatever profit it is making is not enough when it could earn a higher return on capital investment in another industry; the company then exits one industry to enter another.

Third, some plants are closed not because they are inherently unprofitable, but because they are managed badly. Professor Yoshi Tsurumi reports that about 600 failing American factories have been taken over by Japanese companies, who in most cases have been able to turn these plants around in just a few years. American managers have focused almost exclusively on lowering costs of materials and labor as ways to increase productivity and profits. They have sometimes insisted on wage cuts at the same time that they themselves have taken large pay increases. Unions have also contributed to the problems of these factories by insisting on rigid work categories. (Unions legitimately want such categories to protect themselves from the arbitrary power of managers.) In contrast, Japanese managers have pledged to cut their own salaries before they would ask for cuts in workers' salaries. By building more flexibility into production, by providing workers a greater sense of participation and security, and by management's sharing in sacrifices in bad times, Japanese managers have been able to take "failing plants and unproductive and uncooperative workers and turn them into rousing successes."

In all these cases, plant managers may be acting rationally to maximize the company's profits by closing the plant. This does not mean, however, that it is *impossible to* operate the plant profitably. Nor does it mean that profit maximization is a proper measure of social welfare.

Externalities

Private and social costs Plant closings cause substantial externalities, both positive and negative. The company benefits by the closing, as do others if the company transfers its investment to a different economic activity or geographic area. At the same time, many persons other than the parties to the agreement (the workers) are harmed by plant closings. Yet the company may not be legally required to take these negative externalities into account in deciding whether or not to close. If the company is not forced to take into account all the social costs of closing, it may be profitable for the company to close the plant, but the closing may nevertheless produce more social costs than benefits.

Private profits are highly imperfect indicators of what will maximize the general welfare. In *every* plant closing situation, private profit determinations will diverge from social cost/benefit comparisons. If this is true, there is simply no good reason to presume that concentration of economic power in the hands of corporate managers will maximize the general welfare. Private profit is wholly inadequate as a measure of social utility and is even worse as a measure of justice. Substantial regulation of the market is necessary to achieve its own goals of efficiency and satisfaction of human needs.

Labor as a fixed cost When a factory closes, many workers never find new jobs at all. Others are unemployed for long periods of time. Forty percent of the 88,000 steelworkers who lost their jobs between January 1979 and January 1984 because of plant closings were still looking for work at the end of that period. Twenty-five percent of this group left the work force entirely. Those that find jobs

after plant closings often face large reductions in their wages. Steelworkers who found new jobs had a median income 40 percent below their old wages. These difficulties, moreover, are disproportionately visited on older workers, less educated workers, women and racial minorities.

The long-term loss of jobs and substantial reductions in income and wealth of discharged workers also affect the community at large. The loss of work is felt by the public sector in increased unemployment benefits, increased welfare benefits, and increased need for other sorts of public services. It is felt by society generally in the lost contribution of workers who are not working at all or working at jobs that require less than their full talents. Under current law, the company has no enforceable obligation at the time of the plant closing to account to the community for these costs. The company thus partially externalizes onto the community and the public sector the costs of maintaining these people and their families.

In his classic 1923 work, *Studies in the Economics of Overhead Costs,* J. Maurice Clark argued that for some purposes it made sense to think of labor as an overhead or fixed cost, rather than a variable cost. He argues that from the standpoint of the firm, labor appears to be a variable cost. This is because the amount of labor required varies depending on production levels. The firm will either hire more workers or lay off or fire some of its workers as its production levels change. From the standpoint of society, however, labor may be seen as a fixed cost. Workers must be maintained with necessities— food, clothing, shelter, medical care—whether or not they are working. Moreover, they must be trained and their skills maintained and improved.

> There are costs of institutional relief to be borne if maintenance is not met, and much larger losses in productive efficiency. Without attempting to define just where this line comes, we can be quite sure that the laborer does not avoid the cost of maintenance by sleeping on a park bench and living on fifteen cents a day; he deteriorates and both he and the community bear the cost of the deterioration. Plus there is a very large element of maintenance cost, or its equivalent, which goes on whether the laborer is employed or not, and which falls on the laborer if he has reserves to meet it, and on

both laborer and community if his reserves are inadequate.

Someone must bear the cost of maintaining the workers, and if the workers cannot do this themselves, they are taken care of by the government. Thus, the company externalizes the costs of providing for workers by displacing this cost onto the public sector and onto the community directly.

Workers need more than subsistence. They need to maintain or improve their level of skill, morale, and productivity. This is necessary both for the workers themselves and for society. If we do not organize the economy in a way that allows workers to remain productive, we are wasting a valuable social asset—productive labor. Yet plant closings currently produce a large class of discouraged workers who stop looking for work. We lack adequate mechanisms to help workers find new jobs in their own communities.

Workers are often not trained for the jobs that do exist. One of the major problems following a plant closing is the mismatch between the skills of workers who lost their jobs and the available jobs to which they could possibly transfer. This mismatch causes a great many workers to remain unemployed for long periods of times or to accept employment in jobs that require no skills. Workers tend to have skills that are specific to the firm or industry in which they were working. This is especially true if they have been working at the firm for a long time and are middle-aged or older. These firm or industry-specific skills are not always transferable. To the extent it is not possible for a worker to get a new job that utilizes her skills, they will be wasted whether the worker remains unemployed or is underemployed.

Workers are not be able to acquire new skills easily for several reasons. They may have an enormous personal investment in the skills they do possess (they "gave their lives to the steel industry"), or they may hope they will still be able to find work in the industry in which they are skilled. They may lack information about available training programs or available jobs. They may not want to leave their community. Moreover, firms may underinvest in training workers with transferable skills because they would not reap the full rewards of paying for this training. Thus, many workers dis-

placed by plant closings are systematically being shifted from more productive to less productive jobs. This represents a loss of efficiency if the social cost of retraining workers for new jobs is less than the social benefit of this training.

From a social perspective, both individuals and companies may underinvest in retraining when workers lose their jobs as a result of plant closings. If workers were able to get retraining for new jobs and if they were willing to move to other cities or investors were willing to start new businesses in the town where the plant closed, an economic transition could occur that would maintain or increase workers' incomes and produce products that were needed by the community. Most displaced workers, however, do not move, and do not want to move, to other communities. Many communities faced with plant closings find it difficult to attract enough new businesses to make up for the loss.

When we leave workers idle and when we leave plants idle that could profitably produce some needed product, we are wasting useful social resources; we do this both by not using them and by not sufficiently investing in their maintenance and improvement. Allowing the company to externalize these costs onto the workers and the community means that companies may underinvest in employment stability. Because companies are legally entitled to externalize these costs, they have little incentive to organize production in a way that would minimize unemployment. "The result is that those who can do the most to regularize industry do not have the incentive, because they do not bear the worst of the costs of which irregularity is the cause." [Clark] This situation could be changed by requiring companies to pay generous severance payments to workers laid off by plant closings. If companies are not forced to do this, their comparison of costs and benefits of closing the plant are distorted; private and social costs diverge.

Because of barriers to economic readjustment when plants close, we may be faced with a choice between arranging for the workers to continue operating a plant that is profitable (or which at least covers its variable costs) and having both the plant and the workers idle or underemployed for a substantial period of time. In this case, it may be efficient for the plant and workers to be occupied rather than idle. Alternatively, the government could help correct these market failures by helping workers find new jobs, retraining the workers, helping them relocate if they want to move, and taking steps to induce new businesses to open up in the town.

The costs of unemployment are not already taken into account in the wage contract. Workers know they may be laid off and may well have attempted to bargain for severance pay or for increased wages to protect them from the risk of being laid off. Workers, however, may tend to underestimate the chances of the plant closing down, and the difficulty they will have finding a new job. If they had known the chances of the plant closing, they might have bargained for different terms. It may be efficient then to imply into the contract the terms they would have agreed to if they had had perfect information. Their failure to bargain for terms that would sufficiently protect their interests shifts some of the costs of maintaining them onto the public sector and the community itself.

In determining the wisdom of a requirement to compel companies to give severance payments to displaced workers or to require the companies in specific cases to transfer the closed plant to the workers, we must compare the costs and benefits of imposing the regulation with the costs and benefits of not imposing it. If companies were required to consider the social effects of unemployment when they decide whether to close the plant, their decisions would be different, as would the bargain reached by the company and the union. At the same time, it is important to consider the positive externalities of allowing the plant to close without placing further obligations on the company. If we create new obligations on companies or transfer property interests from companies to workers, will this interfere in the creation of new investment and stifle economic growth? Whether these obligations would create better or worse investment and employment decisions is a difficult issue whose answer depends on resolving complicated empirical questions. There is, however, no reason to presume that we are most likely to generate optimum economic activity by allowing companies freely to close plants without imposing on them some obligations to account for the external effects of these decisions.

Third party effects The external impacts of plant closings are enormous. Barry Bluestone and Ben-

nett Harrison have chronicled in detail the social and economic effects of plant closings. These impacts includes losses visited (a) on individual workers and their families; (b) on the city government and its services to the community; (c) on supporting businesses in the community; and (d) on the community at large.

a. *Impacts on workers, their families and the community*. I have already discussed the substantial losses inflicted on workers by unemployment and underemployment. Many workers who lose jobs when a plant closes face long term unemployment and large losses in family income and depletion of family wealth. For example, two years after the Lykes Corporation closed the Youngstown Sheet and Tube Company in Youngstown, 15 percent of the 4,100 workers were still unemployed; 35 percent "retired" prematurely; and 20-40 percent took jobs that involved large wage cuts. Unemployment caused by plant closings is, moreover, associated with large adverse impacts on physical and emotional health. Statistics show increases in specific illnesses such as heart disease, ulcers, alcoholism, mental illness, and hypertension. There is also evidence of increases in suicide, homicide, and child and spouse abuse.

b. *Impacts on city services.* Plant closings often have substantial effects on municipal tax revenues, the main source of funding for local governmental services. After the Youngstown Sheet and Tube closing, it was estimated that the communities around Youngstown would lose up to $8 million in taxes. Loss of property taxes means that city services suffer, including police and fire protection, schools, and libraries. Income taxes are also lost that would have been paid by employed workers to the city, state, and federal governments. This loss of income tax revenue is occurring at the same time that needs for social services from the government are rising.

c. *Impact on supporting businesses.* Closing a major plant in a locality also adversely affects all the business that relied on provision of goods or services to the company itself or to the workers. The United States Chamber of Commerce has estimated that, on the average, a community loses two service jobs for every three manufacturing jobs that are lost. A study of the Youngstown Sheet and Tube closing estimated that the initial loss of 4,100 jobs would expand to 12,000 to 13,000 total jobs lost.

d. *Loss of community*. Major plant closings change everything. When job losses are high, the loss to the community is so great that it is hard to calculate in dollar terms. Some losses are not amenable to easy monetization because there are no markets for them. How much do we value the loss of companionship of large groups of workers that have worked together for twenty years? How much do we value the loss of a healthy economic life in the community? How much do we value the sense of security, the sense of belonging to a productive enterprise, the sense of history? How much do we value the costs of alienation, of disillusionment, of loss of dreams?

I do not mean to argue that things should never change; quite the contrary. I do mean to argue that economists generally tend to undervalue these intangible costs of economic transitions. These costs are very real. If we did consider these costs, we might direct our attention to minimizing hardship on the community during the transition to a new economy.

These externalities are unlikely to be taken care of by the marketplace. Transaction costs are likely to be substantial when thousands of people are affected by the decision to close the plant. The costs include the well-known costs of bargaining, of getting together lots of people, and of strategic moves (holdout and freeloader problems). Freeloader problems are likely to be especially high since many community members are likely to hope that the problem will be taken care of by surrender on the workers' part to demands for wage and benefits concessions.

Moreover, it is unlikely that the workers are adequate proxies for all these affected parties. Although the harm to the workers of destroying the plant is substantial, their ability to bargain with the company is limited by their ability to pay the company to induce it to agree to sell. The outcome of bargaining depends substantially on the relative wealth of the parties and the ability of the more vulnerable persons to bribe the more powerful party to give up its right to destroy the plant. Thus, including in the bargaining process all the adversely affected parties might very well change the outcome. This is especially so if we value the interests of third parties by their asking prices rather than their offer prices. The price third parties would ask

to give up their right to have continued operation of the plant in the community is likely to be much higher than the amount those persons would offer to buy the same right. If we use the asking prices of affected third parties, it is possible that the external costs of allowing the company to destroy the plant would overwhelm its social benefits.

Bargaining Power and Efficiency

The free market argument asserts that any obligations on the company to make unbargained-for severance payments to the workers or to sell the plant to the workers is unlikely to help workers in the long run, if at all. Recognition of these obligations is intended to increase the welfare of the workers either by directly transferring wealth to them from the employer or by increasing their bargaining power in contract negotiations. But the actual result may be quite the opposite. In response to imposition of these obligations, employers and employees may simply bargain around them, even if they are made nondisclaimable. The parties may bargain about other terms of their relationship, including level of employment, job tenure, wages, benefits, and other conditions of employment. Thus, the employer will pass along part of the cost of these obligations onto employees by lowering their wages. Alternatively, it might decrease production and lay off workers. To prevent this from happening, the state would have to regulate *every important provision of the employment contract*. If the state does not do this, then it is not clear that imposition of these obligations will have the intended effect—that is, to give a measure of legal protection to the interests of workers and the community.

This is the familiar "the-landlord-will-raise-the-rent" argument and it is a serious objection to these new entitlements. The conservatives are right to focus attention on it. The argument is, however, more complicated than the simple economic model makes it appear to be. I draw quite different lessons from the argument than the free market enthusiasts.

First, the effects of creating these entitlements are impossible to predict a priori. They depend on the specific labor and product market involved. Whether or not the company can pass on the cost of these new obligations to the workers by lowering their wages or decreasing employment benefits, and whether the company will decrease employment and production depends both on the elasticity of supply and demand for labor in the industry and for the company's products and on the competitive structure of the industry and the labor market.

Second, it is true that a new entitlement in the workers may make the workers worse off, in their own view, if it is not fashioned in a way that significantly alters the distribution of power and wealth between management and labor. It may also make workers worse off if it is adopted in isolation from other remedial legal changes that are necessary to make the entitlement effective in protecting the interests of the persons it is intended to protect.

Whether a new entitlement makes workers better off or not depends on how it is defined. If it is defined correctly, it may substantially increase the bargaining power of the workers and enable them to get a better deal than they would otherwise have gotten. The company knows that it will not be able to do whatever it wants with the plant but will have to negotiate with the workers if the company wants to close the plant; it knows it may be forced to convey the plant to the workers. This may give the company a greater incentive to make the plant more profitable, and this greater profitability may wind up helping the workers. The company is no longer the fee simple owner of the property; the workers have a contingent future interest in the property. The situation is therefore similar to the relation between a life tenant and a remainderperson whose relationship is governed by the law of waste. The life tenant has less freedom to use the property than a fee simple owner precisely because property interests have been divided between the life tenant and the remainderperson. The remainderperson has the right to control, to some extent, the use of the property during the life tenant's regime. Depending on how the right is structured, it may increase the bargaining power of workers tremendously.

For example, the right could be exercisable by the workers only if the company announces that it is closing the plant. If the right is structured in this way, the company is likely to bargain with the workers to get them to give up other benefits, especially if the right is nondisclaimable. On the other hand, the right may be defined to give the workers a continuing legal right of access to financial, investment, and other relevant information about the operation of the business, and the ability to exercise the right whenever the company is

managing the plant badly or failing to engage in reasonable maintenance and modernization needed to keep the plant competitive. If the entitlement were structured in this second way, providing the workers with a right entry for waste, it might dramatically shift the balance of power between the workers and the company. The more property interests or powers that are shifted to the workers, the more the company has to contend with a joint owner of the factory. And if property rights in the plant were defined with the specific intention of transferring both bargaining power and wealth from the company to the workers, it would certainly be possible to achieve the desired effects.

This argument emphasizes the fact that efficiency determinations are relative to background entitlements. The "bargain the parties would have agreed to in the absence of transaction costs" is a function of their relative property and contract rights. If we have to radically redefine or redistribute property entitlements to achieve the desired results, so be it. The argument against radical changes in property law is not one based on efficiency, but on politics. The real issue is the legitimate distribution of power and wealth; who is the right decisionmaker about the future of the workplace community—the shareholders, the board of directors, or some combination of management, workers, and the community? It is certainly *possible* to define property interests in a way that will achieve results that will benefit both the workers and the community. It is not necessary for the regulation to take the form of having the court or the legislature draft the entire contract; it is necessary to regulate only in the sense of defining when power over the plant shifts from management to the workers or how power is divided between them at any given time.

The conservatives are correct in reminding us that we have to be careful how we define property rights. It is true that if we do not shift enough power from the management to the workers, then the workers may in fact not be made better off than they would be without the right. Thus recognition of the right to purchase the plant for its fair market value when the company announces it is going to close the plant may or may not be a good way of helping the workers and the community. For the real balance of power to shift in the desired way, more radical changes may be required.

Would redistribution of property rights be efficient? There is no neutral way to answer this question. Efficiency determinations depend on assuming a particular starting place. If we redefine property rights to protect the interests of the workers in relying on access to the plant, then our determination of what is efficient will change. Efficiency determinations are relative both to the distribution of wealth and background entitlements.

This point gains added strength when one considers that reverses in entitlements change who is offering to buy another's entitlements and who is selling their entitlements. This is because asking prices are likely to be higher, and in some cases, much higher, than offer prices. If the company has the right to blow up the plant, the workers must offer the company more than the company will ask to give up its right. The workers' offer price will be limited by their wealth. But if we reverse entitlements and give the workers a right to assert an ownership interest in the plant when the company wants to close it or when the company fails to manage the plant well, then the company would have to offer the workers more than the workers would ask to give up this right. Because the workers would *own* this right, their wealth would be dramatically higher than if the company had the legal liberty to destroy the plant. Thus the efficiency determination may come out very differently. Under these circumstances, we might conclude that it was efficient for the company not to be able to destroy the plant because it would not be able to bribe the workers to give up their right of security in the plant. This reversal of offer and asking prices may have an enormous impact on the efficiency determination.

This effect would be even more substantial if one were to value third party interests in terms of their asking prices rather than their offer prices. If all the people in the town actually harmed by the plant closing had a right to force a sale of the property to the workers, then the company would have to pay off all these people to induce them not to exercise their rights over the plant. If we use the asking prices of all these people, the efficiency determination looks very different than if we consider what they would pay to induce the company to sell the plant to the workers.

It is of course true that the parties could bargain around any new entitlements granted to the workers. The question then is what their relative bargaining power would or should be when they enter that process. To a large extent, it is contract and property law that will determine their relative bargaining power. If we want to protect the most vulnerable party to the relationship in times of economic stress, we have no alternative but to make them less vulnerable. This means systematically interpreting and changing property and contract principles in ways that effectively redistribute power and wealth to workers. If we do not artificially limit ourselves to examining the consequences of changing one entitlement and no others, it is possible for us to search for the proper structure of property and contract rights that would allow both sufficient flexibility in the marketplace to achieve desirable economic change and would protect those who rely on the continuation of the joint enterprise. That is the challenge for us.

Summary: Reliance and the General Welfare

When a company closes a plant that has been in operation for a substantial period of time and which employs a lot of people, it owes obligations to its workers and to the community. Those obligations may go beyond the terms of its contract with the workers. The company should be legally required to make severance payments to the employees. The workers should also have a right to purchase the plant for its fair market value if they believe they could operate the plant profitably. I come to these conclusions for the following reasons.

The moral principle of protecting reliance on relationships First, and foremost, it is immoral for the company to close the plant without providing for the needs of its employees when the company is capable of providing such help. When a plant closes, the workers are vulnerable to long term unemployment and underemployment, loss of family wealth, and health and family problems. Because the workers are part of the common enterprise, they have earned a right to a measure of protection that may go beyond the terms of their contract. If the company is capable of easing the economic transition for its employees, it has a moral obligation to the workers with whom it has

created a long-term relationship; it may not reproduce within the common enterprise relations of
injustice that may characterize society as a whole.
Thus, the rules of the marketplace should be structured in a way that protects the more vulnerable
party to the relationship to some extent when the
more powerful party ends the relationship.

The mutuality of vulnerability The moral
principle of protecting reliance on relationships is
based on the assumption that both parties to the
relationship have relied on each other. These relations are ones of *mutual dependence.* This mutuality
consists in the fact that each party to the relationship needs what the other offers to their joint enterprise. At the same time, the relationship may not
be one of substantive equality. When the relationship ends, each party faces a world in which they
can no longer rely on the relationship. If one party
wants to end the relationship and the other wants
to continue it, this may indicate that one party
needs what the relationship offered more than the
other does. *But this does not necessarily mean that the
party who is relying on the relationship is the most vulnerable.* The company that is seeking to escape the
obligations of the relationship may be vulnerable, as
well, and may no longer be capable of fulfilling the
obligations of the relationship without undue hardship to itself or without injury to others who also
rely on the company. Moreover, it may be the case
that the workers are relatively well off when the
plant closes. At the same time, the company may be
in rough financial shape such that its very existence
is threatened. Further, the stockholders of the
company may be dominated by pension funds,
charitable foundations, universities, and the like.
Imposing obligations on the company may significantly injure these stockholders at the expense of
relatively wealthy employees of the company. These
stockholders provide benefits to pensioners, students, and low income families. In a case like this,
both parties to the relationship are vulnerable, and
it is a much harder question who should be obligated to whom.

In making moral choices about the mutual
obligations of parties to relationships of mutual
dependence, we must, therefore, be sensitive both
to the mutuality of this dependence, to the relative
vulnerability of the parties during the course of

their relationship and at the point when one wants
to end the relationship, to the relative ability of the
parties to help themselves and the other party in a
time of crisis, and to the nuances of the parties'
relative power in their relationship. As Hale taught
us, each party exercises power, or coercion, over
the other. This does not mean that all exercises of
power are of equal moral significance or equally
legitimate. It does mean that we must carefully
assess the competing moral claims of parties to
ongoing relationships.

To assess the competing claims of the parties,
we must attempt to empathize with each of them,
to see the world from each of their perspectives. It
is imperative that the moral principle of the reliance interest in property not be applied mechanically. We must ask what it would mean to impose
obligations of the company beyond those agreed to
in the contract with the workers. To what extent
would the company, and vulnerable persons who
rely on its financial well-being, be injured by those
obligations? And how do those claims compare to
the claims of the workers and the community in
which the plant is located?

At the same time, we must assess realistically
what the legal remedy would mean for the parties
to the relationship. If the workers have a right of
first refusal to purchase the plant—a legal power to
compel a sale of the plant to them for its fair market value—the company may be harmed very little
by this legal obligation; it can take the money and
reinvest it elsewhere. Moreover, once companies
understand that they have obligations to make
severance payments to workers when they close
plants, they may well adjust to these new obligations in ways that protect the interests of their
shareholders and others dependent on them. If, on
the other hand, these obligations have significant
negative effects on interests of investors, then we
may reach a different conclusion about which party
is most vulnerable. The reliance interest in property
requires us to make realistic judgments of this sort.

Externalities I have argued that the reliance interest in property is the basis of a wide range of currently enforceable legal rules. The difficult question
is how to define the extent of this legal obligation
in the context of plant closings and the circumstances in which it is fairly applicable. Given this

moral starting point, is regulation of plant closings inefficient? Will it decrease social wealth as measured by willingness and ability to pay? Must we sacrifice efficiency to protect the reliance interest? I conclude that regulation will correct the failure of the market to take account of the externalities of plant closings. Such regulation is therefore likely to increase the general welfare as measured by the standard of economic efficiency.

Under current law, companies are free to close plants without taking into account all the social consequences of their decisions. When private and social costs diverge substantially, as they do in every major plant closing, there is no reason to assume that profit-maximizing activity is efficient. The social costs of unregulated plant closings are enormous, including costs of idle plant and equipment, idle labor, health and crime problems, deterioration of public services and secondary businesses. If corporations had to make severance payments to workers when they closed plants, they would take into account, much more than they do now, the social harms caused by their search to maximize profits. In this way their decision to close would more closely approximate an efficient result. At the same time, it is true that regulation of plant closings may prevent substantial positive externalities from emerging. It is not clear whether imposing such obligations on the company would prevent efficient re-allocation of investment.

Ronald Coase argued that there was no objective way to identify who was externalizing costs and who was the victim of those externalities. The polluting factory externalizes the costs of pollution onto homeowners in the area; but it is equally true that if the homeowners object to the pollution, they are externalizing the costs of homeowning onto the factory by making it more difficult or expensive for the factory to use its property. Thus we could as easily argue that, by regulating plant closings, the community and the workers effectively externalize onto the company the costs of economic transitions. Efficiency theorists have concluded from this insight that the only neutral way to determine the balance of costs and benefits was to identify the bargains the parties would have reached in the absence of transaction costs. But this conclusion is unpersuasive for several reasons.

The efficiency determination may be heavily influenced by the initial distribution of entitlements. If we assume that the background rule is that companies have the freedom to close plants with no obligations to make severance payments or sell the plant to the workers when it is closed, our efficiency determination will compare the asking price of the company with the offer price of those who would benefit from such entitlements. On the other hand, if we assume that the rule is the company has such obligations in the absence of agreement to the contrary, then we must compare the asking price of the workers to give up this right with the offer price of the company to acquire a right to destroy the plant. Moreover, the interests of third parties (family members, supporting businesses, others in the community) may be valued either by their offer prices (the amount they would pay to avoid the harm) or their asking prices (the amount they would ask to give up their right to regulate the plant closing). Since asking prices are more likely to be higher, and in some cases, much higher, than offer prices, the formulation of the cost/benefit calculation may determine the outcome. The starting point for analysis will determine the relative bargaining power of the parties in our hypothetical contract, and hence, the efficient result.

Further, we understand the situation as one of joint cost only if we have no moral reason for preferring the interests of one economic actor over another—in other words, if we refuse to make any value judgments about the rights of the parties. But there is simply no reason for us to accept this methodology. We want jobs and products and homes and we may want to make tradeoffs between these social goods. But it is not the case that we are indifferent as between pollution and clean air. To the extent feasible, we want to live in a society that has a clean environment. Pollution is a disfavored activity relative to home-owning or the creation of jobs. We *want* to make it more expensive and difficult for people to pollute the air and water. On the other hand, we have no interest in making it more difficult for people to live in homes. As between the right to clean air and the right to pollute, we have strong preferences for clean air; it is morally wrong to pollute the environment if jobs and houses can be provided without such pollution. It is true that we are not willing to avoid pollution entirely at *any* cost. But we do strongly want to avoid the social cost of pollution. If this is true, the proper way to do an economic analysis may be to insure that this moral preference is reflected in the cost/benefit analysis by comparing the asking price of the favored activity with the offer price of the disfavored activity. *In other words, our social vision of the society we hope to create can aid us in determining how to value the costs and benefits of alternative arrangements.*

Efficiency analysis is indeterminate in the absence of value judgments about the proper distribution of power in the market. We need a moral commitment to one or another distribution of market power to enable us to value the costs and benefits of alternative arrangements. The reliance interest in property gives us a vocabulary for making moral judgments about this issue. The facts indicate that workers and communities are especially vulnerable when companies close plants. To the extent that we can protect those vulnerable persons without significantly harming the interests of others, we should do so. If we have reasons of justice to protect the more vulnerable party who has relied on a relationship of mutual dependence, we have reason to value costs and benefits in a way that favors the more vulnerable party.

How then do we compare the costs and benefits of not regulating plant closings with the costs and benefits of regulation? What are the long-run effects of regulation and how do they compare to the short term effects of regulation? These questions do not have simple answers. One thing is clear: The *assumption* that the costs of regulation outweigh the benefits is unwarranted. It is based on an unjustified faith in the invisible hand. We have plenty of evidence that the invisible hand carries a big stick; the costs and benefits of shifts in investment are not evenly distributed. The faith that things work out for the best for everyone if we steadfastly refuse to regulate market power is touching, but is nothing more than that. It asks us to ignore real victims in times of crisis. It also asks us to have faith in some version of the "trickle-down" theory. Yet the harm to those victims of not regulating market power may or may not be mitigated by later increases in wealth that return to benefit those same victims.

Our goal should be to facilitate desirable economic change without unnecessary misery. Requiring severance payments to workers makes closing a plant more expensive (and may therefore make a

plant close faster than it would otherwise); yet it protects workers and still allows for economic transition. In addition, it allows the company to take into account the benefits of closing the plant and shifting its investment to other areas. Requiring the company to give the workers a first shot at purchasing the plant for its fair market value mitigates the substantial externalities that follow high unemployment. The workers will buy the plant only if it can be operated profitably and if such an arrangement is better for them than any alternative. If the workers are willing to pay the fair market value of the plant, it is likely that the benefits of the forced sale to them and their community outweigh the costs to the company. Such a forced exchange will therefore be wise social policy in the absence of any other remedial legal responses to the plant closing that will better deal with the collapse of the local economy.

The effects of uncertainty on investment The free market ideology claims that shareholders are entitled to returns on their investments because they risked their capital. In the real world, investors are often more secure than workers, and they are secure because they shift many of the risks of investment onto workers and communities by closing plants rather than by bearing the costs of creating profitable and productive enterprises with those workers. It is true that imposing an obligation on the company to sell the plant to the workers will change investment incentives. Uncertainty about this eventuality may have a negative effect on investment. At the same time, the current rules that allow companies to close plants with impunity create a substantial amount of uncertainty *for workers.* Thus, the question is not only whether regulation creates more or less uncertainty, but how that uncertainty is distributed.

Redistribution of power and wealth can be achieved if we design legal rules with this goal in mind While it is true that workers and managers will bargain around compulsory contract terms, the resulting bargain will vary depending on their relative bargaining power. Relative bargaining power, in turn, depends on how we structure the legal rules governing their relationship. The real question is how to regulate both power and wealth between managers and workers to achieve the desired result of protecting the more vulnerable party to the relationship without stifling desirable economic change. It is possible to come closer to this goal than we currently do. If regulation to achieve desired ends has undesirable consequences, we must ask what other legal responses could respond to those unwanted effects. It is not the case that we are unable to alter the relative power of workers and corporations in the market. The current legal rules create that imbalance of power, and they can be altered to equalize it.

Ex ante compensation as a function of bargaining power   The argument that workers are compensated ex ante for being subject to the plant closing by exacting a premium in their contract is flawed. Workers may foolishly sacrifice their long-run well being for higher income in the present. We should protect people from mistakes they will later regret.

There is, moreover, no reason to assume that forcing people to make present decisions about future matters, and holding them to the terms of their contracts, necessarily maximizes wealth in the long-run. As Atiyah explains:

> Because the making of a present exchange, if free and voluntary, is so obviously a Pareto-optimal move, it is assumed that the same holds true of agreements to make a future exchange. This is fallacious. People can and do change their minds. Indeed, one obvious reason why parties sometimes fail to perform contracts is that they have changed their minds on the relative value of the benefits to be exchanged.

At the time the contract was made, both parties thought it would benefit them; at the time the defendant wants to renege on the deal, the benefits to the plaintiff of complying with the contract may or may not outweigh the costs to the defendant of complying with it. It is therefore an *empirical* question whether enforcing contracts in accord with their terms creates more good than harm. There is no reason to *presume* that enforcement of contracts involving future performance maximizes wealth.

Wages are the result of the relative bargaining power of the company and the workers. Even a strong union that is able to bargain for high wages for its employees is often not sufficiently powerful to protect its employees from a company that

abandons a community. It is no answer to say the workers get what they bargained for. Workers lack the power to protect themselves from plant closings when a community is dependent on a single major employer. Nor are they sufficiently powerful to protect themselves from their lack of training for alternate high-paying employment or from the failure of new businesses to move into the community.

Interstate competition   Requiring a company to make severance payments to workers does not prevent the company from shifting its investment elsewhere. If the workers buy the factory, the company is perfectly free to take the money and run to another state. It is only if the plant is given to the workers for free or for a price substantially below the best alternative use that property will have been taken from the company in a way that interferes with new investment elsewhere. A worker buyout subsidized by the government will not interfere in the efficient reallocation of investment because the purpose of the government action is to avoid the substantial costs to the community of idle workers and idle capital that will not be remedied by the private sector.

It is true, however, that if one state adopts regulations that are significantly more burdensome on business than other states, it runs the risk of discouraging new investment. For this reason, national legislation is far superior to state by state plant closing regulation. On the other hand, factors other than severance pay and notice requirements determine where plants are located and may overwhelm these considerations. If that is the case, state regulation may prevent the harmful externalities of plant closings without undue interference in attracting new investment.

Efficiency as a function of wealth and other legal entitlements   Ronald Dworkin has argued that wealth, as measured by willingness and ability to pay, is not, by itself, a social value. He is right about this. We value social wealth because it satisfies human needs. It the market system does not do this, it fails to accomplish its purpose. Thus, the goal of maximizing social utility does not require us to defer to the terms of contracts when we have good reasons to believe that the terms of the contracts are onerous or if the terms are less the result of free choice than of an illegitimate power relationship.

The free market model describes the labor contract as a Pareto superior exchange (in the absence of third-party effects) because each party is better off with the agreement than without it. We presumably increase social wealth to enforce the contract as written. But Robert Hale and Mark Kelman remind us that the parties are better off only in relation to the legally available alternatives. The agreement between the parties is the result not of unconstrained choice, but of the relative power of the parties to withhold from the other party what it needs. Relative withholding power is determined, to a large extent, by the legal definition and allocation of property entitlements. Moreover it is an odd fact of life that those with more power are able to get better terms and thus increase their power and wealth at the expense of others, which further enables them to get even better terms.

We must therefore define the legitimate contours of the power relationship between the parties in order to judge whether enforcement of the

contract as written will increase net welfare or will, instead, increase the concentration of power and wealth in a way that decreases net welfare. Judgments about efficiency therefore become wrapped up in judgments about the proper distribution of power and wealth within corporate enterprises. The agreement between the parties gives us some evidence of the welfare-maximizing result, but it cannot be conclusive. It is necessarily partial and can be reasonably applied only with further examination of the social results of limiting the corporation's obligations to those it voluntarily assumed in the contract.

Plant closings should be regulated to protect the interests of the workers in relying on their relationship with the company; to make more equal—and therefore more democratic—the power relationship between the workers and the company; to force the corporate managers to take into account the externalities of any decision to close the plant; and to alleviate the social harms caused by the plant closing while allowing desirable economic change to occur.

THE ADDICTION OF THE LAYOFF
B. J. Phillips

According to the numbers, everything ought to be hunky-dory for the American economy.

The recession ended, or at least the economy quit shrinking, in the spring of 1991. As 1993 drew to an end, every indicator known to man was up, unemployment was down and overall confidence in the economy, on the part of both corporate leaders and consumers, was the highest it's been since the '80s started to turn sour.

So why does scarcely a day pass without some large corporation announcing that it will lay off thousands of employees? In the last months of 1993, companies announced plans to cut 2,600 jobs a *day* nationwide, a rate that's 5 percent above that for 1991, the last year of the recession.

The big hit this week came at Bristol-Myers Squibb Co., which said it would hack 5,000 more

people off its payroll during the next two years. That represents 10 percent of its workforce—more if you add the 2,200 employees let go in the fall of 1992.

Whatever the economic logic behind the layoffs at Bristol-Myers—and since pharmaceutical companies have shed 34,000 jobs over the last 15 months, there appears to be a sectoral consensus favoring cutbacks—they fit an unhappy pattern that may be as bad for business as it is for the workers who lose their jobs.

LAY OFF ONCE, LAY OFF TWICE

American Management Association studies say that firms laying off workers usually reduce their workforces by 10 percent. Unfortunately, that's usually just an opening salvo.

In fact, layoffs seem to be almost as addictive as crack cocaine. No less than 65 percent of the firms

Reprinted by permission from the *Philadelphia Inquirer*, January 7, 1994, p. C1.

that downsize in a given year do it again the following year. And a quarter of the firms surveyed
that laid off workers since January 1988 have done
it three times or more.

The theory behind all this payroll slashing is
that getting "lean and mean" lowers costs, increases
productivity and enhances profitability.

Well, it ain't necessarily so.

Fewer than half of the firms that downsized
since 1988 report that profits increased after the
cuts, which means that 55 percent either lost
money or merely held their own after layoffs. Only
a third said that worker productivity increased, and
for nearly a quarter of firms, productivity declined
outright.

Doubtless, part of the explanation for this less-
than-stellar performance is that employee morale
goes off the cliff, declining in 71 percent of the
firms that fire workers the first time and in 87
percent of those that do it a third time.

Kenneth P. De Meuse of the University of
Wisconsin at Eau Claire says the outcomes are so
bad that companies don't merely shoot themselves in the foot, "they shoot both feet and the
heart as well."

PERFORMANCE FELL, TOO

One of the bitterest ironies of the layoff logic is that
Wall Street analysts and fund managers urge downsizing on executives, and generally reward it with a

quick uptick in the stock price. But De Meuse
followed a group of downsized companies' financial
performances, instead of their stocks, and found
that two years later, companies that made layoffs
were performing worse than they did before the
cuts—including a lower return on equity.

"Layoffs ought to be the absolute last resort,"
De Meuse says, "to be used only after you've tried
everything else."

There is a growing body of evidence that,
except in the most extreme cases, downsizing is a
rotten idea. Yet executives continue to make it their
first resort. Some companies have even begun to
downsize when they're not under competitive
pressure, as if sacking people were some sort of
vaccine that would prevent a loss of competitiveness
down the line.

Whatever the reasons for the herd instinct—too
many MBA students being taught the same things
about the same case studies, too much short-term-
ism among Wall Street analysts and investors—the
stampede to layoffs is not merely intellectually
bereft, it can be positively damaging to a company's
prospects.

"The people who survive layoffs tend to
emerge both risk-adverse and less productive," says
Davis Noer of the Center for Creative Leadership
and author of a book on the effects of layoffs.
"That's hardly the kind of workers who'll succeed
in the global marketplace."

And if they don't succeed, neither will the
American economy.

Decision Scenario 1
PUBLIC POLICY AND EMPLOYMENT AT WILL

Ray Palmateer worked for International Harvester
for sixteen years, rising from a unionized job at an
hourly rate to a managerial position at a fixed salary.
Palmateer was discharged, and he later sued International Harvester, claiming that his dismissal violated
public policy. Palmateer was fired for reporting a
possible crime to local law enforcement authorities
and agreeing to assist in the investigation of that
crime and to testify at the trial if requested. The
alleged criminal was another International Harvester
employee. Thus Palmateer claimed that he was fired
simply because he was trying to fight crime.

International Harvester claimed that even if
there is a public policy discouraging violation of
the law, it could not be so general as to prevent
employers from dismissing employees. The company held that its sound business judgment is to fire
a managerial employee who so recklessly and pre-
cipitously resorted to the criminal justice system to
handle what was essentially a personnel problem.
This issue, they claimed, would have been better
handled within the company.

The court reasoned that "there is no public
policy more basic, nothing more implicit in the

concept of ordered liberty, than the enforcement of the criminal law." It held that "persons acting in good faith who have probable cause to believe that a crime has occurred should not be deterred from reporting them." In finding for Palmateer, the court concluded that "the law is feeble indeed if it permits IH to take matters into its own hands by retaliating against its employees who cooperate in enforcing the law."

The crime that Palmateer reported was the theft of a $2 screwdriver.

- Was International Harvester justified in dismissing Palmateer?
- Is the public policy of enforcing the criminal law sufficient to override employment at will?
- Would your views differ if this case involved the embezzlement of a large sum of money?

Decision Scenario 2
CLOSING A CHRYSLER PLANT

On January 27, 1988, Chrysler Motors announced plans to shut down most of the operations at its Kenosha, Wisconsin, plant. This former American Motors plant had been building the Omni and Horizon subcompact cars after changing hands the previous year when Chrysler purchased American Motors. Chrysler planned to lay off 5500 of the plant's 6500 workers and to move Omni and Horizon assembly to a Detroit facility. Chrysler chairman Lee Iacocca blamed an inadequate national trade policy with consequent declining sales as the major reason for the closing.

While the plant was still owned by American Motors Corporation (AMC), UAW local unions had agreed to concessions of over $60 million to keep the plant operating. These concessions, given as a loan to AMC, were transferred to Chrysler when it purchased the company in 1987. In addition, the state of Wisconsin paid out over $5 million in 1987 for job training at Kenosha. State officials claimed that these payments had been based upon a Chrysler promise to build Omnis and Horizons at Kenosha for at least five years. State officials were planning a lawsuit over the announced closing.

During this same period, Chrysler was involved in negotiations with the United Auto Workers (UAW) in which the union was seeking a new nationwide contract. Disputes about the Kenosha closing and claims made by the UAW local Kenosha unions threatened to delay or upset the

national union contract, which would cover some 64,000 workers.

On February 16, 1988, Iacocca announced that Chrysler would establish a $20 million trust fund to help some of the 5500 laid-off workers. Calling it a "moral obligation to our people," Iacocca said that the money would be used to provide housing and educational assistance for those who were to lose their jobs. The size of the trust fund would be calculated by a formula based on the average 1987 profit per car and truck and the number of vehicles sold in Wisconsin in 1988. Chrysler had sold 40,000 vehicles in Wisconsin in 1987, and sales in 1988 were expected to rise. National union leaders commended Chrysler for showing "a degree of responsiveness" in attempting to ease the hardship created by the loss of jobs.

Iacocca also said that the trust fund was not a substitute for other obligations owed to the Kenosha workers. Severance pay, extended unemployment payments, and repayment of some money owed to the workers by AMC would not be affected by this plan. The trust fund would continue as long as the money held out, but workers would be eligible only for twelve months after they left their jobs. Further, Iacocca emphasized that this agreement did not establish a precedent for other plant closings:

> I want to reemphasize that this is unique because of the size of the population and so small a town, and for our problem of raising expectations. In came Chrysler from AMC, where people were worrying about their jobs for two decades and expected us to be the miracle

workers, and we blew it, OK? Now we have a moral obligation.

Local union officials were less impressed. A local union president called the Chrysler decision "purely a sales promotion pitch, designed only to boost sales in Wisconsin." In addition, state officials continued their plans for a lawsuit. After a February 18 meeting between Wisconsin Governor Tommy Thompson, U.S. Representative Les Aspin (D-Wisc.), and Iacocca, the governor agreed to delay the lawsuit pending the possibility of Chrysler's extending production at the Kenosha plant through the fall.

In early May, Chrysler reached a tentative agreement with the UAW for a new contract. The agreement included a settlement for the members of the local Kenosha unions. Additional weeks of unemployment benefits for those workers laid off and increased job security for the 1000 workers remaining at the Kenosha plant were included in the settlement. Owen Bieber, UAW president,

would not say whether the Kenosha issue had been the biggest obstacle to a settlement but did say that he was pleased that it was out of the way. "It's a shame that the plant had to close, but we have to face the facts of life. We couldn't let those people in Wisconsin hang in the air. We are now optimistic that we can put a national contract together."

■ Did Chrysler have a moral obligation to the local workers based on the agreements and concessions made while the plant was owned by American Motors?

■ Is it wise for employees or state and local governments to make concessions to corporations in exchange for promises of future corporate conduct, especially when corporate decisions are so influenced by changing economic conditions?

■ Iacocca said that Chrysler had an obligation because it had raised workers' expectations of job security when it bought out AMC. Do you think he believed that? Why or why not?

Decision Scenario 3
UNWRITTEN EMPLOYMENT CONTRACTS

Courts have cited three general exceptions to the doctrine of employment at will. The public policy exception restricts the right to fire when the dismissal would violate a specific law or a well-established principle of public policy. Examples of the public policy exception include an employee's refusal to commit perjury, a refusal to violate a professional code of ethics, and an employee's service on jury duty. The implied covenant of good faith exception restricts the right to fire when doing so is particularly arbitrary or unfair. An example was *Fortune v. National Cash Register,* in which a salesman was fired to avoid paying him a commission that he had earned but not yet received. A third category is based upon the existence of an expressed or implied contract between employer and employee. Since few employees have explicit, written contracts, courts have some latitude in determining the conditions of the implied contract.

Does an employee with a long history of successful service and promotions have an implied

promise not to be fired at will? In *Pugh v. See's Candies,* the California Court of Appeals judged that a contractual promise not to terminate at will could be inferred from the employee's length of service, history of pay raises and promotions, and favorable reviews as well as the employer's past policies and practices.

Employee handbooks and personnel manuals have also been interpreted as establishing a contractual relationship, although not by all courts. In *Gates v. Life of Montana Insurance Co.,* the Supreme Court of Montana decided that an employee handbook, which stated that employees were "subject to reprimand or dismissal with prior warning," had not established a contractual obligation. The court reasoned that because the handbook was distributed after Gates was hired, and because it was issued unilaterally by the employer, the requirement of prior notice was not a contractual right.

However, in *Toussaint v. Blue Cross & Blue Shield of Michigan,* a Michigan court reached the opposite decision. The Blue Cross personnel manual stated: "It is the policy of the company to treat employees leaving Blue Cross in a fair and consistent manner and to release employees for just cause only." The Michigan court decided that despite the absence of negotiation or explicit agreement, the manual did establish contractual rights. Since the handbook produced benefits to the employer, it should produce benefits to the employee as well.

A Nevada court, in *Southwest Gas Corp. v. Ahmad,* explicitly stated the reasoning involved in such cases. The court decided that the employer had violated an implied contract by ignoring an employee handbook statement that employees would be fired only for good cause and only after previous warnings had been issued. The court said:

> The fact that the company issued such handbooks to its employees supports an inference that the handbook formed part of the employ-

ment contract of the parties…by continuing in employment after receiving the handbook, the employee supplied consideration for the promise of job security.

- Contracts usually require mutual consent of the contracting parties. How then can there be such a thing as an "implied contract" if both parties haven't agreed to it? Can there be a promise if only one side is aware of it?

- Suppose an employer unilaterally issued a handbook that *denied* any obligation of due process before dismissal. Should such a disclaimer be contractually valid?

- Would a newspaper job description that promised "career opportunities" constitute a promise not to terminate "at will"?

Decision Scenario 4
"WRONGFUL HIRING"

Most of the discussion and cases in this chapter focus on "wrongful discharge." Courts have held employers legally liable for *terminating* an employee on grounds that have been determined to be, in some sense, "wrongful." Could it be the case that employers can be held liable for *hiring* someone on "wrongful" grounds? A 1984 U.S. Supreme Court case may establish the precedent in this regard.

In *Hishon v. King and Spaulding,* the Supreme Court unanimously agreed that statements made during hiring interviews can create contractual promises. Thus employers can be held liable for representations made at that time, especially if they induce the employee to forgo other opportunities, leave a previous job, or relocate residency. Employers who later determine that the hiring is not working out can be held liable for wrongful hiring in the first place.

Hishon was an attorney hired as an "associate" with King and Spaulding, a large Atlanta law firm. Like many large professional firms, King and Spaulding had a policy of "up or out." If, within a certain time, an associate had been passed over for partnership, "the associate would be notified to

seek employment elsewhere." Hishon alleged that during her interview King and Spaulding had suggested that promotion to partnership was "a matter of course" for associates "who receive satisfactory evaluations" after five or six years. Hishon claimed that she relied on this promise when deciding to accept the job with King and Spaulding.

Recall that in *Pugh v. See's Candies* (mentioned in the previous scenario), a California court ruled that an employee's record of long-term satisfactory service can allow that employee to recover damages if he or she is unfairly fired. In *Hishon,* the Supreme Court allowed a employee to recover damages because she was, in effect, hired under unfair conditions.

A number of states have passed laws that make it illegal to misrepresent a job in the initial hiring process. In other states, and in cases in which the alleged misrepresentation is less clear, serious questions concerning "wrongful hiring" remain to be answered. Consider:

- A person is hired to prevent a competitor from hiring that individual.

- Someone is hired for a position that will soon be phased out or about which internal debates make success in the job unlikely.

- A firm hires an individual who was formerly employed by a competitor in the hope of gaining valuable information.

- Someone who seems "too good to let get away" is hired even though no specific job is open for that person.

- Someone whose training, experience, or even personality makes success unlikely is hired because of an immediate need to fill a position.

In all of these cases, an employee who is terminated may have grounds for charging a "wrongful hiring."

- Do you think that an employee hired under any of these conditions should be allowed to sue for "wrongful discharge"? Can you think of other cases in which this might occur?

- What ethical basis can you see for "wrongful hiring" judgments? Are similar ethical concerns raised by "wrongful discharge"?

- Are too many restrictions being placed upon the authority of employers to hire and fire? Why or why not?

Decision Scenario 5
PLANT CLOSING RESPONSIBILITIES

In 1982, Schlitz Brewing Company was acquired by Stroh's Brewery of Detroit. The acquisition included five modern brewing plants. Subsequently, Stroh's decided to close its Detroit brewery. Stroh's had been brewing beer in Detroit for over seventy years, and the company president, Peter Stroh, felt an obligation to the employees in Detroit.

Unemployment in Detroit at the time was at 9 percent, so Peter Stroh decided to emphasize job placement services for employees. Stroh's announced the shutdown four months early to allow employees to begin their search for new jobs. Peter Stroh personally lobbied other employers in Detroit to find jobs for his displaced workers. With support from the workers' union, Stroh's set up a job placement program that included orientation, counseling, job skills workshops, skills testing, and training in résumé preparation and interviewing.

Stroh's spent $1.5 million on this program. State and local government contributed another $600,000, bringing the total to $2000 spent on

each displaced worker. Thirteen months after the announcement that Stroh's would close its plant, all 125 salaried employees and 98 percent of the 655 hourly employees had found new jobs.

- Critics of plant closing laws that require prior notification of workers claim that advance notice can have serious detrimental effects on the company. A firm can be harmed by a loss of workers and lowered morale, its credit can be affected, it can lose customer confidence, and it can be hurt further by a failure to fill orders, complete jobs, and so on. Weighing the type of program used by Stroh's against these objections, evaluate a legal requirement of advance notice for plant closings.

- Did Stroh's have any obligations to constituencies other than employees? Was the Detroit community treated fairly in the situation described?

- What, if any, further steps would you take to help employees facing a plant shutdown?

Decision Scenario 6
MONTANA'S JUST CAUSE LEGISLATION

In 1987, Montana became the first and only state in the union to adopt a just cause employment termination law. It is interesting that the main support for the law came from business lobbies whose members felt threatened by the possibility of paying large damage awards in the litigation lottery. Just as interesting, organized labor reportedly was not a major player in the legislative activity leading up to the passage of the law.

The Wrongful Discharge from Employment Act requires that nonprobationary employees be dismissed only for "good cause"; that is, there must be "reasonable job-related grounds for dismissal based on a failure to satisfactorily perform job duties, disruption of the employer's operation, or other legitimate business reasons." This legislation also holds that violations of promises made in personnel handbooks are violations of the act. The law, however, does not apply to those employees who are covered by collective bargaining agreements or who have written contracts of employment.

The act limits the ability of workers to sue for damages. It precludes suits for damages based on tort law or contract law (those areas of the law that have generated large damage awards for dismissed employees), and it limits punitive damages to those rare cases where dismissed employees can prove fraud or malice. Instead, it caps the maximum award level at four times annual wages and benefits minus any wages the employee earned (or could have earned with reasonable diligence) in the interim period. The act allows employees to pursue

their cases in the court system, but it encourages the use of cheaper methods of binding arbitration. This is encouraged by a clause that holds that parties who refuse arbitration and then later lose in court must pay the other party's attorney fees. Employees who offer to accept arbitration and later win are to have their costs and fees paid by the employer.

A survey of members of the Montana Bar Association raises some questions about the effectiveness of the law. Most notably, 56.5 percent of respondents felt that the law does not offer adequate incentives for attorneys to take employees' cases. Half of those responding said they had personally declined cases, and their written comments indicated that the foremost reason was that the amount of compensation was not proportionate to the time and difficulty involved in dismissal cases. In addition, a number of attorneys thought that the law had changed employment practices for the worse. Some indicated that with the threat of large damage awards removed, some employers have become less concerned about wrongful discharge actions.

- Do you think that the reduction of damages by subtracting what a person earned or could have earned is appropriate? Why or why not?

- What changes would you have made in personnel practices if you were operating a business in Montana in 1987 when the law was passed?

- Does just cause legislation by itself provide workers increased protection against unfair dismissal, or does it provide protection only when management is committed to the idea?

- Do you believe that the attorneys' opinions show that a law passed primarily with business support will inevitably shortchange employees or that attorneys are interested only in large awards, or both?

This case was prepared from the following sources: the Montana Wrongful Discharge from Employment Act; Alan B. Krueger, "The Evolution of Unjust Dismissal Legislation in the United States," *Industrial and Labor Relations Review*, vol. 44 (1991): 644; Leonard Bierman, et al., "Montana's Wrongful Discharge from Employment Act," *Montana Law Review*, vol. 54 (1993): 367; Leonard Bierman and Stuart Youngblood, "Interpreting Montana's Pathbreaking Wrongful Discharge from Employment Act," *Montana Law Review*, vol. 53 (1992): 53.

6

Employee Responsibilities

Honesty, Loyalty, Whistleblowing

In Chapter Three we spoke of rights as protecting certain central interests. Many philosophers would hold that corresponding to rights are responsibilities or duties of others to respect these rights. If rights are seen as protecting an individual's interests from the actions of others, responsibilities can be seen as establishing limits on my own action. My responsibilities set ethical limits on my own behavior while my rights establish limits on the ethical behavior of others. In this chapter we will examine certain responsibilities of employees.

A helpful starting point for our examination of employee responsibilities is an understanding of the employee–employer relation found in law. Until very recently, this relationship was viewed in terms of what is known as the agency model. In this model, employees are the agents of employers (the "principals") and owe to the employer certain legal duties, including loyalty, obedience, and confidentiality. Thus, employers had a right to expect the loyalty, obedience, and confidence of employees.

In recent decades American law has moved away from a strict adherence to the agency model. Both legislatures and courts have recognized that employees can face responsibilities that override their responsibilities to employers. As we have seen in the discussion of employment at will in the previous chapter, some legislatures have passed laws protecting employees who "blow the whistle" on illegal corporate activity. But this is to say that an employee's responsibility to the public safety overrides the responsibility of loyalty. Likewise, courts have protected employees who have refused to commit perjury at the command of their employers, reasoning that an employee's responsibility to obey the law overrides the responsibility to obey one's employer.

These developments in law parallel the philosophical recognition that autonomous individuals have multiple responsibilities to a variety of other individuals and institutions. We all have general responsibilities to unspecified others: We should be honest, respectful, and so on. We also have responsibilities to specific others: to our families, our community, our friends, our co-workers, as well as to our employers. The serious ethical issues arise when these responsibilities conflict.

HONESTY IN EMPLOYMENT

Few ethical values are as universally recognized as honesty. "Tell the truth" and "don't lie" are responsibilities that most of us learn from our earliest years. But perhaps few rules are so seemingly often broken. "Stretching the truth," telling a "white lie"—deceptive and misleading statements abound. No doubt, dishonesty can sometimes be justified, but this typically occurs when the truth might cause someone harm. Dishonesty is much more troubling, and typically unjustified, when it is done to benefit oneself at the expense of another. In such cases, we normally would hold that our responsibility to be honest overrides our self-interest.

Philosophically, we can identify three general justifications for a responsibility to be honest. Utilitarians typically see honesty as playing a crucial role in social life, particularly in enabling us to communicate with others. Dishonesty undermines the trust necessary for communicating with others; if you could not believe what others were saying to you, social intercourse would be difficult if not impossible. Rights theorists in the Kantian tradition argue that honesty is a fundamental principle of rational ethics. Dishonesty to further our own self-interests irrationally treats our own interests as superior to the equal interests of others. It violates the autonomy of others by, in the words of one commentator, "mugging their intellects." Other ethical theorists would focus on what dishonesty does to the person him- or herself. Dishonesty requires an individual to maintain two "personas": the person who maintains the outward appearance of honesty (dishonesty works only when others believe that you are honest), and the person who, underneath, knows and plans the deception. This "moral schizophrenia" can undermine personal integrity and self-respect.

It is also worth noting the important role that honesty plays in economic markets. Among the very few ethical limits that Milton Friedman places on the pursuit of profits, for example, is the responsibility to avoid deception. Deception in economic transactions threatens the two fundamental ethical goals that justify markets in the first place: social utility and individual liberty. When I am deceived in an economic transaction, I fail to improve my own position; thus, the transaction was inefficient and did not improve social utility. Deception also unjustly interferes with my freedom of choice by manipulating me to do something that I would not have done had I not been deceived.

Nevertheless, the temptation to be dishonest is especially strong in business, where it can lead to great personal benefits. In a classic essay reprinted in this chapter, Albert Carr argues that dishonesty is all part of the "rules of the game" and should not be thought of as unethical. Drawing on an analogy with bluffing in poker, Carr tells us that "falsehood ceases to be falsehood when it is understood on all sides that the truth is not expected to be spoken."

LOYALTY AND WHISTLEBLOWING

Some of the most well-known cases in business ethics have involved situations in which employees chose to inform on unethical or illegal behavior of their employers. Such cases of "whistleblowing" raise questions of conflicting responsibilities. On one hand, the employee would seem to have a responsibility to avoid causing harm to innocent third parties. This responsibility is particularly strong when the employee has specialized expertise that comes from her role as a professional employee, for example, as an engineer or an auditor. So, if an engineer such as Roger Boisjoly believes that the *Challenger*'s booster rockets are unsafe at low temperatures, it would seem obvious that he has a responsibility to try to prevent a launch that might endanger the crew. On the other hand, employees have responsibilities that arise from their role within a firm, including obedience and loyalty to workplace superiors. These professional and workplace responsibilities can limit the moral autonomy of individuals. Thus, whistleblowing occurs when an employee chooses to act disloyally to his or her employer by fulfilling other professional responsibilities to the public.

Of course, whistleblowing carries with it significant costs. In most cases, the whistleblower faces grave harms, ranging from lost jobs and careers to lost friendships and resentment among co-workers. Whistleblowing also jeopardizes the well-being of the firm, disrupting its work and, in some cases, resulting in lost contracts and lost jobs. It also involves one or more individuals asserting that their judgment is superior to those made by many other professionals and managers, sometimes without the full information available to others. In the words of ethicist Sisela Bok, by blowing the whistle, "the whistleblower hopes to stop the game; but since he is neither referee nor coach, and since he blows the whistle on his own team, his act is seen as a violation of loyalty."

In our second reading, Ron Duska argues that much of the debate about whistleblowing assumes an incorrect understanding of the role of loyalty in the workplace. For-profit businesses, according to Duska, are not the kinds of things that can be objects of loyalty. Since one does not owe loyalty to one's corporate employer, the apparent dilemma that confronts whistleblowers really does not exist. On this view, whistleblowing is not only permissible, but something that we can expect from employees. Corporate loyalty cannot limit the moral autonomy of individuals.

Duska recognizes that whistleblowing will always involve costs to the whistleblower. Retaliation is something that most whistleblowers can expect. Mike Martin picks up on this theme in our third reading and focuses on other personal obligations that professionals have. Martin suggests that responsibilities to family can also raise ethical challenges to the whistleblower since these acts can place significant burdens upon one's family as well as on oneself. Furthermore, Martin recognizes that a sense of loyalty to oneself, to personal integrity, can motivate whistleblowers as much as the desire to prevent harm to others. As a result of this analysis, Martin concludes that whistleblowing remains a complex ethical issue that resists easy general and universal resolutions.

CONFLICTS OF INTEREST AND INSIDER TRADING

The personal responsibilities that are discussed in Martin's essay are ethical responsibilities, involving obligations to protect one's family from harm and the commitment to personal integrity. But sometimes one's responsibility to an organization can come into conflict with other personal interests such as profit or personal advancement. "Conflicts of interest" occur when an employee's private interests prevent, or give the appearance of preventing, that employee from making decisions in the best interests of the employer.

We can generalize this account by recognizing that people are often in positions that require them to make independent judgments upon which others rely. For example, business managers, scientists, engineers, accountants, lawyers, politicians, and doctors all fill roles that involve making judgments on behalf of the best interests of others. A wide range of other people—clients, stockholders, customers, citizens—trust the independence and integrity of individuals who fill these roles. A conflict of interest occurs when this independence and integrity clashes with the private interests of the individual making the judgment.

It is common to distinguish between *actual* and *potential* conflicts of interests. An actual conflict of interest occurs when an individual substitutes personal interests for professional responsibility. Thus, for example, a purchasing manager who steers business to a friend's firm even though comparable supplies can be bought for lower prices elsewhere is involved in a conflict of interest. A potential conflict of interest arises when the *appearance* of independent judgment is undermined. For example, consider the politician who accepts a multimillion-dollar book deal from a publishing company owned by an individual who has major interests before his political body. This politician is involved in a potential conflict of interest. While no actual corruption may have occurred, the loss of trust in a political institution created by even the appearance of a conflict raises ethical challenges.

A more complex situation can arise when an individual, in his professional role within a firm or industry, comes to possess information that can be used to give him financial advantage in the marketplace. "Insider trading" refers to situations in which an individual uses inside privileged information to buy or sell securities. Thus, this individual gains an advantage in the market and can receive significant financial rewards due to his position or connections "inside" the business.

But what, exactly, is wrong with insider trading? In our final reading, Jennifer Moore examines this question. Moore reviews many of the arguments against insider trading—that it is unfair, that it violates property rights, that it harms third parties—as well as claims that insider trading can increase the efficiency of markets. Moore concludes that the special duties that arise within fiduciary relationships provide the best reasons for prohibiting insider trading. Fiduciary relationships occur when one party is dependent upon, and must trust, the judgments of another who is obligated to act on behalf of the first party. The attorney–client relationship is a classic example of a fiduciary relationship. According to Moore, insider trading can erode the fiduciary relationship that is necessary in many business organizations.

CASE STUDY   After the *Challenger* Disaster

Under contract from NASA, Morton Thiokol Inc. designs and produces the rocket boosters used to launch the space shuttle. In January 1986, the space shuttle *Challenger* exploded shortly after take-off from the Kennedy Space Center in Florida, killing all seven astronauts aboard. It was the worst disaster in the history of the U.S. space program. Later analysis identified the cause of the explosion to be a failure in the O-rings used to seal the rockets. Evidence shows that prior to the launch both Morton Thiokol and NASA had been concerned about the reliability of the O-rings at low temperatures.

All large institutions confront difficulties when organizing decision-making. In such institutions, two important factors often work at cross purposes: Large institutions develop a wealth of expert and valuable information, yet efficient decision-making can be hampered by too much information. Thus, large institutions usually develop formal organizational structures that assign different responsibilities to different members such that when each member fulfills his or her role, an efficient and rational decision should result. Within such a structure each person has the responsibility of doing what his or her role requires, and nothing more.

Both Morton Thiokol and NASA were typical in this regard. At Morton Thiokol, engineers were responsible for designing and testing the rockets and conveying the relevant information to management. Acting on behalf of the corporation, management would use this information in ways that would advance the best interests of the firm. On this model, engineers provided expert and objective information and managers were responsible for incorporating this information into final decisions.

Various levels of decisions were established, with checks and balances at each level. Likewise, NASA management was organized to protect the best interests of the space program, including the safety of its astronauts. In such complex organizational structures, there is seldom any one individual who is responsible for a decision, either in having the final say, or in being liable for the decision once it is made.

As it normally worked, Morton Thiokol management would accept the recommendations of their engineers and NASA would require contractors to prove the safety and reliability of their products. Just prior to the *Challenger* launch, it appears that both Morton Thiokol and NASA changed the normal decision-making routine.

For over a year prior to this launch, Thiokol engineers had been concerned about the reliability of the O-rings. One engineer who worked closely on the O-rings, Roger Boisjoly, had expressed serious reservations to management on numerous occasions. After an earlier shuttle flight one year before the *Challenger* launch, Boisjoly had found evidence of leakage around the O-rings. Boisjoly later testified that NASA officials had requested that he "soften" his position before presenting his data to a post-launch review board. Boisjoly did, and shuttle flights continued throughout 1985.

After again finding evidence of O-ring leaks in later flights, and believing that his earlier warnings were not being taken seriously, Boisjoly wrote a strongly worded memo to Thiokol management in July 1985. In that memo, marked "company private" to ensure that it remained within the firm, Boisjoly said that he was writing "to insure that management is fully aware of the seriousness of the current O-ring erosion problem." If changes were not made, he predicted, "the result would be a catastrophe of the highest order—loss of human life." He concluded, "It is my honest and very real fear that if we do not take immediate action…then we stand in jeopardy of losing a flight along with all the launch pad facilities." In response to this memo, Thiokol formed an engineering task force to monitor the O-ring problem.

In the days leading up to the January 28 launch of the *Challenger*, Thiokol and NASA were in constant communication concerning the launch. When the weather forecast for launch day showed unusually low temperatures, Thiokol management initially agreed with the recommendations of their engineers and recommended a postponement of the flight.

Normally, NASA would require contractors to prove the safety of their components before going ahead with a launch. However, NASA was under pressure from other sources, including third parties who had contracted to use the shuttle flight, to stay on schedule. It seems in this case that NASA shifted the burden of proof, requiring those with concerns about the O-rings to prove that they were at risk. Without such proof, NASA was inclined to proceed with the launch. Late on the evening before the launch, Thiokol management met to review their recommendation. According to Boisjoly, those present were asked to "make a management decision" and an engineer present was asked to "take off your engineering hat and put on your management hat." The senior management then voted to change their recommendation and advise NASA to go forward with the launch. Again, according to Boisjoly, NASA accepted this recommendation with relief and "without any probing discussion." The next morning, moments after take-off, the *Challenger* exploded.

In the days following this tragedy, management at both Thiokol and NASA denied knowledge of or responsibility for the cause of the disaster. NASA officials discounted "speculation that cold weather might have been a factor," and Thiokol management denied that investigators had focused on "parts of the shuttle for which Morton Thiokol is

responsible." Even weeks later when the evidence was strong that O-ring failure had caused the explosion, Thiokol declared that while this had not been proven, they were working on new designs for the seals.

A presidential commission, chaired by former Secretary of State William Rogers, was formed to investigate this tragedy. Feeling a professional and personal responsibility, and especially in light of the reluctance of Thiokol and NASA management to be forthright in admitting what they knew, Roger Boisjoly agreed to testify before the Rogers Commission with a full disclosure of what he knew. Due in large measure to his testimony, the Rogers Commission concluded that O-ring failure was the cause of the shuttle disaster. Boisjoly later stated that Thiokol management expressed irritation over his decision to tell all. After testifying, his job responsibilities at Thiokol were downgraded and he was continuously isolated at work. After criticism by Rogers, Thiokol later assigned Boisjoly and another engineer to their original jobs. According to Boisjoly, the harassment continued at work until he was forced to take extended sick leave and long-term disability due to the stress and depression brought about by the entire episode.

- Were Roger Boisjoly's responsibilities as an employee different from his responsibilities as an engineer?
- Did Boisjoly go above and beyond his duty by testifying to the Rogers Commission? Could he have just left his responsibilities at the point of writing a strong memo to company management?
- Does Thiokol management have a responsibility to exercise independent judgment on behalf of the firm, or should they always accept the advice of their engineers?
- Given the potential harms to the company by adverse publicity, did Thiokol management do anything wrong when they claimed that O-ring failure had not been proven as the cause? Did they act dishonestly immediately after the disaster?
- Construct a defense of the decisions made by Thiokol management. Construct a similar defense for NASA management.

IS BUSINESS BLUFFING ETHICAL?
Albert Carr

A respected businessman with whom I discussed the theme of this article remarked with some heat, "You mean to say you're going to encourage men to bluff? Why, bluffing is nothing more than a form of lying! You're advising them to lie!"

I agreed that the basis of private morality is a respect for truth and that the closer a businessman comes to truth, the more he deserves respect. At the same time, I suggested that most bluffing in business might be regarded simply as game strategy—much like bluffing in poker which does not reflect on the morality of the bluffer.

I quoted Henry Taylor, the British statesman who pointed out that "falsehood ceases to be falsehood when it is understood on all sides that the truth is not expected to be spoken"—an exact description of bluffing in poker, diplomacy, and business. I cited the analogy of the criminal court, where the criminal is not expected to tell the truth when he pleads "not guilty." Everyone from the judge down takes it for granted that the job of the defendant's attorney is to get his client off, not to reveal the truth; and this is considered ethical practice. I mentioned Representative Omar Burleson, the Democrat form Texas, who was quoted as saying, in regard to the ethics of Congress, "Ethics is a barrel of worms"—a pungent summing-up of the problem of deciding who is ethical in politics. I reminded my friend that millions of businessmen feel constrained every day to say *yes* to their bosses when they secretly believe *no* and that this is generally accepted as permissible strategy when the alternative might be the loss of a job. The essential point, I said, is that the ethics of business are game ethics, different from the ethics of religion.

He remained unconvinced. Referring to the company of which he is president, he declared: "Maybe that's good enough for some businessmen, but I can tell you that we pride ourselves on our ethics. In 30 years not one customer has ever questioned my word or asked to check our figures.

We're loyal to our customers and fair to our supplies. I regard my handshake on a deal as a contract. I've never entered into price-fixing schemes with my competitors. I've never allowed my salesmen to spread injurious rumors about other companies. Our union contract is the best in our industry. And, if I do say so myself, our ethical standards are of the highest!"

He really was saying, without saying it, that he was living up to the ethical standards of the business game—which are a far cry from those of private life. Like a gentlemanly poker player, he did not play in cahoots with others at the table, try to smear their reputations, or hold back chips he owed them.

But this same fine man, at the very time, was allowing one of his products to be advertised in a way that made it sound a great deal better than it actually was. Another item in his product line was notorious among dealers for its "built-in obsolescence." He was holding back from the market a much-improved product because he did not want it to interfere with sales of the inferior item it would have replaced. He had joined with certain of his competitors in hiring a lobbyist to push a state legislature, by methods that he preferred not to know too much about, into amending a bill then being enacted.

In his view these things had nothing to do with ethics; they were merely normal business practice. He himself undoubtedly avoided outright falsehood—never lied in so many words. But the entire organization that he ruled was deeply involved in numerous strategies of deception.

PRESSURE TO DECEIVE

Most executives from time to time are almost compelled, in the interests of their companies or themselves, to practice some form of deception when negotiating with customers, dealers, labor unions, government officials, or even other departments of their companies. By conscious misstatements, concealment of pertinent facts, or exaggeration—in short, by bluffing—they seek to persuade others to agree with them. I think it is fair to say that if the individual executive refuses to bluff from time to time—if he feels obligated to tell the truth, the whole truth, and nothing but the truth—he is ignoring opportunities permitted under the rules and is at a heavy disadvantage in his business dealings.

But here and there a businessman is unable to reconcile himself to the bluff in which he plays a part. His conscience, perhaps spurred by religious idealism, troubles him. He feels guilty; he may develop an ulcer or a nervous tic. Before any executive can make profitable use of the strategy of the bluff, he needs to make sure that in bluffing he will not lose self-respect or become emotionally disturbed. If he is to reconcile personal integrity and high standards of honesty with the practical requirements of business, he must feel that his bluffs are ethically justified. The justification rests on the fact that business, as practiced by individuals as well as by corporations, has the impersonal character of a game—a game that demands both special strategy and an understanding of its special ethics.

The game is played at all levels of corporate life, from the highest to the lowest. At the very instant that a man decides to enter business, he may be forced into a game situation, as is shown by the recent experience of a Cornell honor graduate who applied for a job with a large company:

> This applicant was given a psychological test which included the statement, "Of the following magazines, check any that you have read either regularly or from time to time, and double-check those which interest you most. *Reader's Digest, Time, Fortune, Saturday Evening Post, The New Republic, Life, Look, Ramparts, Newsweek, Business Week, U.S. News & World Report, The Nation, Playboy, Esquire, Harper's, Sports Illustrated.*"
>
> His tastes in reading were broad, and at one time or another he had read almost all of these magazines. He was a subscriber to *The New Republic,* an enthusiast for *Ramparts,* and an avid student of the pictures in *Playboy.* He was not sure whether his interest in *Playboy* would be held against him, but he had a shrewd suspicion that if he confessed to an interest in *Ramparts* and *The New Republic,* he would be thought a liberal, a radical, or at least an intellectual, and

his chances of getting the job, which he needed, would greatly diminish. He therefore checked five of the more conservative magazines. Apparently it was a sound decision, for he got the job.

He had made a game player's decision, consistent with business ethics.

A similar case is that of a magazine space salesman who, owing to a merger, suddenly found himself out of a job:

> This man was 58, and, in spite of a good record, his chance of getting a job elsewhere in a business where youth is favored in hiring practice was not good. He was a vigorous, healthy man, and only a considerable amount of gray in his hair suggested his age. Before beginning his job search he touched up his hair with a black dye to confine the gray to his temples. He knew that the truth about his age might well come out in time, but he calculated that he could deal with that situation when it arose. He and his wife decided that he could easily pass for 45, and he so stated his age on his resume.

This was a lie; yet within the accepted rules of the business game, no moral culpability attaches to it.

THE POKER ANALOGY

We can learn a good deal about the nature of business by comparing it with poker. While both have a large element of chance, in the long run the winner is the man who plays with steady skill. In both games ultimate victory requires intimate knowledge of the rules, insights into the psychology of the other players, a bold front, a considerable amount of self-discipline, and the ability to respond swiftly and effectively to opportunities provided by chance.

No one expects poker to be played on the ethical principles preached in churches. In poker it is right and proper to bluff a friend out of the rewards of being dealt a good hand. A player feels no more than a slight twinge of sympathy, if that, when—with nothing better than a single ace in his hand—he strips a heavy loser, who holds a pair, of the rest of his chips. It was up to the other fellow to protect himself. In the words of an excellent poker player, former President Harry Truman, "If you can't stand the heat, get out of the kitchen." If one shows mercy to a loser in poker, it is a personal gesture, divorced from the rules of the game.

Poker has its special ethics, and here I am not referring to rules against cheating. The man who keeps an ace up his sleeve or who marks the cards is more than unethical; he is a crook, and can be punished as such—kicked out of the game or, in the Old West, shot.

In contrast to the cheat, the unethical poker player is one who, while abiding by the letter of the rules, finds ways to put the other players at an unfair disadvantage. Perhaps he unnerves them with loud talk. Or he tries to get them drunk. Or he plays in cahoots with someone else at the table. Ethical poker players frown on such tactics.

Poker's own brand of ethics is different from the ethical ideals of civilized human relationships. The game calls for distrust of the other fellow. It ignores the claim of friendship. Cunning deception and concealment of one's strength and intentions, not kindness and open-heartedness, are vital in poker. No one thinks any worse of poker on that account. And no one should think any worse of the game of business because its standards of right and wrong differ from the prevailing traditions of morality in our society.

DISCARD THE GOLDEN RULE

This view of business is especially worrisome to people without much business experience. A minister of my acquaintance once protested that business cannot possibly function in our society unless it is based on the Judeo-Christian system of ethics. He told me:

> I know some businessmen have supplied call girls to customers, but there are always a few rotten apples in every barrel. That doesn't mean the rest of the fruit isn't sound. Surely the vast majority of businessmen are ethical. I myself am acquainted with many who adhere to strict codes of ethics based fundamentally on religious teachings. They contribute to good causes. They participate in community activities. They cooperate with other companies to improve working conditions in their industries. Certainly they are not indifferent to ethics.

That most businessmen are not indifferent to ethics in their private lives, everyone will agree. My point is that in their office lives they cease to be private citizens; they become game players who must be guided by a somewhat different set of ethical standards.

The point was forcefully made to me by a Midwestern executive who has given a good deal of thought to the question:

> So long as a businessman complies with the laws of the land and avoids telling malicious lies, he's ethical. If the law as written gives a man a wide-open chance to make a killing, he'd be a fool not to take advantage of it. If he doesn't, somebody else will. There's no obligation on him to stop and consider who is going to get hurt. If the law says he can do it, that's all the justification he needs. There's nothing unethical about that. It's just plain business sense.

This executive (call him Robbins) took the stand that even industrial espionage, which is frowned on by some businessmen, ought not to be considered unethical. He recalled a recent meeting of the National Industrial Conference Board where an authority on marketing made a speech in which he deplored the employment of spies by business organizations. More and more companies, he pointed out, find it cheaper to penetrate the secrets of competitors with concealed cameras and microphones or by bribing employees than to set up costly research and design departments of their own. A whole branch of the electronics industry has grown up with this trend, he continued, providing equipment to make industrial espionage easier.

Disturbing? The marketing expert found it so. But when it came to a remedy, he could only appeal to "respect for the golden rule." Robbins thought this a confession of defeat, believing that the golden rule, for all its value as an ideal for society, is simply not feasible as a guide for business. A good part of the time the businessman is trying to do unto others as he hopes others will *not* do unto him. Robbins continued:

> Espionage of one kind or another has become so common in business that it's like taking a

drink during Prohibition—it's not considered sinful. And we don't even have Prohibition where espionage is concerned; the law is very tolerant in this area. There's no more shame for a business that uses secret agents than there is for a nation. Bear in mind that there already is at least one large corporation—you can buy its stock over the counter—that makes millions by providing counterespionage service to industrial firms. Espionage in business is not an ethical problem; it's an established technique of business competition.

"WE DON'T MAKE THE LAWS"

Wherever we turn in business, we can perceive the sharp distinction between its ethical standards and those of the churches. Newspapers abound with sensational stories growing out of this distinction:

> We read one day that Senator Philip A. Hart of Michigan has attacked food processors for deceptive packaging of numerous products.
>
> The next day there is a Congressional to-do over Ralph Nader's book, *Unsafe at Any Speed,* which demonstrates that automobile companies for years have neglected the safety of car-owning families.
>
> Then another Senator, Lee Metcalf of Montana, and journalist Vic Reinemer show in their book, *Overcharge,* the methods by which utility companies elude regulating government bodies to extract unduly large payments from users of electricity.

These are merely dramatic instances of a prevailing condition; there is hardly a major industry at which a similar attack could not be aimed. Critics of business regard such behavior as unethical, but the companies concerned know that they are merely playing the business game.

Among the most respected of our business institutions are the insurance companies. A group of insurance executives meeting recently in New England was startled when their guest speaker, social critic Daniel Patrick Moynihan, roundly berated them for "unethical" practices. They had been guilty, Moynihan alleged, of using outdated actuarial tables to obtain unfairly high premiums. They habitually delayed the hearing of lawsuits

against them in order to tire out the plaintiffs and win cheap settlements. In their employment policies they used ingenious devices to discriminate again certain minority groups.

It was difficult for the audience to deny the validity of these charges. But these men were business game players. Their reaction to Moynihan's attack was much the same as that of the automobile manufacturers to Nader, of the utilities to Senator Metcalf, and of the food processors to Senator Hart. If the laws governing their businesses change, or if public opinion becomes clamorous, they will make the necessary adjustments. But morally they have in their view done nothing wrong. As long as they comply with the letter of the law, they are within their rights to operate their businesses as they see fit.

The small business is in the same position as the great corporation in this respect. For example:

> In 1967 a key manufacturer was accused of providing master keys for automobiles to mail-order customers, although it was obvious that some of the purchasers might be automobile thieves. His defense was plain and straightforward. If there was nothing in the law to prevent him from selling his keys to anyone who ordered them, it was not up to him to inquire as to his customers' motives. Why was it any worse, he insisted, for him to sell car keys by mail, than for mail-order houses to sell guns that might be used for murder? Until the law was changed, the key manufacturer could regard himself as being just as ethical as any other businessman by the rules of the business game.

Violations of the ethical ideals of society are common in business, but they are not necessarily violations of business principles. Each year the Federal Trade Commission orders hundreds of companies, many of them of the first magnitude, to "cease and desist" from practices which, judged by ordinary standards, are of questionable morality but which are stoutly defended by the companies concerned.

In one case, a firm manufacturing a well-known mouthwash was accused of using a cheap form of alcohol possibly deleterious to health. The company's chief executive, after testifying in Washington, made this comment privately:

We broke no law. We're in a highly competitive industry. If we're going to stay in business, we have to look for profit wherever the law permits. We don't make the laws. We obey them. Then why do we have to put up with this "holier than thou" talk about ethics? It's sheer hypocrisy. We're not in business to promote ethics. Look at the cigarette companies, for God's sake! If the ethics aren't embodied in the laws by the men who made them, you can't expect businessmen to fill the lack. Why, a sudden submission to Christian ethics by businessmen would bring about the greatest economic upheaval in history!

It may be noted that the government failed to prove its case against him.

CAST ILLUSIONS ASIDE

Talking about ethics by businessmen is often a thin decorative coating over the hard realities of the game:

Once I listened to a speech by a young executive who pointed to a new industry code as proof that his company and its competitors were deeply aware of their responsibilities to society. It was a code of ethics, he said. The industry was going to police itself, to dissuade constituent companies from wrongdoing. His eyes shone with conviction and enthusiasm.

The same day there was a meeting in a hotel room where the industry's top executives met with the "czar" who was to administer the new code, a man of high repute. No one who was present could doubt their common attitude. In their eyes the code was designed primarily to forestall a move by the federal government to impose stern restrictions on the industry. They felt that the code would hamper them a good deal less than new federal laws would. It was, in other words, conceived as a protection for the industry, not for the public.

The young executive accepted the surface explanation of the code; these leaders, all experienced game players, did not deceive themselves for a moment about its purpose.

The illusion that business can afford to be guided by ethics as conceived in private life is often fostered by speeches and articles containing such phrases as, "It pays to be ethical," or, "Sound ethics is good business." Actually this is not an ethical position at all; it is a self-serving calculation in disguise. The speaker is really saying that in the long run a company can make more money if it does not antagonize competitors, suppliers, employees, and customers by squeezing them too hard. He is saying that over-sharp policies reduce ultimate gains. That is true, but it has nothing to do with ethics. The underlying attitude is much like that in the familiar story of the shopkeeper who finds an extra $20 bill in the cash register, debates with himself the ethical problem—should he tell his partner?—and finally decides to share the money because the gesture will give him an edge over the s.o.b. the next time they quarrel.

I think it is fair to sum up the prevailing attitude of businessmen on ethics as follows:

We live in what is probably the most competitive of the world's civilized societies. Our customs encourage a high degree of aggression in the individual's striving for success. Business is our main idea of competition, and it has been ritualized into a game of strategy. The basic rules of the game have been set by the government, which attempts to detect and punish business frauds. But as long as a company does not transgress the rules of the game set by law, it has the legal right to shape its strategy without reference to anything but its profits. If it takes a long-term view of its profits, it will preserve amicable relations, so far as possible, with those with whom it deals. A wise businessman will not seek advantage to the point where he generates dangerous hostility among employees, competitors, customers, government, or the public at large. But decisions in this area are, in the final test, decisions of strategy, not of ethics.

THE INDIVIDUAL AND THE GAME

An individual within a company often finds it difficult to adjust to the requirements of the business game. He tries to preserve his private ethical standards in situations that call for game strategy. When he is obliged to carry out the company policies that challenge his conception of himself as an ethical man, he suffers.

It disturbs him when he is ordered, for instance, to deny a raise to a man who deserves it, to fire an employee of long standing, to prepare advertising that he believes to be misleading, to conceal facts that he feels customers are entitled to know, to cheapen the quality of materials used in the manufacture of an established product, to sell as a new product that he knows to be rebuilt, to exaggerate the curative powers of a medicinal preparation, or to coerce dealers.

There are some fortunate executives, who, by the nature of their work and circumstances, never have to face problems of this kind. But in one form or another the ethical dilemma is felt sooner or later by most businessmen. Possibly the dilemma is most painful not when the company forces the action on the executive but when he originates it himself—that is, when he has taken or is contemplating a step which is in his own interest but which runs counter to his early moral conditioning. To illustrate:

> The manager of an export department, eager to show rising sales, is pressed by a big customer to provide invoices, which, while containing no overt falsehood that would violate a U.S. law, are so worded that the customer may be able to evade certain taxes in his homeland.
>
> A company president finds that an aging executive, within a few years of retirement and his pension, is not as productive as formerly. Should he be kept on?
>
> The produce manager of a supermarket debates with himself whether to get rid of a lot of half-rotten tomatoes by including one, with its good side exposed, in every tomato sixpack.
>
> An accountant discovers that he has taken an improper deduction on his company's tax return and fears the consequences if he calls the matter to the president's attention, though he himself has done nothing illegal. Perhaps if he says nothing, no one will notice the error.
>
> A chief executive officer is asked by his directors to comment on a rumor that he owns stock in another company with which he has placed large orders. He could deny it, for the stock is in the name of his son-in-law and he has earlier formally instructed his son-in-law to sell the holding.

Temptations of this kind constantly arise in business. If an executive allows himself to be torn between a decision based on business considera-

tions and one based on his private ethical code, he exposes himself to a grave psychological strain.

This is not to say that sound business strategy necessarily runs counter to ethical ideals. They may frequently coincide; and when they do, everyone is gratified. But the major tests of every move in business, as in all games of strategy, are legality and profit. A man who intends to be a winner in the business game must have a game player's attitude.

The business strategist's decisions must be as impersonal as those of a surgeon performing an operation—concentrating on objective and technique, and subordinating personal feelings. If the chief executive admits that his son-in-law owns the stock, it is because he stands to lose more if the fact comes out later than if he states it boldly and at once. If the supermarket manager orders the rotten tomatoes to be discarded, he does so to avoid an increase in consumer complaints and a loss of good will. The company president decides not to fire the elderly executive in the belief that the negative reaction of other employees would in the long run cost the company more than it would lose in keeping him and paying his pension.

All sensible businessmen prefer to be truthful, but they seldom feel inclined to tell the *whole* truth. In the business game truth-telling usually has to be kept within narrow limits if trouble is to be avoided. The point was neatly made a long time ago (in 1888) by one of John D. Rockefeller's associates, Paul Babcock, to Standard Oil Company executives who were about to testify before a government investigating committee: "Parry every question with answers which, while perfectly truthful, are evasive of *bottom* facts." This was, is, and probably always will be regarded as wise and permissible business strategy.

FOR OFFICE USE ONLY

An executive's family life can easily be dislocated if he fails to make a sharp distinction between the ethical systems of the home and the office—or if his wife does not grasp that distinction. Many a businessman who has remarked to his wife "I had to let Jones go today" or "I had to admit to the boss that Jim has been goofing off lately," has been met with an indignant protest. "How could you do a thing like that? You know Jones is over 50 and will have a lot of trouble getting another job." Or, "You did that to Jim? With his wife ill and all the worry she's having with the kids?"

If the executive insists that he had no choice because the profits of the company and his own security were involved, he may see a certain cool and ominous reappraisal in his wife's eyes. Many wives are not prepared to accept the fact that business operates with a special code of ethics. An illuminating illustration of this comes from a Southern sales executive who related a conversation he had had with his wife at a time when a hotly contested political campaign was being waged in their state:

I made the mistake of telling her that I had had lunch with Colby, who gives me about half my business. Colby mentioned that his company had a stake in the election. Then he said, "By the way, I'm treasurer of the citizens' committee for Lang. I'm collecting contributions. Can I count on you for a hundred dollars?"

Well, there I was. I was opposed to Lang, but I knew Colby. If he withdrew his business I could be in a bad spot. So I just smiled and wrote out a check then and there. He thanked me, and we started to talk about his next order. Maybe he thought I shared his political views. I wasn't going to lose any sleep over it.

I should have had sense enough not to tell Mary about it. She hit the ceiling. She said she was disappointed in me. She said I hadn't acted like a man, that I should have stood up to Colby.

I said, "Look, it was an either-or situation. I had to do it or risk losing the business."

She came back at me with, "I don't believe it. You could have been honest with him. You could have said that you didn't feel you ought to contribute to a campaign for a man you weren't going to vote for. I'm sure he would have understood."

I said, "Mary, you're a wonderful woman, but you're way off the track. Do you know what would have happened if I had said that? Colby would have smiled and said, 'Oh, I didn't realize. Forget it.' But in his eyes from that moment I would be an oddball, maybe a bit of a radical. He would have listened to me talk about his order and would have promised to give it consideration. After that I wouldn't

hear from him for a week. Then I would telephone and learn from his secretary that he wasn't yet ready to place the order. And in about a month I would hear through the grapevine that he was giving his business to another company. A month after that I'd be out of a job."

She was silent for a while. Then she said, "Tom, something is wrong with business when a man is forced to choose between his family's security and his moral obligation to himself. It's easy for me to say you should have stood up to him—but if you had, you might have felt you were betraying me and the kids. I'm sorry that you did it, Tom, but I can't blame you. Something is wrong with business!"

This wife saw the problem in terms of moral obligation as conceived in private life; her husband saw it as a matter of game strategy. As a player in a weak position, he felt that he could not afford to indulge an ethical sentiment that might have cost him his seat at the table.

PLAYING TO WIN

Some men might challenge the Colbys of business—might accept serious setbacks to their business careers rather than risk a feeling of moral cowardice. They merit our respect—but as private individuals, not businessmen. When the skillful player of the business game is compelled to submit to unfair pressure, he does not castigate himself for moral weakness. Instead, he strives to put himself into a strong position where he can defend himself against such pressures in the future without loss.

If a man plans to take a seat in the business game, he owes it to himself to master the principles by which the game is played, including its special ethical outlook. He can then hardly fail to recognize that an occasional bluff may well be justified in terms of the game's ethics and warranted in terms of economic necessity. Once he clears his mind on this point, he is in a good position to match his strategy against that of the other players. He can then determine objectively whether a bluff in a given situation has a good chance of succeeding and can decide when and how to bluff, without a feeling of ethical transgression.

To be a winner, a man must play to win. This does not mean that he must be ruthless, cruel, harsh, or treacherous. On the contrary, the better his reputation for integrity, honesty, and decency, the better his chances of victory will be in the long run. But from time to time every businessman, like every poker player, is offered a choice between certain loss or bluffing within the legal rules of the game. If he is not resigned to losing, if he wants to rise in his company and industry, then in such a crisis he will bluff—and bluff hard.

Every now and then one meets a successful businessman who has conveniently forgotten the small or large deceptions that he practiced on his way to fortune. "God gave me my money," old

John D. Rockefeller once piously told a Sunday school class. It would be a rare tycoon in our time who would risk the horse laugh with which such a remark would be greeted.

In the last third of the twentieth century even children are aware that if a man has become prosperous in business, he has sometimes departed from the strict truth in order to overcome obstacles or has practiced the more subtle deceptions of the half-truth or the misleading omission. Whatever the form of the bluff, it is an integral part of the game, and the executive who does not master its techniques is not likely to accumulate much money or power.

WHISTLEBLOWING AND EMPLOYEE LOYALTY
Ronald Duska

Three Mile Island. In early 1983, almost four years after the near meltdown at Unit 2, two officials in the Site Operations Office of General Public Utilities reported a reckless company effort to clean up the contaminated reactor. Under threat of physical retaliation from superiors, the GPU insiders released evidence alleging that the company had rushed the TMI cleanup without testing key maintenance systems. Since then, the Three Mile Island mop-up has been stalled pending a review of GPU's management.[1]

The releasing of evidence of the rushed cleanup at Three Mile Island is an example of whistleblowing. Norman Bowie defines whistleblowing as "the act by an employee of informing the public on the immoral or illegal behavior of an employer or supervisor."[2] Ever since Daniel Ellsberg's release of the Pentagon Papers, the question of whether an employee should blow the whistle on his company or organization has become a hotly contested issue. Was Ellsberg right? Is it right to report the shady or suspect practices of the organization one works for? Is one a stool pigeon or a dedicated citizen? Does a

person have an obligation to the public which overrides his obligation to his employer or does he simply betray a loyalty and become a traitor if he reports his company?

There are proponents on both sides of the issue—those who praise whistleblowers as civic heroes and those who condemn them as "finks." Glen and Shearer who wrote about the whistleblowers at Three Mile Island say, "Without the *courageous* breed of assorted company insiders known as whistleblowers—workers who often risk their livelihoods to disclose information about construction and design flaws—the Nuclear Regulatory Commission itself would be nearly as idle as Three Mile Island…That whistleblowers deserve both gratitude and protection is beyond disagreement."[3]

Still, while Glen and Shearer praise whistleblowers, others vociferously condemn them. For example, in a now-infamous quote, James Roche, the former president of General Motors said:

> Some critics are now busy eroding another support of free enterprise—the loyalty of a management team, with its unifying values and cooperative work. Some of the enemies of business now encourage an employee to be *disloyal* to the enterprise. They want to create

suspicion and disharmony, and pry into the proprietary interests of the business. However this is labelled—industrial espionage, whistle blowing, or professional responsibility—it is another tactic for spreading disunity and creating conflict.[4]

From Roche's point of view, whistleblowing is not only not "courageous" and deserving of "gratitude and protection" as Glen and Shearer would have it, it is corrosive and not even permissible.

Discussions of whistleblowing generally revolve around four topics: (1) attempts to define whistleblowing more precisely; (2) debates about whether and when whistleblowing is permissible; (3) debates about whether and when one has an obligation to blow the whistle; and (4) appropriate mechanisms for institutionalizing whistleblowing.

In this paper I want to focus on the second problem, because I find it somewhat disconcerting that there is a problem at all. When I first looked into the ethics of whistleblowing it seemed to me that whistleblowing was a good thing, and yet I found in the literature claim after claim that it was in need of defense, that there was something wrong with it, namely that it was an act of disloyalty.

If whistleblowing was a disloyal act, it deserved disapproval, and ultimately any action of whistleblowing needed justification. This disturbed me. It was as if the act of a good Samaritan was being condemned as an act of interference, as if the prevention of a suicide needed to be justified. My moral position in favor of whistleblowing was being challenged. The tables were turned and the burden of proof had shifted. My position was the one in question. Suddenly instead of the company being the bad guy and the whistleblower the good guy, which is what I thought, the whistleblower was the bad guy. Why? Because he was disloyal. What I discovered was that in most of the literature it was taken as axiomatic that whistleblowing was an act of disloyalty. My moral intuitions told me that axiom was mistaken. Nevertheless, since it is accepted by a large segment of the ethical community it deserves investigation.

In his book *Business Ethics,* Norman Bowie, who presents what I think is one of the finest presentations of the ethics of whistleblowing, claims that "whistleblowing…violate[s] a *prima facie* duty of loyalty to one's employer." According to Bowie, there is a duty of loyalty which prohibits one from reporting his employer or company. Bowie, of course, recognizes that this is only a *prima facie* duty, i.e., one that can be overridden by a higher duty to the public good. Nevertheless, the axiom that whistleblowing is disloyal is Bowie's starting point.

Bowie is not alone. Sisela Bok, another fine ethicist, sees whistleblowing as an instance of disloyalty.

> The whistleblower hopes to stop the game; but since he is neither referee nor coach, and since he blows the whistle on his own team, his act is seen as a *violation of loyalty* [italics mine]. In holding his position, he has assumed certain obligations to his colleagues and clients. He may even have subscribed to a loyalty oath or a promise of confidentiality…Loyalty to colleagues and to clients comes to be pitted against loyalty to the public interest, to those who may be injured unless the revelation is made.[5]

Bowie and Bok end up defending whistleblowing in certain contexts, so I don't necessarily disagree with their conclusions. However, I fail to see how one has an obligation of loyalty to one's company, so I disagree with their perception of the problem, and their starting point. The difference in perception is important because those who think employees have an obligation of loyalty to a company fail to take into account a relevant moral difference between persons and corporations and between corporations and other kinds of groups where loyalty is appropriate. I want to argue that one does not have an obligation of loyalty to a company, even a *prima facie* one, because companies are not the kind of things which are proper objects of loyalty. I then want to show that to make them objects of loyalty gives them a moral status they do not deserve and in raising their status, one lowers the status of the individuals who work for the companies.

But why aren't corporations the kind of things which can be objects of loyalty?…

Loyalty is ordinarily construed as a state of being constant and faithful in a relation implying trust or confidence, as a wife to husband, friend to friend, parent to child, lord to vassal, etc. According to John Ladd "it is not founded on just *any* casual relationship, but on a specific kind of relationship or tie. The ties that bind the persons together provide the basis of loyalty."[6] But all sorts of ties bind people together to make groups. I am a member of a group of fans if I go to a ball game. I am a member of a group if I merely walk down the street. I am in a sense tied to them, but don't owe them loyalty. I don't owe loyalty to just anyone I encounter. Rather I owe loyalty to persons with whom I have special relationships. I owe it to my children, my spouse, my parents, my friends and certain groups, those groups which are formed for the mutual enrichment of the members. It is important to recognize that in any relationship which demands loyalty the relationship works both ways and involves mutual enrichment. Loyalty is incompatible with self-interest, because it is something that necessarily requires we go beyond self-interest. My loyalty to my friend, for example, requires I put aside my interests some of the time. It is because of this reciprocal requirement which demands surrendering self-interest that a corporation is not a proper object of loyalty.

A business or corporation does two things in the free enterprise system. It produces a good or service and makes a profit. The making of a profit, however, is the primary function of a business as a business. For if the production of the good or service was not profitable the business would be out of business. Since non-profitable goods or services are discontinued, the providing of a service or the making of a product is not done for its own sake, but from a business perspective is a means to an end, the making of profit. People bound together in a business are not bound together for mutual fulfillment and support, but to divide labor so the business makes a profit. Since profit is paramount if you do not produce in a company or if there are cheaper laborers around, a company feels justified in firing you for the sake of better production. Throughout history companies in a pinch feel no obligation of loyalty. Compare that to a family. While we can jokingly refer to a family as "somewhere they have to take you in no matter what," you cannot refer to a company in that way. "You can't buy loyalty" is true. Loyalty depends on ties that demand self-sacrifice with no expectation of reward, e.g., the ties of loyalty that bind a family together. Business functions on the basis of enlightened self-interest. I am devoted to a company not because it is like a parent to me. It is not, and attempts of some companies to create "one big happy family" ought to be looked on with suspicion. I am not "devoted" to it at all, or should not be. I *work* for it because it pays me. I am not in a family to get paid, but I am in a company to get paid.

Since loyalty is a kind of devotion, one can confuse devotion to one's job (or the ends of one's work) with devotion to a company.

I may have a job I find fulfilling, but that is accidental to my relation to the company. For example, I might go to work for a company as a carpenter and love the job and get satisfaction out of doing good work. But if the company can increase profit by cutting back to an adequate but inferior type of material or procedure, it can make it impossible for me to take pride in my work as a carpenter while making it possible for me to make more money. The company does not exist to subsidize my quality work as a carpenter. As a carpenter my goal may be good houses, but as an employee my goal is to contribute to making a profit. "That's just business!"

This fact that profit determines the quality of work allowed leads to a phenomenon called the commercialization of work. The primary end of an act of building is to make something, and to build well is to make it well. A carpenter is defined by the end of his work, but if the quality interferes with profit, the business side of the venture supercedes the artisan side. Thus profit forces a craftsman to suspend his devotion to his work and commercializes his venture. The more professions subject themselves to the forces of the marketplace, the more they get commercialized; e.g., research for the sake of a more profitable product rather than for the sake of knowledge jeopardizes the integrity of academic research facilities.

The cold hard truth is that the goal of profit is what gives birth to a company and forms that particular group. Money is what ties the group together. But in such a commercialized venture, with such a goal there is no loyalty, or at least none need be expected. An employer will release an employee and an employee will walk away from an employer when it is profitable to do so. That's business. It is perfectly permissible. Contrast that with the ties between a lord and his vassal. A lord could not in good conscience wash his hands of his vassal, nor could a vassal in good conscience abandon his lord. What bound them was mutual enrichment, not profit.

Loyalty to a corporation, then, is not required. But even more it is probably misguided. There is nothing as pathetic as the story of the loyal employee who, having given above and beyond the call of duty, is let go in the restructuring of the company. He feels betrayed because he mistakenly viewed the company as an object of his loyalty. To get rid of such foolish romanticism and to come to grips with this hard but accurate assessment should ultimately benefit everyone.

One need hardly be an enemy of business to be suspicious of a demand of loyalty to something whose primary reason for existence is the making of profit. It is simply the case that I have no duty of loyalty to the business or organization. Rather I have a duty to return responsible work for fair wages. The commercialization of work dissolves the type of relationship that requires loyalty. It sets up merely contractual relationships. One sells one's labor but not one's self to a company or an institution.

To think we owe a company or corporation loyalty requires us to think of that company as a person or as a group with a goal of human enrichment. If we think of it in this way we can be loyal. But this is just the wrong way to think. A company is not a person. A company is an instrument, and an instrument with a specific purpose, the making of profit. To treat an instrument as an end in itself, like a person, may not be as bad as treating an end as an instrument, but it does give the instrument a moral status it does not deserve, and by elevating the instrument we lower the end. All things, instruments and ends, become alike.

To treat a company as a person is analogous to treating a machine as a person or treating a system as a person. The system, company, or instrument get as much respect and care as the persons for whom they were invented. If we remember that the primary purpose of business is to make profit, it can be seen clearly as merely an instrument. If so, it needs to be used and regulated accordingly, and I owe it no more loyalty than I owe a word processor.

Of course if everyone would view business as a commercial instrument, things might become more difficult for the smooth functioning of the organization, since businesses could not count on the "loyalty" of their employees. Business itself is well served, at least in the short run, if it can keep the notion of a duty to loyalty alive. It does this by

comparing itself to a paradigm case of an organization one shows loyalty to, the team.

Remember that Roche refers to the "management team" and Bok sees the name "whistleblowing" coming from the instance of a referee blowing a whistle in the presence of a foul. What is perceived as bad about whistleblowing in business from this perspective is that one blows the whistle on one's own team, thereby violating team loyalty. If the company can get its employees to view it as a team they belong to, it is easier to demand loyalty. The rules governing teamwork and team loyalty will apply. One reason the appeal to a team and team loyalty works so well in business is that businesses are in competition with one another. If an executive could get his employees to be loyal, a loyalty without thought to himself or his fellow man, but to the will of the company, the manager would have the ideal kind of corporation from an organizational standpoint. As Paul R. Lawrence, the organizational theorist says, "Ideally, we would want one sentiment to be dominant in all employees from top to bottom, namely a complete loyalty to the organizational purpose."[7] Effective motivation turns business practices into a game and instills teamwork.

But businesses differ from teams in very important respects, which makes the analogy between business and a team dangerous. Loyalty to a team is loyalty within the context of sport, a competition. Teamwork and team loyalty require that in the circumscribed activity of the game I cooperate with my fellow players so that pulling all together, we can win. The object of (most) sports is victory. But the winning in sports is a social convention, divorced from the usual goings on of society. Such a winning is most times a harmless, morally neutral diversion.

But the fact that this victory in sports, within the rules enforced by a referee (whistleblower), is a socially developed convention taking place within a larger social context makes it quite different from competition in business, which, rather than being defined by a context, permeates the whole of society in its influence. Competition leads not only to winners but to losers. One can lose at sport with precious few serious consequences. The consequences of losing at business are much more serious. Further, the losers in sport are there voluntarily, while the losers in business can be those who are not in the game voluntarily (we are all forced to participate) but are still affected by business decisions. People cannot choose to participate in business, since it permeates everyone's life.

The team model fits very well with the model of the free-market system because there competition is said to be the name of the game. Rival companies compete and their object is to win. To call a foul on one's own teammate is to jeopardize one's chances of winning and is viewed as disloyalty.

But isn't it time to stop viewing the corporate machinations as games? These games are not controlled and not over after a specific time. The activities of business affect the lives of everyone, not just the game players. The analogy of the corporation to a team and the consequent appeal to team loyalty, although understandable, is seriously misleading at least in the moral sphere, where competition is not the prevailing virtue.

If my analysis is correct, the issue of the permissibility of whistleblowing is not a real issue, since there is no obligation of loyalty to a company. Whistleblowing is not only permissible but expected when a company is harming society. The issue is not one of disloyalty to the company, but the question of whether the whistleblower has an obligation to society if blowing the whistle will bring him retaliation. I will not argue that issue, but merely suggest the lines I would pursue.

I tend to be a minimalist in ethics, and depend heavily on a distinction between obligations and acts of supererogation. We have, it seems to me, an obligation to avoid harming anyone, but not an obligation to do good. Doing good is above the call of duty. In-between we may under certain conditions have an obligation to prevent harm. If whistleblowing can prevent harm, then it is required under certain conditions.

Simon, Powers and Gunnemann set forth four conditions:[8] need, proximity, capability, and last resort. Applying these, we get the following.

1. There must be a clear harm to society that can be avoided by whistleblowing. We don't blow the whistle over everything.

2. It is the "proximity" to the whistleblower that puts him in the position to report his company in the first place.

3. "Capability" means that he needs to have some chance of success. No one has an obligation to

jeopardize himself to perform futile gestures. The whistleblower needs to have access to the press, be believable, etc.

4. "Last resort" means just that. If there are others more capable of reporting and more proximate, and if they will report, then one does not have the responsibility.

Before concluding, there is one aspect of the loyalty issue that ought to be disposed of. My position could be challenged in the case of organizations who are employers in non-profit areas, such as the government, educational institutions, etc. In this case my commercialization argument is irrelevant. However, I would maintain that any activity which merits the blowing of the whistle in the case of non-profit and service organizations is probably counter to the purpose of the institution in the first place. Thus, if there were loyalty required, in that case, whoever justifiably blew the whistle would be blowing it on a colleague who perverted the end or purpose of the organization. The loyalty to the group would remain intact. Ellsberg's whistleblowing on the government is a way of keeping the government faithful to its obligations. But that is another issue.

NOTES

1. Maxwell Glen and Cody Shearer, "Going after the Whistle-blowers," *The Philadelphia Inquirer*, Tuesday, Aug. 2, 1983, Op-ed Page, p. 11a.

2. Norman Bowie, *Business Ethics* (Englewood Cliffs, N.J.: Prentice-Hall, 1982), 140. For Bowie, this is just a preliminary definition. His fuller definition reads, "A whistle blower is an employee or officer of any institution, profit or non-profit, private or public, who believes either that he/she has been ordered to perform some act or he/she has obtained knowledge that the institution is engaged in activities which a) are believed to cause unnecessary harm to third parties, b) are in violation of human rights or c) run counter to the defined purpose of the institution and who inform the public of this fact." Bowie then lists six conditions under which the act is justified. 142–143.

3. Glen and Shearer, "Going after the Whistleblowers," 11a.

4. James M. Roche, "The Competitive System, to Work, to Preserve, and to Protect," *Vital Speeches of the Day* (May 1971), 445. This is quoted in Bowie, 141 and also in Kenneth D. Walters, "Your Employee's Right to Blow the Whistle," *Harvard Business Review*, 53, no. 4.

5. Sisela Bok, "Whistleblowing and Professional Responsibilities," *New York University Education Quarterly*, vol. II, 4 (1980), 3.

6. John Ladd, "Loyalty," *The Encyclopedia of Philosophy*, vol. 5, 97.

7. Paul R. Lawrence, *The Changing of Organizational Behavior Patterns: A Case Study of Decentralization* (Boston: Division of

Research, Harvard Business School, 1958), 208, as quoted in Kenneth D. Walters, op. cit.

8. John G. Simon, Charles W. Powers, and Jon P. Gunnemann, *The Ethical Investor: Universities and Corporate Responsibility* (New Haven: Yale University Press, 1972).

WHISTLEBLOWING: PROFESSIONALISM, PERSONAL LIFE, AND SHARED RESPONSIBILITY FOR SAFETY IN ENGINEERING

Mike W. Martin

...I want to take a fresh look at whistleblowing in order to draw attention to some neglected issues concerning the moral relevance of personal life to understanding professional responsibilities. Specifically, the issues concern: personal right and responsibilities in deciding how to meet professional obligations; increased personal burdens when others involved in collective endeavors fail to meet their responsibilities; the role of the virtues, especially personal integrity, as they bear on "living with oneself"; and personal commitments to moral ideals beyond minimum requirements....

Let me bring to mind three well-known cases.

(1) In 1972 Dan Applegate wrote a memo to his supervisor, the vice-president of Convair Corporation, telling him in no uncertain terms that the cargo door for the DC-10 airplane was unsafe, making it "inevitable that, in the twenty years ahead of us, DC-10 cargo doors will come open and I would expect this to usually result in the loss of the airplane."[1] As a subcontractor for McDonnell Douglas, Convair had designed the cargo door and the DC-10 fuselage. Applegate was Director of Product Engineering at Convair and the senior engineer in charge of the design. His supervisor did not challenge his technical judgment in the matter, but told him that nothing could be done because of the likely costs to Convair in admitting responsibility for a design error that would need to be fixed by grounding DC-10's. Two years later, the cargo door on a Turkish DC-10 flying near Paris opened in flight, decompressurizing the cargo area so as to

collapse the passenger floor—along which run the controls for the aircraft. All 346 people on board died, a record casualty figure at that time for a single-plane crash. Ten of millions of dollars were paid out in civil suits, but no one was charged with criminal or even unprofessional conduct.

(2) Frank Camps was a principal design engineer for the Pinto.[2] Under pressure from management he participated in coaxing the Pinto windshield through government tests by reporting only the rare successful test and by using a Band-Aid fix design that resulted in increased hazard to the gas tank. In 1973, undergoing a crisis of conscience in response to reports of exploding gas tanks, he engaged in internal whistleblowing, writing the first of many memos to top management stating his view that Ford was violating federal safety standards. It took six years before his concerns were finally incorporated into the 1979 model Pinto, after nearly a million Pintos with unsafe windshields and gas tanks were put on the road. Shortly after writing his memos he was given lowered performance evaluations, then demoted several times. He resigned in 1978 when it became clear his prospects for advancement at Ford were ended. He filed a law suit based in part on age discrimination, in part on trying to prevent Ford from making him a scapegoat for problems with the Pinto, and in part on trying to draw further attention to the dangers in the Pinto.

(3) On January 27, 1986, Roger Boisjoly and other senior engineers at Morton Thiokol firmly recommended that space shuttle *Challenger* not be launched.[3] The temperature at the launch site was substantially below the known safety range for the

From *Business & Professional Ethics Journal*, vol. 11, no. 2 (1992): 21–40. Reprinted by permission of the author.

O-ring seals in the joints of the solid rocket boosters. Top management overrode the recommendation. Early in the launch, the *Challenger* boosters exploded, killing the seven crew members, to the terrified eyes of millions who watched because schoolteacher Christa McAuliffe was aboard. A month later Boisjoly was called to testify before the Rogers Commission. Against the wishes of management, he offered documents to support his interpretation of the events leading to the disaster—and to rebut the interpretation given by his boss. Over the next months Boisjoly was made to feel increasingly alienated from his coworkers until finally he had to take an extended sick leave. Later, when he desired to find a new job he found himself confronted with companies unwilling to take a chance on a known whistleblower.

As the last two cases suggest, there can be double horrors surrounding whistleblowing: the public horror of lost lives, and the personal horror of responsible whistleblowers who lose their careers. Most whistleblowers undergo serious penalties for "committing the truth." One recent study suggests that two out of three of them suffer harassment, lowered performance evaluations, demotions, punitive transfers, loss of jobs, or blacklisting that can effectively end a career.[4] Horror stories about whistleblowers are not the exception; they are the rule.

THREE APPROACHES TO WHISTLEBLOWING ETHICS

The literature on whistleblowing is large and growing. Here I mention three general approaches. The first is to condemn whistleblowers as disloyal troublemakers who "rat" on their companies and undermine teamwork based on the hierarchy of authority within the corporation. Admittedly, whistleblowers' views about safety concerns are sometimes correct, but final decisions about safety belong to management, not engineers. When management errs, the corporation will eventually pick up the costs in law suits and adverse publicity. Members of the public are part of the technological enterprise which both benefits them and exposes them to risks; when things go wrong they (or their surviving family) can always sue.

I once dismissed this attitude as callous, as sheer corporate egoism that misconstrues loyalty to a corporation as an absolute (unexceptionless) moral principle. *If*, however—and it is a big "if"—the public accepts this attitude, as revealed in how it expresses its will through legitimate political processes, then so be it. As will become clear later, I take public responsibilities seriously. If the public refuses to protect whistleblowers, it tacitly accepts the added risks from not having available important safety information. I hope the public will protect the jobs of whistleblowers; more on this later.

A second approach, insightfully defended by Michael Davis,[5] is to regard whistleblowing as a tragedy to be avoided. On occasion whistleblowing may be a necessary evil or even admirable, but it is always bad news all around. It is proof of organizational trouble and management failure; it threatens the careers of managers on whom the whistle is blown; it disrupts collegiality by making colleagues feel resentment toward the whistleblower, and it damages the important informal network of friends at the workplace; it shows the whistleblower lost faith in the organization and its authority, and hence is more likely to be a troublemaker in the future; and it almost always brings severe penalties to whistleblowers who are viewed by employers and colleagues as unfit employees.

I wholeheartedly support efforts to avoid the need for whistleblowing. There are many things that can be done to improve organizations to make whistleblowing unnecessary. Top management can—and must—set a moral tone, and then implement policies that encourage safety concerns (and other bad news) to be communicated freely. Specifically, managers can keep doors open, allowing engineers to convey their concerns without retribution. Corporations can have in-house ombudspersons and appeal boards, and even a vice-president for corporate ethics. For their part, engineers can learn to be more assertive and effective in making their safety concerns known, learning how to build support from their colleagues. (Could Dan Applegate have pushed harder than he did, or did he just write a memo and drop the matter?) Professional societies should explore the possibility of creating confidential appeal groups where engineers can have their claims heard.

Nevertheless, this second approach is not enough. There will always be corporations and managers willing to cut corners on safety in the pursuit of short-term profit, and there will always be a need for justified whistleblowing. Labelling whistleblowing as a tragedy to be avoided whenever possible should not deflect attention from issues concerning justified whistleblowing.

We need to remind ourselves that responsible whistleblowing is *not* bad news all around: It is very good news for the public which is protected by it. The good news is both episodic and systematic. Episodically, lives are saved directly when professionals speak out, and lives are lost when professionals like Dan Applegate feel they must remain silent in order to keep their jobs. Systematically, lives are saved indirectly by sending a strong message to industry that legally-protected whistleblowing is always available as a last resort when managers too casually override safety concerns for short-term profits. Helpful pressure is put on management to take a more farsighted view of safety, thereby providing a further impetus for unifying corporate self-interest with the production of safe products. (In the DC-10, Pinto, and *Challenger* cases, management made shortsighted decisions that resulted in enormous costs in law suits and damaged company reputations.)

In this day of (sometimes justified) outcry over excessive government regulation, we should not forget the symbolic importance of clear, effective, and enforced laws as a way for society to express its collective vision of a good society.[6] Laws protecting responsible whistleblowing express the community's resolve to support professionals who act responsibly for public safety. Those laws are also required if the public is to meet its responsibilities in the creation of safe technological products, as I will suggest in a moment.

A third approach is to affirm unequivocally the obligation of engineers (and other professionals) to whistleblow in certain circumstances, and to treat this obligation as paramount—as overriding all other considerations, whatever the sacrifice involved in meeting it. Richard De George gave the classical statement of this view.[7] External whistleblowing, he argued, is obligatory when five conditions are met (by an engineer or other corporate employee):

1. "Serious and considerable harm to the public" is involved;

2. one reports the harm and expresses moral concern to one's immediate superior;

3. one exhausts other channels within the corporation;

4. one has available "documented evidence that would convince a reasonable, impartial observer that one's view of the situation is correct"; and

5. one has "good reasons to believe that by going public the necessary changes will be brought about" to prevent the harm.

De George says that whistleblowing is morally *permissible* when conditions 1–3 are met, and is morally *obligatory* when 1–5 are met.

As critics have pointed out, conditions (4) and (5) seem far too strong. Where serious safety is at stake, there is some obligation to whistleblow even when there are only grounds for hope (not necessarily belief) that whistleblowing will significantly improve matters, and even when one's documentation is substantial but less than convincing to every rational person.[8] Indeed, often whistleblowing is intended to prompt authorities to garner otherwise-unavailable evidence through investigations.

Moreover, having a reasonable degree of documentation is a requirement even for permissible whistleblowing—lest one make insupportable allegations that unjustifiably harm the reputations of individuals and corporations. So too is having a reasonable hope for success—lest one waste everyone's time and energy.[9] Hence, De George's sharp separation of requirements for permissibility and obligation begins to collapse. There may be an obligation to whistleblow when 1–3 are met and the person has some reasonable degree of documentation and reasonable hope for success in bringing about necessary changes.

My main criticism of this third approach, however, is more fundamental. I want to call into question the whole attempt to offer a general rule that tells us when whistleblowing is mandatory, *tout court*. Final judgments about obligations to whistleblow must be made contextually, not as a matter of general rule. And they must take into account the burdens imposed on whistleblowers.[10]

THE MORAL RELEVANCE OF PERSONAL LIFE TO PROFESSIONAL DUTY

In my view, there is a strong *prima facie* obligation to whistleblow when one has good reason to believe there is a serious moral problem, has exhausted normal organizational channels (except in emergencies when time precludes that), has available a reasonable amount of documentation, and has reasonable hope of solving the problem by blowing the whistle. Nevertheless, however strong, the obligation is only *prima facie:* It can sometimes have exceptions when it conflicts with other important considerations. Moreover, the considerations which need to be weighed include not only *prima facie* obligations to one's employer, but also considerations about one's personal life. Before they make all-things-considered judgments about whether to whistleblow, engineers may and should consider their responsibilities to their family, other personal obligations which depend on having an income, and their rights to pursue their careers.

Engineers are people, as well as professionals. They have personal obligations to their families, as well as sundry other obligations in personal life which can be met only if they have an income. They also have personal rights to pursue careers. These personal obligations and rights are moral ones, and they legitimately interact with professional obligations in ways that sometimes make it permissible for engineers not to whistleblow, even when they have a *prima facie* obligation to do so. Precisely how these considerations are weighed depends on the particular situation. And here as elsewhere, we must allow room for morally reasonable people to weigh moral factors differently.

In adopting this contextual approach to balancing personal and professional obligations, I am being heretical. Few discussions of whistleblowing take personal considerations seriously, as being morally significant, rather than a matter of nonmoral, prudential concern for self-interest. But responsibilities to family and to others outside the workplace, as well as the right to pursue one's career, are moral considerations, not just prudential ones. Hence further argument is needed to dismiss them as irrelevant or always secondary in this context. I will consider three such arguments.

(i) The *Prevent-Harm Argument* says that morality requires us to prevent harm and in doing so to treat others' interests equally and impartially with our own. This assumption is often associated with utilitarianism, the view that we should always produce the most good for the most people. Strictly, at issue here is "negative utilitarianism," which says we should always act to minimize total harm, treating everyone's interests as equally im-

portant with our own. The idea is that even though engineers and their families must suffer, their suffering is outweighed by the lives saved through whistleblowing. Without committing himself to utilitarianism, De George uses a variation of the impartiality requirement to defend his criteria for obligatory whistleblowing: "It is not implausible to claim both that we are morally obliged to prevent harm to others at relatively little expense to ourselves, and that we are morally obliged to prevent great harm to a great many others, even at considerable expense to ourselves."[11]

The demand for strict impartiality in ethics has been under sustained attack during the past two decades, and from many directions.[12] Without attempting to review all those arguments, I can indicate how they block any straightforward move from impartiality to absolute (exceptionless) whistleblowing obligations, thereby undermining the Prevent-Harm Argument. One argument is that a universal requirement of strict impartiality (as opposed to a limited requirement restricted to certain contexts) is self-demeaning. It undermines our ability to give our lives meaning through special projects, careers, and relationships that require the resources which strict impartiality would demand we give away to others. The general moral right to autonomy—the right to pursue our lives in a search for meaning and happiness—implies a right to give considerable emphasis to our personal needs and those of our family.

As an analogy, consider the life-and-death issues surrounding world hunger and scarce medical resources.[13] It can be argued that all of us share a general responsibility (of mutual aid) for dealing with the tragedy of tens of thousands of people who die each day from malnutrition and lack of medical care. As citizens paying taxes that can be used toward this end, and also as philanthropists who voluntarily recognize a responsibility to give to relief organizations, each of us has a *prima facie* obligation to help. But there are limits. Right now, you and I could dramatically lower our lifestyles in order to help save lives by making greater sacrifices. We could even donate one of our kidneys to save a life. Yet we have a right not to do that, a right to give ourselves and our families considerable priority in how we use our resources. Similarly, engineers' rights to pursue their meaning-giving careers, and the projects and relationships made possible by those careers, have relevance in understanding the degree of sacrifice required by a *prima facie* whistle-blowing obligation.

(ii) The *Avoid-Harm Argument* proceeds from the obligation not to cause harm to others. It then points out that engineers are in a position to cause or avoid harm on an unusual scale. As a result, according to Kenneth Alpern, the ordinary moral obligation of due care in avoiding harm to others implies that engineers must "be ready to make greater personal sacrifices than can normally be demanded of other individuals."[14] In particular, according to Gene James, whistleblowing is required when it falls under the general obligation to "prevent unnecessary harm to others" and "to not cause avoidable harm to others," where "harm" means violating their rights.[15]

Of course there is a general obligation not to cause harm. That obligation, however, is so abstract that it tells us little about exactly how much effort and sacrifice is required of us, especially where many people share responsibility for avoiding harm. I have an obligation not to harm others by polluting the environment, but it does not follow that I must stop driving my car at the cost of my job and the opportunities it makes possible for my family. That would be an unfair burden. These abstract difficulties multiply as we turn to the context of engineering practice which involves collective responsibility for technological products.

Engineers work as members of authority-structured teams which sometimes involve hundreds of other professionals who share responsibility for inherently-risky technological projects.[16] Engineers are not the only team-members who have responsibilities to create safe products. Their managers have exactly the same general responsibilities. In fact, they have greater accountability insofar as they are charged with the authority to make final decisions about projects. True, engineers have greater expertise in safety matters and hence have greater responsibilities to identify dangers and convey that information to management. But whatever justifications can be given for engineers to zealously protect public safety also apply to managers. In making the decision to launch the *Challenger,* Jerald Mason, Senior Vice President for Morton Thiokol, is said to have told Robert Lund, "Take off your engineering hat and put on your management hat." Surely this change in headgear did not alter his moral responsibilities for safety.

Dan Applegate and Roger Boisjoly acted responsibly in making unequivocal safety recommendations; their managers failed to act responsibly. Hence their moral dilemmas about whether to whistleblow arose because of unjustified decisions by their superiors. It is fair to ask engineers to pick up the moral slack for managers' irresponsible decisions—as long as we afford them legal protection to prevent their being harassed, fired, and blacklisted. Otherwise, we impose an unfair burden. Government and the general public share responsibility for safety in engineering. They set the rules that business plays by. It is hypocrisy for us to insist that engineers have an obligation to whistleblow to protect us, and then to fail to protect them when they act on the obligation.

(iii) The *Professional-Status Argument* asserts that engineers have special responsibilities as professionals, specified in codes of ethics, which go beyond the general responsibilities incumbent on everyone to prevent and avoid harm, and which override all personal considerations. Most engineering codes hint at a whistleblowing obligation with wording similar to that of the code of the National Society of Professional Engineers (NSPE):

> Engineers shall at all times recognize that their primary obligation is to protect the safety, health, property and welfare of the public. If their professional judgment is over-ruled under circumstances where the safety, health, property or welfare of the public are endangered, they shall notify their employer or client and such other authority as may be appropriate.[17]

The phrase "as may be appropriate" is ambiguous. Does it mean "when morally justified," or does it mean "as necessary in order to protect the public safety, health, and welfare." The latter interpretation is the most common one, and it clearly implies whistleblowing in some situations, no matter what the personal cost.

I agree that the obligation to protect public safety is an essential professional obligation that deserves emphasis in engineers' work. It is not clear, however, that it is paramount in the technical philosophical sense of overriding all other professional obligations in all situations. In any case, I reject the general assumption that codified professional duties are all that are morally relevant in making whistleblowing decisions. It is quite true that professional considerations require setting aside personal interests in many situations. But it is also true that personal considerations have enormous and legitimate importance in professional life, such as in choosing careers and areas of specialization, choosing and changing jobs, and deciding how far to go in sacrificing family life in pursuing a job and a career.

Spouses have a right to participate in professional decisions such as those involving whistle-blowing.[18] At the very least, I would be worried about professionals who do not see the moral importance of consulting their spouses before deciding to engage in acts of whistleblowing that will seriously affect them and their children. I would be equally worried about critics who condemn engineers for failing to whistleblow without knowing anything about their personal situation.[19]

Where does all this leave us on the issue of engineers' obligations? It is clear there is a minimum standard which engineers must meet. They have strong obligations not to break the law and not to approve projects which are immoral according to standard practice. They also have a *prima facie* obligation to whistleblow in certain situations. Just how strong the whistleblowing responsibility is, all things considered, remains unclear—as long as there are inadequate legal protections.

What is clear is that whistleblowing responsibilities must be understood contextually, weighed against personal rights and responsibilities, and assessed in light of the public's responsibilities to protect whistleblowers. We must look at each situation. Sometimes the penalties for whistleblowing may not be as great as is usually the case, perhaps because some protective laws have been passed, and sometimes family responsibilities and rights to pursue a career may not be seriously affected. But our all-things-considered judgments about whistleblowing are not a matter of a general absolute principle that always overrides every other consideration.

Yes, the public has a right to be warned by whistleblowers of dangers—assuming the public is willing to bear its responsibility for passing laws protecting whistleblowers. In order to play their role in respecting that right, engineers should have a legally-backed *right of conscience* to take responsible action in safety matters beyond the corporate walls.[20] As legal protections are increased, as has begun to happen during the past decade,[21] then the

relative weight of personal life to professional duty changes. Engineers will be able to whistleblow more often without the kind of suffering to which they have been exposed, and thus the *prima facie* obligation to whistleblow will be less frequently overridden by personal responsibilities.

CHARACTER, INTEGRITY, AND PERSONAL IDEALS

Isn't there a danger that denying the existence of absolute, all-things-considered, principles for whistleblowers will further discourage whistleblowing in the public interest? After all, even if we grant my claims about the moral relevance of personal rights and responsibilities, there remains the general tendency for self-interest to unduly bias moral decisions. Until adequate legal protection is secured, won't this contextual approach result in fewer whistleblowers who act from a sense of responsibility? I think not.

If all-things-considered judgments about whistleblowing are not a matter of general rule, they are still a matter of good moral judgment. Good judgment takes into account rules whenever they provide helpful guidance, but essentially it is a product of good character—a character defined by virtues. Character is a further area in which personal aspects of morality bear on engineering ethics, and in the space remaining I want to comment on it.

Virtues are those desirable traits that reveal themselves in all aspects of personality—in attitudes, emotions, desires, and conduct. They are not private merit badges. (To view them as such is the egoistic distortion of self-righteousness.[22]) Instead, virtues are desirable ways of relating to other people, to communities, and to social practices such as engineering. Which virtues are most important for engineers to cultivate?

Here are some of the most significant virtues, sorted into three general categories.[23]

(1) *Virtues of self-direction* are those which enable us to guide our lives. They include the *intellectual virtues* which characterize technical expertise: mastery of one's discipline, ability to communicate, skills in reasoning, imagination, ability to discern dangers, a disposition to minimize risk, and humility (understood as a reasonable perspective on one's

abilities). They also include *integrity virtues* which promote coherence among one's attitudes, commitments, and conduct based on a core of moral concern. They include honesty, courage, conscientiousness, self-respect, and fidelity to promises and commitments—those in both personal and professional life. And *wisdom* is practical good judgment in making responsible decisions. This good moral judgment, grounded in the experience of concerned and accountable engineers, is essential in balancing the aspirations embedded in the next two sets of virtues.

(2) *Team-work virtues* include (a) loyalty: concern for the good of the organization for which one works; (b) collegiality: respect for one's colleagues and a commitment to work with them in shared projects; and (c) cooperativeness: the willingness to make reasonable compromises. Reasonable compromises can be integrity-preserving in that they enable us to meet our responsibilities to maintain relationships in circumstances where there is moral complexity and disagreement, factual uncertainty, and the need to maintain ongoing cooperative activities—exactly the circumstances of engineering practice.[24] Unreasonable compromises are compromising in the pejorative sense: they betray our moral principles and violate our integrity. Only good judgment, not general rules, enables engineers to draw a reasonable line between these two types of compromise.

(3) *Public-spirited virtues* are those aimed at the good of others, both clients and the general public affected by one's work. *Justice virtues* concern fair play. One is respect for persons: the disposition to respect people's rights and autonomy, in particular, the rights not to be injured in ways one does not consent to.

Public-spiritedness can be shown in different degrees, as can all the virtues. This helps us understand the sense of responsibility to protect the public that often motivates whistleblowers. Just as professional ethics has tended to ignore the moral relevance of personal life to professional responsibilities, it has tended to think of professional responsibilities solely in terms of *role responsibilities*—those minimal obligations which all practitioners take on when they enter a given profession. While role responsibilities are sufficiently important to deserve this emphasis, they are not the whole of professional ethics. There are also *ideals* which

evoke higher aspirations than the minimum responsibilities.[25] These ideals are important to understanding the committed conduct of whistleblowers.

Depth of commitment to the public good is a familiar theme in whistleblowers' accounts of their ordeals. The depth is manifested in how they connect their self-respect and personal integrity to their commitments to the good of others. Roger Boisjoly, for example, has said that if he had it all to do over again he would make the same decisions because otherwise he "couldn't live with any self respect."[26] Similarly, Frank Camps says he acted from a sense of personal integrity.[27]

Boisjoly, Camps, and whistleblowers like them also report that they acted from a sense of responsibility. In my view, they probably acted beyond the minimum standard that all engineers are required to meet, given the absence of protective laws and the severity of the personal suffering they had to undergo. Does it follow that they are simply confused about how much was required of them? J. O. Urmson once suggested that moral heroes who claim to be meeting their duties are either muddled in their thinking or excessively modest about their moral zealousness, which has carried them beyond the call of duty.[28]

Urmson, like most post-Kantian philosophers, assumed that obligations are universal, and hence that there could not be personal obligations that only certain individuals have. I hold a different view.[29] There is such a thing as voluntarily assuming a responsibility and doing so because of commitments to (valid) ideals, to a degree beyond what is required of everyone. Sometimes the commitment is shown in career choice and guided by religious ideals: think of Albert Schweitzer or Mother Teresa of Calcutta. Sometimes it is shown in professional life in an unusual degree of *pro bono publico* work. And sometimes it is shown in whistleblowing decisions.

According to this line of thought, whistleblowing done at enormous personal cost, motivated by moral concern for the public good, and exercising good moral judgment is both (a) supererogatory—beyond the general call of duty incumbent on everyone, and (b) appropriately motivated by a sense of responsibility. Such whistleblowers act from a sense that they *must* do what they are doing.[30] Failure to act would constitute a betrayal of the ideal to which they are committed, and also a betrayal of their integrity as a person committed to that ideal.

Here, then, is a further way in which personal life is relevant to professional life. Earlier I drew attention to the importance of personal rights and responsibilities, and to the unfair personal burdens when others involved in collective enterprises fail to meet their responsibilities. Equally important, we need to appreciate the role of personal integrity grounded in supererogatory commitments to ideals. The topic of being able to live with oneself should not be dismissed as a vagary of individual psychology. It concerns the ideals to which we commit ourselves, beyond the minimum standard incumbent on everyone. This appreciation of personal integrity and commitments to ideals is compatible with a primary emphasis on laws that make it possible for professionals to serve the public good without having to make heroic self-sacrifices.[31]

NOTES*

1. Paul Eddy, Elaine Potter, Bruce Page, *Destination Disaster* (New York: Quandrangle, 1976), p. 185.

2. Frank Camps, "Warning an Auto Company About an Unsafe Design," in Alan F. Westin (ed.), *Whistle-Blowing!* (New York: McGraw-Hill, 1981), pp. 119–129.

3. Roger M. Boisjoly, "The Challenger Disaster: Moral Responsibility and the Working Engineer," in Deborah G. Johnson (ed.), *Ethical Issues in Engineering* (Englewood Cliffs, NJ: Prentice Hall, 1991), pp. 6–14.

4. See, e.g., Myron P. Glazer and Penina Migdal Glazer, *The Whistleblowers* (New York: Basic Books, 1989).

5. Michael Davis, "Avoiding the Tragedy of Whistleblowing," *Business & Professional Ethics Journal* Vol. 8, No. 4 (Winter, 1989): 3–19. Davis also draws attention to the potentially negative aspects of laws, as does Sissela Bok in "Whistleblowing and Professional Responsibilities," in D. Callahan and S. Bok (eds.), *Ethics Teaching in Higher Education* (New York: Plenum), pp. 277–295. Those aspects, which include violating corporate privacy, undermining trust and collegiality, and lowering economic efficiency, are serious. But I am convinced that well-framed laws to protect whistleblowers can take them into account. The laws should protect only whistleblowing that meets the conditions for the *prima facie* obligation I state at the beginning of section 3.

6. Robert Nozick drew attention to the symbolic importance of government action in general when he recently abjured the libertarian position he once defended vigorously. *The Examined Life* (New York: Simon and Schuster, 1989), pp. 286–288.

7. The quotes are from Richard T. De George's most recent statement of his view in *Business Ethics*, 3d ed. (New York: Macmillan Publishing, 1990), pp. 208–212. They parallel his view as first stated in "Ethical Responsibilities of Engineers in Large Organizations," *Business & Professional Ethics Journal* Vol. 1, No. 1 (Fall 1981): 1–14. As an example of a far higher demand on engineers see Kenneth D. Alpern, "Moral Responsibility for Engineers," *Business & Professional Ethics Journal* Vol. 2, No. 2 (Winter 1983): 39–47.

8. Gene G. James, "Whistle Blowing: Its Moral Justification," in W. Michael Hoffman and Jennifer Mills Moore (eds.), *Business Ethics,* 2d ed. (New York: McGraw-Hill, 1990), pp. 332–344.

9. David Theo Goldberg, "Tuning in to Whistle Blowing," *Business & Professional Ethics Journal* Vol. 7, No. 2 (Summer, 1988): 85–94.

10. As his reason for conditions (4) and (5), De George cites the fate of whistleblowers who put themselves at great risk: "If there is little likelihood of his success, there is no moral obligation for the engineer to go public. For the harm he or she personally incurs is not offset by the good such action achieves." ("Ethical Responsibilities of Engineers in Large Organizations," p. 7.) Like myself, then, he sees the personal suffering of whistleblowers as morally relevant to understanding professional responsibilities, even though, as I go on to argue, he invokes that relevance in the wrong way.

11. De George, *Business Ethics*, p. 214.

12. See especially Bernard Williams, "A Critique of Utilitarianism" in *Utilitarianism for and Against* (Cambridge: Cambridge University Press, 1973) and "Persons, Character, and Morality," in *Moral Luck* (New York: Cambridge University Press, 1981). For samples of more recent discussions see the special edition of *Ethics* 101 (July 1991), devoted to "Impartiality and Ethical Theory."

13. Cf. John Arthur, "Rights and Duty to Bring Aid," in William Aiken and Hugh La Follette (eds.), *World Hunger and Moral Obligation* (Englewood Cliffs, NJ: Prentice-Hall, 1977).

14. Alpern, "Moral Responsibilities for Engineers," p. 39.

15. James, "Whistle Blowing: Its Moral Justification," pp. 334–335.

16. See Martin and Schinzinger, *Ethics in Engineering*, chapter 3. The emphasis on engineers adopting a wide view of their activities does not imply that they are culpable for all the moral failures of colleagues and managers.

17. National Society of Professional Engineers, Code of Ethics.

18. Cf. Thomas M. Devine and Donald G. Aplin, "Whistle-blower Protection—The Gap Between the Law and Reality," *Howard Law Journal* 31 (1988), p. 236.

19. I am glad that the NSPE and other professional codes say what they do in support of responsible whistleblowing, as long as it is understood that professional codes only state professional, not personal and all-things-considered obligations. Codes provide a backing for morally concerned engineers, and they make available to engineers the moral support of an entire profession. At the same time, professional societies need to do far more than most of them have done to support the efforts of conscientious whistleblowers. Beyond moral and political support, and beyond recognition awards, they need to provide economic support, in the form of legal funds and job-placement.

20. I defend this right in "Rights of Conscience Inside the Technological Corporation," *Conceptus-Studien, 4: Wissen and Gewissen* (Vienna: VWGO, 1986): 179–191.

21. Alan F. Westin offers helpful suggestions about laws protecting whistleblowers in *Whistle-Blowing!* For a recent overview of the still fragmented and insufficient legal protection of whistleblowers see Rosemary Chalk, "Making the World Safe for Whistle-Blowers," *Technology Review* 91 (January 1988): 48–57; and James C. Petersen and Dan Farrell, *Whistleblowing: Ethical and Legal Issues in Expressing Dissent* (Dubuque, Iowa: Kendall/Hunt, 1986).

22. Cf. Edmund L. Pincoffs, *Quandaries and Virtues* (Lawrence, KS: University Press of Kansas, 1986), pp. 112–114.

23. Important discussions of the role of virtues in professional ethics include: John Kultgen, *Ethics and Professionalism* (Philadelphia: University of Pennsylvania Press, 1988); Albert Fiores (ed.), *Professional Ideals* (Belmont, CA: Wadsworth, 1988); and Michael D. Bayles, *Professional Ethics*, 2d edition (Belmont, CA: Wadsworth, 1989). John Kekes insightfully discusses the virtues of self-direction in *The Examined Life* (Lewisburg: Bucknell University Press, 1988).

24. Martin Benjamin, *Splitting the Difference* (Lawrence, KS: University Press of Kansas), 1990.

25. On the distinction between moral rules and ideals see Bernard Gert, *Morality* (New York: Oxford University Press, 1988), pp. 160–178.

26. Roger Boisjoly, ibid., p. 14.

27. Frank Camps, ibid., p. 128.

28. J. O. Urmson, "Saints and Heroes," in A. I. Melden (ed.), *Essays in Moral Philosophy* (Seattle: University of Washington Press, 1958), pp. 198–216.

29. Cf. A. I. Melden, "Saints and Supererogation," in *Philosophy and Life: Essays on John Wisdom* (The Hague: Martinus Nijhoff, 1984), pp. 61–81.

30. Harry Frankfurt insightfully discusses this felt "must" as a sign of deep caring and commitment in *The Importance of What We Care About* (New York: Cambridge University Press, 1988), pp. 86–88.

31. An earlier version of this paper was read in a lecture series sponsored by the Committee on Ethics in Research at the University of California, Santa Barbara (January 1992). I am grateful for the helpful comments of Jacqueline Hynes and Larry Badash, and also for conversations with Roland Schinzinger on this topic. I am especially grateful for the comments I received from the editor of this journal.

WHAT IS REALLY UNETHICAL ABOUT INSIDER TRADING?

Jennifer Moore

"Insider trading," as the term is usually used, means the buying or selling of securities on the basis of material, non-public information. It is popularly believed to be unethical, and many, though not all, forms of it are illegal. Insider trading makes for exciting headlines, and stories of the unscrupulousness and unbridled greed of the traders abound. As it is reported in the media—complete with details of clandestine meetings, numbered Swiss bank accounts and thousands of dollars of profits carried away in plastic bags—insider trading has all the trappings of a very shady business indeed.[1] For many, insider trading has become the primary symbol of a widespread ethical rot on Wall Street and in the business community as a whole.[2]

For a practice that has come to epitomize unethical business behavior, insider trading has received surprisingly little ethical analysis. The best ethical assessments of insider trading have come from legal scholars who argue against the practice. But their arguments rest on notions such as fairness or ownership of information that require much more examination than they are usually given.[3]

From *Journal of Business Ethics* 9 (1990), 171–182. © 1990 Kluwer Academic Publishers. Reprinted by permission of Kluwer Academic Publishers.

Proponents of insider trading are quick to dismiss these arguments as superficial, but offer very little ethical insight of their own. Arguing almost solely on grounds of economic efficiency, they generally gloss over the ethical arguments or dismiss them entirely.[4] Ironically, their refusal to address the ethical arguments on their merits merely strengthens the impression that insider trading is unethical. Readers are left with the sense that while it might reduce efficiency, the prohibition against insider trading rests on firm *ethical* grounds. But can we assume this? Not, I think, without a good deal more examination.

This paper is divided into two parts. In the first part, I examine critically the principal ethical arguments against insider trading. The arguments fall into three main classes: arguments based on fairness, arguments based on property rights in information, and arguments based on harm to ordinary investors or the market as a whole. Each of these arguments, I contend, has some serious deficiencies. No one of them by itself provides a sufficient reason for outlawing insider trading. This does not mean, however, that there are no reasons for prohibiting the practice. Once we have cleared away the inadequate arguments, other, more cogent reasons for outlawing insider trading come to light. In the second part of the paper, I set out what I take to be the real reasons for laws against insider trading.

The term "insider trading" needs some preliminary clarification. Both the SEC and the courts have strongly resisted pressure to define the notion clearly. In 1961, the SEC stated that corporate insiders—such as officers or directors —in possession of material, non-public information were required to disclose that information or to refrain from trading.[5] But this "disclose or refrain" rule has since been extended to persons other than corporate insiders. People who get information from insiders ("tippees") and those who become "temporary insiders" in the course of some work they perform for the company, can acquire the duty of insiders in some cases.[6] Financial printers and newspaper columnists, not "insiders" in the technical sense, have also been found guilty of insider trading.[7] Increasingly, the term "insider" has come to refer to the kind of information a person possesses rather than to the status of the person who trades on that information. My use of the term will reflect this ambiguity. In this paper, an "insider trader" is someone who trades in material, non-public information—not necessarily a corporate insider.

I. ETHICAL ARGUMENTS AGAINST INSIDER TRADING

Fairness

Probably the most common reason given for thinking that insider trading is unethical is that it is "unfair." For proponents of the fairness argument, the key feature of insider trading is the disparity of information between the two parties to the transaction. Trading should take place on a "level playing field," they argue, and disparities in information tilt the field toward one player and away from the other. There are two versions of the fairness argument: the first argues that insider trading is unfair because the two parties do not have *equal* information; the second argues that insider trading is unfair because the two parties do not have equal *access* to information. Let us look at the two versions one at a time.

According to the equal information argument, insider trading is unfair because one party to the transaction lacks information the other party has, and is thus at a disadvantage. Although this is a very strict notion of fairness, it has its proponents[8] and hints of this view appear in some of the judicial opinions.[9] One proponent of the equal information argument is Saul Levmore, who claims that "fairness is achieved when insiders and outsiders are in equal positions. That is, a system is fair if we would not expect one group to envy the position of the other." As thus defined, Levmore claims, fairness "reflects the 'golden rule' of impersonal behavior—treating others as we would ourselves."[10] If Levmore is correct, then not just insider trading, but *all* transactions in which there is a disparity of information are unfair, and thus unethical. But this claim seems overly broad. An example will help to illustrate some of the problems with it.

Suppose I am touring Vermont and come across an antique blanket chest in the barn of a farmer, a chest I know will bring $2,500 back in the city. I offer to buy it for $75, and the farmer agrees. If he had known how much I could get for it back home, he probably would have asked a higher price—but I failed to disclose this information. I have profited from an informational advantage. Have I been unethical? My suspicion is that most people would say I have not. While knowing how much I could sell the chest for in the city is in the interest of the farmer, I am not morally obligated to reveal it. I am not morally obligated to tell those who deal with me *everything* that it would be in their interest to know.

U.S. common law supports this intuition. Legally, people are obligated not to lie or to misrepresent a product they are selling or buying. But they are not required to reveal everything it is in the other party's interest to know.[11] One might argue that this is simply an area in which the law falls short of ethical standards. But there is substantial ethical support for the law on these matters as well. There does seem to be a real difference between lying or misrepresentation on the one hand, and simple failure to disclose information on the other, even though the line between the two is sometimes hard to draw.[12] Lying and misrepresentation are forms of deception, and deception is a subtle form of coercion. When I successfully deceive someone, I cause him to do something that does not represent his true will—something he did not intend to do and would not have done if he had known the truth. Simply not revealing information (usually) does not involve this kind of coercion.

In general, it is only when I owe a *duty* to the other party that I am legally required to reveal all information that is in his interest. In such a situation, the other party believes that I am looking out for his interests, and I deceive him if I do not do so. Failure to disclose is deceptive in this instance because of the relationship of trust and dependence between the parties. But this suggests that trading on inside information is wrong, *not* because it violates a general notion of fairness, but because a breach of fiduciary duty is involved. Cases of insider trading in which no fiduciary duty of this kind is breached would not be unethical.

Significantly, the Supreme Court has taken precisely this position: insider trading is wrong because, and when, it involves the violation of a fiduciary duty to the other parties to the transaction.[13] The Court has consistently refused to recognize the general duty to *all* investors that is argued for by proponents of the fairness argument. This is particularly clear in *Chiarella v. US,* a decision overturning the conviction of a financial printer for trading on inside information:

At common law, misrepresentation made for the purpose of inducing reliance upon the false statement is fraudulent. But one who fails to disclose material information prior to the consummation of a transaction commits fraud *only when he is under a duty to do so.* And the duty to disclose arises when one party has information "that the other party is entitled to know because of a fiduciary or other similar relation of trust and confidence between them." ... The element required to make silence fraudulent—a duty to disclose—is absent in this case....

We cannot affirm petitioner's conviction without recognizing a general duty between all participants in market transactions to forgo actions based on material, nonpublic information. Formulation of such a broad duty, which departs radically from the established doctrine that duty arises from a specific relationship between two parties . . . should not be undertaken absent some explicit evidence of congressional intent....[14]

The court reiterated that "there is no *general* duty to disclose before trading on material nonpublic information" in *Dirks v. SEC.*[15] It is worth noting that if this reasoning is correct, the legal and ethical status of insider trading depends on the understanding between the fiduciary and the party he represents. Insider trading would not be a violation of fiduciary duty, and thus would not be unethical, unless (1) it were clearly contrary to the interests of the other party or (2) the other party had demanded or been led to expect disclosure. We shall return to this point below.

There is a second ethical reason for not requiring all people with informational advantages to disclose them to others: there may be relevant differences between the parties to the transaction that make the disparity of information "fair." Perhaps I invested considerable time, effort and money in learning about antiques. If this is true, I might deserve to reap the benefits of these efforts. We frequently think it is fair for people to benefit from informational advantages of their own making; this is an important justification for patent law and the protection of trade secrets. "Fairness" is often defined as "treating equals equally." But equals in what respect? Unless we know that the two parties to a transaction *are* equal in the relevant way, it is difficult to say that an informational advantage held by one of them is "unfair."

My point here is different from the frequently heard claim that people should be allowed to profit from informational advantages because this results in a more efficient use of information. This latter claim, while important, does not really address the fairness issue. What I am arguing is that the notion of fairness offered by proponents of the equal information argument is itself incomplete. We cannot make the notion of fairness work for us unless we supply guidelines explaining who are to count as "equals" in different contexts. If we try, we are likely to end up with results that seem intuitively *unfair*.

For these reasons, the "equal information" version of the fairness argument seems to me to fail. However, it could be argued that insider trading is unfair because the insider has information that is not *accessible* to the ordinary investor. For proponents of this second type of fairness argument, it is not the insider's information advantage that counts, but the fact that this advantage is "unerodable," one that cannot be overcome by the hard work and ingenuity of the ordinary investor. No matter how hard the latter works, he is unable to acquire non-public information, because this information is protected by law.[16]

This type of fairness argument seems more promising, since it allows people to profit from informational advantages of their own making, but not from advantages that are built into the system. Proponents of this "equal access" argument would probably find my deal with the Vermont farmer unobjectionable, because information about antiques is not in principle unavailable to the farmer. The problem with the argument is that the notion of "equal access" is not very clear. What does it mean for two people to have equal access to information?

Suppose my pipes are leaking and I call a plumber to fix them. He charges me for the job, and benefits by the informational advantage he has over me. Most of us would not find this transaction unethical. True, I don't have "equal access" to the information needed to fix my pipes in any real sense, but I could have had this information had I chosen to become a plumber. The disparity of information in this case is simply something that is built into the fact that people choose to specialize

in different areas. But just as I could have chosen to become a plumber, I could have chosen to become a corporate insider with access to legally protected information. Access to information seems to be a relative, not an absolute, matter. As Judge Frank Easterbrook puts it:

> People do not have or lack "access" in some absolute sense. There are, instead, different costs of obtaining information. An outsider's costs are high; he might have to purchase the information from the firm. Managers have lower costs (the amount of salary foregone); brokers have relatively low costs (the value of the time they spent investigating).... The different costs of access are simply a function of the division of labor. A manager (or a physician) always knows more than a shareholder (or patient) in some respects, but unless there is something unethical about the division of labor, the difference is not unfair.[17]

One might argue that I have easier access to a plumber's information than I do to an insider trader's, since there are lots of plumbers from whom I can buy the information I seek.[18] The fact that insiders have a strong incentive to keep their information to themselves is a serious objection to insider trading. But if insider trading were made legal, insiders could profit not only from trading on their information, but also on selling it to willing buyers. Proponents of the practice argue that a brisk market in information would soon develop—indeed, it might be argued that such a market already exists, though in illegal and clandestine form.[19]

The objections offered above do not show conclusively that *no* fairness argument against insider trading can be constructed. But they do suggest that a good deal more spadework is necessary to construct one. Proponents of the fairness argument need to show how the informational advantages of insider traders over ordinary investors are different in kind from the informational advantages of plumbers over the rest of us—or, alternatively, why the informational advantages of plumbers are unfair. I have not yet seen such an argument, and I suspect that designing one may require a significant overhaul of our traditional ideas about fairness. As it stands, the effectiveness of the fairness argument seems restricted to situations in which the insider trader owes a duty to the person with whom he is trading—and as we will see below, even here it is not conclusive because much depends on how that duty is defined.

The most interesting thing about the fairness argument is not that it provides a compelling reason to outlaw insider trading, but that it leads to issues we cannot settle on the basis of an abstract concept of fairness alone. The claim that parties to a transaction should have equal information, or equal access to information, inevitably raises questions about how informational advantages are (or should be) acquired, and when people are entitled to use them for profit. Again, this understanding of the limits of the fairness argument is reflected in common law. If insider trading is wrong primarily because it is unfair, then it should be wrong no matter *who* engages in it. It should make no difference whether I am a corporate insider, a financial printer, or a little old lady who heard a takeover rumor on the Hudson River Line. But it does make a difference to the courts. I think this is because the crucial questions concerning insider trading are not about fairness, but about how inside information is acquired and what entitles people to make use of it. These are questions central to our second class of arguments against insider trading, those based on the notion of property rights in information.

Property Rights in Information

As economists and legal scholars have recognized, information is a valuable thing, and it is possible to view it as a type of property. We already treat certain types of information as property: trade secrets, inventions, and so on—and protect them by law. Proponents of the property rights argument claim that material, non-public information is also a kind of property, and that insider trading is wrong because it involves a violation of property rights.

If inside information is a kind of property, whose property is it? How does information come to belong to one person rather than another? This is a very complex question, because information differs in many ways from other, more tangible sorts of property. But one influential argument is that information belongs to the people who discover, originate or "create" it. As Bill Shaw put it in a recent article, "the originator of the information (the individual or the corporation that spent

hard-earned bucks producing it) owns and controls this asset just as it does other proprietary goods."[20] Thus if a firm agrees to a deal, invents a new product, or discovers new natural resources, it has a property right in that information and is entitled to exclusive use of it for its own profit.

It is important to note that it is the firm itself (and/or its shareholders), and not the individual employees of the firm, who have property rights in the information. To be sure, it is always certain individuals in the firm who put together the deal, invent the product, or discover the resources. But they are able to do this only because they are backed by the power and authority of the firm. The employees of the firm—managers, officers, directors—are not entitled to the information any more than they are entitled to corporate trade secrets or patents on products that they develop for the firm.[21] It is the firm that makes it possible to create the information and that makes the information valuable once it has been created. As Victor Brudney puts it,

> The insiders have acquired the information at the expense of the enterprise, and for the purpose of conducting the business for the collective good of all the stockholders, entirely apart from personal benefits from trading in its securities. There is no reason for them to be entitled to trade for their own benefit on the basis of such information....[22]

If this analysis is correct, then it suggests that insider trading is wrong because it is a form of theft. It is not exactly like theft, because the person who uses inside information does not deprive the company of the use of the information. But he does deprive the company of the *sole* use of the information, which is itself an asset. The insider trader "misappropriates," as the law puts it, information that belongs to the company and uses it in a way in which it was not intended—for personal profit. It is not surprising that this "misappropriation theory" has begun to take hold in the courts, and has become one of the predominant rationales in prosecuting insider trading cases. In *U.S. v. Newman,* a case involving investment bankers and securities traders, for example, the court stated:

> In *US v. Chiarella,* Chief Justice Burger ... said that the defendant "misappropriated"—stole to

put it bluntly—"valuable nonpublic information entrusted to him in the utmost confidence." That characterization aptly describes the conduct of the connivers in the instant case.... By sullying the reputations of [their] employers as safe repositories of client confidences, appellee and his cohorts defrauded those employers as surely as if they took their money.[23]

The misappropriation theory also played a major role in the prosecution of R. Foster Winans, a *Wall Street Journal* reporter who traded on and leaked to others the contents of his "Heard in the Street" column.[24]

This theory is quite persuasive, as far as it goes. But it is not enough to show that insider trading is always unethical or that it should be illegal. If insider information is really the property of the firm that produces it, then using that property is wrong *only when the firm prohibits it.* If the firm does not prohibit insider trading, it seems perfectly acceptable.[25] Most companies do in fact forbid insider trading. But it is not clear whether they do so because they don't want their employees using corporate property for profit or simply because it is illegal. Proponents of insider trading point out that most corporations did not prohibit insider trading until recently, when it became a prime concern of enforcement agencies.[26]

If insider trading is primarily a problem of property rights in information, it might be argued, then it is immoral, and should be illegal, only when the company withholds permission to trade on inside information. Under the property rights theory, insider trading becomes a matter of *contract* between the company, its shareholders and its employees. If the employment contract forbids an employee from using the company's information, then it is unethical (and illegal) to do so.

A crucial factor here would be the shareholders' agreement to allow insider information. Shareholders may not wish to allow trading on inside information because they may wish the employees of the company to be devoted simply to advancing shareholder interests. We will return to this point below. But if shareholders did allow it, it would seem to be permissible. Still others argue that shareholders would not need to "agree" in any way other than to be told this information when they were buying the stock. If they did not want to hold stock in a company whose employees were permitted to trade in inside information, they would not buy that stock. Hence they could be said to have "agreed."

Manne and other proponents of insider trading have suggested a number of reasons why "shareholders would voluntarily enter into contractual arrangements with insiders giving them property rights in valuable information."[27] Their principal argument is that permitting insider trading would serve as an incentive to create more information—put together more deals, invent more new products, or make more discoveries. Such an incentive, they argue, would create more profit for shareholders in the long run. Assigning employees the right to trade on inside information could take the place of more traditional (and expensive) elements in the employee's compensation package. Rather than giving out end of the year bonuses, for example, firms could allow employees to put together their own bonuses by cashing in on inside information, thus saving the company money. In addition, proponents argue, insider trading would improve the efficiency of the market. We will return to these claims below.

If inside information really is a form of corporate property, firms may assign employees the right to trade on it if they choose to do so. The only reason for not permitting firms to allow employees to trade on their information would be that doing so causes harm to other investors or to society at large. Although our society values property rights very highly, they are not absolute. We do not hesitate to restrict property rights if their exercise causes significant harm to others. The permissibility of insider trading, then, ultimately seems to depend on whether the practice is harmful.

Harm

There are two principal harm-based arguments against insider trading. The first claims that the practice is harmful to ordinary investors who engage in trades with insiders; the second claims that insider trading erodes investors' confidence in the market, causing them to pull out of the market and harming the market as a whole. I will address the two arguments in turn.

Although proponents of insider trading often refer to it as a "victimless crime," implying that no one is harmed by it, it is not difficult to think of examples of transactions with insiders in which ordinary investors are made worse off. Suppose I have placed an order with my broker to sell my shares in Megalith Co., currently trading at $50 a share, at $60 or above. An insider knows that Behemoth Inc. is going to announce a tender offer for Megalith shares in two days, and has begun to buy large amounts of stock in anticipation of the gains. Because of his market activity, Megalith stock rises to $65 a share and my order is triggered. If he had refrained from trading, the price would have risen steeply two days later, and I would have been able to sell my shares for $80. Because the insider traded, I failed to realize the gains that I otherwise would have made.

But there are other examples of transactions in which ordinary investors *benefit* from insider trading. Suppose I tell my broker to sell my shares in Acme Corp., currently trading at $45, if the price drops to $40 or lower. An insider knows of an enormous class action suit to be brought against Acme in two days. He sells his shares, lowering the price to $38 and triggering my sale. When the suit is made public two days later, the share price plunges to $25. If the insider had abstained from trading, I would have lost far more than I did. Here, the insider has protected me from loss.

Not all investors buy or sell through such "trigger" orders. Many of them make their decisions by watching the movement of the stock. The rise in share price might have indicated to an owner of Megalith that a merger was imminent, and she might have held on to her shares for this reason. Similarly, the downward movement of Acme stock caused by the insider might have suggested to an owner that it was time to sell. Proponents of insider trading argue that large trades by insiders move the price of shares closer to their "real" value, that is, the value that reflects all the relevant information about the stock. This makes the market more efficient and provides a valuable service to all investors.[28]

The truth about an ordinary investor's gains and losses from trading with insiders seems to be not that insider trading is never harmful, but that it is not systematically or consistently harmful. Insider trading is not a "victimless crime," as its proponents claim, but it is often difficult to tell exactly who the victims are and to what extent

they have been victimized. The stipulation of the law to "disclose *or* abstain" from trading makes determining victims even more complex. While some investors are harmed by the insider's trade, to others the insider's actions make no difference at all; what harms them is simply *not having complete information* about the stock in question. Forbidding insider trading will not prevent these harms. Investors who neither buy nor sell, or who buy or sell for reasons independent of share price, fall into this category.

Permitting insider trading would undoubtedly make the securities market *riskier* for ordinary investors. Even proponents of the practice seem to agree with this claim. But if insider trading were permitted openly, they argue, investors would compensate for the extra riskiness by demanding a discount in share price:

> In modern finance theory, shareholders are seen as investors seeking a return proportionate with that degree of systematic or market-related risk which they have chosen to incur.... [The individual investor] is "protected" by the price established by the market mechanism, not by his personal bargaining power or position.... To return to the gambling analogy, if I know you are using percentage dice, I won't play without an appropriate adjustment of the odds; the game is, after all, voluntary.[29]

If insider trading were permitted, in short, we could expect a general drop in share prices, but no net harm to investors would result. Moreover, improved efficiency would result in a bigger pie for everyone. These are empirical claims, and I am not equipped to determine if they are true. If they are, however, they would defuse one of the most important objections to insider trading, and provide a powerful argument for leaving the control of inside information up to individual corporations.

The second harm-based argument claims that permitting insider trading would cause ordinary investors to lose confidence in the market and cease to invest there, thus harming the market as a whole. As former SEC Chairman John Shad puts it, "if people get the impression that they're playing against a marked deck, they're simply not going to be willing to invest."[30] Since capital markets play a crucial role in allocating resources in our economy, this objection is a very serious one.

The weakness of the argument is that it turns almost exclusively on the *feelings* or *perceptions* of ordinary investors, and does not address the question of whether these perceptions are justified. If permitting insider trading really does harm ordinary investors, then this "loss of confidence" argument becomes a compelling reason for outlawing insider trading. But if, as many claim, the practice does not harm ordinary investors, then the sensible course of action is to educate the investors, not to outlaw insider trading. It is irrational to cater to the feelings of ordinary investors if those feelings are not justified. We ought not to outlaw perfectly permissible actions just because some people feel (unjustifiably) disadvantaged by them. More research is needed to determine the actual impact of insider trading on the ordinary investor.[31]

II. IS THERE ANYTHING WRONG WITH INSIDER TRADING?

My contention has been that the principal ethical arguments against insider trading do not, by themselves, suffice to show that the practice is unethical and should be illegal. The strongest arguments are those that turn on the notion of a fiduciary duty to act in the interest of shareholders, or on the idea of inside information as company "property." But in both arguments, the impermissibility of insider trading depends on a contractual understanding among the company, its shareholders and its employees. In both cases, a modification of this understanding could change the moral status of insider trading.

Does this mean that there is nothing wrong with insider trading? No. If insider trading is unethical, it is so *in the context* of the relationship among the firm, its shareholders and its employees. It is possible to change this context in a way that makes the practice permissible. But *should* the context be changed? I will argue that it should not. Because it threatens the fiduciary relationship that is central to business management, I believe, permitting insider trading is in the interest neither of the firm, its shareholders, nor society at large.

Fiduciary relationships are relationships of trust and dependence in which one party acts in the interest of another. They appear in many contexts, but are absolutely essential to conducting business in a complex society. Fiduciary relationships allow parties with different resources, skills and information to cooperate in productive activity. Shareholders who wish to invest in a business, for example, but who cannot or do not wish to run it themselves, hire others to manage it for them. Managers, directors, and to some extent, other employees, become fiduciaries for the firms they manage and for the shareholders of those firms.

The fiduciary relationship is one of moral and legal obligation. Fiduciaries, that is, are bound to act in the interests of those who depend on them even if these interests do not coincide with their own. Typically, however, fiduciary relationships are constructed as far as possible so that the interests of the fiduciaries and the parties for whom they act *do* coincide. Where the interests of the two parties compete or conflict, the fiduciary relationship is threatened. In corporations, the attempt to discourage divergences of interest is exemplified in rules against bribery, usurping corporate opportunities, and so forth. In the past few years, an entire discipline, "agency theory," has developed to deal with such questions. Agency theorists seek ways to align the interests of agents or fiduciaries with the interests of those on behalf of whom they act.

Significantly, proponents of insider trading do not dispute the importance of the fiduciary relationship. Rather, they argue that permitting insider trading would *increase* the likelihood that employees will act in the interest of shareholders and their firms.[32] We have already touched on the main argument for this claim. Manne and others contend that assigning employees the right to trade on inside information would provide a powerful incentive for creative and entrepreneurial activity. It would encourage new inventions, creative deals, and efficient new management practices, thus increasing the profits, strength, and overall competitiveness of the firm. Manne goes so far as to argue that permission to trade on insider information is the only appropriate way to compensate entrepreneurial activity, and warns: "[I]f no way to reward the entrepreneur within a corporation exists, he will tend to disappear from the corporate scene."[33] The entrepreneur makes an invaluable contribution to the firm and its shareholders, and his disappearance would no doubt cause serious harm.

If permitting insider trading is to work in the way proponents suggest, however, there must be a direct and consistent link between the profits reaped by insider traders and the performance that benefits the firm. It is not at all clear that this is the case—indeed, there is evidence that the opposite is true. There appear to be many ways to profit from inside information that do not benefit the firm at all. I mention four possibilities below. Two of these (2 and 3) are simply ways in which insider traders can profit without benefiting the firm, suggesting that permitting insider trading is a poor incentive for performance and fails firmly to link the interests of managers, directors and employees to those of the corporation as a whole. The others (1 and 4) are actually harmful to the corporation, setting up conflicts of interest and actively undermining the fiduciary relationship.[34]

1. Proponents of insider trading tend to speak as if all information were positive. "Information," in the proponents' lexicon, always concerns a creative new deal, a new, efficient way of conducting business, or a new product. If this were true, allowing trades on inside information might provide an incentive to work ever harder for the good of the company. But information can also concern *bad* news—a large lawsuit, an unsafe or poor quality product, or lower-than-expected performance. Such negative information can be just as valuable to the insider trader as positive information. If the freedom to trade on positive information encourages acts that are beneficial to the firm, then by the same reasoning the freedom to trade on negative information would encourage harmful acts. At the very least, permitting employees to profit from harms to the company decreases the incentive to avoid such harms. Permission to trade on negative inside information gives rise to inevitable conflicts of interest. Proponents of insider trading have not satisfactorily answered this objection.[35]

2. Proponents of insider trading also assume that the easiest way to profit on inside information is to "create" it. But it is not at all clear that this is true. Putting together a deal, inventing a new product, and other productive activities that add value to the firm usually require a significant investment of time and energy. For the well-placed employee, it would be far easier to start a rumor that the company has a new product or is about to announce a deal

than to sit down and produce either one—and it would be just as profitable for the employee. If permitting insider trading provides an incentive for the productive "creation" of information, it seems to provide an even greater incentive for the non-productive "invention" of information, or stock manipulation. The invention of information is in the interest neither of the firm nor of society at large.

3. Even if negative or false information did not pose problems, the incentive argument for insider trading overlooks the difficulties posed by "free riders"—those who do not actually contribute to the creation of the information, but who are nevertheless aware of it and can profit by trading on it. It is a commonplace of economic theory that if persons can benefit from a good without paying for it, they will generally do so. If there is no way to exclude those who do not "pay" from enjoying a benefit, no one will have an incentive to pay for it, there will be no incentive to produce it, and the good will not be supplied. In the case of insider trading, an employee's contribution to the creation of positive information constitutes the "payment." Unless those who do not contribute can be excluded from trading on it, there will be no incentive to produce the desired information; it will not get created at all.

4. Finally, allowing trading on inside information would tend to deflect employees' attention from the day-to-day business of running the company and focus it on major changes, positive or negative, that lead to large insider trading profits. This might not be true if one could profit by inside information about the day-to-day efficiency of the operation, a continuous tradition of product quality, or a consistently lean operating budget. But these things do not generate the kind of information on which insider traders can reap large profits. Insider profits come from dramatic changes, from "news"—not from steady, long-term performance. If the firm and its shareholders have a genuine interest in such performance, then permitting insider trading creates a conflict of interest for insiders. The ability to trade on inside information is also likely to influence the types of information officers announce to the public, and the timing of such announcements,

making it less likely that the information and its timing is optimal for the firm. And the problems of false or negative information remain.[36]

If the arguments given above are correct, permitting insider trading does not increase the likelihood that insiders will act in the interest of the firm and its shareholders. In some cases, it actually causes conflicts of interest, undermining the fiduciary relationship essential to managing the corporation. This claim, in turn, gives corporations good reason to prohibit the practice. But insider trading remains primarily a private matter among corporations, shareholders, and employees. It is appropriate to ask why, given this fact about insider trading, the practice should be *illegal*. If it is primarily corporate and shareholder interests that are threatened by insider trading, why not let corporations themselves bear the burden of enforcement? Why involve the SEC? There are two possible reasons for continuing to support laws against insider trading. The first is that even if they wish to prohibit insider trading, individual corporations do not have the resources to do so effectively. The second is that society itself has a stake in the fiduciary relationship.

Proponents of insider trading frequently point out that until 1961, when the SEC began to prosecute insider traders, few firms took steps to prevent the practice.[37] They argue that this fact indicates that insider trading is not truly harmful to corporations; if it were, corporations would have prohibited it long ago. But there is another plausible reason for corporations' failure to outlaw insider trading: they did not have the resources to do so, and did not wish to waste resources in the attempt to achieve an impossible task.[38] There is strong evidence that the second explanation is the correct one. Preventing insider trading requires continuous and extensive monitoring of transactions and the ability to compel disclosure, and privately imposed penalties do not seem sufficient to discourage insider trading.[39] The SEC is not hampered by these limitations. Moreover, suggests Frank Easterbrook, if even a few companies allow insider trading, this could make it difficult for other companies to prohibit it. Firms that did not permit insider trading would find themselves at a competitive disadvantage, at the mercy of "free riders" who announce to the public that they prohibit insider trading but incur none of the enforcement costs.[40]

Outlawing the practice might be worth doing simply because it enables corporations to do what is in all of their interests anyway—prohibit trading on inside information.

Finally, the claim that the fiduciary relationship is purely a "private" matter is misleading. The erosion of fiduciary duty caused by permitting insider trading has social costs as well as costs to the corporation and its shareholders. We have already noted a few of these. Frequent incidents of stock manipulation would cause a serious crisis in the market, reducing both its stability and efficiency. An increase in the circulation of false information would cause a general decline in the reliability of information and a corresponding decrease in investor trust. This would make the market less, not more efficient (as proponents of the practice claim). Deflecting interests away from the task of day-to-day management and toward the manipulation of information could also have serious negative social consequences. American business has already sustained much criticism for its failure to keep its mind on producing goods and services, and for its pursuit of "paper profits."

The notion of the fiduciary duty owed by managers and other employees to the firm and its shareholders has a long and venerable history in our society. Nearly all of our important activities require some sort of cooperation, trust, or reliance on others, and the ability of one person to act in the interest of another—as a fiduciary—is central to this cooperation. The role of managers as fiduciaries for firms and shareholders is grounded in the property rights of shareholders. They are the owners of the firm, and bear the residual risks, and hence have a right to have it managed in their interest. The fiduciary relationship also contributes to efficiency, since it encourages those who are willing to take risks to place their resources in the hands of those who have the expertise to maximize their usefulness. While this "shareholder theory" of the firm has often been challenged in recent years, this has been primarily by people who argue that the fiduciary concept should be widened to include other "stakeholders" in the firm.[41] I have heard no one argue that the notion of managers' fiduciary duties should be eliminated entirely, and that managers should begin working primarily for themselves.

III. CONCLUSION

I have argued that the real reason for prohibiting insider trading is that it erodes the fiduciary relationship that lies at the heart of our business organizations. The more frequently heard moral arguments based on fairness, property rights in information, and harm to ordinary investors, are not compelling. Of these, the fairness arguments seem to me the least persuasive. The claim that a trader must reveal everything that it is in the interest of another party to know, seems to hold up only when the other is someone to whom he owes a fiduciary duty. But this is not really a "fairness" argument at all. Similarly, the "misappropriation" theory is only persuasive if we can offer reasons for corporations not to assign the right to trade on inside information to their employees. I have found these in the fact that permitting insider trading threatens the fiduciary relationship. I do believe that lifting the ban against insider trading would cause harms to shareholders, corporations, and society at large. But again, these harms stem primarily from the cracks in the fiduciary relationship caused by permitting insider trading, rather than from actual trades with insiders. Violation of fiduciary duty, in short, is at the center of insider trading offenses, and it is with good reason that the Supreme Court has kept the fiduciary relationship at the forefront of its deliberations on insider trading.

NOTES

1. See, for example, Douglas Frantz, *Levine & Co.* (Avon Books, NY, 1987).

2. This is certainly true of former SEC chair John Shad, one of the leaders of the crusade against insider trading, who recently donated millions of dollars to Harvard University to establish a program in business ethics. Also see Felix Rohatyn of the investment banking house Lazard Frères: "...[A] cancer has been spreading in our industry.... Too much money is coming together with too many young people who have little or no institutional memory or sense of tradition, and who are under enormous economic pressure to perform in the glare of Hollywood-like publicity. The combination makes for speculative excesses at best, illegality at worst. Insider trading is only one result." *The New York Review of Books*, March 12, 1987.

3. An important exception is Lawson. 'The Ethics of Insider Trading', 11 *Harvard Journal of Law and Public Policy* 727 (1988).

4. Henry Manne, for example, whose book *Insider Trading and the Stock Market* stimulated the modern controversy over insider trading, has nothing but contempt for ethical arguments. See *Insider Trading and the Law Professors*, 23 Vanderbilt Law Review 549 (1969): "Morals, someone once said, are a private luxury. Carried into the area of serious debate on public policy, moral arguments are frequently either a sham or a refuge for the intellectually bankrupt." Or see Jonathan R. Macey, *Ethics, Economics and Insider Trading: Ayn Rand Meets the Theory of the Firm,* 11 Harvard Journal of Law and Public Policy 787 (1988): "[I]n my view the attempt to critique insider using ethical philosophy—divorced from economic analysis—is something of a non-starter, because ethical theory does not have much to add to the work that has already been done by economists."

5. *In re Cady, Roberts,* 40 SEC 907 (1961).

6. On tippees, see *Dirks v. SEC,* 463 US 646 (1983) at 659; on 'temporary insiders', see *Dirks v. SEC*, 103 S. Ct. 3255 (1983) at 3261 n. 14, and *SEC v. Musella,* 578 F. Supp. 425.

7. See *Materia v. SEC,* 725 F. 2d 197, involving a financial printer and the Winans case, involving the author of the *Wall Street Journal's* 'Heard on the Street' column, *Carpenter v. US*, 56 LW 4007; *U.S. v. Winans*, 612 F. Supp. 827. It should be noted that the Supreme Court has not wholeheartedly endorsed these further extensions of the rule against insider trading.

8. See Kaplan, '*Wolf v. Weinstein:* Another Chapter on Insider Trading', 1963 *Supreme Court Review* 273. For numerous other references, see Brudney, 'Insiders, Outsiders and Informational Advantages Under the Federal Securities Laws', 93 *Harvard Law Review* 339, n. 63.

9. See *Mitchell v. Texas Gulf Sulphur Co.*, 446 F. 2d 90 (1968) at 101; *SEC v. Great American Industries*, 407 F. 2d, 453 (1968) at 462; *Birdman v. Electro-Catheter Corp.,* 352 F. Supp. 1271 (1973) at 1274.

10. Saul Levmore, 'Securities and Secrets: Insider Trading and the Law of Contracts', 68 *Virginia Law Review* 117.

11. See Anthony Kronman, 'Mistake, Disclosure, Information, and the Law of Contracts' 7 *Journal of Legal Studies* 1 (1978). The Restatement (Second) of Torts § 551 (2)e (Tent. Draft No. 11, 1965) gives an example which is a very similar example to the one above, involving a violin expert who buys a Stradivarius (worth $50,000) in a second-hand instrument shop for only $100.

12. It seems clear that sometimes failure to disclose can *be* a form of misrepresentation. Such could be the case, for example, when the seller makes a true statement about a product but fails to reveal a later change in circumstances

which makes the earlier statement false. Or if a buyer indicates that he has a false impression of the product, and the seller fails to correct the impression. A plausible argument against insider trading would be that failure to reveal the information to the other party to the transaction allows a false impression of this kind to continue, and thus constitutes form of deception. It is not clear to me, however, that insider trading is a situation of this kind.

13. An important question is whether trades involving the violation of *another kind* of fiduciary duty constitute a violation of 10b-5. I address this second type of violation below.

14. *Chiarella v. US,* 445 U.S. 222, at 227–228; 232–233. Italics mine.

15. 445 US at 233. Italics mine.

16. The equal access argument is perhaps best stated by Victor Brudney in his influential article, 'Insiders, Outsiders and Informational Advantages Under the Federal Securities Laws', 93 *Harvard Law Review* 322.

17. Easterbrook, *Insider Trading, Secret Agents, Evidentiary Privileges, and the Production of Information,* 1981 Supreme Court Review 350.

18. Robert Frederick brought this point to my attention.

19. Manne, *Insider Trading and the Stock Market* (Free Press, New York, 1966), p. 75.

20. Bill Shaw, 'Should Insider Trading Be Outside the Law', *Business and Society Review* 66, p. 34. See also Macey, 'From Fairness to Contract: The New New Direction of the Rules Against Insider Trading', 13 *Hofstra Law Review* 9 (1984).

21. Easterbrook points out the striking similarity between insider trading cases and cases involving trade secrets, and cites *Perrin v. US,* 444 US 37 (1979), in which the court held that it was a federal crime to sell confidential corporate information.

22. Brudney, 'Insiders, Outsiders, and Informational Advantages', 344.

23. *U.S. v. Newman,* 664 F. 2d 17.

24. *U.S. v. Winans,* 612 F. Supp. 827. The Supreme Court upheld Winans' conviction, but was evenly split on the misappropriation theory. As a consequence, the Supreme Court has still not truly endorsed the theory, although several lower court decisions have been based on it. *Carpenter v. US,* 56 LW 4007.

25. Unless there is some other reason for forbidding it, such as that it harms others.

26. Easterbrook, 'Insider Trading As An Agency Problem', *Principles and Agents: The Structure of Business* (Harvard University Press, Cambridge, MA, 1985).

27. Carlton and Fischel, 'The Regulation of Insider Trading', 35 *Stanford Law Review* 857. See also Manne, *Insider Trading and the Stock Market.*

28. Manne, *Insider Trading and the Stock Market;* Carlton and Fischel, 'The Regulation of Insider Trading'.

29. Kenneth Scott, 'Insider Trading: Rule 10b-5, Disclosure and Corporate Privacy', 9 *Journal of Legal Studies* 808.

30. 'Disputes Arise Over Value of Laws on Insider Trading', *The Wall Street Journal,* November 17, 1986, p. 28.

31. One area that needs more attention is the impact of insider trading on the markets (and ordinary investors) of countries that permit the practice. Proponents of insider trading are fond of pointing out that insider trading has been legal in many overseas markets for years, without the dire effects predicted by opponents of the practice. Proponents reply that these markets are not as fair or efficient as U.S. markets, or that they do not play as important a role in the allocation of capital.

32. See Frank Easterbrook, 'Insider Trading as an Agency Problem'. I speak here as if the interests of the firm and its shareholders are identical, even though this is sometimes not the case.

33. Manne, *Insider Trading and the Stock Market,* p. 129.

34. For a more detailed discussion of the ineffectiveness of permitting insider trading as an incentive, see Roy Schotland, 'Unsafe at any Price: A Reply to Manne, *Insider Trading and the Stock Market*', 53 *Virginia Law Review* 1425.

35. Manne is aware of the "bad news" objection, but he glosses over it by claiming that bad news is not as likely as good news to provide large gains for insider traders. *Insider Trading and the Stock Market,* p. 102.

36. There are ways to avoid many of these objections. For example, Manne has suggested "isolating" non-contributors so that they cannot trade on the information produced by others. Companies could also forbid trading on "negative" information. The problem is that these piecemeal restrictions seem very costly—more costly than simply prohibiting insider trading as we do now. In addition, each restriction brings us farther and farther away from what proponents of the practice actually want: unrestricted insider trading.

37. Frank Easterbrook, 'Insider Trading as an Agency Problem.'

38. *Ibid.*

39. Penalties did not begin to become sufficient to discourage insider trading until the passage of the Insider Trading Sanctions Act in 1984. Some argue that they are still not sufficient, and that that is a good reason for abandoning the effort entirely.

40. Easterbrook, 'Insider Trading as an Agency Problem.'

41. See Freeman and Gilbert, *Corporate Strategy and the Search for Ethics* (Prentice-Hall, Englewood Cliffs, NJ, 1988).

Decision Scenario 1
BUY AMERICAN, OR ELSE!

During the 1980s the U.S. automobile industry suffered significant sales loss to foreign manufacturers. The once dominant "Big Three" of General Motors, Ford, and Chrysler were losing the competition to Japanese and European firms. As a result, the Big Three were experiencing large financial losses, U.S. autoworkers were losing their jobs, and the American consumer, apparently, was benefitting from this competition by getting quality-built cars at reasonably low prices.

By the early 1990s a major public relations campaign began to encourage U.S. consumers to "Buy American." Supported by industry, labor, and many politicians, the "Buy American" movement promoted the purchase of American cars by appealing to patriotism, loyalty, and a responsibility to one's fellow Americans.

As part of a story on the "Buy American" movement, the CBS news program *60 Minutes* visited the Detroit auto show in January 1992. During this visit, two salesmen working at the General Motors Geo exhibit were questioned about the value of buying American products. One voiced strong support for the view that Americans should buy only American cars. The second, Matt Darcy, disagreed. While the cameras recorded his words, Darcy said, "If America makes a good product, buy it. If they don't, I buy what's good for my money. I don't have to spend money because it's American."

When Darcy returned to his job as a salesman at Gordon Chevrolet in Garden City, Michigan, after the show was aired, he was fired. Gordon Stewart, owner of Gordon Chevrolet, justified this dismissal on the grounds that Darcy's comments offended many customers who worked in the auto industry. Stewart was quoted as saying, "Truth is not the issue. You have to be careful."

Darcy's own parents were both assembly line workers for General Motors. Also, at the time of this incident, many so-called "American" cars were being manufactured at General Motors and Chrysler plants in Canada, while several Japanese manufacturers were producing "foreign" cars in the United States.

- Did Matt Darcy owe any loyalty to American workers, many of whom were his customers? Did he owe more loyalty to Americans who worked for American corporations than to Americans who were employed by Japanese corporations? Did he owe any loyalty to General Motors, the corporation that employed his parents and, indirectly, created his own job?

- How might a defender of the free market such as Milton Friedman respond to the "Buy American" movement? What is the socially responsible position in this case?

- Would it have been wrong for Darcy to lie in this case? Could there have been other things, short of an outright lie, that he could have said that would have pleased his employer? Would it have been ethical for him to do so?

- What might Albert Carr say about this case? What might Ron Duska say? Does it matter that U.S. automakers were manufacturing cars in Canada at the same time that they were encouraging U.S. citizens to "Buy American" in order to support "American" workers and "American" business?

Decision Scenario 2
INSIDE INFORMATION AT THE *WALL STREET JOURNAL*

It is clear that publicity, good or bad, can have profound effects upon a business. Good news can cause stock prices to rise; bad news can cause them to fall. This is particularly true when the news is presented in a trusted national publication like the *Wall Street Journal*. This situation can put journalists in a tempting position. They possess information that, when it becomes public, will likely influence the stock market. Knowing what they know because of their work, they are in a position to profit nicely by making investment decisions before the story breaks.

To prevent such things from happening, most major publications have policies prohibiting reporters from trading on inside information. The *Wall Street Journal*'s policy says:

> It is not enough to be incorruptible and act with honest motives. It is equally important to use good judgment and conduct one's outside activities so that no one—management, our editors, an SEC investigator with power of subpoena, or a political critic of the company—has any grounds for even raising the suspicion that an employee misused a position with the company.[1]

R. Foster Winans was a thirty-six-year-old journalist for the *Wall Street Journal* who wrote a popular column called "Heard on the Street." This column presented stories about happenings in the stock market and included analysis, stock tips, and,

as the title suggests, rumors and "insider" information. In April 1984 Winans was fired from his job when federal investigators charged him with illegally profiting from the material published in his column. Winans had leaked information about upcoming columns to friends who were then able to profit significantly by using this information to buy and sell stocks. Winans's associates made over $500,000 from his inside information, and he personally made about $30,000. Winans was successfully prosecuted on fraud and conspiracy charges.

- What exactly, if anything, was wrong with Winans's behavior? Would your judgment be different if his employer did not have a written policy that seems to prohibit what he did?

- Winans's defense lawyer claimed that he did not trade on inside information at all, but used mere gossip to make his investment decisions. Was Winans involved in insider trading? Was he involved in a conflict of interest?

- If Winans was not working for the *Wall Street Journal* and came by his information through other means, would he have done anything wrong to trade on that information? If a nonemployee, say someone who writes a letter to the editor, was able to accomplish much the same thing as Winans, would she have done something equally wrong? Why or why not?

- Who was harmed by Winans's act?

Decision Scenario 3
LOYALTY AND FREE SPEECH IN THE WORKPLACE

Jerald Schultz worked for Industrial Coils, Inc., at their Baraboo, Wisconsin, plant. In 1982 Schultz wrote a lengthy letter to the editor of a local newspaper that was highly critical of the company and several of its officers. The letter was published, and as a result Schultz was fired. Schultz sued Industrial Coils, claiming that he was wrongfully discharged

since his firing violated the strong public policy of free speech as expressed in Wisconsin's state constitution, which guarantees that "every person may freely speak, write and publish his sentiments on all subjects."

Schultz's letter was written explicitly on the topic of public schoolteachers. Apparently, many in the community felt that the local schoolteachers were being belittled and unfairly criticized within the community. Schultz took the opportunity to castigate the school board president, who also happened to be an officer of Industrial Coils. Schultz went on at great length to criticize the way in which this officer and his fellow managers conducted the company's business.

Industrial Coils acknowledged that Schultz was fired for writing this letter for publication. They claimed that the letter was insubordinate and detrimental to the company's interests. This decision, they claimed, resulted from a valid business judgment and was therefore beyond the reach of the courts. The personnel manager at Industrial Coils testified that he and other managers felt that if Schultz were permitted to continue, they would be hindered in other attempts to discipline employees for similar acts of "disloyalty or insubordination" and, as a result, "productivity would suffer." He further testified that other employees were agitated by the letter and that if Schultz had not been fired there would be "morale problems and a loss of respect for management."

- Should the political right of free speech extend to the workplace? What limitations, if any, should be placed on employee speech?

- What procedures should be followed before dismissing an employee?

- Was management justified in dismissing Schultz? Why or why not? Is the lack of "respect" mentioned by management sufficient for firing someone?

Decision Scenario 4

WHISTLEBLOWING AT THE PHONE COMPANY

Michael J., an employee of the phone company, recognizes that he has divided loyalties. The company has treated him well and, despite some minor disagreements, he gets along quite well with upper management and his own department. However, the phone company is a public utility, regulated for the public interest by the state's Public Utility Commission (PUC). As such, Michael J. recognizes that his firm owes a loyalty to citizens that goes beyond the simple responsibility that other firms owe to their consumers.

Once a year, as part of a major fund-raising drive for a local charity, the phone company encourages its employees to donate their personal time and money to this charity. This year, however, Michael J. discovers that a significant amount of company resources are being used to support the charity. The company is printing posters and sending out mail at its own expense and is using employees on company time to promote the fund-raiser. When Michael J. brought this to the attention of his manager, the whole incident was dismissed as trivial. After all, the resources were going to charity.

After some consideration, Michael J. judged that these charitable efforts were betraying the public trust. The public, and not private individuals acting as their agents, ought to decide for themselves when to contribute to charity. As a result, he notified the PUC of this misallocation of funds. Knowing that records of calls from his desk could easily be traced, Michael J. made the calls from pay phones and from his house.

As required by law, the PUC investigated the charges. Although the facts were as Michael J. reported, the PUC judged that the misallocation was not substantial enough to constitute a violation of the public trust. However, executives of the phone company were less willing to dismiss the incident. They were upset at what they judged to be serious disloyalty among their employees.

Although they suspected that Michael J. was the whistleblower, there was no proof that he was. A check of his office phone records showed no calls placed to the PUC. However, since this was the phone company, it was easy enough to trace calls made from Michael J.'s home and cross-check these against calls made to and from the PUC's offices. They did so, confirmed their suspicions, and disciplined Michael J.

- Do employees of public utilities have special responsibilities to protect the public interest? Why or why not? Should these responsibilities be extended to employees of some private firms, for example, large defense contractors?
- Did the phone company do anything unethical in checking its own records to trace Michael

J.'s phone calls? Should the PUC investigate further?

- Would your opinion of this case change if large sums of money or something other than a charity were involved?

Decision Scenario 5
CONFLICTING INTERESTS

Physicians and other health care professionals have an overriding responsibility to provide appropriate care for their clients. But like many professionals such as lawyers and accountants, physicians are entrepreneurs whose offices are run as small businesses. The interest in patient care and the economic interest of running a business can sometimes create a conflict of interest. Consider the following case.

General practitioners typically earn the lowest salaries of all medical doctors. They often refer patients to specialists for more distinctive care such as surgery and X rays. Surgeons and radiologists can earn three and four times as much as the general practitioner. In recent years, an increasing number of physicians have entered into financial arrangements with health care facilities that provide specialized care. Thus, for example, a physician may be part owner of a radiology center that provides X rays and diagnoses. This investment allows general practitioners to increase their earnings by tapping into the high fees charged for specialized care. Since the profitability of such a center depends on the number of patients referred to it, the general practitioner now has an economic interest in referring patients there, resulting in a potential conflict of interest.

The employee code of conduct at Xerox uses the following example to highlight conflicts of interest. Technical representatives are trained and

employed by Xerox to provide service and advice to customers who lease copy and office equipment from Xerox. Imagine that a spouse of a technical representative opens a small copy center in a town outside of the spouse's service territory. This business was established without using the name of or any money from the Xerox employee. Additionally, this business leases equipment and purchases supplies from Xerox on standard terms that do not differ from those of other Xerox customers.

However, the Xerox employee does help maintain and service the leased equipment, without pay and outside of normal working hours. This outside work does not affect the employee's normal job performance. Nevertheless, this technical representative is providing free-of-charge services that Xerox would ordinarily sell. This representative is using the skills and training that Xerox has provided to help a spouse's business. The spouse is saving money at Xerox's expense. Furthermore, by getting this service free, the spouse's business gains a competitive advantage in the marketplace.

- Identify the ethical issues in these cases. Do the cases raise any issues of honesty? of loyalty?
- What, if any, interests are in conflict in each case?
- If you identify either of these cases as involving a conflict of interest, what would need to be changed to avoid the conflict?

7

Employee Participation

In 1985, when the first edition of this text was published, employee participation in corporate decision-making was a mere blip on the radar screen of America's corporate managers. Involving employees in decisions was sometimes advised by management theorists, but this advice was seldom heeded. In the intervening decade, the number of employee participation programs has expanded geometrically. One study, reported in December 1994 by the federal Commission on the Future of Worker–Management Relations (commonly known as the Dunlop Commission), estimates that perhaps up to 60 percent of American workplaces have some form of employee participation system. That same commission called for expansion of participation programs to cover more workers and more workplaces. The Dunlop Commission and many labor relations experts suggest that increasing the competitiveness of American industry will require abandoning the traditional adversarial American labor relations in favor of a more cooperative style of management. If that suggestion is heeded, as it increasingly appears to be, participation programs will proliferate even further through the workplace.

While the increase in participatory programs is remarkable, it is still true that the vast majority of these programs are limited in both scope and authority. (In fact, American labor law has been interpreted to require limited scope for many programs. See Decision Scenario 5, "Electromation," at the end of this chapter.) Most programs concern well-defined issues such as plant safety or product quality. Also, most function merely as advisory mechanisms with no real authority to make decisions on their own. This chapter considers whether employees should have a right to much stronger forms of participation than those now common in the United States.

ASSESSING THE VALUE OF PARTICIPATION

Since employee participation programs vary so widely, you need to have some idea of the range of possible approaches before engaging in arguments about the value of participation. The case study by David Clowney, which describes AM General's program, as well as the material in the decision scenarios, will provide some specific examples of the variety of possible programs. A more general description is provided in the reading by John McCall, who suggests that participation programs differ both by the amount of institutional authority they possess and by the kinds of issues that they address. You must try to understand these differences before you assess the feasibility and justification of worker participation.

Debates about the wisdom of employee participation in decision-making are presented in the readings by McCall and Jan Narveson. McCall argues that there are five strong ethical reasons that presumptively support recognizing a worker's right to participate. All these reasons derive from a need to protect centrally important human goods such as autonomy and fairness. The arguments suggest that, in practice, protection for these goods is most effective when strong forms of employee participation are seen as important derivative rights. McCall also considers some traditional arguments against participation. Some of those opposing arguments derive from management or owner interests that are seen as conflicting with a right to participate in corporate decisions. For example, an owner's right to control his or her property appears to conflict with employees having strong participation rights that provide some control over corporate policies. McCall suggests, however, that these owner rights do not possess the moral weight necessary to override the presumptive support for participation.

The selection by Narveson argues to the contrary. He claims that mandating participation for all workplaces as a matter of employee right is inconsistent with both the employee's and the employer's right to freedom of association. He argues that such a right to free association is fundamental to our ideal of constitutional democracy. He contends, then, that those who argue for workplace democracy have a flawed conception of democracy. In this chapter we once more have a conflict of right claims that can be settled only if you pursue an investigation into the reasons behind the conflicting right claims. By appeal to what values are the rights to free association and employee participation justified? Which would advance those values more: limiting free association by mandating worker rights or denying workers a right to participate? You need to pursue the same sort of analysis to resolve the conflict between owners' property rights and the claimed worker right to a voice in corporate decisions.

Assessing the desirability of employee participation also requires that you address the practicality of allowing employees to participate in decision-making. Consider the feasibility of participation by asking: How does the economic performance of firms with strong forms of participation compare with the performance of firms without such programs? Are workers competent to make intelligent and informed decisions? Will ordinary workers have any desire for participation rights?

Some data does exist regarding these questions. A 1994 study finds a "participation gap" for workers.* Of American manufacturing workers surveyed, 72 percent reported that they would like to have more influence in workplace decisions. Of those surveyed in other fields, 63 percent reported the same. Nonetheless, the question posed at the end of the case study remains: Should participation programs force "empowerment" on workers who do not desire it?

Some concerns about the efficiency of participation reflect concerns about the attitude of employees. There are fears that if employees are involved in corporate decision-making, they will sack the firm of its profits and underinvest in the capital plant in order to gain short-term wage or benefit increases. There are also fears that employees, while certainly competent to offer suggestions about their immediate work environment, are not competent to make decisions on complex financial matters. Proponents of employee participation regard this last concern as a red herring. Participation need not be equivalent to direct democracy where every worker votes on every issue. It can be instead analogous to representative democracy where employees select (or hire) a competent individual to represent their interests. After all, this is exactly what owners have done in allowing management to make decisions for them.

As for the more general efficiency concerns, the evidence on participatory workplaces is far from clear. It is true that sometimes workers would underinvest in the plant. (It is also true that management sometimes does this, too.) However, that tendency is reduced to the degree that workers can see that their interests and the long-term health of the firm are coincident. In fact, a number of commentators, including the Dunlop Commission and Laura D'Andrae Tyson (a member of the Clinton team of economic advisers), have argued that participation is most likely to increase productivity when it is combined with broad human resources reforms that include a commitment to job security.

Evidence from some of the strongest forms of participation, worker cooperatives, is also mixed. Many newer cooperatives have resulted from worker buyouts of struggling firms. These firms often experience a dual problem of initial undercapitalization and poor competitive position. In other firms, the abrupt introduction of participatory management programs into conflicted workplaces has met with resistance and distrust from workers and managers alike.

These problems are not insurmountable or unavoidable, however. The Avis buyout described in Decision Scenario 2 is a case in point. Long-running lumber cooperatives in the Northwest have demonstrated financial success as well. In addition, more traditionally owned companies have reported profitable results from experiments in participation. The Donnelly Mirrors company has had a "Scanlon Plan" tying bonuses to company performance since the 1950s and has more

---

*Richard Freeman and Joel Rogers, "Worker Representation and Participation Survey" (Princeton Survey Research Associates: 1994).

recently introduced employee councils with wide authority. (See Decision Scenario 6, "Donnelly Mirrors," at the chapter's end.) It would seem that programs of participation experience the same financial and organizational difficulties that most firms do.

Labor and Management Resistance

Some have argued that workplace participation is unnecessary for protecting employee interests because employees can always form unions for that purpose. Others challenge this belief that unions are effective at representing worker interests in the United States today. The proportion of nonagricultural private sector workers who are unionized is now just 11.2 percent. With that low rate of unionization unlikely to rise, many are uncomfortable with the notion that unions should be the primary vehicle for protecting worker interests. Even the economic benefit of union membership has not been great as of late. The 1980s saw a much more aggressive posture towards unions by American business. Unions have often been forced by weak bargaining positions to make concessions or give-backs in contract negotiations. Also, while the wages of union workers remain somewhat higher than those of nonunion workers, unions have not significantly increased labor's proportional share of the national income. As a result, some labor relations theorists, such as Paul Weiler of Harvard, have suggested that it is time for workers in individual enterprises to protect themselves through strong and independent in-house forms of employee participation.

Unions, in fact, have been historically ambivalent about workplace participation. Often they feared that it was a device for weakening work rules and squeezing more work from employees. Union activists have sometimes been cautious about participating in upper-level corporate decisions, worrying that it would threaten the union's adversarial position. Some feared, for example, that union representation on corporate boards would lead the union board members to identify with the perspective of management.

Middle management, of course, has also resisted stronger forms of employee participation. Those forms of participation that give employees some actual decision-making authority directly reduce both the power and the need for middle-management positions. It is small wonder that some participation programs have met with outright hostility from line managers.

These labor and management fears about participation programs reveal that any introduction of employee involvement must be carefully planned and organized if it is to succeed. Both workers and managers need extensive preparation if participation programs are to decrease labor–management tensions and produce a more cooperative and internationally competitive business. The efficiency of employee participation programs, then, continues to be a matter for study.

CASE STUDY   Employee Empowerment at AM General
David Clowney

AM General is a mid-sized company that makes vehicles for the military. Its most well-known product is the HUMMER, the angular, high-riding diesel that has replaced the jeep as the armed services' multipurpose vehicle. Since 1992 AMG has also made a commercial version of the HUMMER.

The Employee Empowerment program at AM General began in 1990, at one of the monthly labor–management meetings initiated by the recently appointed CEO, Jim Armour, to "promote harmonious relations" between labor and management. Labor relations at AMG had been distinctly unharmonious in the seventies and eighties, when it was rare to have a contract negotiation without a strike. When Armour became CEO in 1988, he was determined to make a change.

At the meeting, Armour said that he and the parent company, LTV, were interested in beginning an employee involvement (EI) program, and that the newly acquired contract to build an ambulance version of the HUMMER would be a good place to start. Armour's previous experience at Ford and American Motors had led him to think that such programs could benefit both the company and its employees.

Mike Cinal is chairman of the bargaining committee for the plant union, a unit of UAW Local #5, the oldest existing local in the UAW. Mike and the bargaining committee had their own thoughts about joint labor–management programs. "There's a lot wrong with most of those programs," Mike told Armour. It was not clear that they accomplished anything; many studies, he said, showed no results, or even negative results.[1] The typical management-dominated program, unless it was trivial, could be seen as a company union, and could be illegal under the National Labor Relations Act. Therefore, the illegality would not only be technical. Mike was convinced that most American EI programs undermined the strength of organized labor.[2] They moved negotiable and grievable issues from the collective bargaining setting to small groups run by company facilitators. There workers might have a "voice," but final decision-making

power remained in management hands. The savings and efficiencies that such groups did produce benefitted the company but rarely the work force, who often had to deal with speedups or "downsizing" as a result of their own labor-saving suggestions. Thus, the picture of a "new, nonadversarial" style of labor relations, in which there was "no more us and them," was often more like a management con job. In fact, Mike knew many cases in which EI consultants had been called in by companies as a union-busting strategy.

But Mike, too, was tired of bad labor relations. Like most of the AMG work force, he was proud of the HUMMER. And he certainly understood that labor and management had common interests. If AMG lost an important government contract, half the company's hourly employees could be laid off.

Mike knew of some very different cooperative approaches that he thought were worth a try. These northern European models of "codetermination," rare in the United States, increased the control of work by workers at every level of the company, from shop floor to boardroom. Thus, changes in workplace technology were considered from the viewpoint of their effect on workers (including job loss), as well as their other effects. Savings produced by increased efficiency did not automatically mean that workers would lose jobs.

"That's what interests me," said Mike. "Codetermination. The motivation, and the program, have to come from the shop floor. And the *control* of the program must be equally in the hands of organized labor and management. If you're willing to consider that kind of EI program, I'll try to sell it to my members; and I think they might buy it."

Jim Armour was not threatened by Cinal's suggestion. While he did not think all aspects of the European "codetermination" model could be translated to the U.S. environment, the idea of an equal partnership matched his own ideas closely. AM General retained the services of University of Wisconsin Labor Studies Professor Frank Emspak to help develop a genuine example of such a partnership.

By August of 1990, the pilot Employee Empowerment program was up and running. The "ambo" line was an ideal place to try out the new ideas, since it was self-contained and employed only thirty-seven people. Together, management and labor agreed on a management team of five for the pilot project. Jim Bryant, plant supervisor from a

The author wishes to express his thanks to Jim Armour, Mike Cinal, Gary Wuslich, and the many fine hourly and salaried people at AM General who helped him prepare this article by their interviews and insights. He regrets not being able to include the voices of more of them.

recently closed truck plant (and labor's strongly suggested candidate), headed up the team.

A year later, in August of 1991, the tiny ambulance unit was attracting attention throughout the company. Employees in the unit were off the line for as long as an hour and a half each day for training and for computerized record keeping, job study, and quality control. The results were startling. Workers were enthusiastic. Production was up, quality had improved dramatically, and waste was being eliminated. The finance department calculated that the fledgling program was already saving AM General more than $3000 per unit. It was saving the government money, too, although some numbers had to be shifted around to make this clear. The government's cost review at first showed too many worker hours per vehicle. However, when the hours that the hourly workers spent on quality control and the like were shifted to the "administrative burden" category, both the labor and the administrative costs of the unit were low by the government's standards.

These trends continued through October of 1993. Production doubled from one to two units per day. AMG's costs per vehicle continued to drop, approaching the challenging goal of $10,000 savings per unit. Production speed went up; waste, defects, and administrative costs went down. Jim Bryant became manager of employee relations, and other members of the five-person management team moved to other positions in the company. None of them were replaced. Even before they moved, they were frequently being "borrowed" by other divisions. The ambo line workers had learned to manage themselves.

The ambulance line closed down in October of 1993 for lack of orders. The demand for a medical vehicle built to withstand cold-war risks was drying up. A few orders continue to trickle in from the United States and other governments. Due to the flexibility developed by the EE program, AMG can now profitably allow these orders to collect, then send a group of former ambo line workers over for a few days to make some ambulance bodies. But the days of a full-time ambulance line are over for now.

The reorganization of work at AM General, however, is just beginning. There has not been a strike since 1988. Each new contract has favored an equal partnership more aggressively. Gary Wuslich, the human relations adviser whom Jim Armour hired in 1990, prefers working in a union environment "because that way things can be done by a true consensus."

The most impressive recent result of the developing partnership is a group of major improvements in the areas of health, safety, and worker's compensation. After a year of rigorous training with health care consultant Bill Hembree, a joint union–management team negotiated with local providers to design a "Cadillac" health care package for hourly employees. In the words of Employee Benefits Coordinator Pat Hixenbaugh, "We succeeded where Hillary Clinton failed." Benefits were not only maintained but improved; yet in the first six months the company had cut costs significantly. Even more savings have been realized in the area of health and safety by a greatly improved in-plant ergonomics and safety program, developed and closely monitored by a joint health and safety committee. Accidents and work-related injuries have been drastically reduced. The program includes frequent inspections by hourly workers of health and safety conditions in the plant. They write up problems and code violations as if they were OSHA inspectors, and corrections are made quickly. As a result, OSHA inspectors would not find much wrong should they visit.

The company has saved more than $2 million in the year since these two programs have been instituted. Workers are pleased because their injuries are down and their benefits improved; and the health and safety program has begun to receive both state and national attention.

To get to this point, management opened the company books so that labor could see the actual costs of health care to the company. The company has also paid for workplace changes suggested by the ergonomics committee: for example, they paid $40,000 to raise the floor 18 inches at one point on the paint line, so that workers would not have to reach over their heads to pull out a paint-encrusted pin. (Result: Shoulder injuries at that station dropped from ten times the plant average to below the plant average.) The union, in turn, has helped to identify and eliminate employee abuses of the benefits program.

The lessons of the ambulance line are slowly being applied elsewhere. Together, management and labor developed a proposal for a team-style plant to rebuild Army 2½ ton trucks. Using this plan, AM General outbid a nonunion plant from a state where labor comes much cheaper, and was able to maintain a higher wage than the nonunion bid, plus a full AMG benefits package. (Wages in the truck plant are comparable to others in South Bend, but considerably below those in other AMG plants. New hires get full health benefits, but not, at present, the pension plan.) Two hundred workers have been recalled from layoff to work in this plant, which is managed by Jim Bryant and Mike Nagy from the original ambulance line project. Teams are now being introduced on the civilian HUMMER line as well. A plan has been drawn up to convert the parts warehouse, and the eventual goal is to implement new work systems in every AMG workplace.

The road to full implementation of these new work systems is bumpy enough for the most rugged off-road vehicle. Learning a new way of working is hard for both management and labor. In the words of New Work Systems Coordinator Ann Jones, "It's just as hard to stop taking orders as it is to stop giving them." In addition, outside pressures have been great. Recent drops and fluctuations in military demand have destabilized the work force and scrambled production schedules. It is hard to get a team working together when as soon as team members are trained, they are laid off, moved to another job, or bumped by others with more seniority. While military orders have dropped, a new version of the HUMMER has also been requested; this presents production problems of its own. Trust remains another source of difficulty: Some middle managers are fearful for their jobs and mistrustful of the work force; some workers remain mistrustful of both company and union leadership. The challenges of new projects further complicate the picture. The commercial HUMMER is a daring venture: Most defense contractors have not made a successful transition to commercial production. Likewise, the remanufacture of the 2½ ton truck, tearing down three old trucks and making two new ones from the remains, is a previously unattempted recycling project, which must struggle to overcome unanticipated problems while meeting a demanding production contract.

One other potential difficulty has turned out to be a benefit. New ownership could easily have put an end to the experimentation with new work systems, and in late 1991, to get out of bankruptcy, LTV did put AM General up for sale. But as things turned out, the strength of the labor–management partnership was one of the main features that motivated businessman Ira Rennert to buy the company, and he has aggressively supported it ever since.

The recent history of AM General Corporation shows clearly that labor–management partnerships can benefit both parties to a collective bargaining agreement. The ambulance line and the new health care plan are just two examples of this; neither would have been possible without the aggressive support of top management, union leadership, and the managers and hourly workers directly involved in these projects. Management has also instituted an incentive pay program, based on the number of vehicles produced, plus an incentive for attendance. This program is jointly managed by management

and the union; it has had beneficial effects on production, quality, managerial efficiency, and worker interest in the success of the company.

These are significant results, and they contrast noticeably with those of many "joint" programs. Both managers and union members hope that they can survive, grow, and produce more such results during the next several years.

The case of AM General also demonstrates the difficulty of making such programs work. They are vulnerable to pressures outside the control of their participants, and they require a strong commitment to *equal* partnership by both management and union. The process of change has been slow. It began with a principled commitment to honesty, mutual respect, quality, and joint problem solving by Jim Armour, Mike Cinal, and a small number of other managers and union leaders. In spite of the initial success of the ambulance project, the methods used there are only beginning to be applied in the company's other production lines. But it seems that a solid foundation of earned trust and of experience in joint problem solving has been laid. Both managers and hourly workers speak of a night-and-day change in labor relations. Mutual trust continues to be earned. Management has departed from precedent by informing hourly workers about the state and plans of the company, opening the company books and disclosing other confidential company information to the bargaining committee, and in other ways relinquishing power and seeking instead to solve problems together. On more than one occasion, Jim Armour has chewed out a manager for not being open with employees, or for imposing a solution of his or her own before soliciting employee solutions to a problem. The bargaining committee in turn has worked to improve production and quality, and has been more flexible in contract negotiations than they would otherwise have been.

Is there a cloud to this silver lining? Perhaps there is more than one. Some managerial and supervisory positions will surely be eliminated as new work systems are successfully implemented. The team approach, if successful, reverses a trend that began with the Industrial Revolution, and continued with Frederick Winslow Taylor's scientific management techniques. Taylor *deskilled* workers, turning them into assembly line robots who perform mindless repetitive tasks, and moved knowledge and choices about the task up the organizational hierarchy to where it could be precisely controlled at the top. The team approach can *reskill* workers, giving them a new understanding and control over the work they do. Teams of workers learn to manage themselves. Some middle managers at AMG have seen this cloud on their horizon, and they don't like it. Upper management's policy is that no one will be laid off as a result of implementing new work systems, though some may be moved to new positions or new operations. When layoffs have been necessitated by reduced production demand, management has been careful to make these layoffs before any work system changes are implemented. But it seems likely that maintaining its middle managers' trust and preserving jobs for them will continue to be a challenge for AM General during the next few years.

There may be some clouds for labor as well. The ambulance line was moving toward the point where it could have produced the same number and quality of units with fewer employees. What would AM General do at that point? Because ambulance orders dried up, the question did not arise. But it likely will, when the main HUMMER line is converted to self-managing teams. What will labor and management "codetermine" to do when working smarter and more cooperatively, at a reasonable pace, reduces the need for workers? Perhaps the company will be able to expand in some way. But if not, will low seniority workers have worked themselves out of a job? (The small size of AM General's operations, and the variations in production demands, may keep this from becoming a problem. In larger production operations, like the Big Three auto manufacturers, it has been a serious issue for labor.)

A more pressing issue for AM General is that of seniority and "bumping rights." For labor, such rights are a prized and hard-won feature of collective bargaining agreements, guaranteeing workers a hope for better jobs with more job security the longer they stay with a company. But the workforce movement they generate during cutbacks or production changes can be a production manager's nightmare. If production and quality depend on genuinely self-managing teams, the nightmare can be far worse: Production and quality will suffer as teams are rebuilt at the end of a round of musical jobs. A union suggestion for a preliminary round of "paper bumping" has made this process somewhat less chaotic at AM General, but labor and management are still struggling to find an arrangement that both can live with.

Finally, what about nonparticipators? Some workers don't want to be "participators." The company is not their life: They want to come to work, do their job, and go home. As work teams are implemented throughout AM General, it has

been increasingly difficult to allow this option. Should the company make allowances for nonparticipating workers? If it does not, is it making a fraudulent claim: "We are going to 'empower' you (by our definitions), whether you like it or not"? Is a union selling out its members if it agrees to an arrangement where being a participator in an EE team is part of the job? The current position of AM General and of the union is that AMG is simply redefining jobs, as any company may do, to include more responsible and managerial elements. Hence team participation is written into the contract for the commercial plant.

- Is it a matter of moral justice to even out the power in a workplace so that workers, owners, and managers each have power that matches their contribution? Does a worker have any rights to control the way he or she performs an assigned job?

- Is there anything immoral about a company seeking to control worker attitudes through "work teams" facilitated by a management psychologist?

- What do you think of the slogan, referring to labor and management, "No More Us and Them"? Do the interests of a company's workers, managers, and owners always coincide?

- At what administrative level do you think codetermination could be implemented at GM, Ford, and Chrysler? What would such an arrangement look like, and what sorts of business decisions would it produce?

NOTES

1. See Juravich, Harris, and Brooks, "Mutual Gains? Labor and Management Evaluate Their Employee Involvement Programs," *Journal of Labor Research*, vol. 14, no. 2 (Spring 1993); Harrison and Kelley, "Union, Technology, and Labor–Management Cooperation"; and Eaton and Voos, "Unions and Contemporary Innovations in Work Organization, Compensation and Employee Participation," in Mishel and Voos, eds., *Unions and Economic Competitiveness* (Armonk, N.Y.: M.E. Sharpe, 1992).

2. Among the books Mike had been reading was *Choosing Sides: Unions and the Team Concept* by Mike Parker and Jane Slaughter of *Labor Notes*, a grassroots labor-activist journal published in Detroit. Parker and Slaughter show these problems in case after case of EI programs in the auto industry. One of their chapters is entitled "Management by Stress: Management's Ideal Team Concept."

AN ETHICAL BASIS FOR EMPLOYEE PARTICIPATION
John J. McCall

Until recently, worker participation in corporate decision-making was a topic largely ignored in American management training and practice. Even in recent years, the attention usually given to worker participation by management theory has been confined to small-scale experiments aimed at increasing labor productivity. Little, if any, attention has been given to the possibility that there is an ethical basis for extending a right to participation to all workers.

Numerous explanations for this lack of attention are possible. One is that management sees worker participation as a threat to its power and status. Another explanation may be found in a pervasive ideology underlying our patterns of industrial organization. The ruling theory of corporate property distinguishes sharply between the decision-making rights of ownership and its management representatives on the one hand, and employee duties of loyalty and obedience on the other. The justification for that distinction lies partly in a view of the rights of property owners to control their goods and partly in a perception that nonmanagement employees are technically unequipped to make intelligent policy decisions. The perceived threat to power and this dominant ideology of employment provide for strong resistance even to a discussion of broad worker participation in corporate decisions. But perhaps as strong a source of this resistance comes from a confusion about the possible meanings of and moral justifications for worker participation. The primary aim of this essay is to clarify those meanings and justifications. If the essay is successful, it might also suggest that these sources of resistance to participation should be abandoned.

What people refer to when they use the term *participation* varies widely. We can get a better grasp of that variation in meaning if we recognize that it is a function of variety in both the potential issues available for participatory decisions and the potential mechanisms for that decision-making. The potential issues for participation can be divided into three broad and not perfectly distinct categories. First, employees could participate in decisions involving shop-floor operations. Characteristic shop-floor issues are the schedule of employee work hours, assembly line speed, and the distribution of work assignments. Second, employees could participate in decisions that have been the traditional prerogative of middle management. Issues here are hiring or discharge decisions, grievance procedures, evaluations of workers or supervisors, the distribution of merit wage increases, and so on. Finally, employees might participate in traditional board-level decisions about investment, product diversification, pricing or output levels, and the like. Simply put, employee participation might refer to participation in decision-making over issues that arise at any or all levels of corporate policy.

The mechanisms for participation vary as widely as do the potential issues. These participatory mechanisms vary both in terms of their location within or outside the corporation and in terms of the actual power they possess. For instance, some see employees participating in the shaping of corporate policy by individual acceptance or rejection of employment offers and by collective bargaining through union membership. These mechanisms are essentially external to the particular business institution. Internal mechanisms for participation in corporate policy-making include employee stock ownership plans, "quality circle" consulting groups, and bodies that extend employees partial or total effective control of the enterprise. Employee participation through stock ownership might exist either through union pension fund holdings or through individual employee profit sharing plans.

Internal participation can also exist in ways more directly related to the day-to-day functioning of the corporation. For example, quality circle participation is a recent adaptation of some Japanese approaches to the management of human resources. Employees in these quality circles are invited to participate in round-table discussions of corporate concerns such as improving productivity. It is important to note that these quality circle groups are advisory only; their function within the corporation is consultative and they have no actual authority to implement decisions.

Distinct from these advisory bodies are those mechanisms by which employees share in the actual power to make corporate policy. Among the mechanisms for such partial effective control are worker committees with authority to govern selected aspects of the work environment or worker representatives on the traditional organs of authority. An example of the former would be an employee-run grievance board; an example of the latter received significant notice in the United States when United Auto Workers' President Douglas Fraser assumed a seat on Chrysler's Board of Directors. Either of these mechanisms provides for only partial control, since one has a highly defined area of responsibility and the other provides employees with only one voice among many.

A final form of participation provides employees with full control of the operations of the corporation. Examples of this extensive participation are rare in North America, although some Midwest farm and Northwest lumber cooperatives are organized in this way.

Note that these varied mechanisms combine with the potential issues for participation in numerous ways. We might see union collective bargaining influence merit wage increases or working schedules; worker committee mechanisms of participation might deal with flexible work assignments or with evaluation of supervisors. This brief survey should indicate that discussions of employee participation must be pursued with care, since arguments criticizing or supporting participation might be sufficient grounds for drawing conclusions about one form of participation but not sufficient grounds for conclusions about other forms. That caution brings us to the second major aim of this essay— the clarification of moral arguments in favor of broad extensions of worker rights to participate in corporate decisions. Five justifications, or arguments, for participation will be sketched. Comments about the issues or mechanisms required by each justification will follow each argument sketch.

ARGUMENT 1

The first two ethical justifications for employee participation are applications of points developed in Chapter Two of this text. The first takes its cue from the fundamental objective of any morality— the impartial promotion of human welfare. That requirement of impartiality can be understood as a requirement that we try to guarantee a fair hearing for the interests of every person in decisions concerning policies that centrally affect their lives. Certainly, many decisions at work can have a great impact on the lives of employees. For instance, an employee's privacy and health, both mental and physical, can easily be threatened in his or her working life. Morality, then, requires that there be some attempt to guarantee fair treatment for workers and their interests. We might attempt to institutionalize that guarantee through government regulation of business practices. However, regulation, while helpful to some degree, is often an insufficient guarantee of fair treatment. It is insufficient for the following reasons:

1. Regulation, when it does represent the interests of workers, often does so imprecisely because it is by nature indirect and paternalistic.

2. Business can frequently circumvent the intent of regulations by accepting fines for violations or by judicious use of regulatory appeal mechanisms.

3. Perhaps most importantly, corporate interests can emasculate the content of proposed legislation or regulation through powerful lobbying efforts.

So it seems that an effective guarantee that worker interests are represented fairly requires at least some mechanisms additional to regulation.

We might avoid many of the difficulties of legislation and regulation if workers were allowed to represent their interests more directly whenever crucial corporate decisions are made. Thus, a fair hearing for workers' interests might have a more effective institutional guarantee where workers have available some mechanisms for participation in those decisions. In practice, then, morality's demand for impartiality presumptively may require worker input in the shaping of corporate policies. (This requirement is presumptive since we have not yet investigated what countervailing moral arguments might be offered by opponents of participation.) We have already seen, though, that there are numerous issues and mechanisms for such participation. We need to decide what participatory mechanisms dealing with what issues could satisfy the requirement of fairness.

Clearly, if worker interests are to be guaranteed as much fair treatment as possible, the participatory mechanisms must have actual power to influence corporate decisions. For while workers might receive fair treatment even where they lack such power, possession of real power more effectively institutionalizes a *guarantee* of fairness. Thus, internal participatory mechanisms that serve in a purely advisory capacity (for example, quality circle groups) are obviously insufficient vehicles for meeting the fairness demands of morality.

Less obvious are the weaknesses of individual contract negotiations, union membership, and stock ownership as devices for guaranteeing fairness. None of these devices, in practice, can provide enough power to protect fair treatment for workers. Individual contract decisions often find the prospective employee in a very poor bargaining position. The amount of effective power possessed through union membership varies with the changing state of the economy and with changes in particular industrial technologies. In addition, the majority of workers are not unionized; the declining proportion of union membership in the total work force now stands at about one fifth. Stock ownership plans provide employees very little leverage on corporate decisions because, commonly, only small percentages of stock are held by workers. Moreover, all three of these participation mechanisms most often have little direct power over the important operating decisions that affect worker interests. Those decisions are usually made and implemented for long periods before contract negotiations, union bargaining, or stockholder meetings could have any chance at altering corporate policy.

Thus, a serious moral concern for fairness, a concern central to any moral perspective, presumptively requires that mechanisms for employee participation provide workers with at least partial effective control of the enterprise. Since decisions that have important consequences for the welfare of workers are made at every level of the corporation, employees ought to participate on issues from the shop floor to the board room. Moreover, since a balanced and impartial consideration of all interests is more probable when opposing parties have roughly equal institutional power, employees deserve more than token representation in the firm's decision-making structure. Rather, they should possess an amount of authority that realistically enables them to resist policies that unfairly damage their interests. This first moral argument, then,

provides strong presumptive support for the right of employees to codetermine corporate policy.

ARGUMENT 2

The second moral argument also derives from points that were made in Chapter Two, and its conclusions are similar to those of the preceding argument. Any acceptable moral theory must recognize the inherent value and dignity of the human person. One traditional basis for that belief in the dignity of the person derives from the fact that persons are agents capable of free and rational deliberation. We move towards respect for the dignity of the person when we protect individuals from humanly alterable interferences that jeopardize important human goods and when we allow them, equally, as much freedom from other interferences as possible. Persons with this freedom from interference are able to direct the courses of their own lives without threat of external control or coercion. (Such a view of persons provides for the moral superiority of self-determining, democratic systems of government over oppressive or totalitarian regimes.)

This moral commitment to the dignity of persons as autonomous agents has significant implications for corporate organization. Most of our adult lives are spent at our places of employment. If we possess no real control over that portion of our lives because we are denied the power to participate in forming corporate policy, then at work we are not autonomous agents. Instead we are merely anonymous and replaceable elements in the production process, elements with a moral standing little different from that of the inanimate machinery we operate. This remains true of our lives *at* work even if we have the opportunity to change employers. (Many workers do not have even that opportunity, and if they did it would be of little consequence for this issue, since most workplaces are similarly organized.) The moral importance of autonomy in respecting the dignity of persons should make us critical of these traditional patterns of work and should move us in the direction of more employee participation. However, since autonomy is understood as an ability to control one's activities, the preferred mechanisms of participation should allow employees real control at work. Thus, a commitment to the autonomy and the dignity of persons, just as a commitment to fairness, appears to require that workers have the ability to codetermine any policy that directs important corporate activity.

ARGUMENT 3

These first two arguments for broad worker participation rights have ended in an explicit requirement that workers have real and actual power over corporate policy. The final three arguments focus not on actual power but on the worker's *perception* of his or her ability to influence policy. All of these last arguments concern the potential for negative consequences created when workers see themselves as having little control over their working lives.

The third argument warns that workers who believe themselves powerless will lose the important psychological good of self-respect.[1] Moral philosophers have contended that since all persons should be treated with dignity, all persons consequently deserve the conditions that generally contribute to a sense of their own dignity or self-worth. Psychologists tell us that a person's sense of self is to a large degree conditioned by the institutional relationships she has and the responses from others that she receives in those relationships. A person will have a stronger sense of her own worth and will develop a deeper sense of self-respect when her social interactions allow her to exercise her capacities in complex and interesting activities and when they reflect her status as an autonomous human being. Of course, in contemporary America the development of the division of labor and of hierarchical authority structures leaves little room for the recognition of the worker's autonomy or for the ordinary worker to exercise capacities in complex ways. The consequence of such work organization is the well-documented worker burnout and alienation; workers disassociate themselves from a major portion of their lives, often with the psychological consequence of a sense of their own unimportance. Contemporary American patterns of work, then, often fail to provide individuals with those conditions that foster a strong sense of self-respect; instead, they more often undermine self-respect. Numerous studies have indicated that a reversal of these trends is possible when workers are provided greater opportunities for exercising judgment and for influencing workplace activities.

If we take seriously a demand for the universal provision of the conditions of self-respect, we ought to increase opportunities for satisfying work by allowing workers to participate in corporate policy decisions. It would seem, however, that this argument for worker participation need not conclude that workers be given actual power. All that the argument requires is that a worker's *sense* of self-respect be strengthened, and that is at least a possible consequence of participation in an advisory capacity. In fact, worker satisfaction has been shown to increase somewhat when employees are involved in Japanese-style quality circles that offer suggestions for improving production. Nor does it appear that the self-respect argument requires that workers be able to influence all aspects of corporate activity, since an increased sense of one's own significance could be had through participation only on immediate shop-floor issues.

However, we must be careful to estimate the long-range effects on worker alienation and self-respect of these less extensive forms of participation. Some evidence indicates that, over time, workers can grow more dissatisfied and alienated than ever if they perceive the participatory program as without real power or as simply a management attempt to manipulate workers for increased productivity.[2] We should consider, then, that a concern for long-run and substantial increases in self-respect might require workers to exercise some actual authority, more than a token amount, over the workplace.

ARGUMENT 4

The fourth argument supporting participation also takes its cue from the studies that show repetitive work without control over one's activities causes worker alienation. The specific consequence that this argument focuses on, however, is not a lessening of self-respect but a potential threat to the mental and physical health of workers. Certainly, everyone is now aware that alienated individuals suffer from more mental disturbances and more stress-related physical illnesses. Workers who are satisfied because they feel able to contribute to corporate policy are held to suffer from less alienation. Since mental and physical health are undoubtedly very central human goods, there seems strong presumptive moral reason for minimizing any negative effects on them that institutional organizations might have. Since broader powers apparently help to minimize such effects, we again have an argument for an expansion of worker rights to participate in corporate decisions.

As with the self-respect argument, however, the issues and mechanisms of participation that this requires are unclear. It could be that negative health effects are minimized in the short run through advisory bodies of participation. On the other hand, minimizing threats to mental or physical well-being in the long run might require more actual authority. Which sorts of mechanisms help most is a question only further empirical research can answer. However, since we have already seen presumptive reasons for actual power to codetermine policy from the first two arguments and since that power can have positive effects on self-respect and health, we perhaps have reasons for preferring the stronger forms of participation if we are presented with a choice between alternatives.

ARGUMENT 5

The fifth argument for worker participation also derives from the purported negative consequences of hierarchical and authoritarian organizations of work. This argument, however, focuses on broader social consequences—the danger to our democratic political structures if workers are not allowed to participate in corporate decisions.[3]

Many political theorists are alarmed by contemporary voter apathy. They worry that with that apathy the political process will be democratic in name only, and that the actual business of government will be controlled by powerful and private economic interests. Reversing this trend that threatens democratic government demands that individual citizens become more involved in the political process. However, increased individual involvement is seen as unlikely unless citizens believe themselves to have political power. But an initial increased sense of one's own political power

does not seem possible from involvement in the large macroscopic political institutions of contemporary government. Rather, involvement in smaller, more local and immediate social activities will nurture a sense of political efficacy. Since so much time and attention is devoted to one's work life, the place of employment appears a prime candidate for that training in democracy necessary for development of civic involvement. In fact, powerless and alienated workers can bring their sense of powerlessness home and offer their children lessons in the futility of involvement. Allowing those lessons to continue would only exacerbate the threat to vital democratic institutions. This fifth argument, then, sees participation at work as a necessary condition for the existence of a healthy and lasting system of democracy where citizens have the confidence to engage in self-determining political activities.

Again, since this argument focuses on the worker's perception of his or her own power, it provides presumptive support for those mechanisms that would increase both that sense of power and the tendency for political activity. Just what mechanisms these are can be open to argument. However, as before, if workers feel that their participatory mechanisms lack power, there is the danger that they will become even more cynical about their ability to influence political decisions. And since we have already seen arguments supporting participation with actual power to codetermine policy, there should be a presumption in favor of using mechanisms with real power.

SOURCES OF RESISTANCE

We have, then, five significant reasons for extending to workers a broad right to codetermine corporate policy. Now, in order to determine whether the presumption in favor of worker participation can be overridden, we need only to consider some of the common reasons for resisting this employee right to participate. Common sources of resistance to worker participation are that managers perceive it as a threat to their own status or power, that owners feel entitled to the sole control of their property, and that ordinary employees are believed incompetent to make corporate decisions. We shall consider briefly each of these sources of resistance in turn. Our evaluation of these claims will show them to be unacceptable sources of resistance when measured against the previously described ethical reasons in favor of broad participation.

First, in order for management's perception that participation threatens its power to count as an acceptable moral reason for resistance, management power must have some moral basis of its own. According to even traditional conservative theories of corporate property, management has no basic moral right of its own to control the corporation. Rather, management's authority stems from its position as an agent of the economic interests of shareholders, who are seen as the ultimate bearers of a right to use, control, or dispose of property. On the traditional theory, then, management can find a legitimate moral reason for resisting participation only if it can show that schemes of employee participation are real threats to the economic interests of shareholders. Presently, we shall refer to evidence that this case against participation cannot be supported by the available data. (Management, of course, might still resist even without a moral reason. However, such resistance can have no claim to our support; it is merely an obstacle to be overcome if there are moral reasons to support participation.)

Does participation damage the interests of ownership in a morally unacceptable way? To answer that question, we need to consider what interests ownership has and to what benefits property ownership should entitle one. In the process of confronting these issues, we will also see reasons for suspicion about claims that workers are not capable of participating in the intelligent setting of corporate policy.

In legally incorporated businesses, shareholders commonly have a monetary return on their investment as their principal desire.[4] Moreover, corporate property owners generally have surrendered their interest in day-to-day control of the corporation.[5] The usual owner interest, then, concerns the profitability of the business. Worker participation does not necessarily pose a serious threat to this interest in profit. Evidence shows that worker participation schemes often improve the economic condition of the business by increasing the interest, motivation, and productivity of employees.[6] In addition, corporations seeking qualified and motivated workers in the future might, out of self-interest, have to construct mechanisms for participation to satisfy the

demands of a more slowly growing but more highly educated entry-level labor force.[7] Even when experiments at worker participation have not succeeded, the failures can often be explained by shortcomings of the particular program that are not generic to all forms of participation. In fact, some of those with experience in constructing participatory work schemes believe that employees can be trained to operate most efficiently with expanded responsibilities.[8] When programs are designed carefully and when time is invested in training both former managers and employees, the competence of workers has not been seen as a crucial reason behind examples of participation's lack of success. Thus, in light of both the marked economic successes of broader worker participation programs and the apparent absence of any *generic* threats to profitability (such as employee incompetence), the economic interests of owners do not appear to provide a substantial basis for a justified resistance to an employee right to participate in corporate decision-making.

Some might object, however, on the basis that corporate property owners have other interests at stake. Many see a right to control one's goods as fundamental to the concept of property ownership, for example. Thus, they might claim that shareholders have, because of their property ownership, rights to retain control of the business enterprise even if they fail to exercise those rights on a day-to-day basis. This right to control one's property would effectively eliminate the possibility of an employee right to codetermine policy.

There are two reasons, however, to question whether a right to control property can provide a moral basis for denying workers a right to participate in corporate decisions. First, corporate property owners have been granted by society a limit on their legal liability for their property. If a legally incorporated business is sued, owners stand to lose only the value of their investment; an owner of an unincorporated business can lose personal property beyond the value of the business. Part of the motivation behind making this legal limit on liability available was that society would thereby encourage investment activity that would increase the welfare of its members.[9] It is not unreasonable to suggest that this justification for the special legal privilege requires that corporations concern themselves with the welfare of persons within the society in exchange for limited liability. Society, then, places limits on the extent to which owners can direct the uses of their corporate property. For example, society can require that corporations concern themselves with the environmental health effects of their waste disposal policies. Failure to require such concern is tantamount to allowing some to profit from harms to others while preventing those others from obtaining reasonable compensation for grievous harms. However, if the legal limitation on liability requires corporations to have some ethical concern for the welfare of others, it can also require corporations to protect the welfare of their employees. We have already seen, though, that morally serious goods are at stake when employees are unable to participate significantly in corporate decisions. Thus, if in exchange for limited liability the control of the corporation is to be limited by a concern for others, then the shareholders' interest in controlling corporate property could be limited to allow for an employee right to participate.

A second reason for rejecting the claim that an ownership right to control prohibits employee participation looks not on the legal privileges associated with corporate property but on the very concept of property itself. This argument makes points similar to ones made in the preceding paragraph, but the points apply to property whether it is incorporated or not. It is certainly true that property ownership is meaningless without some rights to control the goods owned. It is equally true, however, that no morally acceptable system of property rights can allow unlimited rights to control the goods owned. You, for example, are not allowed to do just anything you please with your car; you cannot have a right to drive it through my front porch. We accept similar restrictions on the control of business property; we prohibit people from selling untested and potentially dangerous drugs that they produce. The point of these examples is to illustrate that control of property, corporate or not, has to be limited by weighing the constraints on owners against the significance of the human goods that would be jeopardized in the absence of the constraints. Acceptable institutions of property rights, then, must mesh with a society's moral concern for protecting the fundamental human goods of all its members.

We have seen in the first part of this essay that there are significant reasons for thinking that im-

portant moral values are linked to a worker's ability to participate in corporate decision-making. If control of property, personal or corporate, is to override these moral concerns, we need to be presented with an argument showing what more central goods would be jeopardized if employees were granted strong participation rights. The burden of proof, then, is on those who want to deny an employee right to codetermine corporate policy. They must show that an owner's interest in broad control of corporate policy can stand as an interest worthy of protection as a moral right even when such protection would threaten the dignity, fair treatment, self-respect, and health of workers, as well as the continued viability of a democratic polity with an actively self-determining citizenship.

SUMMARY

To summarize: We have seen that there are various understandings of worker participation. The difference between these various understandings is a function of the workplace issues addressed and the participatory mechanisms that address them. We have also seen sketches of five arguments that purport to show a moral presumption in favor of strong worker participation in the form of an ability to actually codetermine policy. We have seen, further, that some traditional sources of resistance to worker participation (a threat to management or owner prerogatives of control, a belief in the incompetence of workers, a fear that profits will suffer) are either not supported by the evidence or are incapable of sustaining a moral basis for rejecting participation. The provisional conclusion we should draw, then, is that our society ought to move vigorously in the direction of a broader authority for all workers in their places of employment.

NOTES

1. This argument has been made by Joe Grcic in "Rawls and Socialism," *Philosophy and Social Criticism*, vol. 8, no. 1 (1980), and in "Rawls' Difference Principle, Marx's Alienation and the Japanese Economy," a paper presented at the Ninth Plenary Session of Amintaphil, 1983. It is also suggested by John Cotter in "Ethics and Justice in the World of

Work: Improving the Quality of Working Life," *Review of Social Economy*, vol. 40, no. 3 (1982).

2. Cf. Daniel Zwerdling, *Workplace Democracy* (New York: Harper and Row, 1980).

3. This argument is made forcefully by Carole Pateman, *Participation and Democratic Theory* (Cambridge: Cambridge University Press, 1970).

4. Of course, the matter is more complex than this simple statement indicates. Some investors might even have interests in losing money if they are attempting to avoid taxes. Others might want to guarantee that their company does not produce immoral goods (as some Dow Chemical investors claimed was the case with Dow's napalm production). Still, in most cases the primary motivation for investment is a monetary return.

5. It is, of course, not always true that shareholders surrender their interest in day-to-day control, since some corporations are headed by their principal stockholders.

6. Additional evidence is found in the experiences of the small but highly publicized experiments of Volvo and of Donnelly Mirrors, Inc. Interviews with heads of both Volvo and Donnelly can be found in *Harvard Business Review*, vol. 55, no. 4 (1977) and vol. 55, no. 1 (1977), respectively. In West Germany, codetermination is mandated by law in some major industries that have been highly competitive with their American counterparts.

7. John Cotter, *op cit.*

8. The Donnelly interview, *op cit.*, and Nancy Foy and Herman Gadon, "Worker Participation: Contrasts in Three Countries," *Harvard Business Review*, vol. 54, no. 3 (1976).

9. Cf. W. Michael Hoffman and James Fisher, "Corporate Responsibility: Property and Liability," in *Ethical Theory and Business*, 1st ed., T. Beauchamp and N. Bowie, eds. (Englewood Cliffs, N.J.: Prentice-Hall, 1979), pp. 187–196.

DEMOCRACY AND ECONOMIC RIGHTS[*]
Jan Narveson

INTRODUCTION

We have long been accustomed to thinking of democracy as a major selling point of Western institutions. That a set of political institutions should be democratic is widely regarded as the *sine qua non* of their legitimacy. So widespread is this belief that even those whose institutions do not look very democratic to us nevertheless insist on proclaiming them to be such (though the number taking this gambit dropped dramatically around the end of 1989). Meanwhile, an adulatory attitude toward democracy has arisen in many quarters, and many theorists have taken up anew[1] the idea that if democracy is the way to go in political institutions,

[*]Work on this paper was carried on both at my home University of Waterloo and at the Social Philosophy and Policy Center, Bowling Green State University, Ohio. I am indebted to the Center for providing an unbeatable workplace—which had the additional merit of sparing me the bother of participatory "democratic decision-making" in the Center's affairs! I wish also to express particular thanks to Ellen Paul for many insightful and helpful editorial comments on the conference version of this paper.

then it must also be the way to go in "other" areas, notably in economic and social institutions. So there has arisen a call for "economic democracy"—which is taken to mean, especially, that the "means of production" should be managed by their constituent workers in concert rather than by some few who own, or act for the owners of, those enterprises. Robert Dahl, in his influential *Preface to Economic Democracy*, sums it up nicely when he proclaims a "stronger justification" for worker participation: "*If* democracy is justified in governing the state, then it must *also* be justified in governing economic enterprises; and to say that it is *not* justified in governing economic enterprises is to imply that it is not justified in governing the state."[2]

It is arguments such as these with which I shall be concerned in this essay....

DEMOCRACY

We had best begin with a brief analysis of democracy, which has long been the essence of Western political ideology. And what is the essence of democracy?

...Democracy, if it has any rationale at all, has its rationale in the idea of *self-rule:* of being one's own boss, doing what one thinks best oneself rather than being forced to do what another directs. Theorists of many persuasions have argued that what democracy is all about is, somehow, freedom. (Aristotle, for example, says that "the underlying idea of the democratic type of constitution is liberty."[3]) Even leftish theorists, such as Frank Cunningham and Carol Gould, whom I shall be considering below, think so. But they have different ideas about the relation between these two contested principles, and much may turn on the discrepancy. Meanwhile, those who think that democracy is an end in itself have a problem when they contemplate ideals of freedom. For democracy *qua* majority rule, which as I have argued is essentially what democracy must be, is nevertheless *rule*, after all. So if the idea was to get away from *being ruled by others,* then we have to appreciate that the central idea of freedom is *not* rule by a majority of one's fellows, but rule *by oneself.* But, in effect, this means that in principle what the free person wants is *no* "rule," in the political sense of the term—in which rule is interpersonal....

...If there is a general objection to being ruled by others, then it is an objection to such rule in any form, democratic or otherwise. It's not as though democracy were so special a form of government that it isn't really a sort of government at all: as though, for example, democracy were *literally* "self-rule." For it is not. Like any form of government, democracy is rule by others—in this case, lots and lots of others. Whatever reasons there are for limiting government, then, apply to democracy as well. The first principle of democracy must therefore be this: that majority rule should only come into play where rule is *needed*—"needed" in the sense that lack of it will defeat people's pursuit of their ends, rather than enabling them to forward them.

CONSTITUTIONALISM: RIGHTS AGAINST GOVERNMENTS— DEMOCRATIC OR OTHERWISE

If we accept freedom as the cornerstone of our argument for government, then democracy makes sense only against a background of *constitutionalism:* the thesis that a just political order obtains only when it is constrained by an understanding of what no government may do, no matter how large a majority supports it. When it nevertheless proceeds to do something impermissible, we don't have the reasonable democracy of the free person, but an unstable tyranny of greater or less degree.

James Buchanan is justly famed for his insistence on this point. He distinguishes three levels of collective action: administrative (the enforcement of existing law), legislative (the creation of new law), and constitutional (the establishment of the fundamental framework within whose limits law may be made and enforced). And he complains,

> In the chaotic intellectual and political settings of the 1980s...the three sets of activities are confusedly intermingled....Modern legal-judicial practice places us all in an ongoing game wherein the umpires themselves continually change the rules and, indeed, openly proclaim this to be their announced social role.... Modern politicians are encouraged to legitimise any and all extensions of legislative activity so long as "democratic" procedures prevail. Majoritarianism is elevated to a position of a normative ideal.[4]

It might be supposed that the idea of constraining the majority is inherently antithetical to democracy. Not so. Quite the converse: democracy depends on constraints operating against majorities.... As a main (and spectacular) case in point, the right to vote itself cannot coherently be thought to be subservient to the majority principle. For imagine what could happen if it were: 51 percent begin by depriving the remaining 49 percent of its vote; then 51 percent of *that* group deprive the remaining 49 percent of *their* vote; and so on, until we wind up with something like a Roman triumvirate. Obviously, this negates the idea of democracy. If The People are to rule, they must have the vote *as a right*, not as the result of a happenstance day-to-day government measure.

For another salient example, consider the question whether you, Ms. Citizen, should be hanged, drawn, and quartered in the public square tomorrow for the general amusement. Is *that* something to be left to a majority? Plainly not. Nor, when you think of it, are such matters as whether the right of *habeas corpus* will be sustained, whether the government may forbid Ms. Smith marrying Mr.

Jones on the ground that they are of differing races, and so forth.

We will not attempt to complete a list at this level of specificity. But we will suggest a general principle, also familiar from recent literature:[5] governments should do nothing, in brief, that can be done at least as well by people acting cooperatively or on their own. Unless it can be demonstrated that people in pursuit of their ends inevitably interfere with each other to the disadvantage of some of them, *and* that they will do better only if a central agency with a monopoly of coercive power intervenes, then government activity is in principle out of order. This, I daresay, is most of the time, if not always.

That principle, admittedly, is wildly far from what contemporary governments tend to claim. What they claim, apparently, is something more like omnipotence, in (some sort of) principle. Is that a hangover from the days of kings, purporting to represent the will of the gods? The *claim* of governments nowadays is that what they do promotes the general good, in some conception or other. Their claim to be democratic is presumably based on the foggy idea that the conception of the good which they allegedly promote is that of "the people."

Of course, there is no conception of the good which is shared by everyone. If what governments claim is true at all, the truth is at best that the conception of the good they claim to promote is one shared, or at least approved, by the majority. As I pointed out above, however, to suppose that is enough is to beg the question posed by freedom.

Indeed, is a "conception of the good" one of the things that governments have any business mucking around with? *Prima facie,* no. At the core of liberalism is just the opposite. That governments should be austerely neutral regarding such matters is a received axiom among people professing to be liberals. The democratic constitution must always acknowledge the rights to freedom of thought, speech, association, and choice of "lifestyle." Yet those who profess their understanding of this concept draw lines, it seems, around a small set of such conceptions, reserving the provision of the "necessities" of life to "the poor," say, or higher education to anyone who can cope with it (and plenty who can't), to the government to finance with everyone's money and to administer as they see fit—thus

promoting those notions of the good in which education plays a large role, and undercutting the wishes of those who may be disinclined to share their wealth for the good of others. Or consider the business of making sure that people don't take drugs—the American obsession with which has lately extended to actual military invasion, the killing of a few hundred Panamanian citizens being evidently thought a modest price to pay for the apprehension of one drug-dealing dictator. The gap between liberal profession and current governmental practice is, in fact, so substantial these days that one really has to conclude that the classic viewpoint of liberal democracy simply has little to do with reality any more. Whether it ever did is perhaps debatable. Yet it is not unfair to suggest that what we have now is a considerable tendency to invoke liberal ideas coupled with a considerable tendency to subvert them in action. The influence of the democratic process, uninhibited by liberal principles, can be pointed to as a major culprit here.

ECONOMIC RIGHTS

Turning now to our central topic, we evidently need a general idea of economic rights. Now, one might have supposed—on analogy with our familiar rights to choose among or reject religions, to speak our minds, without fear of reprisal, to engage in activities expressive of chosen lifestyles, and so on—that we similarly would be free to produce whatever we choose and to trade products on terms agreeable to whomever is interested, without restrictions imposed in the interests of large-scale "social" goals. But ever since Karl Marx thundered his familiar—if fallacious[6]—indictments of capitalism, it has been customary not only for his followers but also, apparently, people who should know better, to go along with him in drawing a strong distinction between private property in consumption goods and private property in the means of production. Liberal freedoms, it seems, are to be restricted to the former, leaving the latter open to essentially unlimited public intervention.

Thus John Rawls famously insists on a general right to "the most extensive system of equal basic liberties compatible with a similar system of liberty for all," insisting even that this right is to be lexically preferred to principles calling for the distribution of other "primary goods" on a basis of equality (unless an unequal distribution does even better for the least favored). Yet in spelling out somewhat more concretely the list of basic liberties intended here, he lists "freedom of the person along with the right to hold (personal) property"[7]—explicitly, though inexplicably, inserting by implication the Marxian distinction and accepting the Marxian restriction. And in his subsequent discussion of "economic systems," he lays it down: "It is evident, then, that there is no essential tie between the use of free markets and private ownership of the instruments of production."[8] One could be forgiven, surely, for wondering what he means by the term "essential tie," in view of the fact that excluding private ownership of the "means of production" from the ambit of the liberty principle means precisely that one keeps such goods—factories, farms, and so on—*off* the free market. That the goods produced by those productive facilities, access to which is excluded from markets, are in their turn to be marketed freely ought to strike people as a paradox rather than as an obvious application of social justice.

That there can be market pricing for some goods and not for others is clear enough. The question is only whether there is any principled way of distinguishing types of goods that would justify imposing this restriction. For it *is* a restriction, after all. From the point of view of the actual or potential owner of a "means of production," it is not at all obvious *to him* that his freedom *isn't* restricted by the State's preventing him from buying, selling, or operating means of production.

Nor is it obvious from the point of view of the actual or potential employee, one would think. If people are allowed to own means of production, then potential employees are allowed a vastly greater array of potential employers to attempt to get employment from, not to mention the possibility of setting up in business themselves.

Indeed, even the very idea of consumer freedom, which one might suppose was entailed by the idea of freedom with regard to the use of consumption (as opposed to productive) goods, is not obviously consistent with the imposition of extensive restrictions on how what is produced shall be produced and by whom. For if individuals may not own productive enterprises, then surely many consumers will not in fact be able to get what they

want: for such productive enterprises as remain (in the hands of cooperatives, say) may not be interested in catering to some of those wants. The fact that it does so eventuate should suggest the bearing of this point.

No one is forced to offer employment, of course. But it is *in the interest* of many people to hire, on a variety of terms, and those people—this is the idea, anyway—don't have to ask anybody else whether they can hire you. If they want to, they just do. Here we are close to the definition of freedom: nobody can tell anybody else what he must do. How, then, can anyone argue that from a point of view sympathetic to *freedom,* there would not be free markets in whatever can be bought and sold?

The standard answer to this is (depressingly) familiar. Free markets give rise to "maldistributions," by which is meant unequal distributions, from which is inferred that they are "inequitable" distributions. And sure enough, we do expect that if all are given the right to do what they please with something, including (then) exchanging it with someone else for what they'd rather have, then after a while some will have more of a lot of things than others. Let us say that this is indeed "unequal." But why should this be thought not merely unequal but *inequitable*? "Inequitable" suggests that there was unfairness here: that some had claims that were overlooked in this process. But how is that to be made out?

If I have no claim over some consumption item of yours, how do I suddenly acquire a claim when you decide instead to produce something with it? Or how do I suddenly come to have a claim if you offer it in exchange for something I happen not to have?

DAHL ON WORKER DEMOCRACY

I turn next to Robert Dahl's argument for worker democracy in some detail. Dahl is by no means the only one to argue for this idea; among mainstream political thinkers, however, he is perhaps the most influential, and his arguments are wholly typical....

...And here is where the argument cited earlier comes into play: that "*if* democracy is justified in governing the state, then it must *also* be justified in governing economic enterprises."[9] Again we should pause to note the difference between the view that democracy is "justified" in the sense of being *permissible* in such contexts, which it obviously is, and the view that it is *obligatory,* which is what Dahl is supposed to be arguing for. The difference is profound.

It is fundamental to politics that political association is *not* essentially voluntary. If it were, there could be no objection in principle to *any* political arrangements (or none). The gatherings of people in the park on a sunny day are voluntary and call for no political arrangements, as such; the gatherings of persons in a church are voluntary despite the (often) total lack of democratic structures in the government of the church; and so on. Once a gathering is plainly voluntary, then there simply is no case for *imposing* "democratic" structures and procedures on it.

...The general principles of politics apply to the *polis* as a whole, and *not* to lesser groups and associations within it. Yet Dahl concludes, in summary, that "members of any association for whom the assumptions of the democratic process are valid have a *right* to govern themselves by means of the democratic process....We...see no convincing reasons why we should not exercise our right to the democratic process in the government of enterprises, just as we have already done in the government of the state."[10] But there *is* a convincing reason: namely, that business enterprises are *not* states, but instead voluntary associations—some of whose members, moreover, in many cases *own* the place and are thus entitled to offer whatever terms of membership to others they may wish, those others being free to take it or leave it.

...What Dahl does *not* consider is...the intrusion of requirements of "democracy" into what were supposed to have been free enterprises....Instead of persons being allowed to offer their services on whatever terms they wish, they will be restricted to firms for whom they must not only do what they claim to be able to do and interested in doing, such as attaching car parts to car bodies, or creating advertising graphics, or whatever, but also *must* get involved in directing the firm—something they may reasonably feel not worth the investment of their time and energies, and/or to which they may feel their talents and interests quite unsuited.

It is interesting that proponents of worker democracy do not see this aspect of the matter. In the view of the intellectuals who dream up these schemes, the right to run things is a self-evident good. How could it possibly be viewed otherwise? Well, to those of us who evade faculty council meetings whenever possible, the answer is remarkably obvious! Of course, if workers have only the *right* and not the *duty* to help run things, they might be able to exercise this right in a similar way, the way familiar to about half the voters in the United States—namely, by not bothering to use it. But it does run into the same problem: my not voting puts me at the mercy of all those who do.[11] And if it is replied that the alternative is being at the mercy of an undemocratic management, the further reply to this is that that could perfectly reasonably be thought to be *better*—especially if one gets paid more! Certainly there's nothing in it that would justify *requiring* that I be at the mercy of my fellow workers rather than a profit-thirsty management.

However, the main objection is more fundamental than this. For the forcibly imposed requirement that all associations within the society be "democratic" is in fact a denial of the right of freedom of association. It has the consequence that people are deprived of the possibility of creating associations, ones that would have been voluntarily entered into or whose services would have been happily taken advantage of by others, whenever the structure of the proposed association would have been nondemocratic. Thus—to take, again, examples whose significance we need to bear in mind— hardly any religions would pass muster, and very few organizations for the carrying on of sport, travel, culture, or education, among many others.

We do indeed have token student representation on faculty councils, left over from the '60s and widely considered a good thing. But this is hardly democratic. Were it to be fully "democratic," students would outnumber faculty on faculty councils by (currently) a ratio of about 25:1. If it is not obvious by this time why students should not have "power" equal or, as would be the case if each student counted equally, vastly superior to their professors at an institution of higher learning, it is probably futile (though entirely relevant) to observe that universities, unlike societies, have a *purpose.* That purpose is not one to which students, who are the consumers of a principal product of these enterprises, have any obvious claim to participate in the administration of. Like consumers, they vote with their feet, and like business executives, those who do administer universities are highly sensitive to that fact. But there is no case for democracy here, for the same reason that there is no fundamental case for it in businesses: the purpose of the firm is set by those who started it, and then those who by agreement acquire control, and not by its customers or its employees. These latter have a different kind of association with the firm: still, crucially, voluntary, but not one that constitutes a claim on its formal control. (Informally, of course, customers have the whip-hand: if they choose not to buy, as is their entire right, then the firm closes down.)

The conclusion, then, is that there are reasons at the constitutional level for objecting to the imposition of democracy on "the workplace." And these reasons stem from the same source as those which give rise in the first place to democracy as a plausible option in the political sphere. In this sense, then, democracy in general politics sits uncomfortably with its imposition on component associations in society.

DEMOCRACY AND ECONOMIC SYSTEMS

Those who insist that a society whose economic institutions are permitted to have undemocratic internal structures is thereby shown to be an undemocratic society need to consider a further point of importance about this relation: namely, that one would have thought that the choice of an "economic system" should, if there were no constitutional reasons of the kind we have been exploring for opposing it, at least be *open* to the voters. In a democracy, the people have the power to rule. Their votes determine who shall govern and, at least roughly, how. They cast those votes as they please—that's what makes it a democracy, after all. Apart from the proper constitutional constraints, they are free to vote for or against measures, or candidates who will support measures, regarding all and sundry matters of common interest. Presented with a choice between, say, free markets and some form of socialism, they could choose the former. If they did (as they evidently have, so far), then they acted in accordance with their democratic rights. This would seem to be a complete refutation of the claim that political democracy *entails* workplace democracy. And thus we must reject the claim that

a society in which people are allowed to form nondemocratic though voluntary associations is an *undemocratic society*.

Why would people fail to see this? One reason is illustrated by Carol Gould's recent book, *Rethinking Democracy,* in which, she says, she will present "the philosophical foundations of a theory that argues that democratic decision-making not only should apply to politics but should be extended to economic and social life as well." "I offer," she writes, "a normative argument for the right of participation in decision-making in all of these domains."[12] But that—as usual—is not in fact what she argues for. Indeed, she needn't have bothered to argue for that, since we already have it. Any association, be it industrial, social, religious, or whatever, may of course adopt democratic procedures if it so chooses. Instead, like Dahl, she argues for *imposing* democracy in the workplace. It's harder to impose on "society," of course: whether every literary tea must become democratic (or else!) under Gould's regime is unclear. What is clear, though, is that society is not democratic in her view unless it makes this "extension." And this brings up the question why she should think that "extension" is the right term to use here.

As her statement implies, she evidently thinks that "politics" is *one* sphere or domain, while economic and social matters are *another*. But that is quite wrong, something very like what used to be called a "category mistake." For politics is not one domain among others. Its domain is *everything* over which political control is possible. The typical legislature spends very little of its time legislating concerning "politics" in the narrowest sense—that is, such things as drawing constituency boundaries, drafting laws about the funding or operation of campaigns, and the like. A great deal of its time is instead spent discussing health, education, welfare, tariffs, crime—all of which are economic and social matters. That democracy is operative over those domains now is perfectly clear.

Those who say that a society, if it is to be democratic, must require that all its constituent groups be democratic as well face a paradox—if they accept that voters have the *liberty* to decide on all these matters. In accepting the right of the electorate to vote, say, in favor of socialism, one accepts that it may overrule individuals and groups who would have wanted it otherwise. But there is also the right to vote against it, in which case it may also overrule individuals (people like Dahl and Gould, say) who wanted it otherwise. Surely if a state is to be democratic, then decisions made by majority voice of *its* people are paradigmatically democratic. But those decisions can call for nondemocratic microstructures: schools, families, churches, and any number of others. And factories and other firms too, then. Thus the claim that if a state is to be democratic, then such component institutions as the workplace *must* be so too is incorrect—even if we don't invoke the stronger thesis of the previous section, according to which these are not even matters that should be put to the vote at all, being preempted by rights of freedom of association and of economic activity.

RAMPANT DEMOCRACY

We'll look at one last reason why people might suppose that political democracy isn't "enough." The thought that comes to mind is that perhaps a society is *more* democratic if more *of* it is democratic, namely, if its microassociations are likewise democratic. One recent writer who takes such a view is Frank Cunningham, who proposes a "degrees of democracy" approach to democratic theory. According to Cunningham,

To say that social unit 'A' is more democratic than 'B' is to say that

1. proportionately *more people* in A have control over the common social environment than do people in B; and/or

2. people in A have control over proportionately *more aspects* of their social environment than do people in B; and/or

3. the aspects of their social environment over which people in A have control are *more important* from the point of view of democracy than those over which people in B have control.[13] [my emphasis]

Now, what does "have control over" mean? Cunningham's own suggestion is that "a person has 'control' over something when what that person wishes to happen to it *does* happen in virtue, at least in part, of actions he or she has taken with this end in view.[14] Very well: but in that case, two points

must be made. The first, which is certainly fundamental, is that a system in which individuals as such can have control over things—namely, by owning them—may be argued to give people more of the kind of control Cunningham has in mind than one in which all matters are politicized.[15] Cunningham would no doubt reply to this by insisting that private ownership denies power over things to all but the owners of those things. But how does he know that the supposed losses of power thus entailed are not more than made up for by the gains?

However, he might also insist that collective control is simply what he is talking about. And it may be agreed that if we are talking about political democracy, then collective control does seem to be the central focus. In that case, however, we have a second point to make: namely, that those who have control could decide that what they should do with what they "have control over" is—nothing! In addressing the question of how various associations within the society should be structured, they might conclude that those associations should be structured in whatever way their members think best.

But if so, then this is enough to show that a society in which the government decides to muck around in the internal doings of its component associations need *not* be reckoned "more democratic" than one that does not. Moreover, a society in which The People decide in favor of a Hands Off Voluntary Associations policy would have its democratic will *thwarted* by some subassociation which democratized as a result of the threat of force against other members by some of its members (or by some non-members). Forced democratization in such a case would be *un*democratic. Those wishing to argue for imposing democracy in the workplace or other institutions, therefore, need other arguments than those calling for general political democracy in the first place.

My argument here does assume that the people ought, in principle, to *have* a choice in such matters. Democracies, after all, have come to grief by depriving themselves, by vote, of the right to vote in the future; if, like Dahl, we want to complain that such a vote was really undemocratic (despite being a majority vote), then perhaps there would be room for Cunningham to take a similar line here, arguing that to fail to impose democracy on such things as workplaces is in fact to act inconsistently with the idea of democracy.[16] That obviously depends on what one thinks that idea is, of course. But it can be countered immediately that unlike the case in which a democracy proceeds to disenfranchise itself, or to eliminate the requirement of periodic submission of elected officials to re-election, or to send people off to jail simply for opposing the re-election of the current regime, a public which elected not to impose democracy on the workplace will still be around tomorrow, able to elect officials and vote on all and sundry matters.

I conclude that the case for democracy's entailing worker democracy again comes, at best, to nothing. At worst, however, it does indeed come to something—something we should surely be loath to accept. To see this, just suppose we interpret Cunningham's "degrees of democracy" approach in such a way that a society is said to be "more democratic" only if it does *not* take the do-nothing option in any given case: it is, we will say, more "democratic" in proportion to the degree to which everything is politicized, everything made subject to detailed majority rulings, and everything required to have a political substructure with equal votes for all "members."

Is this something any rational person could possibly want? Pierre Trudeau famously insisted, in junking previous restrictions against homosexuality, that "the State should keep its nose out of the bedrooms of the nation." On this view, if the State did that, it would be shrinking from its democratic duty. The People would decide, in sexual matters, who should "do what, and with which, and to whom"; The People would decide what you should have for breakfast tomorrow; and so on and so on, without end. What is especially ironic is that the author of so totalitarian an idea should defend it in the name of "freedom." Presumably, he does not really mean this—one hopes! But if he does not, then we are back to seeing that economic rights in the form of the liberty of individuals and voluntary groups to find, make, buy, and sell goods and services as they please[17] are at least consistent with democracy. Or, in the greater wisdom that comes from trying to discern what democracy is all about in the first place, we may be led to embrace a view of democracy that makes it the child, rather than the parent, of liberty, in which case these freedoms are not merely consistent with but really *required* by democracy.

NOTES*

1. The idea isn't new. John Dewey, for instance, was a proponent. See "The Economic Basis of Society," ed. Joseph Ratner, *Intelligence in the Modern World* (New York: Modern Library, 1939), p. 422: "The third phase…is the need of securing greater industrial autonomy, that is to say, greater ability on the part of the workers in any particular trade or occupation to control that industry.…It is so common to point out the absurdity of fighting a war for political democracy which leaves industrial and economic autocracy practically untouched." Dewey's sentence suggests not only that the idea was in the air, but also that the same basic argument was employed that it is a main point of this essay to examine. Before Dewey, there were the guild socialists and the syndicalists. I am not, however, concerned here with the history of the idea, but only with its conceptual structure.

2. Robert A. Dahl, *A Preface to Economic Democracy* (Berkeley: University of California Press, 1985), p. 110.

3. Aristotle, *Politics*, bk. 6, ch. II, tr. Ernest Barker (Oxford: Clarendon Press, 1952), p. 258. I am grateful to the scholarly acumen of Ellen Paul and Fred Miller for bringing my attention to what might be thought support from a surprising quarter. (Lest we go overboard on this, we should take note also of this parenthetical observation: "It may be remarked that while oligarchy is characterized by good birth, wealth, and culture, the attributes of democracy would appear to be the very opposite—low birth, poverty, and vulgarity," p. 259.)

4. James Buchanan, "Contractarian Presuppositions and Democratic Governance," eds. Brennan and Lomasky, *Politics and Process*, pp. 176–77.

5. The literature of the Social Choice school, in particular, should be consulted. Buchanan's now-classic *The Limits of Liberty* (Chicago: University of Chicago Press, 1975) is a major case in point.

6. My own diagnosis of those fallacies is to be found in "Marxism: Hollow at the Core," *Free Inquiry*, vol. 3, no. 2 (Spring, 1983), pp. 29–35.

7. John Rawls, *A Theory of Justice* (Cambridge: Harvard University Press, 1971), p. 61.

8. *Ibid.*, p. 271.

9. *Ibid.*, p. 111.

10. *Ibid.*, p. 135.

11. Aristotle held that the best variety of democracy was the kind that obtains among a population of farmers. Among his main reasons for thinking that democracy would work well there is that "Such people, not having any great amount of property, are busily occupied; and thus they have no time for

_____

*Some notes have been deleted and the remaining ones renumbered.

attending the assembly…indeed they find more pleasure in work than they do in politics or government" (Ernest Barker, *The Politics of Aristotle* (Oxford: Clarendon Press, 1955), p. 263).

12. Carol C. Could, *Rethinking Democracy* (Cambridge: Cambridge University Press, 1988), p. 1.

13. Frank Cunningham, *Democratic Theory and Socialism* (New York: Cambridge University Press, 1987), pp. 26–27.

14. *Ibid.*, p. 27.

15. My thanks again to Ellen Paul for pointing out the aptness of this observation in relation to Cunningham's definitions.

16. This possibility was suggested by John Roemer. The response is mine and, I believe, different from (and an improvement on) my earlier response to him. Unfortunately, Roemer did not have the opportunity for further reply before the published version of this paper needed to be sent in.

17. I have attempted to spell these out somewhat in *The Libertarian Idea* (Philadelphia: Temple University Press, 1989), pt. I, and in the case of "initial acquisition," in a presently unpublished paper, "On Two Arguments About Liberty and Property," read at the American Philosophical Association, Pacific Division meetings, March 29, 1990.

Decision Scenario 1
QUALITY CIRCLES AND LABOR PRODUCTIVITY

In the 1970s, American industry became concerned about declining rates of productivity. That concern was made more acute by the recognition that a new competitor, Japan, had strikingly different productivity performance. As a result, American management began to look at Japanese management techniques for clues that might explain the difference in productivity. One of the "lessons" American management brought home was on the use of "quality circles." Japanese firms often had formally instituted group meetings where workers were given the opportunity to offer suggestions for improving product quality. These advisory quality circle meetings appeared to have the psychological effect of reducing alienation among employees. Management reasoned that improved morale would translate directly into improved productivity.

A decade or so of American experiments with this transplanted Japanese technique has provided rather mixed reviews. Much literature does document improved morale and decreased alienation among workers participating in quality circle programs. However, American organized labor has been largely skeptical of the idea. Labor's leadership often fears that the use of quality circles is an attempt to reduce the rank and file's loyalty to the union. The rank and file sometimes see the programs as a cynical management device for increasing company loyalty, and hence work, without raising wages.

The conflict over quality circles reflects the underlying adversarial nature of American labor relations. While some companies appear to have overcome deep labor–management distrust, other attempts at instituting employee advisory bodies have failed miserably. One commentator who has studied the issue extensively, Daniel Zwerdling, argues that the very nature of employee advisory groups is likely to cause problems. Because quality circles are purely advisory, with no actual decision-making power, they can lead to greater employee frustration and mistrust when management rejects employee proposals. Just because quality circles are a formal part of the institutional structure, the expectation that their deliberations will have some weight is greater. Thus, if management's intent to increase productivity is not combined with a sincere willingness to accept employee recommendations, the use of quality circles is unlikely to have a long-lasting positive effect on productivity.

If this analysis is correct, it raises questions for management that go beyond the difficulties associated with this borrowed Japanese technique. In fact, it raises questions about the very use of "techniques." It also suggests that a management that sees its employees as a resource to be "managed" (in other words, manipulated for greater profitability) is unlikely to reverse a declining productivity trend. Rather, long-term increases in worker morale may have to be tied to a more thorough redefinition of the concept of management.

- Is labor's fear of quality circles justified?
- What mechanisms might offer hope of overcoming the deeply adversarial nature of American labor relations? Do you believe that an adversarial relation is bad?

- Can American middle management learn to follow more participatory and consultative principles of management? What would that do to the authority of middle management?

Decision Scenario 2
AVIS EMPLOYEES PURCHASE THE COMPANY

In 1987 Avis, the number two car rental agency, was purchased by its employees through an employee stock ownership plan (ESOP). Avis was purchased from Wesray capital for $1.75 billion. Wesray, an investment firm, had purchased it in 1986 in a $1.6 billion leveraged buyout that had a mere $10 million capital outlay ensuring the purchase. Wesray managed a $740 million profit on that investment in just over a year.

Wesray sold the company to the ESOP partly because it could get a better price this way. ESOP buyouts receive tax advantages for both the buyer and the lender. For instance, an ESOP's payments on both principal and interest on debts acquired in the purchase are tax deductible. These advantages reduce eventual operating costs and so provide the possibility of greater profits. As a result, ESOPs can afford to take on somewhat more debt in purchasing a company.

The employee-owned stock in Avis will gradually grow as the ESOP pays off its purchase debts. These shares, however, are administered by a trustee. So while workers technically will own stock, their control over that stock is somewhat limited. Nonetheless, Avis's management believes that the change to an ESOP has had tangible benefits for the corporate bottom line. Chairman Joe Vittorio claims that ownership has improved employees' service and productivity. In an era when rising insurance rates and a depressed used car market put pressure on rental agency profits, Avis's profits rose 35 percent in the first six months of ESOP ownership. In addition, Avis's profits are close in dollar value to those of Hertz, even though this competitor has a revenue advantage of almost two to one.

Management believes the increased productivity is the result of more than the new ownership pattern, however. Vittorio has committed the corporation to a more participative management style in which employee representatives meet monthly to discuss ideas for improving productivity. Top management also meets regularly with employee representatives. The employees' greater psychological involvement through this plan has purported beneficial effects on profits. In fact, a research study of ESOPs indicates that those with participation programs will grow an average of 11 percent faster than those without such programs.

There is, of course, some skepticism about the advantages to Avis of the ESOP and quality circle groups. Competitors argue that the Avis program is merely an effective advertising gimmick that will not produce long-term benefits. Also, some of the increased profits may be attributed not to new employee attitudes but to the lower operating costs that come from a tax deduction on the $1 billion debt associated with Avis's new car fleet. Whatever the underlying cause of the profit figures, however, some Avis customers report greater satisfaction with the agency's service. It is also true that Avis's share of the market has grown in important geographical areas.

- What justification is there for giving ESOP-owned companies special tax concessions?
- Do you imagine that quality circle participation groups would increase productivity of workers to the same degree whether the company was ESOP owned or not?
- What are the possibilities for broad ESOP ownership of American industry in the future?

This case was prepared from the following sources: David Kirkpatrick, "How the Workers Run Avis Better," *Fortune*, December 5, 1988; *Business Week*, September 28, 1987 and May 9, 1988; *Fortune*, October 26, 1987.

- Is there likely to be a real difference in relations between management and employees just because of an ESOP or because of more frequent contact between the groups in participation programs?

Decision Scenario 3
THE MONDRAGON COOPERATIVES

The Basque region of Spain contains the world's most successful industrial cooperative, the Mondragon system. The Mondragon system is a group of more than eighty cooperatively owned firms with a combined total of over 18,000 employee owners. These profitable co-ops are the product of a single cooperative firm begun in 1956 under the guidance of a Spanish priest, José Maria Arizmendi.

The system of employee-owned businesses is supported by a cooperative educational system that provides well-educated workers and, most importantly, by a credit union that provides the capital required to sustain cooperative firms in their early years. The credit union's capital is raised from deposits by local residents. Its funds are used to supply loans to cover 60 percent of the startup costs of new cooperative enterprises and also to cover any deficits that accrue during the first two years of the firm's existence. The credit union also supplies invaluable organizational assistance by assigning credit union specialists to assist the cooperative's management in running the new firm. None of the fifty-six new cooperatives begun through the credit union between 1961 and 1976 has failed.

The cooperative firms maintain a maximum disparity between workers' wages of three to one. Since entry-level employees are paid wages comparable to those in noncooperative firms, higher-level employees have wages below the norm in other firms. This may be compensated for by the fact that most profits of the firm eventually return to the worker owners. But the distribution of annual profits is controlled by a policy mandating that 10 to 15 percent of the profits be returned to support community activities such as the school system, 15 percent be reinvested in the firm, and the remaining 70 percent be invested in accounts within the firm in the names of individual employees. These accounts pay employees interest, but the principal cannot be withdrawn until the worker retires. This policy for controlled profit distribution solves one of the most common problems of cooperative enterprises—the lack of operating capital due to too little reinvestment.

Mondragon policies also protect against another tendency of cooperatives—to revert to traditional private ownership by nonemployee stockholders. At Mondragon, the worker owners cannot sell their shares or continue to own stock after leaving the company. In addition, every new employee is required to buy shares in the firm (purchase of those shares can be facilitated by personal loans from the credit union).

Internal governance of the Mondragon cooperatives had until recently been primarily hierarchical and autocratic. Work at Mondragon differed little from the most routinized American factory. However, in the 1970s the Mondragon system began to evolve a more participatory system of governance in response to labor unrest at one of the larger cooperatives. Now most cooperatives have employee-elected boards to oversee management, direct involvement at the shop floor, and employee social councils that consider issues related to working conditions.

- How could a reliable source of initial capital for cooperative firms be created in the United States?
- What do you imagine prevents most U.S. cooperatives from adopting a Mondragon-like policy for controlling shares?
- Is a narrow range of wage levels necessary for maintaining a successful cooperative enterprise?
- The Mondragon system existed for two decades before implementing a more participative governance structure. Is it possible for cooperatives to exist with a hierarchical structure indefinitely?

This case was prepared from the following sources: Ana G. Johnson and William F. Whyte, "The Mondragon System of Worker Production Cooperatives," *Industrial and Labor Relations Review*, vol. 31, no. 1: 18–30; John Simmons and William Mares, *Working Together* (New York University Press, 1985), 136–142.

Decision Scenario 4
THE GERMAN MODEL OF EMPLOYEE PARTICIPATION

German law mandates worker participation in industrial decision-making. Since the 1950s, workers in many industries were guaranteed one-third representation on the board of directors. In the coal and steel industries, workers were guaranteed equal representation on company boards. In 1976 a new law expanded the coal and steel industry policy of codetermination to all companies with over two thousand employees. Critics of this policy of placing worker representatives on company boards have worried that the workers will use their new powers to block management policies. However, studies of over twenty-five years of codetermination in coal and steel indicate that unanimous decisions of the directors were common and that in no case was a tie-breaking vote needed to end an impasse between employee and management representatives.

Although worker representation on boards is now mandated for most large companies in Germany, approximately half of all workers are employed in companies not covered by the 1976 law. For these workers, as well as for all other German workers, participation comes through works councils. These councils are composed of employees only and are mandated for all firms with more than five employees. Employee representatives on these councils are elected for three-year terms. Employers are required to pay costs associated with the operations of the councils. For example, worker representatives must be given release time for their obligations on the councils, and they must have paid leaves available for acquiring the education needed for their duties.

Works councils have broad authorities. They control the employee grievance process. They have the right to codetermine policies governing, among other things, work hours, wages, bonus plans, and safety regulations. They must be consulted about layoffs, plant closures or relocations, mergers, and new work methods. On these matters employers have the final decision, but the employer must codecide with works councils about any social plan for minimizing the effect of such decisions on workers. If the employer and works council cannot reach an agreement, the issue is subjected to binding arbitration. Works councils also are entitled to financial information about the firm.

Again, American management has expressed fears about the likely results of sharing such powers with workers. But numerous commentators argue convincingly that the German system has produced greater labor peace and higher productivity. One report suggests that work stoppages in the United States are seventeen times higher per one hundred thousand workers than in the Federal Republic of Germany. Even German management reports that the councils are an essential ingredient of their conception of effective management.

- Are there conditions in the U.S. industrial relations tradition that would make a successful transplant of the German model impossible?

- What explanations can we give of the failure of U.S. law to have requirements similar to those of Germany?

- Why is there little evidence of significant differences between workers and management on German boards? Would the same experience be expected if American workers were given similar representation?

- Would you expect a deterioration in employee discipline under the German model?

This case was prepared from the following sources: John Simmons and William Mares, *Working Together* (NYU Press, 1985), 283; Paul Blumberg, *Industrial Democracy* (Schocken Books, 1969), 158–160; G. David Garson, "Models of Worker Self-Management: The West European Experience," in *Worker Self-Management in Industry*, edited by G. D. Garson (Praeger, 1977), 12; Alfred Daimant, "Democratizing the Workplace: The Myth and Reality of *Mitbestimmung* in the Federal Republic of Germany," in op. cit., 30–35; Frank Anton, *Worker Participation: Prescription for Industrial Change* (Detselig Enterprises Ltd., 1980), 31–37.

Decision Scenario 5
ELECTROMATION: ILLEGAL EMPLOYEE PARTICIPATION

Electromation is a small nonunion manufacturer of electronic components used in cars and power tools. The company is located in Elkhart, Indiana. In 1989, it instituted an employee participation program, partly in response to employee complaints about new attendance and bonus policies. Separate committees were formed to offer proposals to management on policies for wage scales, absenteeism, bonus pay, and other issues. Management selected the employee members of the committees and also named one supervisor to each committee. The employee benefits manager was also named as an *ex officio* member of every committee. In committee discussions, some fledgling proposals were immediately rejected by the management members, and the teams then created alternate policy suggestions. Before any proposal could be acted on by management, however, a union organizing campaign began in the plant. Management informed workers that it could not interact with the committees until after the union election. In the union certification vote, employees voted against union representation by a vote of 95 to 82.

After the failed unionization campaign, a complaint was lodged with the National Labor Relations Board (NLRB) alleging that the employee participation committees were illegal under the National Labor Relations Act (NLRA), Section 8 (a)(2) (also known as the Wagner Act). When the Wagner Act was passed in 1935, one of its chief targets was the employer-sponsored labor groups that management used as a tactic to discourage employees from choosing representation by independent labor unions. Congress outlawed that tactic by banning "company dominated labor organizations." The act defined a labor organization as one that dealt with management and addressed conditions of work. The act proscribed company domination or interference with the formation or administration of any labor organization, and it also prohibited company financial or other support for a labor organization.

The NLRB found the Electromation committees to be illegal company-dominated labor organizations, and its judgment was affirmed by the United States Supreme Court in 1994. Both the NLRB and the Supreme Court held that the Electromation committees were labor organizations because they involved bilateral discussions of the conditions of work—that is, employee representatives made proposals about wages, benefits, smoking policies, grievance procedures, and the like that were to be accepted or rejected by management. The NLRB and the Court also held that Electromation dominated these labor organizations because it formed the committees, selected the membership and topics for the committees, set the agenda for meetings, gave management representatives implicit veto power over proposals, and paid for the employees' time, as well as for the supplies and space used by the committees. One NLRB member put it this way: "They gave the employees the illusion of a bargaining representative without the reality of one."

In this and subsequent decisions, the NLRB has made it clear that employee involvement committees such as those at Electromation will be found illegal unless and until Congress changes the Wagner Act's language. Through its decisions, the NLRB has also made clear the legality of employee committees that serve as mere "brainstorming" sessions that communicate employee opinions or other information to management. The Supreme Court has said that Section 8 (a)(2) does not foreclose employee committees that do not function in a representative capacity and that focus solely on increasing company productivity, efficiency, and quality control (that is, do not deal with working conditions such as pay, grievances, hours of work, and so on). Additionally, in its later DuPont decision, the NLRB accepted a joint labor–management committee provided that "the committee were governed by majority decision-making, management representatives were in the minority, and the committee had the power to decide matters for itself, rather than simply make proposals to management."

Labor relations specialists are troubled by these decisions. They worry that the decisions allow only for either extreme: weak employee organizations that have very limited scope and no decision-making powers or strong, independent committees that have real authority to make and implement decisions. What appears to run afoul of the law are precisely the sorts of management-sponsored employee participation programs that management theorists have been urging as necessary for the competitiveness of American industry: programs that can discuss the sometimes interrelated issues of productivity and working conditions and that make proposals to management. A number of respected labor relations theorists have called for a revision of Section 8 (a)(2) of the NLRA, as has the recent governmental Dunlop Commission. Union leaders, however, dissent from that call. They still are concerned that in a nation where employers are often hostile to unions, companies will use a change in

the law to revert to the old tactics of in-house, company unions.

- If we allow employee participation in issues of working conditions, what features must the participation programs have to avoid becoming "company dominated unions"?

- Are participation programs helpful or harmful to the goals espoused by unions?

- Can we draw a sharp distinction between issues that relate to productivity and issues that relate to wages and other working conditions?

- Why do some believe that employee involvement is necessary for the competitiveness of American business?

Decision Scenario 6

DONNELLY MIRRORS: FORTY YEARS OF PARTICIPATION

Donnelly Mirrors, Inc., of Holland, Michigan, has been experimenting with worker participation for over four decades. In 1952, the company introduced a Scanlon gain-sharing plan. The plan at Donnelly involved teams of management and elected nonmanagement employees that met to exchange information and suggest cost-saving ideas. Any savings from those ideas were shared among all the workers. The goal of Scanlon plans like the one at Donnelly is to improve productivity, but the plans achieve that goal by engendering a sense of ownership and team cooperation among employees.

Over the years, Donnelly Mirrors introduced a number of new elements to its participation scheme. When they realized that some cost-saving ideas were also job-elimination ideas, they also realized that there were disincentives for employees to offer some money-saving suggestions. So they guaranteed that a worker whose job was eliminated would receive 90 percent of his or her wage for twelve months.

The company also began to use the teamwork concept more broadly. It set up work teams at all levels throughout the company. The teams deal

with all facets of the business. For any given level, the teams would be headed by a supervisor and would include representatives of the employees from that level. The team leaders are chosen by a selection group composed of employees from all levels of the firm. Each team leader is also a member of the team at the next highest level. The teams' overlapping membership is an attempt to ensure a free flow of communication both up and down the corporate structure. It also aims to develop feelings of trust and ownership among the employees. Donnelly must have had an intuitive sense of what works. More recent studies seem to confirm that gain-sharing plans are unlikely to succeed unless significant levels of trust and cooperation are present. After the introduction of this team organization, the company experienced a significant increase in productivity.

Donnelly Mirrors also created another committee that was independent of the work team structure. The committee is known as the Donnelly Committee. The committee has fifteen members, including the company president, who sits *ex officio*. The other members are elected by the employees and come from all parts of the company. The Donnelly Committee governs issues related to working conditions, pay, grievances, and the like. A company spokesperson described the Donnelly Committee as a safety net on issues of fairness and a

---

This case was prepared from the following sources: *Harvard Business Review*, vol. 55, no. 1 (1977): 118; the Dunlop Report; Alan Blinder, ed., *Paying for Productivity* (Washington, D.C.: The Brookings Institute, 1990).

guarantee that all employees have a voice in personnel policies that affect them. Elected members serve a two-year term but are subject to recall by their constituencies if they vote in a manner the electors disapprove. Of interest, the committee takes no action unless there is unanimous agreement, so everyone knows how each member voted. The unanimity requirement, however, does not seem to prevent decisions from being made. Rather, it functions as a consensus builder.

- Donnelly Mirrors is a family-owned business that is still influenced by the values of its founding family. Do you think that the Donnelly approach could work in a corporate culture that did not have that family influence?

- The team concept entails that workers spend a substantial amount of time in meetings. While that work time appears to produce productivity gains at Donnelly, do you believe that it would in all cases? What are the conditions that make productivity gains more probable? What conditions make them less probable?

- How significant in your mind is the presence of the separate Donnelly Committee in the effectiveness of the work team organizational structure?

8

Employee Privacy

What rights of privacy, if any, should employees have? Do employers have a right to know about their employees' activities outside of the workplace? Can an employee legitimately be fired for smoking, or is this decision a purely personal matter? Is the sexual orientation of an employee a legitimate concern of the employer? Can an employer who believes that abortion is unethical fire an employee who chooses to have an abortion? Can employers conduct drug tests on job applicants? On present employees? Are polygraph tests for employees ethically legitimate? Are psychological tests? What about screening for genetic disorders? Should an employer be allowed to screen job applicants and employees for AIDS? Are employers justified in using electronic surveillance in the workplace?

Each of these questions was raised by actual cases in recent years. Each asks about the extent to which an employee maintains her or his privacy in the workplace. This chapter examines the issue of workplace privacy by examining the nature, value, and extent of employee privacy.

In one sense the controversy returns to the familiar tension between an employer's goal of controlling costs and an employee's concern with being free from unwarranted interference. In simple terms, the more an employer knows about an employee, the better able she'll be to control (or "manage") the workplace. For example, statistics show that employees who smoke will have higher health care costs than employees who do not. For an employer who provides health insurance, this fact can have major financial implications. Management can significantly reduce health care costs by eliminating smokers from the work force. A similar claim can be made about employer knowledge of employee drug use, criminal records, HIV test results, and genetic makeup, as well as more mundane information like work experience, work habits, personality, and educational background.

Yet privacy issues can also raise questions about the very nature of work. Are jobs merely the property of employers who can dispose of them as they choose, hiring and firing at will? What rights do employers have in this regard? Can employers establish just any criteria as job qualifications? Shouldn't employers be allowed the freedom to employ people of their own choosing? Would an employer be ethically justified in deciding to hire only heterosexuals? Only Christians? The law sets some limits to this, of course. People cannot legally be denied jobs solely on the basis of race or sex, for example. But are these legal restrictions themselves ethically valid? In deciding what information is job relevant and what information should remain personal and private, we are also deciding the limits of control that employers can exercise over the workplace.

THE NATURE OF PRIVACY

As we begin to examine these questions, we need to think more carefully about privacy itself. What is privacy, and why is it important? Two, not altogether different, conceptions of privacy are common. One understanding of privacy, most common in legal debates, centers around the notion of being "let alone." In this sense, privacy is closely related to individual liberty and autonomy: There are some areas of a person's life that should remain totally a matter of the person's discretion. These legal discussions of privacy are usually traced to an essay written for the *Harvard Law Review* in 1890 by Samuel Warren and Louis Brandeis. In their article, Warren and Brandeis were troubled that certain technological advances and business practices, particularly the practice of some newspapers of printing stories and photographs of private parties (today called "tabloid journalism"), were causing an increasing threat to the solitude of individual citizens. In the face of what they saw as increasingly intrusive technology and business activities, they defended privacy as "the next step which must be taken for the protection of the person, and for securing to the individual...the right 'to be let alone.'"

Over the past one hundred years, the U.S. Supreme Court has debated the extent of this right "to be let alone." It was not until 1965, however, that the Court explicitly recognized a constitutionally protected right of privacy. In *Griswold v. Connecticut* the Court ruled that the Constitution established a "zone of privacy" around each citizen that is created by certain constitutional rights. This particular ruling invalidated a Connecticut law that prohibited the use of contraceptives by married couples. That decision, the Court ruled, is best left to the discretion of individual conscience.

At first glance, this might seem much too vague and broad an understanding of privacy. It is difficult to see how a general claim to be let alone can be maintained by anyone who wishes to participate in any social arrangement, particularly an essentially social and cooperative activity like work. Thus, debates concerning privacy usually focus on drawing the boundary between those decisions that are personal and those that are legitimately the concern of others. Historically, these legal cases have involved decisions concerning the family, the home, raising and educating children, sexuality, reproduction, abortion, and the decision to forgo life-sustaining medical treatment.

A second understanding of privacy focuses not so much on personal *decisions* as on personal *information*. This view understands privacy as involving information about oneself and the right of privacy as the right to control that personal information. We can return to the concerns of Warren and Brandeis to appreciate the informational sense of privacy.

It would seem that the journalism practices that troubled Warren and Brandeis did not threaten the interest in being "let alone" as much as they violated the interest in keeping personal information private. People attending social events, after all, don't want to be let alone; they simply wish to prevent the general public from knowing the details of their private life. Informational privacy is violated when a person loses control over information that is rightfully personal, as when news reporters and newspaper readers come to know the intimate details of a person's social life.

The philosopher George Brenkert has suggested that this right of privacy involves a three-place relation between a person (A), some information about that person (X), and another person (Z). The informational right of privacy is violated only when Z comes to possess information X, *and* no relationship between A and Z exists that would justify Z's coming to know X. Following Brenkert, we shall say that the informational sense of privacy is "the right of individuals, groups, or institutions that access to and information about themselves is limited in certain ways by the relationships in which they exist to others."[*]

Thus, to understand informational privacy in employment we need to return to the nature of the employer–employee relationship. What, exactly, is this relationship, and what does it justify an employer coming to know about employees? On one hand, if the work relationship simply involves the property rights of employers to hire and fire "at will," then it would seem that employers have little claim to privacy in the workplace. On the other hand, if employment is viewed on a contractual model between equals, then employee consent would place major limits on what an employer can come to know about employees. On this view, employers would have a claim to know only information that is job relevant and for which employees have consented to their coming to know. This issue is picked up in the reading by DesJardins and Duska in this chapter.

THE VALUE OF PRIVACY

Understanding what privacy is will not be sufficient for a complete evaluation of privacy in the workplace. Even if we could establish that employees do maintain a right of privacy in the workplace, we need to know something about its value

[*]George Brenkert, "Privacy, Polygraphs, and Work," *Business and Professional Ethics Journal*, vol. 1, no. 1 (Fall 1981): 19–35.

before deciding if employee privacy overrides the concerns of employers. Why should privacy be desirable? Is it so important that it should be protected by legal and ethical rights?

Let us begin by considering the value of informational privacy. What would be wrong, what values would be lost, if, for example, the content of your diary was published in the local newspaper? Why should we so value controlling our most personal thoughts and feelings?

One source of concern would be the embarrassment and anxiety we would no doubt feel if our most personal thoughts became public. But what explains this anxiety? Why don't we want others to know our most personal thoughts? Part of the reason may be a fear about what others might do with this information. We are made vulnerable by others knowing a great deal about us. Part also is the desire to maintain some basic core of personal integrity. To maintain a sense of personal identity—*this* is who I am—requires some boundary between self and others. Maintaining that boundary, whether by control of the personal information or by reserving certain decisions for the individual, is an important element of protecting the integrity of our own selves. Certainly it is part of what we mean by the ethical commitment to respect the dignity of individuals.

Another aspect of this concerns the relationships that we have with other people. Consider for a minute the differences between strangers, acquaintances, friends, "best" friends, family, lovers. Cannot these differences be explained in terms of the amount of information shared? Isn't the difference between an acquaintance and a friend due in large measure to the fact that friends know more about you? We confide in friends, we trust them, we let them see who we "really" are. Thus it seems our social identity—the roles we fill, the relationships that we have with others—also depends on privacy.

When we compare this to the kinds of decisions that the Supreme Court has considered to involve privacy—decisions about family, children, sexuality, reproduction, abortion, even death—we can see that these all deeply affect our very identity as an individual. These decisions seem fundamental to establishing the persons that we are: parent, spouse, lover, even the person who is unwilling to exist dependent on a respirator.

Thus the value of privacy seems connected to respecting and protecting the integrity of individuals. Respecting others as individual persons seems to commit us to maintaining a boundary between the *personal* and the public. Privacy, whether it concerns certain basic decisions we make or controlling personal information, would appear to be a major element in the ethical responsibility to respect other persons. Thus, a reasonable case could be made that the *right* of privacy is derived from the more fundamental right to being treated with respect. A person whose privacy is violated is being treated with a lack of respect.

How others might use the personal information that they come to possess is the final consideration. We said earlier that a person who loses privacy often feels vulnerable. Typically, we have a reason for keeping personal information private. We are put into a fundamentally coercive position when someone possesses personal information about us, *and* they know that we had a reason not to divulge that information. Blackmail is perhaps the most dramatic example of a situation in which an individual can be coerced by a threat to disclose personal information.

THE EXTENT OF PRIVACY

With this examination of the nature and value of privacy in general, we turn next to the extent of privacy in the workplace. If we adopt Brenkert's understanding of informational privacy as our model, we can develop conclusions about workplace privacy by starting with an examination of the employer–employee relationship. Following the reasoning in Chapter Five, we can assume here that this relationship is a contractual relationship. In general, then, we can say that employee privacy is violated whenever personal information is collected or used by an employer for any purpose that is irrelevant to or in violation of the employment contract.

More specifically, there are three conditions of any valid contract: (a) It must arise out of the informed consent of both parties; (b) it must be free from fraud or coercion; and (c) it presupposes a legal system to be enforceable. Thus, we have a framework for determining the extent of employee privacy. Information that ensures that the contract is free from fraud (such as misinformation about past employment experience or educational background), that has been gathered with the informed consent of employees, or that is required by law would seem not to be rightfully private.

A helpful exercise is to apply this framework to information requested prior to employment. (For example, should a job applicant be required to supply his Social Security number?) Or apply this framework to the use to which employers can put personal information. (For example, can information gathered for health insurance purposes be used to deny jobs or dismiss employees?) Are all methods of gathering information (such as polygraph tests, drug tests, and electronic surveillance), even job-relevant information, equally valid?

Finally, there are a number of ethical reasons why an employee might wish to keep personal information from her employer. On one hand, of course, if an employee does have a legitimate ethical claim to a right of privacy, then the burden of proof rests on the employer to justify any infringement on this right. But as we've seen, employers can make the claim that they have a justification: Economic efficiency is served by this increase in employer knowledge. How might employees respond?

Two responses deserve note. First, as we've said, privacy is important for maintaining the boundaries that establish our personal identity. For many people it is important to maintain a distinction between work and home, between their life as an employee and their life outside of work. Very few people desire to be completely identified with their work. Most of us, whether we work at jobs we love or at jobs full of drudgery and toil, need to be able to "punch out" and leave work behind. There are good psychological as well as ethical reasons for being able to separate our role as employee from our roles as parent, spouse, citizen, neighbor, and so on. Privacy is a necessary part of maintaining this boundary.

Second, many employees have good reason to fear the uses to which personal information will be put by employers. Most obviously, the personal information that employers seek will be used to affect one's job status. Employers seek personal information about employees to improve managerial decisions. These personnel decisions ultimately rest on the ability to hire, fire, demote, and transfer employees. An employee's ability to protect his job can be a function of his ability to protect his privacy.

CASE STUDY Genetic Screening in the Workplace

The Humane Genome Project is a worldwide multi-billion-dollar project aimed at mapping and sequencing the entire human genome, the approximately one hundred thousand individual genes that form the molecular basis of human life. "Mapping" genes involves identifying and locating all the individual genes on a particular chromosome; "sequencing" involves identifying the particular sequence of DNA base pairs, thought to be perhaps three billion, that make up the human genome. Within the last decade thousands of genes have been located at specific sites on chromosomes, and dozens of major diseases have been linked to particular genes. Among those identified are genes linked to Huntington's chorea, cystic fibrosis, inherited forms of colon cancer and breast cancer, and Alzheimer's disease. Some evidence also suggests a genetic basis for heart disease, high blood pressure, diabetes, and arthritis. Claims have even been made that link genes to alcoholism, homosexuality, and criminality.

But the language of a genetic "link" or a genetic "basis" is ambiguous. In some cases, like sickle-cell anemia, Huntington's chorea, and Down syndrome, there is a direct causal connection between the presence of a particular gene and the resultant disease. The presence of a specific genetic structure causes the disease. But in other cases, like cancer and heart disease, the linkage is more a matter of a predisposition or a susceptibility than a cause. People with a specific genetic makeup are predisposed or susceptible to the disease, but many other factors like environment and diet also seem to be necessary. In still other cases where the gene is linked to complex phenomena like alcoholism, intelligence, schizophrenia, or homosexuality, the linkage amounts to little more than a statistical correlation: The presence of specific genes is statistically related to those phenomena.

The Human Genome Project has tremendous implications for medicine. It has already provided significant new knowledge for understanding and diagnosing disease. Unfortunately, therapy and treatment for these diseases often lag many years behind knowledge of their genetic basis. Nevertheless, significant therapeutic advances will certainly follow in coming years.

To some observers, the project raises serious ethical issues as well. Many fear that employers and insurance companies, in particular, would use genetic screening as a means for denying jobs and insurance. Even a small statistical correlation between a certain gene and cancer would provide a strong incentive for an insurance company to reduce its risks by denying insurance to carriers of this gene. Likewise, business can reduce its risk by not hiring people with a genetic susceptibility to disease, or whose genes suggest a predisposition to alcoholism, crime, or a psychological disorder.

Since most of the Human Genome Project is funded by the federal government, the Office of Technology Assessment (OTA) of the U.S. Congress was charged with examining some of these issues. The OTA's report, *Genetic Monitoring and Screening in the Workplace*, found very few employers who were using genetic screening in the workplace. While only twelve of the 330 Fortune 500 companies surveyed reportedly used genetic monitoring or screening, half thought that genetic screening is acceptable and almost half report that the costs of insuring a job applicant would affect their decision to hire someone.

As the Human Genome Project progresses, new and less expensive techniques for genetic screening will no doubt be developed. This will provide employers and insurance companies with an added incentive to use these tools for screening employees. Since most people receive health insurance through work, both insurers and employers have incentives to work together to gather this information and reduce their risks.

One preliminary study found several cases in which individuals were denied jobs because of their genetic conditions.[1] One case involved the brother of a person with Gaucher Disease (a disease affecting fat metabolism) who was denied a job after including this information on a job application. The brother was labeled a "carrier" and denied the job as a result. In another case, a woman was denied employment because she had Charcot-Marie-Tooth disease (a nonfatal, genetically based neuromuscular disease).

Several states have considered laws that would restrict the use of genetic information. The federal Americans with Disabilities Act (1990) prohibits employment discrimination on the basis of past and current disabilities. But the law says nothing about future disabilities or people with only a susceptibility to some disease. Insurance companies, of course, are free to treat people with preexisting conditions differently than those without. Additionally, there seems to be no legal protection for people identified as having predispositions to disease or behavioral traits such as alcoholism or crime.

The increasingly likely use of genetic screening in the workplace raises many ethical questions. In coming years, society must decide if employers have a legitimate claim to conduct genetic tests, to possess information about employees' genetic makeup, and to deny jobs or insurance to people on the basis of this information.

Additionally, as in other privacy issues, we need to acknowledge the important role of consent. The most obvious way to justify diminishing privacy rights is to obtain the consent of the people affected. Society needs to decide if employees should be free to refuse genetic tests without fear of reprisal and if they should have the right to be informed of the results of any tests. In essence, we need to resolve the question of ownership. Does the information obtained by genetic tests belong to the employer or the employee? Even if the test results suggest a susceptibility to some risk, does it necessarily follow that employers should have the right to exclude others from taking that risk? Perhaps employees should have the freedom to take a job that, given their genetic makeup, increases health risks.

Finally, a number of concerns can be raised about the economics of the tests themselves. Employers will always want to reduce costs, and this will likely mean that the best available tests, as well as follow-up techniques to verify test results, will not always be used. The cost to follow up screening with genetic counseling and medical advice means that it will probably not be provided. Also, genetic tests will likely be used as screening devices rather than as monitoring tools because genetic screening is typically a one-time occurrence, whereas genetic monitoring is conducted on an ongoing basis to determine if the condition is worsening. Since monitoring is both more expensive and more likely to indicate that the workplace itself is contributing to the health risk, employers are more likely to rely on genetic screening to filter out "undesirable" employees.

NOTES

1. Paul Billings et al., "Discrimination as a Consequence of Genetic Testing," *American Journal of Human Genetics* 50 (1992): 476–482.

FAIR HIRING TESTS
Robert Ellis Smith

In this age of high tech, employers are increasingly relying on some rather low-tech, and often unreliable, methods for selecting employees. They seem no longer interested in experience, skills, and character to determine whether an individual is qualified for a particular job. Instead they have delegated the task of screening applicants to impersonal measurements—urinalysis, blood tests, fingerprints, psychological tests, pen-and-pencil honesty tests, computerized criminal-record checks, and even handwriting analysis and astrology.

Each of these methods has what many people in the high-tech era consider a benefit: the tests void the necessity to confront other people directly. This has profound implications for the individuality, dignity, and privacy of employees in America.

"We are frisking each other," *New York Times* columnist William Safire once wrote. "Picture yourself going to work tomorrow, handing over blood and urine samples, taking a quick turn with the house polygraph, turning out your pockets and walking through some new fluoroscope. You object? Whatsamatter, you got something to hide?"

Each of these methods has different levels of reliability and intrusiveness (and legality), and so employers and employees have to be discriminating. Applicants must know the attributes of each screening device and decide whether the job is worth the indignity.

The most fraudulent of these devices is the poly-graph, or so-called lie detector. Federal law now virtually bans the devices for screening applicants.

CURRENT TESTING FAD

The current fad—and that is what it is—is the use of urinalysis tests to detect the presence of drugs. The sudden popularity of this methodology in the early 1980s was due directly to a test developed and aggressively marketed by the California-based Syva Corporation. The test is simple and cheap. It produced what seemed to be a perfect weapon in the war on drugs: a way to determine the presence of drugs by analyzing a person's urine.

The trouble is that it also picks up the presence of substances besides illegal drugs, like aspirin, codeine, or herbal diet products. It does not distinguish between one-time use and habitual abuse. (In fact, there is medical evidence that the Syva test is more likely to pick up the one-time user, not the addict.) Nor does the test measure impairment on the job, only the possible presence of drugs within the past several days. The manufacturers warn that the test is not valid without a confirming test using a different methodology, but many employers and laboratories ignore this. A judge in Massachusetts, citing expert testimony, concluded flatly that Syva's test "is never conclusive."

Unlike the case of the polygraph, there seem to be alternative methods of analyzing urine that have a higher reliability rate than the readily available Syva product. But these alternatives are expensive and, except in major league baseball, not often used by employers. Commonly, applicants and employees are simply rejected or disciplined on the basis of the once-over-lightly Syva test or its clones.

Here the development of the polygraph is instructive. It was developed as a means of measuring stress in highly structured interrogations; it was never intended as an absolute indicator of truth or falsity, especially in the hands of inexperienced examiners. The Syva urinalysis test was intended to measure marijuana use in large groups. It was never thought to be precise enough to determine the fate of one individual.

Whereas the polygraph was favored by small, often shaky businesses, the urinalysis test is favored by large corporations and shunned by small opera-

tions. Nearly a fifth of Fortune's 500 largest corporations reported using drug testing in the mid-1980s.

TEST USE WANING?

There is new evidence that use of the tests has peaked. A 1991 study by the U.S. Department of Labor found that one out of three companies that had urinalysis tests in 1988 had discontinued them by 1990. It was mostly companies with fewer than fifty employees that were discovering that urinalysis programs were not worthwhile. Large companies were continuing their programs largely because federal law required them to do so in order to continue to do federal contract work. A study of the American Medical Association at the same time showed that drug testing is not cost-effective unless drug use in the workplace is known to be high.

A leading laboratory involved in this distasteful work, SmithKline-Beecham, reported fewer and fewer positive test results in the past five years. In federal agencies and in college athletics, drug testing has succeeded only in showing that drug use there is minuscule (one half of 1 percent). Was this because the threat or reality of drug testing has successfully deterred drug use, or was it because drug use was never a major problem in most workplaces in the first place?

While the fad was hot, thirteen states moved to restrict it: California, Florida, Hawaii, Iowa, Maine, Maryland, Minnesota, Montana, Nebraska, New Mexico, Oregon, Rhode Island, and Vermont.

We can now see that during the drug-testing mania many people got hurt. Their dignity and their self-esteem were irreparably damaged.

For instance, a flight attendant in California suffered medical complications because of federal transportation requirements that compel drug-testing monitors to have employees drink water until they can provide a urine sample. The 40-year-old woman was pressured to drink more and more water—three quarts of it—and expected to urinate in a crowded room. She couldn't. After three hours she was sent home. That night she couldn't sleep and she couldn't urinate. She was hospitalized with water intoxication.

A husky oil rig worker was so humiliated about having to urinate in front of coworkers that he began to weep when testifying about it before a jury. He was awarded compensatory damages in his lawsuit.

A woman employed at a nuclear plant in Georgia described her experience: "The first day I went in I could not give enough urine. The second day, the nurse made me stand in the middle of the bathroom with one hand in the air, with my pants around my ankles, and a bottle between my legs. She walked real close behind me and leaned over. I was scared she was going to touch me. She screamed at me that I had not followed procedure, and I was going to have to do it again. Well, needless to say, I did not do it again, and I will never, if it means that I will never have a job again, I will never do that again."

PUBLIC SUPPORT

Yet most Americans supported drug testing in the workplace and still do. Isn't this based on their misunderstanding of the actual humiliation involved in the process, on their misguided faith in the reliability of the methodology, on their abhorrence of drug use at work, and on their fear of being suspected of being tolerant of drug use? This is reminiscent of the McCarthyism era in the 1950s, another time when Americans abandoned their good judgment and accepted a cure worse than the disease.

The blood test for the HIV AIDS virus, like nearly all tests, is not 100-percent reliable. There are many "false positives" in any test. These are results that falsely show the presence of the virus. Any test also produces the opposite effect, "false negatives." And it is important to remember that a confirmed positive test will show that the individual has the virus, not the AIDS condition itself. Still, the HIV test, when confirmed, is reliable enough for its purposes, to advise individuals of their health condition.

But, in view of the Public Health Service's unequivocal advisory that AIDS is not transmitted by other than sexual contact or blood transference, is there any rationale for employers to require AIDS tests of applicants or employees? Most employers at present have answered no.

The states of Montana, Nebraska, New Mexico, Vermont, Washington, and Wisconsin ban AIDS testing in the workplace. Most states prohibit AIDS testing without consent.

Some companies have begun testing applicants' and employees' blood for the presence of genetic traits that are said to make one susceptible to certain substances in the workplace or to have a likelihood of developing certain inherited diseases. Genetic screening will detect certain diseases that are inherited or a susceptibility to certain diseases that are not directly inherited. For example, a certain gene seems to show a propensity for Alzheimer's disease, but not a direct inheritance of the disease; not everyone with the gene seems to get Alzheimer's disease.

Genetic screening can also expose vulnerabilities to certain environmental exposures. For example, some people with a particular gene that results in a deficiency of an enzyme may face a destruction of their red blood cells if they take an antimalarial drug. Some scientists believe that there are many substances used in manufacturing that have properties similar to the antimalarial drug. People identified with this condition, therefore, should be warned against exposure to these substances on the job.

At present, according to the Congressional Office of Technology Assessment, "The power to identify biological risks (that is, the exposure to infectious disease or genetic vulnerability to chemicals in the environment) often outstrips the capability to remove or reduce those risks. This raises a demand for social control measures that sometimes impinge on constitutional freedoms."

During this interim period when there is a gap between our ability to identify genetic conditions and our inability to do much about them, is it fair to deprive a person of making a living based on genetic screening? And is it any business of an employer to know sensitive medical conditions that the individual himself or herself may not be aware of yet and that may have no effect on one's ability to do a job? Wisconsin has moved to regulate genetic testing, but no other state has yet. With benign motives, employers could use test results to assign employees to safe environments and to warn them of risks, not to bar them from jobs.

The danger is that this new DNA technology will be used in unsophisticated ways in the workplace, just as polygraphs, urinalysis, and other developments have been. It could be used as an absolute denial of employment, rather than a red flag or a guide to safe assignments. It could be used merely to reject applicants who may cause concern to the employer's health insurance provider. Used as a shortcut to selecting employees, DNA screening will be disastrous for many innocent people.

HONESTY TESTS

Now that polygraph testing is prohibited, some companies use pen-and-pencil honesty tests, designed to elicit responses that betray a dishonest personality. The problem for the job applicant is that no one knows the right answer to questions like, "Do most people steal?" or "Should a judge dismiss a minor stealing charge against a poor person?" That includes the authors of the "tests." They don't know the right answers either, but they purport to tell companies which employees will be trustworthy based on answers to these questions.

Many state laws prohibiting polygraphs in employment—including those in Connecticut, Maryland, Michigan, Minnesota, Nebraska, and Wisconsin—also prohibit honesty testing. Massachusetts and Rhode Island prohibit them explicitly.

No laws specifically address psychological tests in the workplace, although nearly every state human rights commission has declared that use of the most popular test violates state antidiscrimination requirements. That test is the controversial Minnesota Multiphasic Personality Inventory (MMPI).

Because of such attention to the MMPI, questions about sexual activities, religious beliefs, and bladder and bowel functions have been eliminated from a revised version.

The test is used regularly in the selection and assignment of employees. It had never been revised since it was first published in 1942. Think of the changes in the American workplace since then.

The old version of the Minnesota test asked job applicants for true or false responses to statements like these: "I have never had any black tarry-looking bowel movements." "I have never noticed any blood in my urine." "I pray several times a week." "Christ performed miracles." "I like mannish women." "I have diarrhea once a month or more." "My sex life is satisfactory."

Can you imagine job applicants sitting through this insulting exercise? No wonder they found the questions offensive. The authors of the test, who are affiliated with the University of Minnesota, admitted this. It took them thirty-seven years to figure that out.

The MMPI test has been the target of a lengthy class action lawsuit for invasion of privacy and discrimination, filed in 1989 against Target Stores in California by an applicant for a security job.

IN THE DARK AGES

The authors of the MMPI may have deleted some offensive questions, but they are still in the dark ages. To test the validity of their questions they go to rural Minnesota, somewhere just south of Lake Wobegon. Is this any way to determine whether a test has any relevance to the diverse American work force?

The authors have included some curious true-false queries in the revised test: "I am very seldom troubled by constipation." "I love my father." "I have never vomited or coughed up blood." "There is very little love and compassion in my home." "I like to talk about sex."

Here's another, to be answered true or false: "I have wished I were a girl." (Or if you are a girl) "I have never been sorry that I am a girl." It's hard to imagine that question getting by any enlightened state human rights commission—or past any self-respecting woman who is applying for work, and does not consider herself a girl.

IMAGINATIVE SHORTCUTS

It should be no surprise that some employers have resorted to more imaginative shortcuts, including using handwriting analysis to assign or evaluate applicants. It is astounding that sophisticated companies—the same companies that insist on detailed fact finding before making a major marketing or investment decision—will rely on the unexamined views of a graphologist (some call themselves "graphoanalysts") in the crucial decisions about hiring employees.

A few companies, though not those in the terrestrial mainstream, rely on astrology for selecting and assigning employees.

FEDERAL CHECKS

A more serious threat to civil liberties is the federal government's push to require fingerprints and computerized criminal records checks of certain employees who work with children or the elderly—or who work with our apparently next-ranking national asset, nuclear power. The flaw in this effort is that, according to the federal government's own studies, the accuracy and timeliness of computerized criminal records are at an unacceptably low level. Beyond that, few child abusers or sex offenders are in these files; they are family members and friends who have not been prosecuted. (Nor do potential nuclear terrorists generally register with the police under their correct names and social security numbers.)

If a man can rise to become secretary general of the United Nations with a sordid history of Nazi collaboration on file, how effective can we expect computerized criminal checks to be in purifying certain workplaces?

As in the case of testing applicants for drugs to keep addicts out of the workplace and demanding identity papers from applicants to confront the problem of undocumented aliens, we seem to impose restrictions on the law-abiding segment, causing the problem we are trying to solve. The consequence is that the innocent majority is hampered by restrictions on their liberties with no apparent deterrent effect on crime or drug use or illegal immigration.

All of these high-tech shortcuts have lulled personnel executives and supervisors into a false sense of security. All of this is also intrusive and degrading to the individual. It has created a pool of workers who are intimidated and unsophisticated. No longer are close supervision, job-performance testing, and careful auditing valued highly by companies. The inclination is to hire the persons who survive the gauntlet of tests—and to assume that they are free from temptation and irresponsibility once they are on the job. An employee with nothing to hide may well be an employee with nothing to offer.

BLIND FAITH

In the 1990s we seem to have developed a blind faith that objective measuring devices—preferably those that plug into an electrical socket and produce cathode-ray lettering—are less risky ways of selecting good people than are subjective human judgments.

A flat ban on all of these devices might be as unwise as an insistence that they all work equally well. Still, we can legislate that no person be deprived of employment solely for declining to submit to any of these tests. Informed experts are split on assessing the effectiveness of these methodologies; we should support the right of an employee or applicant to decline to have a crucial job decision based on them.

DRUGS IN THE WORKPLACE

Two of the largest drug-testing companies, Roche Biomedical Labs and SmithKline-Beecham Clinical Laboratories, estimate that fifteen million Americans or 13 percent of the work force are being required to give urine samples for testing annually, up from half that five years ago. Between 5 percent and 8 percent of those tested by the two big labs are found to have drugs in their system. Of those, 40 percent to 50 percent have been using marijuana, 20 percent occasionally heroin. The rest test positive for either [sic] amphetamines, an animal tranquilizer known as PCP or angel dust, or a variety of mainly prescription drugs that are sometimes abused.

DRUG TESTING IN EMPLOYMENT
Joseph DesJardins and Ronald Duska

We take privacy to be an "employee right," by which we mean a presumptive moral entitlement to receive certain goods or be protected from certain harms in the workplace.[1] Such a right creates a prima facie obligation on the part of the employer to provide the relevant goods or, as in this case, refrain from the relevant harmful treatment. These rights prevent employees from being placed in the fundamentally coercive position where they must choose between their jobs and other basic human goods.

Further, we view the employer–employee relationship as essentially contractual. The employer–employee relationship is an economic one and, unlike relationships such as those between a government and its citizens or a parent and a child, exists primarily as a means for satisfying the economic interests of the contracting parties. The obligations that each party incurs are only those that it voluntarily takes on. Given such a contractual relationship, certain areas of the employee's life remain his or her own private concern, and no employer has a right to invade them. On these presumptions we maintain that certain information about an employee is rightfully private, in other words, that the employee has a right to privacy.

THE RIGHT TO PRIVACY

George Brenkert has described the right to privacy as involving a three-place relation between a person A, some information X, and another person B. The right to privacy is violated only when B deliberately comes to possess information X about A and no relationship between A and B exists that would justify B's coming to know X about A.[2] Thus, for example, the relationship one has with a mortgage company would justify that company's coming to know about one's salary, but the relationship one has with a neighbor does not justify the neighbor's coming to know that information.

Hence, an employee's right to privacy is violated whenever personal information is requested,

collected, or used by an employer in a way or for any purpose that is *irrelevant to* or *in violation of* the contractual relationship that exists between employer and employee.

Since drug testing is a means for obtaining information, the information sought must be relevant to the contract if the drug testing is not to violate privacy. Hence, we must first decide whether knowledge of drug use obtained by drug testing is job relevant. In cases in which the knowledge of drug use is *not* relevant, there appears to be no justification for subjecting employees to drug tests. In cases in which information of drug use is job relevant, we need to consider if, when, and under what conditions using a means such as drug testing to obtain that knowledge is justified.

IS KNOWLEDGE OF DRUG USE JOB-RELEVANT INFORMATION?

Two arguments are used to establish that knowledge of drug use is job-relevant information. The first argument claims that drug use adversely affects job performance, thereby leading to lower productivity, higher costs, and consequently lower profits. Drug testing is seen as a way of avoiding these adverse effects. According to some estimates $25 billion are lost each year in the United States through loss in productivity, theft, higher rates in health and liability insurance, and similar costs incurred because of drug use.[3] Since employers are contracting with an employee for the performance of specific tasks, employers seem to have a legitimate claim upon whatever personal information is relevant to an employee's ability to do the job.

The second argument claims that drug use has been and can be responsible for considerable harm to individual employees, to their fellow employees, and to the employer, and third parties, including consumers. In this case drug testing is defended because it is seen as a way of preventing possible harm. Further, since employers can be held liable for harms done to employees and customers, knowledge of employee drug use is needed so that

From *Business and Professional Ethics Journal* (1989). Reprinted by permission.

employers can protect themselves from risks related to such liability. But how good are these arguments?

THE FIRST ARGUMENT: JOB PERFORMANCE AND KNOWLEDGE OF DRUG USE

The first argument holds that drug use lowers productivity and that consequently, an awareness of drug use obtained through drug testing will allow an employer to maintain or increase productivity. It is generally assumed that the performance of people using certain drugs is detrimentally affected by such use, and any use of drugs that reduces productivity is consequently job relevant. If knowledge of such drug use allows the employer to eliminate production losses, such knowledge is job relevant.

On the surface this argument seems reasonable. Obviously some drug use, in lowering the level of performance, can decrease productivity. Since the employer is entitled to a certain level of performance and drug use adversely affects performance, knowledge of that use seems job relevant.

But this formulation of the argument leaves an important question unanswered. To what level of performance are employers entitled? Optimal performance, or some lower level? If some lower level, what? Employers have a valid claim upon some *certain level* of performance, such that a failure to perform at this level would give the employer a justification for disciplining, firing, or at least finding fault with the employee. But that does not necessarily mean that the employer has a right to a maximum or optimal level of performance, a level above and beyond a certain level of acceptability. It might be nice if the employee gives an employer a maximum effort or optimal performance, but that is above and beyond the call of the employee's duty and the employer can hardly claim a right at all times to the highest level of performance of which an employee is capable....

If the person is producing what is expected, knowledge of drug use on the grounds of production is irrelevant since, by this hypothesis, the production is satisfactory. If, on the other hand, the performance suffers, then to the extent that it slips below the level justifiably expected, the employer has preliminary grounds for warning, disciplining, or releasing the employee. But the justification for

this action is the person's unsatisfactory performance, not the person's use of drugs. Accordingly, drug use information is either unnecessary or irrelevant and consequently there are not sufficient grounds to override the right of privacy. Thus, unless we can argue that an employer is entitled to optimal performance, the argument fails.

This counterargument should make it clear that the information that is job relevant, and consequently is not rightfully private, is information about an employee's level of performance and not information about the underlying causes of that level. The fallacy of the argument that promotes drug testing in the name of increased productivity is the assumption that each employee is obliged to perform at an optimal or at least quite high level. But this is required under few if any contracts. What is required contractually is meeting the normally expected levels of production or performing the tasks in the job description adequately (not optimally). If one can do that under the influence of drugs, then on the grounds of job performance at least, drug use is rightfully private. An employee who cannot perform the task adequately is not fulfilling the contract, and knowledge of the cause of the failure to perform is irrelevant on the contractual model.

Of course, if the employer suspects drug use or abuse as the cause of the unsatisfactory performance, then she might choose to help the person with counseling or rehabilitation. However, this does not seem to be something morally required of the employer. Rather, in the case of unsatisfactory performance, the employer has a prima facie justification for dismissing or disciplining the employee....

THE SECOND ARGUMENT: HARM AND THE KNOWLEDGE OF DRUG USE TO PREVENT HARM

The performance argument is inadequate, but there is an argument that seems somewhat stronger. This is an argument that takes into account the fact that drug use often leads to harm. Using a variant of the Millian argument, which allows interference with a person's rights in order to prevent harm, we could argue that drug testing might be justified if such testing led to knowledge that would enable an employer to prevent harm.

Drug use certainly can lead to harming others. Consequently, if knowledge of such drug use can prevent harm, then knowing whether or not an employee uses drugs might be a legitimate concern of an employer in certain circumstances. This second argument claims that knowledge of the employee's drug use is job relevant because employees who are under the influence of drugs can pose a threat to the health and safety of themselves and others, and an employer who knows of that drug use and the harm it can cause has a responsibility to prevent it.

Employers have both a general duty to prevent harm and the specific responsibility for harms done by their employees. Such responsibilities are sufficient reason for an employer to claim that information about an employee's drug use is relevant if that knowledge can prevent harm by giving the employer grounds for dismissing the employee or not allowing him or her to perform potentially harmful tasks. Employers might even claim a right to reduce unreasonable risks, in this case the risks involving legal and economic liability for harms caused by employees under the influence of drugs, as further justification for knowing about employee drug use.

This second argument differs from the first, in which only a lowered job performance was relevant information. In this case, even to allow the performance is problematic, for the performance itself, more than being inadequate, can hurt people. We cannot be as sanguine about the prevention of harm as we can about inadequate production. Where drug use may cause serious harms, knowledge of that use becomes relevant if the knowledge of such use can lead to the prevention of harm and drug testing becomes justified as a means for obtaining that knowledge.

Jobs with Potential to Cause Harm

In the first place, it is not clear that every job has a potential to cause harm—at least, not a potential to cause harm sufficient to override a prima facie right to privacy. To say that employers can use drug testing where that can prevent harm is not to say that every employer has the right to know about the drug use of every employee. Not every job poses a threat serious enough to justify an employer coming to know this information.

In deciding which jobs pose serious-enough threats, certain guidelines should be followed. First the potential for harm should be *clear* and *present*. Perhaps all jobs in some extended way pose potential threats to human well-being. We suppose an accountant's error could pose a threat of harm to someone somewhere. But some jobs—like those of airline pilots, school bus drivers, public transit drivers, and surgeons—are jobs in which unsatisfactory performance poses a clear and present danger to others. It would be much harder to make an argument that job performances by auditors, secretaries, executive vice-presidents for public relations, college teachers, professional athletes, and the like could cause harm if those performances were carried on under the influence of drugs. They would cause harm only in exceptional cases.[4]

Not Every Person Is to Be Tested

But, even if we can make a case that a particular job involves a clear and present danger for causing harm if performed under the influence of drugs, it is not appropriate to treat everyone holding such a job the same. Not every jobholder is equally threatening. There is less reason to investigate an airline pilot for drug use if that pilot has a twenty-year record of exceptional service than there is to investigate a pilot whose behavior has become erratic and unreliable recently, or one who reports to work smelling of alcohol and slurring his words. Presuming that every airline pilot is equally threatening is to deny individuals the respect that they deserve as autonomous, rational agents. It is to ignore their history and the significant differences between them. It is also probably inefficient and leads to the lowering of morale. It is the likelihood of causing harm, and not the fact of being an airline pilot per se, that is relevant in deciding which employees in critical jobs to test.

So, even if knowledge of drug use is justifiable to prevent harm, we must be careful to limit this justification to a range of jobs and people where the potential for harm is clear and present. The jobs must be jobs that clearly can cause harm, and the specific employee should not be someone who has a history of reliability. Finally, the drugs being tested should be those drugs that have genuine potential for harm if used in the jobs in question.

LIMITATIONS ON DRUG-TESTING POLICIES

Even when we identify those situations in which knowledge of drug use would be job relevant, we still need to examine whether some procedural limitations should not be placed upon the employer's testing for drugs. We have said when a real threat of harm exists and when evidence exists suggesting that a particular employee poses such a threat, an employer could be justified in knowing about drug use in order to prevent the potential harm. But we need to recognize that so long as the employer has the discretion for deciding when the potential for harm is clear and present, and for deciding which employees pose the threat of harm, the possibility of abuse is great. Thus, some policy limiting the employer's power is called for.

Just as criminal law imposes numerous restrictions protecting individual dignity and liberty on the state's pursuit of its goals, so we should expect that some restrictions be placed on employers to protect innocent employees from harm (including loss of job and damage to one's personal and professional reputation). Thus, some system of checks upon an employer's discretion in these matters seems advisable.

A drug-testing policy that requires all employees to submit to a drug test or to jeopardize their jobs would seem coercive and therefore unacceptable. Being placed in such a fundamentally coercive position of having to choose between one's job and one's privacy does not provide the conditions for a truly free consent. Policies that are unilaterally established by employers would likewise be unacceptable. Working with employees to develop company policy seems the only way to ensure that the policy will be fair to both parties. Prior notice of testing would also be required in order to give employees the option of freely refraining from drug use. Preventing drug use is morally preferable to punishing users after the fact, because this approach treats employees as capable of making rational and informed decisions.

Further procedural limitations seem advisable as well. Employees should be notified of the results of the test, they should be entitled to appeal the results (perhaps through further tests by an independent laboratory), and the information obtained through tests ought to be kept confidential. In summary, limitations upon employer discretion for administering drug tests can be derived from the nature of the employment contract and from the recognition that drug testing is justified by the desire to prevent harm, not the desire to punish wrongdoing.

THE ILLEGALITY CONTENTION

At this point critics might note that the behavior which testing would try to deter is, after all, illegal. Surely this excuses any responsible employer from being overprotective of an employee's rights. The fact that an employee is doing something illegal should give the employer a right to that information about his or her private life. Thus it is not simply that drug use might pose a threat of harm to others, but that it is an *illegal* activity that threatens others. But again, we would argue that illegal activity itself is irrelevant to job performance. At best, *conviction* records might be relevant, but since drug tests are administered by private employers we are not only ignoring the question of conviction, we are also ignoring the fact that the employee has not even been arrested for the alleged illegal activity.

Further, even if the due process protections and the establishment of guilt are acknowledged, it still does not follow that employers have a claim to know about all illegal activity on the part of their employees.

Consider the following example: Suppose you were hiring an auditor whose job required certifying the integrity of your firm's tax and financial records. Certainly, the personal integrity of this employee is vital to adequate job performance. Would we allow the employer to conduct, with or without the employee's consent, an audit of the employee's own personal tax return? Certainly if we discover that this person has cheated on a personal tax return we will have evidence of illegal activity that is relevant to this person's ability to do the job. Given one's own legal liability for filing falsified statements, the employee's illegal activity also poses a threat to others. But surely, allowing private individuals to audit an employee's tax returns is too intrusive a means for discovering information about that employee's integrity. The government certainly would never allow this violation of an employee's privacy. It ought not to allow drug testing on the same grounds. Why tax returns should be protected in ways that urine, for example, is not, raises interesting questions of fairness. Unfortunately, this question would take us beyond the scope of this paper.

VOLUNTARINESS

A final problem that we also leave undeveloped concerns the voluntariness of employee consent. For most employees, being given the choice between submitting to a drug test and risking one's job by refusing an employer's request is not much of a decision at all. We believe that such decisions are less than voluntary and thereby hold that employers cannot escape our criticisms simply by including with the employment contract a drug-testing clause.[5] Furthermore, there is reason to believe that those most in need of job security will be those most likely to be subjected to drug testing. Highly skilled, professional employees with high job mobility and security will be in a stronger position to resist such intrusions than will less skilled, easily replaced workers. This is why we should not anticipate surgeons and airline pilots being tested and should not be surprised when public transit and factory workers are. A serious question of fairness arises here as well.

Drug use and drug testing seem to be our most recent social "crisis." Politicians, the media, and employers expend a great deal of time and effort addressing this crisis. Yet, unquestionably, more lives, health, and money are lost each year to alcohol abuse than to marijuana, cocaine, and other controlled substances. We are well advised to be careful in considering issues that arise from such selective social concern. We will let other social commentators speculate on the reasons why drug use has received scrutiny while other white-collar crimes and alcohol abuse are ignored. Our only concern at this point is that such selective prosecution suggests an arbitrariness that should alert us to questions of fairness and justice.

In summary, then, we have seen that drug use is not always job relevant, and if drug use is not job relevant, information about it is certainly not job relevant. In the case of performance it may be a cause of some decreased performance, but it is the performance itself that is relevant to an employee's position, not what prohibits or enables that em-

ployee to do the job. In the case of potential harm being done by an employee under the influence of drugs, the drug use seems job relevant, and in this case drug testing to prevent harm might be legitimate. But how this is practicable is another question. It would seem that standard motor dexterity or mental dexterity tests given immediately prior to job performance are more effective in preventing harm, unless one concludes that drug use invariably and necessarily leads to harm. One must trust the individuals in any system for that system to work. One cannot police everything. Random testing might enable an employer to find drug users and to weed out the few to forestall possible future harm, but are the harms prevented sufficient to override the rights of privacy of the people who are innocent and to overcome the possible abuses we have mentioned? It seems not.

Clearly, a better method is to develop safety checks immediately prior to the performance of a job. Have a surgeon or a pilot or a bus driver pass a few reasoning and motor-skill tests before work. The cause of the lack of a skill, which lack might lead to harm, is really a secondary issue.

NOTES

1. "A Defense of Employee Rights," Joseph DesJardins and John McCall, *Journal of Business Ethics* 4 (1985). We should emphasize that our concern is with the *moral* rights of privacy for employees and not with any specific or prospective *legal* rights. Readers interested in pursuing the legal aspects of employee drug testing should consult "Workplace Privacy Issues and Employer Screening Policies" by Richard Lehr and David Middlebrooks in *Employee Relations Law Journal*, vol. 11, no. 3, 407–421; and "Screening Workers for Drugs: A Legal and Ethical Framework," Mark Rothstein, in *Employee Relations Law Journal*, vol. 11, no. 3, 422–436.

2. "Privacy, Polygraphs, and Work," George Brenkert, *Journal of Business and Professional Ethics*, vol. 1, no. 1 (Fall 1981). For a more general discussion of privacy in the workplace see "Privacy in Employment" by Joseph DesJardins, in *Moral Rights in the Workplace*, edited by Gertrude Ezorsky (SUNY Press, 1987). A good resource for philosophical work on privacy can be found in "Recent Work on the Concept of Privacy" by W. A. Parent, in *American Philosophical Quarterly*, vol. 20 (Oct. 1983), 341–358.

3. *U.S. News and World Report*, 22 Aug. 1983; *Newsweek*, 6 May 1983.

4. Obviously we are speaking here of harms that go beyond the simple economic harm that results from unsatisfactory job

performance. These economic harms are discussed in the first argument above. Further, we ignore such "harms" as providing bad role models for adolescents, harms often used to justify drug tests for professional athletes. We think it unreasonable to hold an individual responsible for the image he or she provides to others.

5. It might be argued that since we base our critique upon the contractual relationship between employers and employees, our entire position can be undermined by a clever employer who places within the contract a privacy waiver for drug tests. A full answer to this would require an account of the free and rational subject that the contract model presupposes. While acknowledging that we need such an account to prevent just any contract from being morally legitimate, we will have to leave this debate to another time. Interested readers might consult "The Moral Contract between Employers and Employees" by Norman Bowie in *The Work Ethic in Business*, edited by W. M. Hoffman and T. J. Wyly (Cambridge, MA: Oelgeschlager and Gunn, 1981), 195–202.

AIDS TESTING MANDATED BY INSURERS AND EMPLOYERS

Martin Gunderson, David Mayo, and Frank Rhame

AIDS is costly as well as deadly. Estimates of the cost of treating an individual with AIDS vary widely. One study places the mean cost of treating a person with AIDS in Massachusetts in 1986 at $46,505 per year. Another study estimated the costs of hospital care alone run as high as $147,000. Interestingly, a survey of 372 insurance corporations indicated that in 1986 the average health insurance claim paid for people with AIDS was $36,159 and that the average life insurance claim was $33,471. The cost of treatment with zidovudine is between $8,000 and $10,000 per patient per year. Apart from the cost of medical treatment, there are indirect costs (e.g., loss of earnings and the cost of needed support services other than medical treatment) as well as the costs of research and education. One estimate figured the total direct and indirect costs of AIDS in 1986 to have been nearly 8.7 billion dollars, and costs of over 66 billion dollars were projected for 1991.

This has dramatic implications for the insurance industry. Few individuals with AIDS are wealthy enough to pay for their own treatment. As a result, people who believe that they are at risk for AIDS may attempt to offset the direct health care costs of the disease through private health insurance. In addition, individuals may attempt to offset indirect costs associated with loss of future income through life and disability insurance. The cost of AIDS also has dramatic implications for employers. Employers who provide group insurance to their employees may find their insurance rates increasing rapidly if they have employees with AIDS. In addition, employers of persons with AIDS are faced with all of the costs associated with employees who become ill and eventually die. Such costs include lost work time due to illness and the costs of retraining new employees as employees with AIDS eventually become unable to work.

Both insurers and employers have good reason to try to protect themselves by finding out who is at risk of contracting AIDS. Methods for protection include attempting to determine who is in a high-risk group (e.g., who is gay), attempting to determine who engages in high-risk behavior, and attempting to determine who is HIV infected by checking medical records or by requiring HIV testing. The fact that insurers and employers are gravely tempted to protect themselves from the costs of AIDS is not lost on the various state legislatures and insurance commissioners, and several states have enacted legislation or regulations forbidding insurance companies and employers from using HIV antibody tests for the purpose of determining insurability or employability.[1]

We are primarily concerned with whether insurers and employers ought to be forbidden from requiring HIV testing as a precondition of insurance or employment. In asking this question, we will be primarily concerned with privacy issues. Concerning insurers, we argue (1) that insurers do not violate individual privacy rights by requiring

From Martin Gunderson, David Mayo, and Frank Rhame, *AIDS: Testing and Privacy* (Salt Lake City: University of Utah Press, 1989), 165–188. © 1989 University of Utah Press. Reprinted by permission.

HIV testing or inquiring into high-risk behavior, (2) that such tests and inquiries do intrude into privacy even if they do not constitute a violation of the right to privacy, (3) that the costs of the treatment of AIDS should be borne by the state. Concerning employers, we argue that employers should not be allowed to require HIV tests as a condition of employment because of both privacy and public policy considerations. We consider the issue of insurance first and then turn to the issue of employment.

BACKGROUND VALUES

Our insurance system has evolved to meet several important and sometimes competing values. The first is the value which we place on providing health care. As a society, we are committed to providing necessary health care to citizens who are unable to finance their own health care. Conservatives as well as liberals agree on this commitment, though they differ over what care is necessary and over who can afford to finance their own health care. Few conservatives argue that we should allow those who are desperately sick and unable to afford health care to die without treatment....

In the case of insurance, there is another general value which needs to be taken into account. This second value is sometimes called *contractual freedom* or *freedom of contract*.[2] As a society we believe that, other things being equal, people ought to be allowed to enter freely into agreements with others. We believe that this freedom is enhanced when all of the contracting parties know the relevant facts concerning the agreement. We also believe that this freedom is enhanced when both parties are in a roughly equal bargaining position. Such values are reflected in the law of contracts. Courts may modify or even refuse to enforce contracts which are so one sided as to be unconscionable. In addition, courts will typically allow minors and mental incompetents to void contracts into which they have imprudently entered. There are also cases in which courts will modify or refuse to enforce a contract because one or both of the parties were mistaken as to the relevant terms of the contract. Thus, if one party relies on fraud or misrepresentation of the other party to enter into a contract, courts will not enforce the contract against the victim of the fraud.

In the specific case of health insurance, these values are sometimes in tension. The insurance company that knows all of the relevant facts about a person's health may refuse to enter into an insurance contract with that person, leaving him or her without financial access to adequate health care. It is arguable that states which forbid insurers to require HIV tests are in effect placing a higher priority on freedom of contract than on provision of health care. While these values may conflict, such conflict is not necessary, and it is reasonable to hope for resolutions which enable us to achieve both values.

ECONOMIC INCENTIVES

Before getting down to specific moral arguments concerning whether insurers should be forbidden to consider HIV seropositivity and high-risk behavior in underwriting insurance, it needs to be noted that there are significant economic pressures on insurance companies to determine who is at risk for AIDS. First, there are economic pressures to treat people with roughly equal risks in a roughly equal manner for purpose of insurance underwriting.[3] Indeed, this is the single most fundamental principle of underwriting. This principle is given legal instantiation in the National Association of Insurance Commissioners Model of Unfair Trade Practices Act, some version of which has been adopted by every state. If an insurance company requires healthy persons to subsidize those who are less healthy, then, in a free market system, the healthy will either band together to insure themselves or choose insurance companies which base premiums on risk. Thus, in a free market system, insurance companies are forced to treat people at roughly equal risk equally. Of course, such pressure can be avoided by state legislation that forbids any insurance company from denying insurance to specific groups. For example, a state law forbidding all insurers from using AIDS or HIV seropositivity as a factor in underwriting will prevent competitive advantage from being gained by companies who do not insure those who are infected with HIV. Whether such legislation is justified will be explored shortly. For now, it is enough to note that without such legislation, insurance companies have an economic incentive to try to determine who is at risk for AIDS and to base underwriting decisions on the test results.

A second economic consideration arises from the fact that people who are HIV infected can in most states find out that they are positive at anonymous test sites. Such people, of course, have good reason to purchase large quantities of life and health insurance. Purchasing insurance when one knows that a claim will likely be made while keeping this from the insurance company is called *antiselection* or *adverse selection*. Antiselection has already occurred among persons with AIDS and HIV. According to a 1985 survey conducted by the American Council on Life Insurance and the Health Insurance Association of America, 44 percent of the total amount paid on AIDS life insurance claims are for claims made within two years of the issuance of the life insurance policy. By contrast, only 7.6 percent of the total amount paid on non-AIDS claims are for claims made within two years of the issuance of a policy....

The third economic factor which motivates insurance companies to determine a prospective insuree's risk for AIDS is the simple fear that insurance companies will be overwhelmed with AIDS-related claims. In his report "AIDS and Life Insurance," Michael Cowell projects that the total amount for AIDS-related life insurance claims could reach $2 billion annually, or about 15 percent of individual life insurance claims for all U.S. companies by the mid-1990s....

SPECIFIC MORAL PROBLEMS

Insurers present three arguments based on fairness for requiring HIV testing and for inquiring about high-risk behavior. The arguments differ depending on which groups are being compared. The first argument is that since people can determine for themselves whether or not they are infected with HIV, it is unfair not to allow insurers also to make this determination before insuring a person for risks including those associated with HIV seropositivity. We have already seen that there is evidence of antiselection and that those who find that they are HIV infected have good reason to load up on

insurance. This provides at least a reason for allowing insurers to require HIV testing before granting insurance. There are other reasons as well.

We have noted that it is a fundamental principle of insurance that equal risks should be treated in the same fashion for purposes of insurance underwriting. We have also seen that in a free underwriting market there is an economic reason for using this principle. Moral reasons might be offered as well. It has been argued, for instance, that it is unfair for low-risk insurees to pay higher rates to subsidize high-risk insurees. The alleged unfairness here is that people who are relevantly different are being treated in the same fashion. Those who use this argument may find such inequitable treatment especially galling when it is a person's voluntary behavior which leads to the higher risk. It might be replied, however, that it is not unfair to any significant degree, because insurees voluntarily sign insurance policies knowing full well what the costs are. If I know that in a game of blackjack the odds are in favor of the house but I choose to play anyway, I can hardly complain that the game is unfair when I lose.

There is another argument based on fairness. If smokers, diabetics, and others with great health risks are forced to pay higher premiums, it might be claimed that it is unfair to them not to take HIV positivity into account, for HIV positives are also at high risk. Here the alleged unfairness results from treating classes which are not relevantly different in radically different ways. Of course, a major disanalogy between HIV-infected persons and people who pay higher rates because of health risks is that HIV seropositivity, if taken into account, would result not merely in higher rates or, in the case of health insurance, exclusion of a pre-existing condition, but in denial of any insurance whatever. The argument is thus better stated in terms of the unfairness of treating people denied insurance coverage because of, for example, a previous severe heart attack differently from people infected with HIV.

Assuming that there are no relevant differences between people with health risks resulting from their HIV status and people who are denied insurance coverage for other health-related reasons, it could plausibly be claimed that an insurer who did not also exclude HIV-infected persons from health coverage is acting unfairly. Of course, there is little danger that the insurance companies will act unfairly in this manner if left to their own devices. Insurers would gladly exclude HIV-infected persons, as well as others at extreme risk, from various forms of insurance coverage. The real question is whether those states which forbid screening for HIV infection are acting unfairly in protecting some people at extreme health risk, but not others.

Whether the difference in protection accorded persons with HIV and others who have serious health risks is in fact unfair depends on whether there are morally relevant differences between the two groups. Consider, first, questions concerning high-risk behavior. There is a significant disanalogy between dangerous sexual practices and other forms of high-risk behavior. I would feel perfectly free to ask the man sitting next to me on the city bus whether he engaged in rock climbing but not whether he engaged in anal intercourse. What accounts for the difference, of course, is that, at least in our culture, asking whether he climbs mountains, sky dives, or the like does not require an answer involving a great sacrifice of privacy. In fact, such activities are usually carried out in public. We do, however, seek an answer which would involve considerable sacrifice of privacy when we ask about someone's sexual behavior.

The disanalogy is not so great when insurance companies require HIV tests or check medical records for the results of any HIV testing. It could be argued that just as insurance companies have a right to know whether a prospective insuree suffers from cancer or heart disease, insurance companies also have a right to know whether a prospective insuree suffers from AIDS or is HIV infected. That someone has cancer or heart disease is nearly as much a private matter as whether someone has AIDS or is infected with HIV. The difference seems to be more one of degree than of kind. The degree of difference can be significant, however, if the information becomes general knowledge. People who are HIV infected have been evicted from their homes and fired from their jobs. In one case, townspeople destroyed the home of three boys who were HIV infected. Cancer and heart patients, whatever their problems, do not face such serious discrimination.

In short, there are significant privacy claims which can be offered against the fairness claims made by insurance companies and in favor of state laws prohibiting insurers from HIV testing or making underwriting decisions based on HIV status. There are, however, several reasons for thinking that such privacy considerations are not, in fact, overriding.

To begin with, even though there may be a sacrifice of privacy, there is no violation of the right to privacy, since in answering questions concerning high-risk activity or in consenting to HIV testing, a person waives the right to privacy. This, of course, assumes that the consent is genuine and not in some sense coerced. It might be claimed that the consent is in fact not voluntary, at least in the case of health insurance, because insurance is a necessity given the high cost of medical treatment. People have no choice but to purchase insurance and therefore no choice but to do what is necessary to purchase it. A similar, though less forceful, argument could be given concerning life insurance. It could be argued that it is necessary to provide for dependents in the case of death and that, for most people, life insurance is the only way in which this can be done. This argument is less forceful, because there are more ways to provide for dependents than through insurance. Also, AIDS is most prevalent among gays, who are less likely than heterosexuals to have such typical dependents as children and spouses, though certainly some gays have married and have children.

There are several problems with the above argument. First, it is by no means clear that health and life insurance are in fact necessities. In those states that have assigned risk pools for health insurance, people who otherwise would have been denied health insurance are provided with health insurance at an increased rate. Even in those states without assigned risk pools, Medicaid and Aid to Families with Dependent Children ensure that at least the minimal health and sustenance requirements will be met. The benefits are provided by welfare programs administered by the states, though, as we noted, eligibility is restricted to those whose assets and income fall below a certain level (which varies among the states). As a result, those who would rely on these benefits must first exhaust their resources. Nonetheless, the existence of such programs means that private health insurance is being used not so much to provide needed health financing as to ensure a certain level of income.

This in turn means that it is difficult to argue that health insurance, much less life insurance, is required for meeting genuine necessities.

Second, even if health insurance were necessary for adequate health care, it would not follow that someone's consent to insurance company requirements is not voluntary. People who are in the position of being the sole suppliers of something which someone needs do not necessarily coerce that person by demanding that conditions be met before receipt is made. Suppose, for example, that a starving person walks out of the wilderness into a restaurant and orders a meal. The fact that the starving man must pay a reasonable price for the meal does not mean that he did not pay voluntarily. If, however, the restaurant owner demanded that the starving man have sex with her before she would feed him, then there would be coercion. The difference is that in one case the price is reasonable and in the other it is not. In the case of insurance, the question turns on whether requiring an HIV test or asking whether the person engages in high-risk behavior is reasonable in light of the insurance sought. There are three considerations which suggest that it is in fact reasonable. First, the insurance companies are setting requirements concerning the very conditions for which insurance is being sought. Second, there is a high likelihood of antiselection if insurance companies do not screen. Third, there is a safety net for those denied insurance, even if it is not what it should be.

What follows from the above is that insurance companies do not violate the right to privacy by requiring HIV testing and inquiring about high-risk behavior before granting insurance. This is because the right to privacy is voluntarily waived by those seeking insurance. Even if the right to privacy is waived, however, it is nonetheless true that insurance must be purchased at a sacrifice of privacy. The fact that this privacy is voluntarily sacrificed does not mean that it is not a genuine cost. It is not pleasant revealing one's sexual activities to an insurance agent. Nor is it pleasant to reveal one's HIV status to others, even if they are medical professionals. Given that the loss of privacy is a genuine cost, it is an important question how the interests of insurance companies should be balanced against such a loss, even if the right to privacy is not violated....

EMPLOYMENT

Like insurers, employers have a number of reasons for screening people who are infected with HIV or at risk for AIDS. Some of these reasons concern insurance. Employers themselves may provide insurance to their employees, in which case the economic benefit of keeping out those at risk for AIDS is obvious. If, on the other hand, the employer relies on group insurance, the insurance rates may rise to unacceptable levels if there are too many claims against the insurance company.

Employers who hire persons infected with HIV or people at high risk for contracting AIDS face costs associated with an ill employee. These include the costs associated with lost work time due to illness and eventually the cost of training a new employee. Sadly, in some cases it also includes the cost of prejudicial reaction by other employees or by customers. Perhaps the most obvious example is a restaurant which would lose customers if it became generally known that one of its employees was infected with HIV. In very few cases, however, will HIV infection itself be relevant to job performance. The most notable exception to this are certain medical occupations....

With the possible exception of employers who are self-insurers, it is arguable that it is unreasonable for employers to demand that a person take an HIV test or answer questions about his or her sexual history before being accepted for employment. In fact, HIV seropositivity and sexual behavior are seldom relevant for employment. The fairness considerations which form a significant part of the justification for insurance screening those at risk for AIDS do not apply to employment. There is no analogy to antiselection. Potential employees are contracting with employers concerning matters to which their sexual behavior and HIV status is by and large irrelevant. In addition, other employees are not being asked to subsidize the employee infected with HIV. If an employer screens out health risks generally, it may be unfair not to screen out those at risk of AIDS as well, but it is by no means clear that employers are justified in screening out health risks in the first place.

Regarding employers who are self-insurers, it might be claimed that the insurance aspect justifies screening for those at risk for AIDS. The obvious solution is to keep the insurance and employment aspects separate. Thus, applicants could be hired without regard to whether they are at risk for AIDS, but they could be screened before being offered insurance. An equally obvious problem is that when those in the firm responsible for the insurance learn that a new employee is HIV positive or engages in high-risk behavior, they are likely to inform others in the firm. There are two ways in which this could be prevented through legislation. First, legislation could require that screening by self-insurers be done by people outside the firm who inform the firm whether the person should be granted insurance but do not give the reason. Second, legislation could forbid employers from firing those infected with HIV.

In short, there do not seem to be compelling arguments to support the view that employers are justified in using HIV tests as a means of screening potential employees. There are, however, two general arguments which can be given to support the view that employers are not justified in HIV screening. The first is an economic argument. If employers generally were to screen applicants for HIV infection, it would put otherwise able people on welfare, thereby increasing an already serious state problem. It would also make it impossible for people at risk to arrange their finances to be able to withstand the financial burden of eventual treatment for AIDS. This would mean even greater state expenses incurred for the treatment of AIDS.

The second argument is based on considerations of fairness. As a society we have committed ourselves to protecting the handicapped from employment discrimination. At the federal level this protection is embodied in the federal Rehabilitation Act of 1973. As far as reasons for protecting he handicapped are concerned, there is no significant difference between handicapped persons and those who have HIV infection. Thus, it would be unfair not to accord those who are HIV infected the same protections afforded others who have medical problems which do not significantly affect their job performance.

There is a strong analogy between HIV infection and more traditional handicaps as far as employment discrimination is concerned. Just as many people with handicaps can perform their jobs competently, so too can many people with HIV infection. Just as handicapped persons pose no threat to their co-workers because of their handicaps, those who are infected with HIV pose no threat to their co-workers because of their infection.... Just as handicapped persons typically need employment in order to achieve a high level of personal autonomy, HIV-infected persons typically need employment to achieve autonomy. Finally, both HIV-infected persons and handicapped persons are likely to be subjected to irrational discrimination unless they are given legal protection.

On the basis of the analogy between HIV infection and traditional handicaps, it can be argued that those who are HIV infected ought to be given protection under the legislation which protects handicapped persons. We begin by asking whether current legal analysis allows us to apply federal protections to those who are HIV infected. The Rehabilitation Act of 1973 promises protection, especially in light of recent case law. If this act, which prohibits discrimination against the handicapped by certain employers, can be interpreted to cover persons with HIV infection, it will protect privacy in two ways. It will help prevent outright discrimination against those with HIV infection, since such discrimination would be illegal. It will also protect privacy by undercutting the temptation of certain employers and administrators to test those they supervise for the HIV antibodies. Employers who cannot discriminate against those with AIDS, ARC, or HIV infection will have less motive to test for the HIV antibodies. However, if AIDS and ARC are covered but not HIV infection, then employers will be motivated to require tests, since they can then get rid of employees who are HIV infected before they develop AIDS or ARC and receive the protection of the rehabilitation act.

The rehabilitation act provides that no person who is handicapped and otherwise qualified shall "be subjected to discrimination under any program or activity conducted by any Executive agency or by the United States Postal Service." The crucial question concerns who is a handicapped individual for purposes of the act. Section 794, formerly Section 504, of the act defines a handicapped person as "any person who (i) has a physical or mental impairment which substantially limits one or more of such person's major life activities, (ii) has a record of such an impairment, or (iii) is regarded as having such an impairment."

A plaintiff bringing suit under the rehabilitation act must show four things. First, the plaintiff must show that the person who discriminated against the plaintiff was covered by the rehabilitation act. Not all private employers are covered, but only those who receive federal funds. Employment by executive agencies such as the State Department are covered. Thus, the rehabilitation act is relevant to the HIV screening of State Department employees and their families.

Second, the plaintiff must show that he or she is handicapped. Section 794, quoted above, makes it clear that it is sufficient to show that the plaintiff has a physical or mental impairment which substantially limits at least one major life activity. For our purposes it is relevant to note that impairments include physiological disorders of the reproductive, genitourinary, hemic, and lymphatic systems. Major life activities include "functions such as caring for one's self, performing manual tasks, walking, seeing, hearing, speaking, breathing, learning, and working." A plaintiff can also be shown to be handicapped if he or she has a record of such an impairment even when the plaintiff has been misclassified as having an impairment. A plaintiff can also be shown to be handicapped if it can be shown that the plaintiff is treated by an employer as having an impairment which substantially limits major life activities even when the plaintiff has no such impairment. Finally, a plaintiff can be shown to be handicapped if it can be shown that the plaintiff has an impairment and that impairment substantially limits life functions because of the attitudes of others even when the impairment would not otherwise substantially limit life functions.

Third, the plaintiff must show that he or she was discriminated against solely because of the handicap. Fourth, the plaintiff must show that he or she is otherwise qualified for the job or program. This means that the plaintiff can perform the job with reasonable accommodation by the employer....

Certainly many persons suffering from AIDS or ARC meet the definition of a handicapped person. All persons with AIDS and ARC have disorders of the hemic and lymphatic systems which count as impairments for purposes of the rehabilitation act. In addition, many persons with AIDS have one or more of the debilitating diseases (e.g., pneumocystis pneumonia) that substantially limit major life func-

tions (e.g., the ability to breathe). People with ARC have one of several severe physical symptoms, such as serious weight loss (wasting) and prolonged fever, that also affect major life activities, such as the ability to work. Even when persons with AIDS or ARC are not substantially limited by their disease, they are often regarded as being substantially limited by their employers or are treated by others in such a way that they are substantially limited in major life activities. In spite of these limitations, persons with AIDS and ARC are often qualified for employment with reasonable accommodations by their employers....

CONCLUSION

There are a number of reasons for allowing insurance companies to require HIV testing as a condition of insurability, and these reasons are not overridden by privacy concerns. The various values at stake can best be balanced by federal legislation modifying Medicare to provide for AIDS treatment in the manner in which it now provides for dialysis. While employers also have self-interested reasons for requiring HIV testing as a condition of employment, these reasons do not override the privacy and public policy considerations which militate against such screening.

NOTES*

1. States which have such laws or regulations include Arizona, California, Delaware, District of Columbia, Massachusetts, Michigan, New Jersey, and New York. See Ruth Faden and Nancy Kass, "Health Insurance and AIDS: The Status of State Regulatory Activity," *American Journal of Public Health* 78 (1988): 438. This study updates a survey of state regulations conducted by the National Gay Rights Advocates.

2. For an article which places significant emphasis on the contractual freedom of insurance companies, see Joyce Nixson Hoffman and Elizabeth Zieser Kincaid, "AIDS: The Challenge to Life and Health Insurers' Freedom of Contract," *Drake Law Review* 35 (1986-1987): 709–71.

3. Underwriting is the process by which degree of risk is assessed for the purpose of determining insurability and setting premiums.

*Some notes have been deleted and the remaining ones renumbered.

Decision Scenario 1
DRUG TESTING OF RAILROAD EMPLOYEES

On August 2, 1985, the Federal Railroad Administration (FRA) issued regulations requiring mandatory blood and urine tests of railroad employees after certain accidents, incidents, and rule violations. After initial legal challenges by the Railroad Labor Executives' Association (RLEA), an association representing all crafts of railroad workers, these regulations went into effect on February 10, 1986. The RLEA sued the Department of Transportation, and on February 11, 1988, the United States Court of Appeals ruled in favor of the RLEA and invalidated these regulations.

The regulations required alcohol and drug testing for all employees involved in accidents that resulted in fatalities, release of hazardous materials, injuries, or damage to railroad property exceeding $50,000. Further, the regulations required that employees submit to breath or urine tests when a supervisor has a reasonable suspicion that an employee is under the influence or impaired by alcohol or drugs. To require a urine test, two supervisors must have a reasonable suspicion, and if drug use is suspected, one of them must have been trained in spotting drug use. The railroads may also require testing when an employee violates certain rules of train operation. Refusal to provide a sample would result in a nine-month suspension.

The appeals court reasoned that these regulations constituted a violation of the Fourth Amendment's prohibition of "unreasonable searches." The railroad industry argued that since the regulations authorized testing by *private* companies and did not involve government action, the Fourth Amendment should not apply. The court rejected this argument, reasoning that "the government participates in a significant way" in the railroad industry and in the formulation of these regulations. Thus these regulations were held to involve a "search" in the relevant sense.

But are these regulations "reasonable"? Ordinarily, a warrant is needed to make a search "reasonable," but the Supreme Court has ruled that certain warrantless searches are constitutional. The appeals court ruled that the railroad case failed to meet the necessary standards for warrantless searches on two grounds. First, the standard of reasonableness requires that the search be based upon "individualized" or "particularized" suspicion. The court decided that accidents, incidents, and rule violations were not themselves sufficiently reasonable grounds for testing any one railroad employee, much less an entire train crew. Further, these tests were found not to be reasonable on grounds relating to the very goals that justified interfering with employees in the first place. Specifically, the court ruled that the goal of the testing is to measure *present* intoxication or impairment, but the tests themselves can detect only metabolites of drugs, which may remain in the body's system for days or weeks after the intoxication or impairment. The court left some room for testing, but only when individualized suspicion and observable symptoms of present impairment exist. The drug test could then provide confirming evidence and a sound basis for disciplinary action.

The Department of Transportation appealed this decision to the Supreme Court. On March 21, 1989, in a 7 to 2 decision, the Supreme Court overturned the appeals court judgment and ruled that drug testing was constitutionally valid. The majority opinion stated that the employees' expectation of privacy can be overridden by the safety concerns of the railroads. The Court also ruled that in this case "individualized suspicion" was not necessary, thus allowing drug tests for the entire crew of a train involved in an accident.

In November 1988 the Department of Transportation announced plans to require drug tests for over four million workers in the trucking, airline, and mass transit industries. This Supreme Court decision would seem to remove the last obstacle to this program.

- Railroad workers are subject to drug tests because their jobs put them in a position where public safety is at risk. Can you think of other jobs where the health and safety of third parties is at risk? Would mandatory drug testing be justified for all these jobs? Why or why not?

- Some observers have claimed that mandatory punishment for refusal to submit to drug tests amounts to a presumption of guilt until proven innocent. Do you agree?

- If an employee is not presently impaired by alcohol or drugs and is therefore presently able to perform his or her job, why should past alcohol or drug use be relevant?

- Would alcoholism or past alcohol abuse be legitimate grounds for firing someone? Why or why not? In what ways is alcohol abuse different from drug abuse? In what ways are they similar?

Decision Scenario 2
SEARCH AND SEIZURE IN THE WORKPLACE

The Fourth Amendment to the U.S. Constitution grants to citizens the right "to be secure in their persons, houses, papers, and effects, against unreasonable searches and seizures." Since this right, like all constitutional rights, protects individual citizens against government action, employees cannot expect the same legal protection against unreasonable search and seizures. "Papers and effects," along with desks, lockers, files, and even automobiles, can be searched by a private employer.

Courts have developed two general tests to determine whether a government search violates the Fourth Amendment: Did the individual have a "reasonable expectation of privacy"? If so, was the search "unreasonable"? For example, an individual has a reasonable expectation of privacy while making a phone call from a public phone booth, but not while walking down a public street carrying a gun. Even if the individual does have a reasonable expectation of privacy, a government search will not violate the Fourth Amendment if it is "reasonable." A search of a tax evader's bank records is reasonable; random searches of black males walking in predominantly white neighborhoods are not.

In a recent case, the U.S. Supreme Court was asked to decide whether a public employee's

Fourth Amendment rights were violated by the search of his office. In *O'Connor v. Ortega,* the Court ruled against a psychiatrist who claimed that his office was illegally searched by officials of the public hospital in which he worked. In this case, the psychiatrist was director of the psychiatric residency program at a state hospital. Other employees complained that he had coerced residents into contributing to the purchase of a computer for the office and that he had sexually harassed women who worked for him. Pending the outcome of an internal investigation, the hospital administrator placed the psychiatrist on a paid leave of absence. The administrator then had investigators search the psychiatrist's office and collect evidence from desks an files. This evidence was used in a hearing that resulted in the dismissal of the psychiatrist. He then sued, claiming that his Fourth Amendment rights were violated.

- Do employees have a reasonable expectation of privacy in their office, desk, and files? Is a complaint by co-workers sufficient to establish a "reasonable" basis for the search?

- Should these standards be extended to employees in the private sector? Why or why not?

Decision Scenario 3
PRIVACY IN EMPLOYMENT

As the personnel director of a manufacturing firm with about 500 employees, you have the responsibility for establishing all company policies concerning personnel files. The company is in the process of computerizing all its past and present files, and

this will be a convenient time to review your company's privacy policies.

The first issue you confront concerns the older files. How long should you retain information after a person has left the firm? (For that matter, is there some information about present employees that you no longer should keep?) In the past you have used these older files to supply information to landlords and banks who want to verify the individual's creditworthiness. One time you also were required to supply information for a lawsuit against your company. Although in general you would prefer not to be bothered by the extra work, computer technology has greatly reduced the trouble of long-term storage.

You also would prefer not to be bothered by credit checks on present employees. You have always verified information to landlords and credit grantors as a courtesy to employees. After all, if they did not want this information released they could have withheld it originally. Since it is a burden to you, and since you see it as a favor to the employee, you have never thought it necessary to get the employee's consent before releasing this information. Besides, you have asked other personnel people to verify information about a potential employee, and you recognize the necessity and benefits of this practice.

Recently, however, you have received an offer from a credit agency that causes you some concern. This agency, which you often have used to do background checks on potential employees (especially those in the security office), has made a new policy available to clients who have computerized personnel files. Rather than charge a fee for its service, this agency will now accept information as payment. Specifically, for each report it compiles for you, the firm requests access to information in

your personnel files. Since this agency is in the information collection business, this practice makes sense to them.

What makes this offer particularly attractive is the ease of the entire process. With your new computerized system, the exchange of information is as easy as one telephone call. When the agency staff has the information you have requested, they call up your computer and, using the access code you supplied, simply transfer the relevant information into your files. Next, using another access code number, the agent types in the Social Security number of an individual whose records are sought, and that employee's file is transferred into the credit firm's computer files. In the more likely case that no specific employee is being sought at present, a file can be chosen at random or the access permission can be saved for future use. Of course, you can easily program a limit to the number of times the firm can access your files.

Although this firm has promised to respect whatever standards of confidentiality you set, you are worried by this practice. However, it seems to be no more than an extension of present practices, and it will likely save you money.

- What policies should you establish for the privacy of the personnel files in your keeping?
- Are personnel files the property of the employer? If not, why not? If so, should employers be allowed to sell their property?
- In what ways have computers affected privacy in the workplace?

Decision Scenario 4
SURVEILLANCE AT WORK

"Report Says Computers Spy on 7 Million Workers in the U.S." read the *New York Times* headline on September 28, 1987. According to a report prepared by the Congressional Office of Technology Assessment for Rep. Don Edwards (D-Calif.), over seven million American workers are being monitored at work by computers. For many of

these workers, this surveillance occurs without their knowledge.

Computers monitor such things as rest breaks, use of telephones, presence at work stations, and frequency of errors. Some computers count individual typewriter keystrokes, eavesdrop on customer service calls, and count the number of incoming phone calls. The computers can then be programmed to evaluate job performance against a norm established by monitoring other workers.

■   If you were an office manager and had this service offered to you, would you take advantage of it?

■   Would it depend on the type of workers that you were supervising?

■   Would there be a difference if most of your workers were in the secretarial pool? If most of your workers were professionals, such as accountants or loan officers?

■   How, if at all, is this any different from more traditional methods of monitoring employees?

■   Would it make any difference if the employees were told about these procedures beforehand?

Decision Scenario 5

IF YOU WORK HERE, DON'T SMOKE

In 1991, Ford Meter Box Co., a small manufacturing firm in Indiana, prohibited employees from smoking both on the job and away from work. Janice Bone worked for Ford Meter Box, and when a routine urinalysis detected nicotine in her system, she was fired for violating company policy. Bone sued, arguing that her off-work activities were private and should not be the basis for employment decisions.

Ford Meter is on a growing list of companies that are placing employment restrictions on smokers. The most obvious restriction is the prohibition of smoking on the job. A number of considerations have led companies to go further than this, leading up to policies like Ford Meter's, which prohibits smoking altogether. Companies argue that increased health care and insurance costs associated with smoking justify these restrictions. Smokers use health care insurance more often, they have greater rates of absenteeism, and tend to retire earlier than other workers due to health issues such as emphysema, lung cancer, and heart disease. In the opinion of many employers, these factors make smoking a job-relevant activity.

Some companies, like Texas Instruments and U-Haul, require smokers to pay higher rates—an insurance surcharge—for health insurance. In 1994 a Lockheed plant in Georgia joined companies like

Turner Broadcasting in refusing to hire people who smoke. In defending their policy, a Lockheed spokesperson referred to an American Lung Association study that showed companies pay up to $5000 per year in additional health care costs for employees who smoke. The Lockheed policy applied only to new employees.

In response to Janice Bone's lawsuit, the state of Indiana passed a law protecting employees from dismissal because they smoke outside of the workplace. By 1993, twenty-eight states had passed legislation protecting the rights of smokers.

■   Is smoking an activity that is job relevant? Are all employee activities that can increase employer costs relevant for employment decisions?

■   Ford Meter Box conducted routine urinalysis tests to check for traces of nicotine. Is this means of enforcing company policy reasonable?

■   Should governments get involved in these issues, or should they be left to the individual bargaining between employers and employees?

■   Ford Meter fired a present employee for smoking. Lockheed refused to hire smokers, but left alone present employees. Texas Instruments and U-Haul placed additional conditions on employees who smoke. Are all of these policies justified? Some of these policies? None of them?

Decision Scenario 6
PREEMPLOYMENT PSYCHOLOGICAL TESTING

Target Stores, a division of Dayton Hudson Corporation, routinely used a psychological examination called "Psychscreen" as a preemployment test for all applicants for store security positions. Three applicants for such a position sued Target Stores, claiming that this test violated their privacy and should not be a condition of employment.

Psychscreen is a combination of two widely used psychological profile tests, the Minnesota Multiphasic Personality Inventory and the California Psychological Inventory. The test asks 704 true–false questions that are later evaluated by an independent consulting firm of psychologists. The test was used to ensure careful hiring of security guards, seeking to provide a profile of applicants' attitudes, personality, values, character, and emotional makeup. Target's own employees did not see answers given to these questions, but based their hiring decisions on the assessments provided by the outside consultants. While the scientific validity of these tests is open to debate, defenders claim that they are more objective and valid than the similar judgments that would be made intuitively during an interview.

The job applicants who filed suit, Sibi Soroka, William d'Arcangelo, and Sue Urry, found many of the questions intrusive. Questions included: "I feel very strongly attracted to members of my own sex....I have never indulged in any unusual sex practices....I feel sure that there is only one true religion....I go to church almost every week.... I·

wish that I were not bothered by thoughts about sex....I have had no difficulty starting or holding my urine.....I believe that my sins are unpardonable."

The state of California grants a specific constitutional right of privacy and has laws prohibiting preemployment questions concerning religious beliefs and sexual orientation. A trial court found in favor of Target, but a California Court of Appeal issued an injunction against the use of this test. Before the case returned to trial, Target settled out of court, agreeing to pay more than $2 million in class-action damages. Target discontinued the use of Psychscreen in 1991.

- Do you think that psychological testing violates an employee's privacy?
- Is personality a valid reason for refusing to hire someone? Is it a valid reason for firing someone? Which personality traits would justify refusal to hire someone as a store security officer?
- Would your views of these tests change if they were shown to be scientifically valid?
- Is sexual orientation a legitimate basis for making hiring decisions? Do devoutly religious people make better employees?
- Do you object more to the goals of these tests, or to the tests themselves as inappropriate means for attaining the goals? Or do you object to neither?

Decision Scenario 7
DISMISSAL FOR AN ABORTION?

Robin Flanigan was a twenty-one-year-old unmarried hairdresser working at a salon in suburban Maryland in 1990 when she faced a decision that many young women confront: Should she choose to end her pregnancy through an abortion? According to Ms. Flanigan, she approached one of the salon owners, Patrice Davidson, for advice. Shortly

thereafter Mrs. Davidson and her husband (the other salon owner) began, in the words of Ms. Flanigan, an "endless assault" to convince her not to go through with her decision to have an abortion. On December 11, 1990, Ms. Flanigan went through with her decision. On December 15 she was fired from her job. Ms. Flanigan filed a civil suit against the Davidsons, claiming that she was wrongfully fired for choosing to have an abortion.

In her suit, Ms. Flanigan alleged that the Davidsons aimed to "coerce and intimidate her into not having the abortion." Their activities included phone calls to her family, offers to help raise the child, letters, and, at one point, hanging pictures of aborted fetuses at her workplace. The Davidsons denied all of Ms. Flanigan's allegations. They claimed that she was fired for unsatisfactory work and that the timing of her dismissal was simply coincidental.

- Assume that the facts are as Ms. Flanigan claims. What, if anything, would be wrong with the Davidsons' activities? Assume that there was no campaign of harassment, but simply that the Davidsons fired Ms. Flanigan when they discovered that she had had an abortion. What, if anything, would be wrong with their action?

- Imagine a parallel case in which an employer encouraged an employee to have an abortion. Would the same issues be involved if the employee was fired for refusing?

- Shouldn't employers be allowed to make personnel decisions based upon their own judgments of moral character? Why or why not?

9

Health and Safety in
the Workplace

What responsibilities does a business have for the health and safety of its
workers? What role does government have in protecting worker health
and safety? Should policies be aimed at preventing injury at all costs,
or should these decisions be made in terms of both the costs and benefits to
safety? Should employers be free to exclude workers who might be prone to accidents, or those genetically susceptible to disease? This chapter examines issues
of workplace health, safety, and risk.

THE VALUE OF HEALTH

Everyone is in favor of a healthy and risk-free workplace; nevertheless, significant
controversy surrounds issues of workplace health and safety. For this reason it will
prove helpful first to consider the value of health and safety. If anything can be
said to be *intrinsically* good, it would be health and safety. Except in the most extreme circumstances, life is better than death, health is better than illness, and bodily integrity is better than injury. Besides this intrinsic value, health and safety also
have significant *instrumental* value. That is, they are very useful, seemingly necessary, for acquiring other things of value. Whatever one desires, chances are that
being healthy and safe will greatly improve one's chances for satisfying that desire.

But health and safety also function as ideals, seldom fully attainable (at least
for any extended time) during our lives. It would be odd to claim that one is

perfectly healthy, or completely safe. We seem to face risks to our health and safety at all times. When I kiss my child good-night, I risk being infected with his flu. As I sit here typing at my word processor, I risk getting carpal tunnel syndrome from typing too much.

Many of the debates concerning workplace health and safety focus not on those issues as such, but on reducing risks faced by workers. Risk can be understood as the probability of harm. Risk therefore can be measured and compared. Protecting worker health and safety, therefore, will involve questions of risk assessment and risk assumption: How high are the risks, and how do they compare with alternatives? Who shall bear the risks, and how much risk is acceptable? The first two questions are technical and can be answered by scientists and engineers. The last two questions are ethical and best not left to technicians.

Assessing risks involves making judgments on the magnitude or seriousness of the harm involved. There is an important difference between a low probability of minor harm and a high probability of major harm. Again, scientists and engineers can determine the probabilities of various harms, but judging whether or not these risks are worth taking and making judgments about the nature of potential harms require ethical thinking.

These distinctions often get confused in debates about workplace health and safety. In many cases, highly technical and mathematical studies are done to evaluate workplace safety standards. In effect, these studies measure the probability of various harms and compare those probabilities to other risks taken in other circumstances. For example, workers might be told that they stand a higher risk of being in a car accident on their way to work than contracting cancer from airborne chemicals in the workplace. We should always be careful to distinguish the factual questions from the normative ones, however. It may well be, as a matter of fact, more risky to drive on a busy highway than to inhale workplace carcinogens. But this fact alone does not answer the questions of whether employees *ought* to take such risks, of who should decide which risks are taken, of whether or not the benefits of these risks are worth it. Determining relative risks does not, in itself, decide the ethical questions.

While the value of health and safety is uncontroversial, there is wide disagreement over the best means for pursuing these goals. One view would leave these decisions to be reached through a bargaining process between employer and employee. Accordingly, acceptable risk is determined by individual employees and their employers. Those who place a high value on health and safety would presumably demand a relatively safe workplace and be willing to sacrifice wages and other benefits to get it. Those who are willing to take risks would presumably bargain for higher wages as a trade-off for accepting greater workplace risk. In each case, all involved get what they most want and society maximizes happiness. Individual bargaining is the method favored by defenders of free market economics.

In recent decades, another view has emerged as consensus in the United States concerning workplace health and safety. This consensus has concluded that workplace safety should not be left totally to individual employees and employers. History suggests that this approach may place too many workers at significant risk and does little to prevent workplace harms for occurring in the first place. The reading from Mark MacCarthy reviews some challenges to this approach.

The consensus has determined that government has a legitimate role in establishing regulations to protect workers. In 1970, Congress established the Occupational Safety and Health Administration (OSHA) to set standards for workplace health and safety. Since that time, most debates have focused on how OSHA should determine these standards.

OSHA

The primary mission of the Occupational Safety and Health Administration is to promulgate safety standards and conduct inspections to determine compliance with these standards. (The U.S. Supreme Court has ruled, however, that if a company objects to an inspection, OSHA must first obtain a search warrant.) Companies found in violation of OSHA standards can be fined. Working through the federal courts, OSHA can also close a workplace for serious safety violations if the management refuses either to comply with safety standards or to voluntarily suspend operations.

Since OSHA initially had no studies of its own on which to base its standard, the first standards established were adopted from those prevailing in industry at the time. However, as the agency matured and began to issue new standards of its own, its actions were criticized by many in business. These complaints fall into two categories: complaints about the specific standards and complaints about the methods and procedures used in establishing these standards.

In one famous case concerning specific standards, OSHA held that there was insufficient data available to draw a reasonable conclusion about the precise level of benzene exposure that constituted a cancer hazard. As a consequence, the agency adopted a rule that limited benzene exposure to what it considered the lowest feasible level. The rule created vigorous petroleum-industry resistance. The industry complained that setting a standard requiring the lowest feasible levels of exposure, when there was no evidence that such a measure was necessary to protect health, unfairly imposed substantial costs on business. In 1980, as a result of a series of appeals, the Supreme Court held that OSHA must show substantial evidence that its standards are necessary for reducing significant risk. The Court rejected the benzene standard as having insufficient evidence in its support.

Another major case challenged OSHA's interpretation of its duty under the Occupational Safety and Health Act to ensure health by regulating exposure to toxins "to the extent feasible." OSHA had set standards for the exposure to another carcinogen, cotton dust, by interpreting the word *feasible* to mean "technologically and economically feasible." Under this interpretation OSHA argued that it did not have to perform a cost–benefit analysis to prove that a proposed standard optimally balanced costs and benefits. Again, industry took OSHA to court to challenge the stringent cotton dust standard because regulations based on cost–benefit analysis would likely result in fewer expenses. In 1981, the Supreme Court upheld OSHA's interpretation of "feasible."

Recent criticisms have focused on OSHA's effectiveness in protecting workers and on its general methods and procedures for setting standards. Some critics point to well-known studies indicating that aggregate injury rates have shown no substantial decline since the implementation of OSHA standards. The conclusion drawn is that OSHA is ineffective in protecting workers.

These criticisms have come from both the right and the left. Right-wing opponents of OSHA charge that we are not getting any benefits from the many dollars spent supporting the OSHA bureaucracy and complying with the agency's standards. According to this perspective, we would be better off if we eliminated the agency. Left-wing critics take a different perspective. They argue that protective standards characteristically are introduced with public relations fanfare, but the necessary enforcement mechanisms soon fall prey to corporate influence in the political process. For instance, under the Reagan administration the OSHA budget was cut and its staff reduced by 25 percent. Workplace inspections have therefore declined. Fewer inspections provide less incentive for business to comply with safety standards. (Inspectors annually visit fewer than 4 percent of the nation's businesses.)

Defenders of OSHA respond to both criticisms as follows: First, the data about injury rates fail to account for the effectiveness of OSHA standards aimed not at reducing injury and accidents but at workplace related illnesses such as cancer. Second, while the overall injury rates have not changed substantially, two things are worth noting. In certain categories of injury, such as having a hand caught in machinery, rates of injury have shown a decline. Of course, this fact means other categories of injury have increased. Proponents claim that this fact reflects increased reporting due to a greater awareness of safety and a fear of fines for failure to report injuries. Hence, the real effect of OSHA may be understated by both the overall and the category-specific data because reporting in both areas may have increased.

These debates have led some conservative critics to propose two separate changes in agency policy. The more radical proposal is to abandon the approach of setting standards and to rely instead on an injury tax. Under this proposal, business would have an economic incentive to provide a safe workplace since unsafe workplaces would be required to pay higher taxes. Critics charge that this is tantamount to allowing businesses to purchase a license to injure; at least the present policy of mandatory standards clearly states that our public policy goal is to protect worker health and safety.

The other proposed change urges government to adopt economic criteria for establishing regulations and standards. This was the approach favored by many in the Reagan and Bush administrations and by many in the recently elected Republican majorities in the U.S. House and Senate. The reading by James Chelius, for instance, argues that public policy ought to be guided by a criteria of optimality that would require a formal balancing of costs and benefits. According to this view, since there is no such thing as a risk-free workplace, government policy should aim to minimize risk and optimize safety. Any workplace could always be made safer, but at a certain point it simply becomes too expensive to do so. The decrease in risks is not worth the increase in costs. This point of equilibrium is the point of optimal safety, and it can be found through cost–benefit analysis.

Chelius's approach is explicitly rejected by Mark MacCarthy. MacCarthy presents complex but powerful arguments for the conclusion that it is theoretically impossible to use economic criteria adequately for determining public safety policy. The implication of MacCarthy's argument is that such public policy questions are inescapably questions of ethics and politics and that we delude ourselves if we pretend that technicians can provide clear, unproblematic solutions to safety problems. (These disputes between Chelius and MacCarthy should be compared to the disputes between William Baxter and Mark Sagoff in Chapter Twelve.)

RISKY WORK OR RISKY WORKERS?

As early as the 1930s, biologists had recognized that different workers exposed to the same workplace toxins responded differently. The geneticist J. B. Haldane speculated in 1938 that these differences could be explained by genetic differences between workers. Some workers were genetically more susceptible to disease than others. Thus, Haldane concluded, it would be advisable to screen out workers who were more susceptible to these harms.[*]

This represents a common and reasonable strategy for reducing workplace injury. If an employee is accident-prone, it seems reasonable to reduce accidents by eliminating the employee. Recent developments in genetics make this a more far-ranging strategy. Genetic research does suggest that some people are more susceptible to specific diseases than others. Given similar exposure to workplace carcinogens, not every worker gets cancer. This difference may lie in the different genetic makeup of individuals. Thus, one strategy for reducing workplace disease is to genetically screen workers to identify those most susceptible to disease, and not hire them in the first place or transfer or fire them from hazardous jobs.

This strategy raises significant ethical issues. It shifts the focus of workplace health and safety from the workplace to the workers. Instead of asking if a particular *workplace* is too risky, we now ask if a particular *worker* is too risky. Instead of focusing energies on eliminating workplace toxins, we eliminate workers. This is troublesome for several reasons.

Even assuming that the scientific basis of such claims is valid, genetic "susceptibility" and "predispositions" are just that: They are possibilities and not at all certain. Thus, we have a real likelihood of unfairly discriminating against people who would not suffer from exposure. This is also unfair because such discrimination is based on things over which people exercise no control. Unlike our genetic makeup, we can control the workplace environment. Fairness would hold that responsibility for reducing harm rests with the workplace and not with the workers.

We see this general strategy at work in two readings in this chapter. Some workplace toxins pose threats to fetuses if the mother is exposed to the toxin. Thus, in the American Cyanamid/Johnson Controls case study, employers excluded women of child-bearing age from jobs that might expose them to toxins

---

[*]J. B. S. Haldane, *Heredity and Politics* (London: Allen and Unwin, 1938).

that could harm their fetuses. In the Johnson Controls case, the U.S. Supreme Court concluded that such exclusionary policies unfairly discriminated against women. The reading from Hubbard and Wald considers the issues raised by workplace genetic screening. Since the subject of genetic screening also raises serious questions about employee privacy, you should integrate this discussion with the questions raised in the previous chapter.

CASE STUDY American Cyanamid and Johnson Controls

In the beginning of 1978, Glen Mercer, an officer of American Cyanamid Company's Willow Island plant in West Virginia, held meetings with groups of the plant's female employees. The subject of the meetings was the presence in the plant of numerous chemicals known to be hazardous to the health of fetuses. Mr. Mercer announced a new corporate policy that would exclude women of childbearing age from those areas of the plant where these chemicals were present. The exclusion would apply to every woman between the ages of 16 and 50 unless the woman presented documents proving that she had been sterilized. At the meetings the women were given information about the ease of sterilization procedures and about the local availability of those procedures.

Initially, the company's exclusionary policy was to apply to all but seven jobs in the plant. Mercer informed the approximately thirty women who would be subject to the policy that those who either were not sterilized or were not awarded the remaining nonhazardous jobs would be dismissed. After several months, American Cyanamid modified its policy so that it applied to only one department. Of the seven women in that department, five were sterilized and two were assigned to other jobs with reduced wages.

The final exclusionary policy applied to a department where there was environmental exposure to airborne lead. American Cyanamid claimed that it was unable to reduce the lead levels in the air to comply with Occupational Safety and Health Administration standards. OSHA believed that those standards were safe even for fetuses. When American Cyanamid failed to reduce lead levels, OSHA issued a citation and proposed a fine of $10,000 on the ground that the policy of sterilization or reassignment/termination was itself a hazard to the health of the women. On appeal, an administrative law judge exempted the plant from the OSHA

standards on the ground that compliance was not "economically feasible."

The Oil, Chemical and Atomic Workers Union, which represented the female employees, brought two suits against the company. One alleged that the administrative law judge erred in determining that the exclusionary policy was not itself a health hazard prohibited by the intent of the Occupational Safety and Health Act of 1970 since, according to the union, sterilization is a serious harm. The other suit alleged that the exclusionary policy was a form of discrimination prohibited by the 1964 Civil Rights Act.

In the first case, Judge Robert Bork, then sitting on the District of Columbia Court of Appeals, wrote a decision upholding the original decision of the administrative law judge. Bork, in a characteristically clear and narrow decision, ruled that the precedent from previous court cases and legislative history of the OSHA act both indicate that the term *hazard* refers only to the physical or environmental conditions of the workplace. Thus, Cyanamid's exclusionary policy was not a hazard covered by the OSHA act.

The sex discrimination suit was settled out of court, and therefore no clear precedent emerged from this case. However, a few years later a similar case did make its way to the U.S. Supreme Court. In *Automobile Workers v. Johnson Controls*, the Court had to decide if policies that excluded women from certain jobs in order to protect their potential children constituted unfair and illegal discrimination.

Johnson Controls Inc. manufactures batteries, a major component of which is lead. Exposure to lead affects the reproductive abilities of both men and women, and poses additional health risks to all adults, children, and fetuses. Evidence suggests that a fetus is more vulnerable to harm than an adult.

Prior to the Civil Rights Act of 1964, Johnson Controls did not employ any women in jobs that involved exposure to lead. The company's first official policy regarding women in such positions strongly advised women capable of bearing children against taking these jobs. Women who applied for jobs involving exposure to lead were required to sign a statement informing them that "women exposed to lead have a higher rate of abortion...not as clear as the relationship between cigarette smoking and cancer...but medically speaking, it just makes good sense not to run that risk if you want children and do not want to expose the unborn child to risk, however small."

In 1982 Johnson Controls went further and excluded all women who were capable of bearing children from jobs involving lead exposure. This change resulted from the discovery that several employees who had recently become pregnant had

tested for blood lead levels above the OSHA critical-level category. The new policy defined women capable of bearing children as "all women except those whose inability to bear children is medically documented."

In response to this policy, several employees filed suit, including a woman who chose to be sterilized rather than lose her job, a woman who was a single parent and who had been transferred to a lower-paying job, and a man who had been denied a leave of absence so that he could lower the level of lead in his system before he and his wife tried to become parents. This case was decided by the U.S. Supreme Court in 1991. The following reading contains excerpts from this decision.

AUTOMOBILE WORKERS V. JOHNSON CONTROLS, INC.
United States Supreme Court

Justice Blackmun delivered the opinion of the Court.

In this case we are concerned with an employer's gender-based fetal-protection policy. May an employer exclude a fertile female employee from certain jobs because of its concern for the health of the fetus the woman might conceive?

I

Respondent Johnson Controls, Inc., manufactures batteries. In the manufacturing process, the element lead is a primary ingredient. Occupational exposure to lead entails health risks, including the risk of harm to any fetus carried by a female employee.

Before the Civil Rights Act of 1964, 78 Stat. 241, became law, Johnson Controls did not employ any woman in a battery-manufacturing job. In June 1977, however, it announced its first official policy concerning its employment of women in lead-exposure work....

Johnson Controls "stopped short of excluding women capable of bearing children from lead exposure," *id.,* at 138, but emphasized that a woman who expected to have a child should not

choose a job in which she would have such exposure. The company also required a woman who wished to be considered for employment to sign a statement that she had been advised of the risk of having a child while she was exposed to lead....

Five years later, in 1982, Johnson Controls shifted from a policy of warning to a policy of exclusion. Between 1979 and 1983, eight employees became pregnant while maintaining blood lead levels in excess of 30 micrograms per deciliter. Tr. of Oral Arg. 25, 34. This appeared to be the critical level noted by the Occupational Health and Safety Administration (OSHA) for a worker who was planning to have a family. See 29 CFR § 1910.1025 (1989). The company responded by announcing a broad exclusion of women from jobs that exposed them to lead:

> "...[I]t is [Johnson Controls'] policy that women who are pregnant or who are capable of bearing children will not be placed into jobs involving lead exposure or which could expose them to lead through the exercise of job bidding, bumping, transfer or promotion rights." App. 85–86.

The policy defined "women...capable of bearing children" as "[a]ll women except those whose inability to bear children is medically documented."

From *Supreme Court Reporter* 111 (March 20, 1991): 1196–1217.

Id., at 81. It further stated that an unacceptable work station was one where, "over the past year," an employee had recorded a blood lead level of more than 30 micrograms per deciliter or the work site had yielded an air sample containing a lead level in excess of 30 micrograms per cubic meter. *Ibid.*

II

In April 1984, petitioners filed in the United States District Court for the Eastern District of Wisconsin a class action challenging Johnson Controls' fetal-protection policy as sex discrimination that violated Title VII of the Civil Rights Act of 1964, as amended, 42 U. S. C. § 2000e *et seq.* Among the individual plaintiffs were petitioners Mary Craig, who had chosen to be sterilized in order to avoid losing her job....

III

The bias in Johnson Controls' policy is obvious. Fertile men, but not fertile women, are given a choice as to whether they wish to risk their reproductive health for a particular job. Section 703(a) of the Civil Rights Act of 1964, 78 Stat. 255, as amended, 42 U. S. C. § 2000e-2(a), prohibits sex-based classifications in terms and conditions of employment, in hiring and discharging decisions, and in other employment decisions that adversely affect an employee's status. Respondent's fetal-protection policy explicitly discriminates against women on the basis of their sex. The policy excludes women with childbearing capacity from lead-exposed jobs and so creates a facial classification based on gender. Respondent assumes as much in its brief before this Court. Brief for Respondent 17, n. 24.

Nevertheless, the Court of Appeals assumed, as did the two appellate courts who already had confronted the issue, that sex-specific fetal-protection policies do not involve facial discrimination....

...The court assumed that because the asserted reason for the sex-based exclusion (protecting women's unconceived offspring) was ostensibly benign, the policy was not sex-based discrimination. That assumption, however, was incorrect.

First, Johnson Controls' policy classifies on the basis of gender and childbearing capacity, rather than fertility alone. Respondent does not seek to protect the unconceived children of all its employees. Despite evidence in the record about the debilitating effect of lead exposure on the male reproductive system, Johnson Controls is concerned only with the harms that may befall the unborn offspring of its female employees....Johnson Controls' policy is facially discriminatory because it requires only a female employee to produce proof that she is not capable of reproducing.

Our conclusion is bolstered by the Pregnancy Discrimination Act of 1978 (PDA), 92 Stat. 2076, 42 U. S. C. § 2000e(k), in which Congress explicitly provided that, for purposes of Title VII, discrimination "on the basis of sex" includes discrimination "because of or on the basis of pregnancy, childbirth, or related medical conditions." "The Pregnancy Discrimination Act has now made clear that, for all Title VII purposes, discrimination based on a woman's pregnancy is, on its face, discrimination because of her sex." *Newport News Shipbuilding & Dry Dock Co. v. EEOC,* 462 U. S. 669, 684 (1983). In its use of the words "capable of bearing children" in the 1982 policy statement as the criterion for exclusion, Johnson Controls explicitly classifies on the basis of potential for pregnancy. Under the PDA, such a classification must be regarded, for Title VII purposes, in the same light as explicit sex discrimination. Respondent has chosen to treat all its female employees as potentially pregnant; that choice evinces discrimination on the basis of sex....

The beneficence of an employer's purpose does not undermine the conclusion that an explicit gender-based policy is sex discrimination under § 703(a) and thus may be defended only as a BFOQ [bona fide occupational qualification].

The enforcement policy of the Equal Employment Opportunity Commission accords with this conclusion. On January 24, 1990, the EEOC issued a Policy Guidance in the light of the Seventh Circuit's decision in the present case....

In sum, Johnson Controls' policy "does not pass the simple test of whether the evidence shows 'treatment of a person in a manner which but for that person's sex would be different.'"...

IV

Under § 703(e)(1) of Title VII, an employer may discriminate on the basis of "religion, sex, or national origin in those certain instances where religion, sex, or national origin is a bona fide occupational qualification reasonably necessary to the normal operation of that particular business or enterprise." 42 U. S. C. § 2000e-2(e)(1). We therefore turn to the question whether Johnson Controls' fetal-protection policy is one of those "certain instances" that come within the BFOQ exception....

The PDA's amendment to Title VII contains a BFOQ standard of its own: unless pregnant employees differ from others "in their ability or inability to work," they must be "treated the same" as other employees "for all employment-related purposes." 42 U. S. C. § 2000e(k). This language clearly sets forth Congress' remedy for discrimination on the basis of pregnancy and potential pregnancy. Women who are either pregnant or potentially pregnant must be treated like others "similar in their ability...to work." *Ibid.* In other words, women as capable of doing their jobs as their male counterparts may not be forced to choose between having a child and having a job....

V

We have no difficulty concluding that Johnson Controls cannot establish a BFOQ. Fertile women, as far as appears in the record, participate in the manufacture of batteries as efficiently as anyone else. Johnson Controls' professed moral and ethical concerns about the welfare of the next generation do not suffice to establish a BFOQ of female sterility. Decisions about the welfare of future children must be left to the parents who conceive, bear, support, and raise them rather than to the employers who hire those parents. Congress has mandated this choice through Title VII, as amended by the Pregnancy Discrimination Act. Johnson Controls has attempted to exclude women because of their reproductive capacity. Title VII and the PDA simply do not allow a woman's dismissal because of her failure to submit to sterilization.

Nor can concerns about the welfare of the next generation be considered a part of the "essence" of Johnson Controls' business....

Johnson Controls argues that it must exclude all fertile women because it is impossible to tell which women will become pregnant while working with lead. This argument is somewhat academic in light of our conclusion that the company may not exclude fertile women at all; it perhaps is worth noting, however, that Johnson Controls has shown no "factual basis for believing that all or substantially all women would be unable to perform safely and efficiently the duties of the job involved." *Weeks v. Southern Bell Tel. & Tel. Co.,* 408 F. 2d 228, 235 (CA5 1969), quoted with approval in *Dothard,* 433 U. S., at 333. Even on this sparse record, it is apparent that Johnson Controls is concerned about only a small minority of women. Of the eight pregnancies reported among the female employees, it has not been shown that any of the babies have birth defects or other abnormalities. The record does not reveal the birth rate for Johnson Controls' female workers but national statistics show that approximately nine percent of all fertile women become pregnant each year. The birthrate drops to two percent for blue collar workers over age 30. See Becker, 53 U. Chi. L. Rev., at 1233. Johnson Controls' fear of prenatal injury, no matter how sincere, does not begin to show that substantially all of its fertile women employees are incapable of doing their jobs....

It is no more appropriate for the courts than it is for individual employers to decide whether a woman's reproductive role is more important to herself and her family than her economic role. Congress has left this choice to the woman as hers to make.

The judgment of the Court of Appeals is reversed and the case is remanded for further proceedings consistent with this opinion.

It is so ordered.

THE OCCUPATIONAL SAFETY AND HEALTH PROBLEM
James Chelius

THE NATURE OF THE PROBLEM

One of every ten workers in private industry each year suffers the effects of an accident or disease incurred while working.[1] Only one-third of these incidents involve lost worktime, but lost time totals over 31 million days per year in the United States.[2] Naturally, these accidents and diseases have aroused public concern.

Without slighting the seriousness of the work-injury problem, it is helpful to place it in perspective by considering other activities which give rise to similar harm. The National Safety Council estimates that many more deaths result from non-work automobile accidents than from all work accidents. Accidents in the home and accidents in "public-place" activities, which include swimming and hunting, also produce more deaths than working.[3] Walter Oi has estimated that "...fully a third of all employed persons confront a risk of being injured on the job that is lower than the risk of living in general."[4] Thus, while work injuries are a serious concern, they do not represent a unique or isolated phenomenon. Work is simply one of the many activities which yields injuries. Although there are certain aspects of work which make it different from other activities, there is much that is common to all injury-producing endeavors.

Safety as an Economic Commodity

Although work deaths and injuries are occurrences everyone would like to eliminate, unfortunately this is not possible. Many of these accidents and diseases cannot be prevented if we also want the desirable goods, services, and incomes which accompany them. All of life's activities entail the possibility of being injured or catching a disease but people do not choose just the least risky activities. Relatively hazardous activities such as working, driving, and consuming new products are freely chosen because people feel the benefits of participation outweigh the risks. Since there are benefits

as well as risks to participation in all activities, the problem of risk control can be most usefully analyzed within the economist's framework of costs and benefits.

The moral anguish associated with accidents and disease notwithstanding, it must be understood that prevention is an economic commodity. Prevention can be "produced" only by the use of scarce resources which, if not allocated to prevention, could serve other beneficial purposes. The resources used for prevention usually have an obvious economic character. For example, heavy-duty automobile bumpers, protective headgear, and safety experts use resources that could be devoted to other beneficial purposes than accident and disease prevention. Of all the resources available to us for accident prevention, the most expensive is abstaining from a risky activity. Each of us avoids many activities which could give us some form of satisfaction. However desirable the satisfaction, many of us feel that activities such as riding motorcycles or building skyscrapers are far too risky compared with the rewards of participation. The fact that there are many risky activities which we do not choose to avoid simply means that we savor the rewards of these activities more than we fear the risks.

Why Occupational Safety and Health Are Special

Although working is often no more dangerous than other activities, work risks receive attention disproportionate to their impact. To understand why, it is useful to consider how people decide whether to participate in a risky activity. This choice is often very difficult. However, people usually feel comfortable with these decisions, once made, because they did have a choice and were aware of the rewards and risks when they chose. The same decision process occurs in both work and nonwork settings, but there are substantial differences. In a nonwork situation the rewards of exposure to risk typically accrue directly to the participant. Furthermore, control over the decision is usually direct and immediate. In deciding whether to drive to the beach, an individual implicitly weighs the risks of

From James Chelius, *Workplace Safety and Health* (Washington, D.C.: American Enterprise Institute, 1977).

driving against the pleasures of visiting the beach. If the anticipated pleasure outweighs the anticipated risks, the individual goes to the beach. If not he stays home.

A work situation with exactly the same risks and rewards may present a more difficult decision. Whereas the worker driving to the beach to deliver food supplies exposes himself directly to the same risks as the vacationer, the direct rewards of his drive accrue to the consumers of the food he delivers. If consumers desire the benefits created by having the food at the beach, they must pay the employee's company, and the company in turn rewards the employee. Therefore, even in an ideal situation where the company pays extra wages for exposure to risk, the rewards for such risks are more indirect than in the typical nonwork situation.

In addition, the decisions controlling individual exposure to risks in the workplace frequently have a less immediate impact than nonwork decisions. An individual who considers going to the beach for his own recreation can quickly make a decision or change it if conditions change, whereas an individual in the work situation must negotiate with his employer for changes in the level of risk or benefits. An individual planning a family trip to the beach can change his mind if weather conditions change and he feels the drive is too risky. If a worker encounters such a change in driving conditions, however, he may not be able to alter his schedule to accommodate the increase in risk. A worker's recourse is to negotiate with his employer, individually or through his union, to lower the level of risk or to increase wages. If the situation is not corrected the individual may have to search for a new job. Certainly the process of bargaining with an employer or changing jobs is a more difficult and complicated method of responding to a change in the level of risk than is typical in a nonwork setting.

Another factor making work safety an object of special public attention is the availability of a relatively small group to serve as scapegoats. Employers serve this function admirably. They serve as an object of blame and scorn out of proportion to their responsibility for accidents and disease simply because there are fewer employers than employees. Just as "middlemen" are almost invariably blamed for food price increases, because there are fewer of them than there are farmers or retailers, so perhaps must employers serve as the objects to be blamed for occupational injuries. Since there is no readily available scapegoat for hunting or swimming accidents, we will probably always pay less attention to these sources of injuries than to injuries which arise from work. Thus, because the benefits of risk-taking on the job are indirect, because the immediate situation is often less controllable, and because there is a readily available group to blame, the risks of work have generated special concern. It is a difficult and sensitive issue which most people feel deserves extraordinary attention.

The Concept of Optimal Safety

Since both benefits and costs are associated with risky activities, it is desirable to balance them so as to achieve an ideal or optimal amount of risk. For each individual, this desired level of risk is one in which the value placed on benefits minus costs is at a maximum. In other words, the goal is the largest level of satisfaction net of all costs including risks. Since virtually all activities entail some degree of risk, it follows that we would not want to eliminate all risks, because this would entail avoiding all rewarding activities. What is needed is a compromising balance of prevention efforts, activity benefits, and activity risks. It is therefore desirable to have arrangements by which these trade-offs can be achieved in a manner satisfactory to the individuals who comprise our society.

The desirability of accepting some positive level of risk runs counter to many people's initial reaction to the subject. At first glance, accident and disease prevention are usually seen as an unmitigated benefit whose value is infinite. It therefore is seen as something that should not be constrained by the cost of the resources required for its accomplishment. Individuals who voice this opinion should ask themselves whether they act as if this were the value they placed on prevention. To do so, they would have to go through most of life's activities with prevention as their primary goal. Of course, very few (if any) people actually behave in this manner. However, one may place whatever value one wants on prevention. The goal, again, is to provide arrangements under which individuals may trade off risks and benefits in the manner that maximizes their personal satisfactions.

If all the costs and benefits of accidents and diseases accrued to the same person, determination of the appropriate exposure to risk would be relatively straightforward. A well-informed decision maker would participate in an activity if the value of expected benefits exceeded the value of expected costs. However, the costs and benefits of certain activities, such as work, generally accrue to different decision makers. For example, products go to customers while injuries go to workers. In these cases, it is necessary to devise mechanisms which allow the balancing of costs and benefits not directly and immediately borne by the individual participants. It follows from this that the ultimate goal of government intervention in safety and health affairs should be to facilitate the arrangements by which individuals and groups seek to achieve an optimal level of risk.

Many people of high purpose are offended by the expression of the occupational safety and health problem in terms of costs and benefits. However, it must be remembered that this is not a normative structure imposed by economists but a formalization of the factors which concern individuals. To ignore the cost/benefit framework does not change the nature of the problem or the attributes of possible solutions. Such avoidance simply increases the likelihood that certain features of our desires or the constraints on our desires will be ignored. The use of cost/benefit labels merely categorizes and explicitly considers factors which might otherwise be ignored. Ignoring such factors does not cause them to go away, nor does it make difficult decisions easier.

We have defined the optimal level of risk as that at which the net value of benefits over costs is at a maximum for each individual. This goal is met by continuing to reduce the incidence of accidents and disease until the costs of achieving the reduction are equal to the extra benefits derived. After the equality of marginal benefits and costs has been achieved, further reduction in accidents and diseases will cost more than it is worth, which represents a net social loss. The difficulty of translating this abstract decision process into concrete identifiable terms should not deter us from recognizing the appropriateness of optimal risk as a public policy goal. To ignore this goal, because of its abstract character, can only lead to policy decisions that waste the limited resources at our disposal. While we cannot concretely and precisely define the "ideal" incidence of accidents and diseases, we must understand the nature of the trade-offs involved and make recognition of these realities an integral part of public policy.

THE ROLE OF PUBLIC POLICY

For a broad range of activities our society trusts private decision makers such as workers, consumers, unions, and firms to achieve through their interaction the desired amount of goods and services. The quantity of such varied "commodities" as travel, garbage, and books is largely determined by individuals deciding how much they care to produce and consume in view of how much is received or forgone in a trade. We rely on these decisions because, in making them, people at least implicitly balance the costs and benefits of production and consumption thus satisfying themselves while preserving freedom of choice for others. An important question to ask ourselves, therefore, is whether we can trust the decisions individuals make about the production and consumption of occupational safety and health.

Our society relies on private decisions for most commodities because the costs and benefits facing individuals are the same as the costs and benefits to society. In most cases, the optimal amount for society is simply the sum of the optimal amounts for each member of society. A problem arises, however, when the full value of either costs or benefits are not known or felt by the decision maker. If the cost which accrues to the decision maker is less than the true social cost of a product or activity, then the individual will consume or produce more than is appropriate from society's point of view since the individual is ignoring costs which others must bear. A classic example of this social cost problem is pollution. We know that, because the producers who pollute have not had to bear the total costs of polluting, their production exceeds optimal levels. Steel producers, for example, have not always borne their full costs, which include the aesthetic loss of clean waterways, ill health generated by polluted air, and extra cleaning bills for families living in the vicinity of the mills. From society's viewpoint these costs are as much a part of steel production as the costs of iron ore and coal for which steel companies pay. Because these pollution costs are not paid by steel companies, the cost of steel appears to be less than it truly is. Hence, the price of steel is less than it should be, and too much steel—and pollution—are produced.

Under certain conditions private market forces will eliminate the distortion caused by ignoring these social costs. If rights are well-defined, markets are competitive, decision makers are aware of all costs, and the costs of making and enforcing contracts are negligible, then there will be no distortions due to these social costs.[5] In the case of steel pollution, its effect on the company's neighbors would be borne by the steel producers if: (1) the neighbor was aware of the problem and its cost to him; and (2) the neighbor could bargain and enforce contracts with the steel company at negligible costs. Although few would contend that this is a likely situation, the point is important because the degree to which these conditions are met will determine the extent of the distortion in production due to the divergence between social and private costs.

In occupational safety and health, the issue is whether there are any differences in costs to decision makers and in social costs which will cause a nonoptimal amount of safety to be supplied in the absence of government regulation. A social cost problem might arise if the party bearing the costs of accident prevention is not the one who receives all the benefits of prevention. In many situations, the worker receives most of the benefits of accident prevention while both the worker and his employer have a substantial role in prevention. To the extent that the employer does not receive adequate benefits from safety measures, his prevention expenditures will not fully reflect the total benefits of prevention. This situation, of course, parallels the case where a steel firm does not bear the costs of pollution and hence produces a socially undesirable amount of pollution.

Just as economic theory predicts that the amount of pollution may be optimized even with differential private and social costs, it also predicts that the amount of safety and health may be optimized under analogous circumstances. If workers accurately perceive the risks of accidents and disease and if there are negligible costs of bargaining with employers, an optimal safety level can be achieved. Under such circumstances the cost of taking risks would be reflected in the wage structure. That is, in order to attract workers to risky

work the employer would have to pay a wage premium. The extra wages reflecting compensation for danger are the mechanism by which the firm is made to carry the burden of not preventing accidents and disease. Insofar as the employer devotes resources to prevention, the wage premium needed to attract workers will decrease. Thus, true social costs are made to be the employer's private costs. By preventing accidents for employees, an employer receives a benefit for himself—a reduction in his wage bill. This arrangement, based on a private exchange between employers and employees, would yield the optimal amount of safety and health because the relevant decision makers feel the full burden and rewards of both costs and benefits.

Are workers and employers likely to be fully aware of injury and prevention costs? It is difficult to answer this question. Many observers feel that workers do not accurately perceive the risks and cost of injury. The typical worker is often viewed as having the philosophy, "It will never happen to me." Although this view is intuitively no more appealing than the contrary view that the average worker is inappropriately fearful of his environment, neither view is based on compelling evidence.[6]

As to the ease of bargaining and enforcing contracts, it is again difficult to make a judgment. Certainly bargaining between parties with an ongoing contractual relationship, such as employers and employees, is cheaper and easier than bargaining between a steel factory manager and a neighboring home owner. Unfortunately there is no solid empirical evidence to guide us on these issues. Even if we had direct evidence there would be no reliable standard by which to judge it. For example, how much information is necessary before an accurate system of risk-compensating wage premiums will develop? At what point do bargaining and enforcement mechanisms become too costly to facilitate health and safety agreements? There are no a priori standards by which to judge these matters. The need for empirical evidence is obviously great; however, we do not have firm answers to any of these critical questions. Whether private individual and group exchange can optimize safety and health remains an unanswered question, although the longstanding assumption by public policy makers is that it cannot. It is this unsupported assumption that has led to the conclusion that the government has a positive role to play in this area.

Even if it were determined that the private interactions of employees and employers do not yield an optimal amount of safety, it does not necessarily follow that government could improve the situation. Theoretical or practical misfunctionings in private markets should not be compared with a theoretical ideal of perfect government intervention, that is, socially optimal production by government fiat. The relevant comparison is between the practical realities of the marketplace and the practical realities of government regulation.

WHO CAUSES ACCIDENTS?

One of the important factors that shapes policy is the actual source of industrial accidents. Who, or what, causes them? Various studies have found a startlingly wide range in the proportion of work accidents caused by employees (2 to 88 percent). Perhaps this is not so surprising given the lack of rigorous design in most of the studies.

The most thorough and credible analysis of accidents on the job appears to be a recent study sponsored by the state of Wisconsin.[7] The Wisconsin study found that approximately 45 percent of work injuries are due to careless behavior by workers, such as misuse of hand tools. An additional 30 percent are attributable to momentary physical hazards like open file drawers and wet floors. The remaining 25 percent of work injuries are caused by permanent physical factors like improperly guarded machines. The last category is the only one we might reasonably expect to reduce by the compulsory safety rules and inspection approach to regulation. Although there have been no formal studies, it would appear that the employee's role in disease prevention is not as critical as it is in accident prevention. The employee, of course, still has a role in disease prevention through careful use of the available prevention equipment, conscientious adherence to prescribed procedures, and monitoring of individual health.[8]

The employee's role in prevention is crucial because an effective policy must consider the underlying causes of accidents and diseases.[9] The current methods of regulation—both safety rules and workers' compensation—are geared toward the employer's role in prevention. Since many accidents and illnesses are not caused by the employer,

the potential effectiveness of such regulation is limited. As an example of such policy ineffectiveness, consider the federal government's effort to make driving safer by mandating head rests on all new cars. There is no doubt that such head rests can help passengers avoid injuries from a crash. The National Safety Council, however, estimates that 80 percent of all drivers do not bother to adjust these head rests so that they will do any good. Similarly, in occupational safety regulation via controls on work environment, there will be little impact unless workers have incentives to act carefully.

Government officials have been reluctant to design public policies that recognize the employee's critical role in accident prevention. For example, in its concern about the impact of noise on workers' hearing, the government unhesitatingly requires expensive changes in the physical environment rather than less expensive worker-protection gear. A kind interpretation of the government's approach to prevention is the paternalistic one that workers must be protected from their own indiscretions. A cynic might argue that workers have far more votes than employers.

THE GOALS OF PUBLIC POLICY

Although we have concentrated on the role of public policy in achieving an optimal quantity of accident and disease prevention, workers' compensation has an additional goal. This goal is to alleviate a worker's financial hardship resulting from an injury.[10] This objective is usually labeled income maintenance or income security. Although income maintenance is viewed by many as the sole purpose of workers' compensation, this is not a compelling foundation for such a policy. It makes little sense to have a separate and rather complicated system that distinguishes work injuries from nonwork injuries and other sources of poverty unless the system also serves the goal of encouraging an appropriate amount of safety and health.

There is, unfortunately, a conflict between the efficient prevention and the income-maintenance objectives of workers' compensation. The conflict is best illustrated by considering two extremes—one in which the income-maintenance goal is completely ignored and one in which workers suffer absolutely no penalty from an injury.

If all forms of insurance against financial loss due to injury were prohibited, the incentive for employees to avoid accidents would certainly be maximized. Employees would take extraordinary measures to avoid uninsured losses caused by injury. Some observers feel that the potential physical suffering of an injury already provides a maximum safety incentive, but there can be little doubt that financial incentives are also important. For example, avoiding personal injuries is an important motive in home fire prevention. However, the importance of this incentive should not distract us from the role played by the financial protection of fire insurance. If insurance were not available, most of us would surely take additional measures to protect our homes with smoke detectors, electrical wiring checkups, and decreased use of fireplaces, candles, and matches. Similarly, in a work setting a complete lack of insurance protection would surely eliminate some horseplay and reckless driving and increase the use of safety equipment like hardhats, goggles, and gloves.

On the other hand, if there were 100 percent protection against all losses due to accidents, including full compensation for lost salary, pain, and loss of leisure, a worker would tend to be indifferent to accident prevention. This policy extreme would satisfy the income-maintenance goal, but it would have a most undesirable effect on safety since workers would lose nothing from injury.

Certainly a generous insurance plan will not cause many people to take risks that they think will cause death or serious injury. However, such financial protection might induce people to take risks that involve the possibility of minor injuries. Unfortunately, these minor risks sometimes turn out to have very serious consequences. A worker might for convenience remove the guard from a machine because he "knows" the only risk is a bruised hand. However, it is just such actions that too often result in severed hands rather than bruises.

The extremes of no income protection and complete income protection illustrate the conflict between the prevention and the income-maintenance objectives of workers' compensation. As income-maintenance benefits increase, the cost of an accident to an employee decreases. Accordingly, his incentive to avoid an accident also decreases. Conversely, while low income-maintenance benefits give employees added incentive to avoid accidents, they do not satisfy the demand for income maintenance or provide any additional prevention incentives for employers. As a practical matter, low income-maintenance benefits might not even yield the extra prevention incentives for employees, since other forms of income maintenance, such as welfare benefits financed by general tax revenues, would likely be used to prevent an injured worker from suffering the full financial consequences of an injury. Our society does have a general income-maintenance goal, and any specific regulatory effort that ignores this objective will in all probability be displaced or supplemented by other programs.

The achievement of adequate income maintenance does not, of course, mean that workers must have full protection against every financial consequence of an injury. Some current workers' compensation laws, and proposals for reforming these laws, appear not to recognize the nature of the conflict between income maintenance and injury prevention and opt for virtually unrestrained fulfillment of the income-maintenance goal. A continuing theme of this [article] is that while income maintenance and efficient prevention are both desirable goals, there unfortunately is a conflict between them. As a result, a compromise must be reached between them. It is a further theme of this analysis that the compromise embodied in the current system and suggested reforms overemphasizes income maintenance, while not being sufficiently sensitive to efficient accident and disease prevention.

NOTES

1. Throughout this [article], the term *injury* will be used to cover the result of both accidents and disease.

2. Data are from a news release by the U.S. Department of Labor, Bureau of Labor Statistics, *BLS Reports Results of Occupational Injuries and Illnesses for 1974* (Washington, D.C., 1975).

3. National Safety Council, *Accident Facts* (1975 ed.), 3.

4. Walter Oi, "An Essay on Workmen's Compensation and Industrial Safety," *Supplemental Studies for the National Commission on State Workmen's Compensation Laws,* vol. 1 (Washington, D.C., 1973), 72.

5. Ronald Coase, "The Problem of Social Cost," *Journal of Law and Economics,* vol. 3 (October 1960), 1–44.

6. Studies of the wage-premium issues include: R. Thaler and S. Rosen, "The Value of Saving a Life: Evidence from the Labor Market" (Paper presented at the National Bureau of Economic Research Conference, Washington, D.C., November 30, 1973); R. Smith, "The Feasibility of an 'Injury Tax' Approach to Occupational Safety," *Law and Contemporary Problems* (Summer–Autumn 1974), 730–744; and J. Chelius, "The Control of Industrial Accidents: Economic Theory and Empirical Evidence," *Law and Contemporary Problems* (Summer–Autumn 1974), 700–729.

7. Wisconsin State Department of Labor, Industry, and Human Relations, *Inspection Effectiveness Report* (1971).

8. As an example of the worker's role in disease prevention, there is anecdotal evidence that textile workers are reluctant to wear available face masks, which offer some protection from lung diseases. This reluctance is apparently due to the discomfort associated with the masks.

9. Sam Peltzman, *Regulation of Automobile Safety* (Washington, D.C.: American Enterprise Institute, 1975), finds that the National Highway Safety Administration has been ineffective in reducing auto accidents for lack of recognition of their underlying causes.

10. Some literature on workers' compensation further differentiates the system's goals. For example, the National Commission on State Workmen's Compensation Laws distinguished between the provision of income and medical care to injured workers. The notion of "income maintenance" in this volume is intended to encompass all forms of benefits to injured workers. Similarly, a distinction is sometimes made between encouragement of safety and the allocation of injury costs to the productive process. Any system that achieves the goal of "efficient prevention" as described in this [article] would also allocate injury costs to the appropriate productive process.

A REVIEW OF SOME NORMATIVE AND CONCEPTUAL ISSUES IN OCCUPATIONAL SAFETY AND HEALTH

Mark MacCarthy

I. INTRODUCTION

Controversy has surrounded public policy toward occupational safety and health at least since the establishment of the Occupational Safety and Health Administration (OSHA) in 1971. Political, legal, and economic conflicts have surfaced in debates over the existence and nature of rights to safety and health on the job, the use of economic criteria in setting safety and health standards, and the principles that are to guide public policy in this area. Many of these issues were raised in recent court cases. In *Industrial Union Department, AFL-CIO v. American Petroleum Institute* (the benzene case), the Supreme Court decided that OSHA must make a threshold determination of significant risk before lowering the permissible exposure level of a toxic substance. In *American Textile Manufacturers Institute, Inc. v. Donovan, Secretary of Labor* (the cotton dust case), the Supreme Court upheld OSHA's policy of setting exposure levels for toxic substances at the lowest feasible level. In February 1981, the Reagan Administration issued an Execu-

tive Order addressing these problems. It sets the maximization of net benefits to society as the goal for all regulatory agencies and bars any major regulatory action unless its potential benefits to society outweigh its potential costs. Controversy continues over the appropriateness of this cost-benefit approach to occupational safety and health.

Although legal, political, and economic perspectives dominate these debates, the best means of improving the quality of public policy decisions concerning occupational safety and health is by clearly understanding the philosophical issues involved. This article identifies and describes the major issues of occupational safety and health that are in need of and amenable to philosophical clarification....

II. THE NATURE OF OCCUPATIONAL RISK

Before addressing the major philosophical questions, several preliminary remarks may help to identify the special nature of the occupational safety and health problem. First, individual risks must be distinguished from group outcomes. Risk, in general, is the probability of an adverse outcome. Occupational risk is the probability of an injury or illness due to hazards in the workplace. These hazards, such as noise, toxic substances, or unguarded machinery, often produce a regular, predictable number of injuries and illnesses in the exposed worker population. At the individual level, the outcome is hypothetical; an individual worker may or may not be killed, injured, or made ill by workplace hazards. At this level, workers take their chances. In many situations, however, the outcome at the group level can be accurately predicted, and one may, then, expect a certain number of illnesses and injuries to appear in the exposed worker population as a whole. At this level, chance gives way to certainty.

A. The Individual and the Group

This distinction between the risk each individual takes and the overall outcome for the group is a conceptual distinction, related to the difference between statements about individuals and statements about the groups to which individuals belong. This distinction raises two questions regarding many kinds of risks. Consider, for example, coffee, which is allegedly involved in cancer of the pancreas. If coffee is involved in producing half of all pancreatic cancers, a non-coffee drinker aged fifty to fifty-four has seven chances in one hundred thousand of developing cancer of the pancreas in any single year. A coffee drinker's chances are doubled or tripled to approximately fourteen to twenty-one out of one hundred thousand. Should a person, then, avoid this extra risk by not drinking coffee? A different question arises with respect to the population as a whole. If coffee is implicated in producing half of all pancreatic cancers, then the consumption of coffee in the United States produces about twelve thousand of these cancers annually. Should steps be taken to reduce this number?

In the first example, we focus on the decision of the individual agent. His or her choice is essentially a private one. In the second case, we are concerned with the balance between two collective goals: the protection of public health and the provision of other social goods, including individual freedom of choice. This is a paradigm problem in public decision making.

This example illustrates the logical difference between the question, "Is this risk too great for

me?" and the question, "Does the social value of this risky activity balance the certain harm that can be expected to result from it?" An answer to the first question is not necessarily an answer to the second. The distinction between questions concerning individual risk and questions concerning group outcomes (and group responsibility for these outcomes) parallels the difference between private and public choice.

In the area of occupational safety and health, the distinction between individual risk and group outcome is reflected in the difference between two approaches to public health. Economists typically take an individualistic approach. They are concerned with the rational choices individuals might make when confronted with a probability or an uncertainty about some harm. The other approach, more typical of doctors and other public health professionals, concerns predictable group outcomes and whether they are acceptable. The difference in focus is related to a difference in public policy goals: in the one instance, the problem is that the probability of an actual outcome is too large for the individual to accept; in the other, the aggregate outcome is too severe for society to tolerate.

It is fair to suggest that the label "risk" encourages, even if it does not strictly imply, an individualistic self-regarding (as distinct from group-regarding) approach to occupational safety. That may seem appropriate. Individuals face risks; it is they who bear them. The most familiar context in which people evaluate risks is personal—are the chances of being killed in an automobile or airplane accident too great for me? Will cigarettes give me cancer? Is this job too risky for me? Will coffee ruin my pancreas? These are familiar questions which we, as individuals, ask ourselves.

Yet there are other questions concerning risk which we may ask ourselves not as self-regarding individuals but as members of a society. We may wonder, for example, whether the yearly toll of automobile deaths is socially acceptable. Are risks imposed by various products—cigarettes and coffee among them—of the sort that should be left to individual discretion? The problem of workplace safety, at least as much as the problem of highway safety or product safety, has a public dimension.

The sheer amount of injury or death may be an appropriate cause of public as well as individual concern. From the individual point of view, a probability of death or injury, say one in a thousand, remains the same whether ten or ten million people take the same risk. From the social point of view, however, the difference is important: it could mean the loss of a thousand lives. How should we respond as a nation to these numbers? When occupational safety and health information is presented in terms of individual probabilities only, an evaluation typically follows in terms of the individual, not the group. By describing the problem this way—in terms of individual risks rather than community costs—we may commit ourselves to a subtle but powerful bias toward individualistic rather than community norms and values.

B. Hazards to Health

Occupational hazards are threats to health. These threats are special in that what may be lost—life or functional capacity—is irreplaceable. In the case of loss of life or limb, the irreplaceability is obvious. But the functional impairment of lungs or ears caused by exposure to hazards is also often irreversible, and the impairment becomes permanent. Techniques to reverse these effects are sometimes available, but in many instances, for example, chelation therapy for lead poisoning, the cure can be worse than the disease.

In addition, people cannot always be compensated for a loss of health. Damage to one's health is not altogether like damage to one's automobile. The insurance received for a damaged car, in principle at least, restores the owner to the earlier level of well-being. Compensation, in short, can be paid in full. In occupational fatalities, however, the precondition for any compensation is precisely what is lost. Any payment that could feasibly be made to workers with permanent disabilities, moreover, would not be compensatory in the technical sense that the workers would just as soon have the compensation payment as their ability to walk or breathe. Normally, spending money, or what money can buy someone with diminished capacities, on disabling injuries and illnesses may be better than not doing so, but prevention may be better still.

Health is a precondition for a wide variety of other activities; it is an instrumental good. In fact, health is a precondition for such a wide variety of other activities that it is best viewed not simply as a value in itself, but as a condition of many or most other values. As such, it is not only an individual good, but also an element of social infrastructure, that is, an item that is needed to make possible the basic social and economic activities we engage in. From this point of view, maintaining an adequate public health system is in the same category as providing an adequate transportation system: widespread defects in either would have serious consequences for almost everything else we do. In contrast, other commodities have a much smaller range of activities that depend on them. If bicycles, three-piece suits, and garbage cans are not available, then certain desirable and socially worthwhile activities are foreclosed. But the range of such activities is small compared to the range of activities that depend upon public health or an adequate transportation system.

Health and physical integrity are also intrinsically valuable. They are social requirements not only in the sense that they are needed for other activities, but in the sense that they are desirable in and of themselves. They are primary goods in that they are things that all rational people want regardless of whatever else they want. This does not imply that risk minimization is a primary good, for this entails that people who risk their lives for good reason, for example, to conquer Mt. Everest or to free others from oppression, are irrational. Rather, the idea is that what is being risked—health—is a primary good that even risk takers would prefer not to lose.

C. Risk in the Workplace

The conditions under which risks occur in the workplace differ from those associated with other activities, for example, participation in recreational sports. People sometimes seek or actively court danger. The danger itself is sometimes satisfying because, among other things, it provides an opportunity for people to test themselves. Hence, dangerous sports like hang gliding are popular. In this sport—as in other risks people seek—the participants feel that their responses are crucial and they are engaged by and prove themselves against challenging conditions.

Risks encountered on the job are typically quite different. First, while it is possible that police officers, fire fighters, and other workers sometimes seek and take satisfaction in the dangers they face, this is not true of most workers. Those put at risk by toxic chemicals, for example, hardly feel challenged by the hazards they confront. These risks do not call upon workers to show special strength or dexterity. They may feel as if they were sitting ducks instead. In general, workers would like to avoid or minimize occupational hazards they face.

Secondly, risks on the job typically have no natural consequences that are desired. Coffee and cigarettes produce feelings of well being. Hence, despite the risks involved, people are willing to spend large amounts of money to consume these items. Occupational risks are quite different in that, by and large, they have only undesirable natural consequences. Natural consequences of occupational risk that are genuinely relished are hard to locate, and certainly are not sufficient in themselves to outweigh these risks in the minds of those who must bear them. For this reason, workers, perhaps like financial investors, would have to be compensated in some way to be persuaded to take risks.

A third distinction can be made between risks encountered on and off the job. Many risks, from children's games to casino gambling, have a social meaning. When risk taking has trappings of moral import, what is at stake is less important than the fact that undergoing the risk helps to structure social life. Esteem, honor, dignity, respect, and status all flow from withstanding symbolic gambles. In unusual occupations, such as airplane testing, occupational risks can become symbolically important in just this way. For most workplace risks, however, such "status gambling" may have less to do with heightening the meaningfulness of life and more to do with manipulation and self-deception. The transformation of occupational risks into symbolic risks can either be imposed deliberately on workers as a way of avoiding hazard control or can be spontaneously generated by workers themselves as a defense mechanism to cope with their powerlessness. What seems clear, however, is that typical occupational hazards are not deliberately sought and that, if they were suddenly removed or greatly reduced, the "status gambling" attitudes fostered by the hazards would either wither away or find another focus.

Finally, exposure to occupational hazards is, by and large, involuntary. For most people in our society, work is unavoidable. If individual workers find themselves facing unacceptable occupational risks they cannot simply withdraw from the market. They must choose among available occupations—and so some must accept risky jobs. This does not mean that workers are coerced into taking risky jobs in the same way that draftees are. But external conditions frequently limit options so severely that coercion is not needed. The labor market sometimes structures risks so that those who bear them are not the informed, mobile risk-bearers of economic theory. Adequate information is often lacking; the power to insist on less risk does not exist; and there is no possibility of mobility. These limitations on choice characterize occupational as opposed to recreational or aesthetic risks.

D. The Distribution of Occupational Risk

Those who gain from risky work are not always those who do it. When hazardous working conditions lead to lower production costs, consumer prices go down and profits of business firms go up. But workers may suffer as a result. The distribution of risks among various industries, moreover, is plainly unequal. Some occupations and industries are extremely dangerous, while others are comparatively safe. This unequal distribution of risk is made all the more problematic because the burden of occupational risk apparently falls hardest on the comparatively disadvantaged.

Those who bear occupational risks, moreover, sometimes form small specific groups—vinyl chloride workers and native American uranium miners are examples. Others form large, but identifiable, social groups, as is the case with cotton textile workers, coal miners, and steelworkers. These workers tend to share common attitudes and interests that make them recognizable as a group. They are likely to regard occupational risk reduction as a matter of group interest. Risks associated with riding in automobiles or consuming saccharin-sweetened drinks or breathing polluted air, on the other hand, are likely to cut across recognizable social divisions. People face these latter risks either as isolated individuals or as members of rather more abstract and encompassing aggregates. This fact raises questions concerning the distribution of risk, not only among individuals, but also among groups.

Finally, the circumstances of occupational risk are unique because of the political dimension they introduce. Labor and management approach each other as adversaries on a wide variety of workplace issues. Very often an issue concerning occupational safety will also be an issue concerning the control of the workplace. The presence of job hazards is then used as an example of how things can go wrong if management is allowed unrestricted discretion in making decisions concerning the organization and pace of work. On the other hand, militant action in favor of reducing occupational risks can sometimes be resisted, not because management is opposed to risk reduction, but because of a feeling that labor is too forcefully infringing upon management prerogatives to organize production. The general issue concerning control over the workplace therefore colors the issue of occupational risk.

III. ETHICS AND GOVERNMENTAL INVOLVEMENT IN OCCUPATIONAL SAFETY AND HEALTH

The previous discussion suggests that occupational safety and health is at least partly a matter of moral and social concern. But the justification of government involvement in the area is more and more frequently being stated in terms of market failure, not moral principle. The labor market, it is argued, does not provide sufficient information for workers and management to make informed decisions about occupational risk…

This justification of government involvement is based upon considerations of efficiency in the satisfaction of personal preferences. According to this view, the labor market does not provide an amount of safety on the job that maximizes the satisfaction of these individual preferences. Behind the market failure justification for government involvement there lies a utilitarian principle. Several other ethical bases for government involvement exist, however, that are not derived from a utilitarian tradition. For analytical purposes, the following discussion divides these justifications into those based on workers' rights, those based on distributive justice, and those based on public values.

A. Workers' Rights
The framework of individual rights provides one ethical perspective on the problem of occupational safety and health. This framework emphasizes that

people should be treated as ends and not as mere means. People have rights that protect them from others who would enslave them or otherwise use them for their own purposes. In bringing this idea to bear on the problem of occupational safety, many people have thought that workers have an inalienable right to earn their living free from the ravages of job-caused death, disease, and injury. Philosophers have offered strong defenses of the right to be free of the infliction of cancer on the job. Behind this contention lies the idea that people need rights to protect them from unreasonable health hazards where they earn their living. If the unrestricted market does not automatically satisfy this right to safety on the job, then the government must intervene in order to protect it.

What does it mean to say that someone has a right to safety and health on the job? According to one view, people have rights to something when they have a valid claim upon society to protect them in the possession of it. This general idea does not specify whether the entitlement in question is negative (noninterference) or positive (recipience), or partly both. The right to safety and health on the job has sometimes been seen as derivative from the right not to be killed or severely injured by others. From this perspective, workers would have a negative right to noninterference and protection against persons who threaten life or limb in a direct way. On the other hand, a right to safety and health on the job can be construed as a species of a positive right to life. From this perspective, workers are entitled to that share of society's resources needed to provide a minimum level of protection against hazards on the job. This minimal level of protection obviously varies with the available resources of the community. For a given amount of resources, the minimal standard may not be the optimal level at which to provide safety and health on the job, but it provides a floor below which protection should not be allowed to fall.

This right to minimum protection on the job is held by workers but it imposes duties on employers. These duties require employers to refrain from the use of hazardous materials or processes that would impose a significant risk of killing or seriously injuring workers—a negative duty corresponding to a negative right. Additionally, or alternatively, these duties could be construed to require adequate levels of protection against serious threats to worker safety and health—a positive duty corresponding to a positive right. These employer duties call for the expenditure of resources to provide safety on the job, either in the form of opportunity costs or actual expenditures. The allocation of resources to the fulfillment of this duty has a certain priority over the allocation to the production of other commodities. The existence of a right to safety on the job, then, implies that the pursuit of private interest must take the provision of safety and health on the job as something of a side-constraint, although not necessarily an absolute one.

A right to occupational safety would also have a certain priority over collective or social goals. According to one popular theory, rights are political trumps to the effect that the collective good is not a sufficient justification for imposing some loss or injury on the individuals holding these rights. A more moderate view would allow some compromises between the satisfaction of rights and the satisfaction of common goals. Even if a more moderate view is adopted, however, a right to occupational safety and health could not be overridden by relatively minor increases in the satisfaction of some collective interest.

The assignment of a safety right to workers still allows the possibility of trading the right for additional wages. A right to safety, however, could also be viewed as inalienable. On this view, market transactions involving the exchange of *minimum* safety and health protections for wages would not be allowed. The reason for this is to ensure that everyone would enjoy the substance of the right. This restriction does not necessarily prohibit *all* wage/risk transactions. One possibility would be to permit employers to charge workers (via lower wages) for the provision of extra safety over and above the social minimum. A further possibility would be to allow employers to charge for the provision of the social minimum. One could argue that just as a right to safe consumer products allows manufacturers to charge extra to make their products free of unreasonable risks, so a right to occupational safety allows employers to charge extra to make their workplaces free of unreasonable risks. On the other hand, one could argue that the unavoidability of work makes the consumer product analogy inappropriate. On this view, the cost of providing worker safety is a cost of doing business, and must be passed on to the consumer or taken out of profits.

Some people propose that jobs with unreasonable risks should be made available to workers if the alternative is unemployment. On the average, let us say, workers will be better off taking these risky jobs than being unemployed. It would therefore be rational for them to accept these jobs. Why prohibit them from doing so? This way of stating the issue may be misleading. A better way may be to ask whether these risky jobs should be made available at all. In effect, the provision of unsafe jobs offers one way of providing employment for the unemployed. It has to be evaluated, therefore, against other strategies for reducing unemployment, including a deliberate national policy of full and safe employment. One argument for such a policy might be that, in its absence, workers would face a choice between jobs with unreasonable risks and no jobs at all.

The framework of individual rights, then, may provide principles that justify government intervention in the area of occupational safety and health. Furthermore, the principle of ensuring minimal levels of safety and health protection provides some guidance in setting levels of effort in mandated programs....

B. Distributive Justice

A second reason for the government to be involved in the area of occupational safety and health is to eliminate or reduce inequities in the distribution of occupational risks. The following example may clarify our intuitions about the idea of equal protection against occupational threats. Suppose firms were taxed at a fixed rate for each unit of worker exposure to a toxic substance. The result of this would be to encourage firms to control exposures up to the point where it becomes cheaper to pay the tax. Firms that could reduce toxic exposures cheaply would provide more protection for their workers than would firms that could reduce toxic exposures only at great expense. Workers would therefore receive unequal protection against toxic substances depending upon whether their employing firm faced high or low marginal abatement costs.

Why is this example unsettling? Certain intuitions about distributive justice are touched, but exactly what are they? Suppose that different plants provide unequal protection, but none is so lax that it violates the threshold level of protection guaranteed by right. Is any worker being treated unfairly?

What if no rights were being violated, but there were extreme inequalities in protection? What if the extra risks were borne disproportionately by the powerless and the poor?...

...The following are several possible principles of justice in the distribution of occupational risk that could be examined in...an egalitarian framework.

The first principle declares that extreme inequality in the dangers associated with different jobs is in itself objectionable. It is not fair on this view that illnesses and injuries should be concentrated in particular jobs, occupations, and industries. The mere inequality in risk, and not just its distribution among nonoccupational groups, is objectionable. Some policy implications of this view are that high-risk industries should be targeted first, that exposure levels to toxic substances should be set at background levels, and that where risks cannot be eliminated they should be spread more equally among a larger population.

A second principle objects to extreme inequality in the prevalence of occupational illnesses and injuries among certain nonoccupational groups. It is not fair, on this view, that occupational illnesses and injuries should fall disproportionately on the poor, minorities, and the powerless. Nor should extra risks fall on people in morally irrelevant groups such as those who work in medium-size establishments or those for whom abatement costs are especially high. The difference between the two principles is that the first objects to any unequal distribution of occupational risks while the second objects only when the distribution has been determined in what seems an unjust way. A policy implication of the second principle is that special attention and effort should be given to those groups that experience extra occupational risk because they are poor, powerless, or victims of illegitimate discrimination.

These two principles each suggest that large increases in efficiency would be needed to balance the loss in equity resulting from the application of market principles such as a "toxic exposure" tax. A third principle might propose that, if occupational risk is concentrated in groups that are already disadvantaged, programs for the reduction of occupational risk should have priority over programs to reduce risks that are spread more evenly throughout the general population. Thus, if we have to choose between saving an equal number of asbestos workers and motorists, equity considerations should make us favor the asbestos workers.

All three distributive principles are in need of further theoretical support. They do not, moreover, specify the extent to which these egalitarian goals should be pursued in the face of conflicts with other goals. In addition, they are silent on the overall level of protection we should provide. They, therefore, do not determine the level of effort at which government programs in this area should operate. More complete guidance for occupational safety and health policy might be found by referring to widely shared public values that lie behind the concern over workplace safety.

C. Public Values

The concept of public values provides an important ethical justification for government involvement in occupational safety and health. This perspective is based on a distinction between individuals' preferences for their own personal welfare and their values and moral principles concerning the kind of society they think desirable or the collective policies they think worthwhile. These public values can concern the rules to be followed in the pursuit of private interests (such as property rights) or they can address some concrete common concern like national defense or environmental quality. When adopted by the community these public values become collective goals.

Not all public values are well defined. There is often no consensus supporting them; the criteria for community acceptance are not always clear. Yet in the case of occupational safety and health these concerns are not always problematical. One public value at stake in the question of government involvement in occupational safety and health, for example, is the uncontroversial belief that a society in which fewer people killed or seriously disabled on the job is, other things being equal, better than a society in which more people are killed or seriously disabled on the job. This value may derive from a more basic judgment that people have a dignity and a worth that make it wrong to use them as mere means to any end including efficiency. This judgment leads to the idea that a special regard for the health and safety of workers is required to avoid treating them simply as components in the production process. This moral ideal underlies the passage of the Occupational Safety and Health Act, which established job safety and health as a national goal.

From the perspective of public values, the problem of occupational safety and health is not simply that occupational risks are inequitably distributed and that individuals are receiving less protection against threats to their safety and health on the job than they are entitled to by right. The problem is, in addition, that the level of injury and illness may be unacceptably high, even if rights are respected and the distribution of job risk is equitable. Both rights and justice are important public values. But if too many workers are killed or disabled on the job, the public may determine that the meager level of effort devoted to the reduction of this toll displays a disregard for the value we place on human life.

This evaluation of occupational safety is not necessarily accomplished by examining risks at the individual level. We may want to prohibit hazardous activities that are fully rational for each individual even when there are no violations of rights or justice involved. Recall the coffee example mentioned earlier. For a more extreme example, imagine a nonoccupational death lottery in which people could accept a risk of death in return for a cash payment. The death risks and the payments could probably be arranged so that many people would play. But deliberation regarding whether to allow such a death lottery would concern more than the size of the death risk, the monetary compensation involved, and the individuals or groups likely to play. It would also concern such matters as whether a sufficient respect for the value of life was displayed by this type of transaction, and whether the value of individual choice in the matter outweighed the damage done to the value of life. Also relevant would be the purposes behind the death lottery and the social outcomes to be expected, which would vary even if the individual-level death risks did not.

In the occupational risk market, where the group outcomes are often regular and predictable, the perspective of public values would similarly require a direct consideration of the importance of the activities producing these outcomes. The role of government would be to reflect this evaluation and to regulate or prohibit certain activities on the job when the outcomes that would result violate this public judgment.

To approach occupational safety on the basis of public values, however, is to encounter a familiar problem. The approach justifies some degree of government involvement, but does not specify the level. Moreover, it has a special difficulty in explaining why society has more of an interest in regulating the outcomes of occupational risks than in regulating other risk-taking behavior. The beginnings of an answer are to be found in the social nature of employment, the fact that it is not an avoidable activity, and the irreversible and non-compensable nature of injury and death. But more work would have to be done to distinguish the cases so as to avoid the use of principles that would also justify intrusiveness and intolerance.

IV. ECONOMIC CRITERIA

While moral principles involving rights, justice, and public values may help to justify centralized programs regulating occupational safety and health, they do not completely determine the level of government effort required. It has been suggested that various *economic* criteria may be used to supplement these moral principles in determining a desirable level of effort. This section examines the economic approach to occupational safety and health. It focuses on the difficulties in applying economic techniques in this area, notes some tensions between the use of these techniques and the normative considerations just discussed, and attempts to sketch an appropriate role for these techniques.

According to this economic approach, the goal of occupational safety and health policy should be to minimize the sum of workplace accident costs and workplace accident prevention costs, or equivalently, to maximize the difference between the benefits of workplace safety programs and the costs of these programs. A number of techniques have been proposed to achieve this goal. They divide into cost-effectiveness and cost-benefit rules. A program is cost-effective when it maximizes its objectives for a given cost, or minimizes its cost for a given objective. A program is cost-beneficial when its benefits exceed its costs. The cost-benefit criterion goes beyond the cost-effectiveness criterion in assigning a monetary value to the benefits involved, thereby allowing direct comparisons of the positive and negative consequences of a program in monetary terms. In examining the economic approach it is helpful to treat these criteria separately.

A. Cost-Effectiveness

Cost-effectiveness criteria were never intended to determine levels of safety. They presuppose that the desirable level of effort has already been set or that some cost constraint has already been imposed. The major use for cost-effectiveness approaches is not in setting levels, then, but in achieving in an efficient way goals determined on some other basis. Even this role, however, is limited by the need to balance efficiency against other values.

Despite this inherent limitation, cost-effectiveness can be a useful measure of the desirability of alternative workplace safety and health programs. Consider, for example, the problem of what to do about noise in the workplace. Suppose that one program calls for the use of engineering controls as a way of preventing cases of hearing impairment; another calls for the use of hearing protectors that prevent the same number of cases of hearing impairment, but at a much lower cost. In this hypothetical example, a cost-effectiveness approach would favor the use of the less expensive hearing protectors. Only rarely, however, is the choice quite that simple. The actual controversy in the case of noise in the workplace is whether hearing protectors do in fact provide the same level of protection as engineering controls. If the less expensive hearing protectors provide less protection, then the fact that they are less expensive does not make them more cost-effective. Alternative programs can be compared with respect to cost-effectiveness only when they achieve the same level of effect or impose the same costs.

Some misunderstandings of this point have resulted in the idea that a program that imposes the lowest average or marginal cost per accident avoided is cost-effective, while programs with higher unit costs are not cost-effective. This is not so. If the program that avoids more accidents or injuries has higher unit costs, this may reflect the familiar fact of diminishing returns, and indicates that if we want to avoid more incidents it will simply cost us more per incident to do it. Relative to our objectives, each program may be equally efficient.

Some analysts who use a cost-effectiveness framework propose to equalize the marginal cost per incident avoided. An example of this approach would be to set different levels of exposure to toxic substances for different industry segments depending upon the cost required to control exposures. If this is done, then the number of cases avoided will be maximized for any given level of expenditure. However, the distribution of cases avoided will differ from that determined by a policy that requires equal protection for all. To equalize the marginal cost of safety conflicts with considerations of distributive justice that could motivate government programs. More telling, perhaps, in the context of trying to determine levels, is that this cost-effectiveness rule does not specify at what level marginal costs should be set, or what should be the total social cost of the regulation.

Another cost-effectiveness rule would concentrate attention on the accidents or injuries that can be avoided most cheaply. The policy recommendation here is to set priorities and levels for safety programs on the basis of the lowest unit costs. The rationale is this: if we proceed up the supply curve for lives saved in this way, then no matter where we stop spending, we will have maximized the number of lives saved for the amount spent. One difficulty with this recommendation is that it is likely to conflict both with the goal of targeting high risk industries and groups first and with the goal of providing equal protection across groups. Moreover, it does not take account of the total number of lives saved by a particular safety program. For example, when we choose which of two toxic substances to regulate first, it may be better to give priority to the substance that produces more illnesses and fatalities rather than the one that has the lowest per unit prevention costs. This would maximize the number of lives saved in a given period of time although it would be at an increased cost per life saved. Finally, the policy of saving the "cheapest" lives first does not solve the problem of levels since it does not specify at what point we should stop spending to save lives.

B. Cost-Benefit

From within a cost-benefit framework, the limitations on cost-effectiveness criteria appear to stem from the lack of a monetary value for the benefits of occupational safety and health programs. The cost-benefit approach attempts to move beyond the cost-effectiveness approach by placing a monetary value on these benefits. Cost-effectiveness analysis measures the benefits of safety and health programs in their natural units—lives saved, number of cases of hearing impairment avoided, and overall reductions in occupational illnesses and injuries. Cost-benefit analysis transforms these "naturally" measured benefits into monetary terms by specifying an appropriate monetary value. Since the economic costs of safety and health programs are already in dollar units, a direct comparison of benefits and costs is possible in terms of a single common measure. With this common metric, it is possible to examine clearly whether the benefits of a safety and health program exceed the costs.

A formal cost-benefit analysis, then, requires monetary values for the lives saved and illnesses avoided by safety and health programs. But these items are not typically bought and sold on markets, and so there is no prevailing price to use as a measuring rod. There has been much research, therefore, attempting to measure these benefits indirectly. However, a review of the two principal methods used to value the benefits of programs that save lives reveals severe technical and theoretical difficulties. The first method attempts to assess the social cost of lost lives. Essentially, this amounts to estimating the future earnings of those whose lives would be saved by the program and discounting this estimate to its present value. The benefits of life-saving programs are then measured as reductions in these social costs. Critics argue cogently that the social cost approach confuses the contribution people make to the gross national product with their social worth; the value of their livelihood with the value of their lives. It has the ethically unacceptable implications that poor people are worth less than the rich, women are worth less than men, blacks worth less than whites, and old people who have no income worth nothing at all. To remedy these difficulties, it has been suggested that a second approach be tried that uses the traditional economic criterion of willingness to pay.

This willingness-to-pay approach is the favored approach in the economics profession, largely because it has a solid basis in welfare economics. A straightforward application of this traditional criterion is blocked, however, by the fact that there appears to be little sense in asking what payment an individual would make to escape certain death. The accepted solution to this problem is to ask a different question: what would individuals be willing to pay to reduce the probability of death when these probabilities are very small? The monetary value of a person's life is not determined by this procedure, but a monetary value of personal safety is. Once this value is available, then a monetary value of the benefits of a life-saving program can be calculated as the number of people at risk times the probability of death times the value of safety.

The most widespread method of calculating the value of safety is based upon labor market studies. The labor market is assumed to function as an occupational risk market in which worker demand curves for safety and management safety supply curves intersect in a series of equilibrium points. Attempts are then made to measure the slope of the curve that these market equilibria trace out. This slope represents the wage differential for extra risk and is used as a measure of the value of safety.

There are some technical problems with this approach. First, the evidence is mixed on the existence of these compensating wage differentials. Some studies show the expected positive coefficient, indicating that hazardous work pays more; some show a negative one, indicating that hazardous work pays less; and some show a coefficient that cannot be statistically distinguished from zero at the usual levels of confidence, suggesting that level of risk has *no* influence on wage rates. It is not even clear that there is a risk market then. Second, even if a positive coefficient is found, it does not represent a worker demand curve for safety, but the intersection of worker demand curves and management supply curves. For small changes in the risk of death this does not matter, since, at market equilibrium, the amount workers are willing to pay for safety is theoretically the same as the amount management is willing to spend on it. But, conceptually, it is important to note that the estimated coefficient measures management willingness to supply safety as much as it measures worker demand for it. Third, the estimated coefficient may or may not represent an adequately functioning risk market. Lack of knowledge, power, or mobility may prevent workers from expressing their full desire for compensation. Fourth, since the loss of life cannot be measured objectively, there is no way to tell whether the observed compensation is adequate or not.

Further, a dilemma threatens the entire wage differential approach to estimating the value of safety. If risk markets are fully functioning, then workers receive full compensation for bearing risk, and there is no need for government intervention, because any mandated program above and beyond those already in place would cost management more than the fully compensated workers are willing to pay for it. On the other hand, if the markets are not fully functioning, then the estimated value of safety bears no systematic relation to the real value. It would then be illegitimate to value the benefits of a program designed to increase occupational safety in a malfunctioning occupational risk market on the basis of unreliable estimates of the value of safety drawn from these very same malfunctioning markets.

There is an even more fundamental objection to the wage differential measure. A formal cost-benefit analysis needs a measure of what people are willing to pay for a program that saves lives. What the wage differential coefficient represents, however, is willingness to pay for personal safety, not life-saving programs. The two are by no means the same. The value we want is what people are willing to spend for a social program that will fundamentally alter the options available on the occupational risk market; we, therefore, want to measure individual preferences for structural changes in the labor market. Wage differentials, however, represent people's preferences within a given structure of occupational risk, not what they would prefer in a labor market with an altered structure. It is possible that valuation under the present and the altered structure are systematically related, but individual preferences for structural change in the occupational risk market would have to be measured somehow before this could be established. But if they can be estimated directly, why bother with a surrogate measure?

These difficulties apply to estimates of the wage differentials for injury and non-fatal illness as well. It appears then that the attempt to value the benefits of occupational safety and health programs via wage differentials is not likely to produce useful estimates. If so, the option of using cost-benefit criteria to set levels of effort for government occupational safety and health programs is considerably less attractive.

Economic cost-benefit criteria in general suffer from a more basic limitation that makes them less desirable as public policy guides. They are designed to promote efficiency in the satisfaction of personal preferences. The notions of Pareto optimality and Kaldor-Hicks efficiency that underlie these criteria are admittedly one-sided in their neglect of individual rights, distributive justice, and public values. For this reason, economic criteria may underdetermine the level of governmental effort required in the area of occupational safety and health. Only if some further reason justifies giving pride of place to efficiency in the satisfaction of private preferences can economic criteria, as traditionally applied, be the principal basis for setting levels of effort in this area.

It may be possible to use ingenious techniques to incorporate distributional considerations and other public values into cost-benefit analyses. Even so, economic criteria may still have a limited role in occupational safety and health decisions. The political preferences and moral ideals of citizens are poorly represented in a market or surrogate market approach. People sometimes want certain social goals to be achieved, not because there is any personal gain in it for them, but simply because they think it is the right thing to do. The only way an economic analysis can capture these public ideals is by first pricing them. The defect in this procedure is not simply that people are not used to placing a monetary value on their ideals, but that it substitutes a measure of the strength of a preference for an evaluation of an ideal. The evaluation of an ideal, however, is a completely normative undertaking, and is properly done through public discussion, argument, and debate, rather than by assessing the intensity of people's preferences. It might be better, then, to see if the ideals that stand behind our public commitment to occupational safety and health can enter materially into public policy without first being priced by economic techniques.

If economic criteria are not to be the sole basis for occupational safety and health policy, what role should they play in this area? Some economists recommend that cost-benefit criteria be used as basic guidelines in standard-setting, qualified, if necessary, by equity and other considerations. Others recommend that cost-benefit analysis be done to measure the efficiency impact of policies only. The idea would be to balance economic efficiency as one of a number of perhaps equally important social values. This multidimensional approach may be attractive; it requires us, however, to specify techniques other than those available within cost-benefit analysis to balance efficiency against other normative considerations. The following section examines some possible ways in which this may be done.

V. ALTERNATIVE PUBLIC POLICY PRINCIPLES

Economic criteria cannot be the sole basis for public policy toward occupational safety and health because they do not adequately take into account the public concerns that motivated government involvement in this area. The Occupational Safety and Health Act was passed to make the workplace *safer,* not necessarily *more efficient.* The public remains concerned, moreover, with the nature of workplace hazards, their distribution, and the degree to which workers have a say in controlling the risks they face on the job. However, in attempting to carry out its mandate, OSHA has been criticized for failing to take into account important economic constraints. If we accept the conclusion of the previous section, that economic criteria cannot be the sole basis for occupational safety and health policy, the question arises whether principles can be devised or guidelines suggested that would both respect economic limits and satisfy public values.... A final approach is the OSHA strategy of feasibility analysis....The policy of OSHA under Dr. Eula Bingham was to set standards regulating exposure to toxic substances based upon a criterion of feasibility. This feasibility approach...provides a way of directly setting desirable levels of protection.... [It] generally attempts to minimize threats to safety and health on the job, and...it provides...guidance in the area of weighing economic costs against health benefits.

The policy, in the most general terms, calls for the lowest *feasible* level of toxic exposure in the workplace, which is consistent with a literal reading of section 6(b)(5) of the Act. The approach of the agency to regulation may be pictured, roughly and generally, as follows. The agency asks first whether a substance is hazardous, that is, whether any material impairment to health would follow from exposure to it. If no, the agency does nothing. If yes, OSHA tries to determine the level of exposure at which no material impairment would take place. OSHA's generic policy for carcinogens

sets this level at zero in the absence of proof to the contrary. If this zero-level is not technologically feasible, the agency then selects the lowest exposure level that can be met with reasonably available technology. If the affected industries cannot afford to achieve this level, the agency then requires the lowest economically feasible exposure standard. The criterion of economic feasibility might require some firms to close down, namely, those that could not remain profitable and at the same time meet the standard. The industry as a whole, however, could not be crippled or destroyed.

In principle, the constraint of feasibility is simply a matter of what can be done, and the goal of the regulation of toxic substances is to provide the maximum possible protection against material impairment of health. Notice that this approach does not countenance an explicit balancing of costs and benefits in *particular* cases. This is not because the advantages of safety and health on the job do not have to be compared to economic costs and other losses. The reason no trade-offs are permitted in determining particular permissible exposure levels is that the balance between occupational safety and health and other values has already been set by Congress when it in effect declared that lowest feasible level standards are worth whatever trade-offs are necessary in terms of economic costs and other values. Balancing worker health against other values, in short, must be done as part of overall national policy, but the agency cannot substitute its judgment of the proper balance in particular cases for the congressional directive to promulgate lowest feasible level standards.

Despite its consideration of costs, feasibility analysis clearly allows the promulgation of extremely protective standards. Affected industries contend that some of the standards passed under the feasibility criterion are overly stringent....

The notion of feasibility, that provides the equivalent of a cost constraint in this approach, is also far from clear. How seriously must an industry be harmed before a standard is no longer economically feasible? Are there criteria for feasibility that impose an effective constraint on the agency? Beyond these questions of clarity, the idea that no trade-offs are allowed in particular cases raises questions of balance. For example, when several toxic substances are used in the same industry it may be economically feasible to control each substance individually, but not all at the same time. Surely some trade-offs would have to be made in instances like this. The lack of clarity in the concept of feasibility and the likely need to balance costs and benefits in particular rule-making cases may lead to a situation in which balancing judgments are in fact made, but are publicly justified in terms of feasibility.

There is still, therefore, a pressing need for principles that will help to make these balancing judgments. This does not mean, however, that formal cost-benefit analysis is the most desirable approach. The use of economic information is absolutely essential in the occupational safety and health area, and cost-benefit criteria can be useful in assessing the effect of standards on economic efficiency. But cost-benefit analysis does not provide a proper framework for balancing all the relevant values that have to be taken into consideration in setting health and safety standards. It is crucial to recognize, then, that not all balancing need be based exclusively on cost-benefit comparisons. A distinction must be drawn between justifying a level of effort in an occupational safety and health program on the basis of a comparison of the monetary value of the associated costs and benefits, and justifying such a program by weighing the reasons for and against it and deciding that, all things considered, the level of effort in the program is worthwhile. The first method is simply the cost-benefit approach and in effect treats efficiency as the only, or the most important, consideration. The second method considers efficiency, and might sometimes give it pride of place, but also considers individual rights, justice, and competing public values as reasons for or against a level of effort in a program. In the first case, the basis of decision is already given, and the crucial questions are technical. In the second case, most of the technical questions remain, although some are less urgent (for example, the monetary value of safety), but the bases for decision making are unclear. It is here that much further work needs to be done.

VI. CONCLUSION

By calling attention to the fact that occupational safety and health is one of many desirable goals of public policy, proponents of cost-benefit analysis

have opened the door for integrating job safety into the framework of a coherent, overall industrial policy. However, the cost-benefit approach... discussed earlier [is] inherently unable to incorporate all the considerations relevant to occupational safety and health.... [F]easibility analysis [is] also incomplete. In formulating a new approach to occupational safety and health policy within an industrial policy framework, the conceptual and normative issues raised earlier cannot be ignored. Hazards in the workplace do not merely increase the chances of injury for individuals—they also increase the overall toll of injury and illness for the nation. Moreover, workplace risks are fundamentally different from the voluntarily assumed risks of everyday life because they do not typically challenge the skills of those who must withstand them, they are rarely intrinsically enjoyable or symbolically important, and they normally involve a conflict of interest between labor and management characterized by imbalances of power, information, and mobility. Finally, the distribution of occupational risks among individuals and groups is arbitrarily unequal.

These points suggest that safety on the job is a matter of community interest, not individual discretion, and they lead to several normative guidelines for collective action. First, there is a need to preserve people's rights to protection against unreasonable health threats while they are earning their livelihood. Second, efforts should be made to achieve a more equitable distribution of the occupational risks that cannot be easily eliminated. Finally, social action is required to realize widely shared public values, such as the conviction that conditions of work should reflect a concern and respect for workers' dignity and autonomy, that lie behind the group interest in workplace safety. Although these normative considerations do not determine an overall level of effort, much less the details of particular regulatory actions, their neglect by decision makers will inevitably lead to an impoverished occupational safety and health policy.

EXPLODING THE GENE MYTH
Ruth Hubbard and Elijah Wald

GENETIC DISCRIMINATION
IN THE WORKPLACE

In workplaces genetic tests are used to screen workers and to monitor them. *Genetic screening* is done in order to find out whether job applicants are more likely than an "average person" to develop medical conditions that are thought to be inherited biologically and that might reduce their effectiveness as workers. Such screening is likely to be done just once. *Genetic monitoring,* by contrast, is done periodically to find out whether some chemical or other hazard in the workplace is altering the chromosomes or genes (DNA) of the workers.

Employers usually shy away from genetic monitoring, since it tends to implicate workplace chemicals as the source of harm. However, employers have economic reasons to screen prospective or actual workers in order to keep people with potential health problems out of the workplace. Since businesses are run to make a profit, employers try to minimize labor costs. Such costs include time spent training employees and paying employees' benefits, such as health and disability insurance. Nearly all but the smallest firms offer health and disability insurance as part of their benefits program, and large businesses have begun to cover the costs of their employees' health care themselves rather than contracting with insurance companies. According to Nelkin and Tancredi, "employment benefits exceeded 39 percent of total payroll costs in 1986, and over 21.1 percent of that total went for medical benefits....Where companies buy insurance from commercial carriers, premiums are experience rated [and] higher claims mean higher costs." So, insurance costs are one reason that employers may try to minimize health insurance claims by employees.

It is also in the interest of employers not to spend time training employees whom they will lose through sickness or death, as well as to reduce the cost of disability benefits. However, while it is costly to have workers become ill, it is also costly to keep workplaces uncontaminated by toxic chemicals used in the manufacturing process, and to take the various safety precautions that may be necessary to preserve workers' health and well-being. Employers will therefore want to use tests that promise to predict the future health of prospective employees, in order to weed out job applicants who might be unusually sensitive to hazards in the workplace.

Employers have used the concept of the "accident-prone" worker to shift responsibility for industrial accidents onto the people who are injured. For example, though there are consistently more accidents on the graveyard shift, such accidents are often blamed on the carelessness of individual workers rather than on the difficulty of working through the night. By the same token, many employers now embrace the concept of genetic "hypersusceptibility" to explain why some workers respond to lower levels of dusts or other contaminants than the "average worker" does.

In a 1984 article I [Hubbard] wrote with Mary Sue Henifin, an attorney trained in public health, we discussed problems inherent in the notion of "hypersusceptibility" to contaminants. For one thing, it is difficult to decide on appropriate criteria: How low (or high) must the level of exposure be before someone who is harmed is labeled "hypersusceptible"?

Another point is that the same industrial chemical or other toxic agent can provoke acute reactions in some people in the short term, while other workers may slowly develop chronic conditions, such as cancers, without ever exhibiting an immediate, acute reaction. Most screening tests in current use detect only those workers likely to develop the short-term reactions, but not those who may experience long-term effects. However, molecular biologists are now laying the groundwork for genetic tests said to predict "tendencies" for the more slowly developing, chronic conditions. When such tests become available, they will be even less reliable in their predictions than the tests that currently

From Ruth Hubbard and Elijah Wald, *Exploding the Gene Myth* (Boston: Beacon Press, 1993), 133–144. © Ruth Hubbard and Elijah Wald. Reprinted by permission of Beacon Press. All notes have been deleted.

promise to identify "hypersusceptible" individuals, since so many factors can contribute to chronic conditions.

Predictive tests should never be used to screen out workers who are considered "hypersusceptible," whether to short- or long-term effects. Whatever their individual "susceptibility" may be, all workers who are exposed to toxic agents risk developing a chronic condition sooner or later.

For example, formaldehyde is a common contaminant in the plastics industry, among others. It can evoke acute allergic reactions such as asthma or skin rashes in some people, and is also known to be a human carcinogen. Once predictive tests are available, employers will want to screen out workers who might have allergic reactions or be at greater than average risk of developing cancer. This could then allow them to expose everyone else to high levels of this carcinogen. It would be far better to find a chemical substitute for formaldehyde or change the procedures so as to lessen the risks of both types of effects for all the workers, but to a cost-conscious industry that sounds like a more expensive proposition.

Genetic tests, far from being safety measures, can lead to a relaxing of existing precautions. However, the scientists involved in developing such tests often stress only the potential benefits. An opinion piece in the British scientific weekly *Nature,* which criticizes those of us who warn that the Human Genome Initiative will increase the potential for discrimination, asks editorially: "Would it not be profitable to keep the plants [which use vinyl chloride, a carcinogen that produces liver cancers and to which some people are supposedly 'hypersusceptible'] going and to use part of the economic wealth created to compensate those with the bad luck to be susceptible?" Such questions can only be asked in an academic ivory tower. Of course such a policy would make economic sense, just as it would make economic sense to share the profits of mechanization with the workers who are replaced by machines, but that is not how our society works.

It is encouraging that in October 1991, the Council on Ethical and Judicial Affairs of the American Medical Association published a set of guidelines "to help physicians assess when their participation in genetic testing [by employers] is appropriate and does not result in unwarranted discrimination against individuals with disabilities." In its statement, the Council stresses that genetic tests are poor at predicting diseases and even poorer at predicting whether a specific health problem will interfere with an individual's work performance. The Council therefore considers it inappropriate for physicians to participate in testing that assesses anything beyond a worker's ability to perform the actual tasks that are part of the job. The Council also states categorically that "testing must not be performed without the informed consent of the employee or applicant for employment."

Although a number of genetic traits have been implicated as possible predictors of "hypersusceptibility" and others will be suggested as more genetic tests become available, there are no adequate data to link any genetic trait to a specific industrial disease. What is more, little, if any, research is being done to explore the parameters within which such predictions might conceivably be valid. Despite this, the Office of Technology Assessment (OTA) of the U.S. Congress published a report in 1990 that includes a table entitled, "Identification and Quantification of Genetic Factors Affecting Susceptibility to Environmental Agents." This table lists twenty-seven "high-risk groups" of people who are described as genetically "hypersusceptible" to environmental contaminants. The authors tone down that claim by stating that these groups only "may be" at risk, but why publish such a table at all when it is based on little, if any, reliable information?

According to surveys the OTA conducted in 1982 and 1989, few employers are using predictive genetic tests. But these surveys had only a 6 percent response rate. Even if the survey results are representative, the process of testing is still new and relatively expensive, in some cases running into thousands of dollars. Many an employer who does not use tests now might act rather differently if prices come down.

Larry Gostin, an attorney and the executive director of the American Society for Law and Medicine, predicts that "market forces may be the single greatest factor motivating genetic testing." He points out that "market researchers project that U.S. genetic test sales will reach several hundred million dollars before the decade's end" and that this will lower the cost of testing and encourage its use by employers and insurance companies. As some insurers or employers become more sophisticated in their use of genetic predictions, this will put economic pressure on others to do the same. When many more tests are available and they are cheaper to administer, employers are likely to try to use them to screen out potentially costly workers, whether or not the tests are reliable.

As always, the discriminatory potential will not be felt equally in all jobs or by all applicants. A highly skilled person with unique qualifications will be less likely to be screened out than an applicant for a more routine job, for which many others could be hired. So here as elsewhere, the least powerful segments of society are most likely to be exposed to discrimination.

Although preemployment genetic discrimination is not yet an everyday occurrence, Paul Billings and his colleagues have already come across it in their preliminary research. One of their respondents listed *Charcot-Marie-Tooth Disease (CMT),* which is a heritable neuromuscular disorder known for its highly variable clinical manifestations, on a preemployment form. The interviewer asked her what CMT was, looked it up in a medical book, and did not hire her. In another instance, a healthy young man who carries one allele associated with a recessive condition called *Gaucher disease* was not permitted to enlist in the Air Force, though this condition is never manifested in the carrier state. Billings's relatively informal survey has turned up two instances of genetic discrimination in employment, even though few employers are yet geared up to administer genetic tests. We may expect to see many more cases when genetic testing becomes widespread, unless legal safeguards are put into place.

If genetic tests could predict a person's health status with fair accuracy, and if employers did not use them primarily to save expenses of training people who might get sick, predictive tests might benefit some workers. But these are very big "ifs." Since the test results can jeopardize a worker's future employment possibilities, genetic tests are not likely to meet the health needs of workers or further their welfare. This is why during the past decade, trade unions and their allies have been outspoken in their opposition to the use of genetic

screening tests. They have noted that tests that emphasize inborn genetic differences as the causes of potential disabilities are by their very nature discriminatory, because they sort people on the basis of factors that are beyond their control. At present there are no safeguards to limit the future use of such information. Also, in weighing the potential benefits of such testing it is often assumed that workers who are denied employment in one kind of job or industry because of a given physical condition can turn elsewhere for work, but this is far from true in the present state of the U.S. economy.

Unless there are sufficient numbers of adequate jobs for everyone who needs or wants to work, so that people can find not only a job but one that is suitable, and until workers and management jointly have exhausted the possibilities to reduce workplace hazards, genetic screening will threaten the health of workers, not improve it. At present, predictive tests are more likely to divert attention from the unnecessarily dismal conditions of most workplaces and so only benefit management. Even when workplace conditions are improved, the results of such tests must be privileged information that is available only to the tested worker.

We will be looking at such privacy issues in the next chapter, but first let us see to what extent such legislative measures as the Americans with Disabilities Act of 1990 (ADA) can reduce the risk of genetic discrimination in the workplace.

MEASURES TO COUNTER EMPLOYMENT-RELATED DISCRIMINATION

In its report, *Genetic Monitoring and Screening in the Workplace,* the Office of Technology Assessment (OTA) of the U.S. Congress states that without protective contracts or legislation an employer has "virtually unlimited authority to terminate the employment relationship at any time….[This] includes the right to refuse to hire an individual because of a *perceived* physical inability to perform the job and the right to terminate employment because of a *belief* that the employee is no longer able to perform adequately" (italics mine). The report goes on to point out that "even if test results were inaccurate or unreliable, the employer would be protected in basing employment decisions on them."

Though courts have begun to create precedents based on antidiscrimination law that limit this "right" of employers, genetic testing is so new that as yet there is no relevant body of judicial attitudes or opinions to regulate its use. Meanwhile, the OTA report estimates that the tests that are at present available to detect simple Mendelian traits or inherited chromosomal aberrations could affect some 800,000 people in this country, while "potential future tests" could affect some ninety million people. Included are tests for so-called genetic conditions that confer a "tendency" or "predisposition" to develop hypertension, dyslexia, cancer, and seven other common physical or behavioral disabilities.

Various federal laws may provide some protection for workers by restricting the right of employers to impose mandatory genetic tests, to use test results to discriminate against workers, or to breach confidentiality. These include the Occupational Safety and Health (OSH) Act which set up the Occupational Safety and Health Administration (OSHA), Title VII of the Civil Rights Act of 1961, the Rehabilitation Act of 1973, the National Labor Relations Act, and the Americans with Disabilities Act (ADA) of 1990. Unfortunately, there are problems with all of these.

To come under the protection of the Rehabilitation Act, which prohibits employers who receive federal contracts or other federal subsidies from discriminating against persons with disabilities, employees must be able to prove that their genetic condition constitutes a genuine impairment, but that they are otherwise qualified to do the job. If they can do that, the employer must provide them with "reasonable accommodations." The ADA extends this protection to the private sector and, by 1994, is supposed to cover all employers with fifteen or more employees. The ADA stipulates that preemployment medical examinations or inquiries may be used only to determine an applicant's ability to perform the actual job in question. In other words, an applicant cannot be disqualified unless the condition interferes with specific tasks required as part of his or her job. This is very important for people with all kinds of disabilities. However, since the ADA does not make specific reference to inherited conditions or to tests designed to detect or predict them, it is not clear how the courts will apply these provisions to now-healthy people said to have a "tendency" to develop a disability at some undefined future time.

The OTA report suggests that OSHA is the most likely federal agency to monitor genetic testing in the workplace, since it has dealt with other biological tests in the past, but it is not clear what form its monitoring will take. In fact, the OSH Act takes no position on genetic testing and is not concerned with protecting employment rights. Besides, OSHA has been so chronically understaffed that it is unrealistic to expect it to monitor yet another set of workplace practices effectively.

Individual states are likely to address the issue of genetic discrimination by virtue of their involvement with workers' compensation programs. The OTA found that in 1983, four states (Florida, Louisiana, North Carolina, and New Jersey) had statutes restricting the use of genetic information in employment decisions, but all except New Jersey mentioned only genetic screening for the sickle-cell gene. Only New Jersey has a law banning employment discrimination on the basis of genetic tests.

Gostin has done a detailed analysis of the extent to which the provisions of the ADA are likely to be useful to prevent genetic discrimination. He believes that "persons currently disabled by a genetic disease are undoubtedly covered under the ADA," but since the courts define "disability" as a "'substantial' limitation of one or more life activities," it is not clear whether a genetic condition that can be argued not to cause "substantial" impairment will count as a disability.

As far as predictive diagnoses are concerned, it is not clear whether a currently healthy person who has been shown to carry the allele implicated in Huntington disease, and who will therefore become disabled at some unspecified future time, can be classified as "disabled" within the meaning of the ADA and is therefore protected against genetic discrimination. Gostin thinks the ADA covers the "healthy ill" and that such people would be protected in the same way as people who test positive for HIV are protected even before they develop symptoms of AIDS. The same reasoning should also apply to people who have genetic tests that show them to be "predisposed" or "susceptible" to develop heart disease or cancer.

The ADA was intended to protect anyone who has or is *perceived* to have a disability. Therefore, Gostin argues, it would betray the spirit of the Act to interpret it as permitting discrimination against individuals who have had genetic tests that predict they or their children may become disabled, simply because they have not yet experienced the predicted disability. In enacting the ADA, Congress ruled specifically that "an inquiry or medical examination that is not job-related serves no legitimate employer purpose, but simply serves to stigmatize the person with a disability." Congress also made it clear that, even when there is reason to think that applicants may become too ill to work in the future, employers cannot cite training costs as valid reasons to discriminate against them in hiring or other employment decisions.

Employers also cannot cite increased costs of health care or insurance benefits. Gostin believes that these safeguards will be effective in limiting the ability of employers to use genetic tests before offering someone a job. The ADA allows employers to require medical examinations once a person has been hired, but only if the same tests are given to every new employee and if all medical information is kept confidential. Even then, the examination must be relevant to the job and justifiable as serving business interests.

These measures appear to offer protection against genetic discrimination. However, employers are exempted from some of these provisions if they themselves also serve as insurers, which increasing numbers of large employers do. As we will see shortly, the antidiscrimination provisions do not apply to insurers.

Despite his generally optimistic reading of the ADA, Gostin points out that while the Act prohibits "discrimination based upon past disability ('record of impairment'), current disability ('impairment'), or perception of disability ('regarded' as impaired)…[it] is silent about discrimination based upon future disability." Gostin suggests that the ADA could easily be strengthened if its definition of disability were broadened to include: "having a genetic or other medically identified potential of, or predisposition toward, an impairment." This change would be extremely important. At present, if a healthy person is predicted to develop a condition such as Huntington disease, a court could rule

that she or he is not currently impaired and therefore not protected by the ADA.

There are also other problems. An employer does not have to give reasons why a particular applicant is not hired. If employers can conduct predictive or other medical tests as part of the preemployment process, they may use medical information from these tests to make hiring decisions, but claim to have based their decisions on reasons unrelated to health. It is easy to imagine how this practice could be extended to genetic conditions, so it is important that the ADA prohibit employers from requiring medical examinations or inquiries before hiring a job applicant, except as they relate to that person's present ability to do a specific job. (Drug testing is excepted because drug tests are not considered medical examinations.) Yet, here again, these restrictions will not apply to employers who self-insure. To be effective in preventing genetic discrimination, state laws need to be directed more specifically against discrimination based on predictions of genetically mediated disabilities that might become manifest at some unspecifiable time in the future.

There is no question that the U.S. Congress and state legislatures could improve this situation by passing laws that specifically prohibit genetic discrimination in hiring and employment, but we must recognize that laws can address only part of the problem. Although civil rights legislation in other areas has been important and has curbed many abuses, civil rights laws have not ended discrimination. When people are oppressed, and have few resources at their disposal, they are often unable to resort to legal remedies. Furthermore, prospective employers are not accountable to people they interview for job openings. At a time when there is no shortage of applicants, employers will have no difficulty concealing discriminatory reasons for their decisions about hiring and firing.

As for the right to refuse tests, such a right has only a limited value. Job applicants or employees are at an even greater disadvantage in dealing with employers than prospective parents are with physicians or parents are with school authorities. Even if job applicants or workers have the right to refuse predictive tests, they may not know they have that right. If they do know, they may not be in a position to exercise it. Even though it seems that most medical geneticists favor voluntary over mandatory testing in the workplace, the distinction may be largely academic. As we will see in the next chapter, someone applying for a job can easily be made to sign away rights to privacy and confidentiality.

Because of the impact genetic discrimination could have on people's health and well-being, people need access to education and information about these issues. Unions and public interest groups must insist that protective legislation and contract language are enforced. Model laws must be developed to counter this new form of discrimination. Mechanisms must be put into place that regulate the ways in which decisions are made about what scientific research is appropriate in this area and the rate at which it should be done. Also, as scientific capabilities to offer individuals fateful predictions of uncertain validity keep expanding, we must decide how best to anticipate and minimize the economic and social damage such predictions will produce.

GENETIC DISCRIMINATION IN INSURANCE

In his preface to *The Doctor's Dilemma,* George Bernard Shaw satirized the situation of the medical profession, which is supposedly in the business of healing, but derives its livelihood from sickness. To quote:

> It is not the fault of our doctors that the medical service of the community…is a murderous absurdity. That any sane nation, having observed that you could provide for the supply of bread by giving bakers a pecuniary interest in baking for you, should go on to give a surgeon a pecuniary interest in cutting off your leg, is enough to make one despair of political humanity. But that is precisely what we have done. And the more appalling the mutilation, the more the mutilator is paid. He who corrects the ingrowing toenail receives a few shillings: he who cuts your inside out receives hundreds of guineas, except when he does it to a poor person for practice….I cannot knock my shins severely without forcing on some surgeon the difficult question, "Could I not make a better use of a pocketful of guineas than this man is making of his leg? Could he not

> write as well—or even better—on one leg than on two? And the guineas would make all the difference in the world to me just now. My wife—my pretty ones—the leg may mortify—it is always safer to operate—he will be well in a fortnight—artificial legs are now so well made that they are really better than natural ones—evolution is onwards towards motors and leglessness, &c., &c., &c.

The for-profit health insurance industry raises this contradiction by several notches. Insurance companies make money only so long as people pay more to buy health insurance than it costs the insurance company when these people feel so ill that they consult a physician. So, to make a healthy profit, insurance companies should sell most of their insurance to people who won't get sick.

In the real world, insurers get around this dilemma by using actuarial and other sources of information to estimate the probability that someone will get sick on the basis of his or her membership in a specific group, identified by age, sex, profession, and other criteria. The insurance industry therefore is in the business of discrimination, since it sorts people into groups on the basis of criteria over which they have no control, and then sets their premiums on the basis of that group's statistical risk of developing specific illnesses. The idea is to make money despite the fact that insured people will get ill and the insurer may have to pay out quite a lot before some of them get well or die.

Insurance companies also use various means to identify those applicants who are more likely to develop a medical condition than their group membership might suggest. The use of this information to determine a person's insurability is known as "underwriting." If the insurance company has reason to believe someone will turn out to be a costly client, it may charge that person higher premiums. If the company believes a person is likely to develop a specific condition, it can also refuse to insure him or her for that condition, or cancel the relevant coverage. Already in 1989, pediatrician and epidemiologist Neil Holtzman was able to list nine conditions, including sickle-cell anemia, arteriosclerosis, Huntington disease, type 1 diabetes, and Down syndrome, for which insurers had denied medical or disability insurance, and six others for which they granted only conditional or partial coverage.

Insurers want to have as much and as accurate predictive information as they can lawfully get before they insure anyone. By the same token, it is in a client's interest to withhold any information that makes her or him appear other than "average."

Along with individual insurance policies such as I have been discussing, insurance companies also issue group policies to businesses. The price of these policies is set on the basis of the health care costs the business has experienced in previous years. This process is called "experience-rating." Employees in such businesses are eligible for the group plan without being tested individually, unless they admit they have certain, specific medical conditions. If they have an excludable health problem, they must buy an individual insurance policy, which is usually written so that it excludes coverage for their "pre-existing" condition.

Insurance companies point out that, owing to the way insurance currently works, people who pay their premiums without getting sick pay for the medical expenses of the ill. Therefore, the companies say, it is only fair that people who are already sick, or who are more likely to get sick than the "average" person, should pay higher premiums, rather than making other people pay their health care costs. They also argue that it should be within their rights to renegotiate contracts so as to eliminate certain coverages if an insured person's health status changes, as for example if the person tests positive for HIV. Such rewriting defeats the purpose of health insurance. If the terms of a policy change as soon as one gets sick or is predicted to become sick, the insurance is worthless.

If exclusionary practices are allowed, the existence of supposedly predictive tests for an increasing number of common conditions such as cancer, high blood pressure, or diabetes will surely exclude people outright or force them to pay more for insurance. Not only will these tests permit a glimpse into someone's distant future (however fogged that glimpse may be) but they may suggest something about the health of that person's future children, who might be covered by the same insurance policy. Widespread use of predictive genetic tests is bound to exacerbate the injustices inherent in for-profit health insurance. More people will join the pool of "uninsurables" who must rely on public social insurance, which we pay for out of social security and other taxes. Clearly, nothing short of universal coverage by a national health plan similar to those in Canada and the European nations will remedy this situation. Such a plan must guarantee access to health care for everyone, irrespective of their present or future health status and their ability to pay for health insurance or medical care.

Insurers are not yet making extensive use of predictive genetic tests but, like employers, they are likely to use them once such tests become less expensive than they are at present. Legislation and organizing are needed to forbid this form of discrimination. Let us remember that it took years of court battles based on prohibitions against sex discrimination in employment to stop employers and insurers from using actuarial grounds to pay women lower retirement benefits than men, which they had done on the grounds that, statistically, women live longer. The same effort will be required here.

Already there are documented instances of genetic discrimination by insurance companies. Just as Paul Billings and his colleagues uncovered pre-employment discrimination, they also came across a man who was denied automobile insurance because he had a predictive genetic diagnosis of Charcot-Marie-Tooth disease (CMT), although he had never had an automobile accident in twenty years of driving and his physician certified that he had no symptoms of this condition. Another person with CMT could not buy life insurance, despite the fact that CMT does not affect life expectancy.

In two instances, "women carrying fetuses, which had been diagnosed as having genetic disorders, decided to continue their pregnancies. They then had to fight to retain full insurance coverage for the future care of their babies." Billings and his colleagues also cite insurance discrimination against someone who was still healthy, but was known to carry the allele involved in Huntington disease, and Gostin cites the instance of someone who was not allowed to buy insurance because he had a diagnosis of *hemochromatosis,* which is a controllable malfunction of iron metabolism. In a "60 Minutes" interview in May 1992, Jamie Stephenson described having her entire family's health insurance cancelled after two of her children were diagnosed to have *fragile X syndrome,* a variable condition involving mental retardation.

Insurance practices such as exempting "preexisting conditions," limiting coverage, charging higher premiums for higher perceived risks, or changing existing insurance policies are bound to have a serious impact on people said to have a genetic "predisposition" to develop cancer or some other condition. As Gostin points out: "If insurers have actuarial data demonstrating a likelihood of future illness, they can limit coverage [of that illness]. More worrisome would be a decision by an insurer to view a genetic predisposition as a preexisting condition." He adds that the greater the predictive value of tests gets to be, "the more likely …that insurers will regard the condition as uninsurable or preexisting." This would not be unlike the reaction some insurance companies have had to HIV infection, which has been to require HIV testing and to consider persons who test positive uninsurable.

The only limitation the Americans with Disabilities Act places on insurance companies is that it does not allow them to refuse coverage to someone for other health conditions because that person has a specific genetic prediction. They can refuse, cap, or limit insurance, but only for the predicted condition. Obviously, this can have a devastating effect on someone who becomes ill and is denied insurance. Already, insurers have rewritten policies to exclude coverage for AIDS after a policyholder has become ill with AIDS-related conditions, thus denying him or her health insurance at the time when it is most needed. Some states have passed legislation prohibiting this practice, but most allow it.

The ADA forbids employers to ask non-work-related questions about their employees' health. However, now that large companies increasingly serve as their own insurance carriers, they can ask for information as insurers that the ADA would prevent them from asking in their role of employer. Also, as insurers, they have access to the Medical Information Bureau in Westwood, Massachusetts, a centralized data bank of health information for all of North America. While they are not supposed to use this information to make employment decisions, once they have it there is no way to control the ways in which they may use it.

In September 1991, the California legislature passed an amendment to the California Civil Rights Act that provided for an eight-year ban on the use of genetic information by health insurers and employers and on the use of such information to limit access to group life and disability insurance. Although this amendment had bipartisan support, Governor Pete Wilson vetoed it.

Also in 1991, Wisconsin passed legislation forbidding any person or organization to require an individual to take a genetic test or reveal whether she or he has taken such a test. Moreover, the results of such a genetic test for any individual or family member cannot be a condition of insurance coverage, rates, or benefits. Unfortunately, this legislation defines "genetic test" narrowly, to mean "a test using deoxyribonucleic acid extracted from an individual's cells in order to determine the presence of a genetic disease or disorder or the individual's predisposition for a particular genetic disease or disorder." Other ways to "determine the presence of a genetic disease…" are currently used to test for PKU, sickle-cell anemia, and other conditions, and it is not clear that they are covered by this legislation.

We need strong laws at the federal level to control genetic discrimination in employment and insurance. Scientists involved in predictive genetics and the Human Genome Project have promised that genetic predictions will improve preventive measures and so make us healthier. However, if insurance companies can use results of genetic tests to limit or deny coverage, such predictions will have the opposite effect. Without coverage, people will have less access to preventive care, thus will be more likely to become ill and less able to get appropriate medical treatments.

Since much of the scientific research that can lead to genetic discrimination is being done in this country, Americans have a special responsibility to develop ways to counteract this insidious new form of discrimination. I hope that scientists will join in the effort, and devote as much energy to preventing genetic discrimination as they do to developing the technologies that make such discrimination possible.

Decision Scenario 1
OSHA'S COTTON DUST STANDARD

The Occupational Safety and Health Act directs the Secretary of Labor to establish standards for control of toxic materials in the workplace. It requires the secretary to set the standard "which most adequately assures, to the extent feasible, on the basis of the best available evidence" that no employee will suffer impairment of health. On December 28, 1976, OSHA proposed a new permanent standard to replace existing cotton dust standards. After holding public hearings around the country and soliciting comments from industry, workers, physicians, economists, scientists, and others, OSHA issued its final standard on June 23, 1978. Including an accompanying statement of findings and reasons, the standard was 69 pages long.

Byssinosis, commonly known as "brown lung" disease in its more severe forms, is a respiratory disease primarily caused by inhaling cotton dust. Cotton dust is present in the air during the processing, weaving, knitting, or handling of cotton. Estimates have at least 35,000 present or former cotton mill workers, or 1 in 12 such workers, suffering from the most disabling form of byssinosis. Other estimates have 100,000 active and retired workers suffering from some form of the disease. Byssinosis was not recognized as a distinct occupational hazard associated with cotton mills until the early 1960s.

Cotton industry groups, including the American Textile Manufacturers Institute and the National Cotton Council of America, filed suit to challenge the validity of the cotton dust standard. Their major challenge was that OSHA had not, but should have, used cost–benefit analysis in determining the appropriate standard.

In establishing the cotton dust standard, OSHA interpreted the law to require adoption of the most stringent standard possible to protect health, bounded only by technical and economic "feasibility." "Feasible" was taken to mean "capable of being done." Legislative history indicates that Congress itself mandated that worker health should

override considerations of cost. The Congress had specifically chosen "feasible" rather than "cost–benefit" when enacting the OSHA law. The U.S. Court of Appeals upheld OSHA's interpretation of the law in all major respects and rejected the industry's contention that the benefits of the standard must outweigh its costs.

Much of the Supreme Court debate that followed centered upon the phrase "to the extent feasible." The majority, which ruled in favor of the OSHA standard, reasoned that cost–benefit analysis is not required of OSHA regulations. The majority ruled that "feasible" meant that the most stringent standard should be used wherever technologically and economically possible. The implication was that only economic viability, and not simply high costs, could count against the health and safety of employees.

In a dissenting opinion, Justice William Rehnquist argued that "economic feasibility" was too vague to decide the issue either way. He argued that OSHA's legislative history showed that the phrase "to the extent feasible" was a compromise between those who favored and those who rejected cost–benefit analysis. As such, it masked a fundamental policy disagreement in Congress. Since Congress "abdicated its responsibility for making a fundamental and most difficult policy choice," interpretation of this phrase is nothing other than a bureaucratic decision of the Executive Branch. Since "economic feasibility" clearly implies that costs should be considered, OSHA should not ignore cost–benefit analyses.

- Should cost–benefit analysis be used in cases of health and safety? Is feasibility too vague?

- Are standards, rather than compensation or a market solution, the best way to protect employee health and safety?

- Is "economic viability" too strict a standard when protecting employee health and safety?

Decision Scenario 2
MANVILLE'S BANKRUPTCY AND ASBESTOS LITIGATION

In August of 1982 the Manville Corporation, formerly Johns-Manville, filed for protection from creditors under Chapter 11 of the federal bankruptcy code. Since the turn of the twentieth century the Manville Corporation had been one of the principal producers of asbestos, a mineral fiber that had wide use as an insulator and fireproofing material. Its uses ranged from pipe insulation to ceiling tiles to brake shoe insulation. The mineral's fibers, when inhaled, cause a debilitating form of lung cancer. Evidence indicates that only a very small quantity of inhaled fiber can have devastating long-term health effects. Manville's bankruptcy appeal was the consequence of the potential legal liability from thousands of lawsuits filed by industrial workers exposed to Johns-Manville's asbestos. The Chapter 11 filing froze all pending asbestos suits against Manville and required injured employees to seek their compensation through the bankruptcy court.

This escape from the asbestos lawsuits seemed to benefit the corporation and to harm the asbestos claimants. In liability suits, individual claimants stood to recover much greater damages because there was evidence of Manville's having known about and covered up the health dangers of asbestos. Documents presented in prebankruptcy lawsuits revealed that Manville had evidence of asbestos-related disease as early as the 1930s. In fact, an appeals court ruled that asbestos industry correspondence from those years showed a conspiracy by the industry to hide the links between asbestos and lung disease. On the basis of this information, asbestos plaintiffs whose suits were settled outside of a bankruptcy proceeding might have received large punitive damage awards.

Manville's management had been preparing for years before the actual bankruptcy filing. Manville's president at the time, John McKinney, oversaw a Manville defense against the asbestos suits that continued to deny company knowledge of the

dangers of asbestos. McKinney also pursued policies that minimized the proportion of Manville's debt that was secured. When the bankruptcy filing finally came, Manville hoped to be able to cut its losses substantially.

However, the eventual bankruptcy settlement potentially ceded control of the corporation to a trust fund established for the asbestos victims and their families. In addition to cash payments, the settlement provided the trust at least 50 percent of Manville's common stock and 20 percent of its annual future profits for an indeterminate time. If the administrators of the trust felt funds were insufficient to compensate the victims, they would eventually have the power to liquidate the company's assets. Obviously, Manville's stockholders were not pleased with the reorganization plan. In fact, they voted against it, but their vote was overruled by the court.

The primary beneficiaries of the bankruptcy plan appear to have been the executives in charge of Manville. The settlement shielded them from personal liability for the asbestos injuries. Moreover, they retained control of the corporation during the reorganization negotiations. Those same officers who directed Manville's defense against asbestos lawsuits arranged for themselves to receive large salary increases; some ranged as high as 88 percent between 1982 and 1988. In addition, management received bonuses that were as high as 97 percent of salary. McKinney's severance pay when he was removed in 1986 was $1.3 million. Other long-term officers also received severance settlements in the millions.

- In a bankruptcy case that involves commercial creditors, shareholders, and injured victims, who should have priority in the settlement?

- Should management have been shielded from personal liability if they knew of the harms caused by asbestos and hid those harms from workers and consumers?

- What opinion do you have of the procedure for setting up "golden parachutes" for executives of a company undergoing bankruptcy proceedings?

This case was prepared from information in the following sources: *The Product Safety and Liability Reporter*, vol. 16, no. 16, 351; Arthur Sharplin, "Manville Lives on as Victims Continue to Die," *Business and Society Review* (Spring 1988): 25–29; Eugene Bucholz, *Fundamental Concepts and Problems in Business Ethics* (Englewood Cliffs, N.J.: Prentice-Hall, 1989), 152–166.

Decision Scenario 3
OSHA AND THE BENZENE STANDARD

Benzene is a carcinogenic chemical produced as a by-product of gasoline refining. When inhaled, it leads to leukemia. During its early days, the Occupational Safety and Health Administration (OSHA) adopted a standard for exposure to benzene. The initial standard limited the presence of benzene in air to 10 parts per million (ppm). In 1978, however, OSHA issued a new standard, reducing permissible exposure levels to 1 ppm. OSHA's reasoning was that there was insufficient data for a reasonable determination about the level of benzene exposure that produced no significant risk: Wildly different conclusions about the effects of benzene exposure could be drawn from different but equally reasonable studies and assumptions. Consequently the agency adopted a policy of limiting exposure to the lowest technically and economically feasible level in order to minimize the possibility of health hazards. OSHA determined that the lowest feasible level was 1 ppm.

The American Petroleum Institute challenged OSHA's new standard in court. In a preliminary ruling, an appeals court struck down the OSHA standard. The appeals court mandated that OSHA issue regulations only on the basis of quantifiable benefits expected from such regulation. The court also required that OSHA compare any such benefits against the costs of the regulation before proceeding.

OSHA appealed the court ruling, and on July 2, 1980, the U.S. Supreme Court handed down its decision. The Supreme Court upheld the lower court's decision to vacate the OSHA standard, but the Supreme Court's reasoning was different. Its ruling did not require OSHA to perform a cost–benefit study before proceeding with the regulation of a carcinogen. However, it did require that OSHA provide some substantial and quantifiable evidence that a standard would eliminate some significant risk.

The Supreme Court decision, then, struck down OSHA's policy of reducing exposure to the lowest feasible levels when uncertainty exists about the effects of a carcinogen at higher levels. A "lowest feasible level" policy would not meet the requirement that standards be justified on substantial evidence as reducing significant risk. However, the Supreme Court ruling left OSHA wide discretion in assessing when it had substantial evidence of significant risk. The court recognized that it is often not possible to prove conclusively that human health is at risk at specific levels of exposure. The decision, then, required that OSHA attempt to quantify risk on the basis of epidemiological studies, but it did not prevent OSHA from issuing strict standards based on controversial studies.

- OSHA had a study indicating that sixty to eighty yearly cases per 100,000 population of leukemia would be caused by exposure to 1 part per *billion*. Should OSHA have simply repromulgated its standard on the basis of this study?

- Stricter standards are obviously more costly to comply with. What priority should be given to health when there are contrary studies about human health effects at low levels of exposure?

- Of course, scientific judgments about carcinogens must often be based on animal studies in which effects of large doses are calculated. Is the Supreme Court correct in requiring some effort to quantify risk when there is such wide disagreement about methods for extrapolating to human health the consequences of lower exposure levels?

This case was prepared from information in the following sources: U.S. Supreme Court's decision in *Industrial Union Department v. American Petroleum Institute* 448 U.S. 607 (1980); Mark Rothstein, *Occupational Safety and Health Law* (West Publishing, 1983), 71–77; Benjamin Mintz, *OSHA: History, Law and Policy* (Bureau of National Affairs, 1984), 253–288.

Decision Scenario 4

CRIMINAL CONVICTIONS FOR AN EMPLOYEE DEATH:
FILM RECOVERY SYSTEMS, INC.

Film Recovery Systems, Inc., made a business out of recycling small amounts of silver found in used X-ray film. The company used a process that bathed used film in a solution of water and sodium cyanide. After a few days, the silver separated from the film. The solution was then passed through a tank with electrode plates. The silver in the solution adhered to the plates, which were removed and scraped. The cyanide-tainted film remaining in the tanks was removed with shovels by undocumented Polish workers who spoke little English.

Exposure to cyanide through inhalation or contact with the skin can cause convulsions leading to death. A number of Film Recovery Systems employees became ill from cyanide poisoning. In 1983 a worker named Stefan Golab, a Polish immigrant who had worked at Film Recovery for about a year, collapsed over a tank of cyanide and died. The medical examiner ruled that acute cyanide poisoning caused by inhaling cyanide had caused his death. The state attorney's office said that Golab and his co-workers were never informed of the chemicals that they were working with, were given no protective equipment, and were not aware of their rights under OSHA. The corporation and its president, plant manager, and plant foreman were charged in a criminal indictment with the death of Stefan Golab.

The prosecution argued that workers were knowingly and willfully placed in danger by the company and its officers; that corporate officers concealed the risk from workers; that their officers were negligent in areas of safety training and health monitoring. In 1985 the individuals were convicted of murder and reckless homicide and were sentenced to nearly twenty-six years in prison. The corporation was convicted of involuntary manslaughter and fined over $40,000.

The corporation was subject to criminal prosecution because it had the status of a person before the law. As such, it had legal rights but also statutory duties. In this case, state law permitted criminal punishment of a corporation if violations of criminal statutes were approved by executives of the corporation. The individual executives were also subject to prosecution since the state law, as in most jurisdictions, does not permit a defense based solely on the claim that the individual's illegal actions were performed in his or her capacity as corporate employee.

In 1990 an Illinois state appeals court overturned these convictions on the technical grounds that conviction for murder was inconsistent with the involuntary manslaughter convictions of the other defendants. As the second trial was about to begin, the defendants pleaded guilty to manslaughter charges. Under this agreement, Steven O'Neil, former president and part owner of Film Recovery, was sentenced to three years in prison, and Daniel Rodriquez, plant foreman, was sentenced to thirty months probation, four months home confinement, and five hundred hours of community service. Another part owner of Film Recovery, Michael McKay, moved to Utah to avoid prosecution. Utah authorities repeatedly denied Illinois's request to extradite him for prosecution.

- Is criminal prosecution an effective and fair way to deter cases of gross corporate disregard for the health and safety of employees, consumers, or citizens at large?

- Would this case have been decided differently if cost–benefit analysis had been used by OSHA in setting safety standards?

- What would you say if the defense in this case had argued that the business would not have been economically viable if more effective precautions had been taken?

- Is there a difference, ethically or legally, between jeopardizing the life of another to make profits in business and jeopardizing the life of another in a robbery?

Decision Scenario 5
VIDEO DISPLAY TERMINALS AND WORKER HEALTH

In May 1988 the County Council of Suffolk County, New York, enacted the first U.S. law regulating the working conditions of video display terminal (VDT) operators in the private sector. Twenty-six state and local governments had considered similar legislation but had rejected it. In fact, the Suffolk County legislation was enacted only after a council override of the county executive's veto.

For over thirty years it has been known that electrical devices like home appliances and VDTs give off magnetic fields. Besides the obvious visible light, VDTs give off ultraviolet, infrared, microwave, and magnetic fields. Since the intensity of these emissions falls off dramatically after a few feet, little health concern was generated by the early use of VDTs. It is now estimated that there are over 40 million VDTs in use in the United States, many used in jobs that require workers to spend most of their work hours sitting in front of the screen at close range. As this use has increased, so have fears that VDTs present significant risks to worker health.

Beginning in the 1970s, some European studies suggested that VDT operators faced a higher risk than other workers for eye injuries. About this time, the Newspaper Guild of New York, on behalf of some members who were experiencing cataract and vision problems, complained to the National Institute for Occupational Safety and Health (NIOSH). Several studies at newspapers over the next few years produced no evidence that prolonged exposure to VDT screens would cause vision problems.

During the 1980s reports began to emerge of a variety of pregnancy problems among women who worked with VDT screens. Stories of miscarriages, birth defects, and premature births gave rise to investigations by government and industry in both the United States and Canada. The United States House Committee on Science and Technology held public hearings in 1982 on the health risks posed by VDTs, but no conclusions or recommendations resulted. The scientific data on VDT health risks seem, at this point, inconclusive. A NIOSH study, published in the *New England Journal of Medicine* in 1991, concluded that long-term exposure to VDT screens did not increase the risk of miscarriage among the 730 telephone operators studied.

The 1988 law in Suffolk County regulates the conditions in workplaces with twenty or more VDTs where operators average twenty-six or more hours a week in front of the terminals. The law requires fifteen-minute breaks after every three hours at a VDT, and it mandates nonglare screens and adjustable desks and chairs for equipment purchased after 1990. In addition, the law requires the employer to pay 80 percent of the cost of eye examinations and needed eyeglasses.

The Communications Workers of America lobbied hard on behalf of this legislation. VDT operators had reported health problems ranging from back disorders and eye-strain headaches to chronic and disabling pain in the hands, arms, and shoulders. Numerous operators have been diagnosed with carpal tunnel syndrome, a condition in which ligaments in the wrist enlarge and press against nerves in the arm; this condition is most common in occupations in which individuals are required to perform repetitive movements of the hands and arms.

Business groups lobbied hard against this bill as an illegitimate intrusion into workplace labor relations. They argued that many businesses were already in compliance with the standards and therefore the law was unnecessary. Business also argued that the law imposes costs that would make Suffolk County locations less attractive to business, and thus could cost the community jobs and tax revenues. One major employer, Metropolitan Life Insurance Company, has reportedly reconsidered locating an additional two hundred jobs at its local operations.

- How should health and safety decisions be made in light of inconclusive and contradictory evidence? Should cost–benefit analysis be used to establish health standards for VDT workers?

- What aspects of the Suffolk County law are the businesses most discontented with?

- How could safety standards be implemented without discouraging business from locating in the area covered by the law?

PART III

Business and Consumers

10

Product Liability
and Safety

THE HISTORY OF PRODUCT LIABILITY

NEWS FLASH: Woman spills coffee and sues McDonald's for $2.8 million! That case, perhaps more than any other, stimulated a growing national feeling that the court system has lost all connection to common sense. This feeling has prompted calls for change in the way the law compensates persons for injuries caused by products—products liability law.

Product liability policies have for decades been under attack from business and the insurance industry. However, with the change in congressional balance of power in the 1994 elections, it is also now under a legislative assault. Democrats and Republicans alike are clamoring for reforms. Advocacy ads by groups with names like "Citizens for a Sound Economy" (along with competing ads by the Trial Lawyers Association) have flooded airwaves in states with swing vote legislators. Sifting through all the arguments about reform is a daunting task. Before we try to assess the current debate, it is best to have an understanding of how the law on product liability has developed over the years.

The earliest legal approach to product liability was a system known as "caveat emptor," or "Let the buyer beware." It meant that a consumer injured by a defective product was unable to sue the manufacturer and recover damages. Gradually individual states, which have primary jurisdiction over liability law, began to shift away from caveat emptor as the economy became less agricultural and more industrial. By the turn of the twentieth century, the usual state law on product liability had become a conjunction of two doctrines: "privity of contract" and the "negligence standard." The privity of contract doctrine allowed suits over product-related injuries only when the parties to the suit had a contractual relationship between them. In practice, this meant that consumers were typically unable to bring product liability suits against manufacturers since most products purchased by the consumer were obtained from a retailer, not from the manufacturer. Since there was no direct economic transaction between consumer and manufacturer, the privity doctrine disallowed liability suits against the producers of defective products. Moreover, if a consumer was allowed to bring a suit against a seller, the consumer had to establish negligence in order to prevail. In the law, negligence generally is understood as a failure to exercise due care. If a product defect had its source in the manufacturing process, and if the defect was not easily apparent on visual inspection, then the retailer who sold the product would not be negligent in most cases. (The first reading in this chapter is the 1928 *Palsgraf* decision from New York's Court of Appeals. It presents an interesting discussion that reveals the difficulties surrounding determinations of negligence and causation.)

In 1916, the New York Court of Appeals issued a ruling that over time came to be adopted as the law in most other states. In the case of *MacPherson v. Buick Motors,* the court held a manufacturer negligent and hence liable for failure to inspect the wooden spokes of its automobile wheels for defects. The case was one of the first to remove the privity doctrine's requirement of a direct contractual relationship between plaintiff and defendant. As a result of this decision, plaintiff consumers had merely to establish the following to sue and recover damages from a manufacturer of a defective product: (1) an injury occurred; (2) the product was defective; (3) the injury was the result of the product defect; (4) the product came from the defendant; and (5) the defendant was negligent in letting the defective product onto the market. Proving negligence was, however, often difficult. Negligence requires that the plaintiff establish facts about the defendant's state of mind or conduct. In many cases, the information required for proof is not available. The situation in the famous Ford Pinto case—where the plaintiffs secured internal Ford memoranda that indicated Ford executives knew about the risk of gas tank explosions, yet calculated it was not cost beneficial for Ford to correct the problem—is perhaps unusual in the degree of evidence available about the defendant's state of mind.

Another watershed case was decided in 1960. A New Jersey court, in the case of *Henningsen v. Bloomfield Motors,* decided that an injured consumer should be entitled to recover damages because the axle of the car she was riding in broke. The court held that the axle was defective and the product was not reasonably fit for its intended use. The court reasoned that consumers have a right to expect that a car, as a durable good, will not have such serious defects. The court's decision announced a new doctrine of liability law—the "doctrine of implied warranty." It establishes that manufacturers implicitly warrant their products to be fit for intended use by the very act of offering them for sale. The crucial aspect of this case is that it removed the previously stated fifth requirement for a successful product liability suit: Consumers under this doctrine would not have to establish negligence.

In 1963, a California court announced a similar decision in the case of *Green-man v. Yuba Power Products* (see Decision Scenario 3 at the end of the chapter). That case, decided on principles of tort law (the area of the law covering injuries between private parties), issued in the doctrine of "strict liability." From the consumer plaintiff's position, it was practically equivalent to the implied warranty theory since both approaches removed the negligence requirement.

The strict liability approach has become the dominant approach to product liability in most states since that 1963 California decision. The shift in the law from negligence to strict liability is perhaps even greater than the shift away from the privity doctrine. Whereas the negligence standard focuses on the conduct and state of mind of the defendant, the strict liability standard concerns only the quality of the product. If the product is defective (usually defined as unreasonably dangerous), the manufacturer can be required to pay damages regardless of whether it was at fault. Essentially, with the adoption of the strict liability approach, product liability law has gone from a fault-finding exercise to a mechanism for compensating those injured by product defects.

This shift from a fault-based to a compensatory standard has been defended on two grounds. First, strict liability is seen as a mechanism for spreading the costs of accidental product defects. Under negligence, if a product is defective but the manufacturer is not negligent, the cost of the injury is located entirely on the injured party. (Defects can exist without negligence because, even with the strictest design and quality control standards, a defective product can slip through the net into the stream of commerce. The only way to guarantee zero defects is to cease all production.) With a strict liability standard, such a case would result in the manufacturer or, more likely, the manufacturer's insurance company, paying the injured consumer. The cost of that payment would eventually be turned back on other consumers of the injuring product.

The second traditional defense of strict liability is that it provides an incentive for manufacturers to make their products safer. If manufacturers know that they will be liable for any defect that causes injury, then they will take extra steps to ensure that products are safe and defect free. (Some have claimed that strict liability will not increase safety since manufacturers are held liable for unforseen product defects, which they cannot prevent. This, of course, makes some sense. However, it seems to apply more to design defects than to defects that are the result of the manufacturing process. Some of the latter could still be eliminated if producers had financial incentives to exercise stricter quality controls.)

The law has obviously shifted away from protection for producers and more towards protection for consumers. Some have even suggested that we now have a legal system of "Seller beware." While it is true that manufacturers are now greatly more exposed to financial liability for products that cause injury, it is not the case that manufacturers are without legal defenses or that we have reached a stage of "absolute liability." First, plaintiffs in product liability cases must still establish that there was a defect. Second, even if that is established, there are many legal doctrines and tactics available for defendant manufacturers. Manufacturers can argue that the consumer misused the product (although the misuse cannot be one that was reasonably forseeable, for that again makes the producer liable). They can prove that the consumer was contributorily negligent, for example, by showing that the defect was obvious and that the consumer used the product anyway. They can argue that the product's inherent risks were patently known and that the consumer therefore voluntarily assumed the risk. (This has been quite a successful line of defense used by tobacco manufacturers. See Decision Scenario 1, "Tobacco Companies Under Fire.") Producers can argue that the product contained a warning. Finally, they can claim that although the product risk cannot be eliminated, the product provides great social utility. (Drugs are often placed in this last category.)

If we reflect on this brief historical sketch, we can imagine four broad policy alternatives for how to assign liability for defective products that cause injury. At one extreme, we could adopt a policy of caveat emptor. Under this policy consumers would be unable to recover damages and business would be totally insulated from liability suits.

Next, we can imagine a negligence approach similar to the one that predominated in the law between 1916 and 1963. Under this standard, consumers have increased opportunity to receive compensation relative to the first approach. Business, however, would be that much more exposed to financial liability for the consequences of its products.

Then, we can imagine the strict liability system of the recent past. Under this approach, a business would be held strictly liable for *any* injuries caused by a defective product. The costs of such injuries would initially be located on the business itself through its insurance premiums. Ultimately, those costs would be reflected in product prices.

Finally, we can imagine a hybrid policy that has been suggested as an alternative to the current approach. It would locate financial responsibility for injuries on the individual business when the defect was the result of negligence. However, if the defect were a pure accident, that is, not the result of corporate negligence, the consumer would still recover, but the monies would come from a general fund to which we all, as taxpayers, contribute. The idea of this hybrid is to retain the compassionate compensation for the injured found under strict liability but to lessen the financial burden on business.

As you read the cases and articles of this chapter, try to identify the advantages and disadvantages of each of these broad policies. For instance, caveat emptor might provide for a greater variety of products and for cheaper products because insurance for liability would not be a cost of doing business. It would also allow more consumer injuries to occur. Alternatively, strict liability with businesses purchasing private insurance to cover the costs of defect-related injuries would increase product costs. But it would also maximize the manufacturer's incentive to produce safe products because the more numerous the injury-causing defects, the higher its insurance premiums will be. We encourage you to identify other costs and benefits of these four alternatives. The article by Peter Huber, for example, is critical of strict liability. He presents a number of serious charges about the costly consequences of that system. We urge you to consider carefully Huber's arguments and to imagine what hidden costs are present for the other approaches as well. Only after such an analysis can you arrive at an adequately informed decision about which alternative is the best public policy.

REFORMING LIABILITY LAW

Before addressing the specific legal reforms now under discussion in Congress, we should discuss a few criticisms that have been levelled against the current strict liability approach. Opponents of the current American system deride it as the most costly in the world. They maintain that it harms American industry's competitiveness and costs the United States jobs. They argue that American business pays ten to fifty times more for product liability insurance than does its international competition. Our largest trading partner, Canada, for instance, does not have the costs of a strict liability system. There, manufacturers are generally liable only for negligently caused product defects.

Opponents also charge the liability system is partly responsible for a decline in the willingness of Americans to accept responsibility for their actions. They point to a cultural climate where whatever bad that happens to a person must be someone else's fault. Critics also claim that the system, with its potential for large awards, encourages fraudulent or frivolous suits that are filed as fishing expeditions by greedy lawyers and their clients. (In Philadelphia, which is known for its high number of insurance fraud cases, a woman recently filed a fraudulent suit against the public transit agency for injuries purportedly sustained in a train accident. Unfortunately for the woman, the "train accident" she saw reported on the news, and in which she claimed to be injured, was merely a report on an emergency preparedness drill!) As a result, critics claim we have experienced a flood of product liability lawsuits in recent years.

Those in favor of strict liability must admit that with every reduction in what a plaintiff must prove to win an award, more frivolous or fraudulent suits are possible. They also need to recognize a concern about the effect of the legal system on cultural attitudes. However, they argue that a return to negligence would be a draconian overreaction that penalizes those who are the greatest victims, the seriously injured. Additionally, they contend, strict liability has not created the difficulties alleged. They note that much of the recent litigation is against a small number of defendants. If one removes the mass tort cases for damaging products such as asbestos or the Dalkon Shield (see Decision Scenario 5 on that case), the litigation flood slows remarkably. For instance, a University of Wisconsin law professor notes that in 1988 there were 8,200 nonasbestos product liability suits filed; in 1991 there were 5,200. Proponents also point to two reports that suggest the costs of the system are often overstated. A Rand study found that only 10 percent of those injured in product accidents ever bring suit, and a business research group, the Conference Board, found in 1987 that product liability costs were only about 1 percent of gross receipts. The board also said that liability law had small effect on jobs or international market share.

Still, a problem must be recognized for small businesses that operate on small profit margins and yet have radically increasing insurance costs. There are questions, though, about whether the increase in insurance premiums is justified by the amount paid out in damage awards to victims. It is certainly true that many of the large jury verdicts that are reported in the news are subsequently reduced on appeal. The question, then, is whether the problems of the product liability system are severe enough to justify abandoning a strict liability approach in favor of one of the other alternatives. Some argue that whatever problems exist can be addressed by marginal changes in the law. Others hold that adequate corrections demand a more wholesale change in liability rules.

Those in favor of a more wholesale change often charge that the system of strict liability is unfair to business. They argue that business ought not be held responsible for accidents that are beyond its control. No matter how rigid the quality control standards of a business, a defective product might still slip through. As we have seen, that business will be financially liable for injuries that its product causes. Business lobbyists, however, point out that the business in that instance is not morally responsible for the injuries. Being forced to pay for negligence is one thing, they argue; being forced to pay for unforseen and perhaps unforseeable defects is quite another.

The articles by George Brenkert and John McCall both address this question of fairness. Brenkert raises some serious considerations about the sufficiency of the traditional two justifications of strict liability. He goes on, however, to defend the practice on new grounds. McCall suggests that many of Brenkert's objections to the traditional defenses are ultimately questions about fairness. He argues that an adequate understanding of fairness will show that strict liability is compatible with fairness, and perhaps even required by it. He contends that when the traditional justifications of safety and cost sharing are conjoined with an adequate understanding of fairness, they are sufficient justification for adopting strict liability as our overall public policy. McCall notes, however, some problematic cases in which the legitimacy of the current standard may be called into question.

Even those sympathetic to strict liability as a general principle are now often urging reform of liability law. In fact, the current reform proposals under consideration by both the House and Senate are more tinkering at the margins of the law rather than an abandoning of strict liability entirely. (This is somewhat surprising in that much past criticism was aimed at strict liability itself.)

As of May 1995, both the House and Senate have passed their respective bills and are working in conference on removing any differences between them. House Rule 956 limits punitive damage awards to successful plaintiffs to the greater of $250,000 or three times the award for lost wages and medical expenses. It would cap pain and suffering awards in medical and drug cases at $250,000. It requires plaintiffs in some federal liability cases to pay the defendant's legal fees if the plaintiff rejected a settlement offer and the jury award was less than that offer. Finally, it prohibits punitive damage awards in cases where a drug or medical device had Food and Drug Administration (FDA) approval. Senate Bill 565 differs from the House version in capping punitive damage awards at $250,000 or two times the award for economic damages and pain and suffering. The Senate bill does not have the pain and suffering limits, the FDA defense, or the "loser pays" clause. Both bills place a greater legal burden on juries before they may award punitive damages, and both place restrictions on plaintiffs' lawyers' fees.

Those in favor of the reforms claim that they are needed to restore fairness to the liability system and to remove stifling burdens on the competitiveness of American business. Critics of the reforms see the "loser pays" clause and the limits on legal fees as effectively removing access to the court system for many consumers. They also find the limits on punitive damages to be unnecessary and insufficient to deter wrongdoing by larger corporations. They note that punitive damage awards are relatively rare: There were 355 nationally between 1965 and 1990, with one quarter of those for asbestos cases.

Whatever the House–Senate resolution and whatever the presidential response to the proposed reforms, it seems likely now that federal and state legislatures will continue to institute changes in product liability law. We hope that the material in this chapter will allow you to assess both the current and future debates.

PRODUCT SAFETY REGULATION

If product liability law is about how and when to assess damages once a product injury has occurred, product safety regulation is about preventing accidents from happening. The current legal approach to product safety regulation is known as a standards enforcement approach. The government, through executive agencies such as the Consumer Product Safety Commission and the Food and Drug Administration, mandate that products meet certain safety standards if they are to be available for sale. The agencies have the authority to ban products from the market, to order recalls, and to impose fines for violations of mandated standards. (As with all administrative agencies' decisions, these actions of the CPSC and FDA are subject to appeal; the agencies are not the final authorities in these matters.)

This form of government regulation of consumer products has met with some resistance. One of the main complaints against safety standards is that those standards take too little notice of the costs that they impose on business and on society generally. Often, critics charge, business is made less efficient, products more costly, and jobs more scarce because of safety-oriented regulations. Obviously, we cannot eliminate product risks. What we must decide is when levels of risk are acceptable, which is a rough definition of "safety." Those critical of current safety regulation would have us answer this question by engaging in a formal cost–benefit analysis before promulgating any new safety standard. In fact, a bill currently before Congress, the Job Creation and Wage Enhancement Act, would require all federal agencies to conduct a complex review of regulatory costs and benefits that would be subject to corporate comments and judicial review. (For a discussion of the adequacy of cost–benefit analysis as a public policy tool, see the readings by Chelius and MacCarthy in Chapter Nine and by Sagoff in Chapter Twelve.)

Another major criticism against safety regulation is that it expresses a paternalistic attitude towards consumers. Since the agencies set standards that all products in a given market must meet, the agencies also prevent consumers from choosing for themselves just what mix of safety features they are willing to pay for. Critics maintain that protecting consumers from their own choices is a paternalistic interference with consumer autonomy. Given the value placed on autonomy in Chapters Two and Three (and elsewhere throughout this text), that is a most serious charge. It is a charge made more serious since most protective legislation follows this same standards enforcement approach. (Consider the EPA, OSHA, and other agencies.) If the charge holds, and protective regulation is unjustifiably paternalistic, we would have an argument for dismantling much of the federal bureaucracy and for letting consumer demand determine safety levels through free market bargaining.

A number of responses to this charge are possible. One could admit that regulation is paternalistic and claim that the paternalism is justified either because citizens are incapable of making intelligent choices (the justification for treating children paternalistically) or because the social benefits of paternalism are great enough to justify it. In our society, neither of these justifications is compatible with deep-seated commitment to individual autonomy.

A second argument against the charge of paternalism is provided by those who contend that consumer choice in the marketplace is not really free. Proponents of regulatory standards who argue this way will claim that there are significant enough market imperfections that government intervention is needed in order to protect consumers. The pure market approach, they argue, places individual consumers in an unequal bargaining position that in fact jeopardizes their autonomy.

A third response would be to defend regulatory action as a way of protecting the rights of third parties. Laws requiring motorcyclists to wear safety helmets, for example, have been urged as a way of reducing the need for taxation to support the care of individuals who suffer severe brain damage in accidents. Similar arguments are obvious in the case of gun regulations.

A fourth response is the one pursued in the reading by Steven Kelman, who argues that safety regulation is not really paternalistic. Kelman attempts to prove that it is economically rational for the consumer to autonomously surrender to the government his or her authority to choose. Such surrender is rational, he claims, when the costs of making the decision oneself are great. Note that Kelman's argument is not intended as a particular defense of every instance of government regulation.

Recently, one of the oldest federal consumer safety agencies, the FDA, has come under fire in a different way. Critics of the agency charge that its drug and medical device approval process is still too slow, despite recent attempts to streamline the process and get life-saving medications onto the market more quickly. House Speaker Newt Gingrich, in fact, has called the FDA "America's leading job-killer." Critics have proposed both more streamlining of the approval process and a narrowing of the agency's charter. Now, the agency is responsible for assuring that drugs and medical devices are safe *and* efficacious. Reformers are suggesting that the agency limit its review to ensuring safety and let consumers in the market determine if products are effective. That way, they argue, life-saving drugs and devices will be available sooner. Opponents of the reform worry that the narrowed charter will result in consumer purchases of useless products that may sometimes delay effective treatments. As you can see from this brief survey, the advisability and effectiveness of government safety regulation will continue to be subject to debate.

Ethics and the Marketing of Dangerous Products

Whatever view you take on the issue of government regulatory action, there remains a further question for you to address. It is the question of what *ethical* standards should be used in assessing the marketing of dangerous products. We need to remember that it is possible for an act to be legal and yet not morally appropriate. It is possible, then, that the sale of some products would be legal but immoral. Some critics of the tobacco industry consider the sale of cigarettes to be an instance of this.

One reason for the difference between an action's legality and its moral acceptability is that the law is not always a desirable method for enforcing moral norms. For example, sometimes the law should not attempt to enforce a moral norm because that attempt will cause more moral problems than it solves, as some would say resulted with the Prohibition Era's attempt to enforce abstinence from alcohol. So, before we use law to enforce a moral norm, we need to ask whether the enforcement will be effective, whether it will lead to a decline in respect for law generally, and whether it will predictably cause other, significant harms.

This caution about using the law to enforce all of morality only makes more pressing the need to supplement your assessment of government safety regulation with a parallel moral assessment of the practice of marketing dangerous products. One possible moral assessment would be to argue that the autonomy of both consumer and seller generates a moral right to sell any product for which there is market demand.

This use of autonomy will not work, however. It merely is an application of the extreme laissez-faire understanding of liberty that was discarded in Chapter Three. Autonomy does not mean having a right to do whatever one pleases. Rather, autonomy must be linked to areas of life that are of crucial importance for an adequate human existence. Buying or selling a particular product seems unlikely to qualify for that lofty status. There are intuitively reasonable cases where the sale of products is limited but where the extreme understanding of autonomy would object to those limits. The most addictive and dangerous of the currently illegal drugs are examples. Moreover, as was also pointed out in Chapter Three, even if we admitted a right to sell any product we wished, that does not automatically mean that selling it is morally appropriate. Having a right to do something does not entail that you ought to do it, all things considered.

At the other extreme is the view holding that it is unethical to market any product that predictably causes harm or whose net social impact is negative. This, too, seems unacceptable. While the harmful consequences of products are a matter of serious concern, this method of assessment is merely the utilitarian approach that was challenged in Chapter Two. And, while the first approach gives too much weight to consumer and seller desires, this utilitarian approach appears to give too little weight to consumer sovereignty.

Another approach to the moral evaluation of the sale of harmful products would be to say that it is acceptable to sell products that are dangerous only if consumers are adequately warned about those dangers. However, there is evidence that warnings are often not processed by consumers or are not forceful enough. Also, some question whether mere warnings are enough to morally justify marketing a dangerous product when the seller spends millions in advertising and public relations to counteract the effect of any warnings. Hence, some who accept the sale of harmful products argue that it is not morally appropriate to promote and advertise those products.

Others suggest that while it may be acceptable to sell potentially harmful products, with appropriate warnings, to wary adults, producers have a moral obligation to ensure that those products are not sold in ways that provide easy access for minors.

We urge you to morally assess if, when, and how dangerous products should be sold. In developing such a position, you need to make specific reference to all the different products that people claim are dangerous. Should the sale of tobacco, guns, alcohol, heroin, and crack cocaine all be assessed similarly? Or are there differences in the products that justify reaching a different moral conclusion for each of them? Whatever the law says about these products, or whatever you believe the law *ought* to say, an ethical evaluation of their sale is still essential.

CASE STUDY Diethylstilbestrol (DES)

Diethylstilbestrol (DES) is a synthetic estrogen hormone that was first produced by British medical researchers in the 1930s. The formula for the drug was not patented, so the drug was available for manufacture by any company. U.S. drug companies applied to the Food and Drug Administration (FDA) for permission to market the drug in the United States as a remedy for symptoms of menopause. FDA approval was granted in 1941 on the basis of clinical data developed by a joint project of a number of interested drug companies. Further FDA approval for the use of the drug in the prevention of miscarriages was granted in 1947. Diethylstilbestrol was used throughout the 1950s and 1960s for the treatment of pregnancies that presented the danger of miscarriage. As many as three hundred companies produced the drug during that period. The drugs produced by those companies were essentially identical in manufacture and medicinal action; the only differences between the drugs of different manufacturers were inessential differences in packaging. Therefore, DES is legally considered a "fungible" product.

In 1971 a statistical connection was found between the use of DES during pregnancy and the appearance of certain forms of vaginal cancer in

the female children of women treated by the drug. It is now considered well established that DES caused those cancers, which developed after at least ten years had lapsed since the consumption of the drug. In 1972 the FDA prohibited all marketing of the drug for use during pregnancy.

Given both the long period before the appearance of the side effects and the unexpected place of occurrence (in the offspring rather than in the person treated), it seems that the difficulties with the drug were not forseen by the companies that marketed it, especially during the earlier 1950s period.

The two most common approaches to product liability law are the negligence and strict liability standards of liability. The negligence standard would normally allow a consumer injured by a product to recover damages from the company only on condition of proving that the injury resulted from the company's negligence. Under the strict liability standard, the consumer could recover damages without proving the company's negligence in cases of products that were nonetheless defective and unreasonably dangerous.

In the DES cases, the female victims of the drugs taken by their mothers could possibly have argued to the satisfaction of a jury that the companies were negligent for insufficiently testing the product or that the product was unreasonably dangerous.

This case was prepared from the decisions of the relevant state courts.

Under the standard requirements for bringing liability suits, however, the injured consumer must also establish that the defendant company was the source of the injuring product. In the DES cases, this requirement would effectively bar the victims from bringing suits successfully. Generally, the drug companies, the pharmacists who provided the prescriptions, and the women who took the drug could not establish which particular manufacturer was the source of the drugs any given woman had taken. Pharmacists, for example, often had supplies from different manufacturers that were used inter-changeably. In addition, less than precise record-keeping and the passage of time also made it nearly impossible to determine which manufac-turer's drugs were the cause of specific cancers. Consequently, state courts, in whose jurisdiction product liability suits fall, had a dilemma. Fairness to the injured victims seemed to at least allow them the opportunity to make their case in court. Tradi-tional standards of proof for causation in product liability cases, however, would lead to the summary dismissal of suits against the DES manufacturers. There are only two ways out of this dilemma: Courts could pass a "hard-luck" judgment on the victims, or they could offer new theories of liability law that would allow some chance of recovery. Some states adopted the former approach, but some adopted the latter.

California, Wisconsin, and Michigan are three of the states in which proof of causation requirements were relaxed. A Michigan appellate court reversed the decision of a lower court and allowed a DES suit on the ground that the plaintiff had named all the known manufacturers that distributed DES in the area and at the time her mother had taken the drug. In the famous *Sindell* case, the California Supreme Court allowed a suit on the condition that the named defendants together constitute a "sub-stantial" share of the market. If the drug companies lost the suit, they would be apportioned damages in direct proportion to their market share. The Wisconsin Supreme Court allowed an injured victim to sue just one company, even though she could not prove that company was the source of her mother's DES. The Wisconsin court required only that the plaintiff prove by a preponderance of the evidence that the defendant company marketed the type (according to characteristics such as pill or capsule form, shape, color) of DES taken by her mother.

On March 31, 1988, the California Supreme Court issued a decision that limits the scope of its previous *Sindell* market-share theory of liability. The court held that in cases involving drug manufacturers, consumers can sue only under a negligence standard of liability and not under a strict liability standard. In addition, the court held that damages for an injury in a market-share case can be assessed only in proportion to the defendant's share of the market. This means that unless the consumer sues all manu-facturers who distributed the drug in the relevant area (an unlikely event, since many companies are no longer operating), the consumer can recover only partial costs of her injury.

The California Supreme Court reasoned that applying strict liability to drug companies, especially in a climate allowing market-share liability, might lead to company reluctance to develop and market new drugs that could provide great social benefits. In addition, the court was concerned that the needed drugs that do get produced might be pro-hibitively expensive if drug companies were subject to increasingly expensive product liability insurance. In essence, the California court declared that, as a class, prescription drugs fall into a category of products that are necessary yet unavoidably dan-gerous. The traditional approach to strict liability exempts such products, requiring instead that negli-gence be proved before damages are recovered.

Interestingly, the Wisconsin Supreme Court in its 1984 decision came to exactly the opposite conclu-sion after considering some of the same arguments. It reasoned that imposing strict liability on drug companies would still allow the production of so-cially beneficial drugs but would encourage their being produced with greater care. The Wisconsin court, then, explicitly refused to classify all prescrip-tion drugs as unavoidably dangerous. It left open the possibility that some drugs are unreasonably danger-ous. The court preferred for public policy reasons (encouraging adequate testing and safety) to judge harms caused by drugs on a case-by-case basis.

HELEN PALSGRAF V. THE LONG ISLAND RAILROAD COMPANY
Court of Appeals of New York

Syllabus: A man carrying a package jumped aboard a car of a moving train and, seeming unsteady as if about to fall, a guard on the car reached forward to help him in and another guard on the platform pushed him from behind, during which the package was dislodged and falling upon the rails exploded, causing injuries to plaintiff, an intending passenger, who stood on the platform many feet away. There was nothing in the appearance of the package to give notice that it contained explosives. In an action by the intending passenger against the railroad company to recover for such injuries, the complaint should be dismissed. Negligence is not actionable unless it involves the invasion of a legally protected interest, the violation of a right, and the conduct of the defendant's guards, if a wrong in relation to the holder of the package, was not a wrong in its relation to the plaintiff standing many feet away.

Judges: Cardozo, Ch. J. Pound, Lehman and Kellogg, JJ., concur with Cardozo, Ch. J.; Andrews, J., dissents in opinion in which Crane and O'Brien, JJ., concur.

Opinion by: Cardozo

Opinion: Plaintiff was standing on a platform of defendant's railroad after buying a ticket to go to Rockaway Beach. A train stopped at the station, bound for another place. Two men ran forward to catch it. One of the men reached the platform of the car without mishap, though the train was already moving. The other man, carrying a package, jumped aboard the car, but seemed unsteady as if about to fall. A guard on the car, who had held the door open, reached forward to help him in, and another guard on the platform pushed him from behind. In this act, the package was dislodged, and fell upon the rails. It was a package of small size, about fifteen inches long, and was covered by a newspaper. In fact it contained fireworks, but there

From 248 N.Y. 339; 162 N.E. 99; 59 A.L.R. 1253. February 24, 1928, argued; May 29, 1928, decided.

was nothing in its appearance to give notice of its contents. The fireworks when they fell exploded. The shock of the explosion threw down some scales at the other end of the platform, many feet away. The scales struck the plaintiff, causing injuries for which she sues.

The conduct of the defendant's guard, if a wrong in its relation to the holder of the package, was not a wrong in its relation to the plaintiff, standing far away. Relatively to her it was not negligence at all. Nothing in the situation gave notice that the falling package had in it the potency of peril to persons thus removed. Negligence is not actionable unless it involves the invasion of a legally protected interest, the violation of a right. "Proof of negligence in the air, so to speak, will not do" (Pollock, Torts [11th ed.], p. 455;…), "Negligence is the absence of care, according to the circumstances" (Willes, J., in Vaughan v. Taff Vale Ry. Co., 5 H. & N. 679, 688;…). The plaintiff as she stood upon the platform of the station might claim to be protected against intentional invasion of her bodily security. Such invasion is not charged. She might claim to be protected against unintentional invasion by conduct involving in the thought of reasonable men an unreasonable hazard that such invasion would ensue. These, from the point of view of the law, were the bounds of her immunity, with perhaps some rare exceptions, survivals for the most part of ancient forms of liability, where conduct is held to be at the peril of the actor.…If no hazard was apparent to the eye of ordinary vigilance, an act innocent and harmless, at least to outward seeming, with reference to her, did not take to itself the quality of a tort because it happened to be a wrong, though apparently not one involving the risk of bodily insecurity, with reference to someone else. "In every instance, before negligence can be predicated of a given act, back of the act must be sought and found a duty to the individual complaining, the observance of which would have averted or avoided the injury" (McSherry, C. J., in W. Va. Central R. Co. v. State, 96 Md. 652, 666;…). "The ideas of negligence and duty are strictly correlative" (Bowen, L. J., in Thomas v. Quartermaine, 18 Q. B.

D. 685, 694). The plaintiff sues in her own right for a wrong personal to her, and not as the vicarious beneficiary of a breach of duty to another.

A different conclusion will involve us, and swiftly too, in a maze of contradictions. A guard stumbles over a package which has been left upon a platform. It seems to be a bundle of newspapers. It turns out to be a can of dynamite. To the eye of ordinary vigilance, the bundle is abandoned waste, which may be kicked or trod on with impunity. Is a passenger at the other end of the platform protected by the law against the unsuspected hazard concealed beneath the waste? If not, is the result to be any different, so far as the distant passenger is concerned, when the guard stumbles over a valise which a truckman or a porter has left upon the walk? The passenger far away, if the victim of a wrong at all, has a cause of action, not derivative, but original and primary. His claim to be protected against invasion of his bodily security is neither greater nor less because the act resulting in the invasion is a wrong to another far removed. In this case, the rights that are said to have been violated, the interests said to have been invaded, are not even of the same order. The man was not injured in his person nor even put in danger. The purpose of the act, as well as its effect, was to make his person safe. If there was a wrong to him at all, which may very well be doubted, it was a wrong to a property interest only, the safety of his package. Out of this wrong to property, which threatened injury to nothing else, there has passed, we are told, to the plaintiff by derivation or succession a right of action for the invasion of an interest of another order, the right to bodily security. The diversity of interests emphasizes the futility of the effort to build the plaintiff's right upon the basis of a wrong to someone else. The gain is one of emphasis, for a like result would follow if the interests were the same. Even then, the orbit of the danger as disclosed to the eye of reasonable vigilance would be the orbit of the duty. One who jostles one's neighbor in a crowd does not invade the rights of others standing at the outer fringe when the unintended contact casts a bomb upon the ground. The wrongdoer as to them is the man who carries the bomb, not the one who explodes it without suspicion of the danger. Life will have to be made over, and human nature transformed, before prevision so extravagant can be accepted as the norm of conduct, the customary standard to which behavior must conform.

The argument for the plaintiff is built upon the shifting meanings of such words as "wrong" and "wrongful," and shares their instability. What the plaintiff must show is "a wrong" to herself, i.e., a violation of her own right, and not merely a wrong to someone else, nor conduct "wrongful" because unsocial, but not "a wrong" to anyone. We are told that one who drives at reckless speed through a crowded city street is guilty of a negligent act and, therefore, of a wrongful one irrespective of the consequences. Negligent the act is, and wrongful in the sense that it is unsocial, but wrongful and unsocial in relation to other travelers, only because the eye of vigilance perceives the risk of damage. If the same act were to be committed on a speedway or a race course, it would lose its wrongful quality. The risk reasonably to be perceived defines the duty to be obeyed, and risk imports relation; it is risk to another or to others within the range of apprehension.... This does not mean, of course, that one who launches a destructive force is always relieved of liability if the force, though known to be destructive, pursues an unexpected path. "It was not necessary that the defendant should have had notice of the particular method in which an accident would occur, if the possibility of an accident was clear to the ordinarily prudent eye" (Munsey v. Webb, 231 U.S. 150, 156;...). Some acts, such as shooting, are so imminently dangerous to anyone who may come within reach of the missile, however, unexpectedly, as to impose a duty of prevision not far from that of an insurer. Even today, and much oftener in earlier stages of the law, one acts sometimes at one's peril.... Under this head, it may be, fall certain cases of what is known as transferred intent, an act willfully dangerous to A resulting by misadventure in injury to B.... These cases aside, wrong is defined in terms of the natural or probable, at least when unintentional.... The range of reasonable apprehension is at times a question for the court, and at times, if varying inferences are possible, a question for the jury. Here, by concession, there was nothing in the situation to suggest to the most cautious mind that the parcel wrapped in newspaper would spread wreckage through the station. If the guard had thrown it down knowingly and willfully, he would not have threatened the plaintiff's safety, so far as appearances could warn him. His conduct would not have involved, even then, an unreasonable probability of invasion of her bodily security. Liability can be no greater where the act is inadvertent.

Negligence, like risk, is thus a term of relation. Negligence in the abstract, apart from things related, is surely not a tort, if indeed it is understandable at all....Negligence is not a tort unless it results in the commission of a wrong, and the commission of a wrong imports the violation of a right, in this case, we are told, the right to be protected against interference with one's bodily security. But bodily security is protected, not against all forms of interference or aggression, but only against some. One who seeks redress at law does not make out a cause of action by showing without more that there has been damage to his person. If the harm was not willful, he must show that the act as to him had possibilities of danger so many and apparent as to entitle him to be protected against the doing of it though the harm was unintended. Affront to personality is still the keynote of the wrong. Confirmation of this view will be found in the history and development of the action on the case. Negligence as a basis of civil liability was unknown to mediaeval law....For damage to the person, the sole remedy was trespass, and trespass did not lie in the absence of aggression, and that direct and personal....Liability for other damage, as where a servant without orders from the master does or omits something to the damage of another, is a plant of later growth....When it emerged out of the legal soil, it was thought of as a variant of trespass, an offshoot of the parent stock. This appears in the form of action, which was known as trespass on the case....The victim does not sue derivatively, or by right of subrogation, to vindicate an interest invaded in the person of another. Thus to view his cause of action is to ignore the fundamental difference between tort and crime....He sues for breach of a duty owing to himself.

The law of causation, remote or proximate, is thus foreign to the case before us. The question of liability is always anterior to the question of the measure of the consequences that go with liability. If there is no tort to be redressed, there is no occasion to consider what damage might be recovered if there were a finding of a tort. We may assume,

without deciding, that negligence, not at large or in the abstract, but in relation to the plaintiff, would entail liability for any and all consequences, however novel or extraordinary....There is room for argument that a distinction is to be drawn according to the diversity of interests invaded by the act, as where conduct negligent in that it threatens an insignificant invasion of an interest in property results in an unforseeable invasion of an interest of another order, as, e.g., one of bodily security. Perhaps other distinctions may be necessary. We do not go into the question now. The consequences to be followed must first be rooted in a wrong.

The judgment of the Appellate Division and that of the Trial Term should be reversed, and the complaint dismissed, with costs in all courts.

Dissent by: Andrews

Dissent: Andrews, J. (dissenting). Assisting a passenger to board a train, the defendant's servant negligently knocked a package from his arms. It fell between the platform and the cars. Of its contents the servant knew and could know nothing. A violent explosion followed. The concussion broke some scales standing a considerable distance away. In falling they injured the plaintiff, an intending passenger.

Upon these facts may she recover the damages she has suffered in an action brought against the master? The result we shall reach depends upon our theory as to the nature of negligence. Is it a relative concept—the breach of some duty owing to a particular person or to particular persons? Or where there is an act which unreasonably threatens the safety of others, is the doer liable for all its proximate consequences, even where they result in injury to one who would generally be thought to be outside the radius of danger? This is not a mere dispute as to words. We might not believe that to the average mind the dropping of the bundle would seem to involve the probability of harm to the plaintiff standing many feet away whatever might be the case as to the owner or to one so near as to be likely to be struck by its fall. If, however, we adopt the second hypothesis we have to inquire only as to the relation between cause and effect. We deal in terms of proximate cause, not of negligence.

Negligence may be defined roughly as an act or omission which unreasonably does or may affect the rights of others, or which unreasonably fails to protect oneself from the dangers resulting from such acts. Here I confine myself to the first branch of the definition. Nor do I comment on the word "unreasonable." For present purposes it sufficiently describes that average of conduct that society requires of its members.

There must be both the act or the omission, and the right. It is the act itself, not the intent of the actor, that is important.…In criminal law both the intent and the result are to be considered. Intent again is material in tort actions, where punitive damages are sought, dependent on actual malice—not on merely reckless conduct. But here neither insanity nor infancy lessens responsibility.…

As has been said, except in cases of contributory negligence, there must be rights which are or may be affected. Often though injury has occurred, no rights of him who suffers have been touched. A licensee or trespasser upon my land has no claim to affirmative care on my part that the land be made safe.…Where a railroad is required to fence its tracks against cattle, no man's rights are injured should he wander upon the road because such fence is absent.…An unborn child may not demand immunity from personal harm.…

But we are told that "there is no negligence unless there is in the particular case a legal duty to take care, and this duty must be one which is owed to the plaintiff himself and not merely to others" (Salmond Torts [6th ed.], 24). This, I think too narrow a conception. Where there is the unreasonable act, and some right that may be affected there is negligence whether damage does or does not result. That is immaterial. Should we drive down Broadway at a reckless speed, we are negligent whether we strike an approaching car or miss it by an inch. The act itself is wrongful. It is a wrong not only to those who happen to be within the radius of danger but to all who might have been there—a wrong to the public at large. Such is the language of the street. Such the language of the courts when speaking of contributory negligence. Such again and again their language in speaking of the duty of some defendant and discussing proximate cause in cases where such a discussion is wholly irrelevant on any other theory.…As was said by Mr. Justice Holmes many years ago, "the measure of the defendant's duty in determining whether a wrong

has been committed is one thing, the measure of liability when a wrong has been committed is another" (Spade v. Lynn & Boston R. R. Co., 172 Mass. 488). Due care is a duty imposed on each one of us to protect society from unnecessary danger, not to protect A, B, or C alone.

It may well be that there is no such thing as negligence in the abstract. "Proof of negligence in the air, so to speak, will not do." In an empty world negligence would not exist. It does involve a relationship between man and his fellows. But not merely a relationship between man and those whom he might reasonably expect his act would injure. Rather, a relationship between him and those whom he does in fact injure. If his act has a tendency to harm someone, it harms him a mile away as surely as it does those on the scene. We now permit children to recover for the negligent killing of the father. It was never prevented on the theory that no duty was owing to them. A husband may be compensated for the loss of his wife's services. To say that the wrongdoer was negligent as to the husband as well as to the wife is merely an attempt to fit facts to theory. An insurance company paying a fire loss recovers its payment of the negligent incendiary. We speak of subrogation—of suing in the right of the insured. Behind the cloud of words is the fact they hide, that the act, wrongful as to the insured, has also injured the company. Even if it be true that the fault of father, wife or insured will prevent recovery, it is because we consider the original negligence not the proximate cause of the injury.…

In the well-known Polemis Case…, Scrutton, L. J., said that the dropping of a plank was negligent for it might injure "workman or cargo or ship." Because of either possibility the owner of the vessel was to be made good for his loss. The act being wrongful the doer was liable for its proximate results. Criticized and explained as this statement may have been, I think it states the law as it should be and as it is.…

The proposition is this. Everyone owes to the world at large the duty of refraining from those acts that may unreasonably threaten the safety of others. Such an act occurs. Not only is he wronged to whom harm might reasonably be expected to result, but he also who is in fact injured, even if he be outside what would generally be thought the danger zone. There needs be duty due the one complaining but this is not a duty to a particular individual because as to him harm might be expected. Harm to someone being the natural result of the act, not only that one alone, but all those in fact injured may complain. We have never, I think, held otherwise. Indeed in the Di Caprio case we said that a breach of a general ordinance defining the degree of care to be exercised in one's calling is evidence of negligence as to everyone. We did not limit this statement to those who might be expected to be exposed to danger. Unreasonable risk being taken, its consequences are not confined to those who might probably be hurt.

If this be so, we do not have a plaintiff suing by "derivation or succession." Her action is original and primary. Her claim is for a breach of duty to herself—not that she is subrogated to any right of action of the owner of the parcel or of a passenger standing at the scene of the explosion.

The right to recover damages rests on additional considerations. The plaintiff's rights must be injured, and this injury must be caused by the negligence. We build a dam, but are negligent as to its foundations. Breaking, it injures property down stream. We are not liable if all this happened because of some reason other than the insecure foundation. But when injuries do result from our unlawful act we are liable for the consequences. It does not matter that they are unusual, unexpected, unforeseen and unforeseeable. But there is one limitation. The damages must be so connected with the negligence that the latter may be said to be the proximate cause of the former.

These two words have never been given an inclusive definition. What is a cause in a legal sense, still more what is a proximate cause, depend in each case upon many considerations, as does the existence of negligence itself. Any philosophical doctrine of causation does not help us. A boy throws a stone into a pond. The ripples spread. The water level rises. The history of that pond is altered to all eternity. It will be altered by other causes also. Yet it will be forever the resultant of all causes combined. Each one will have an influence. How great only omniscience can say. You may speak of a chain, or if you please, a net. An analogy is of little aid. Each cause brings about future events. Without each the future would not be the same. Each is proximate in the sense it is essential. But that is not what we mean by the word. Nor on the other

hand do we mean sole cause. There is no such thing.

Should analogy be thought helpful, however, I prefer that of a stream. The spring, starting on its journey, is joined by tributary after tributary. The river, reaching the ocean, comes from a hundred sources. No man may say whence any drop of water is derived. Yet for a time distinction may be possible. Into the clear creek, brown swamp water flows from the left. Later, from the right comes water stained by its clay bed. The three may remain for a space, sharply divided. But at last, inevitably no trace of separation remains. They are so commingled that all distinction is lost.

As we have said, we cannot trace the effect of an act to the end, if end there is. Again, however, we may trace it part of the way. A murder at Serajevo may be the necessary antecedent to an assassination in London twenty years hence. An overturned lantern may burn all Chicago. We may follow the fire from the shed to the last building. We rightly say the fire started by the lantern caused its destruction.

A cause, but not the proximate cause. What we do mean by the word "proximate" is, that because of convenience, of public policy, of a rough sense of justice, the law arbitrarily declines to trace a series of events beyond a certain point. This is not logic. It is practical politics. Take our rule as to fires. Sparks from my burning haystack set on fire my house and my neighbor's. I may recover from a negligent railroad. He may not. Yet the wrongful act as directly harmed the one as the other. We may regret that the line was drawn just where it was, but drawn somewhere it had to be. We said the act of the railroad was not the proximate cause of our neighbor's fire. Cause it surely was. The words we used were simply indicative of our notions of public policy. Other courts think differently. But somewhere they reach the point where they cannot say the stream comes from any one source.

Take the illustration given in an unpublished manuscript by a distinguished and helpful writer on the law of torts. A chauffeur negligently collides with another car which is filled with dynamite, although he could not know it. An explosion follows. A, walking on the sidewalk nearby, is killed. B, sitting in a window of a building opposite, is cut by flying glass. C, likewise sitting in a window a block away, is similarly injured. And a further illustration.

A nursemaid, ten blocks away, startled by the noise, involuntarily drops a baby from her arms to the walk. We are told that C may not recover while A may. As to B it is a question for court or jury. We will all agree that the baby might not. Because, we are again told, the chauffeur had no reason to believe his conduct involved any risk of injuring either C or the baby. As to them he was not negligent.

But the chauffeur, being negligent in risking the collision, his belief that the scope of the harm he might do would be limited is immaterial. His act unreasonably jeopardized the safety of anyone who might be affected by it. C's injury and that of the baby were directly traceable to the collision. Without that, the injury would not have happened. C had the right to sit in his office, secure from such dangers. The baby was entitled to use the sidewalk with reasonable safety.

The true theory is, it seems to me, that the injury to C, if in truth he is to be denied recovery, and the injury to the baby is that their several injuries were not the proximate result of the negligence. And here not what the chauffeur had reason to believe would be the result of his conduct, but what the prudent would foresee, may have a bearing. May have some bearing, for the problem of proximate cause is not to be solved by any one consideration.

It is all a question of expediency. There are no fixed rules to govern our judgment. There are simply matters of which we may take account. We have in a somewhat different connection spoken of "the stream of events." We have asked whether that stream was deflected—whether it was forced into new and unexpected channels.... This is rather rhetoric than law. There is in truth little to guide us other than common sense.

There are some hints that may help us. The proximate cause, involved as it may be with many other causes, must be, at the least, something without which the event would not happen. The court must ask itself whether there was a natural and continuous sequence between cause and effect. Was the one a substantial factor in producing the other? Was there a direct connection between them, without too many intervening causes? Is the effect of cause on result not too attenuated? Is the cause likely, in the usual judgment of mankind, to produce the result? Or by the exercise of prudent

foresight could the result be foreseen? Is the result too remote from the cause, and here we consider remoteness in time and space.... Clearly we must so consider, for the greater the distance either in time or space, the more surely do other causes intervene to affect the result. When a lantern is overturned the firing of a shed is a fairly direct consequence. Many things contribute to the spread of the conflagration—the force of the wind, the direction and width of streets, the character of intervening structures, other factors. We draw an uncertain and wavering line, but draw it we must as best we can.

Once again, it is all a question of fair judgment, always keeping in mind the fact that we endeavor to make a rule in each case that will be practical and in keeping with the general understanding of mankind.

Here another question must be answered. In the case supposed it is said, and said correctly, that the chauffeur is liable for the direct effect of the explosion although he had no reason to suppose it would follow a collision. "The fact that the injury occurred in a different manner than that which might have been expected does not prevent the chauffeur's negligence from being in law the cause of the injury." But the natural results of a negligent act—the results which a prudent man would or should foresee—do have a bearing upon the decision as to proximate cause. We have said so repeatedly. What should be foreseen? No human foresight would suggest that a collision itself might injure one a block away. On the contrary, given an explosion, such a possibility might be reasonably expected. I think the direct connection, the foresight of which the courts speak, assumes prevision of the explosion, for the immediate results of which, at least, the chauffeur is responsible.

It may be said this is unjust. Why? In fairness he should make good every injury flowing from his negligence. Not because of tenderness toward him we say he need not answer for all that follows his wrong. We look back to the catastrophe, the fire kindled by the spark, or the explosion. We trace the consequences—not indefinitely, but to a certain point. And to aid us in fixing that point we ask what might ordinarily be expected to follow the fire or the explosion.

This last suggestion is the factor which must determine the case before us. The act upon which defendant's liability rests is knocking an apparently harmless package onto the platform. The act was negligent. For its proximate consequences the defendant is liable. If its contents were broken, to the owner; if it fell upon and crushed a passenger's foot, then to him. If it exploded and injured one in the immediate vicinity, to him also as to A in the illustration. Mrs. Palsgraf was standing some distance away. How far cannot be told from the record— apparently twenty-five or thirty feet. Perhaps less. Except for the explosion, she would not have been injured. We are told by the appellant in his brief "it cannot be denied that the explosion was the direct cause of the plaintiff's injuries." So it was a substantial factor in producing the result—there was here a natural and continuous sequence—direct connection. The only intervening cause was that instead of blowing her to the ground the concussion smashed the weighing machine which in turn fell upon her. There was no remoteness in time,

little in space. And surely, given such an explosion as here it needed no great foresight to predict that the natural result would be to injure one on the platform at no greater distance from its scene than was the plaintiff. Just how no one might be able to predict. Whether by flying fragments, by broken glass, by wreckage of machines or structures no one could say. But injury in some form was most probable.

Under these circumstances I cannot say as a matter of law that the plaintiff's injuries were not the proximate result of the negligence. That is all we have before us. The court refused to so charge. No request was made to submit the matter to the jury as a question of fact, even would that have been proper upon the record before us.

The judgment appealed from should be affirmed, with costs.

LIABILITY: THE LEGAL REVOLUTION AND ITS CONSEQUENCES
Peter W. Huber

UNCOMMON LAW

It is one of the most ubiquitous taxes we pay, now levied on virtually everything we buy, sell, and use. The tax accounts for 30 percent of the price of a stepladder and over 95 percent of the price of childhood vaccines. It is responsible for one-quarter of the price of a ride on a Long Island tour bus and one-third of the price of a small airplane. It will soon cost large municipalities as much as they spend on fire or sanitation services.

Some call it a safety tax, but its exact relationship to safety is mysterious. It is paid on many items that are risky to use, like ski lifts and hedge trimmers, but it weighs even more heavily on other items whose whole purpose is to make life safer. It adds only a few cents to a pack of cigarettes, but it adds more to the price of a football helmet than the cost of making it. The tax falls especially hard on prescription drugs, doctors, surgeons, and all things

From Peter W. Huber, *Liability: The Legal Revolution and Its Consequences* (New York: Basic Books, Inc., 1990), 3–44. © 1990 Peter W. Huber. Reprinted by permission of Basic Books.

medical. Because of the tax, you cannot deliver a baby with medical assistance in Monroe County, Alabama. You cannot buy several contraceptives certified to be safe and effective by the Food and Drug Administration (FDA), even though available substitutes are more dangerous or less effective. If you have the stomach upset known as hyperemesis, you cannot buy the pill that is certified as safe and effective against it. The tax has orphaned various drugs that are invaluable for treating rare but serious diseases. It is assessed against every family that has a baby, in the amount of about $300 per birth, with an obstetrician in New York City paying $85,000 a year.

Because of the tax, you cannot use a sled in Denver city parks or a diving board in New York City schools. You cannot buy an American Motors "CJ" Jeep or a set of construction plans for novel airplanes from Burt Rutan, the pioneering designer of the *Voyager*. You can no longer buy many American-made brands of sporting goods, especially equipment for amateur contact sports such as hockey and lacrosse. For a while, you could not use public transportation in the city of St. Joseph, Missouri, nor could you go to jail in Lafayette County in the same state. Miami canceled plans for an experimental railbus because of the tax. The tax has curtailed Little League and fireworks displays, evening concerts, sailboard races, and the use of public beaches and ice-skating rinks. It temporarily shut down the famed Cyclone at the Astroland amusement park on Coney Island.

The tax directly costs American individuals, businesses, municipalities, and other government bodies at least $80 billion a year, a figure that equals the total profits of the country's top 200 corporations. But many of the tax's costs are indirect and unmeasurable, reflected only in the tremendous effort, inconvenience, and sacrifice Americans now go through to avoid its collection. The extent of these indirect costs can only be guessed at. One study concluded that doctors spend $3.50 in efforts to avoid additional charges for each $1 of direct tax they pay. If similar multipliers operate in other areas, the tax's hidden impact on the way we live and do business may amount to a $300 billion dollar annual levy on the American economy.

The tax goes by the name of *tort liability*. It is collected and disbursed through litigation. The courts alone decide just who will pay, how much, and on what timetable. Unlike better-known taxes, this one was never put to a legislature or a public referendum, debated at any length in the usual public arenas, or approved by the president or by any state governor. And although the tax ostensibly is collected for the public benefit, lawyers and other middlemen pocket more than half the take.

The tort tax is a recent invention. Tort law has existed here and abroad for centuries, of course. But until quite recently it was a backwater of the legal system, of little importance in the wider scheme of things. For all practical purposes, the omnipresent tort tax we pay today was conceived in the 1950s and set in place in the 1960s and 1970s by a new generation of lawyers and judges. In the space of twenty years they transformed the legal landscape, proclaiming sweeping new rights to sue. Some grew famous and more grew rich selling their services to enforce the rights that they themselves invented. But the revolution they made could never have taken place had it not had a component of idealism as well. Tort law, it is widely and passionately believed, is a public-spirited undertaking designed for the protection of the ordinary con-

sumer and worker, the hapless accident victim, the "little guy." Tort law as we know it is a peculiarly American institution. No other country in the world administers anything remotely like it.

From Consent to Coercion

Tort law is the law of accidents and personal injury. The example that usually comes to mind is a two-car collision at an intersection. The drivers are utter strangers. They have no advance understanding between them as to how they should drive, except perhaps an implicit agreement to follow the rules of the road. Nor do they have any advance arrangement specifying who will pay for the damage. Human nature being what it is, the two sides often have different views on both these interesting questions. Somebody else has to step in to work out rights and responsibilities. This has traditionally been a job for the courts. They resolve these cases under the law of *torts* or civil wrongs.

But the car accident between strangers is comparatively rare in the larger universe of accidents and injuries. Just as most intentional assaults involve assailants and victims who already know each other well, most unintended injuries occur in the context of commercial acquaintance—at work, on the hospital operating table, following the purchase of an airplane ticket or a home appliance. And while homicide is seldom a subject of advance understanding between victim and assailant, unintentional accidents often are. More often than not, both parties to a transaction recognize there is some chance of misadventure, and prudently take steps to address it beforehand.

Until quite recently, the law permitted and indeed promoted advance agreement of that character. It searched for understandings between the parties and respected them where found. Most accidents were handled under the broad heading of *contract*—the realm of human cooperation—and comparatively few relegated to the dismal annex of tort, the realm of unchosen relationship and collision. The old law treated contract and tort cases under entirely different rules, which reflected this fairly intuitive line between choice and coercion.

Then, in the 1950s and after, a visionary group of legal theorists came along. Their leaders were thoughtful, well-intentioned legal academics at some of the most prestigious law schools, and judges on the most respected state benches. They were the likes of the late William Prosser, who taught law at Hastings College, John Wade, Professor of Law at Vanderbilt University, and California Supreme Court Justice Roger Traynor. They are hardly household names, but considering the impact they had on American life they should be. Their ideas, eloquence, and persistence changed the common law as profoundly as it had ever been changed before. For short, and in the absence of a better term, we will refer to them as the founders of modern tort law, or just the *Founders*. If the name is light-hearted, their accomplishments were anything but.

The Founders were to be followed a decade or two later by a much more sophisticated group of legal economists, most notably Guido Calabresi, now Dean of the Yale Law School, and Richard Posner of the University of Chicago Law School and now a federal judge on the Seventh Circuit Court of Appeals. There were many others, for economists seem to be almost as numerous as lawyers, and the application of economic theory to tort law has enjoyed mounting popularity in recent years as tort law has itself become an industry. An economist, it has been said, is someone who observes what is happening in practice and goes off to study whether it is possible in theory. The new tort economists were entirely true to that great tradition. Indeed, they carried it a step forward, concluding that the legal revolution that had already occurred was not only possible but justified and necessary. Mustering all the dense prose, arcane jargon, and elaborate methodology that only the very best academic economists muster, they set about proving on paper that the whole new tort structure was an efficient and inevitable reaction to failures in the marketplace. Arriving on the scene of the great tort battle late in the day, they courageously congratulated the victors, shot the wounded, and pronounced the day's outcome satisfactory and good.

Like all revolutionaries, the Founders and their followers, in the economics profession and elsewhere, had their own reasons for believing and behaving as they did. Most consumers, they assumed, pay little attention to accident risks before the fact. Ignoring or underestimating risk as they do, consumers fail to demand, and producers fail to supply, as much safety as would be best. As a result, manufacturers, doctors, employers, municipalities, and other producers get away with undue carelessness, and costly accidents are all too frequent. To make matters worse, consumers buy less accident insurance than they really need, so injuries lead to unneeded misery and privation and some victims become public charges.

With these assumptions as their starting point, the new tort theorists concluded that the overriding question that the old law asked—how did the parties agree to allocate the costs of the accident?—was irrelevant or worse. The real question to ask was: How can society best allocate the cost of accidents to minimize those costs (and the cost of guarding against them), and to provide potential victims with the accident insurance that not all of them currently buy or can afford? The answer, by and large, was to make producers of goods and services pay the costs of accidents. A broad rule to this effect, it was argued, can accomplish both objectives. It forces providers to be careful. It also forces consumers to take accident costs into account, not consciously but by paying a safety-adjusted price for everything they buy or do. And it compels the improvident to buy accident insurance, again not directly but through the safety tax. It has a moral dimension too: People should be required to take care before the accident and to help each other afterward, for no other reason than that it is just, right, and proper to insist that they do so.

The expansive new accident tax is firmly in place today. In a remarkably short time, the Founders completely recast a centuries-old body of law in an entirely new mold of their own design. They started sketching out their intentions only in the late 1950s; within two short decades they had achieved virtually every legal change that they originally planned. There were setbacks along the way, of course; the common law always develops in fits and starts, with some states bolder and others more timid, and the transformation of tort law was no exception. But compared with the cautious incrementalism with which the common law had changed in centuries past, an utter transformation over a twenty-year span can fairly be described as a revolution, and a violent one at that.

The revolution began and ended with a wholesale repudiation of the law of contract. Until well into the 1960s, it was up to each buyer to decide how safe a car he or she wanted to buy. Then as now, the major choices were fairly obvious: large, heavy cars are both safer and more expensive; economy cars save money but at some cost in safety. In case after case today, however, the courts struggle to enforce a general mandate that all cars be *crashworthy*. That term is perfectly fluid; it is defined after the accident by jury pronouncements; it is defined without reference to preferences and choices deliberately expressed by buyer and seller before the transaction. A woman's choice of contraceptives was once a matter largely under the control of the woman herself and her doctor, with the FDA in the background to certify the general safety and efficacy of particular drugs or devices. Today tort law has shifted that authority too from the doctor's office to the courtroom. Balancing the risks and benefits of childhood vaccination was once a concern of parents, pediatricians, the FDA, and state health authorities. But here again, the views of the courts have become the driving force in determining what may be bought and sold. Not long ago, workplace safety was something to be decided between employer and employees, often through collective bargaining, perhaps with oversight from federal and state regulators, while compensation for accidents was determined by state workers' compensation laws. Today the courts supervise a free-for-all of litigation that pits employees against both employers and the outside suppliers of materials and equipment, the latter two against each other, and both against their insurers.

What brought us this liability tax, in short, was a wholesale shift from consent to coercion in the law of accidents. Yesterday we relied primarily on agreement before the fact to settle responsibility for most accidents. Today we emphasize litigation after the fact. Yesterday we deferred to private choice. Today it is only public choice that counts, more specifically the public choices of judges and juries. For all practical purposes, contracts are dead, at least insofar as they attempt to allocate responsibility for accidents ahead of time. Safety obligations are now decided through liability prescription, worked out case by case after the accident. The center of the accident insurance world has likewise shifted, from *first-party* insurance chosen by the expected beneficiary, to *third-party* coverage driven by legal compulsion.

Paralleling this shift from consent to coercion has been a shift from individual to group responsibility. The old contract-centered law placed enormous confidence in individuals to manage the risks of their personal environments. The new, tort-

dominated jurisprudence prefers universal rules with no opt-out provisions. Tort law now defines acceptable safety in lawn mower design, vaccine manufacture, heart surgery, and ski slope grooming, without regard to the preferences of any individual consumer or provider. If the courts declare there is to be a safety tax on a vaccine at such and such a level, the tax will surely be paid, whatever other arrangements the buyer or user of the vaccine or the FDA, let alone the manufacturer, may prefer or can afford. In a similar spirit, the old law relied on the political branches of government to make those safety choices that only a community as a whole can responsibly oversee. The new again prefers control through the instrument of the lawsuit. Safety standards have been entirely socialized, but in a peculiar sort of way that freezes out not only private choice but also public prescription through all government authority other than the courts. The new accident insurance is likewise furnished on a universal and standardized plan, whether or not one or another of us might prefer a different set of policy terms or a different insurance carrier....

Backfire

If you pay a steep, unsettling, and broad-based tax, you expect something in return. The Founders promised the world that their tax would bring measurable progress toward two deeply held social goals: protecting life and limb, and helping the injured when accidents do happen nevertheless. How well has the tort tax achieved these goals? The record is a mountain of pretentious failure.

High taxes drive up some prices, and the new tort system has certainly done that. Taxes drive other things off the market altogether, and that too has happened. The immediate impact of the new legal rules has been a marked increase in price and a decline in the availability of a wide range of goods and services. That much was expected, indeed welcomed, by the Founders. Hazardous goods should cost more, they felt, to reflect the risk; too-hazardous goods should not be sold at all.

What was unexpected was the propensity of the tort tax to fall where it is least needed and most difficult to bear. Contrary to all original expectations, the first major casualties of the new legal regime have been many of the methods by which society pursues safety itself. Hospital emergency-room services are perilous in liability terms because emergency-room patients are in trouble to begin with. Vaccines are hazardous (again, from the legal perspective) because the children who receive them are susceptible to a host of diseases and reactions often indistinguishable from vaccine side effects. Running a municipal police department, ambulance service, town dump, or waste cleanup service invites litigation because these activities are aimed at situations that are risky from the beginning. Selling an antimiscarriage drug, contraceptive, abortion, or obstetrical service is legally dangerous because pregnancy itself is risky for both mother and child. And modern tort law has written an altogether new conclusion to the parable of the Good Samaritan, making it unwise to stop at the roadside accident without first checking in with your local insurance agent and lawyer. In its search for witches, the modern tort system has undoubtedly found a few and reduced them to ashes. But too many wonder drugs have also been gathered into the flames.

How could a tort system so committed to increasing safety have landed some of its first punches on the very persons who work on the front line of helping others? Why does it so often fail to distinguish risks that are part of the problem from risks that are part of the solution? The answers are complex. For one thing, juries have often (and quite understandably) proved unskilled at distinguishing the various parties found at the scene of the crime. They are too prone to arrest the firefighter along with the arsonist, the ambulance driver along with the drunk who made the ambulance necessary in the first place. Another part of the reason lies in a slip between theoretical cup and real-world lip. The Founders were committed to deterring hazardous practices. But judges and juries were, for the most part, committed to running a generous sort of charity. If the new tort system cannot find a careless defendant after an accident, it will often settle for a merely wealthy one. But the wealthy defendant is more often part of the safety solution than the safety problem.

The larger fallacy in the Founders' grand scheme was the idea that the most attractive defendants would stick around to be sued, in case after case, after it became clear what was happening. As our right to sue the butcher, brewer, and baker after the sale has grown, our freedom to make the purchase in the first place has declined. The purveyors

of meat, beer, and such withdraw only partially, by demanding a higher price; the purveyors of rare drugs, Yellowstone hiking, and rural obstetrical services have often been driven from the market altogether. An unbounded and impossible-to-waive right to sue necessarily overtakes and destroys the right to make deals with people who place a high premium on staying in business and out of court. While the consumer has indeed acquired a new and sometimes valuable right to sue, he has done so only by surrendering an older right, the right to contract, which in the long run is worth far more.

What about the aim of providing more and better insurance against accidents? It has fared no better than the goal of improving safety, and for much the same reason. How much insurance we get depends not only on how much we want to buy but on how much others are willing to sell. The Founders sought to increase the demand for liability insurance, and they undoubtedly did just that. But at the same time they decimated the supply. The net effect was less insurance all around.

The key to providing private insurance is to seek out reasonably narrow, well-defined risk groups, whose membership can be precisely described and whose future claims can be predicted with some accuracy. If an insurer cannot distinguish the young Corvette enthusiast from the middle-aged driver of a weekend Oldsmobile, high-risk drivers will stock up on bargain coverage while low-risk drivers will cut back, and the insurer will eventually have to charge everyone something approaching a Corvette rate. Less insurance will be sold as a result. Every major change in legal rules implemented by the Founders aggravated problems of exactly this kind, by requiring a looser definition of risk and responsibility, which led to higher rates, which led to lower coverage.

As it became less and less clear whose policy would have to pay for whose injury, liability insurance became scarce. In more than a few markets it disappeared altogether. For day care centers, orthopedists, neurosurgeons, and countless others, insurance became wholly unavailable at any price. Some insured activities were discontinued, which turned the shortage of insurance into a shortage of goods and services. Some among the bolder liability targets chose to go bare, deliberately undercapitalizing and underinsuring their operations, and then daring the tort system to do its worst. Many others wound up doing what amounted to the same thing on a more modest scale, still carrying some insurance but far less than they needed or wanted. The liability insurance crisis has hit the smallest enterprises the hardest. While larger players always survive the assault one way or another, the smaller ones often cannot. The system does succeed in paying some of the people some of the time, and on occasion paying them handsomely. But though munificent for a very few, it has been profoundly destabilizing for many more. The financial security of most people, most of the time, has declined.

In both its safety and its insurance effects, the new tort system is highly regressive; those who have the least to begin with are hurt the most. The affluent woman in this country today goes abroad for the IUD, once-a-month pill, or for the exotic eye drug driven off the U.S. market by liability too heavy to be borne; the poor woman stays at home and does without. The highly skilled worker need not be concerned when employers retrench their hiring because of liability concerns; the borderline worker has everything to lose. The well-to-do escape contagious disease entirely or survive with expert medical care; those who live in crowded squalor are far more likely to succumb to an unchecked epidemic that only aggressive distribution of vaccines or medicines could halt. The city dweller continues to enjoy ready access to specialty medical services; her less fortunate country cousin travels great distances or does without.

The insurance picture is more regressive still. The mandatory accident insurance required by modern tort law is funded by an excise tax on goods and services, but its benefits, such as they are, are strongly linked to income and social status. The car—and the implicit insurance contract that must go along with it—is sold at one price, whether the buyer is the president of the First National Bank or its janitor. Yet when disabled in a crash, the president can expect to receive a far higher award than the janitor for loss of future wages. The deal may be a good one for the president (though she undoubtedly has obtained comprehensive direct insurance elsewhere); for the janitor it is a cruel fraud. We would find it unthinkable to require all citizens to pay the same rate for a type of life insurance that gave far higher benefits to affluent beneficiaries. Nor would we charge the same fire insurance premium for a

bungalow in Watts as for a mansion in Beverly Hills. Yet that is precisely how modern tort law operates. A more regressive scheme of social welfare could hardly be imagined.

Although the legal revolution has assumed the mantle of public interest, it has paradoxically put a damper on communal enterprise as well. Many things that can only be accomplished collectively are no longer even attempted, because the private right to sue has eclipsed the public power to act and serve. Sometimes the consequences are comparatively minor, as when public transportation is curtailed or a public beach shut down. Sometimes they are grave, as when a mass vaccination initiative is delayed or abandoned altogether. And again the worse-off are hit harder. The wealthy community always finds a way to ship its smokestack factories and wastes elsewhere; the poor one, when prevented by the courts from reaching an understanding with its own citizens, must entirely surrender the communal benefits that such activities make possible.

Across the board, modern tort law weighs heavily on the spirit of innovation and enterprise. The Founders confidently expected that their reforms would provide a constant spur to innovate. The actual effect has been quite the opposite. The old tort rules focused on the human actors, inquiring whether the technologist was careful, prudently trained, and properly supervised. The new rules place technology itself in the liability dock. But jurors, who generally can reach sensible judgments about people, perform much less well when they sit in judgment on technology.

Under jury pressure, the new touchstones of technological legitimacy have become age, familiarity, and ubiquity. It is the innovative and unfamiliar that is most likely to be condemned. One feature after another of the new system presses in the same direction. Consider the gilt-edged safety warnings that the new tort rules demand. Honing a warning to a fine point of perfection requires years of market and litigation experience, which means that established products now do comparatively well in tort suits based on warnings, while innovative challengers are vulnerable. The new rules also force providers to sell not only a product or service but also an accident insurance contract with it. But the availability of reasonably priced insurance depends on the accumulation of actuarial experience—

something that all established technologies have but no truly innovative one ever does.

As a result of these and other similar forces, it is far safer, in liability terms, to sell an old, outdated oral contraceptive than a new IUD or sponge. It is more prudent, at least from the legal perspective, to stick with the tried-and-true technologies for car frame design, or aircraft engines, or vaccine formulation than to experiment boldly with something new. Does a pesticide manufacturer wish to steer clear of the courts? Any lawyer knows that the best legal bet is an old, familiar chemical, which has been used for years by every farmer in the community, rather than the latest exotic breakthrough in genetic engineering. Is the electric power company seeking at all costs to avoid liability? It will find coal to be the safest possible fuel in those terms, and uranium the most dangerous, though the ranking of actual risks may be the reverse.

The result is to ingrain a bias against innovation at all levels of the economy—for which we pay a heavy price, not just in money and in our nation's competitive position in the world, but in safety once again. The lay mind is accustomed to equate familiarity with safety, but newer, more often than not, is in fact safer than older. Life expectancy in this country has increased at the astonishing rate of three months per year throughout the twentieth century, not because of the proliferation of litigation but because of the constant press of technological innovation—innovation that is now being slowed and sometimes even reversed by the ongoing legal assault....

As we have seen, tort law had been around for ages—even longer than the law of contracts. The very earliest tort law in medieval England provided remedies for intentional wrongdoing—the barroom assault and things of that sort. And if a landowner, clearing his land with all due care, felled a tree trunk that struck a passerby on the adjacent highway, he would have to pay at least nominal damages, even if there had been no actual injury. The insult the passerby suffered in being hit was harm enough. Indirect injuries more remote in time or place were treated less strictly. If another passerby stumbled over the errant log soon after it fell, he could win damages only if he suffered real injury and also showed that the landowner was negligent or had intended to cause harm. And if a passerby *bought* the log from the landowner and managed to hurt himself with it

later, tort law was out of the picture entirely; all that counted then was the contract.

The ancients, in short, had fairly modest and limited notions about liability from the beginning. As industrial accidents became more common in the nineteenth century, the courts introduced a new principle of tort that was still more restrictive: Neither direct nor indirect injuries would give rise to liability unless there had been *fault* in some sense of that word. And what was fault? Malicious intent counted, of course. But otherwise, the person seeking recovery would have to prove *negligence*.

Endless pages have since been written about just what the fuzzy concept of negligence means. It is commonly defined with reference to terms that are no more exact, such as ordinary prudence. In 1888, for example, ten-year-old Carl Brown went to play in a railroad yard with his friends. He climbed on a car containing coal and was standing on it with his feet on the drawhead, holding on to the brake wheel, between two stationary cars, when a switch engine kicked several cars against the two stationary cars, catching his foot and crushing it. The railroad had given no signal that the cars were approaching, even though a municipal ordinance expressly required that locomotives ring their bells when moving within city limits. Young Carl sued the railroad, charging negligence. The court agreed. "[I]t becomes the duty of the railway company to use such care to avoid injury to such person as a man of ordinary prudence would have used under like circumstances." "Ordinarily prudent" railroads comply with municipal ordinances.

In the end the layperson's understanding of negligence is as good as the lawyer's, and is all that counts in the jury room anyway. A jury scrutinizes the defendant's character, reconstructs her conduct leading up to the accident, and asks if an ordinarily prudent person standing in her shoes would have avoided the accident by exercising greater care. Did the railway give its employees proper training and supervision? Did the obstetrician take normal, reasonable precautions in helping deliver the baby? Did the maker of a vaccine exercise all the care of an ordinarily prudent manufacturer in that line of business? If so, there was no legal case, no matter how gruesome the injuries that materialized anyway. If not, the defendant was negligent, even if he acted from the purest and kindest of motives. Good faith did not ward off liability. But good care did.

Negligence standards were extended to product manufacturers in the early decades of this century, at least for injuries not covered by any contract. The key opinion was written in 1916 by the great Benjamin Cardozo, then a judge on New York's highest court. Donald MacPherson bought a Model 10 runabout from Close Brothers, a Buick dealer in Schenectady, New York. On July 25, 1911, MacPherson's car was found wrapped around a telephone pole near Saratoga Springs. MacPherson himself was discovered "under the hind axle of the machine," and he was released "with some difficulty." The accident had apparently been caused by the collapse of all twelve wooden spokes on one of the car's wheels. MacPherson had dealt entirely with the independent dealer, but he sued Buick anyway. There was, of course, no contract in the picture, since the two parties had never dealt with each other directly. But Cardozo declared Buick negligent in failing to inspect the car's wheels. "If the nature of a thing is such that it is reasonably certain to place life and limb in peril when negligently made," Cardozo declared, it is a "thing of danger." Irrespective of contract, "the manufacturer of this thing of danger is under a duty to make it carefully."

The *MacPherson* decision injected a bit of tort law at the edges of the marketplace for goods and services. But throughout the mid-1950s, hazardous product or no, the manufacturer would lose only if a person ultimately injured by his product could show negligence or worse. And protection for the immediate buyer of the product, if there was to be any at all, came from her contract, not some independent theory of tort liability.

The negligence standard was frugal. Accidents are vastly more common than accidents caused by negligence. Ordinary prudence, which is what negligence law demands, is what ordinary people ordinarily exercise. The butcher, baker, and fluorescent-bulb maker generally *are* prudent by this standard, as are the majority of surgeons, automotive designers, architects, and others who stand in the foreground or background of life's calamities. In addition, under the old negligence standard courts scrutinized conduct on both sides of the lawsuit. A person who came willingly to a risky situation, such as a fenced-off construction project, assumed the risk of his activities and couldn't blame someone else later for his accident. Nor could an injured

party collect if he himself had been negligent in any contributing way.

The system, in short, dealt with most accidents by refusing to deal with them outside the terms of advance private agreement. Oliver Wendell Holmes summarized the philosophy in his 1881 classic, *The Common Law*. "Unless my act is of a nature to threaten others, unless under the circumstances a prudent man would have foreseen the possibility of harm, it is no more justifiable to make me indemnify my neighbor against the consequences, than to make me do the same thing if I had fallen upon him in a fit, or to compel me to insure him against lightning.... The state might conceivably make itself a mutual insurance company against accidents, and distribute the burden of its citizens' mishaps among all its members." But the courts of the time would not.

This, by and large, was still the prevailing tort law when contracts were suddenly dismantled and discarded eighty years later.

Strict Liability

The old negligence rules had always been open to the reproach of stinginess. With the death of contract, they now promised to be hopelessly cumbersome as well. The prospect of running an ever-growing number of cases through a full postaccident inquest on how all the players had performed was discouraging; the sheer task threatened to overwhelm the courts, and the outcome would too often be compensation deferred or denied altogether. This was most vexing. The Founders had labored hard to cross the high mountains of contractual language, only to find that the valley of tort below was not exactly flowing with milk and honey.

As we saw earlier, their initial response was to rely on the contractual material already at hand, using it to spin out liability through the implied warranty. If the Mammoth Corporation had somehow *promised* to pay for any and all accidents involving its product, everything else was simple. No one had to worry about whether there had been negligence; somewhere or other down there between the lines the contract itself promised payment. The content was novel, but the forms were reassuringly familiar.

For a while, then, the reinterpretation of contract terms sufficed as a basis for inventing liability standards much stricter than negligence. And a while was all the Founders really needed. Most people are eager to believe good news, even when it is too good to be true. The public and press didn't at all mind the idea that manufacturers had suddenly begun promising (tacitly, mind you) to pay for accidents resulting from all defects in their products, regardless of negligence. Within a few years, this legal notion of "strict" producer liability had become familiar and obvious. At that point, several state courts were ready to discard the roundabout legal fictions and take a more direct route to the same result. In 1962, the California Supreme Court led the way.

For Christmas in 1955, William Greenman's wife had bought her husband a Shopsmith, a new power tool that served as a combination saw, drill, and wood lathe. Greenman was making a wooden chalice on his Shopsmith one day when a piece of wood flew out of the machine and struck him on the forehead. He sued the manufacturer, maintaining that "inadequate[ly] set screws were used to hold parts of the machine together so that normal vibrations caused the tailstock of the lathe to move away from the piece of wood being turned, permitting it to fly out of the lathe." No contract claim was possible: Greenman was not the actual buyer of the lathe, and he had failed, in any event, to comply with California contract rules that require timely notice of a pending claim. By 1962, however, when the case reached it, the California Supreme Court was already growing tired of contracts and all their troublesome formalities and rules. It contemptuously brushed aside the notice requirement as a "booby trap for the unwary." Strict liability, the court bluntly declared, would no longer be rationalized in terms of implied warranties, fictional contracts, or anything of that sort. Product manufacturers would instead be held "strictly liable" to consumers for accidents caused by a "defect in manufacture" of their product.

This was a great leap. The need to find implied warranties and such had been a bothersome and often embarrassing barrier to contractual theories of liability. The need to find negligence had been an equally troublesome barrier to tort theories of liability. Now, at one bound, the courts could leap directly to the desired goal, at least so long as a product defect was at issue.

But there was important work still to be done. Though somewhat obscure on the point, *Greenman* seemed to cover *manufacturing defects,* which are in fact quite rare. *Design defects,* however, were quite another matter, and had not yet been officially incorporated into the new doctrine. So Barbara Evans learned in 1966. Driving her station wagon across an intersection one day, Barbara's husband was broadsided by another car and killed. The 1961 Chevrolet had an X-shaped frame; at the time, other manufacturers still used a box frame. Barbara sued General Motors, claiming misdesign. Her suit was quickly dismissed. "Perhaps it would be desirable to require manufacturers to construct automobiles in which it would be safe to collide," the court of appeals declared, "but that would be a legislative function, not an aspect of the judicial interpretation of existing law." Errors in manufacture were one thing. But in 1966 the courts were not yet ready to examine product design and declare it defective.

Greenman, however, had its own inexorable logic. If General Motors can be held liable for leaving a frame strut loose accidentally, why shouldn't it be liable for leaving it out deliberately? By mid-decade the design defect barrier was beginning to crumble.

David Larsen broke through this last major conceptual wall in 1968, just two years after Barbara Evans lost her case. His 1963 Chevrolet Corvair collided head on with another car, thrusting the steering column into his head. He sued General Motors, complaining that "the design and placement of the solid steering shaft, which extends without interruption from a point 2.7 inches in front of the leading surface of the front tires to a position directly in front of the driver, exposes the driver to an unreasonable risk of injury from the rearward displacement of that shaft in the event of a left-of-center head-on collision." This time, a federal appeals court was ready to move ahead. Thereafter, the court announced, juries would be free to pin liability on defects in design as well as manufacture.

Like so many other changes in the tort rules, the step from manufacturing defects to design defects was presented as the soul of modesty. But with that simple change the courts plunged into a new and daunting enterprise. To begin with, the stakes in design defect cases are much higher. A manufacturing-defect verdict condemns only a single item coming off the assembly line. But a defect of design condemns the entire production, and a loss in one case almost inevitably implies losses in many others. Moreover, design is a much more subtle business than manufacture, and identifying deficiencies is vastly more difficult.

Before long, juries across the country were busy redesigning lawn mowers, electrical switches, glass and plastic bottles, pesticides, and consumer and industrial products of every other description. A product can be defectively designed because a safety device has been omitted (e.g., a paydozer without rearview mirrors) or because certain parts are not as strong as they might have been (e.g., a car roof is not strong enough to withstand a rollover, or the impact of a runaway horse that lands on the roof after a front-end collision). A jury can find that a single-control shower faucet is defective because if one turns it on all the way to one side, it will allow only hot water to spray, or that children's cotton sleepwear is defective because it has no flame-retardant chemicals added. Sears lost a $1.2 million judgment to a man who suffered a heart attack caused (he alleged) by a lawn mower rope that was too hard to pull. The Bolko Athletic Company paid $92,500 for defectively designing the second base on a baseball diamond; a concrete anchor, the jury concluded, was unsafe for amateur-league players. Recent cases have attempted to extend strict liability (at least for the condition rather than the design of a product) to persons who sell used goods, even ordinary citizens selling cars through the classified ads, though so far most courts have declined to take this seemingly logical step.

Drugs and pharmaceutical devices were among the last products to be swept up in design defect litigation. Until well into the 1970s, most courts accepted that potent drugs often have unavoidable side effects, and they declined to repeat the difficult balancing of risks and benefits already conducted by the FDA. But this line was crossed in the end as well. Courts began to find design defects in contraceptive pills (one brand contained more hormone than another, making it both more effective and riskier), vaccines (the live but weakened polio virus is both more effective and more dangerous than the killed virus), morning sickness drugs, and intrauterine devices.

Blaming the Product, Not the People

The courts thus slipped gently from telling people how to behave to redesigning cars, tractors, drugs, and second bases. The single-minded new search for product defects left no room for inquiry into the human element of accidents. Larsen, injured in a car manufactured by General Motors, did not have to prove that the company employees had been negligent in their work; he only had to persuade a jury that the car itself ended up defective for whatever reason. But if the car maker's negligence or good care didn't matter, why should the driver's? Symmetry seemed to suggest that it shouldn't, so the once broad defense of "contributory negligence" was abandoned too.

A driver pushed his Mercury Cougar to more than 100 miles per hour and was killed when one of its Goodyear tires exploded. The tires were designed for a maximum safe speed of 85 miles per hour, but Goodyear and Ford were held liable nonetheless; the product was defective in failing to protect against foreseeable consumer negligence of this sort. A Pennsylvania farmer ordered a skid loader but specifically asked the International Harvester Company to remove a standard protection cage around the driver's seat so that the loader could pass through his low barn doors. Harvester honored the request; the operator was later crushed in an accident that the standard-issue cage would have prevented. A court ruled the loader defective as delivered. The preferences, foolishness, or wickedness of third parties no longer counted for much either. An unknown psychopath deliberately placed cyanide in a bottle of Tylenol capsules; the subsequent suits turned only on whether the bottle was defective in failing to protect against the peril. A labor dispute inspired some arsonists to firebomb a Puerto Rico hotel, killing a hundred guests; the subsequent suits focused on the alleged defectiveness of the building's design and materials in succumbing to this kind of attack.

Where once it had inquired into the frailties of the people who manufactured, used, or abused a product, the law now focused relentlessly on the product alone. The legal inquiries began to take on the color of an inquisition, with the product as the lonely heretic. A car, contraceptive, or lawn mower was either correctly and safely designed or it was unreasonably dangerous and defective. A plaintiff no longer had to contend with the natural ebb and flow of jury sympathy between two human parties. She merely had to impugn a product. And in weighing the case against the product, the original contract between seller and buyer could not, of course, count at all.

Both Weapon and Tool

In his whimsical poem "The Objection to Being Stepped On," Robert Frost recounts how he accidentally "stepped on the toe of an unemployed hoe," whereupon the implement "rose in offense" and struck Frost a blow "in the seat of [his] sense." Yes, there was once a prophecy that weapons would one day be beaten into tools. "But what do we see? The first tool I step on / Turns into a weap-on."

There is a great insight here. The line between tools and weapons is exceedingly fine. Knives cut, irons scorch, dynamite blasts, poison kills. In the wrong hands or under the wrong foot, the tamest and most domestic object quickly becomes an instrument of assault and battery.

Wherever possible, the old tort law had left it up to each individual to distinguish between weapons and tools in her own private universe. If someone wanted to buy a fast horse, lightweight canoe, sharp knife, or strong medicine, that was her business and her risk, or, more precisely, it was a risk that she and her seller could allocate between themselves as they chose. But new tort theorists had clearly declared that it was for the courts to draw the line between tools and weapons, and to draw it without reference to anything but the implement itself.

Just how does one go about locating a defect in a complex product? Sometimes the job is easy. Defects in manufacture are immediately apparent when we compare the car without a critical bolt in the steering column to hundreds of others that came off the same assembly line with it. In effect, the mass manufacturer establishes his own standards, by which any one of his products can be gauged. Manufacturing-defect cases are straightforward. They are also comparatively rare. Far more difficult are cases in which the product is said to be defective in design, where there is no such simple point of comparison. Fully 80 percent of product liability cases today are of this kind.

The search for design defects often requires a jury to compare real with hypothetical products. What is a jury to do, for example, when a lawyer for

a sick child claims that a whooping cough vaccine was defective in that it was based on a whole virus rather than a virus extract? The whole-virus vaccine is the only one sold in this country. An alternative formulation has indeed been tested in Japan, but the FDA does not approve its use here.

And how is a jury to decide whether a whole class of products—say, the intrauterine device (IUD) contraceptive—is inherently defective? The new tort system has apparently reached that conclusion, having driven from the market not only the notorious Dalkon Shield, but also its far safer substitutes, the Copper-7 and the Lippes Loop IUDs. The FDA, Planned Parenthood, and the vast majority of doctors do not endorse that sweeping verdict, but the verdict stands, nonetheless.

It is not enough to identify a safety shortcoming; the jury must also weigh the cost of remedying it. In the early 1970s, the Ford Pinto was to car crashworthiness cases what the Dalkon Shield later became to contraceptive designs. The Pinto weighed under 2,000 pounds and cost less than $2,000. Ford's own tests revealed that its gas tank was vulnerable to rear-end collisions, but the company decided not to spend an extra $10 per car to reinforce the structure—a calculation on which plaintiffs' lawyers subsequently grew very rich. But did they really deserve to? Ten dollars is not much, but full-force rear-end collisions aren't common either, and there are innumerable equally rare hazards that could also be averted for $10 or thereabouts. Protecting against every one of them would cost thousands. But people with thousands to spare don't buy a Pinto in the first place, they buy a Mercedes. What about other cars in Pinto's class? Some certainly had safer gas tanks, but that is not to say they were safer cars. A jury later fined Honda $5 million for its "reckless" act of using lighter-gauge materials than some other manufacturers in a 1971-model vehicle. (The driver of that car admitted he had bought it for its economy.) Toyota lost a $3 million judgment on similar grounds. The subtle message here may be that *all* economy cars are inherently defective for tort purposes. But millions of consumers, all major car companies, and NHTSA, the federal agency that regulates car safety, seem to view the matter quite differently.

With lawn mowers, kitchen appliances, airplanes, and safety valves, the conclusion is almost always the same: Safety is no exception to the golden rule that buyers can pay more and get more. Design is an infinitely variable and subtle process. It is always possible to strengthen an airplane wing or a column in a building; it is always possible to reduce the dosage of a drug or change the method or timing of its administration. But the follow-up questions are the difficult ones. There are questions of function: Will the plane still fly? Will it fly as fast? There are questions of cost: At what point is an incremental benefit in the car's safety no longer worth the price increase it would entail? There are questions of safety itself: Has the therapeutic drug really been improved, or has one risk just been traded off for another, possibly a more serious one?

The rule of thumb for American engineers is that the perfect device will be too late, too heavy, or too expensive. "We make do with the third best," the British said in World War II, "because the second best is always too late, and the first best never gets built." The perfectly safe vaccine, birth control pill, or airplane is also perfectly ineffectual or non-functional. Whether the objective is to cure disease, or alter the body's chemistry, or travel at 600 miles per hour, some trade-off between safety and functionality is always in order. Disquieting though these judgments may be, they are what real-world design is all about. In fact, they constitute the full-time business of countless design experts in both industry and government.

To give them their due, principled keepers of the new tort faith never denied any of this. To the contrary, they toiled to incorporate these realities in their new jurisprudence. The intellectual effort took the form of interminable discussion, most of it in densely footnoted law review articles, on how jury guidelines could be precisely crafted to steer the design defect inquest through court. A verbal blueprint eventually emerged. It has since become a standard in jury instructions and appellate decisions.

A jury is to consider, first, "the usefulness and desirability of the product—its utility to the user and to the public as a whole." It should then assess "the likelihood that [the product] will cause injury and the probable seriousness of the injury," considering, of course, "the user's ability to avoid danger by the exercise of care in the use of the product." Here, to be sure, the jury should take into account "the user's anticipated awareness of

the dangers inherent in the product and their avoidability, because of general public knowledge of the obvious condition of the product, or of the existence of suitable warnings or instructions." Also relevant are "the availability of a substitute product which would meet the same need and not be as unsafe, [and] the manufacturer's ability to eliminate the unsafe character of the product without impairing its usefulness or making it too expensive to maintain its utility." Finally, the tireless jury must determine "the feasibility, on the part of the manufacturer, of spreading the loss by setting the price of the product or carrying liability insurance."

By 1975, this was pretty much the state of the law. Only a lawyer could love the mind-numbing profusion of words. There was, however, a nagging concern. Perhaps the torrent of verbiage conveyed the right sorts of signals, but could any jury really follow the wonderfully complex directives in any intelligent way? At the very least, trials would have to become advanced seminars in economics, engineering, pharmacology, and industrial design.

They soon did. Experts lined up in hordes, on both sides of the courtroom, to educate juries on the finer points of designing a morning sickness drug, a crashworthy car, or a safe playground swing. The old tort law refused to hear this kind of hired-gun testimony in all but the most exceptional cases. But new, relaxed federal rules of evidence were put on the books in 1975, and just in time as far as the new tort doctrines were concerned. Today one referral service in Pennsylvania maintains a nation-wide list of about 10,000 experts grouped in 4,000 categories, and reports a 15 percent annual growth in its listings. Classified ads in the back pages of legal journals offer counsel on bicycle mishaps, grain dust blasts, playground traumas, battery or bottle explosions, hot-air balloon calamities, radiation incidents, and accidents involving lawn mowers, toys, and beer barrels. Car crashworthiness cases now routinely inquire into the relative frequency and severity of the different sorts of accidents that can and do occur with a given model, the probable extent of the injuries, the types of precautions that might have been taken, how those precautions might have impaired overall design and performance of the car, and how they might have affected the vehicle's price and the protection it affords against other types of accident hazards.

By the late 1970s, the technical and economic questions being raised in design defect cases were triggering titanic courtroom struggles. But these struggles remained, all the while, mere parodies of the actual process of real-world design. The original design of a car, drug, or appliance takes years, as does review, when required, by a government agency like the FDA. With or without help from two camps of hired experts, a jury typically has a few days, seldom more than a few weeks.

So the courts were now wholeheartedly in the business of trying technologies, not technologists.

But they weren't doing it very well, for fairly obvious reasons. "'The theory of the adversary system,'" George Bernard Shaw caustically observed, "is that if you set two liars to exposing each other, eventually the truth will come out." As the new tort jurisprudence picked up momentum, the paid experts and other hired hands multiplied the numbers far beyond two. But despite all the courtroom frenzy and expense there were few signs that much new truth was emerging.

STRICT PRODUCTS LIABILITY AND COMPENSATORY JUSTICE
George G. Brenkert

I

Strict products liability is the doctrine that the seller of a product has legal responsibilities to compensate the user of that product for injuries suffered due to a defective aspect of the product, even though the seller has not been negligent in permitting that defect to occur.[1] Thus, even though a manufacturer, for example, has reasonably applied the existing techniques of manufacture and has anticipated and cared for nonintended uses of the product, he may still be held liable for injuries a product user suffers if it can be shown that the product was defective when it left the manufacturer's hands.[2] To say that there is a crisis today concerning this doctrine would be to utter a commonplace observation which few in the business community would deny. The development of the doctrine of strict products liability, they say, financially threatens many businesses.[3] Further, strict products liability is said to be a morally questionable doctrine since the manufacturer or seller has not been negligent in the occurrence of the injury-causing defect in the product. On the other hand, victims of defective products complain that they deserve full compensation for injuries sustained in

using a defective product whether or not the seller is at fault. Medical expenses and time lost from one's job are costs no individual should have to bear by himself. It is only fair that the seller share such burdens.

In general, discussions of this crisis focus on the limits to which a business ought to be held responsible to compensate the injured product user. Much less frequently do discussions of strict products liability consider the underlying question of whether the doctrine of strict products liability is rationally justifiable. But unless this question is answered it would seem premature to seek to determine the limits to which businesses ought to be held liable in such cases. In the following paper I discuss this underlying philosophical question and argue that there is a rational justification for strict products liability which links it to the very nature of the free enterprise system.

II

It should be noted at the outset that strict products liability is not absolute liability. To hold a manufacturer legally (and morally) responsible for any and all injuries which product users might sustain would be morally perverse. First, it would deny the product user's own responsibility to take care in his actions and to suffer the consequences when he does not.

As such, it would constitute an extreme form of moral and legal paternalism. Second, if the product is not detective, there is no significant moral connection between anything that the manufacturer has done or not done and the user's injuries other than the production and sale of the product to its user. But this provides no basis to hold the manufacturer responsible for the user's injuries. If, because of my own carelessness, I cut myself with my pocket knife, the fact that I just bought my knife from Blade Manufacturing Company provides no moral reason to hold Blade Manufacturing responsible for my injury. Finally, though the manufacturer's product might be said to have harmed the person,[4] it is wholly implausible, when the product is not defective and the manufacturer not negligent, to say that the manufacturer has harmed the user. Thus, again there would seem to be no moral basis upon which to maintain that the manufacturer has any liability to the product user. Strict products liability, on the other hand, is the view that the manufacturer can be held liable when the product can be shown to be defective even though the manufacturer himself is not negligent.[5]

There are two justifications of strict products liability which are predominant in the literature. Both justifications are, I believe, untenable. They are:

a. To hold producers strictly liable for defective products will cut down on the number of accidents and injuries which occur, by forcing manufacturers to make their products safer.

b. The manufacturer is best able to distribute to others the costs of injuries which users of his defective products suffer.

There are several reasons why the first justification is unacceptable. First, it has been plausibly argued that almost everything that can be attained through the use of strict liability to force manufacturers to make their products safer can also be attained in other ways through the law.[6] Hence, to hold manufacturers strictly liable will not necessarily help reduce the number of accidents. The incentive to produce safer products already exists without invoking the doctrine of strict products liability.

Second, at least some of the accidents which have been brought under strict liability have been due to features of the products which the manufacturers could not have foreseen or controlled. At the

time the product was designed and manufactured, the technological knowledge required to discover the hazard and take steps to minimize its effects was not available. It is doubtful that, in such cases, the imposition of strict liability upon the manufacturer could reduce accidents.[7] Thus, again, this justification for strict products liability fails.[8]

Third, the fact that the imposition of legal restraints and/or penalties would have a certain positive effect, viz., the reduction of accidents, does not show that the imposition of those penalties would be just. It has been pointed out before that the rate of crime might be cut significantly if the law would imprison the wives and children of men who break the law. Regardless of how correct that claim may be, to use these means in order to achieve a significant reduction in the rate of crime would be unjust. Thus, the fact, if fact it be, that strict liability would cut down on the amount of dangerous and/or defective products placed on the market, and thus reduce the amount of accidents and injuries, does not thereby justify the imposition of strict liability on manufacturers.

Finally, the above justification is essentially a utilitarian appeal which emphasizes the welfare of the product users. It is not obvious, however, that those who use this justification have ever undertaken the utilitarian analysis which would show that greater protection of the product user's safety would further the welfare of product users. If emphasis on product user safety would cut down on the number and variety of products produced, the imposition of strict liability might not, in fact, enhance product user welfare but rather lower it. Furthermore, if the safety of product users is the predominant concern, massive public and private education safety campaigns might just as well lower the level of accidents and injuries as strict products liability.

The second justification given for strict products liability is also utilitarian in nature. Among the considerations given in favor of this justification are the following:

a. "An individual harmed by his/her use of a defective product is often unable to bear the loss individually";

b. "Distribution of losses among all users of a product would minimize both individual and aggregate loss";

c. "The situation of producers and marketers in the marketplace enable them conveniently to distribute losses among all users of a product by raising prices sufficiently to compensate those harmed (which is what in fact occurs where strict liability is in force)."[9]

This justification is also defective.

First, the word "best" in the phrase "best able to distribute to others the cost" is usually understood in a non-moral sense; it is used to signify that the manufacturer can most efficiently pass on the costs of injuries to others. Once this use of "best" is recognised, then surely the question may correctly be asked: Why ought these costs be passed on to other consumers and/or users of the same product or line of products? Even if the imposition of strict liability did maximize utility, it might be the case that it was still unjust to use the producer as the distributor of losses.[10] Indeed, it has been objected that to pass along the costs of such accidents to other consumers of products of a manufacturer is unjust to them.[11] The above justification is silent to these legitimate questions.

Second, it may not be, as a matter of fact, that manufacturers are always in the best (i.e., most efficient and economical) position to pass costs on to customers. This might be possible in monopoly areas, but even there there are limitations. Further, some products are subject to an "elastic demand" and as such the manufacturer could not pass along the costs.[12] Finally, the present justification could justify far more than is plausible. If the reason for holding the manufacturer liable is that the manufacturer is the "best" administrator of costs, then one might plausibly argue that the manufacturer should pay for injuries suffered not simply when he is not negligent but also when the product is not defective. That is, theoretically this argument could be extended from cases of strict liability to absolute liability. Whether this argument could plausibly be made would depend upon contingent facts concerning the nature and frequency of injuries people suffer using products, the financial strength of businesses, and the kinds and levels of products liability insurance available to them. The argument would not depend on any morally significant elements in the producer/product user relation. Such an implication, I believe, undercuts the purported moral nature of this justification. It

reveals it for what it is: an economic, not a moral justification.

Accordingly, neither of the major, current justifications for the imposition of strict liability appears to be acceptable. If this is the case, is strict products liability a groundless doctrine, willfully and unjustly imposed on manufacturers?

III

This question can be asked in two different ways. On the one hand, it can be asked within the assumptions of the free enterprise system. On the other hand, it could be raised such that the fundamental assumptions of that socio-economic system are also open to revision and change. In the following, I will discuss the question *within* the general assumptions of the free enterprise system. Since these are the assumptions which are broadly made in legal and business circles it is interesting to determine what answer might be given within these constraints. Indeed, I suggest, it is only within these general assumptions that strict products liability can be justified.

To begin with, it is crucial to remember that what we have to consider is the relation between an entity doing business and an individual.[13] The strict liability attributed to business would not be attributed to an individual who happened to sell some particular product he had made to his neighbor or a stranger. If Peter sold an article which he had made to Paul, and Paul hurt himself because the article had a defect which occurred through no negligence of Peter's, we would not normally hold Peter morally responsible to pay for Paul's injuries. Peter did not claim, we may assume, that the product was absolutely risk free. Had he kept it himself, he too might have been injured by it. Paul, on the other hand, bought it. He was not pressured, forced, or coerced to do so. Peter mounted no advertising campaign. Though Paul might not have been injured if the product had been made differently, he supposedly bought it with open eyes. Peter did not seek to deceive Paul about its qualities. The product, both its good and bad qualities, became his through his purchase of it. In short, we assume that both Peter and Paul are morally autonomous individuals capable of knowing their own interests, that such individuals can legitimately exchange their ownership of various products, that the world is not free of risks, and that not all injuries one suffers in such a world can be blamed on others. To demand that Peter protect Paul from such dangers and/or compensate him for injuries resulting from such dangers, is to demand that Peter significantly reduce the risks of the product he offers to Paul. He would have to protect Paul from encountering those risks himself. However, this smacks of paternalism, and undercuts our basic moral assumptions about such relations. Hence, in such a case, Peter is not morally responsible for Paul's injuries, or, due to this transaction, obligated to aid him. Perhaps Peter owes Paul aid because Paul is an injured neighbor or person. Perhaps simply for reasons of charity Peter ought to aid Paul. But Peter has no moral obligation, stemming from the sale itself, to provide aid.

It is different in the case of businesses. They have been held to be legally and morally obliged to pay the victim for his injuries. Why? What is the difference? The difference has to do with the fact that when Paul is hurt by a defective product from corporation X, he is hurt by something produced in a socio-economic system purportedly embodying free enterprise. To say this is to say, among other things, that (a) each business and/or corporation produces articles or services which they sell for profit; (b) each member of this system competes with other members of the system in trying to do as well as he can for himself not simply in each exchange but through each exchange for his other values and desires; (c) competition is to be "open and free, without deception or fraud"; (d) exchanges are to be voluntary and undertaken when each party believes he can thereby benefit. One party provides the means for another party's ends if the other party will provide the first party the means to his ends[14]; (e) the acquisition and disposition of ownership rights, i.e., of private property, is permitted in such exchanges; (f) no market or series of markets constitutes the whole of a society; (g) law, morality, and government play a role in setting acceptable limits to the nature and kinds of exchange in which people may engage.[15]

What is it about such a system which would justify claims of strict products liability against businesses? Calabresi has suggested that the free enterprise system is essentially a system of strict liability.[16] Thus, the very nature of the free enterprise system justifies such liability claims. His argu-

ment has two parts. First, he claims that "bearing risks is both the function of, and justification for, private enterprise in a free enterprise society."[17] Free enterprise is prized, in classical economics, precisely because it fosters the creation of entrepreneurs who will take such uninsurable risks, who will, in other words, gamble on uncertainty and demonstrate their utility by surviving—by winning more than others."[18] Accordingly, the nature of private enterprise requires that individual businesses assume the burden of risk in the production and distribution of its products. However, even if it be granted that this characterisation of who must bear the risks "in deciding what goods are worth producing and what new entrants into an industry are worth having" is correct, it would not follow that individual businesses ought to bear the burden of risk in cases of accidents. Calabresi himself recognises this. Thus, he maintains, in the second part of his argument, that there is a close analogy which lets us move from the regular risk bearing businesses must accept in the marketplace to the bearing of risks in accidents: "although...(the above characterisation) has concerned *regular* entrepreneurial-product risks, not accident risks, the analogy is extremely close."[19] He proceeds, however, to draw the analogy in the following brief sentence: "As with product-accident risks, our society starts out by allocating ordinary product-production risks in ways which try to maximize the chances that incentives will be placed on those most suited to 'manage' these risks."[20] In short, he simply asserts that the imposition of strict products liability on business will be the most effective means of reducing such risks. But such a view does not really require, as we have seen in the previous section, any assumptions about the nature of the free enterprise system. It could be held independently of such assumptions. Further, this view is simply a form of the first justificatory argument we discussed and rejected in the previous section. We can hardly accept it here under the guise of being attached to the nature of free enterprise.

Nevertheless, Calabresi's initial intuitions about a connection between the assumptions of the free enterprise system and the justification of strict products liability are correct. However, they must be developed in the following, rather different, manner. In the free enterprise system, each person and/or business is obligated to follow the rules and understandings which define this socioeconomic system. Following the rules is expected to channel competition among individual persons and businesses so that the results are socially positive. In providing the means to fulfill the ends of others, the means to one's own ends also get fulfilled. Though this does not happen in every case, it is supposed that, in general, this happens. Those who fail in their competition with others may be the object of charity, but not of other duties. Those who succeed, *qua* members of this socio-economic system, do not have moral duties to aid those who fail. Analogously, the team which loses the game may receive our sympathy but the winning team is not obligated to help it so that it may win the next game, or even play better the next game. Those who violate the rules, however, may be punished or penalized, whether or not the violation was intentional and whether or not it rebounds to the benefit of the violator. Thus, a team may be assessed a penalty for something a team member unintentionally did to a member of the other team but which, by violating the rules, nevertheless injured the other team's chances of competition in the game.

This point may be emphasized by another instance involving a game but one which brings us closer to strict products liability. Imagine that you are playing table tennis with another person in his newly constructed table tennis room. You are both avid table tennis players and the game means a lot to both of you. Suppose that after play has begun, you are suddenly and quite obviously blinded by the light over the table—the light shade has a hole in it which, when it turned in your direction, sent a shaft of light unexpectedly into your eyes. You lose a crucial point as a result. Surely it would be unfair of your opponent to seek to maintain his point because he was faultless—i.e., he had not intended to blind you when he installed that light shade. You would correctly object that he had gained the point unfairly, that you should not have to give up the point lost, and that the light shade should be modified so that the game could continue on a fair basis. It is only fair that the point be played over.

Businesses and their customers in a free enterprise system are also engaged in competition with each other.[21] The competition here, however, is multifaceted as each tries to gain the best agreement he can from the other with regard to the buying and selling of raw materials, products, services, and labour. Such agreements, however, must be voluntary. The competition which leads to them cannot involve coercion. In addition, such competition must be fair and ultimately result in the benefit of the entire society through the operation of the proverbial "invisible hand." Crucial to the notion of fairness of competition is not simply the demands that the competition itself be open, free, and honest, but also that each person in a society be given an equal opportunity to participate in the system in order to fulfill his own particular ends. Friedman formulates this notion in the following manner: "the priority given to equality of opportunity in the hierarchy of values…is manifested particularly in economic policy. The catchwords were free enterprise, competition, laissez-faire. Everyone was free to go into any business, follow any occupation, buy any property, subject only to the agreement of the other parties to the transaction. Each was to have the opportunity to reap the benefits if he succeeded, to suffer the costs if he failed. There were to be no arbitrary obstacles. Performance, not birth, religion, or nationality, was the touchstone."[22]

What is obvious in Friedman's comments is that he is thinking primarily of a person as a producer. Equality of opportunity requires that one not be prevented by arbitrary obstacles from participating (by engaging in a productive role of some kind or other) in the system of free enterprise, competition, etc. in order to fulfill one's own ends ("reap the benefits"). Accordingly, monopolies are restricted, discriminatory hiring policies have been condemned, and price collusion is forbidden. However, each person participates in the system of free enterprise *both* as a worker/producer *and* as a consumer. The two roles interact; if the person could not consume he would not be able to work, and if there were no consumers there would be no work to be done. Even if a particular individual is only (what is ordinarily considered) a consumer, he too plays a theoretically significant role in the competitive free enterprise system. The fairness of the system depends upon the access to information, which is available to him, about goods and services on the market, the lack of coercion imposed on him to buy goods, as well as the lack of arbitrary restrictions imposed by the market and/or government on his behavior. In short, equality of opportunity is a doctrine with two sides which applies both to producers and to consumers. If, then, a person as a consumer or a producer is injured by a defective product, which is one way in which his activities might be arbitrarily restricted by the action of (one of the members of) the market system, surely his free and voluntary participation in the system of free enterprise will be seriously affected. Specifically, his equal opportunity to participate in the system in order to fulfill his own ends will be diminished.

It is here that strict products liability enters the picture. In cases of strict liability the manufacturer does not intend that a certain aspect of his product injures a person. Nevertheless, the person is injured. As a result, his activity both as a consumer and as a producer is disadvantaged. He cannot continue to play the role he might wish either as a producer or consumer. As such he is denied that equality of opportunity which is basic to the economic system in question just as surely as he would be if he were excluded from employment by various unintended consequences of the economic system which nevertheless had certain racially or sexually prejudicial implications. Accordingly, it is fair that the manufacturer compensate the person for his losses before proceeding with business as usual. That is, the user of a manufacturer's product may justifiably demand compensation from the manufacturer when a product of his which can be shown to be defective has injured him and harmed his chances of participation in the system of free enterprise.

Hence, strict liability finds a basis in the notion of equality of opportunity which plays a central role in the notion of a free enterprise system. This is why a business which does *not* have to pay for the injuries which an individual suffers in the use of a defective article made by that business is felt to be unfair to its customers. Its situation is analogous to a player's unintentional violation of a game rule which is intended to foster equality of competitive opportunity. A soccer player, for example, may unintentionally trip an opposing player. He did not mean to do it: perhaps he himself had stumbled and consequently tripped the other player. Still, he is to be penalised. If the referee looked the other way, the tripped player would rightfully object that he had been treated unfairly. Similarly, the manufac-

turer of a product may be held strictly liable for a product of his which injures a person who uses that product. Even though he be faultless, it is a causal consequence of his activities that renders the user of his product less capable of equal participation in the socioeconomic system so as to fulfill his (the user's) own ends. The manufacturer too should be penalised by way of compensating the victim. Thus, the basis upon which manufacturers are held strictly liable is compensatory justice.

In a society which refuses to resort to paternalism or to central direction of the economy and which turns, instead, to competition in order to allocate scarce positions and resources, compensatory justice requires that the competition be fair and losers be protected.[23] Specifically no one who loses should be left so destitute that he cannot reenter the competition. Further, those who suffer injuries traceable to the defective results of the activities of others which restrict their participation in the competitive system should also be compensated. As such, compensatory justice does not presuppose negligence or evil intentions on the part of those to whom the injuries might ultimately be causally traced. It is not perplexed or incapacitated by the relative innocence of all parties involved. Rather it is concerned with correcting the disadvantaged situation an individual experiences due to accidents or failures which occur in the normal working of that competitive system. It is on this basis that other compensatory programs which alleviate the disabilities of various minority groups are founded. It is also on compensatory justice that strict products liability finds its foundation.

An implication of the preceding argument is that business is not morally obliged to pay, as such, for the physical injury a person suffers. Rather, it must pay for the loss of equal competitive opportunity—even though it usually is the case that it is because of a (physical) injury that there is a loss of such equal opportunity. This, however, corresponds to actual legal cases in which the injury which prevents a person from going about his/her daily activities may be emotional or mental as well as physical. If it were the case that a person were neither mentally nor physically harmed, but still rendered less capable of competitively participating due to a defective aspect of a product, then there would still be grounds for holding the company liable. For example, suppose I purchased and used a cosmetic product guaranteed to last a month. When used by most people it is odorless. On me, however, it has a terrible smell. I can stand the smell, but my co-workers, and most other people, find it intolerable. My employer sends me home from work until it wears off. The product has not physically or mentally harmed me. Still, on the above argument, I would have reason to hold the manufacturer liable. Any cosmetic product with this result is defective. As a consequence my opportunity to participate in the socio-economic system so as to fulfill my own ends is disadvantaged. I should be compensated....

NOTES

1. This characterization of strict products liability is adapted from Weinstein et al., *Products Liability and the Reasonably Safe Product* (New York: John Wiley & Sons, 1978), ch. 1. I understand "the seller" to include the manufacturer, the retailer, as well as distributors and wholesalers. For convenience sake, I will generally refer simply to the manufacturer.

2. Cf. John W. Wade, "On Product 'Design Defects' and Their Actionability," 33 *Vanderbilt Law Review* 553 (1980). Weinstein, et al., *Products Liability and the Reasonably Safe Product*, 8, 28–32. Reed Dickerson, "Products Liability: How Good Does a Product Have to Be?" 42 *Indiana Law Journal* 308–316 (1967). Section 402A of the Restatement (Second) of Torts characterises the seller's situation in this fashion: "the seller has exercised all possible care in the preparation and sale of his product."

3. Cf. John C. Perham, "The Dilemma in Product Liability," *Dun's Review*, 109 (1977), 48–50, 76. W. Page Keeton, "Products Liability—Design Hazards and the Meaning of Defect," 10 *Cumberland Law Review* 293–316 (1979). Alvin S. Weinstein et al., *Products Liability and the Reasonably Safe Product* (New York: John Wiley & Sons, 1978), ch. 1.

4. More properly, of course, the person's use of the manufacturer's product harmed the product user.

5. Clearly one of the central questions confronting the notion of strict liability is what is to count as "defective." With few exceptions, it is held that a product is defective if and only if it is unreasonably dangerous. There have been several different standards proposed as measures of the defectiveness or unreasonably dangerous nature of a product. However, in terms of logical priorities, it really does not matter what the particular standard for defectiveness is unless we know whether we may justifiably hold manufacturers strictly liable for defective products. It is for this reason that I concentrate in this paper on the justifiability of strict products liability.

6. Marcus L. Plant, "Strict Liability of Manufacturers for Injuries Caused by Defects in Products—An Opposing View," 24 *Tennessee Law Review* 945 (1957). William L. Prosser, "The Assault Upon the Citadel (Strict Liability to the Consumer)," 1114, 1115, 1119.

7. Keeton, "The Meaning of Defect in Products Liability—A Review of Basic Principles," 594–595. Weinstein et al., *Products Liability and the Reasonably Safe Product*, 55.

8. It might be objected that such accidents ought not to fall under strict products liability and hence do not constitute a counterexample to the above justification. This objection is answered in Sections III and IV. [Section IV is not included in this anthology.]

9. These three considerations are formulated by Michael D. Smith, "The Morality of Strict Liability in Tort," *Business and Professional Ethics Newsletter*, 3 (1979), 4. Smith himself, however, was drawing upon Guido Calabresi, "Some Thoughts on Risk Distribution and the Law of Torts," 70 *Yale Law Journal* 499–553 (1961).

10. Michael D. Smith, "The Morality of Strict Liability in Tort," 4. Cf. George P. Fletcher, "Fairness and Utility in Tort Theory," 85 *Harvard Law Review* 537–573 (1972).

11. Rev. Francis E. Lucey, S. J., "Liability Without Fault and the Natural Law," 24 *Tennessee Law Review* 952–962 (1957). Perham, "The Dilemma in Product Liability," 48–49.

12. Marcus L. Plant, "Strict Liability of Manufacturers for Injuries Caused by Defects in Products—An Opposing View," 946–947. By "elastic demand" is meant "a slight increase in price will cause a sharp reduction in demand or will turn consumers to a substitute product" (946–947).

13. Cf. William L. Prosser, "The Assault Upon the Citadel" 69 *Yale Law Journal* 1140–1141 (1960). Wade, "On Product 'Design Defects' and Their Actionability," 569. Michel A. Coccio, John W. Dondanville, Thomas R. Nelson, *Products Liability: Trends and Implications* (AMA, 1970), 19.

14. F. A. Hayek emphasizes this point in "The Moral Element in Free Enterprise," in *Studies in Philosophy, Politics, and Economics* (New York: Simon and Schuster, 1967), 229.

15. Several of these characteristics have been drawn from Milton Friedman and Rose Friedman, *Free to Choose* (New York: Avon Books, 1980).

16. Calabresi, "Product Liability: Curse or Bulwark of Free Enterprise," 325.

17. Ibid., 321.

18. Ibid.

19. Ibid., 324.

20. Ibid.

21. Cf. H. B. Acton, *The Morals of Markets* (London: Longman Group Limited, 1971), 1–7, 33–37. Milton Friedman and Rose Friedman, *Free to Choose*.

22. Milton Friedman and Rose Friedman, *Free to Choose*, 123–124.

23. I have heavily drawn, in this paragraph, on the fine article by Bernard Boxhill, "The Morality of Reparation," reprinted in *Reverse Discrimination*, ed. Barry R. Gross (Buffalo, New York: Prometheus Books, 1977), 270–278.

FAIRNESS, STRICT LIABILITY, AND PUBLIC POLICY
John J. McCall

The recent insurance crisis has intensified the public debate over product liability law. Business and insurance industry lobbyists have pressured for state and federal reform of the current strict liability standards. The main complaints about strict liability center on two claims: (1) the cost of a strict liability system is exorbitant and (2) holding business strictly liable for product-related injuries is unfair. This brief comment evaluates only the second of these claims.

The charge that strict liability is unfair to business gains credibility from an often unspoken underlying principle of fairness: Individuals should not be penalized (or, for that matter, advantaged) for things that are beyond their control and, hence, not their fault. This principle, or something like it, lies behind our intuition that the harms caused by severe mental incompetents do not deserve punishment. Something similar also explains the great attraction of John Rawls's recent theory of justice.

If we apply this principle to the case of product liability, it certainly appears unfair to adopt a strict liability approach when compensating for injuries due to defective products. For, according to strict liability, a business is held financially liable for harms caused by its products even when the defect is not the result of negligence. For example, if a defective product is released on the market despite a strict quality control inspection program, the business can still be held liable according to this standard. Because no quality control system can prevent all defects, a company could escape financial jeopardy only by ceasing production. A corporation, then, can suffer serious economic damage under a strict liability standard for something that is not, in any morally significant sense, its fault.

We should look a bit closer, however, before concluding that strict liability is unfair. By defini-

tion, a strict liability standard applies to cases of accidental injury related to product defects. A consumer who is injured by a defective product is not at fault for the injury just as the business is not at fault. In an equally important way, then, the consumer is harmed by something beyond his or her control. (Ignore the complexities associated with contributory negligence on the part of the consumer since those complexities have no bearing on the general question of the fairness of any strict liability standard.)

If we accept the argument that strict liability is unfair to business, the paradoxical conclusion is that the alternative for cases of non-negligent defects is also unfair to the injured consumer. So, rather than drawing conclusions on the basis of the above fault/control principle about the fairness of strict liability, we instead should recognize that this principle is simply inapplicable when no one bears moral responsibility for the harm, that is, when the harm is purely accidental.

We need not abandon, however, any attempt to discuss the fairness of strict liability just because one common principle of fairness does not apply. We could, for instance, adapt another interpretation of fairness that is also associated with the work of John Rawls. Imagine a hypothetical choice of product liability policy under impartial and unbiased conditions. Suppose we ask an ordinary rational person to suspend her current views on product liability policy and to imagine two mutually exclusive alternative situations: one in which she is injured by a non-negligent-caused product defect and has no legal possibility of compensation; the other in which she is harmed by higher consumer prices or lower dividend return as a shareholder because the corporation must pay for strict liability product insurance. I suspect the first alternative is distasteful enough that the ordinary citizen would agree to accept the second alternative as a way of precluding the first.

If we develop this argument more completely by taking account of all associated costs, we may be able to construct a forceful argument for the conclusion that strict liability, far from being unfair, is actually *required* by fairness. Whatever we think of such an argument, the failure of the initial argument against strict liability is clear enough. At the very least, we ought to allow that a strict liability standard is, prima facie, *not unfair*.

If we do grant that strict liability is at least compatible with fairness, we still need to provide reasons for adopting it over other standards that may also be compatible with fairness. There are two such reasons frequently offered for a strict liability policy. First, proponents claim that a strict liability policy would reduce the number of product-related injuries. Because businesses would be exposed to greater financial jeopardy by a strict liability standard, they would have greater economic incentive to guarantee the safety of their products. The less cautious a company is, the more it can expect to have product liability judgments against it.

George Brenkert argues that this is not a sufficient reason for adopting a strict liability policy. Brenkert suggests (a) that strict liability will not achieve any greater safety results than could be achieved through, say, legislated product safety standards; (b) some accidents are unpreventable; and (c) strict liability may be analogous to the unfair policy of imprisoning the wives (not husbands?) of criminals. Even though I agree that accident reduction is not, in itself, a sufficient justification for strict liability, I also believe that none of these objections is compelling. For instance, lobbying and the appeals process may weaken congressional safety legislation so that fines become a less than effective deterrent. Moreover, even though some accidents will still occur under strict liability, this does not prove that strict liability will not eliminate other injuries when compared, say, with a negligence standard. Finally, the unfair imprisoning of wives who are not at fault is not analogous to compensation for a non-negligent, injury-causing product defect, which, for reasons stated above, is not unfair.

A second policy reason traditionally used in support of strict liability is that it distributes the cost of injuries in a way that minimizes their im-

pact. It also distributes the costs to those who have benefitted from the availability of the injury-causing product. Ordinarily, the cost of product liability insurance is passed on in the form of higher product prices to those who demand the product. But even in cases in which an individual business in an elastic market has markedly higher insurance premiums, costs are still assigned to those who benefitted—the shareholders. (Why might one manufacturer have higher insurance premiums? Does this situation suggest a negligent failure to operate by the best available industry practice? One also wonders about entire industries with high insurance costs where the demand for the product is elastic. Does that indicate that the product is both dangerous and unnecessary?)

I would argue that the costs are more appropriately assigned to other consumers or to shareholders than to either the injured consumer or to society at large. Making the injured bear the full economic cost of the injury seems too harsh. Making society at large bear the cost through some form of socialized product liability insurance violates the principle of "user pays" and lessens the incentive to manufacture safe products. In ordinary circumstances, then, a strict liability standard is preferable to its alternatives.

A number of caveats for this conclusion are in order, however. First, if the social costs of a private insurance system under a strict liability policy were too great (for example, high unemployment, shortages of socially necessary products), perhaps some public subsidy for that insurance would be in order. I hesitate to acknowledge this qualification, though, because recent history indicates that such a policy exception could be manipulated by business and the insurance industry into a policy norm.

Second, cases arise in which the corporation that supplied the product no longer exists or the harms caused go beyond the available assets of the corporation and, hence, full recovery by the victim from the corporation is precluded. Perhaps in such cases public subsidy to complete the compensation of the victim is preferable to partial compensation. About whether the same subsidy should be available to the families of victims, I am less sure. About joint and several liability cases in which the harms are caused by more than one agent but some of the harm causers no longer exist and the remaining are liable for full compensation of the victim, I am also unsure. These cases indicate the difficulties in fashioning a fair, reasonable, and effective public policy on product liability. However, I hope to have suggested that any such policy ought to start from a strict liability basis.

REGULATION AND PATERNALISM
Steven Kelman

Opposition to paternalism plays an important role in the current national debate over the appropriate scope for government regulation, especially consumer protection regulation on behalf of safety and health. It is frequently summoned in condemning calls to ban saccharin or laetrile. It is pronounced likewise against proposals to require people to wear seatbelts or motorcycle helmets. And it appears in criticisms of safety standards for lawnmowers or autos, since such standards, although they neither ban nor mandate use of the product in question, do require that consumers pay for certain safety features if they wish to buy the product. The antipaternalistic contention is simple. If people know the risks of, say, saccharin and choose to run these risks for themselves in order to obtain the benefits they believe they will gain, who are we to interfere with that choice?

I believe that it is correct to oppose paternalism, but incorrect to tar most government consumer protection health and safety regulations with a paternalistic brush....

There are, in other words, good nonpaternalistic arguments for such regulation, although these arguments are often mistaken for paternalistic ones. In the final section, I will discuss explicitly the question of whether there are ever any occasions when regulation might be justified on avowedly paternalistic grounds.

The force of the argument to be made and most of the examples selected involve regulation of consumer products for purposes of safety or health. Some of the arguments will, however, also be applicable to other public policy domains that raise issues of paternalism, such as the use of in-kind as opposed to cash transfer payments....

From *Public Policy*, vol. 29, no. 2 (Spring 1981). Copyright © 1981 by the President and Fellows of Harvard College. Reprinted by permission of John Wiley & Sons, Inc.

DECISION-MAKING COSTS AND VOLUNTARY RENUNCIATION OF CHOICE AUTHORITY

In this section, I argue that when there are costs associated with deciding what choice to make, it is rational in some situations for an individual to renounce his authority to make the choice for himself, and to hand over such authority to a third party who will make the choice in the individual's interest. Such third-party choices are not paternalistic, because they are not made against the person's wishes. They introduce a new category, separate both from choices one makes oneself and from choices made paternalistically. Much government safety regulation of consumer products, I believe, falls into this category.

The probability that one would want to renounce the authority to choose increases (1) the more that the decision-making costs for the person exceed those for the third party, and (2) the closer the choice the third party makes is to the choice the person would have made.[1]

The situation where voluntary renunciation of the authority to choose is rational may be illustrated by a simple example. Imagine that a person could, without bearing any decision-making costs, simply go out and choose, off the top of his head, to buy a product with certain general features. Let us say that such a choice would produce a net benefit of ten units of satisfaction for him. Imagine further that he could gain perfect information about the specific features of the different types of the product that are available. If he had this information and processed it, he would be able to make a better choice—say, one that gives him 15 units of satisfaction. But if gathering and processing the information cost him eight units of satisfaction, his net benefit from the choice, after decision-making costs are taken into account, would be only seven units. In such a case, the "off the top of the head" choice, yielding ten units of satisfaction, would be preferable to the "better" but decision-costly choice, which yields only seven units of satisfaction.

But these may not be the only two alternatives. Let us say someone else can gather and process the same information *much more cheaply than the person himself*—for two units of satisfaction (units that presumably would be billed to the person in some way). Armed with this information, the third party would make a decision for the person yielding only 13 units of satisfaction. The third party has gathered and processed the same information that the person did, but the decision he makes may not yield as much satisfaction, even though he is supposed to act in his person's best interest. This may be because he makes a faulty judgment about exactly what those interests are. It may be because he takes advantage of the opportunity and imposes his own judgment of what he thinks is best for the person, or acts in his own self-interest and imposes a decision that better satisfies his own interests. The net benefits of authorizing the third party to make the decision in this case would be 11 units (13 units for the decision minus two units of decision-making costs). Of the three alternatives—uninformed choice by consumer, informed choice by the consumer, and informed choice by third party—the last yields the highest net benefits. This is so despite the fact that if one looks simply at the benefits of the choice itself and not at decision-making costs, the informed choice by the consumer himself would have appeared to be the most advantageous one.

The costs of decision-making include information-gathering costs, information-processing costs, and possibly psychological costs of choice. Information-gathering costs are the costs of determining the existence of all the relevant features across which the different types of a product can vary and the different values these variables take across the different types of a product. Information-processing costs are the costs of calculating the implication of the different values for a judgment of the benefits of the product, given one's preferences. Psychological costs are the frustration that may be felt from information overload or the trauma that may be experienced from having to make difficult choices.

An immense disservice to intelligent discussion of the safety regulation of consumer products occurs because of the tendency to base such discussions on a small number of dramatic instances—

saccharin, seatbelts, laetrile. A statement such as, "People know that it's more risky to drive without seatbelts than with them, and if they choose to take that risk to avoid the discomfort of wearing the belts, that should be up to them," may be made with a straight face. People know the feature they are making a choice about (that is, they know what seatbelts are). They know what values the variable can take (the seatbelts may be worn or not worn). They know the implications of these different values for their judgments about the choice (wearing seatbelts decreases risk but may increase discomfort).

The problem is that such individual dramatic examples are unrepresentative of the universe of choices that consumers would have to make for themselves in a world where they had to make all decisions about the safety features of products they buy themselves. Statements about consumers knowing the risks of failing to use seatbelts or consuming saccharin and choosing to bear them are plausible. Statements such as the following are far less so: "People know that if the distance between the slats on the infant crib is 2⅜th inches there is little risk that an infant will strangle himself falling through the slats, while if the distance is 3¼th inches the risk is much greater, and if they choose to take this risk to get a crib that is less expensive, that should be up to them." The reader may ask himself if he would feel confident identifying which one of the four following substances that may be present in food is far more risky than the other three: calcium hexametaphosphate, methyl paraben, sodium benzoate, and trichloroethylene. Or he may ask himself how confident he would feel making decisions about what safety features to buy in order to guard against power lawnmower accidents or to protect against a radio exploding or electrocuting him. If he does know, how confident does he feel that he understands the risks associated with various levels of the substance? Is five parts per million of benzene hexachloride a lot or a little? If the bacteria count in frozen egg is one million per gram, should we be alarmed?

What these examples suggest—and they could be multiplied manyfold—is that consumers do not ordinarily have anything approaching perfect information for judging the safety of most consumer products themselves, the misleading examples from widely publicized regulatory controversies over issues such as seatbelts and saccharin to the contrary notwithstanding. Compared with their knowledge of product features such as appearance, convenience, or taste, knowledge of safety features is typically very small.

One conclusion sometimes drawn is that lack of knowledge demonstrates lack of concern. If people do not know about safety features, it is sometimes argued, that means they do not care about them. This conclusion does not follow from the premise. When information-gathering costs something, the amount of information gathered depends not only on the perceived benefits of the information but also on how costly it would be to gather. I may "care" about two product features equally, but if information on one is cheap to obtain and information on the other is expensive, I will gather more information on the first feature than on the second. Information on product features such as appearance or convenience is often relatively easy to get. Information on a product's appearance is garnered by simple observation. For a product that does not cost very much and that is frequently repurchased, experience is a cheap way to gain information about the product's convenience or taste.[2] I may buy a certain brand of orange soda or paper tissue and try it. Then I will know whether I like it.

By contrast, gathering information on safety features is often very costly. Frequently, arcane or technical facts must be understood, and the recourse to experience is not available in the same way as with many other product features. Using a risky product does not always lead to an accident. Drinking a brand of orange soda will always lead to information on taste, but not on its additives. To go through the pain of an injury or illness is a very high cost to pay for gathering information about a product's safety. As Victor Goldberg (1974) has noted sardonically, "Learning from one's own experience is even more impractical if the injury is a very serious one. In the extreme case of a fatal accident, of course, the learning experience might be profound, but the learning curve is abruptly truncated."

The first criterion for a situation in which it would be rational for an individual to hand over decision-making authority to a third party is when the third party can gather the information more cheaply than the individual can. This criterion often applies in the case of safety features. The per consumer cost of gathering safety information is likely to be much less for an expert third party gathering it for a large group of consumers than for an individual. An expert has an easier time finding out about and evaluating different technical safety features. Since only one gathering process need occur, its cost can be divided among the large group for whom it is undertaken, rather than having to be separately borne by each individual consumer assembling similar information for himself.

The second cost associated with the act of choosing is the cost in information-processing. This involves taking information about a product feature and evaluating its significance in light of one's preferences. Memory and other cognitive limitations make it costly or simply impossible to process large amounts of information about a product, even if the information is available. Information-processing costs clearly vary across people and situations, but the more information that must be processed, the higher the processing costs. Furthermore, there is evidence that at some point "information overload" occurs, where the brain has too much information to process. Under the circumstances, one's skill at evaluating information can decrease so much that the choice reflects one's preferences worse than a choice made where less information was available, but could be processed better (see, e.g., Jacoby et al., 1974). Overload may appear not only when we must process a lot of information for a single choice, but also when we must process little information for many choices.

Choice may carry with it psychological costs as well. To be sure, there are many instances, as noted earlier, where people relish the opportunity to choose. In other instances, people might not relish the process, but believe that a choice made by a third party is likely to be so inferior to the choice they make themselves that they are willing to pay possible psychological costs. But this is not always the case. Life would be unbearable if we constantly had to make all decisions for ourselves. Information overload may produce not only evaluations poorer in quality but also feelings of frustration growing out of the realization that our brains are not processing information as well as they usually do. Furthermore, people can find some kinds of decisions very unpleasant to make. These might include thinking about distasteful things, or ones where all the alternatives are disagreeable. Everyday experience is filled with instances where people try to avoid making unpleasant decisions—if this were not the case, Harry Truman would never have placed the sign "The buck stops here" in his office. Linus, the Peanuts comic strip character, expressed the trauma that can accompany difficult choice when he said, "No problem is so big or so complicated that it can't be run away from." Yet, as Irving Janis and Leon Mann have noted, "In the extensive writings by social scientists on decision making we find hardly any mention of this obvious aspect of human choice behavior" (Janis and Mann, 1977). (Some of the same people who argue against proposals for, say, greater employee participation in choices currently made by management in the workplace, on the grounds that most workers would prefer not to be burdened psychologically with such choices, forget about this burden when proposals for government regulation of consumer products are made.)

As with costs of information-gathering, the costs of information-processing and the psychological costs of choice are likely frequently to be lower for an expert third party, as far as safety is concerned, than for the individual. Decisions about safety, because they involve so much technical information, are likely to be those where information overload makes processing costly. They are also likely to be decisions that many people find unpleasant to make. They require that one contemplate the prospect of illness, disfigurement, or even death. They also necessitate thought about tradeoffs between saving money and taking risks—thoughts that most people also find unpleasant, as can be seen by looking at how politicians, agency officials, and even business spokesmen themselves squirm when such topics are raised. In fact, I believe this uneasiness is one of the main reasons why safety decisions are handed over to government. (The argument that people do not like to think about injury is sometimes used as a justification for paternalistic interventions in the safety area, on the grounds that "people don't like to think about these things, so they won't take safety into account enough." The argument here is different. It depends on a judgment by the person *himself* that thinking about illness or injury is unpleasant and that therefore he wishes to renounce his authority to choose to a third party.) An expert third party can generally process information much more cheaply per consumer, both because of his expertise and because the cost of processing can be divided among a large group. A third party's per consumer charge for bearing any psychological costs of choice (presumably in the form of a wage premium required to attract people to such work) is also likely to be far less than the cost an individual would have to bear himself. These costs are lowered further because the third party's expertise and experience reduce possible frustration from information overload. Furthermore, the trauma of dealing with difficult choices is counterbalanced by the satisfaction that arises from power to make decisions affecting many people. Also, there may be some self-selection into such kinds of work of people who find it less traumatic to make difficult choices.

One point ought to be made about decision-making costs before proceeding. It is unrealistic to believe that many consumers consciously tote up the difference between their own and third-party decision-making costs in making a judgment about whether to renounce voluntarily the authority to choose. If a consumer does not even know about the existence of a feature along which he might judge a product, it is hard to conceive of his "deciding" how much it would cost him to gather information. Instead, the judgment consumers might reasonably be thought to make is of a much grosser sort, namely, that they know enough to know that they are quite ignorant about the whole area of product safety and that finding out will be costly. They might also conclude that they know they do not find thinking about illness or injury pleasant. On this basis, they know enough to make the general judgment that they want product safety choices *as a whole* to be turned over to a third party. This is why Milton Friedman's objection that government safety regulation "amounts to saying that we in our capacity as voters must protect ourselves in our capacity as consumers against our own ignorance" is unconvincing (Friedman, 1969). In our capacity as voters we need know only that we are ignorant or reluctant in our capacity as consumers about certain areas.

Another consideration was cited earlier as influencing the probability that it would be rational to renounce voluntarily the authority to choose: How similar is the choice the third party would make to the person's own fully informed choice?

Insofar as safety choices are concerned, there are reasons to believe that government officials often attach a higher weight to safety than the average consumer (does in deciding what safety features to mandate). This is because the organizational mission of these agencies is to promote safety and because many agency officials are recruited from safety or health professions whose ideology stresses such protection.[3] On the other hand, there is also reason to believe that the disparity normally will not be extreme. "Safety" is a value attributed high weight whenever people discuss it consciously; indeed, environmentalists have shifted the focus of their political efforts from woods and streams to safety and health out of a conviction that this strikes the most responsive chord among large numbers of Americans. I shall return to the subject of the weight people attach to safety at the end of this section. But the possibility of large disparities between the weight many consumers attach to safety and the weight government officials attach to it is the strongest reason why consumers might not wish to renounce to the government their authority to choose the safety features of products they buy. In most cases, however, the disparity in weights is not likely to be large enough to outweigh the benefits in lower decision-making costs.

Objections to the Information Argument for Intervention

Different objections might be made to the argument developed so far. One that is frequently heard runs something like this: if the consumer has difficulty making choices about safety features because he lacks information, then let the government see that the requisite information is provided, rather than mandating safety features or banning products. To do more, the argument goes, would be to throw out the baby of individual choice with the bathwater of imperfect information. (A more radical argument could be made as well: Market forces will see to it that consumers are provided with appropriate information and that there is thus no need even for government to provide or mandate information.)

Another objection is sometimes raised: Voluntary renunciation of consumer choice to *some* third party need not justify *government* standards or product bans. Consumers might hire a personal agent to make the choice for them. Or the government might be limited to certify that a product meets whatever safety standards the agency determines to be appropriate. All these methods, it is argued, allow voluntary renunciation of the authority to choose without mandatory government regulation.

I will first consider arguments claiming that the government's role should be limited to information provision—or even that such an information provision role is unjustified. For the government to mandate provision of information or to provide it itself does indeed lower information-gathering costs. To require its dissemination in nontechnical form lowers these costs further. And to make the information conveniently available (as part of labeling) lowers it still further. These steps sometimes do lower decision-making costs enough to make it worthwhile for consumers to retain their authority to choose. An example would be in the area of product quality, where the psychological costs of choice are low and preferences differ widely across consumers. In these cases, government should stick to such tasks. But in other situations, all these steps still would not lower decision-making costs enough to make it rational for a consumer to retain his authority to choose. Under such a regime, consumers still might be confronted frequently with columns of fine print presenting large numbers of product features and risk information about each. The information-processing costs of evaluating this information in the light of one's preferences remain unaffected by the cheaper information-gathering. Any psychological decision-making costs are unaffected as well.

A more radical argument against any government role even in information provision suggests that whenever products vary along a feature that some group of consumers would find relevant, the producers of the product with the more attractive features themselves have an incentive, if markets are competitive, to provide consumers with information about that attractive feature. With competitors whose products lack such features unable to make similar claims, consumers will become informed, through producer efforts, about whatever features a significant number of people value.[4]

The operation of such a mechanism is clearly seen sometimes. Manufacturers of low-tar cigarettes or margarines with a high polyunsaturated fat content advertise these features of their products widely. Manufacturers who have removed antioxidants from their potato chips promote them as being additive-free. But to show that this mechanism works sometimes is not to show that it is sufficient to obviate any need for a government role. It has a chance of working mainly where consumers *already know* something about the feature in question. Most consumers know that cigarettes and saturated fats are hazardous. This makes it much easier for producers to advertise their product's good performance on such dimensions. In cases where producers would need to create knowledge of the feature itself from scratch, such advertising is far less likely. This is because, in part, if one producer advertises, some of the benefits of creating such consumer awareness would be reaped by competitors whose products also perform well on the relevant dimension, without the competitors having to share the significant costs of educating consumers. Furthermore, the distrust consumers have of self-serving claims by producers might discourage them from accepting the information.

Alternatively, it may be argued that if ways exist to make information-gathering cheaper by using experts to gather the information and sharing the costs among large numbers of people, market incentives would also exist for private firms to arise to perform such information-gathering functions, thus making a government role unnecessary. Again, this mechanism does indeed operate to an extent. *Consumer Reports* tests products and reports the results, but this information is not as accessible as, say, information on a product label, and the cost to the consumer of locating it must thus be added to the information-gathering costs the private organization bears. Also, the decreasing marginal cost of disseminating information once it is gathered means that marginal cost pricing will not meet a private firm's cost, while pricing at higher than marginal cost will mean that an inefficiently small amount will be produced. This market failure suggests the preferability of public provision.[5] There are, then, still likely to be instances where individuals would wish to renounce voluntarily to a third party their authority to choose.

Let us turn now to objections that the third party need not be the government. Consumers might choose to let decisions be made for them by friends they trust or by expert agents they hire to make the decisions in their interests (Stigler, 1975). Mandatory government regulation, the argument continues, is a poor vehicle for making decisions

that a consumer chooses to renounce, because it binds not only those who choose *not* to make the choice themselves, but also those who *would* have wanted to do so.

Certainly there are instances where choice by agents that a consumer seeks out might be preferable to decisions by government. Consumers use doctors as agents, for instance, and to some limited extent retail stores act as agents as well. One advantage such choices have is that the agent can be apprised of the client's individual preferences. By contrast, a government agency must make a single choice, despite the existence of diverse preferences among citizens. But in other instances, looking for, paying, and monitoring a privately hired agent would be more expensive than having the government undertake the same tasks. This greater expense might outweigh the advantages of a choice personally tailored to the client's preferences. Furthermore, the private provision of the information-gathering aspect of the agent's job creates the same public goods problems as any private provision of information. And for a person to seek an agent in any individual instance, he must have enough knowledge of the existence of dimensions along which he wishes to judge the product in question to know that he needs an agent in the first place.

Another way for a person to renounce his authority to choose without requiring mandatory government regulation is for the government to certify the safety of products and for the consumer, who wished to renounce his authority, to choose simply to buy the certified product. In certifying a product, the government would decide on appropriate safety features. The only difference would be that it would not be mandatory that all products comply with the features. Only those that did comply, however, would be certified. If a consumer decides to buy a certified product, he in effect has let the government make his decision for him. But those who wish to decide for themselves would have the choice of buying a product without the certified safety feature package.

Choosing to buy certified products might be an appropriate form for voluntary renunciation of the authority to choose. But it might not be a consumer's preferred alternative either. Most important as a reason for preferring mandatory regulation to certification is the fear that despite one's general resolution to buy only certified products, one might be tempted in individual cases to depart from one's resolution and buy noncertified ones. The concept of "temptation"—of doing something one does not "really" want to do—is a difficult one for the standard economic paradigm where, if John has voluntarily chosen *x* over *y,* he has become better off because the choice shows a preference for *x* over *y.* Therefore, he should be glad he had the opportunity to make the choice. In fact, though, it is common for people to fear that at some future moment they might act "in a moment of weakness" in a way that under normal circumstances they would not. Even if we end up not giving in to temptation, we might wish to be spared temptation so as to avoid the anxiety costs of realizing that one might, at any time, give in. Thus, a person might well prefer mandatory regulation to certification out of fear that in many specific instances, with one lawnmower in front of him that is certified and another that is not, he might "take a chance" and get the cheaper, noncertified one, although as a general matter of considered reflection he would wish to buy only certified products.[6] People frequently choose to have an alternative withheld from them at later times just to avoid temptation.

If there are psychological costs to the very *thought* of choosing something that one would ordinarily shun, the most tragic aspect of temptation is that once one has been tempted, one may be better off giving in. This may well be the case in situations where one is being tempted to risk life and limb to save a few dollars. Imagine a situation where at the moment of temptation the perceived net benefits of choosing a cheaper, more dangerous product over a more expensive but safer one is one unit. But the pangs from just considering the choice cost two units. Since these pangs are experienced whether the choice is made one way or the other, once the situation is clearly in front of you, you are better off choosing the cheaper but more dangerous product, because you then "cut your losses." But you are still one unit worse off than you otherwise would have been had the possibility of choice never been presented.

A consumer may have other reasons as well to prefer regulation to certification. If he must decide in each case whether to buy a certified or noncertified brand, the decision-making costs are still significant. Even if a consumer decides that he will buy

only certified brands, he still must remember to check for the certification every time he buys an unfamiliar product. Given the number of times that people buy unfamiliar products, this may add up to a not insignificant annoyance. Imagine also the situation of the consumer buying an unfamiliar product who sees no certification on the product. This may be because the product has no significant safety or health aspects that need to be regulated, and thus it has not been subject to certification. The consumer who wishes simply to trust the judgment of the government agency and buy only certified (or regulated) products need not check if the product is subject to mandatory regulation. Either the product will possess the safety features the regulation requires or it will not have been regulated because it was deemed that the product had no safety aspects that needed regulation. In either case, the consumer can proceed without further ado to buy the product. If the signal to the consumer is *only* a certification, however, absence of certification requires further investigation by the consumer who wishes to buy only certified products. He must check whether the product type has been subject to certification (in which case the particular product in question has not been certified) or whether the product type has not been subject to certification. Again, extra effort is required that a consumer may prefer not to expend. He may thus favor regulation to certification. (This might be dealt with by placing the certification on products that were not required to meet any standards in order to gain the certification, but this would probably reduce the general perceived value of the certification in the eyes of many consumers.) Lastly, a consumer who wants to see the government demonstrate a higher level of concern for his welfare might prefer regulation to certification because the former provides that demonstration.

It may be accepted that there are people who would rather have government set mandatory safety standards than hire private agents or have the government certify product safety. Yet it still might be protested that others who would prefer to make the decisions themselves (or to hire their own agents or choose with the help of government certification) should not be forced to pay for safety features they do not want.

Under the circumstances, one group or the other will end up being hurt. Either those opposed to mandatory safety standards are harmed by being forced to buy products with mandated features, or those favoring mandatory standards are hurt by having to do without the mandatory standards they seek. Whether the social decision finally made responds to the wishes of the first group or the second has, then, external effects on the group whose wishes are denied. I shall return to the question of how social determinations may be made in such situations when dealing with external effects, in a different context, in the next section. Those seeking mandatory regulation are demanding something that will help themselves and hurt those who would prefer to choose for themselves. The latter group, then, may be seen as passive victims of the acts of those demanding regulation. The *prima facie* duty to do justice suggests sympathy with passive victims against active encroachers. Nevertheless, considerations of the size of the groups seeking and wishing to avoid regulation, as well as of the nature of the interference contemplated, are relevant to such judgments. In regard to the size of the groups in the case of government safety regulation, there exist unambiguous survey data. In a 1974 poll, respondents were asked whether the government should "make sure that each packaged, canned, or frozen food is safe to eat." An overwhelming 97% agreed, a degree of unanimity hard to replicate for any government policy. In a 1976 poll, respondents were asked a similar question about government product safety standards and 85% agreed.[7] As for the extent of interference, it is not generally great. Those opposed to regulation are interfered with to the extent of having to pay some extra money for safety features they would have preferred to avoid. Their homes are not broken into. They are not restrained by physical force from moving around where they wish. Their fortunes are not decimated. My own conclusion is that it would be wrong to prevent the vast majority of Americans who prefer to turn the general run of decisions about product safety over to the government from doing so.[8]

The figures on the percentages of those who wish to turn safety decisions over to the government also shed light on the earlier brief examination of whether decisions made by government safety regulators were likely to be sufficiently similar to those that consumers would make themselves, if fully informed, to make it rational for consumers voluntarily to hand such choices over to regulators.

If government agencies did make decisions frequently that wildly departed from those that consumers would make themselves, one would expect the survey results to have been dramatically different. Instead, they show a broad vote of confidence for the efforts of government agencies regulating product safety.

There remain instances of public outcry over issues such as saccharin. A wise agency official might well conclude that such outcries signify withdrawal in the specific instances of consumer's general delegation to government of the authority to choose. It is not irrational for a consumer to decide as a general matter to renounce that authority but wish to reclaim it when he feels himself sufficiently informed and/or when the agency would make a decision sufficiently different from his own.

Not to allow people the option of delegating to government agencies decisions they would prefer not to make is to do liberty a disservice. Those who oppose such an option appear to place choice on a pedestal as a supreme value. But in doing so they set it up for a fall. Erich Fromm wrote almost 40 years ago about the desire among some people to "escape from freedom" which the support for Nazi and Communist totalitarian movements showed (Fromm, 1941). People might want to escape from freedom, Fromm wrote, if they felt overwhelmed by constant demands to make choices they did not feel they could handle. If the only options perceived are either having to make too many choices they would prefer to delegate or giving up their freedom entirely, many might choose the course—horrible to all who value liberty—of giving up freedom. Ironically, those who would refuse to allow people the option of delegating choices to the government often end up themselves making paternalistic arguments—that liberty of choice is such an important value that people must be required to give it priority under all circumstances, whether they wish to or not, or that people must be protected against the long-term erosion in ability to choose that might result from choosing to give up too many choices. Those who truly value liberty of choice will be eager to allow people to delegate to the government choices they do not wish to make, so that they can better husband their choice-making resources for decisions they genuinely wish to make for themselves.

EXTERNAL EFFECTS AND THE OVERRULING OF A PERSON'S OWN CHOICE

John Stuart Mill affirmed in *On Liberty* that the restriction against interference with a person's authority to choose applied to acts that affected only the individual himself and not to those acts affecting others. Ever since Mill, however, this distinction has come under withering attack. Government intervention in people's choices may occur not out of a desire to overrule paternalistically an individual's choices insofar as they regard only himself, but out of a desire to protect others against the negative consequences of those choices. Thus, banning saccharin or requiring people to wear seatbelts might be justified on nonpaternalistic grounds even if people did not want to hand these decisions to the government, because of the effects bladder cancer or auto accidents have, not on the individual himself, but on others. The distinction between intervention on paternalistic grounds and intervention on the grounds that others must be protected against the negative consequences of a person's behavior is often lost in the general public debate on regulation, where opposition to both kinds of intervention tends to get lumped together as complaints against "government interference." Thus, the resentment of businessmen against OSHA or EPA regulations should not be confused with resentment against a bureaucrat who believes he knows what is good for a person better than the person does himself.

The discussions of external effects, such as pollution, in introductory economics textbooks tend to obscure the issue, because they imply that most actions lack external effects. That "no man is an island" dashes any attempt to make such neat categorizations. Clearly the argument for freedom of political speech, an argument often made in terms similar to the one against paternalism, can hardly be made on the grounds that free speech affects no one else. The famous argument by Lord Devlin against allowing pornography was based on its external effects on social cohesion (Devlin, 1971).

The inevitability of external effects extends to actions in the private sphere as well. Words we speak every day, small gestures we make, even the tone of our voices all may profoundly affect the feelings of those around us who value our friendship or our love. The clothes we wear, the opinions we express, the plays we attend, the colors we paint our houses all may give joy to or offend those around us. If I choose to patronize a new business in town, my action has an effect on other businesses that lose my patronage. Even if we are passive, our passivity affects others. Words we fail to say or gestures we fail to make can affect another person as much as words we do say or gestures we do make. Whenever we are passive, we affect others who could have benefited from our aid. The person who sees a fire starting in a building and goes on his way without calling the fire department is hardly in a position to say that his failure to act had no external effects.

If a person becomes sick or is injured or if he dies because he purchased an unsafe product, clearly his action in buying the product had external effects on friends and loved ones. If a person is insured, other policyholders ultimately foot the bills.[9] If a person is not insured and suffers great financial hardship, other members of society still end up paying. When the victim appears before us after a sad fate has befallen him, the rest of us pay cash to help the uninsured victim out—or pay in the form of the guilty feelings occasioned by turning our backs on the victim, even if we attempt the justification that the victim made his bed and now should have to lie in it. The fact that we end up either saving people from the really bad consequences of their choices or feeling guilty if we do not is an argument, based on external effects and not on paternalism, for intervening in the original choices. Consequently, we require people to provide for their old age through Social Security, give the poor in-kind rather than cash transfers, or mandate safety regulations....

To decide in a given case whether an individual should have the right to make decisions about what risks to take, despite the harm that the bad consequences of such decisions can cause others, raises difficult questions to which answers cannot be cranked out deductively. It will not do to argue, as is sometimes done, that external effects arguments must never be used to justify restricting risks because it would be possible to use such arguments to eradicate all exercises of liberty. For the fact is that *everyone,* even libertarians, recognizes that at some point the external effects of an individual's acts become great enough to justify taking away the individual's right to act. Thus, all agree that murder or assault are not rightful displays of liberty. We cannot escape a controversial balancing process in which the extent of the external effects that the person's actions produce, the importance of the act for the individual, and possible deontological considerations regarding *prima facie* duties, are weighed against one another....

The purpose of this article has not been to defend or criticize any specific example of government safety regulation. Rather, I have attempted to defend the justifiability, in principle, of such regulation against the specific accusation that it inevitably involves paternalism and hence should be condemned. I have agreed with the general condemnation of paternalism, while suggesting nonpaternalistic justifications for such intervention and arguing that there are certain cases where cautious paternalistic intervention might be justified.

That government safety regulation can be justified in principle does not necessarily mean that the safety regulatory activities of the Food and Drug Administration, the Consumer Product Safety Commission, and the Federal Trade Commission on balance have been justified in practice. My own belief, though, is that they clearly have been. Establishing the case for such a proposition would require going through a representative sample of the regulatory interventions these agencies have undertaken and analyzing them in light of the conceptual criteria for intervention presented here. This does not imply that there are not individual regulations that are excessively or insufficiently protective, or that some things that have been regulated should never have been regulated while others not regulated should have been. The view that such regulation is to be condemned in principle as paternalistic has constituted a not insignificant part of the attack on consumer product safety regulation. That bulwark of the case against such regulation thus falls.

BIBLIOGRAPHY

Brandt, Richard (1959): *Ethical Theory*, Englewood Cliffs, NJ: Prentice-Hall. chaps. 15–17.

Calabresi, Guido and Malamed, A. Douglas, "Property Rights, Liability Rules, and Inalienability," *Harvard Law Review, 85* (April 1972).

Cornell, Nina W., et al. (1976): "Safety Regulation," in Henry Owen and Charles L. Schultz, eds., *Setting National Priorities: The Next Ten Years*, Washington, DC: The Brookings Institution, 465–66.

Cyert, Richard and March, James (1963): *A Behavioral Theory of the Firm*, Englewood Cliffs, NJ: Prentice-Hall, p. 118.

Demsetz, Howard, "Toward a Theory of Property Rights," *American Economic Review, 57* (May 1967).

Devlin, Lord Patrick (1971): "Morals and the Criminal Law," reprinted in Richard A. Wasserstrom, ed., *Morality and the Law*, Belmont, CA: Wadsworth.

Food and Drug Administration (1976): *Consumer Nutrition Knowledge Survey, Report 1*, Washington, DC: FDA, 39.

Friedman, Milton (1962): *Capitalism and Freedom*. Chicago, IL: Univ. Chicago P., 148.

Fromm, Erich (1941): *Escape from Freedom*. New York: Rinehart.

Goldberg, Victor, "The Economics of Product Safety and Imperfect Information," *The Bell Journal of Economics and Management Science, 5* (Spring 1974), 686.

Hart, H. L. A. (1964): *Law, Liberty and Morality*, Stanford, CA: Stanford U.P.

Jacoby, Jacob, et al., "Brand Choice Behavior as a Function of Information Load," *Journal of Marketing Research, 11* (February 1974), 65.

Janis, Irving L. and Mann, Leon (1977): *Decision Making: A Psychological Analysis of Conflict, Choice, and Commitment*, New York: The Free Press, 3.

Kelman, Steven (1979): "The Psychological Costs of Markets" (stencil).

Kelman, Steven (1981): *Regulating America, Regulating Sweden: A Comparative Study of Occupational Safety and Health Policies*, Cambridge, MA: MIT Press, chap. 3.

Lieberman, Jethro. "The Relativity of Injury," *Philosophy and Public Affairs, 6* (Summer 1977).

Lipset, Seymour Martin and Schneider, William, "The Public View of Regulation," *Public Opinion, 2* (January 1979), 11.

Nelson, Philip, "Information and Consumer Behavior," *Journal of Political Economy, 78* (March 1970).

Posner, Richard A. (1979): "The Federal Trade Commission's Mandated Disclosure Program," in Harvey J. Goldschmid, ed., *Business Disclosure: Government's Need to Know*, New York: McGraw-Hill.

Ross, W. D. (1930): *The Right and the Good*, London: Oxford U.P.

Stigler, George (1975): *The Citizen and the State*, Chicago, IL: Univ. Chicago P., 12.

Tversky, Amos, "Intransitivity of Preferences," *Psychological Review, 76* (January 1969).

Tversky, Amos and Kahneman, Daniel (1974): "Judgment under Uncertainty: Heuristics and Biases," in Richard Zeckhauser et al., eds., *Benefit-Cost and Policy Analysis*, Chicago, IL: Aldine.

Wikler, Daniel, "Paternalism and the Mildly Retarded," *Philosophy and Public Affairs, 8* (Summer 1979).

NOTES

1. Throughout this part of the discussion I will consider the case of an individual consumer. Both decision-making costs and the gap between the fully informed decision an individual would have made and the choice a third party makes may of course vary among individuals. I discuss the aggregation question in a situation with variation across individuals at the end of this section.

2. This point is made in Nelson (1970).

3. For a discussion of these points, see Kelman (1981).

4. This argument appears in Posner (1979).

5. On this point, see Cornell et al. (1976).

6. Another alternative is possible in the case of products not subject to certification. Such products might carry a statement such as "This product not subject to certification." Note, however, that this alternative would require relearning behavior on the part of consumers whenever certification was newly introduced, either because the government finally got around to looking at the product in question or because of a change in knowledge about the product's safety that led to development of certification criteria where none had previously existed.

7. These figures are from Food and Drug Administration (1976) and Lipset and Schneider (1979).

8. A case could probably be made for allowing establishment of certain stores, with warnings prominently posted, that sell only products that do not meet regulatory standards. This would allow those who wish to buy such products the opportunity to do so without subjecting others to serious temptation problems. There would be important implementation problems with such proposals, however, especially with fraud at the manufacturer level (labeling noncomplying products as complying ones) or at the distributor level. Also, if an important part of the justification for regulation in a specific instance is the external effects of choices a person makes (to be discussed below), then the individual's own choice might be overridden. These problems make the establishment of such outlets for noncomplying products hardly a top priority item on the consumer protection regulation agenda.

9. That situation is only partly remedied if the policyholder falls into an experience category with a higher premium. It is sometimes argued that only the existence of government-provided health insurance creates the external effect from accidents that may be used to justify government intervention. This contention is then used to illustrate the general view that government regulation pyramids on itself, one regulation soon requiring another, with the implication being that the process should never have started. The use of government-provided health insurance to argue for this contention is unwarranted. First, there exist important external effects from an accident other than bills paid by fellow insurance policyholders. Second, this problem exists whether insurance is governmental and mandatory or private and voluntary.

Decision Scenario 1

TOBACCO COMPANIES UNDER FIRE

On June 13, 1988, the tobacco industry suffered its first real loss in over three hundred product liability cases. In previous suits, the industry was able to emerge victorious. The industry usually carried the day through appeals to smokers' voluntary assumption of the risks of smoking, to the clear warnings present on the cigarette package since 1966, and to the "lack of conclusive scientific proof of a causal link between smoking and lung disease." In the case of Rose Cipollone, deceased, a Newark, New Jer-

sey, jury found a single tobacco company partially responsible for injuries suffered by a consumer of its products. It awarded her husband $400,000 in damages.

The plaintiff's lawyer in the Cipollone case brought suit on a number of separate grounds. The Liggett Group, Inc., producers of the L&Ms and Chesterfields smoked by Mrs. Cipollone, was charged with failure to warn consumers prior to 1966 about the dangers of their product and with a breach of express warranty that the product was healthful. Those warranties were purportedly presented through ads associating cigarettes with health; some of those ads touted the brands as those most

This case was prepared from the Bureau of National Affairs' *Product Liability Reporter*, vol. 16, no. 25 (June 17, 1988); *Cipollone v. Liggett*, 893 F. 2d 541 (1990); *New York Times*, Feb. 18, 1995, p. 1.

smoked by doctors. Liggett, together with two other tobacco companies, was also charged with conspiracy to conceal evidence about the health effects of smoking and with fraudulent misrepresentation.

The jury did not accept the charges of conspiracy or misrepresentation against any of the three companies. After the verdict, lawyers for the plaintiff argued that the jury's failure to return a guilty verdict on these charges should not be read as a rejection of the charge of conspiracy; they contended that the jury simply decided that prior to 1966, when warnings were first required on cigarettes by order of the surgeon general, no compensable conspiracy occurred. (The lawyer for the Cipollones was among the first to present documents obtained from tobacco industry files as evidence that the companies covered up data about the health effects of smoking.)

On the charge of failure to warn, the jury found Liggett guilty but responsible only for 20 percent of the subsequent harm to Mrs. Cipollone. The jury held that Mrs. Cipollone was 80 percent responsible for her own death. Because of a New Jersey law, no damages were assessed against the company on this verdict because Mrs. Cipollone was more than 50 percent responsible for her own condition.

On the final item, breach of express warranty, New Jersey allows damages on a proportional basis even when the victim is more than 50 percent responsible. The $400,000 award was compensation for Liggett's partial role in the harm caused to Mrs. Cipollone because of its breach of warranty.

The judgment of the jury was appealed, and in 1990 the Third Circuit Court of Appeals returned the case for retrial on a number of grounds. It held that the jury improperly considered Mrs. Cipollone's post-1965 behavior (after cigarette package warnings) in assessing her 80 percent responsible for her own injury. The Appeals Court also held that Liggett should have been permitted to argue that Mrs. Cipollone did not believe the advertising health claims. Court observers predicted that a retrial would still find Liggett guilty. However, the Cipollones' attorney gave up the case. He said that the litigation had already cost his small firm more

than it could ever recoup and that his firm could no longer afford to press the case. It has not been retried.

The U.S. Surgeon General has recently declared publicly that nicotine in tobacco is an addictive drug. In 1994, David Kessler, Commissioner of the FDA, began investigating charges that the tobacco companies knew for years that nicotine was addictive and that they manipulated the levels of the drug to keep smokers hooked. As a result, a Louisiana judge cleared the way for a class action suit against tobacco companies for allegedly hiding the fact that nicotine was addictive. The class action suit joins together sixty large law firms whose combined assets will make the conclusion of the Cipollone case unlikely to be repeated. Tobacco companies are also being sued by several state attorney generals who are attempting to recover state moneys spent on Medicare costs for smokers.

- Does heavy advertising of cigarettes have any bearing on the tobacco industry's defense that smokers have "voluntarily assumed a risk"? Would the age at which an individual begins to smoke make any difference to your answer?

- What explains the relatively strict government regulation of alcohol consumption, given that the effects of tobacco are as harmful to the user? Is prohibition of any product legitimate?

- Are companies entitled to market any good for which there is demand, or do they have a responsibility to market only goods which provide a net benefit to consumers? Some authors point to psychic benefits associated with products, such as an enhanced self-image. Does this make tobacco a product that arguably produces net benefits?

- The tobacco industry pursues vigorous investigations into the background of plaintiffs who have brought suit. There are reports of unannounced visits in late evening hours to take depositions from family members. The industry also steadfastly denies any link between tobacco and cancer. Is the industry justified in the activities it uses to defend itself?

Decision Scenario 2
THE MICHIGAN TOY BOX COMPANY

The Michigan Toy Box Company of Detroit, Michigan, has established a reputation of producing durable, high-quality toy chests for children. Recently, however, they have discovered that the very durability of their toy chest can pose serious threats to the children who use them. The toy chests are constructed of prime hardwoods with a thickness of three quarters of an inch. The lids of these chests alone weigh eight pounds. Reports have returned to the company that nationally nearly one hundred children a year are either killed or seriously injured when a toy box lid falls on their heads or necks while they are reaching into the chest.

Consumer advocates have suggested a solution to the problem. It involves installing a friction hinge on the lid that prevents the lid from falling freely. The hinge functions by providing a resistance that causes the lid to close by dropping slowly. If all toy chests had such a safety device, consumer safety experts claim, the deaths and injuries suffered by children using toy chests would decline to almost zero. The recent nature of the safety problem and the slowness of government regulatory agencies concerned with safety, however, have prevented any mandatory safety standards for toy chests from being established as law. The Michigan Toy Box Company must decide whether to install the suggested safety device voluntarily.

The production costs associated with the addition of the safety hinge are clear. The cost per unit for the hinges is rather small, under $1.50. However, the company has determined that installation of the hinge will require an additional quarter-hour of labor time in the production of each chest. Salaries of workers at the plant are higher than national averages for unskilled laborers because of the competition for labor in the Detroit area and because of the strength of unions in the local labor scene. The additional quarter-hour will cost the company $1.25 for each chest produced. Although the hinges would require no major retooling for the production line, the installation of the hinges will also entail capital and maintenance expenditures associated with the purchase of additional tools and the creation of a new work station in the assembly process. The company estimates that in-

stallation of the hinges will raise costs by about $5.00 per chest.

Although the company's reputation and sales are strong, there is increasing competition from other manufacturers because inflation has made the Michigan Toy Box product appear high priced to parents of young children. The company doubts whether it could increase retail prices by $5.00 and retain an important segment of its consumer population. In fact, the relatively infrequent rate of injury associated with the toy chests makes it less than probable that marketing that emphasized the new safety feature could offset expected sales losses due to increased prices. The infrequent injury rate also makes less likely any major liability settlements against the company and in favor of families whose children were injured. (The expectation is that the courts will not find the product defective and that liability insurance will not increase because of large settlements.)

Management of the company has decided for the interim to forgo installation of the hinges because of an impending recession that will dampen sales. They do not wish to exacerbate that decline in sales by installing the hinges, although the addition of the hinges would not threaten the continued viability of the company.

The company's sales remained stable, though not as strong as expected, throughout the recession. The result was that the company had a backlogged stock of toy chests in its storage facilities. During the recession, however, consumer advocates succeeded in having mandatory safety standards requiring the hinges passed into law. To sell the boxes in the United States the company would have to remove them from storage, transport them to the factory, and install the hinges. The additional labor and transportation costs would add further to the list price of the chests. Rather than install the hinges, the company sold the chests to another company (which it has frequently supplied) in neighboring Windsor, Ontario. Canadian law does not require the safety hinge.

- Was the company's financial judgment not to produce toy chests with safety hinges ethically acceptable? What about its decision to supply the stored chests to another legal jurisdiction to avoid installing the hinges on the chests in stock?

■ When should financial considerations be sufficient to override a concern for the safety of the product? Does the frequency of injury have any implications for an answer to the preceding question?

■ Would your judgment about the morality of the management decision have been any different were the injured from the adult consumer population? Does this indicate that standards of product safety should differ between types of products and types of consumers who use those products?

Decision Scenario 3
GREENMAN V. YUBA POWER PRODUCTS

Greenman v. Yuba Power Products is a landmark case in product liability law because it was the first product liability case to be decided as a case in tort law rather than contract law. This distinction may seem subtle at first, but it has far-ranging implications.

Mr. Greenman saw a Shopsmith power tool, a combination saw, drill, and wood lathe, demonstrated at a retail store and studied a sales brochure prepared by the manufacturer, Yuba Power Products, Inc. He decided he wanted a Shopsmith for his home workshop, and his wife gave him one for Christmas 1955. In 1957, Mr. Greenman purchased the necessary attachments to use the Shopsmith as a lathe for turning large pieces of wood. After he had used the machine in this way several times, a piece of wood suddenly flew out of the machine and struck him on the head, inflicting serious injuries. Ten-and-a half months later, Mr. Greenman filed suit against both the retailer and manufacturer claiming negligence and a breach of warranty.

An earlier New Jersey case, *Henningsen v. Bloomfield Motors,* had established a consumer's right to recover damages from a manufacturer on the basis of an implied warranty. But warranties are a matter of contract, implied or otherwise, and contract law sets certain restrictions upon an individual's ability to recover damages. In contract law: (a) An individual must give written notice of breach of warranty within a specified time limit; (b) the statute of limitations begins at the time of the sale; and (c) recovery of damages can be limited or precluded by a contract disclaimer.

Unfortunately for Mr. Greenman, he gave written notice of the alleged breach of contract after the time limit had expired. (His case could have been further damaged if the injury had occurred after the statute of limitations on contracts had expired, or if the warranty had contained a simple disclaimer like "the manufacturer assumes no liability for injuries resulting in the use of this product.") The California court judged the manufacturer to be liable anyway. They reasoned that "the purpose of such liability is to ensure that the costs of injuries resulting from defective products are borne by the manufacturers that put such products on the market rather than by the injured parties who are powerless to protect themselves.... The remedies of injured consumers ought to be made to depend upon the intricacies of the law of sales. To establish the manufacturer's liability it was sufficient that plaintiff proved that he was injured while using the Shopsmith in a way it was intended to be used as a result of a defect in design and manufacture...."

■ Was this decision fair? Could the manufacturer claim it was unfair since, in effect, the rules were changed after the fact?

■ Are disclaimers legitimate even in contract law? Can you think of situations in which such disclaimers are unfair?

■ The court decided it was unfair to hold the consumer liable because consumers "are powerless to protect themselves." Is this true? How might a defender of caveat emptor respond?

Decision Scenario 4
CHILDREN AND REASONABLY SAFE PRODUCTS

When children are involved, how safe need a "reasonably safe" product be? How vigilant should manufacturers be in forseeing misuse? Consider two cases.

In *Ritter v. Narragansett Electric Co.,* a four-year-old girl was injured when she used an oven door as a stepstool to stand on so that she could peek into a pot on the top of the stove. Her weight caused the stove to tip over, causing serious injury to the child. The first question concerns a possible defective design. Was the stove defective because it could not support thirty pounds on the oven door without tipping? A forseeable use of the stove could involve placing a heavy roasting pan on the oven door while checking food during preparation. If the stove tipped over and injured the cook during this use, it is very likely that a court would rule against the manufacturer on the grounds of a design defect. The manufacturer should have forseen the use of the door as a shelf. Could the manufacturer forsee the use of the door as a stepstool? Should it matter, since the product was defective in this regard anyway?

Vincer v. Esther Williams Swimming Pool Co. concerned a two-year-old boy who climbed the ladder of an above-ground swimming pool at his grandparents' house and fell into the pool. He remained under water for some time before being rescued. As a result, he suffered severe and permanent brain damage. His family sued the manufacturer, claiming that the pool should have had a self-closing gate and/or an automatically retractable ladder. Knowing that children are attracted to swimming pools and knowing that many children drown each year because of such accidents, should the manufacturer have forseen this possibility? Was it "unreasonable" not to include protections against such an accident in the design of the swimming pool?

- Courts ruled against the manufacturer in *Ritter* and in favor of the manufacturer in *Vincer*. Do you agree? Why or why not?
- Does your determination of "reasonably safe product" depend on the person who is using it? If so, are any products "reasonably safe" where children are concerned? If so, who decides what is "reasonable"?

Decision Scenario 5
A. H. ROBINS AND THE DALKON SHIELD

The A. H. Robins Company of Richmond, Virginia, marketed an intrauterine contraceptive device (IUD) known as the Dalkon Shield in the early 1970s. The company pursued an aggressive marketing program for the potentially profitable IUD despite early reports of medical complications in women who used the device. However, in 1974 the company stopped marketing the Dalkon Shield in the face of mounting suits against the company from women who were harmed by the product. The device, which was implanted in the uterus and

could be removed by an attached string, caused serious infections, infertility, perforations of the uterine wall, and in some cases, damage to the stomach when it worked its way through the wall of the uterus and attached itself to the stomach.

Robins's response to product liability suits was as aggressive as its marketing program had been. It used its legal resources to delay litigation, and it subjected female plaintiffs to humiliating investigations of their sexual histories. Eventually, however, Robins began to lose in its courtroom battles. A Minnesota court ordered a search of company files and found evidence that the management of Robins marketed the Dalkon Shield with sketchy research and despite knowledge at an early stage

This case was prepared from the following sources: *Product Safety and Liability Reporter,* vol. 16, nos. 4 and 29; *The Nation,* February 13, 1989; and *The MacNeil–Lehrer Report.*

that infectious bacteria could migrate up the attached string into the uterus. In these pretrial discovery proceedings, Robins claimed several significant documents had been lost; a company attorney later admitted to destroying documents.

After the company lost several large awards in product liability suits, it filed for bankruptcy under Chapter 11 of the U.S. bankruptcy code, arguing that its possible liability exposure was greater than the net assets of the company. The Chapter 11 filing froze all suits against the company until the court could determine the potential combined value of the liability suits that were either pending or expected.

Eventually, Robins's stock was priced in a way that made it an attractive takeover target. American Home Products, a New York–based company, reached an agreement to buy Robins. This agreement, which was approved by the bankruptcy court, establishes a $2.5 billion trust fund for victims of the Dalkon Shield. Victims can collect by merely showing medical proof of injury; no lawyers or litigation will be required. Damage awards are predicted to be approximately $1,000 to $10,000 for the large majority of victims and $50,000 to $200,000 for those with the most serious injuries. The settlement also precludes further suits against Robins's officers and insulates them from punitive damage awards.

In addition, American Home Products will pay about $700 million to Robins's stockholders. Since Robins was about 40 percent family owned, much of that award will go to the Robins family and to

E. Claiborne Robins Senior and Junior, who were executives of the company. These two Robins family officers must each pay $5 million into the trust fund. The settlement, however, will provide each of them many millions more than their respective contributions to the trust fund.

The Robins settlement has been criticized for inadequately compensating injured victims, for shielding the company's executives from personal liability, and for providing substantial profits to shareholders, especially members of the controlling family. The settlement's benefits for shareholders stand in marked contrast to the bankruptcy settlement in the case of Johns-Manville, the asbestos producer.

- Should companies faced with potentially large damage awards follow Robins's example and pursue every legal mechanism within their power to avoid those awards?
- Should Chapter 11 settlements insulate corporate officers from personal liability for tortious actions performed in the exercise of their corporate authorities?
- What should be the priorities in a bankruptcy settlement that involves both traditional commercial debtors and persons injured by the company's products?
- If the bankruptcy or takeover settlement does not fully compensate consumers injured by a company's products, should the federal government subsidize such compensation?

Decision Scenario 6
CAUTION: MCDONALD'S COFFEE IS *HOT!*

On February 27, 1992, seventy-nine-year-old Stella Liebeck was burned after spilling on her lap a cup of coffee that she had purchased at a McDonald's drive-through window. She brought suit against McDonald's and was awarded a jury verdict of $2.86 million—$160,000 in compensatory damages

This scenario was prepared from the following sources: *Dateline NBC*, April 28, 1995; *Consumer Reports*, May 1995, p. 312; and *Jury Verdict Research*, Liebeck v. McDonald's Restaurants, Case # CV 932419.

and $2.7 million in punitive damages. A judge reduced the punitive damage award to $480,000, or three times the amount of the award for the injury. McDonald's and Liebeck subsequently settled out of court for an undisclosed amount.

The initial jury award received quite a bit of media attention—most of it critical. The award became a rallying cry for those interested in reform of the current product liability law. Advocacy ads excoriating the award as an example of the legal system gone haywire appeared on radio and television as Congress was beginning debate on liability reform.

The legal case began when Ms. Liebeck requested $10,000 for medical expenses and an additional amount for pain and suffering. McDonald's refused a settlement. Liebeck's initial demand in court was for $300,000. The company argued, however, that the coffee was not unreasonably dangerous and that Liebeck was responsible for her own injuries. The jury obviously evaluated the case differently than did McDonald's or much of the media.

The jury's verdict was driven by a number of factors. McDonald's served its coffee at 185 degrees Fahrenheit, far higher than the temperature of typical home-brewed coffee. The jury found that coffee at that temperature was both undrinkable and more dangerous than a reasonable consumer would expect (part of the definition of a defective product). The coffee was hot enough to cause third-degree burns over an extensive portion of Liebeck's thighs and buttocks. The injury required skin grafting and resulted in scarring.

Testimony at trial revealed that McDonald's had over seven hundred past burn claims lodged against it. The company claimed that it served the coffee at that temperature in response to consumer demand, but it had done no survey to assess the sales impact of coffee served at lower temperatures. As a result of past claims, McDonald's had put a warning on the cup and had designed a tighter fitting lid. The latter,

ironically, may have been a factor in Liebeck's injury; she held the cup between her legs in order to pry the lid off.

The jury found that Liebeck was 20 percent responsible for her own injury, but it also found McDonald's warning was not sufficiently noticeable to alert consumers to the danger. The punitive damage award of $2.7 million was, jurors later said, an attempt to send a message to fast-food chains. The amount was approximately two days of coffee sales for McDonald's. The judge reduced that punitive damage award. In doing so, however, he said that McDonald's action was "willful, wanton, reckless, and callous."

- Punitive damage awards exist in order to deter future harmful actions. What level of award do you believe is necessary to achieve that deterrence effect? When would a cap on such awards undercut the purpose of the awards?

- How can a jury apportion responsibility for injury? What principles could be used to establish percentage responsibility, as was done in this case?

- Was McDonald's action reckless, as the judge claimed? Can a corporation legitimately block such a charge if it has evidence of customer preferences to explain its actions?

- Given the facts as presented, if you were on the jury, would you have voted with all the other jurors to award Liebeck damages? Would you have awarded the same amount?

11

Advertising

Two main topics are addressed in this chapter on advertising: deceptive advertising and the effect of nondeceptive advertising on consumer autonomy.

All advertising aims to influence us. Attempted influence is obviously not, in itself, morally objectionable. We all attempt at times to influence the desires and opinions of others. When we attempt to influence another by reasons and argument, our rational persuasion is perfectly acceptable. Some other attempts to influence, though, count as undue and morally inappropriate. The challenge is to find some consistent and principled way to identify those attempts at influence that are unacceptable.

We can start that search by attending to the characteristics of deception. Certainly, deceptive influences are presumptively immoral. But deception is presumed wrong because it attempts to interfere with a person's autonomy. It tries to prevent the person from making a rational choice by having that person unknowingly act on false beliefs. If this is what makes deceptive advertising wrong, then there will be other techniques of influence used by advertisers that are also wrong, namely, those that attempt to manipulate an individual in a way that tries to disable that person's critical judgment.

When we consider advertising influences, then, we should keep in mind that there are different categories of influence. Reasonable persuasion is one; manipulation and its subspecies, deception, are others. In your moral assessment of advertising, you will need to identify which techniques of advertisers fall into which of these categories. The readings in the chapter will help in your analysis.

The first reading, by John McCall, explains in more detail the grounds for presuming that deception is wrong. It argues that, regardless of the effect, any attempt to deceive in advertising is presumptively immoral. The reading goes on to apply that analysis to a number of advertising techniques, and it concludes that advertisers and the public are insufficiently critical of contemporary advertising practices.

The next three readings focus on another aspect of deceptive ads. Whereas McCall's article concerned an ethical assessment of deceptive intent, these three readings discuss when government should regulate deceptive ads.

GOVERNMENT REGULATION
OF ADVERTISING

The Federal Trade Commission is the primary administrative agency charged with policing advertising practices. The five FTC commissioners have broad authority to regulate commercial speech. The commission can require advertisers to conform to uniform language standards. It did this, for example, in its detailed 1994 "enforcement policy statement" that defined acceptable use of nutritional terms such as *fat free* in advertisements and on food packaging. It can require advertisements to contain affirmative disclosures such as health warnings on cigarettes. It can also effectively ban classes of advertisements by issuing cease and desist orders. Advertisers in violation of FTC orders are subject to fines.

These administrative powers of the FTC and other federal agencies that regulate ads, such as the FDA, have led some conservative critics to label the regulatory actions an unconstitutional violation of First Amendment free speech rights. Unfortunately for that view, the U.S. Supreme Court has not agreed. In the second reading, by DesJardins and McCall, the difference in constitutional treatment between commercial speech and, for example, political speech is considered. The authors briefly recount some of the traditional justifications for this difference and then go on to consider a potential public policy problem arising from a Supreme Court decision that allows corporations to engage in advocacy on political issues. Decision Scenario 6 on political advocacy also raises questions about the role of corporations in contemporary policy debate.

The readings by Ivan Preston and James Miller more directly address the question of when government should regulate potentially deceptive advertisements. Most would agree that individual consumers, as autonomous decision-makers, ought not always be protected against their own foolish choices. Also, some degree of advertising "puffery" or hyperbole is expected and allowed; just where the government should draw the line between harmless hyperbole and objectionable deception is not a matter on which all agree.

According to one position, regulation of advertising should be based on whether the advertiser intended to mislead consumers. Although the advertisers' intent is certainly relevant in judging their morality, it would appear that even an ad not intended to deceive could be a reasonable subject for regulation if its net effect is to mislead or harm consumers. If a large enough number of consumers purchased Sunlight dishwashing detergent as lemon juice concentrate because of the presence of a lemon on the label, the FTC might legitimately intervene even if the intent of the advertisers was benign. For public policy decisions, then, the *effect* of an advertisement is perhaps more relevant than the intent of the advertiser.

Ivan Preston and James Miller present two different pairs of criteria for when to regulate. Both sets of criteria are based on the effect of an ad. Preston distinguishes between regulating to protect the reasonable, informed consumer (the reasonable man standard) and regulating to protect the foolish consumer (the ignorant man standard). Preston seems to believe that the FTC has occasionally flirted with too extreme an ignorant man standard. Preston's most recent work suggests that he is rather in favor of a modified reasonable/ignorant man standard that moves the FTC to act when a substantial minority of consumers are misled.

James Miller offers a different pair of standards for determining when to regulate. Miller, himself an FTC commissioner when he wrote this article, chastises the commission for sometimes regulating when it merely expects consumers to be misled. Miller argues that this quick action by the FTC unjustly imposes increased costs on business. Miller, in place of what he considers armchair predictions, would allow the FTC to intervene only when market research has proven that consumers were deceived.

If we take these two authors' alternatives, we could construct a simple matrix as follows:

	Proven Deception	Expected Deception
Reasonable Man Deceived	A	B
Ignorant Man Deceived	C	D

A regulatory approach defined by box D, where FTC action occurs when commissioners merely expect that the more ignorant consumer would be misled, allows more frequent government regulation. An approach defined by box A, on the other hand, would place strict conditions on when the FTC could regulate ads. Currently, the approach most usual for the FTC is that defined by box C, where the "ignorant man" standard refers to deception of about 20 percent of consumers. You should decide whether any of the four approaches defined by this matrix could be universally appropriate as FTC policy. What complexities are ignored by the simple choice of one of these four alternatives? Do differences in target market or product advertised require different regulatory approaches?

NONDECEPTIVE ADS AND CONSUMER AUTONOMY

Debate on the other major issue of the chapter, the effect of nondeceptive ads on consumer autonomy, had its source in the classic John Kenneth Galbraith book *The Affluent Society*. His argument may be stated as three simple propositions. First, Galbraith claimed that advertising creates wants in the consumer. Second, he suggested that this shaping of consumer demand by marketers is a violation of the consumer's autonomy. Third, Galbraith contended that this want creation encourages consumers to demand, and the economy to produce, less important goods instead of goods necessary for satisfying important needs. In a striking passage, Galbraith claimed that advertising causes an irrational economy that produces luxury autos but allows the pollution of the environment through which we drive. (We will not pursue a discussion of this final point in the text. We leave assessment of that to you.)

Attacks on Galbraith have continued for over three decades. Those attacks have taken a number of forms, which we can separate into two categories. Empirical criticism of Galbraith claims that advertising is simply not all that effective at controlling consumer behavior. Studies of new product success rates have been used to indicate that advertisers are unable to guarantee success even for heavily advertised new products. This criticism has meager success itself because historical evidence consistently indicates that new products that are actively introduced into the marketplace have a success rate of about 60 percent. That figure is sufficiently ambiguous, providing neither conclusive support nor conclusive refutation for Galbraith's contentions. Galbraith himself said that he did not believe that the power of advertisers was "plenary." In addition, Galbraith may be interpreted as claiming not that advertisers have control over consumer *behavior* but that they have unacceptable influence on consumer *desire*. If Galbraith is interpreted this way, evidence about sales of new products (consumer behavior) would be irrelevant.

Another, more common, category of criticism of Galbraith focuses on purported conceptual errors in his argument. Critics have noted that advertising cannot create wants out of nothing. Rather, advertisers must appeal to some preexisting desire and then convince the consumer that their products are the means for best satisfying that original desire. Thus, deodorant ads may stimulate consumers to associate Arrid with their desire to be attractive to (or not to offend) the opposite sex. But this ad can be successful only if that desire to be attractive already exists. So, critics argue, ads merely persuade consumers to want products as vehicles for satisfying their already existing wants. This is still consistent with the consumer's remaining autonomous. The consumer is free, after all, to buy or not buy the product.

One possible response those more sympathetic to Galbraith would make at this point would be to distinguish two senses of autonomy. We can obviously speak of behavior as autonomous, as the preceding criticism of Galbraith does. But his defenders hold that it is also sensible to speak of desires as autonomous. Even when an ad does not compel behavior, it might still interfere with autonomy in the way it shapes our desires. As an example of this, consider the desire a person might acquire for a Coke after being subjected to a subliminal ad during a movie presentation. (A famous New Jersey case similar to this generated quite a bit of controversy a few decades back.) Even if the moviegoer decides not to act on the newly acquired desire, many of us have the vague feeling that the person's autonomy has been violated if he so much as desires the Coke. This feeling persists in the face of the recognition that the moviegoer freely chose not to buy a soft drink. We need some way of analyzing this feeling to assess its validity. One approach to that assessment involves getting some clarity about what it might mean to say a desire is autonomous.

A classic account of autonomous desire is provided by philosopher Gerald Dworkin. Dworkin contends that for a desire to be autonomous, it must have two elements like the following: (1) It must be such that we do not try to renounce the desire and (2) it must be such that we are able effectively to step back and critically evaluate the desire. That is, we must not only accept the desire as our own but we must be able to do so on the basis of rational reflection.

Dworkin names these conditions the "authenticity condition" and the "independence condition." For him, autonomy demands that a person retain some independence. Desires obviously can be acquired both from a multitude of sources and through a multitude of influence mechanisms. As a result, Dworkin believes that independence can exist only if those acquired desires can be subjected to rational evaluation. Thus, Dworkin finds desires that are acquired based on deception are not autonomous because they fail to satisfy the independence condition. He also suspects desires that are the product of other forms of manipulation.

This account of Dworkin's may provide some way of understanding that vague feeling about subliminally acquired desires. If we are unaware of how the desire came to be, we are less likely or able to critically evaluate it. When we know a desire has been acquired through some advertising pitch, on the other hand, we are more likely to take a critical and skeptical stance towards it. All of us have had the experience of catching ourselves being seduced by a particularly effective ad presentation.

Consider the alternative account of "autonomous desire" provided in the reading by Robert Arrington. Arrington's analysis resembles the first part of Dworkin's. Arrington claims that his desire for A-1 Steak Sauce is autonomous so long as he does not kick himself for impulsively pouring the stuff over a choice steak. He does not find it necessary to include in his account a condition similar to Dworkin's second condition. As a consequence, Arrington's analysis would judge the moviegoer's desire for a Coke to be an autonomous one. Evaluating which of these competing accounts of "autonomous desire" is the more appropriate one will be a complex process of achieving some balance between the reasoned analyses themselves and our own considered intuitions about methods of influence.

Whichever perspective you adopt, it is clear that Galbraith is not correct if he intended to say that all advertisements individually threaten the consumer's autonomy. As Arrington points out, the question is *when* a particular nondeceptive ad crosses the line between acceptable persuasion and manipulation, between influence and undue influence. You should be careful in assessing Arrington's definitions of "control" and "manipulation" in reaching an answer to that question. Does he define them so strictly that anything, short of absolute domination, would be acceptable? For example, how would deception satisfy Arrington's analysis of control and manipulation as requiring that the advertiser intended to assure *all* conditions necessary for getting a person to act in a desired way? Can there be unacceptable manipulation that falls short of full control?

The article by Richard Lippke carries the discussion of advertising's impact on consumer autonomy to a different level. His concern is not the impact of single ads but the cumulative impact of what he calls "persuasive mass–advertising." He argues that it, along with a number of other features of our economy and culture, leads to a suppressing of our capacities for autonomous choice. He uses an analysis of autonomy similar to Dworkin's to conclude that mass–advertising ought to be restricted. In reading Lippke's article, ask yourself whether the cumulative impact of advertising leads, as he suggests, to an unreflective desire for a lifestyle of conspicuous consumption.

The final article of the chapter is by Lynn Sharp Paine. It raises a question about the propriety of advertising to children. If advertising must respect the autonomy of consumers and if children are not yet capable of reasoned judgment, serious questions arise for children's advertising. Note that a common response to critics of children's ads is not available as a response to Paine's approach. Sometimes, people say that advertising to children is acceptable because parents can simply tell a child no when the child requests some advertised item. However, parental control of the purse strings is not a response if the original complaint is one about how the ads affect the desires and the mind of the child. This issue about desires cannot be addressed solely by noting that parents can refuse to satisfy those desires. Rather, this is an issue that forces you back to the relationship between desire and autonomy. It is an issue that once again forces you to decide what methods of influence are consistent with autonomy, fairness, and respect for the person.

CASE STUDY   Advertising Tobacco

ADVERTISING ON THE OFFENSE: CHILDREN AND TOBACCO

Each year in the United States, nearly one million adult tobacco smokers either die or quit. Critics claim that the tobacco industry needs to replace those lost sales by recruiting minors to pick up the habit. Cigarette sales to minors are illegal in most states, however.

Historically, children have been exposed to a variety of tobacco ads. Even though the industry cooperated with a ban on television and radio ads in 1971, advertising and promotion of cigarettes is significant. Print ads in magazines and newspapers, and on billboards, sponsorship of sporting events, and promotional items with brand logos effectively enable tobacco companies to reach wide audiences that include children. While the days of ubiquitous

This case was prepared from the following sources: *Mangini v. Reynolds*, 22 Cal. App. 4th 628 (1993); Sally Venverloh, "The Harkin Amendment," 13 *St. Louis Univ. Public Law Rev.* 787 (1994); *Philip Morris Magazine*, May/June 1990, July/August 1989; *New York Times*, November 19, 1989; *Philadelphia Inquirer*, July 21, 1995, March 3, 1995, July 3, 1994; *Consumer Reports*, March and June 1995.

candy cigarettes are over, critics claim that many of these advertising or promotional campaigns directly target children. Singled out for particular criticism is the Camel cigarette campaign featuring the cartoon character Cool Joe Camel.

Company spokespersons deny that the Joe Camel campaign is aimed at children, and they contend that the nearly $5 billion spent each year on advertising and promotion is aimed at getting adults to switch brands. (Others note, however, that few adults, less than 10 percent, switch brands and that market shares of brands change very little from year to year.) Whatever the intent of the campaigns, however, there is strong evidence that ads reach kids effectively. One study reported that 91 percent of six-year-olds were able to match Camel brand logos to cigarettes, a percentage equal to the recognition level for Mickey Mouse. Evidence from market share and sales information indicates that when the Joe Camel campaign began in 1988, only 0.5 percent of those teenagers who smoked used Camel. In 1992, Camel's market share was nearly 33 percent of teenage smokers, with sales to them of $476 million.

The effect of ads is also evident from studies of adolescent opinion and behavior. Adolescents consistently overestimate the percentage of the population that smokes, and those exposed to more advertising overestimate more. Experts on adolescent behavior say that ads are certainly not the greatest influence on teens who start to smoke. They say peer pressure is the greatest influence. Teens with close peers who smoke are thirteen times more likely to experiment with smoking than the average. Experts, however, suggest ads make teens more susceptible by making them view smoking as socially acceptable.

Critics are concerned because, while smoking among adults is declining, it is on the increase among teens. Only 10 percent of smokers begin after age twenty; 75 percent begin before age eighteen, and 57 percent begin before age fourteen. The average age of new smokers is twelve and a half years. A just released study by the National Institute on Drug Abuse reported that the number of eighth-graders who smoke had jumped nearly one third in three years, to 18.6 percent.

ADVERTISING ON THE DEFENSE: SECOND-HAND SMOKE
Public tolerance of cigarette smoking has declined appreciably over the last decade. Complaints by nonsmokers about being subjected to second-hand, or "sidestream," smoke have led many restaurants to severely limit smoking areas or to ban smoking entirely. Corporations have declared workplaces "smoke-free zones," and it is now common to see smokers huddled outside office buildings, under doorways in the rain because they are prohibited from lighting up in their offices. Airlines have banned smoking on some international flights, and Congress has banned it on all domestic flights. State governments are also promulgating broad prohibitions on smoking in public places. Recently, the state of Maryland issued a ban on smoking in all workplaces, including bars, hotels, and restaurants.

This decreased tolerance of smoking is largely a function of reports emanating from the EPA, OSHA, the Surgeon General, and other sources. Some reports assert that "passive smoking" causes cancer. Other studies charge that second-hand smoke is linked to heart disease and to asthma in children. The response to these reports poses a serious problem for the tobacco industry. At a time when many current smokers say they wish they could quit and when the rate of adult smoking is dropping, restrictions that make smoking more difficult and less socially acceptable are likely to further depress demand for cigarettes.

Tobacco industry advertising campaigns have been crafted to defend the industry's market. Philip Morris paid $600,000 to the National Archives to sponsor a bicentennial campaign for the Bill of Rights. It simultaneously launched an advertising campaign that featured arguments about individual freedom and smokers' rights.

As the movement to limit smoking grew, the tobacco companies became more explicit in their defensive strategy. R. J. Reynolds and Philip Morris both bought full-page ads to reprint an article from *Consumer Research* that was critical of the scientific reliability of studies linking sidestream smoke to health problems. Philip Morris's ad was three full-length pages, and it ran in major papers, including the *New York Times* and *Philadelphia Inquirer*. In the *Inquirer*, the ad appeared during the July Fourth Independence Day celebrations. The first page of the ad was blank above the fold except for the boldface words "Were you misled?"

The *Consumer Research* article reprinted in the ads charged that the EPA study linking second-hand smoke to cancer had made these errors: illegitimately combining data from several small-scale studies that were not individually statistically significant; ignoring more recent, contrary data; and neglecting to investigate other possible variables (diet, socioeconomic status, and so on) that might account for increased incidence of cancer among those exposed to sidestream smoke. *Consumer Reports* (not associated with *Consumer Research*) published a review of the scientific criticisms made by the tobacco industry ads, with the assistance of two Harvard epidemiologists. They concluded that the charges were without merit. *Consumer Reports* alleged that the ads were part of the long history of tobacco industry attempts to create public doubt about the harmful health effects of cigarettes.

FURTHER THREATS
Numerous recent legal developments further threaten the industry. Legislation, introduced in 1993 and sure to be reintroduced, proposes to remove the full tax deduction tobacco companies receive for their advertising and promotion expenditures. The Supreme Court has cleared the way for a California case against R. J. Reynolds that alleges the company unfairly entices minors to smoke illegally. A class action suit alleging the tobacco companies hid data from the public about the addictiveness of nicotine is proceeding in Louisiana. The FDA appears poised to declare tobacco an addictive drug and to regulate the conditions of its sale. Possible actions include the licensing of tobacco vendors and a ban on vending machine sales in order to deter illegal sales to minors.

DECEPTIVE ADVERTISING
John J. McCall

MORAL PRESUMPTIONS AGAINST DECEPTION

Every society has rules against deception and lying. It is easy to understand this presumption against deception by imagining what a society would be like if its members could never expect that others were being honest and truthful. A group that so completely lacked trust would never be able to engage in the ongoing cooperative activities that are the hallmark of human social life. For one example that is relevant to this text, consider what business would be if there were not background expectations that others would abide by their prior agreements. No business could be done on credit; all transactions would have to be "cash on the barrel" exchanges. (To those who suggest that the law could be used to enforce the terms of an exchange on credit: Imagine what it would be like to assume that every transaction was likely to require instituting legal process.)

The conditions necessary for coordinated and cooperative social life, then, explain why all societies will have some presumptions against deception. The difficulty for applying this analysis to specific questions of advertising deception is that social life can obviously go on even where the presumption against deception is a very bounded presumption. That is, society can tolerate defined areas of deception as long as most of its members understand where the rules against deception operate and, more importantly, where they do not operate.[1]

This analysis of the reasons for a presumption against deception, therefore, does not allow us easily to conclude that any given act of deception is presumptively wrong. It might be that the specific deceptive act in question is one that takes place in an arena where the parties do not expect honesty and trustworthiness. In our culture, a very narrowly bounded exception to the presumption against deception exists in the game of poker. There, everyone expects the other players to misrepresent their current hands of cards. In a given culture, the same bounded exception to expectations of honesty might exist in the marketplace. (Though, of course, that culture's marketplace might never advance much beyond a bazaar. The evolution to more complex transactions seems to require a higher level of trust between parties, as do certain circumstances where the same individuals engage in repeated transactions over time.) In any case, the need for cooperation and trust does not entail a general presumption against deception *in advertising*. It only entails that societies have some rules against deception.

The morality of our culture, happily, also contains nonconsequentialist standards that can generate stronger and less bounded presumptions against deception. If, as we have argued in Chapters Two and Three, the ideas of individual rights and dignity rest in part on the autonomy of persons, then there are additional reasons to reject acts of lying and deception.[2]

Deception cuts at the core of another's autonomy because it is an attempt to short-circuit that person's ability to engage in free, reasoned choice. It is an attempt to manipulate another's decision by getting that person unknowingly to act on false beliefs. Even so conservative a picture of business responsibility as Milton Friedman's sees the relationship between deception and autonomy when it enjoins both coercion *and* deception. Thus, the contemporary moral commitment to individual rights and dignity allows us to derive a stronger and less bounded presumption against deception than we could if we depended only on the social necessity of some unspecified rule against deceit. We can argue now that any attempt to deceive is presumptively wrong because it attempts manipulatively to undermine the capacity for reasoned choice.

Of course, even this argument against deception will admit that there are instances of deception that can be justified. We cannot identify all possible exceptions to the rule against lying here, but we can identify three typical cases where lies and deception are acceptable. Perhaps the clearest case is the first one, where the deception is needed to save a life. No one, that is no one with moral sensitivity, seriously believes that Dutch villagers were acting wrongly when they deceived the Nazis about the presence of Jews among them. That elaborate deception was necessary to prevent an even greater wrong, an even greater violation of someone's autonomy.

Second, we generally accept harmless deceit where no unfair advantage is sought through the deception. "You look nice today!" when a person really doesn't may be a case in point. Such deception might merely be understood as appropriate sociability. (However, there are cases where falsely telling someone they look fine might be inappropriate—for example, when a person is on his way to a job interview and needs an honest opinion rather than reassurance. Telling when a lie is sociable and when it is inappropriate requires subtle skill and moral sensitivity.)

We also accept deception in the third case, where the parties involved *all* know that deception is likely. The poker game mentioned earlier is an example. So also is the labor negotiation where a party puts forward its "best offer." Even in these cases, however, the areas of permissible deception are narrowly defined. The poker player cannot legitimately deceive by slipping hidden cards into his hand; the negotiator cannot legitimately deceive by accepting a negotiated settlement and then later refusing to comply with the terms of the agreement.

Do these categories of exception have any implications for our topic of deceptive advertising? Can advertising be counted as an exception to the general rule against deception? Clearly, it cannot count as an instance of the first two types of acceptable deception. Typically, deceptive advertising is not required to save a life or to protect some equally important interest of another party from unjust harm. Nor is deceptive advertising usually a harmless act without any attempt to gain an unfair advantage. More typically, deception in advertising is calculated to create an unfair advantage for the advertiser both against the consumer targeted by the ad and against the business's competitors. It also intends some loss or harm to both of those parties. A consumer who buys one brand of product because she or he was deceived into thinking it a better value than a competitive product is harmed, as is the competitor.

It is frequently claimed, though, that deceptive advertising counts as an instance of the third category of deception—that is, it is deception in a case where everyone expects (or ought to expect) deception to occur. The frequency of this opinion does not alter the fact that it is confused on both factual

and conceptual grounds. There is ample evidence that consumers are in fact regularly tricked by deceptive advertising and marketing practices. (Why would those practices be used if those employing them did not believe they would be successful?) While this discussion is a discussion of the morality of deceptive advertising rather than one about government regulation of ads, a comment about the Federal Trade Commission is in order here. The FTC frequently concludes on the basis of market study that ads trick a significant number of consumers. Ivan Preston's most recent book, *The Tangled Web: Truth, Falsity and Advertising,* provides numerous examples where the FTC has found that 20 to 25 percent of the surveyed consumer population was misled by an intentionally deceptive advertising practice. So it seems as if the claim that consumers expect deception runs counter to the evidence from consumer research.

One possible, and I think very weak, retort to this is to point out that there is no logical inconsistency between saying that consumers expect deception and saying that they are simultaneously taken in by an act of deception. After all, some claim, in activities such as poker and labor negotiations the parties expect deception yet are sometimes successfully bluffed nonetheless. This is true enough. That mere logical possibility, however, is insufficient to convince me that consumers generally expect to be deceived. Here is where the second, conceptual confusion arises for those thinking that deceptive ads fall into the third exception category.

Consumers, having been burned once or twice by a particular deceptive practice, learn to be wary of falling for that practice again. Once you learned that "economy size" merely meant bigger but not cheaper per unit, you learned to compare unit prices for packages of different quantity. That alone, of course, suggests that you were not expecting that particular form of deception the first few times it happened to you.

Moreover, the attempt to assimilate deceptive advertising into the third category ignores the fact that for deception to be expected, it has to be expected in relatively well defined areas. It may be possible, after learning, to expect deception in the use of a word like *economy.* It is not possible, however, to expect deception to occur in all the places where advertisers might conceivably use it. Expecting deception to that degree is both conceptually and psychologically impossible. It's conceptually impossible because the available deceptive techniques are infinite in number and a consumer logically cannot expect all of them. In addition, a consumer who even attempted to guard against a significant number of those possible avenues of deception would soon experience overload and decision-making paralysis. Imagine pushing your cart down the supermarket aisle and looking out for the innumerable ways you might be deceived.

It seems clear, then, that deceptive marketing and advertising is not a case of deception everyone knows about and expects. The fact that many of us are cynical about advertising practices does not in the least diminish the conclusion that it is conceptually and factually confusing to place ads in the third exception category. Deceptive marketing and advertising practices should be subject to a strong presumption of immorality.

Another common retort to that conclusion is the view that the consumer has a responsibility to act warily and protect him- or herself against deception. A consumer foolish enough to be taken in by some intentionally deceptive scheme is at fault for failing to be adequately vigilant.

But even if we accept that consumers have responsibility and can be at fault for falling prey to the more obvious tricks of advertisers, the retort still misses the point. If the intent to deceive is present, as it is assumed by those who use this retort, and if advertisers trade upon the fact that some consumers will fail to process the deception, then the advertiser is still subject to the charge of moral impropriety. It is the mere intent to deceive that supports that moral judgment. If I walk onto a used car lot and the salesperson has illegally turned back the odometer so the car appears to have fewer miles than it actually does, I might be able to catch the deception. I might, for instance, take note of the excessive wear on the seats and note the discrepancy between that and the odometer's mileage. The fact that the attempted deception was unsuccessful does not diminish its immorality. And if I failed to detect the deception and bought the car, even if I bear some responsibility for believing the sales pitch, that personal responsibility does not amount to absolving the car salesperson of ethical wrong. The consumer's behavior is simply not relevant one way or the other to the principle that intentional deception is immoral.[3]

DECEPTIVE ADVERTISEMENTS

This principle of assessment for the morality of advertising is not an easy one to apply, however. Any particular judgment will require speculation about the largely private mental states of the advertiser. We need to have some skepticism about our interpretation of a person's intentions. These mental states are not completely inaccessible, though, and there are reasonable presumptive judgments we can make about many advertisements just from their design and content. As a first step in evaluating whether ads are intentionally deceptive, we can categorize some techniques of deception and discuss some examples.

All ads attempt to communicate a message that intends to influence us. The vehicle of that communication can take a variety of forms. There is the linguistic element of the communication, of course—what is said, implied, and omitted. But of equal importance is the visual communication (at least for ads other than those on radio!). An anecdote from the political arena can help emphasize the importance of this category of communication. During Ronald Reagan's second presidential campaign, news reports were often critical of his policies. One such report had a visual of Reagan on the campaign trail. He was on a bandstand, surrounded by American flag bunting, cheerleaders, a pep band, and a cheering crowd. The news reader's voice-over was presenting a criticism of a Reagan policy. After the news spot aired, a Reagan press aide purportedly called the network to thank it for the helpful news story. He said that what the viewer would carry away was the positive image from the video footage, not the critical commentary. This point about the power of visual images can be even more true for commercials.

Examples where we can presume intended use of visuals to deceive are easy to find. Some classic ones are the following: (1) A shaving cream commercial that claimed the cream was so good at softening beards that it could even be used to shave sandpaper. The camera showed a razor apparently removing the grit from sandpaper that was sprayed with the foam. What was actually photographed was a piece of glass set against a tan background and sprinkled with loose sand. The razor had no blade. (2) A soup commercial touting its new chunky style loaded with vegetables. The picture showed a bowl with the vegetables mounded high above the broth. What was not disclosed was that the bowl had marbles in it to raise the vegetables for better display. (3) A car commercial that advertised the safety of the car, especially in rollovers where the roofs of many vehicles collapse onto the passengers. The car was the only one in a group to withstand a "monster truck" rolling over them. The vehicle was not a stock model but was rather one with a specially reinforced roof.

In each of these examples, we can presume that the advertiser intended to deceive with the visuals because in each case the product was made to appear as something it was not. This is true regardless of whether the shaving cream was more effective than competitors at softening beards, whether the soup was indeed chunky, whether the car was safer than others in rollovers. It will not do, either, for the advertisers to defend themselves by saying that they merely intended to visualize a real product attribute, because that intended goal was achieved by a means that intentionally misrepresented the product in its visual display. Agents are, of course, responsible for the means they use as well as the ends they pursue.

More contemporary, and perhaps more controversial, examples of presumptive intent to deceive with visuals (and with language) have been proposed by students in business ethics classes. You should consider each of the following examples and decide whether it is reasonable to conclude that there was deceptive intent.

One example concerns a commercial for a child's action toy that is displayed against a background that makes the toy look larger, more realistic, and capable of more movements than it actually is.[4]

A second contemporary example is an ad for a brand of fat-free cookie. The ad shows a group of, shall we say, physically imposing women pursuing a cookie delivery man. The cookies are fat free but they are definitely not low calorie. Yet the visuals may be taken to suggest that the women are interested in the product for weight loss reasons. It is certainly true that the choice of women of this particular body type was a conscious decision by the ad team. (Note that most products try to associate themselves with more svelte body types.)

Another recent example might be frozen dinner packages with cover photos of a "serving suggestion." In reality, it would be difficult to make the contents of the package appear on the plate as does the food in the photo. All of these cases were proposed as cases where it is the advertiser's intentional decision to visually communicate messages that can be described as misleading. While those judgments are surely speculative to some degree, the conscious design of the ads makes it reasonable to question the intent of those creating them.

Similar questions can be raised about misleading intent based on the linguistic element of advertisements. Few ads these days make directly false statements. Ads can be designed, though, to deceive by ambiguity in their actual statements, by what advertisers hope the public, or some portion of it, will take as an implication of what was said, or by the intentional omission of pertinent information.

Food nutrition claims of the past decade have been notorious for misleading with carefully crafted use of language. (In fact, they have been so notorious that both the FDA and FTC have issued guidelines in the last two years to stop the use of deceptive nutrition claims on labels and in ads.) Some of the most notable of the claims surround the use of terms such as *fat free, low fat, lite/light, low calorie,* and *cholesterol free.* A manufacturer of potato chips, for example, has advertised its chips as cholesterol free, which was technically true. However, the chips were high in fat and even in saturated fat (which the body processes into cholesterol). The claim was true, but we can surmise that the intent was to depend on a confusion in the consumer's mind about fats, cholesterol, and body chemistry. The ad clearly hoped some consumers would take away the message that the chips would not raise cholesterol. What else could the intent have been?

The plastics industry has been proposed as a more subtle example where we might reasonably conclude intent to deceive. The industry has, of course, come under criticism from environmentalists who are concerned that our "throw-away" society uses too much nonrenewable fossil fuel in its consumption of nonrecyclable plastic. Industry commercials defend plastic by praising its value for artificial limbs, automobile air bags, and the like. Some critics claim that the ads, like a shell game at a carnival, intend to deceive by obfuscating the issue and attempting to imply a generalized false conclusion that plastics are, in all their uses, essential.

Ads might intend to deceive even when they provide full and accurate information. Auto lease advertisements do disclose the terms of the lease that qualify the highly attractive monthly payment figures that dominate the ads. But those qualifying terms, when presented on television commercials, are displayed so quickly that even the speediest readers will be unable to process the information. Some suggest that the design of the ads suggests an intentional deception that depends on consumers being unable to assimilate the government-required disclosures.

Assessing intended deception is perhaps most difficult for ads that omit information. One might try to say that an ad is deceptive if an advertiser intentionally omits information that might lead the consumer to a different decision. The difficulty with this principle, however, is that it might require too much disclosure. Certainly, the principle would seem to require advertisers to disclose *all* the negative features of their products. It also seems to require disclosure of deficiencies of a product relative to competitor products. Not hiding major flaws is one thing; it is quite another to suggest that ads disclose everything that might be relevant to consumer judgment. Exactly where we should draw the line concerning what can knowingly be omitted without intending to mislead is a difficult question.

The difficulty of drawing that line should not obscure the obvious cases that intend to deceive by omission, however. Political campaign ads are perhaps the most corrupt example of misleading by omission. Often opponents will charge that "Senator Smith voted against funding for [choose a popular hot button issue]." While it is usually true that "Smith" did vote against a bill containing funding, what the ads fail to disclose is that the bill was a complex appropriation bill that dealt with a number of other appropriations as well. Political ads also fail to disclose instances where "Smith" supported the popular project. Despite the general difficulty in determining when omissions intend to deceive, then, there are cases where that intent is clearly present. Commercial examples of deceptive omission might be found in ads that omit reference to hidden charges or costs, for instance, points paid on a mortgage, or that omit to say that a sale price applies only to a very small number of products.

The preceding examples are meant to illustrate some of the main ways in which ads can intend to deceive. Any controversy surrounding the examples should not cloud the main point: There are reasonable presumptive judgments of intended deception that we can make about ads based on the facts of their design, language, and context. Consumers have legitimate moral grounds for complaining about any ad where such reasonable presumption exists. More importantly, advertisers themselves have obligations to assess their own intentions self-critically. They should reject as inappropriate any technique whereby they hope to mislead by statement, implication, omission, or visual image. Intent is one main criterion by which ads should be evaluated. Both the public and advertisers need to apply that standard of evaluation more strictly. Currently advertisers too frequently engage in a corrupt cat and mouse game with consumers, and the public too frequently tolerates that corruption.

With that conclusion drawn, one final question needs to be posed. Are there cases where, lacking intent to deceive, advertisers nevertheless have a moral responsibility for consumers being misled? There are at least two kinds of case where the answer to that question is yes. The first is one where the false impression in the mind of the consumer was a reasonably foreseeable result of an ad. Even if the advertiser did not intend that result, he or she can still be responsible for a negligent failure to exercise appropriate forethought in the design of the advertisement. Some examples of visual representations that aim to highlight the positive features of a product would be of this kind. If we refer back to the classic cases of chunky soup or sturdy cars, even if the advertiser intended no deception, the false ideas carried away by consumers were predictable. Omissions that we cannot conclude are intentionally deceptive may often fall into this category. (So, even though it is hard to determine when omissions intend to deceive, we still have resources for concluding that advertisers sometimes bear responsibility for false impressions caused by omissions, intentional or not.)

The second kind of case is perhaps more common. On occasions where an ad intends no deception, it may be that consumers unpredictably misread the meaning of the ad. If an advertiser knows this has been the result and yet continues to use the same ad, there is reason for claiming the continued use of the ad is intentionally deceptive. For even if the ad in its debut did not intend to deceive, an advertiser who knowingly trades on a miscommunication knowingly allows a future false impression to be created. Thus, there are cases where, absent initial intent to deceive, the deceptive effect of an ad is nonetheless the ethical responsibility of the advertiser. Further discussion of deceptive effect (and the role it plays in government regulatory action) is left for later readings in this chapter.

NOTES

1. Some suggest that where no one expects honesty, there can be no deception. The reading by Albert Carr in Chapter Six contains such a claim. Even if that were true, which it is not, it cannot apply to the point that societies can operate with bounded rules against deception. All that such bounded prohibition against deception requires is that *most* members understand where the rules operate, not that *all* members do. And, in any case, the claim is false. Even where the social rules against deception are suspended, one person may still attempt to mislead another. The example of the poker game makes this

point. Suspending the presumption against deception, then, means only that deception in that area is not considered wrong. It does not mean that deception is impossible.

2. Lying, by definition, is the intentional utterance of a falsehood with the intent to deceive another. As such, lying is a species of deception, and it is the element of *intended* deception that makes a lie presumptively wrong. Jokes or pieces of fiction, after all, are intentional falsehoods. They simply do not intend deception.

3. This analysis also points out the difference between standards of moral evaluation and standards for legal regulation of deceptive advertising. In regulatory matters it is of some importance whether the ad actually misleads the reasonable or only the ignorant consumer, that is, if the ad misleads many or only a very few. If it is few, and if the consequent harm to those few is also small, a government regulatory response may not be appropriate. However, regardless of the number or nature of those misled, if the ad intends to deceive some portion of the public, then there is a strong reason to say the behavior of the advertiser is immoral.

4. See the article by Lynn Sharp Paine later in this chapter for another criticism of advertising to children.

ADVERTISING AND FREE SPEECH
Joseph R. DesJardins and John J. McCall

I

Commercial speech is significantly constrained by a wide variety of Federal Trade Commission regulations. When compared with the relative absence of constraints placed on other forms of speech, this fact reveals that our political institutions apply widely different standards for determining the constitutional limits of government interference with speech. There are a number of reasons why the different treatments given to commercial speech and, for example, that given to political speech should concern marketers and ordinary citizens alike.

First, and most generally, understanding this difference and the reasons offered in its support will force any citizen to examine the basis of our society's belief that free speech is important enough to warrant constitutional protection.

Second, when any speech is subjected to constraints, there is always the danger that precedents set in the restraint of that form of speech might

evolve into a justification for future restraints on other, perhaps more important, forms of speech. Reasons offered to regulate commercial speech today might be offered tomorrow for regulating journalistic or religious speech.

Finally, understanding the basis for treating commercial speech differently from other forms of speech might provide us with a guide for deciding future social policy with respect to regulating corporate political advertising.

These three reasons for being concerned with the special constitutional status of commercial speech will provide the framework for our discussion of advertising regulation. In the next section, we sketch reasons why a right of free speech is an important component of any acceptable political structure. We then explain the precise differences between the treatment given to commercial speech and that given to other forms of speech. We will outline and reject certain justifications offered for this dissimilarity. However, we will defend the different treatment by explaining how the general justification for a right of free speech can allow for the regulation of advertising in ways that are unacceptable for other forms of speech. In addition, we use that defense of free speech to underscore some constitutional limitations on regulating advertisements. In the final section, we note some implications that our analysis has for corporate political advertising and sketch some potential solutions to the practical political problems raised by that analysis.

II

Freedom of speech is important both because of the specific values it promotes and because of the general moral attitude towards persons that the promotion of these values encourages. Historically, political and constitutional theory have recognized a practical connection between the existence of free speech on the one hand, and the values of political autonomy, individual development, and the discovery of truth on the other.[1]

Free speech clearly is a means towards greater political autonomy for the citizens of a society. Where institutions allow freedom of speech, citizens are able to raise critical questions concerning the policies of their government. Open discussions of political questions provide citizens with a powerful opportunity for influencing the direction of those policies. Alternatively, where speech is suppressed, government authorities have greater power to set the public agenda, to indoctrinate the populace by promoting only approved opinions, and to stifle public criticisms of their actions. Collective self-rule by the citizens is thus furthered when those citizens are provided a constitutional guarantee of free speech.

Persons living in a society with such guarantees also possess an opportunity for individual self-development not possessed by other persons. The capacity for rational and deliberative choice is an important component of adult human existence. In fact, the capacity for deliberative choice is often offered as one characteristic that distinguishes persons from mere animals. This important human capacity certainly has a much higher chance of being realized when individuals are able to freely speak their minds. In circumstances allowing freedom of speech, speakers have an opportunity through discussions with others for

refining the ideas they express. (We all recognize the improvement in our own deliberations that is provided by criticisms received from others.) In addition, listeners are presented an opportunity for receiving and evaluating new points of view when others are able to express their opinions freely. Even from the perspective of the listener, then, freedom of speech provides an opportunity for improving the human capacity for informed and critical deliberation. Thus, free speech has an important instrumental value in that it promotes political autonomy and the development of central human capacities.

Freedom of speech also has been defended as an effective means for the discovery of truth. John Stuart Mill, for example, claimed that a long-term competition in the marketplace of ideas will be won by those ideas that are most true. Since true ideas are understood as a benefit to society and as a necessary component in reasonable deliberations by individuals, the value of free speech would be increased if it led to greater discovery.

Finally, these three values (political autonomy, self-development, and the discovery of truth), which have played a significant role in First Amendment theory, all exhibit a particular attitude towards human beings. A concern with promoting each of these values can be seen as an outgrowth of the attempt to treat each person with respect, since each of these values expresses a belief in persons as rational autonomous agents capable of directing the courses of their own lives. Thus, we move towards respect for persons when we allow them to govern themselves. The defense of freedom of speech based upon these three historically important values, then, expresses as a fundamental tenet of our political morality that all persons are to be treated with equal respect.

First Amendment rights to free speech are thus important political rights whose interpretation should be a matter of concern for all. Moreover, the fact that one form of speech, commercial speech, is significantly regulated should be a special concern, since the precedents for regulation in that area are potentially available as justifications for new restriction on speech in other areas. We need, then, to understand the precise way in which commercial speech is accorded different treatment, as well as to understand the potential justifications for that different treatment.

III

Until quite recently, commercial speech was provided with little or no constitutional protection under the First Amendment. The source of modern constitutional theory on this issue is found in the 1942 Supreme Court decision in *Valentine v. Chrestensen,* where the Court decided that commercial speech was undeserving of protected status.[2] The basis of that decision was that the presence of an economic motive was sufficient to disqualify an expression from having protected status. More recent decisions have moderated this position somewhat, but commercial speech is still without full protected status. For instance, in the 1976 *Virginia State Board of Pharmacy v. Virginia Citizens Consumer Council, Inc.* decision, the Supreme Court expressly asserted that commercial speech is entitled to a lesser degree of protection. The same comment occurs in a landmark case in 1978, *Ohralik v. Ohio State Bar Association,* which freed regulators to prohibit broad classes of commercial speech.[3] Thus, while the Supreme Court has recently expanded the protections offered to commercial speech, it still has steadfastly refused to judge the regulation of such speech by the same strict standards applied to regulation of, for example, political speech.[4] The following specific differences in the extent of allowable regulation are instructive.

Ordinarily, other forms of speech, such as political speech, are provided protection regardless of their truth; commercial speech, however, must be true in order to gain even its limited protected status. We prosecute advertisers for false claims made within their advertisements. On the other hand, we all recognize that even intentionally false statements made by political candidates are ordinarily beyond prosecution. But constitutionally acceptable differences in treatment extend well beyond this. Commercial speech that is not strictly false is subject to broad regulation if government regulatory agencies deem it to possess a significant tendency to deceive. Thus, regulation can include even cases of harmless speech if regulating those cases is an effective means for eliminating other potentially deceptive instances of commercial speech.

This court-sanctioned regulation applies a significantly different standard than is applied to other forms of speech. Regulation in other areas is subject to a relatively strict requirement that the regulation not be "overbroad"—that it not discourage speech beyond the extent necessary to solve a particular difficulty. This "overbreadth" or "least restrictive means" doctrine has not been applied with the same rigor in commercial speech cases.[5]

Moreover, advertisements are subject to compliance with regulatory standards that set requirements of unfair language in order to avoid possible deception and misunderstanding.[6] Government regulatory agencies also can impose requirements of affirmative disclosure by requiring advertisers to include health warnings or by requiring them to correct misleading impressions that may have been created by previous advertisements.[7] Further, the Federal Trade Commission, through cease and desist orders for classes of advertisements, also has a further court-recognized power of prior restraint over advertising speech. None of these regulatory powers ordinarily are acceptable for limiting other forms of speech in advance of their utterance.

More recent Supreme Court decisions have carried the current doctrine requiring a lesser burden of proof in order to justify restricting commercial speech even further. In *Friedman v. Rogers* (1979), the Court allowed regulation prohibiting even true information (about manufacturers' trade names) from being used in ads because of the possibility that such information *might* mislead and because trade names have little intrinsic meaning.[8] The *Central Hudson Gas and Electric v. Public Service Commission* (1980) decision even recognized the legitimacy of a state action suppressing nondeceptive commercial speech in order to promote a state interest in lessening a demand for a legally available product (electricity).[9]

Thus commercial speech, unlike other forms of speech, must be true to have constitutional protection. However, even nondeceptive commercial speech is subject to significant regulation. The dissimilarity in constitutional treatment for commercial speech and other forms of speech is striking.

IV

Any number of explanations and justifications for this different treatment have been offered, some by the Supreme Court in its own rulings, and others by legal theorists. Not all of these justifications are sufficiently convincing. For instance, the previously cited basis of the *Chrestensen* doctrine (that economic motive disqualifies speech from constitutional protection) seems overbroad in itself, since paid political speakers and newspapers have economic motive for their speech.[10] Similarly, the Court in the *Virginia Board* decision argued that commercial speech is, because of its economic motivation, more "hardy" (less likely to be totally discouraged) than other forms of speech and, hence, can withstand greater restraints. The difficulty with this justification, however, is that it seems clear that threats of government regulation do in fact deter advertisers.[11] In addition, since some accepted regulations actually *prohibit* some types of commercial speech, it seems inappropriate to claim that such speech is "hardier" and can resist such regulation.

The *Virginia Board* decision also justifies government regulation of commercial speech because such speech is factually more verifiable than political or religious speech and, thus, the possibility of government bias does not arise as easily in the area of advertising regulation. However, this justification exhibits a naive understanding of advertisements. Certainly many advertisements are at least as unverifiable or open to dispute as are statements in the area of politics or religion. In fact, political speech is often more verifiable than statements in commercials, and yet no Supreme Court Justice would argue that similar regulation of political speech is therefore justifiable.[12]

Serious problems also exist in a number of other potential justifications for this special treatment accorded commercial speech. Some have argued that this dissimilar treatment is justified because advertisers possess an unequal power to influence, because advertisements involve emotional appeals, or because advertising is not a truth-seeking or self-correcting process.[13] Since each of these beliefs can equally as well describe certain political debates, it would appear inappropriate to use them as justification for a difference in treatment between the two classes of speech. There is a difficulty, then, in constructing an explanation for why commercial speech ought to be treated differently. The difficulty lies in the possibility that the proposed explanations would also justify restrictions on forms of speech that we would not want to regulate.

Another plausible explanation for the different treatment accorded commercial speech lies in the state interest in regulating commerce and contracts. As implicit contract offers, advertisements might justifiably be regulated in ways that all contracts are. Unfortunately, this explanation also is insufficient to explain completely the different treatment accorded religious and commercial speech because it presupposes that the state has a legitimate interest in regulating commerce for the welfare of its citizens, and it implicitly denies that the state has an equal interest in regulating religious expression for the welfare of its citizens.

But, of course, a citizen's welfare might well be endangered by certain religious practices just as it could be by certain advertising or contract practices that are now subject to regulation. What needs explaining, then, is why commerce and commercial speech are accorded a status of lesser importance. Presupposing that status fails to carry the explanation far enough.

V

A more plausible, if controversial, explanation can be found by appealing to the values cited in traditional defenses of free speech and in the attitude of respect towards persons evidenced by those values. For example, it seems unlikely that free commercial speech is as practically necessary for promoting political autonomy as is free political speech. Certainly there is an obvious danger in allowing a government regulatory body to regulate the very political speech that concerns the evaluation of government policy. The open debate necessary for real political autonomy appears less than likely unless there is a strong presumption against government interference with political speech.

The absence of such an equally strong presumption against government regulation of commercial speech would not similarly threaten the existence of political autonomy. Hence, one of the traditional values provides a substantial reason for treating regulation of commercial speech according to standards different from those used for regulating political speech. We should note, however, that this reason does not claim that commercial speech should be without protection. It only argues for a status of lesser protection.

Nevertheless, this reason fails to explain why the speech of advertisers ought to be treated differently than, say, speech about religious or moral matters, which is protected in a manner similar to political speech. Free religious or moral speech seems no more practically required for political autonomy than does free commercial speech. (There *may* be a reason for treating moral speech in a manner similar to political speech, in that one of the legitimate interests of the government is to promote the welfare of its citizens, and moral speech often is about what constitutes that welfare. Thus, there may be a threat to political autonomy in allowing government control over moral speech.) Accordingly, if we grant religious and moral speech a protected status equal to political speech and greater than commercial speech, and if serving the value of political autonomy is not a relevant difference between religious or moral speech and commercial speech, then we must defend the special status given religious and moral speech by appeal to some other value.

It also appears that without some amending, the other traditional values cannot offer a reason for treating either moral or religious speech differently than commercial speech. One cannot, for example, argue that commercial speech leads to less development of rational capacities for choice, since much moral and religious speech makes the same use of emotional appeals and has the same paucity of reasoned or factual analysis as is found in many advertisements. Of course, emotionally based religious or moral speech is protected to a greater extent than is commercial speech.

Why, then, do moral and religious speech deserve special constitutional protection? It seems that the greater protection depends upon a particular view concerning the sorts of discussions that are most central to human experience. Some types of speech might be more valuable to human life than others. No doubt, any such view contains significant bias in its judgment that certain issues are of more momentous human concern. However, that need not imply that the bias is unreasonable or unacceptable.

The elevation of discussions of moral and religious issues to full constitutional protection indicates that investigations into those issues are more valuable than other investigations. Religious and moral questioning is part of what provides human life with its special status. Religious and moral speech contribute to the pursuit of meaning and

value in human existence. Freedom of expression in offering an item for sale, in comparison, appears a rather mundane concern. (The Court implicitly adopted this view in the *Chrestensen* decision.[14])

Thus, while freedom for commercial speech might promote the development of a human capacity for deliberative choice, the manner in which it promotes this development differs markedly from the manner in which human development might be promoted by deliberation about other choices that are seen as more central to human existence. On one hand, commercial speech promotes the capacity for rational choice by encouraging us to deliberate about various and competing consumer choices. Religious and moral speech, on the other hand, promotes this capacity by encouraging us to deliberate about the very meaning and value of human life. Thus, on the basis of this idea of what makes a human life valuable, a respect for the humanity of each person might dictate a stronger presumption against restrictions on moral or religious speech than against restrictions on commercial speech.

None of this, however, is to say that commercial speech is without significant value. Inasmuch as it promotes, to some degree, important values, it too deserves a measure of protection. The preceding analysis offers only an explanation of why the protection for it ought to be less.

In its recent decisions the Supreme Court seems to agree with the conclusion that commercial speech deserves increasing protection. The Court has overturned government prohibitions on certain particular types of factual advertising by lawyers, pharmacists, and abortion services, arguing that there is no legitimate state interest that would justify preventing the public from having such information available.[15] In addition, the strong presumption in favor of free political speech would be consistent with the Court's decision in the 1980 *First National Bank of Boston v. Bellotti* case, where the Court ruled against state prohibition of corporate advocacy advertisements on current political issues. If we wish to prevent government from controlling political debate, from setting the public agenda, or from stifling political criticism, then there seems no good reason to allow it to prohibit outright any political expression.

This last Court decision raises a number of new and potentially significant problems for future government policy, however. By granting strong protection to corporate political advertising, this decision presents the problem of distinguishing between corporate "image" advertising (which apparently deserves only the limited protection accorded commercial speech) and more mainstream political advocacy advertisements (which deserve stronger constitutional protection). It also raises an important question concerning the ability of powerful and monied interests to influence inordinately the political agenda and debate by heavy promotional campaigns. A comment about each of these potential problems is in order.

VI

Most observers of television and radio advertising trends have recognized that large corporations have begun to advertise more frequently in ways that do not directly present any specific products for sale but which, rather, present a positive image of the corporation as a loyal and concerned member of the community. Since such image advertisements do not provide consumers with the factual information necessary for informed consumer choice, it is not clear in which direction recent precedents will move the Court. As was noted above, some of the recent Court decisions have expanded protection for commercial speech. As also noted above, however, in its *Friedman* decision the Court found the use of trade names to be undeserving of protection, since trade names were thought to have little intrinsic significance of their own. Likewise, image advertising seems to lack the intrinsic significance of informative product advertising. The *Friedman* decision, then, might provide some grounds for government regulation of non-product-related and noninformational image advertising. Thus, there seem to be opposing tendencies in the Court's recent history that make its direction regarding cases of image advertising ambiguous.

Of course, it may turn out that the Court need not decide whether the constitutional status of image advertising would preclude certain forms of government regulation. However, there is a significant possibility that cases dealing with image advertising might come before the Court in conjunction with cases dealing with corporate political advertising. This possibility becomes increasingly probable

when corporate image advertising not only presents positive images of the corporation but when it also, by implication, suggests that certain political positions are more appropriate than others. Instances of this might be seen in image ads that argue, at least implicitly, for a free enterprise economy with less government regulation. Other instances can be found in recent ads by energy companies that promote the virtues of expanding production of untapped oil reserves or the positive features of nuclear electric power plants. Since these are important contemporary political issues as well as issues of economic concern to the corporate world, there is some sense in which corporate image advertising can be seen as increasingly political in nature. Thus, whatever might give rise to Court deliberation on corporate political advertising might also give the Court reasons for ruling on corporate image advertising. We ought to consider what responses to political advocacy advertising by corporations would be appropriate.

In the *Bellotti* decision referred to above, the Supreme Court has already issued a ruling that prevents the state from *prohibiting* corporate political advertising. The Court's ruling in *Bellotti* seems particularly appropriate when we recognize the grave dangers to political autonomy present when the state is able to determine the direction or content of political debates. However, we should not misread the *Bellotti* decision as one which prevents state *regulation* of political advocacy advertisements by corporations. (Prohibition and regulation, of course, are not identical.) In fact, there are strong reasons for suggesting that the recognition of the value of political autonomy should encourage state regulation of such corporate advertising.

If promoting political autonomy is tied to maintaining a free and open system of expression in which opposing points of view can be offered and received, then there might be a danger to political autonomy other than that presented when the government can control political debate. The ability of citizens to autonomously determine the direction of their political institutions could also be threatened if powerful private interests were capable of dominating media discussions of political issues. In fact, with the increasing influence and cost of advertising, in the electronic media especially, there is a very real danger that unregulated political advertising by corporations might render meaningless the right of free expression of opinion for ordinary citizens or unmonied groups.[16] Thus, if traditional constitutional theory supports the right to free speech by connecting it to the value of political autonomy, the Court ought to recognize the legitimacy and potential need for some regulation of corporate political advocacy advertising.

In fact, there are already precedents for such limitations on corporate speech in the Court's sanctioning of FCC fairness rulings requiring equal time for presentation of opposing views after presidential broadcasts on television and radio. Thus, possible regulations requiring equal time (perhaps with public financing) and/or limiting the frequency of political advocacy advertising might be both needed and appropriate if citizens are to have fair value for their rights to freedom of speech.

In summary, consistent with traditional justifications for freedom of speech, recent Supreme Court decisions have expanded the rights of commercial speakers to disseminate factual product information. However, also consistent with appropriate approaches to free speech, these same decisions have made clear that commercial speech deserves less constitutional protection than that provided political or religious speech. On the basis of the appropriateness of these decisions, any future Court decisions ought also to reaffirm the government's right to apply a fairness doctrine to corporate political advertising. Hence, corporate rights to commercial speech should not preclude government activity necessary to ensure both that a fair value for the right to free speech is available to all citizens and that corporate monied interests are unable to set the agenda for public discussion.

NOTES

1. See John Stuart Mill, *On Liberty* (New York: Bobbs-Merrill, 1956); D. A. J. Richards, *The Moral Criticism of Law* (Belmont, CA: Wadsworth, 1977); Thomas Scanlon, "A Theory of Freedom of Expression," *Philosophy and Public Affairs* 1 (1972); Jonathan Weinberg, "Constitutional Protection of Commercial Speech," 82 *Columbia Law Review* 720 (1982).

2. Daniel Farber, "Commercial Speech and First Amendment Theory," 74 *Northwestern University Law Review* 377 (1979).

3. Weinberg, 726.

4. Tracy Westen, "The First Amendment: Barrier or Impetus to FTC Advertising Remedies?" 46 *Brooklyn Law Review* 501.

5. Weinberg, 727, 747; Westen, 503; Farber, 390.

6. Westen, 505.

7. Ibid., 506.

8. Farber, 397; Westen, 496.

9. Weinberg, 728.

10. Ibid., 20; Michael Davis, "Should Commercial Speech Have First Amendment Protection?" *Social Theory and Practice* 6:2 (Summer, 1980) 127; Farber, 382.

11. Farber, 385.

12. Ibid., 386; Davis, 128.

13. Westen, 493–498.

14. Weinberg, 722–723.

15. The *Ohlarik*, *Virginia Board*, and *Bigelow* decisions respectively.

16. Westen, 508–512; Thomas Emerson, "The Affirmative Promotion of Freedom of Expression: Radio and Television," in *Freedom of Expression,* Fred Berger, ed. (Belmont, CA: Wadsworth, 1980) 163–177.

REASONABLE CONSUMER OR IGNORANT CONSUMER? HOW THE FTC DECIDED
Ivan Preston

Is the Federal Trade Commission obligated to protect only reasonable, sensible, intelligent consumers who conduct themselves carefully in the marketplace? Or must it also protect ignorant consumers who conduct themselves carelessly?

Since its origin in 1914 the Commission has varied its answer to these questions. It has committed itself at all times to prohibit seller's claims which would deceive reasonable people, but has undergone changes of direction on whether to ban

From *The Great American Blow-Up*, by Ivan Preston, 1975, The University of Wisconsin Press. Reprinted by permission of The University of Wisconsin Press.

claims which would deceive only ignorant people. At times it has acted on behalf of the latter by invoking the "ignorant man standard."[1] At other times it has been ordered by courts to ignore these people and invoke the "reasonable man standard." In still other cases it has chosen to protect certain ignorant persons but not others.

The significance of the issue is that the FTC will rule against the fewest types of seller's claims under the reasonable man standard, and against the most under the ignorant man standard. The latter guideline therefore means, in the eyes of many, the greatest protection for the consuming public. Consumerists may feel, in fact, that such a standard should be mandatory on the grounds that a flat prohibition is needed against all seller's deceptions which would deceive anyone at all.

The FTC, however, works under a constraint which makes it necessary to temper its allegiance to the ignorant man standard. The constraint is that the Commission may proceed legally only in response to substantial public interest.[2] Over the years the Commissioners have been sensitive to the argument that there is no public interest in prohibiting messages which would deceive only a small number of terribly careless, stupid, or naive people. To explain the compelling nature of this argument, I would like to describe a deception of that sort.

In my hometown of Pittsburgh, Pennsylvania, there appears each Christmastime a brand of beer called Olde Frothingslosh. This quaint item is nothing but Pittsburgh Brewing Company's regular Iron City Beer in its holiday costume, decked out with a specially designed label to provide a few laughs. The label identifies the product as "the pale stale ale for the pale stale male," and there is similar wit appended, all strictly nonsense. One of the best is a line saying that Olde Frothingslosh is the only beer in which the foam is on the bottom.

My old friend at Pittsburgh Brewing, John deCoux, the ad manager there, once told me about a woman who bought some Olde Frothingslosh to amuse friends at a party, and was embarrassed to find the claim was nothing but a *big lie:* the foam was right up there on top where it was on every other brand of beer she'd ever seen! She wanted her money back from the beer distributor (another quaint Pennsylvania custom), but he told her Hell, no, so she went to her lawyer with the intention of bringing suit. The story (and it's true) ended right

there; the lawyer told her to forget it…nobody in earth's history ever saw a beer with the foam on the bottom. The reasonable man (woman! person!) standard would be applied to her suit, her reliance on the belief about the foam would be judged unreasonable, and that would be the end of that.

Had the ignorant man standard applied she would possibly have succeeded, which illustrates the difference the choice of standards makes. It also illustrates the essential weakness (in conjunction with definite strengths) possessed by a legal standard which sets out to protect everybody from everything. Many of the prohibitions it produces would eliminate only infinitesimal amounts of deception.

There are other reasons, too, for the FTC's cautious attitude toward the ignorant man standard. One problem is that the Commission does not have the resources to prosecute all cases,[3] therefore those which are investigated might better be ones which endanger greater numbers of people. Another problem is that an extreme concern for the ignorant could lead to repression of much communication content useful to consumers, and could lead as well to possible violation of the First Amendment's freedom of speech guarantee.[4]

Probably the most important objection to the ignorant man standard is that the reasonable man standard was traditional in the common law which preceded the development of the FTC in 1914. The common law held that to avoid being negligent a person must act as a reasonable person would act under like circumstances.[5] Mention of the reasonable or prudent person first appeared in an English case of 1837[6] and has been in widespread use since….

The question is whether something called contributory negligence may be charged against the plaintiff, the person deceived. He brings a suit against the deceiver, and the rules require him to assert and show that he relied upon the misrepresentation, and that the damages suffered were a result of such reliance. In addition, he must show that his reliance was justified—that is, his reliance must pass the test of the conduct of a reasonable person. He may not claim to have relied on a statement which sensible and prudent people would recognize as preposterous. If he does, he is guilty of contributory negligence which the deceiver may use as a defense which can result in having the suit dismissed.[7]

This rule usually does not apply in the case of a fraudulent misrepresentation, where the deceiver consciously knows it was false and intentionally seeks to deceive with it. If that is shown, the person deceived is entitled to rely without having to justify his reliance as reasonable.[8] But an exception to the exception comes with puffery and the other false but legally nondeceptive claims which are the topic of this book. The law states that people know and understand they are not to rely on such misrepresentations, even when stated fraudulently. Therefore with these kinds of statements the reasonable man standard, when it is the prevailing standard, applies.

At the time the FTC was created, the only specific law on these matters was the common law just described. The FTC Act said nothing explicitly about what persons the Commission was authorized to protect; it said only that proceedings must "be in the interest of the public."[9] The most obvious way of pursuing this mandate would have been to follow the common law precedents and embrace the reasonable man standard. Instead, the FTC did the unexpected and flaunted the reasonable man standard in many of its early cases. Neither that concept nor a replacement standard were discussed explicitly, but numerous cases show that the Commission was applying an ignorant man standard or a close approximation of it. In 1919 it ordered a manufacturer to stop advertising that its automobile batteries would "last forever."[10] One might assume that no reasonable person even in that year would have relied upon the claim literally, especially when the same ads offered a service by which "the purchaser pays 50 cents per month and is entitled to a new battery as soon as the old one is worn out." The FTC saw the latter phrase, however, as confirming the falsity and deceptiveness rather than the sheer frivolousness of "last forever." The case indicates the Commission was developing a deliberate policy of stopping deceptions which would deceive only a minority.[11]

This switch to the ignorant man standard appeared questionable legally; precedent did not support it. But before we describe the eventual court considerations of this matter, we should acknowledge that there was much argument against the reasonable man standard in common sense if not in law. The legal conception of the buyer who failed to be reasonable in the marketplace was that of a person who made a stupid purchase through his own

fault—he should have known better.[12] It was this conception with which common sense could disagree. Some so-called stupid choices may be made not through carelessness but through the impossibility of obtaining and assessing information even when great caution and intelligence are applied. The world of goods and services was once simple, but has become terribly technical. Many poor choices are made by persons who *couldn't* know better.

These problems might have been incorporated into the reasonable man standard by adjusting that standard to the realities of the market. Consider a store scene in which a product is available at six cans for a dollar while one can is sixteen cents. In considering whether a reasonable person would be deceived, the law might have taken into account that many people are slow at arithmetic, and that the bustle of a market and the need to make many other choices in the same few minutes render it unlikely they would fully use the mathematical capacity they possess. The competence assumed of a "reasonable person" might have been reduced accordingly, and the traditional standard, altered in this way, might still have been applied.

What actually occurred in legal actions was something bordering on the opposite. The reasonable person came to be regarded as a *better* than average person, as someone who was never negligent and who therefore was entirely fictitious outside the courtroom.[13] He was "an ideal creature… The factor controlling the judgment of [his] conduct is not what *is*, but *what ought to be*."[14] The law, apparently, had created an unreasonable conception of the reasonable person.

It was this problem the FTC sought to correct. We do not know, because the point was not discussed as such, whether the Commission regarded its new conception as a move to the ignorant man standard or as a redefinition of the reasonable man standard by the method described above. But the practical effect was the same either way—the Commission moved toward protecting the public from deceptions which regulators previously had ignored because they did not harm the fictitiously reasonable person.

Considerations of the reasonable and ignorant man standards eventually were made explicit through the intervention of appeals court decisions into FTC affairs. In *John C. Winston* of 1924,[15] the Commission outlawed a sales method which offered an encyclopedia "free" provided a purchaser paid $49 for two supplementary updating services. The seller appealed and won a reversal on the grounds that no deception was involved: "It is conceivable that a very stupid person might be misled by this method of selling books, yet measured by ordinary standards of trade and by ordinary standards of the intelligence of traders, we cannot discover that it amounts to an unfair method of competition..."[16]

The FTC did not adopt the reasonable man standard as a result of this ruling; its subsequent activities reflected instead a posture of resistance.[17] When it stubbornly invoked a similar restraint against a different encyclopedia company, Standard Education Society, in 1931,[18] it was again reversed by an appeals court.[19] Circuit Judge Learned Hand was most adamant in declaring that "a community which sells for profit must not be ridden on so short a rein that it can only move at a walk. We cannot take seriously the suggestion that a man who is buying a set of books and a ten year's 'extension service,' will be fatuous enough to be misled by the mere statement that the first are given away, and that he is paying only for the second. Nor can we conceive how he could be damaged were he to suppose that that was true. Such trivial niceties are too impalpable for practical affairs, they are will-o'-the-wisps which divert attention from substantial evils."

This time, however, the FTC took the case to the Supreme Court, where a new justice delivering his first opinion told Learned Hand that the encyclopedia decision *was* a substantial evil. Hugo Black's opinion in *FTC v. Standard Education* of 1937[20] restored the Commission's use of the ignorant man standard: "The fact that a false statement may be obviously false to those who are trained and experienced does not change its character, nor take away its power to deceive others less experienced. There is no duty resting upon a citizen to suspect the honesty of those with whom he transacts business. Laws are made to protect the trusting as well as the suspicious. The best element of business has long since decided that honesty should govern competitive enterprises, and that the rule of caveat emptor should not be relied upon to reward fraud and deception."

Though Black mentioned the name of neither standard, his words suggest he was rejecting the reasonable man standard rather than proposing merely to adjust it. Black's words, above all, led to the concept of an "ignorant man standard" for the FTC in place of what went before.

Just how *Standard Education* was supported by precedent is a curious question. Justice Black's opinion cited none. It affirmed that the sales method not merely had deceptive capacity but clearly deceived many persons, and it also stated that the deception was committed knowingly and deliberately.[21] This suggests that the Supreme Court was invoking the common law notion that the reasonable man standard should not apply in case of deliberate deception. Something left unclarified, however, is what significance such a ruling should have for an agency such as the FTC which routinely did not make findings of deliberate deception. Deliberate intent to deceive undoubtedly occurs in many cases where no one can prove it. The whole advantage of FTC procedure, in comparison with what went before, was that it could rule seller's messages out of the marketplace *without* bothering with the traditional requirement of proving intent. What was the advantage, then, of obtaining the right to use the ignorant man standard only in conjunction with proving intent to deceive?

The result, strangely, was that the FTC, on the basis of *Standard Education,* began applying the ignorant man standard liberally without regard for determining intent, and in some cases without regard for the fact that intent to deceive was almost surely absent. The appeals courts, also via *Standard Education,* approved this procedure. The trend was thoroughly questionable but was pursued decisively, particularly by the Second Circuit Court of Appeals, the court which *Standard Education* had reversed. In *General Motors v. FTC* of 1940,[22] a case involving a "6% time payment plan" which actually charged 11.5 percent interest, the Second Circuit's Judge Augustus Hand concluded: "It may be that there was no intention to mislead and that only the careless or the incompetent could have been misled. But if the Commission, having discretion to deal with these matters, thinks it best to insist upon a form of advertising clear enough so that, in the words of the prophet Isaiah, 'wayfaring men, though fools, shall not err therein,' it is not for the courts to revise their judgment."

The influence of the *Standard Education* reversal was unmistakable on the one Hand—and on the other Hand as well. When Judge Learned Hand considered an appeal to the Second Circuit of the Commission's finding of deception in an admittedly untrue claim that "one Moretrench wellpoint is as good as any five others,"[23] he said: "It is extremely hard to believe that any buyers of such machinery could be misled by anything which was patently no more than the exuberant enthusiasm of a satisfied customer, but in such matters we understand that we are to insist upon the most literal truthfulness. Federal Trade Commission v. Standard Education Society..."

Turning to another literally untrue Moretrench claim, that its product had an advantage to which "contractors all over the world testify," Hand stated: "It is again hard to imagine how anyone reading it could have understood it as more than puffing; yet for the reasons we have just given, if the Commission saw fit to take notice of it, we may not interfere."

It was clear that the Second Circuit's Hands were tied. Substitution of the ignorant man standard for the reasonable man standard proceeded in additional Second Circuit cases,[24] and in others as well.[25] Under these liberal interpretations the FTC appeared during most of the 1940s to be knocking down right and left every advertising claim it thought had the slightest chance of deceiving even the most ignorant person. There was a good bit of unchecked exuberance in this spree, including the action against Charles of the Ritz's use of "Rejuvenescence" as a name for its face cream.[26] The FTC outlawed the term on the grounds that it referred literally to the restoration of youth and the appearance of youth. The company protested that it was merely a "boastful and fanciful word" used nondeceptively, but the Second Circuit agreed with the Commission. I find it amusing that Charles of the Ritz has been using the trade name "Revenescence" ever since, avoiding the literal meaning but apparently retaining some of the persuasive value it once received from "Rejuvenescence."

The Second Circuit's thoughtfulness toward the ignorant man reached an extreme when it agreed with the FTC in forbidding Clairol to say that its dye will "color hair permanently."[27] The FTC thought the public would take that as a claim that all the hair a person grows for the rest of her life will emerge in the Clairol color. That expectation was based on the testimony of a single witness who

said she thought somebody might think that—although she added that *she* wouldn't.

On Clairol's appeal one judge of the Second Circuit, Clark, agreed fully with the FTC: "Petitioner's [Clairol's] actual defense is that no one should be fooled—a defense repudiated every time it has been offered on appellate review, so far as I know, since it is well settled that the Commission does not act for the sophisticated alone."

The majority of judges, Swan and Augustus Hand, disagreed with this reasoning. They said they couldn't imagine *anybody* believing the Clairol claim: "There is no dispute that it imparts a permanent coloration to the hair to which it is applied, but the commission found that it has 'no effect upon new hair,' and hence concluded that the representation as to permanence was misleading. It seems scarcely possible that any user of the preparation could be so credulous as to suppose that hair not yet grown out would be colored by an application of the preparation to the head. But the commission has construed the advertisement as so representing it..."

Nonetheless, the majority said, they had to support the FTC position no matter what they personally thought: "Since the Act is for the protection of the trusting as well as the suspicious, as stated in Federal Trade Commission v. Standard Education Society...we think the order must be sustained on this point."

In basing the decision on *Standard Education,* the Second Circuit offered no judgment that the Clairol claim was used with intent to deceive, and made no acknowledgment that *Standard Education* might have been intended by the Supreme Court to apply only where such intent was evident. The inclination to apply the ignorant man standard appears to have overridden any other consideration. We may speculate that if the Olde Frothingslosh matter had been appealed to the Second Circuit in the same year as the Clairol case, 1944, the purchaser might have recovered damages because the beer's foam wasn't on the bottom!

This [selection] thus far has discussed the development of a strong emphasis on the ignorant man standard. The next task is to describe how this emphasis came to be diluted, a matter which involved additional curious events. One of the arbitrary facts of life in American law is that the various circuit courts of appeal are sometimes inconsistent in their rulings. They need not take each other's decisions into account, so a case may be decided differently in one than in another. The Second Circuit was the one reversed by *Standard Education,* and we have seen that this court in subsequent cases applied the ignorant man standard assiduously. This included the prohibition of puffery in *Moretrench,* even though puffery had traditionally been called nondeceptive. With its long-standing immunity, puffery might have been expected to resist the courts even if nothing else did, but under the ignorant man standard the Second Circuit moved to eliminate this kind of falsity along with everything else.

But the time came, in 1946, when a puffery case was appealed to the Seventh Circuit rather than the Second, and the difference was significant. *Carlay*[28] involved a claim that Ayds candy mints make weight-reducing easy, which the FTC said was false. On appeal the Seventh Circuit[29] which had tended earlier to object to the ignorant man standard,[30] decided, "What was said was clearly justifiable…under those cases recognizing that such words as 'easy,' 'perfect,' 'amazing,' 'prime,' 'wonderful,' 'excellent,' are regarded in law as mere puffing or dealer's talk upon which no charge of misrepresentation can be based." The court cited previous non-FTC cases which allowed puffery, and completely ignored the cases stemming from Justice Black and the Second Circuit, which would have supported the FTC's outlawing of "easy."

As a result the FTC had a contradiction on its hands. The Second Circuit told it to protect the ignorant man; the Seventh Circuit told it to permit puffery which could deceive the ignorant man. The contradiction might have been resolved by the Supreme Court, but was never considered there. The FTC's resolution was to allow puffery thereafter, which tended to dilute the ignorant man standard.

The trend away from the extreme ignorant man standard had begun, but only slightly. Cases followed in which the FTC retained a strong protective stance on behalf of ignorant consumers.[31] But in 1963 the Commission finally commented that the standard could be carried too far. *Heinz v. Kirchner*[32] was a case about an inflatable device to help a person stay afloat and learn to swim. Called Swim-Ezy, it was worn under the swimming suit and advertised as being invisible. It was not invisi-ble, but the FTC found it to be "inconspicuous," and ruled that that was all the claim of invisibility would mean to the public: "The possibility that some person might believe Swim-Ezy is, not merely inconspicuous, but wholly invisible or bodiless, seems to us too far-fetched to warrant intervention."

What about the few persons who would accept this "far-fetched" belief? The Commission made clear it no longer intended to protect such ignorant persons:

> True…the Commission's responsibility is to prevent deception of the gullible and credulous, as well as the cautious and knowledgeable…. This principle loses its validity, however, if it is applied uncritically or pushed to an absurd extreme. An advertiser cannot be charged with liability in respect of every conceivable misconception, however outlandish, to which his representations might be subject among the foolish or feeble-minded…A representation does not become "false and deceptive" merely because it will be unreasonably misunderstood by an insignificant and unrepresentative segment of the class of persons to whom the representation is addressed.

That is the position the FTC has followed since. It holds no longer to the strict ignorant man standard by which it would protect everyone from everything which may deceive them.[33] It would reject consideration, for example, of the Olde Frothingslosh claim which apparently fooled only one stray individual. Perhaps we may call the new stance a modified ignorant man standard which protects only those cases of foolishness which are committed by significant numbers of people.

Some readers may protest that any behaviors which are customary for a substantial portion of the population shouldn't be called "ignorant." They might rather call the new stance a modified reasonable man standard in which what is reasonable has been equated more closely than before with what is average or typical.[34] Whatever the name, however, the FTC's present position appears to remain closer to the spirit and practice of the strict ignorant man standard of the 1940s than to the reasonable man standard of tradition.[35]

NOTES

1. "Ignorant man standard" is my own term, which I feel is correctly blunt. The terms "credulous man standard" and "lowest standard of intelligence," which lack semantic punch, have been used elsewhere; see *Truth in Advertising: A Symposium of the Toronto School of Theology*, 2–3, 30–34 (1972); Ira M. Millstein, "The Federal Trade Commission and false advertising," 64 *Columbia Law Rev.* 439, 458–462 (1964).

2. FTC Act, § 5(b); Millstein, "False advertising," 483–487; "Developments in the law—deceptive advertising," 80 *Harvard Law Rev.* 1005, 1023–1025 (1967).

3. "Deceptive advertising," 1082; Millstein, "False advertising," 494; Edward F. Cox, Robert C. Fellmuth, and John E. Schulz, *Nader's Raiders: Report on the Federal Trade Commission* (1969).

4. Millstein, "False advertising," 462–465; "Deceptive advertising," 1027–1038; Peter B. Turk, "Justice Hugo Black and advertising: the stepchild of the First Amendment," in *For Freedom of Expression: Essays in Honor of Hugo L. Black*, ed. Dwight L. Teeter and David Grey (in press).

5. *Restatement of the Law of Torts (Second)*, § 283 (1965). Section 283A adds that a child must act as would a reasonable person of like age, intelligence, and experience under like circumstances.

6. *Vaughan v. Menlove*, 3 Bing, N.C. 468, 132 Eng. Rep. 490 (1837). For other cases and references see Reporter's Notes to § 283 of *Restatement of Torts (Second)*.

7. The term *contributory negligence* is not always used, but the idea of denying recovery for unreasonable reliance on misrepresentations is based on that concept; William L. Prosser, *Handbook of the Law of Torts*, 4th ed., 717 (1971).

8. Ibid., 716.

9. FTC Act, § 5(b).

10. *FTC v. Universal Battery*, 2 FTC 95 (1919).

11. See also *FTC v. A. A. Berry*, 2 FTC 427 (1920); *FTC v. Alben-Harley*, 4 FTC 31 (1921); *FTC v. Williams Soap*, 6 FTC 107 (1923); *Alfred Peats*, 8 FTC 366 (1925).

12. See discussion above at note 5 ff.

13. *Restatement of Torts (Second)*, § 283, comment c.

14. Francis H. Bohlen, "Mixed questions of law and fact," 72 *Univ. of Pennsylvania Law Rev.* 111, 113 (1923).

15. 8 FTC 177 (1924).

16. *John C. Winston v. FTC*, 3 F.2d 961 (3rd Cir., 1925).

17. *Nugrape*, 9 FTC 20 (1925); *Ostermoor*, 10 FTC 45 (1926), but set aside in *Ostermoor v. FTC*, 16 F.2d 962 (2d Cir., 1927); *William F. Schied*, 10 FTC 85 (1926); *Good Grape*, 10 FTC 99 (1926); *Hobart Bradstreet*, 11 FTC 174

(1927); *Frank P. Snyder*, 11 FTC 390 (1927); *Dr. Eagan*, 11 FTC 436 (1927); *Berkey & Gay Furniture*, 12 FTC 227 (1928), but set aside in *Berkey & Gay Furniture v. FTC*, 42 F.2d 427 (6th Cir., 1930); *Northam-Warren*, 15 FTC 389 (1931), but set aside in *Northam-Warren v. FTC*, 59 F.2d 196 (2d Cir., 1932); *Fairyfoot Products* 20 FTC 40 (1934), affirmed in *Fairyfoot v. FTC*, 80 F.2d 684 (7th Cir., 1935).

18. *Standard Education Society*, 16 FTC 1 (1931).

19. *FTC v. Standard Education Society*, 86 F.2d 692 (2d Cir., 1936).

20. 302 U.S. 112, 58 S.C. 113 (1937).

21. Ibid., 116: "It was clearly the practice of respondents through their agents, in accordance with a well matured plan, to mislead customers…"

22. 114 F.2d 33 (2d Cir., 1940).

23. *Moretrench v. FTC* 127, F.2d (2d Cir., 1942). This was the same judge who once had rejected similar claims on the grounds that "there are some kinds of talk which no man takes seriously…"; *Vulcan Metals v. Simmons*.

24. See notes 26 and 27 below.

25. *D.D.D. v. FTC* (1942); *Aronberg v. FTC* (1942); *Gulf Oil v. FTC*, 150 F.2d 106 (5th Cir., 1945); *Parker Pen v. FTC*, 159 F.2d 509 (7th Cir., 1946). In the latter case the FTC's role was said to be to "protect the casual, one might say the negligent, reader, as well as the vigilant and more intelligent…" A much-used quotation, cited in *Aronberg*, *Gulf Oil*, and *Gelb* (see note 27 below), stated, "The law is not made for the protection of experts, but for the public— that vast multitude which includes the ignorant, the unthinking, and the credulous, who, in making purchases, do not stop to analyze, but are governed by appearances and general impressions"; *Florence v. Dowd*, 178 F. 73 (2d. Cir., 1910). This was a pre-FTC case with evidence of deliberate deception.

26. *Charles of the Ritz v. FTC*, 143 F.2d 676 (2d Cir., 1944), following *Charles of the Ritz*, 34 FTC 1203 (1942).

27. *Gelb v. FTC*, 144 F.2d 580 (2d Cir., 1944), following *Gelb*, 33 FTC 1450 (1941).

28. 39 FTC 357 (1944).

29. *Carlay v. FTC*, 153 F.2d 493 (1946).

30. *Allen B. Wrisley v. FTC*, 113 F.2d 437 (7th Cir., 1940); also later in *Buchsbaum v. FTC*, 160 F.2d 121 (7th Cir., 1947).

31. *Lorillard v. FTC* (1950); *Independent Directory*, 47 FTC 13 (1950) (but see dissent by Commissioner Mason); *Goodman v. FTC*, 244 F.2d 584 (9th Cir., 1957); *FTC v. Sewell*, 353 U.S. 969, 77 S.C. 1055 (1957); *Bantam Books v. FTC*, 275 F.2d 680 (2d Cir., 1960) (but see questions raised by Judge Moore); *Exposition Press v. FTC*, 295 F.2d 869 (2d Cir., 1961); *Giant Food v. FTC*, 322 F.2d 977 (D.C. Cir., 1963);

FTC v. Colgate, 380 U.S. 374, 85 S.C. 1035 (1965).

32. 63 FTC 1282 (1963).

33. In *Papercraft*, 63 FTC 1965, 1997 (1963), Commissioner MacIntyre protested that the retreat from the extreme ignorant man position was unfortunate. The majority opinion had withdrawn from protecting the "foolish or feeble-minded," and MacIntyre dissented: "Should this observation be construed as a retreat from our long-held position that the public as a whole is entitled to protection, including even 'the ignorant, the unthinking, and the credulous,' then the result may well be confusion."

34. *Truth in Advertising*, 31.

35. "It might be said that the test of consumer competence generally employed by the Commission appears to approximate the least sophisticated level of understanding possessed by any substantial portion of the class of persons to whom the advertisement is addressed." Personal correspondence to Peter B. Turk from Gale T. Miller, law clerk, Bureau of Consumer Protection, Federal Trade Commission, December 6, 1971. The "class of persons" assumed generally consists of adults. Special consideration for representations made to children (see note 5) was recognized in *FTC v. Keppel*, 291 U.S. 304, 54 S.C. 423 (1934). As for other groups, Miller wrote: "It is the position of the staff that advertising geared towards other special audiences, such as the ghetto dweller, the elderly, and the handicapped, might also be subjected to a more rigorous test than is applied to advertisements addressed to the public at large."

WHY FTC CURBS ARE NEEDED
James C. Miller

When the Federal Trade Commission began its children's advertising rule making, the advertising community moved to eliminate the FTC's jurisdiction over unfair advertising. The "kidvid" experience revealed that the only limit on the commission's powers under the unfairness standard was the imagination of those in charge.

It is time to describe, that is, to specify the FTC's basic mission. It is time Congress set limits on what is now virtually unlimited authority. Broad power in the hands of a few nonelected officials is neither in the public's interest nor, paradoxically, in the agency's interest. Indeed, I believe that one reason the agency has been under so much fire recently is that under Section 5 of the FTC Act three commissioners could just as easily wreak havoc as pursue the interest of the public.

The commission's authority needs to be narrowed and redefined. That, in my view, is the right approach, not exempting special interest groups. A more directed FTC would mean a clearer focus on real problems and more benefits for individual consumers, for providers of goods and services and for the advertising industry.

Should advertisers achieve their goal—the elimination of our unfairness jurisdiction over commercial speech—they would discover they had won a battle but lost the war. Unfairness is only half the critical phrase of our statute. The other half is deception. It too, needs attention as a legal concept. Indeed, with respect to advertising, almost anything the agency has ever done, or proposed to do under its fairness jurisdiction, could have been addressed under a deception theory.

The very proceeding that demonstrated the breadth of the commission's unfairness doctrine—children's advertising—might well have been based on a deception theory. Indeed, the initial staff report proposed the rule making on the basis of *both* unfairness and deception.

The report argued that advertising to young children is inherently deceptive because children can't distinguish between ads and programs. Based on this alleged deception, as well as upon unfairness, commission lawyers asserted that the ads should be banned. As for sugared products, the staff argued that the ads' failure to mention the adverse health effects of sugar was deceptive.

In sum, the staff believed that the commission could proceed with the children's advertising rule under either the deception standard or under an unfairness theory. (When the staff recommended ending "kidvid," it was because of the difficulties in defining which ads would be covered, not because they thought the legal basis was inadequate.)

Another example of the breadth of the commission's deception jurisdiction involves the staff's proposal for rotational warnings to advise consumers on the specific health hazards of smoking. The proposed legal basis for commission action is that if some consumers do not know that smoking causes heart attacks, then it is deceptive to advertise cigarets without disclosing that fact.

No one argues that current advertisements imply that cigarets *don't* cause heart attacks. Instead, they argue that some consumers do not have the requisite information linking cigarets with heart attacks. Let me make clear that I'm not addressing whether Congress should impose a rotational warning scheme. My point is that if the commission can require cigaret health warnings under a deception theory, what couldn't it do in other areas of advertising?

Deception seems to be a concrete word, one independent of the perceptions of individual commissioners. Perhaps it is because the meaning of the word seems obvious that the central element of the current definition is circular—that an ad is deceptive if it has a "tendency or capacity to deceive." Within this broad definition, the commission's law of deception has few limits. For example, the commission need not interpret an ad's claim as would a reasonable consumer.

Consider the case against Ford. The company produced an ad describing a mileage test. The test covered how the cars were broken in, how fast they were driven and so forth. The ads also said, "You yourself might actually average less, or for that matter more. Because mileage varies according to maintenance, equipment, total weight, driving habits and road conditions. And no two drivers, or even cars, are exactly the same." Nevertheless, the FTC read this carefully qualified claim to mean that the *average* driver would get the advertised mileage and demanded substantiation. Quick-on-the-trigger action of this type may keep valuable information from being disseminated.

The Ford case illustrates an additional problem. The commission can evaluate claims with only its own "expertise." Sometimes how a reasonable consumer will interpret an ad is obvious. I believe that the commission should be bound to consult research evidence, such as surveys of consumer responses.

Of course it is occasionally inappropriate to base deception only on whether reasonable consumers are misled. Certain groups are particularly vulnerable. An example would be a miracle cure aimed at the terminally ill.

There is another major problem with the commission's discretion with respect to deception. The commission doesn't have to consider if consumers have actually been harmed. The Poli-Grip denture cream case is illustrative. The ad claimed users could eat "problem" foods. Although this product was inexpensive, frequently purchased and, by its nature, something each consumer could easily evaluate, the commission took issue with the ads. As then-commissioner Thompson put it: "It is inconceivable to me that any denture wearer who applied Poli-Grip or Super Poli-Grip and bit into a red apple and then saw his dentures smiling back at him would ever purchase the gripper again."

Finally, under current law the commission can find an ad deceptive not only for what it says but for what it does not say. For example, the commission has required sellers of salt substitutes to state that the products are not appropriate for those on potassium-restricted diets. The commission found the ads to be deceptive and required this disclosure even though the ads made no claims regarding potassium.

As I've argued elsewhere, the commission needs new legislation defining the term "unfair." I've tried to show here the need for a similar clarification of our deceptive jurisdiction.

Legislation is needed to provide a clear mission for the FTC now and in the future. If Congress acts, the commission will be able to give more specific guidance to its staff. Advertisers will have a better indication of what is permitted and what is prohibited. And consumers will receive more accurate information on which to base their purchasing decisions.

ADVERTISING AND BEHAVIOR CONTROL
Robert L. Arrington

Consider the following advertisements:

1. "A woman in *Distinction Foundations* is so beautiful that all other women want to kill her."

2. Pongo Peach color for Revlon comes "from east of the sun...west of the moon where each tomorrow dawns." It is "succulent on your lips" and "sizzling on your finger tips (and on your toes goodness knows)." Let it be your "adventure in paradise."

3. "Musk by English Leather—The Civilized Way to Roar."

4. "Increase the value of your holdings. Old Charter Bourbon Whiskey—The Final Step Up."

5. Last Call Smirnoff Style: "They'd never really miss us, and it's kind of late already, and it's quite a long way, and I could build a fire, and you're looking very beautiful, and we could have another martini, and it's awfully nice just being home...you think?"

6. A Christmas Prayer. "Let us pray that the blessing of peace be ours—the peace to build and grow, to live in harmony and sympathy with others, and to plan for the future with confidence." New York Life Insurance Company.

These are instances of what is called puffery—the practice by a seller of making exaggerated, highly fanciful or suggestive claims about a product or service. Puffery, within ill-defined limits, is legal. It is considered a legitimate, necessary, and very successful tool of the advertising industry. Puffery is not just bragging; it is bragging carefully designed to achieve a very definite effect. Using the techniques of so-called motivational research, advertising firms first identify our often hidden needs (for security, conformity, oral stimulation) and our desires (for power, sexual dominance and dalliance, adventure) and then they design ads which respond to these needs and desires. By associating a product, for which we may have little or no direct need or desire, with symbols reflecting the fulfillment of these other, often subterranean interests, the advertisement can quickly generate large numbers of consumers eager to purchase the product advertised. What woman in the sexual race of life could resist a foundation which would turn other women envious to the point of homicide? Who can turn down an adventure in paradise, east of the sun where tomorrow dawns? Who doesn't want to be civilized and thoroughly libidinous at the same time? Be at the pinnacle of success—drink Old Charter. Or stay at home and dally a bit—with Smirnoff. And let us pray for a secure and predictable future, provided for by New York Life, God willing. It doesn't take very much motivational research to see the point of these sales pitches. Others are perhaps a little less obvious. The need to feel secure in one's home at night can be used to sell window air conditioners, which drown out small noises and provide a friendly, dependable companion. The fact that baking a cake is symbolic of giving birth to a baby used to prompt advertisements for cake mixes which glamorized the "creative" housewife. And other strategies, for example involving cigar symbolism, are a bit too crude to mention, but are nevertheless very effective.

Don't such uses of puffery amount to manipulation, exploitation, or downright control? In his very popular book *The Hidden Persuaders*, Vance Packard points out that a number of people in the advertising world have frankly admitted as much:

> As early as 1941 Dr. Dichter (an influential advertising consultant) was exhorting ad agencies to recognize themselves for what they actually were—"one of the most advanced laboratories in psychology." He said the successful ad agency "manipulates human motivations and desires and develops a need for goods with which the public has at one time been unfamiliar—perhaps even undesirous of purchasing." The following year *Advertising Agency* carried an ad man's statement that psychology not only holds promise for understanding people but "ultimately for controlling their behavior."[1]

From *Journal of Business Ethics* 1 (1982): 3–12. Copyright © 1982 by D. Reidel Publishing Co., Dordrecht, Holland. Reprinted by permission.

Such statements lead Packard to remark: "With all this interest in manipulating the customer's subconscious, the old slogan 'let the buyer beware' began taking on a new and more profound meaning."[2]

B. F. Skinner, the high priest of behaviorism, has expressed a similar assessment of advertising and related marketing techniques. Why, he asks, do we buy a certain kind of car?

> Perhaps our favorite TV program is sponsored by the manufacturer of that car. Perhaps we have seen pictures of many beautiful or prestigeful persons driving it—in pleasant or glamorous places. Perhaps the car has been designed with respect to our motivational patterns: the device on the hood is a phallic symbol; or the horsepower has been stepped up to please our competitive spirit in enabling us to pass other cars swiftly (or, as the advertisements say, "safely"). The concept of freedom that has emerged as part of the cultural practice of our group makes little or no provision for recognizing or dealing with these kinds of control.[3]

In purchasing a car we may think we are free, Skinner is claiming, when in fact our act is completely controlled by factors in our environment and in our history of reinforcement. Advertising is one such factor.

A look at some other advertising techniques may reinforce the suspicion that Madison Avenue controls us like so many puppets. T.V. watchers surely have noticed that some of the more repugnant ads are shown over and over again, *ad nauseum.* My favorite, or most hated, is the one about A-1 Steak Sauce which goes something like this: Now, ladies and gentlemen, what is hamburger? It has succeeded in destroying my taste for hamburger, but it has surely drilled the name of A-1 Sauce into my head. And that is the point of it. Its very repetitiousness has generated what ad theorists call *information.* In this case it is indirect information, information derived not from the content of what is said but from the fact that it is said so often and so vividly that it sticks in one's mind—i.e., the information yield has increased. And not only do I always remember A-1 Sauce when I go to the grocers, I tend to assume that any product advertised so often has to be good—and so I usually buy a bottle of the stuff.

Still another technique: On a recent show of the television program "Hard Choices" it was demonstrated how subliminal suggestion can be used to control customers. In a New Orleans department store, messages to the effect that shoplifting is wrong, illegal, and subject to punishment were blended into the Muzak background music and masked so as not to be consciously audible. The store reported a dramatic drop in shoplifting. The program host conjectured whether a logical extension of this technique would be to broadcast subliminal advertising messages to the effect that the store's $15.99 sweater special is the "bargain of a lifetime." Actually, this application of subliminal suggestion to advertising has already taken place. Years ago in New Jersey a cinema was reported to have flashed subthreshold ice cream ads onto the screen during regular showings of the film—and, yes, the concession stand did a landslide business.[4]

Puffery, indirect information transfer, subliminal advertising—are these techniques of manipulation and control whose success shows that many of us have forfeited our autonomy and become a community, or herd, of packaged souls?[5] The business world and the advertising industry certainly reject this interpretation of their efforts. *Business Week,* for example, dismissed the charge that the science of behavior, as utilized by advertising, is engaged in human engineering and manipulation. It editorialized to the effect that "it is hard to find anything very sinister about a science whose principle conclusion is that you get along with people by giving them what they want."[6] The theme is familiar: businesses just give the consumer what he/she wants; if they didn't they wouldn't stay in business very long. Proof that the consumer wants the products advertised is given by the fact that he buys them, and indeed often returns to buy them again and again.

The techniques of advertising we are discussing have had their more intellectual defenders as well. For example, Theodore Levitt, Professor of Business Administration at the Harvard Business School, has defended the practice of puffery and the use of techniques depending on motivational research.[7] What would be the consequences, he asks us, of deleting all exaggerated claims and fanciful associations from advertisements? We would be left with literal descriptions of the empirical characteristics of products and their functions. Cosmetics

would be presented as facial and bodily lotions—
and powders which produce certain odor and color
changes; they would no longer offer hope or adventure. In addition to the fact that these products
would not then sell as well, they would not, according to Levitt, please us as much either. For it is
hope and adventure we want when we buy them.
We want automobiles not just for transportation,
but the feelings of power and status they give us.
Quoting T. S. Eliot to the effect that "Human kind
cannot bear very much reality," Levitt argues that
advertising is an effort to "transcend nature in the
raw," to "augment what nature has so crudely
fashioned." He maintains that "everybody everywhere wants to modify, transform, embellish, en-
rich and reconstruct the world around him."
Commerce takes the same liberty with reality as the
artist and the priest—in all three instances the
purpose is "to influence the audience by creating
illusions, symbols, and implications that promise
more than pure functionality." For example, "to
amplify the temple in men's eyes, (men of cloth)
have, very realistically, systematically sanctioned the
embellishment of the houses of the gods with the
same kind of luxurious design and expensive deco-
ration that Detroit puts into a Cadillac." A poem, a
temple, a Cadillac—they all elevate our spirits,
offering imaginative promises and symbolic interpretations of our mundane activities. Seen in this
light, Levitt claims, "Embellishment and distortion
are among advertising's legitimate and socially
desirable purposes." To reject these techniques of
advertising would be "to deny man's honest needs
and values."

Phillip Nelson, a Professor of Economics at
SUNY-Binghamton, has developed an interesting
defense of indirect information advertising.[8] He
argues that even when the message (the direct
information) is not credible, the fact that the brand
is advertised, and advertised frequently, is valuable
indirect information for the consumer. The reason
for this is that the brands advertised most are more
likely to be better buys—losers won't be advertised
a lot, for it simply wouldn't pay to do so. Thus even
if the advertising claims made for a widely advertised product are empty, the consumer reaps the
benefit of the indirect information which shows
the product to be a good buy. Nelson goes so far as
to say that advertising, seen as information and
especially as indirect information, does not require

an intelligent human response. If the indirect information has been received and has had its impact,
the consumer will purchase the better buy even if
his explicit reason for doing so is silly, e.g., he
naively believes an endorsement of the product by a
celebrity. Even though his behavior is overtly irrational, by acting on the indirect information he is
nevertheless doing what he ought to do, i.e., getting his money's worth. "'Irrationality' is rational,"
Nelson writes, "if it is cost-free."

I don't know of any attempt to defend the use
of subliminal suggestion in advertising, but I can
imagine one form such an attempt might take.
Advertising information, even if perceived below
the level of conscious awareness, must appeal to
some desire on the part of the audience if it is to
trigger a purchasing response. Just as the admoni-
tion not to shoplift speaks directly to the superego,
the sexual virtues of TR-7's, Pongo Peach, and
Betty Crocker cake mix present themselves directly
to the id, bypassing the pesky reality principle of
the ego. With a little help from our advertising
friends, we may remove a few of the discontents of
civilization and perhaps even enter into the paradise
of polymorphous perversity.[9]

The defense of advertising which suggests that
advertising simply is information which allows us
to purchase what we want, has in turn been challenged. Does business, largely through its advertising efforts, really make available to the consumer
what he/she desires and demands? John Kenneth
Galbraith has denied that the matter is as straightforward as this.[10] In his opinion the desires to
which business is supposed to respond, far from
being original to the consumer, are often themselves created by business. The producers make
both the product and the desire for it, and the
"central function" of advertising is "to create desires"? Galbraith coins the term "The Dependence
Effect" to designate the way wants depend on the
same process by which they are satisfied.

David Braybrooke has argued in similar and
related ways.[11] Even though the consumer is in a
sense, the final authority concerning what he
wants, he may come to see, according to Braybrooke, that he was mistaken in wanting what he
did. The statement "I want x," he tells us, is not
incorrigible but is "ripe for revision." If the consumer had more objective information than he is
provided by product puffing, if his values had not

been mixed up by motivational research strategies (e.g., the confusion of sexual and automotive values), and if he had an expanded set of choices instead of the limited set offered by profit-hungry corporations, then he might want something quite different from what he presently wants. This shows, Braybrooke thinks, the extent to which the consumer's wants are a function of advertising and not necessarily representative of his real or true wants.

The central issue which emerges between the above critics and defenders of advertising is this: do the advertising techniques we have discussed involve a violation of human autonomy and a manipulation and control of consumer behavior, *or* do they simply provide an efficient and cost-effective means of giving the consumer information on the basis of which he or she makes a free choice. Is advertising information, or creation of desire?

To answer this question we need a better conceptual grasp of what is involved in the notion of autonomy. This is a complex, multifaceted concept, and we need to approach it through the more determinate notions of (a) autonomous desire, (b) rational desire and choice, (c) free choice, and (d) control or manipulation. In what follows I shall offer some tentative and very incomplete analyses of these concepts and apply the results to the case of advertising.

(a) Autonomous desire Imagine that I am watching T.V. and see an ad for Grecian Formula 16. The thought occurs to me that if I purchase some and apply it to my beard, I will soon look younger—in fact I might even be myself again. Suddenly want to be myself! I want to be young again! So I rush out and buy a bottle. This is our question: was the desire to be younger manufactured by the commercial, or was it "original to me" and truly mine? Was it autonomous or not?

F. A. von Hayek has argued plausibly that we should not equate nonautonomous desires, desires which are not original to me or truly mine, with those which are culturally induced.[12] If we did equate the two, he points out, then the desires for music, art, and knowledge could not properly be attributed to a person as original to him, for these are surely induced culturally. The only desires a person would really have as his own in this case would be the purely physical ones for food, shelter, sex, etc. But if we reject the equation of the

nonautonomous and the culturally induced, as von Hayek would have us do, then the mere fact that my desire to be young again is caused by the T.V. commercial—surely an instrument of popular culture transmission—does not in and of itself show that this is not my own, autonomous desire. Moreover, even if I never before felt the need to look young, it doesn't follow that this new desire is any less mine. I haven't always liked 1969 Aloxe Corton Burgundy or the music of Satie, but when the desires for these things first hit me, they were truly mine.

This shows that there is something wrong in setting up the issue over advertising and behavior control as a question whether our desires are truly ours *or* are created in us by advertisements. Induced and autonomous desires do not separate into two mutually exclusive classes. To obtain a better understanding of autonomous and nonautonomous desires, let us consider some cases of a desire which a person does not *acknowledge* to be his own even though he *feels* it. The kleptomaniac has a desire to steal which in many instances he repudiates, seeking by treatment to rid himself of it. And if I were suddenly overtaken by a desire to attend an REO concert, I would immediately disown this desire, claiming possession or momentary madness. These are examples of desires which one might have but with which one would not identify. They are experienced as foreign to one's character or personality. Often a person will have what Harry Frankfurt calls a second-order desire, that is to say, a desire *not* to have another desire.[13] In such cases, the first-order desire is thought of as being nonautonomous, imposed on one. When on the contrary a person has a second-order desire to maintain and fulfill a first-order desire, then the first-order desire is truly his own, autonomous, original to him. So there is in fact a distinction between desires which are the agent's own and those which are not, but this is not the same as the distinction between desires which are innate to the agent and those which are externally induced.

If we apply the autonomous/nonautonomous distinction derived from Frankfurt to the desires brought about by advertising, does this show that advertising is responsible for creating desires which are not truly the agent's own? Not necessarily, and indeed not often. There may be some desires I feel which I have picked up from advertising and which

I disown—for instance, my desire for A-1 Steak Sauce. If I act on these desires it can be said that I have been led by advertising to act in a way foreign to my nature. In these cases my autonomy has been violated. But most of the desires induced by advertising I fully accept, and hence most of these desires are autonomous. The most vivid demonstration of this is that I often return to purchase the same product over and over again, without regret or remorse. And when I don't, it is more likely that the desire has just faded than that I have repudiated it. Hence, while advertising may violate my autonomy by leading me to act on desires which are not truly mine, this seems to be the exceptional case.

Note that this conclusion applies equally well to the case of subliminal advertising. This may generate subconscious desires which lead to purchases, and the act of purchasing these goods may be inconsistent with other conscious desires I have, in which case I might repudiate my behavior and by implication the subconscious cause of it. But my subconscious desires may not be inconsistent in this way with my conscious ones; my id may be cooperative and benign rather than hostile and malign.[14] Here again, then, advertising may or may not produce desires which are "not truly mine."

What are we to say in response to Braybrooke's argument that insofar as we might choose differently if advertisers gave us better information and more options, it follows that the desires we have are to be attributed more to advertising than to our own real inclinations? This claim seems empty. It amounts to saying that if the world we lived in, and we ourselves, were different, then we would want different things. This is surely true, but it is equally true of our desire for shelter as of our desire for Grecian Formula 16. If we lived in a tropical paradise we would not need or desire shelter. If we were immortal, we would not desire youth. What is true of all desires can hardly be used as a basis for criticizing some desires by claiming that they are nonautonomous.

(b) Rational desire and choice Braybrooke might be interpreted as claiming that the desires induced by advertising are often irrational ones in the sense that they are not expressed by an agent who is in full possession of the facts about the products advertised or about the alternative products which might be offered him. Following this line of thought, a possible criticism of advertising is that it leads us to act on irrational desires or to make irrational choices. It might be said that our autonomy has been violated by the fact that we are prevented from following our rational wills or that we have been denied the "positive freedom" to develop our true, rational selves. It might be claimed that the desires induced in us by advertising are false desires in that they do not reflect our essential, i.e., rational, essence.

The problem faced by this line of criticism is that of determining what is to count as rational desire or rational choice. If we require that the desire or choice be the product of an awareness of *all* the facts about the product, then surely every one of us is always moved by irrational desires and makes nothing but irrational choices. How could we know all the facts about a product? If it be required only that we possess all of the *available* knowledge about the product advertised, then we still have to face the problem that not all available knowledge is *relevant* to a rational choice. If I am purchasing a car, certain engineering features will be, and others won't be, relevant, *given what I want in a car*. My prior desires determine the relevance of information. Normally a rational desire or choice is thought to be one based upon relevant information, and information is relevant if it shows how other, prior desires may be satisfied. It can plausibly be claimed that it is such prior desires that advertising agencies acknowledge, and that the agencies often provide the type of information that is relevant in light of these desires. To the extent that this is true, advertising does not inhibit our rational wills or our autonomy as rational creatures.

It may be urged that much of the puffery engaged in by advertising does not provide relevant information at all but rather makes claims which are not factually true. If someone buys Pongo Peach in anticipation of an adventure in paradise, or Old Charter in expectation of increasing the value of his holdings, then he/she is expecting purely imaginary benefits. In no literal sense will the one product provide adventure and the other increased capital. A purchasing decision based on anticipation of imaginary benefits is not, it might be said, a rational decision, and a desire for imaginary benefits is not a rational desire.

In rejoinder it needs to be pointed out that we often wish to purchase subjective effects which in being subjective are nevertheless real enough. The feeling of adventure or of enhanced social prestige and value are examples of subjective effects promised by advertising. Surely many (most?) advertisements directly promise subjective effects which their patrons actually desire (and obtain when they purchase the product), and thus the ads provide relevant information for rational choice. Moreover, advertisements often provide accurate indirect information on the basis of which a person who wants a certain subjective effect rationally chooses a product. The mechanism involved here is as follows.

To the extent that a consumer takes an advertised product to offer a subjective effect and the product does not, it is unlikely that it will be purchased again. If this happens in a number of cases, the product will be taken off the market. So here the market regulates itself, providing the mechanism whereby misleading advertisements are withdrawn and misled customers are no longer misled. At the same time, a successful bit of puffery, being one which leads to large and repeated sales, produces satisfied customers and more advertising of the product. The indirect information provided by such large-scale advertising efforts provides a measure of verification to the consumer who is looking for certain kinds of subjective effect. For example, if I want to feel well dressed and in fashion, and I consider buying an Izod Alligator shirt which is advertised in all of the magazines and newspapers, then the fact that other people buy it and that this leads to repeated advertisements shows me that the desired subjective effect is real enough and that I indeed will be well dressed and in fashion if I purchase the shirt. The indirect information may lead to a rational decision to purchase a product because the information testifies to the subjective effect that the product brings about.[15]

Some philosophers will be unhappy with the conclusion of this section, largely because they have a concept of true, rational, or ideal desire which is not the same as the one used here. A Marxist, for instance, may urge that any desire felt by alienated man in a capitalistic society is foreign to his true nature. Or an existentialist may claim that the desires of inauthentic men are themselves inauthentic. Such concepts are based upon general theories of human nature which are unsubstantiated and perhaps incapable of substantiation. Moreover, each of these theories is committed to a concept of an

ideal desire which is normatively debatable and which is distinct from the ordinary concept of a rational desire as one based upon relevant information. But it is in the terms of the ordinary concept that we express our concern that advertising may limit our autonomy in the sense of leading us to act on irrational desires, and if we operate with this concept we are driven again to the conclusion that advertising may lead, but probably most often does not lead, to an infringement of autonomy.

(c) Free choice It might be said that some desires are so strong or so covert that a person cannot resist them, and that when he acts on such desires he is not acting freely or voluntarily but is rather the victim of irresistible impulse or an unconscious drive. Perhaps those who condemn advertising feel that it produces this kind of desire in us and consequently reduces our autonomy.

This raises a very difficult issue. How do we distinguish between an impulse we *do* not resist and one we *could* not resist, between freely giving in to a desire and succumbing to one? I have argued elsewhere that the way to get at this issue is in terms of the notion of acting for a reason.[16] A person acts or chooses freely if he does so for a reason, that is, if he can adduce considerations which justify in his mind the act in question. Many of our actions are in fact free because this condition frequently holds. Often, however, a person will act from habit, or whim, or impulse, and on these occasions he does not have a reason in mind. Nevertheless he often acts voluntarily in these instances, i.e., he could have acted otherwise. And this is because if there *had been* a reason for acting otherwise of which he was aware, he would in fact have done so. Thus acting from habit or impulse is not necessarily to act in an involuntary manner. If, however, a person is aware of a good reason to do x and still follows his impulse to do y, then he can be said to be impelled by irresistible impulse and hence to act involuntarily. Many kleptomaniacs can be said to act involuntarily, for in spite of their knowledge that they likely will be caught and their awareness that the goods they steal have little utilitarian value to them, they nevertheless steal. Here their "out of character" desires have the upper hand, and we have a case of compulsive behavior.

Applying these notions of voluntary and compulsive behavior to the case of behavior prompted by advertising, can we say that consumers influenced by advertising act compulsively? The unexciting answer is: sometimes they do, sometimes not. I may have an overwhelming, T.V. induced urge to own a Mazda Rx-7 and all the while realize that I can't afford one without severely reducing my family's caloric intake to a dangerous level. If, aware of this good reason not to purchase the car, I nevertheless do so, this shows that I have been the victim of T.V. compulsion. But if I have the urge, as I assure you I do, and don't act on it, or if in some other possible world I could afford an Rx-7, then I have not been the subject of undue influence by Mazda advertising. Some Mazda Rx-7 purchasers act compulsively; others do not. The Mazda advertising effort *in general* cannot be condemned, then, for impairing its customers' autonomy in the sense of limiting free or voluntary choice. Of course the question remains what should be done about the fact that advertising may and does *occasionally* limit free choice. We shall return to this question later.

In the case of subliminal advertising we may find an individual whose subconscious desires are activated by advertising into doing something his calculating, reasoning ego does not approve. This would be a case of compulsion. But most of us have a benevolent subconsciousness which does not overwhelm our ego and its reasons for action. And therefore most of us can respond to subliminal advertising without thereby risking our autonomy. To be sure, if some advertising firm developed a subliminal technique which drove all of us to purchase Lear jets, thereby reducing our caloric intake to the zero point, then we would have a case of advertising which could properly be censured for infringing our right to autonomy. We should acknowledge that this is possible, but at the same time we should recognize that it is not an inherent result of subliminal advertising.

(d) Control or manipulation Briefly let us consider the matter of control and manipulation. Under what conditions do these activities occur? In a recent paper on "Forms and Limits of Control" I suggested the following criteria.[17]

A person C controls the behavior of another person P if

1. C intends P to act in a certain way A;

2. C's intention is causally effective in bringing about A; and

3. C intends to ensure that all of the necessary conditions of A are satisfied.

These criteria may be elaborated as follows. To control another person it is not enough that one's actions produce certain behavior on the part of that person; additionally one must intend that this happen. Hence control is the intentional production of behavior. Moreover, it is not enough just to have the intention; the intention must give rise to the conditions which bring about the intended effect. Finally, the controller must intend to establish by his actions any otherwise unsatisfied necessary conditions for the production of the intended effect. The controller is not just influencing the outcome, not just having input; he is as it were guaranteeing that the sufficient conditions for the intended effect are satisfied.

Let us apply these criteria of control to the case of advertising and see what happens. Conditions (1) and (3) are crucial. Does the Mazda manufacturing company or its advertising agency intend that I buy an Rx-7? Do they intend that a certain number of people buy the car? *Prima facie* it seems more appropriate to say that they *hope* a certain number of people will buy it, and hoping and intending are not the same. But the difficult term here is "intend." Some philosophers have argued that to intend A it is necessary only to desire that A happen and to believe that it will. If this is correct, and if marketing analysis gives the Mazda agency a reasonable belief that a certain segment of the population will buy its product, then, assuming on its part the desire that this happen, we have the conditions necessary for saying that the agency intends that a certain segment purchase the car. If I am a member of this segment of the population, would it then follow that the agency intends that I purchase an Rx-7? Or is control referentially opaque? Obviously we have some questions here which need further exploration.

Let us turn to the third condition of control, the requirement that the controller intend to activate or bring about any otherwise unsatisfied necessary conditions for the production of the intended effect. It is in terms of this condition that we are able to distinguish brainwashing from liberal education. The brainwasher arranges all of the necessary conditions for belief. On the other hand, teachers (at least those of liberal persuasion) seek only to influence their students—to provide them with information and enlightenment which they may absorb *if they wish*. We do not normally think of teachers as controlling their students, for the students' performances depend as well on their own interests and inclinations.

Now the advertiser—does he control, or merely influence, his audience? Does he intend to ensure that all of the necessary conditions for purchasing behavior are met, or does he offer information and symbols which are intended to have an effect only *if* the potential purchaser has certain desires? Undeniably advertising induces some desires, and it does this intentionally; but more often than not it intends to induce a desire for a particular object, *given* that the purchaser already has other desires. Given a desire for youth, or power, or adventure, or ravishing beauty, we are led to desire Grecian Formula 16, Mazda Rx-7's, Pongo Peach, and Distinctive Foundations. In this light, the advertiser is influencing us by appealing to independent desires we already have. He is not creating those basic desires. Hence it seems appropriate to deny that he intends to produce all of the necessary conditions for our purchases, and appropriate to deny that he controls us.[18]

Let me summarize my argument. The critics of advertising see it as having a pernicious effect on the autonomy of consumers, as controlling their lives and manufacturing their very souls. The defense claims that advertising only offers information and in effect allows industry to provide consumers with what they want. After developing some of the philosophical dimensions of this dispute, I have come down tentatively in favor of the advertisers. Advertising may, but certainly does not always or even frequently, control behavior, produce compulsive behavior, or create wants which are not rational or are not truly those of the consumer. Admittedly it may in individual cases do all of these things, but it is innocent of the charge of intrinsically or necessarily doing them or even, I think, of often doing so. This limited potentiality, to be sure, leads to the question whether advertising should be abolished or severely curtailed or regulated because of its potential to harm a few poor souls in the above ways. This is a very difficult question, and I do not pretend to have the answer. I only hope that the above discussion, in showing some of the kinds of harm that can be done by advertising and by indicating the likely limits of this harm, will put us in a better position to grapple with the question.

NOTES

1. Vance Packard, *The Hidden Persuaders* (Pocket Books, New York, 1958), 20–21.

2. Ibid., 21.

3. B. F. Skinner, "Some Issues Concerning the Control of Human Behavior: A Symposium," in Karlins and Andrews (eds.), *Man Controlled* (The Free Press, New York, 1972).

4. For provocative discussions of subliminal advertising, see W. B. Key, *Subliminal Seduction* (The New American Library, New York, 1973), and W. B. Key, *Media Sexploitation* (Prentice-Hall, Inc., Englewood Cliffs, N.J., 1976).

5. I would like to emphasize that in what follows I am discussing these techniques of advertising from the standpoint of the issue of control and not from that of deception. For a good and recent discussion of the many dimensions of possible deception in advertising, see Alex C. Michalos, "Advertising: Its Logic, Ethics, and Economics" in J. A. Blair and R. H. Johnson (eds.), *Informal Logic: The First International Symposium* (Edgepress, Pt. Reyes, Calif., 1980).

6. Quoted by Packard, op. cit., 220.

7. Theodore Levitt, "The Morality (?) of Advertising," *Harvard Business Review* 48 (1970), 84–92.

8. Phillip Nelson, "Advertising and Ethics," in Richard T. De George and Joseph A. Pichler (eds.), *Ethics, Free Enterprise, and Public Policy* (Oxford University Press, New York, 1978), 187–198.

9. For a discussion of polymorphous perversity, see Norman O. Brown, *Life Against Death* (Random House, New York, 1969), chapter III.

10. John Kenneth Galbraith, *The Affluent Society*; reprinted in Tom L. Beauchamp and Norman E. Bowie (eds.), *Ethical Theory and Business* (Prentice-Hall, Englewood Cliffs, 1979), 496–501.

11. David Braybrooke, "Skepticism of Wants, and Certain Subversive Effects of Corporations on American Values," in Sidney Hook (ed.), *Human Values and Economic Policy* (New York University Press, New York, 1967); reprinted in Beauchamp and Bowie (eds.), op. cit., 502–508.

12. F. A. von Hayek, "The *Non Sequitur* of the 'Dependence Effect,'" *Southern Economic Journal* (1961); reprinted in Beauchamp and Bowie (eds.), op. cit., 508–512.

13. Harry Frankfurt, "Freedom of the Will and the Concept of a Person," *Journal of Philosophy* LXVIII (1971), 5–20.

14. For a discussion of the difference between a malign and a benign subconscious mind, see P. H. Nowell-Smith, "Psycho-analysis and Moral Language," *The Rationalist Annual* (1954); reprinted in P. Edwards and A. Pap (eds.), *A Modern Introduction to Philosophy*, Revised Edition (The Free Press, New York, 1965), 86–93.

15. Michalos argues that in emphasizing a brand name—such as Bayer Aspirin—advertisers are illogically attempting to distinguish the indistinguishable by casting a trivial feature of a product as a significant one which separates it from other brands of the same product. The brand name is said to be trivial or unimportant "from the point of view of the effectiveness of the product or that for the sake of which the product is purchased" (op. cit., 107). This claim ignores the role of indirect information in advertising. For example, consumers want an aspirin *they can trust* (trustworthiness being part of "that for the sake of which the product is purchased"), and the indirect information conveyed by the widespread advertising effort for Bayer aspirin shows that this product is judged trustworthy by many other purchasers. Hence the emphasis on the name is not at all irrelevant but rather is a significant feature of the product from the consumer's standpoint, and attending to the name is not at all an illogical or irrational response on the part of the consumer.

16. Robert L. Arrington, "Practical Reason, Responsibility and the Psychopath," *Journal for the Theory of Social Behavior* 9 (1979), 71–89.

17. Robert L. Arrington, "Forms and Limits of Control," delivered at the annual meeting of the Southern Society for Philosophy and Psychology, Birmingham, Alabama, 1980.

18. Michalos distinguishes between appealing to people's tastes and molding those tastes (op. cit., 104), and he seems to agree with my claim that it is morally permissible for advertisers to persuade us to consume some article *if* it suits our tastes (105). However, he also implies that advertisers mold tastes as well as appeal to them. It is unclear what evidence is given for this claim, and it is unclear what is meant by *tastes*. If the latter are thought of as basic desires and wants, then I would agree that advertisers are controlling their customers to the extent that they intentionally mold tastes. But if by molding tastes is meant generating a desire for the particular object they promote, advertisers in doing so may well be appealing to more basic desires, in which case they should not be thought of as controlling the consumer.

ADVERTISING AND THE SOCIAL CONDITIONS OF AUTONOMY
Richard L. Lippke

In *The New Industrial State,* John Kenneth Galbraith charged that advertising creates desires rather than responds to them.[1] His thesis raised in stark terms the issue of who is controlling whom in the marketplace. Yet, Galbraith did not provide a rigorous analysis of autonomy, and his remarks about the effects of advertising on individuals were often more suggestive than carefully worked out.

The claim that advertising is inimical to the autonomy of individuals has been taken up and discussed by philosophers, economists, and social theorists. Typically, these discussions provide first, an analysis of autonomy, and second, some empirical conjecture about whether or not advertising can be said to subvert it. The focus of most of these discussions has been on whether or not advertising can be justly accused of manipulating individuals into wanting and therefore purchasing specific products or services. Less attention has been paid to what I believe is another major theme in Galbraith's writings—that mass-advertising induces in individuals beliefs, wants, and attitudes conducive to the

economic and political interests of corporations in advanced capitalist societies like the United States. Galbraith's concern seems to be not only that advertising is hostile to individual autonomy, but that it is an aspect of the ability of corporations to dominate the lives of other members of society.

What the effects of mass-advertising are on individuals is, it must be admitted, ultimately an empirical question. In spite of this, I will try to show how we might reasonably conclude that advertising undermines autonomy, especially under the social conditions that exist in advanced capitalist countries like the United States.[2] Recent discussions of advertising have not only failed to consider one crucial way in which advertising might subvert autonomy; they have also ignored important aspects of the broader social context of advertising. Specifically, they have paid scant attention to the ways in which other social conditions also undermine autonomy. My analysis will emphasize the complex interplay between and amongst the various social conditions that affect the autonomy of individuals.

In addition to providing an analysis of autonomy, I will show how autonomy requires social

From *Business & Professional Ethics Journal,* vol. 8, no. 4 (1988): 35–58. Reprinted by permission of the author.

conditions for its development and continued viability. I will show how the content and methods of *persuasive* mass-advertising are likely to suppress the development of the abilities, attitudes and knowledge constitutive of dispositional autonomy. Yet, my view is that its full impact on autonomy should be considered in light of the ways in which political and economic institutions distribute the other social conditions of autonomy.

My primary focus will be on persuasive as opposed to informational advertising. Though the distinction is not a sharp one, I take the latter to involve information about the features, price, and availability of a product or service. Persuasive advertising, in contrast, often contains very little direct informational content about a product or service. Whereas the former presupposes some interest on the part of individuals in the product or service, the latter seeks to cultivate an interest. This typically involves tying the product or service to the satisfaction of individuals' other, sometimes subconscious desires. It seems fair to say that current informational advertising is woefully deficient. The information that is presented is often incomplete or misleading, or both. As a result, even informational ads are deceptive or manipulative at times.[3] To that extent, they undercut the abilities of persons to make informed choices and may be destructive to the intellectual honesty that is one of the constituents of dispositional autonomy. Also, in the context of massive persuasive advertising, informational advertising is likely to reinforce the content of its persuasive counterpart. Nonetheless, the two can be roughly distinguished and my remarks will be predominantly directed against persuasive advertising.

Implicit in my analysis will be the claim that one criterion for judging social orders is the extent to which they provide all of their members with the social conditions of autonomy. I will not attempt to argue for this claim here, though it is by no means an uncontroversial one. I note only that my claim is a relatively modest one—that this is *one* criterion for judging social orders. Critics of my approach may point out that many individuals seem to lack a strong desire for the sort of autonomous life I elucidate. We should not, however, be misled by this appearance. Many persons will assent to the principle that, *ceteris paribus,* the choices of individuals ought to be respected. Yet, as Lawrence Haworth shows, it makes little sense to urge such

respect where peoples' choices do not reflect an autonomous way of living.[4] This suggests there may be sound reasons to hold that autonomy is a central value. Its value may be obscured for many people by, among other things, persuasive mass-advertising.

One reason that we value autonomy is relevant to Galbraith's thesis that advertising is an aspect of the dominance of large corporations over the lives of individuals in advanced capitalist societies. Persons who are nonautonomous seem much more likely to be dominated by others. Such domination need not be consciously intended or effected by the more powerful.[5] They may simply act in ways that they perceive to be in their own interests. Nonautonomous individuals may respond by passively assimilating the interests of the more powerful. I suspect that something like this is true when it comes to corporations, advertising, and its effects on individuals. Though I cannot hope to fully support Galbraith's thesis here, I will touch on it in numerous places throughout my discussion.[6]

I

Recent discussions of advertising and autonomy are inadequate because they fail to isolate the crucial way in which the content of advertising might be subversive to autonomy. Roger Crisp, a critic of advertising, develops and tries to support the claim that ads are manipulative in an objectionable fashion. He argues that advertising "links, by suggestion, the product with my unconscious desires for [for instance] power and sex."[7] Crisp claims that persuasive advertising leaves persons unaware of their real reasons for purchasing a product, and so precludes their making rational purchasing decisions. Crisp then argues that "many of us have a strong second-order desire not to be manipulated by others without our knowledge, and for no good reason."[8] If persons become aware of how persuasive advertising affects them, by locking onto their unconscious desires, they will likely repudiate the desires induced by advertising. Such repudiated desires will not be regarded by individuals as theirs. Hence, Crisp believes he has shown how advertising is subversive to autonomy.

Crisp's approach seems to attribute both too much and too little power to advertising. Too much, because there is reason to doubt that most adults are manipulated by particular ads in the way

Crisp describes. Perhaps children are so manipulated at times, and this is cause for concern. Most adults, though, seem quite able to resist what I will call the "explicit content" of ads. The explicit content of ads is the message to "buy X," along with information about where it may be purchased, its features, and how much it costs. Most individuals learn at an early age that many ads are out to persuade them, even manipulate them. They become wary of ads and this explains why they often resist their explicit consent quite easily. Even if persons do have the second-order desire Crisp attributes to them, it is not the explicit content of ads that manipulates them *without their knowledge*. The challenge is to develop an account of how advertising can have power over individuals who very often realize ads are designed to manipulate them.

This brings us to the way in which Crisp's account attributes too little power to advertising. In addition to encouraging persons to buy Brand X, many ads have what I will term an "implicit content" that consists of messages about, broadly speaking, the consumer lifestyle. This lifestyle consists of a set of beliefs, attitudes, norms, expectations, and aspirations that I will, in due course, attempt to summarize. While individuals may be aware that they are being sold particular products, the crucial issue is the extent to which they are aware of being "sold" this implicit content. As Samuel Gorovitz remarks, "it is an error to focus too narrowly on the cognitive content of advertising by looking at the truth of its claims and the validity of its inferences."[9] Instead, we should consider how the images and emotional content of ads affect our beliefs, aspirations, expectations, and attitudes. Crisp does not really consider where some of the unconscious desires ads supposedly lock onto might originate.

In an important defense of advertising, Robert Arrington argues that it rarely, if ever, subverts the autonomy of individuals. He maintains that a desire is autonomous so long as it is endorsed by an individual on reflection. In other words, the (first-order) desire is autonomous if the person has a second-order desire to have and satisfy it.[10] Advertising, he contends, rarely leads persons to have first-order desires for products that they subsequently repudiate. Perhaps, as we saw earlier, this is because many individuals resist the explicit content of even the most manipulative ads.

Arrington also argues that ads do not violate autonomy by inducing persons to make irrational choices based on faulty or inadequate information. The only information needed for a rational choice, on his view, is information relevant to the satisfaction of individuals' particular desires. He claims that ads often provide the information relevant to the satisfaction of such desires.

Even if we accept his arguments as stated, Arrington's defense of advertising is seriously incomplete. He ignores the very real possibility that it violates autonomy *not* by manipulating persons' desires and choices with respect to particular products, but by suppressing their capacities to make rational choices about the implicit content of ads. If advertising induces uncritical acceptance of the consumer lifestyle as a whole, then Arrington's vindication of it with respect to the formation of particular desires or the making of particular choices *within* that lifestyle is hardly comforting. Arrington consistently ignores the possibility that the beliefs, attitudes, and desires particular ads cater to may themselves be influenced by ads in ways that ought to trouble anyone who values human autonomy.

II

As a first step in building my case, I offer an account of autonomy that draws on recent work on the concept. Robert Young notes that a person has "dispositional autonomy" to the extent that the person's life is "ordered according to a plan or conception which fully expresses [that person's] own will."[11] In a similar vein, Gerald Dworkin suggests that autonomy is a "global" concept: "It is a feature that evaluates a whole way of living one's life and can only be assessed over extended periods of a person's life...."[12] Autonomy is a matter of degree, an achievement that depends in part on the capacities and virtues of individuals, and in part, as we shall see, on the existence of certain social conditions.[13]

Dworkin's analysis employs the well-known distinction between first and second-order desires and abilities. He summarizes his account as follows:

> Putting the various pieces together, autonomy is conceived of as a second-order capacity of persons to reflect critically upon their first-order preferences, desires, wishes, and so forth and the capacity to accept or attempt to change these in light of higher-order preferences and values.[14]

Similarly, Lawrence Haworth interprets autonomy in terms of the notion of "critical competence."[15] Autonomous persons are competent in the sense of being active and generally successful in giving effect to their intentions. They are critical in that they deliberate not only about means to their ends, but about the ends themselves, including those of central significance in their lives. While not engaged in continuous ratiocination, they are nonetheless disposed to critically examine their beliefs, desires, attitudes, and motivations. They subject claims they are confronted with and norms others urge on them to rational scrutiny.

Importantly for our purposes, autonomous individuals should be understood as ones who scrutinize the political, social, and economic institutions under which they live. These institutions, and the patterns of habit and expectation they establish, shape the possibilities individuals can envision and determine the areas in which they can exercise their autonomy. Autonomous individuals want to shape their own lives. Hence, of necessity they will be interested in the social forces and institutions that significantly affect their lives, especially since these forces and institutions are often humanly alterable.

Autonomy is not a capacity that develops in isolation from the social conditions that surround individuals. It requires individuals to have certain abilities, motivations, and knowledge (or at least awareness) of alternative belief-systems and lifestyles. It also requires venues in which they can reasonably expect to display these abilities and act on these motivations. Obviously, individuals must not be subjected to things like coercion, deception, brainwashing, and harassment. Being shielded from these is a necessary social condition of the development and exercise of autonomy. Yet, there are other social conditions that while perhaps not, strictly speaking, necessary ones, are such that they foster and support autonomy in vital ways. Societies differ in the extent to which they provide these conditions for all individuals, and thus in the extent to which they enable autonomy.

III

What is the importance of noting the numerous social conditions of autonomy in the context of an analysis of persuasive mass-advertising? Very simply that advertising, as a possible threat to autonomy, does not exist in a social vacuum. We cannot assume that individuals encounter mass-advertising with already finely-honed skills of critical competence. The extent to which they do so is a function of the distribution of other social conditions of autonomy. The absence of social conditions of autonomy in one area will often reinforce or exacerbate the effects of their absence in other areas. Thus, in any attempt to gauge how much of a threat to autonomy persuasive mass-advertising represents, we must consider these and other background social conditions of autonomy.

In advanced capitalist countries like the United States, many individuals spend significant portions of their working lives in conditions destructive to autonomy. As Adina Schwartz and others have argued, hierarchical, authoritarian management structures, typical in such industrialized countries, thwart the autonomy of workers in obvious ways.[16] Very few have meaningful input into the decisions affecting their working lives. The tasks they perform are determined by management, as are the methods used in carrying them out. Work technology is decided by management, as are productivity quotas, discipline procedures, and criteria for evaluation. Workers are not allowed or expected to exercise even the *minimal* autonomy of determining the ends they will pursue or the means used to pursue them. This is one way in which the institutions of advanced capitalism enable corporations to impose their interests on individuals.

Often connected with the character of work is unequal access to quality education. While certain ways of organizing work may simply deny individuals avenues along which to exercise their autonomy, lack of education or poor quality education undermines it in more basic ways.[17] Reduced educational and cultural experiences often result in restricted intellectual abilities and dispositions. The kinds of rational skills needed for autonomy and the motivation to employ them seem to be the products of a liberal education in the classic sense. Individuals who lack ready access to such education are likely to have an impoverished awareness of different ways of conceiving of their lives and their social relations. This makes them ideal candidates for the tutelage in the consumer lifestyle effected by mass-advertising.

Much of that which is sponsored by advertising on TV, radio, and in magazines is hardly such as to encourage the development of autonomy.[18] Program content on commercial networks is often mindless, melodramatic, simplistic in its approach to the problems of human life—or worse, violent, sexist, or subtly racist. Even commercial network news programs seem to emphasize entertainment. Dramatic visual images, "sound bites," and fifteen second summaries of events are the rule. Commercial sponsorship of the media opens the way for the exercise of subtle control over program content. But the more likely effect of that sponsorship is an emphasis on gaining and holding an audience. That which cannot do so does not get sponsored. Yet, I think we should be wary of those who claim that what the public does not choose to consume in the way of mass media reflects its autonomous choices. Other factors, such as lack of education, mindless work, and the impact of advertising may figure in such choices. In any case, what ads are wrapped around must be factored into any analysis of their likely effects.

We should also pay attention to the ways in which institutions distribute political power, and therefore the abilities of individuals to act on and realize their interests. In this regard, the existence of formally democratic political structures is often misleading. Notoriously, access to political power depends on wealth or economic power in various ways. Here again, the political and economic institutions of advanced capitalism facilitate the dominance of corporations and their constituents.

IV

I come, at last, to the central argument of my paper. My strategy in what follows will be to amass considerations that make a plausible case for the claim that persuasive mass-advertising is detrimental to autonomy. If there is a case to be made, it is not one that can be made by showing how advertising falls into categories that are traditionally viewed as hostile to autonomy—coercion, deception, manipulation, and brainwashing. While advertising is sometimes deceptive and often manipulative, and in some ways akin to brainwashing, its overall character is not easily assimilable to any of these. I am inclined to think that the way to conceptualize its

character is in terms of the notion of *suppression*. Advertising suppresses autonomy by discouraging the emergence of its constitutive skills, knowledge, attitudes, and motivations.

One general feature of mass-advertising is simply its pervasiveness. Individuals are inundated with ads, no matter where they go or what activities they engage in. David Braybrooke refers to the "aggregative and cumulative effects" of ads.[19] The quantity of ads and their near inescapability are such that even the most diligent will be hard-pressed to avoid absorbing some of their implicit content. Many television shows and magazines feature or cater to the consumer lifestyle and this reinforces the implicit content.

The pervasiveness of ads is often coupled with an absence of views that challenge or reject their implicit content. In assessing the likely impact of mass-advertising, we must pay attention to societal measures to counter its effects. For instance, in the United States, there are few if any public service announcements urging individuals to be wary of ads, exposing the tactics of manipulation and seduction ads employ. Also, it is unlikely that such announcements would ever be repeated often enough, or have anything like the appeal of ads which promise persons sex, power, prestige, etc., if only they will buy the associated products. It seems clear that our society's educational and religious institutions, which might serve to counter ads, are ill-equipped to raise and deal with complex issues such as the nature of the good life. These are issues which ads greatly oversimplify and offer a virtual unanimity of opinion about. In many cases, attempts to educate children (and adults) about ads are sporadic and unsophisticated. To the extent that this is so, it is unlikely that such education will be forceful enough to effectively counter the advertising barrage.

Stanley Benn writes that one of the unique features of rational suasion is that it invites response and criticism.[20] It presupposes the possibility of a dialogue between or amongst the parties involved. Yet, we might wonder how far most individuals are from having a meaningful dialogue in their lives with advertising. What competing conceptions of the good life has advertising vanquished in an open, rational dialogue? If individuals lack appealing and coherent alternatives to what ads tell them about how to live, they cannot make critical, rational choices about such matters.

It is bad enough that advertising has the character of a loud, persistent bully. What is worse is that it often is not directed only at adults who might be capable of responding critically. The concern about the effects of advertising on the vulnerable, especially children, is not simply that many ads are so manipulative that they trick the vulnerable into wanting things they do not need or which are not good for them. It is also that the implicit content of ads gets absorbed by children, and habits are set up that *carry forward* into their adult lives. The ways in which they habitually perceive their lives and the social world, the alternatives they see as open to them, and the standards they use to judge themselves and others, are all shaped by advertising, perhaps without their ever being aware of it.[21]

I now turn to an analysis of the implicit content of persuasive mass-advertising. This content is a function of both the methods of conveying messages in ads and the messages conveyed. What follows are some of the key facets of this implicit content. I do not claim that my analysis is exhaustive, only that it is thorough enough to support my contention that the character of advertising is such as to suppress autonomy.

I begin with that facet of the content and methods of ads that Jules Henry refers to as the encouragement of "woolly mindedness."[22] Ads subtly encourage the propensity to accept emotional appeals, oversimplification, superficiality, and shoddy standards of proof for claims. Evidence and arguments of the most ridiculous sorts are offered in support of advertising claims. Information about products is presented selectively (i.e. bad or questionable features are ignored), the virtues of products are exaggerated, and deception and misinformation are commonplace. The meanings of words are routinely twisted so that they are either deceptive or wholly lost (e.g. consider the use of words like 'sale' or 'new and improved'). Also, ads encourage the belief that important information about our lives must be entertainly purveyed and such that it can be passively absorbed.

All of these are what we might term "meta-messages." They are messages about how to deal with messages, or more precisely, about how to approach claims made by others. They are messages that tell individuals, among other things, that they cannot believe or trust what others say, that anything (or nothing!) can be proved, that evidence contrary to one's claims may be ignored, and that words can mean whatever anyone wants them to mean. They tell persons that success in communication is a matter of persuading others *no matter how it is done*. Such attitudes about thought and communication starkly oppose the habits and attitudes constitutive of critical competence: clarity, rigor, precision, patience, honesty, effort, etc. Henry remarks that advertising would never succeed in a world filled with logicians.[23] Though we may not want such a world, we should be aware of how advertising promotes sophistry and attitudes supportive of it.

Complementing the meta-messages is the pervasive emphasis on ease and gratification. As Henry points out, austerity and self-restraint are anathema to advertisers.[24] Mass production requires the existence of ready and willing consumers. Lifestyles contrary to consumption are either absent from ads (and from TV shows) or are ridiculed in them. Predominant messages in ads are "take it easy," "relax and enjoy yourself," and most especially "buy it now!" In moderation, there may be nothing objectionable about such messages. However, where not balanced by other messages, and so not made liable to critical examination, they encourage attitudes subversive to autonomy. In order to formulate, assess, and carry out life-plans of their own choosing, individuals must possess self-control and seriousness of purpose. They must also have the capacity to resist temptations or momentary distractions.

More insidious, though, is a further implied message—that persons ought to let advertisers show them how to live the good life. What could be more inviting than a life that demands so little beyond ease and gratification (especially to children, who are less attuned to the values of self-control and delayed gratification)? Freedom is divorced from self-direction and equated with passivity and consumption. Control over one's life becomes simply the ability to satisfy one's consumer desires. Alternative conceptions of freedom are drowned out. Opposing lifestyles are saddled with a burden of justification. Those who resist the easy gratifications of the consumer marketplace are likely to be perceived as square, eccentric, boring, or life-denying. The scorn of others thus becomes a barrier to the critical examination of life.

While one of the main messages of advertising is to accept a lifestyle of ease and gratification, individuals who buy into that lifestyle cannot be allowed to relax if that means not buying products. Fear and insecurity are the motifs of advertising. There are always new products and services to be sold and individuals must be convinced that they will not experience true or complete gratification until they buy this or that product. As John Waide remarks, advertising cultivates and thrives on "sneer group pressure."[25] Other persons are portrayed as constantly ready to judge negatively those who have not tried the newest product that promises to make their lives more appealing in some fashion. Advertising is fundamentally divisive in this regard. It encourages the view that social relationships are competitive, that persons are out to "top" one another rather than help and support one another. The internalization of this competitive model is likely to deprive individuals of the care and counsel of others, two things that vitally contribute to the sustained critical examination of their lives. Individuals need others to provide them feedback about their conduct and projects, as well as to present them with alternative beliefs, outlooks, and commitments.[26]

Numerous writers have commented on the confusion about values ads promote. Many ads tell individuals that if they will only buy X, they will acquire friendship, self-esteem, sex appeal, power, etc. Collectively, these ads tell individuals that they will be able to satisfy some of their most important desires (ones Waide refers to as being for "non-market goods"[27]) through the purchase and use of consumer products. Where they have bought these products and still not found the relevant satisfactions, advertising has a ready answer: buy more or better products!

It is doubtful that there are areas of peoples' lives where clear thinking is of more importance. It is equally doubtful that consumer products can make a significant contribution to the satisfaction of the desires for such nonmarket goods. More to the point, at best ads can only *distract* individuals from clear thinking about such things as why they lack self-esteem, or why they feel powerless, or why their friendships or marriages are unsatisfactory. At worst, they can fill individuals' minds with pseudo-truths or pseudo-values bearing on issues of central significance in their lives. Numerous examples come to mind: how women are encouraged by ads to conceive of their self-worth in terms of

unrealistic standards of physical beauty; how having fun is portrayed in ads for beer, wine, and alcohol; ideas about nutrition courtesy of the junk food industry; how racial disharmony, homosexuality, and poverty are missing from the social world of ads; and so on.

Finally, in light of my earlier claim that autonomous individuals will be disposed to critically scrutinize the institutions they live under, it is important to point out how the portrayal of consumption as the good life serves a political function. This portrayal provides individuals with standards and expectations against which to judge not only their own lives, but the institutions that shape and mold their lives. Consumption is presented as the reward for "making it," and as a way of ameliorating, if not curing, boredom, powerlessness, lack of self-esteem, etc. Political and economic institutions then come to be measured by the extent to which they provide individuals access to consumer goods. Of course, there is no guarantee that, judged against this criterion, a society's political and economic institutions will fare well. In this way, even mass-advertising may provide individuals with a basis for criticizing their institutions.

However, the basis is a very limited one. Individuals may only be concerned with whether they might get more or less consumer goods if institutions were organized differently (or run by members of a different political party). Other, competing criteria against which to judge institutions are likely to have a hard time getting a hearing in societies dominated by mass-advertising. In this way, advertising serves as a force that *legitimizes* the political and economic status quo. It deadens individuals to a more extensive critical scrutiny of the institutions they live under. The ways in which their political and economic institutions distribute the social conditions of autonomy, and therefore allow the economic interests of corporations to dominate their lives, are rarely considered or seriously discussed.

One of the supposed virtues of advanced capitalist societies where mass-advertising is ubiquitous is that they afford individuals a wide range of choices. Within the ambit of the consumer lifestyle, that may be so. But, what about some of the more basic choices individuals have about how to live their lives or about how to organize their political and economic affairs? Are these choices many individuals in such societies realize they have, let alone can conceive of an array of alternatives about? My contention is that many in such societies are in no position to make critically competent choices about these more basic issues and that advertising significantly contributes to their inability to do so.

V

It is not enough for defenders of advertising to respond to the preceding analysis by pointing out that *some* individuals seem to resist absorbing much of its implicit content. No doubt this is true. It is also true that many interactions of a more mundane sort between and amongst individuals fall short of being fully autonomous ones. The use of emotional appeals is widespread, as are other forms of manipulation. There are many insecure or servile individuals who are influenced by others in ways that likely fail the tests of critical competence. Few would suggest that societies be judged harshly for allowing such interactions to go on. Yet, it might be argued, why should we think societies ought to treat persuasive mass-advertising any differently? Why not, instead, think it reasonable to let individuals watch out for themselves in the face of mass-advertising? After, all some seem to.

This is a formidable objection, but it fails to take account of the differences between individuals' encounters with advertising and their encounters with other individuals. The latter typically have three features that the former lack. First, encounters with other individuals are often either voluntarily sought out or at least voluntarily maintained. Yet, advertising is not easily avoided. It begins to work its influence on individuals when they are young and it never lets up. It is omni-present. Second, even where individual encounters with other individuals are not fully voluntary (e.g. familial or work relationships), they typically serve some important value or function in individuals' lives. This is less obviously true with respect to persuasive mass-advertising. Third, encounters with other individuals, if found unsatisfactory, can be altered by the participants. Individuals can ask, or insist, that others not deceive or manipulate them. Sometimes this works. With advertising, individuals can, at best, try to shut it out or be wary of it. It is not an agent whose "conduct" can be altered by direct appeals.

Also, the fact that some individuals manage to resist the effects of persuasive mass-advertising might be explained by their having greater access to the other social conditions of autonomy (e.g. education). Surely that does not show that a society need do nothing about an institution in its midst that arguably plays a very significant role in suppressing the autonomy of what is perhaps a very large majority of its members. As Tom Beauchamp notes, a source of influence need not be completely controlling in order to be an object of concern.[28]

Defenders of advertising might at this point argue that the actions of corporations are protected by the moral right of free speech. Joseph DesJardins and John McCall maintain, however, that we should distinguish commercial speech from moral, religious, and political speech. They argue that some types of speech are more valuable to human life than others. Moral, religious, and political speech "contribute to the pursuit of meaning and value in human existence," while commercial speech "in offering an item for sale appears a rather mundane concern."[29] The latter only encourages persons to deliberate about various and competing consumer choices.

DesJardins and McCall are mostly concerned about providing a rationale for governmental efforts to regulate deceptive commercial speech. Their argument relies on a conception of human autonomy similar to my own. Still, it seems to me that there exists a simpler and more straightforward justification for attempts to regulate deceptive commercial speech, one that appeals to the notion of the sorts of voluntary informed exchanges which are supposed to be the backbone of free enterprise economic systems. Deceptive commercial speech vitiates the *informedness* of such exchanges and it is often possible to prove ads deceptive.

Additionally, DesJardins and McCall fail to distinguish between the explicit and implicit content of persuasive mass-advertising. The latter, as we have seen, is rich in moral and political content. Thus, by their argument, if we should reject restrictions on political, religious, and moral speech, we should equally reject the curtailment of persuasive mass-advertising.[30] Nevertheless, I think that most of the traditional arguments for free speech will not serve defenders of persuasive advertising. Frederick Schauer develops and assesses several of these arguments.[31] I will concentrate on three central ones.

First, there is what Schauer calls the "argument from truth." This argument alleges that there is a causal link between freedom of speech and the discovery of truth. Schauer suggests we modify this argument to emphasize the elimination of error so as to avoid the complications that attend the notion of "objective truth."[32] The modified argument suggests that allowing the expression of contrary views is the only rational way of recognizing human fallibility, thus making possible the rejection or modification of erroneous views. It holds that we can increase the level of rational confidence in our views by comparing them to other views and seeing whether ours survive all currently available attacks. The suppression of speech, as John Stuart Mill noted, is inconsistent with a recognition of human fallibility.

A second argument is what Schauer refers to as the "argument from democracy." It is an argument that presupposes the acceptance of democratic principles for the organization of the state. It then consists of two parts:

1. In order for the people as sovereign electorate to vote intelligently, all relevant information must be available to them; and
2. as political leaders are to serve their citizens' wishes, the latter must be able to communicate their wishes on all matters to the government.

In short, since democracy implies that government is the servant of the people, the people must retain the right to reject and criticize their government. Yet, this requires no prior restrictions by the government on information available to the citizens.

A third argument has been developed by Thomas Scanlon, and is referred to by Schauer as the "argument from autonomy."[33] This argument claims that the province of thought and decision-making is morally beyond the reach of the state's powers. The state is alleged to have no ultimate authority to decide matters of religious, moral, political, or scientific doctrine. Autonomous persons cannot accept, without independent consideration, the judgment of others as to what they should believe or do, especially on these matters. Thus, it is held that individuals must be free from governmental intrusion into the process of choice.

It is important to note, in general, that all three of these arguments presuppose that it is government suppression of speech that threatens individual thought-processes and choices. Historically, this may have been true, but the development of persuasive mass-advertising poses a different sort of threat. Schauer repeatedly claims that the province of individual thought and decision-making is inherently (as a causal matter) beyond the control of the state. He claims that the area of individual conscience is "under the exclusive control of the individual" because of the "internal" nature of thought.[34] While this may only underestimate the power of the state to influence thoughts and feelings, it surely ignores the possibility that persuasive mass-advertising significantly influences these in the ways detailed earlier.

With regard to the argument from truth, it is not fair to portray advertising as simply offering "truths" for consideration that compete against other beliefs in the marketplace of ideas. Whatever "truths" it offers (and I suspect they are small ones) threaten to drown out all other claims, or to render them tedious or irrelevant by comparison. Worse, as we have seen, its implicit content encourages beliefs and attitudes about thought and decision-making that are hostile to those necessary to sort through claims and weed out the false or misleading ones.

Similar remarks hold for the argument from democracy. Especially relevant here is the political content of persuasive mass-advertising, with its emphasis on consumption-as-the-good-life as *the* standard against which to measure political and economic systems. More insidious than its insistence on this essentially status quo-preserving standard is its implicit denial of the value of political debate and activity. Consumption is where individuals are told they will find satisfaction, and a host of pseudo-issues about such a life are offered as the central focus for individuals' care and concern.

Finally, if advertising is inimical to autonomy in the ways I have claimed throughout this paper, it is obvious that the argument from autonomy cannot be invoked on its behalf. Those who defend persuasive mass-advertising on the basis of its contribution to individual choice would seem to have an extremely limited notion of the range of choices that individuals have about their lives.

Virginia Held makes the important point that in societies like the United States, it is no longer adequate to construe the right to free expression simply as a right not to be interfered with:

> But in a contemporary context this leaves those with economic resources free to express themselves through the media: they can buy time on TV or own a station, they can buy up or start a newspaper, and so on. At the same time, those without economic resources can barely be heard.[35]

Held's concern is with a society's taking steps to *enable* its members to freely express themselves. Though she does not directly address the issue of persuasive mass-advertising, it is likely that she would view the nearly unchecked power of corporations to express their interests through the media with alarm.

VI

What to do about persuasive mass-advertising is, I think, a daunting problem. Throughout my analysis, I have insisted that we consider the effects of advertising in conjunction with the effects of other social conditions that might impact on autonomy. The question we must ask ourselves, then, is what changes in our political and economic institutions are necessary in order to provide all persons with the social conditions of autonomy. Since advanced capitalist countries like the United States are now plagued in various ways by the dominance of corporate interests, we might hope that enhancing the social conditions of autonomy for all persons will result in the cultivation, expression, and realization of more varied (and autonomous) interests.

While some will think that the only way to accomplish this result is to abandon capitalism altogether, I want to consider changes that are somewhat more modest. First, in order to modify the organization of work so as to provide a venue for the realization of worker autonomy, we might adopt the sorts of worker participation mechanisms institutionalized in countries like West Germany and Sweden.[36] These mechanisms guarantee workers participation in the economic decisions that vitally affect their lives. Second, we would need to guarantee to all individuals the level and quality of education necessary for them to develop the skills, dispositions, and knowledge constitutive of disposi-

tional autonomy. Third, we would need to take steps to lessen if not eliminate the influence of wealth and economic power over the decisions of democratically elected political officials. This might include such things as the development of a public financing scheme for all political campaigns and the institutionalization of mechanisms to guarantee the independence of government officials from those they regulate or purchase products and services from. Fourth, steps must be taken to divorce the media from their almost exclusive reliance on commercial financial support and to provide individuals with increased access to the means of expression. Virginia Held offers a number of valuable proposals about how to effect these ends.[37] These include having more public financing of the media and having commercial sponsors buy nonspecific time on the airwaves. Both measures would reduce the pressure to produce programming that is successful according to narrow commercial criteria. The hope is that this will lead to greater experimentation in the media, and thus to the creation of a more diverse cultural life.

Obviously, the preceding changes would need to be considered at greater length. But, let me instead turn to advertising and its role in the suppression of autonomy. As an aspect of the dominance of corporate interests in advanced capitalist societies, it is important to neither over-estimate nor under-estimate its significance. On the one hand, without complementary changes of the sort just discussed, attempts to regulate or restrict advertising seem likely to have only minimal impact on the development and maintenance of autonomy. At most, such regulation or restriction would eliminate one barrier to autonomy. On the other hand, it may be argued that the salutary effects of such complementary changes will be undermined if no steps are taken to regulate or restrict persuasive mass-advertising. Workers might remain imbued with the mentality promulgated in ads and so unwittingly express views conducive to corporate interests. Attempts to cultivate a more educated populace would still be opposed by the barrage of ads with its implicit content.

Unfortunately, it is hard to come up with a feasible approach to the regulation or restriction of advertising. Since the thrust of my argument has been against persuasive advertising, it might be suggested that we attempt to legislate a distinction between it and informational advertising. The idea would then be to restrict if not eliminate the former while permitting the latter. Perhaps simply providing information about the price, character, and availability of products and services poses little threat to autonomy and may even facilitate it.

One serious problem with this approach will be that of defining "persuasive." For instance, if individuals are shown using and enjoying a product, will that have to be considered an attempt at persuasion? Or, if a product is displayed in a pictorially pleasing manner, will that be considered persuasive? Also, assuming this difficulty can be overcome in a reasonable manner, won't the amount of regulation required necessitate the creation of a massive bureaucracy? It should be noted that corporations confronted with restrictions on persuasive advertising are likely to respond creatively in attempts to circumvent the rules.

An alternative approach would be to try to restrict the overall quantity of advertising without regard to a distinction between informational and persuasive types. It might be feasible to restrict the number of ads on TV to a certain number per hour, but can we do something similar with magazines, radio, and newspapers? Even if we had the will to do so, at least two serious problems remain:

1. a mere reduction in the quantity of ads (persuasive and otherwise) may not greatly lessen their impact in terms of selling the consumer lifestyle—especially in the absence of steps to counter this implicit content;
2. the difficulties in formulating and enforcing such restrictions would be formidable.

On the latter point, think about the enormous number of venues for advertising (currently existing as well as those that might soon be available) that we would have to regulate.

It is not easy to avoid drawing a pessimistic conclusion from the preceding remarks. Perhaps those more inventive than I can come up with proposals to restrict persuasive advertising that evade these problems and others like them. What cannot be evaded is the political reality that any proposed restrictions will be steadfastly, and I suspect effectively, resisted by corporations and advertisers. On this score, the only hope may lie with the sorts of institutional changes sketched earlier. It is possible that a better educated populace with more democratic control over its corporations can

take the necessary steps to curtail the suppression of autonomy effected by current mass-advertising.

NOTES

1. John Kenneth Galbraith, *The New Industrial State* (Boston, MA: Houghton Mifflin, 1967), especially pp. 198–218. See also the selection by Galbraith, "Persuasion—and Power," in Joseph R. DesJardins and John J. McCall (eds.), *Contemporary Issues in Business Ethics* (Belmont, CA: Wadsworth, 1985): 142–147.

2. I will limit my claims to countries with schemes of political and economic organization like those in the United States. Obviously, my claims would have to be weakened or modified if they were to be made applicable to countries with significantly different institutions.

3. On the ways in which many ads deceive by presenting information in misleading ways, see, for instance, Tom L. Beauchamp, "Manipulative Advertising," *Business and Professional Ethics Journal* 3 (Spring/Summer 1984): 1–22.

4. Lawrence Haworth, *Autonomy: An Essay in Philosophical Psychology and Ethics* (New Haven, CT: Yale University Press, 1986), especially Chapter 8.

5. Tom Beauchamp distinguishes between the responses of individuals to advertising and the intentions of those who create the advertising. My remarks in what follows concern the responses of individuals. I do not wish to suggest that corporations consciously intend all of the effects I delineate. See Beauchamp, "Manipulative Advertising," p. 7.

6. Virginia Held has also touched on the theme of the dominance of corporate interests. See her *Rights and Goods: Justifying Social Action* (New York: The Free Press, 1984), especially Chapter 12.

7. Roger Crisp, "Persuasive Advertising, Autonomy, and the Creation of Desire," *Journal of Business Ethics* 6 (1987): 413–418, p. 414.

8. Ibid., p. 414.

9. Samuel Gorovitz, "Advertising Professional Success Rates," *Business and Professional Ethics Journal* 3 (Spring/Summer 1984): 31–45, p. 41.

10. Robert Arrington, "Advertising and Behavior Control," reprinted in DesJardins and McCall, *Contemporary Issues in Business Ethics*, pp. 167–175.

11. Robert Young, *Personal Autonomy: Beyond Negative and Positive Liberty* (New York: St. Martin's Press, 1986), p. 8.

12. Gerald Dworkin, *The Theory and Practice of Autonomy* (Cambridge: Cambridge University Press, 1988), pp. 15–16.

13. Young distinguishes between internal constraints on autonomy (e.g. lack of self-control) and external constraints (e.g. lack of liberty). See his *Personal Autonomy*, p. 35.

14. Dworkin, *The Theory and Practice of Autonomy*, p. 20.

15. Haworth, *Autonomy*, pp. 42–43.

16. Adina Schwartz, "Meaningful Work," *Ethics* 92 (July 1982): 632–646. See also Edward Sankowski, "Freedom, Work, and the Scope of Democracy," *Ethics* 91 (January 1981): 228–242; and Carole Pateman, *Participation and Democratic Theory* (Cambridge: Cambridge University Press, 1970).

17. Of course, the lack of avenues for the exercise of autonomy will often result in atrophy of the abilities and motivations that are its constituents.

18. For more on advertising and program content, see Virginia Held, "Advertising and Program Content," *Business and Professional Ethics Journal* 3 (Spring/Summer 1984): 61–76. See also the accompanying commentaries by Clifford Christians and Norman Bowie.

19. David Braybrooke, *Ethics and the World of Business* (Totowa, NJ: Rowman and Allanheld, 1983), pp. 327–328.

20. Stanley I. Benn, "Freedom and Persuasion," *Australasian Journal of Philosophy* 45 (December 1967): 259–275.

21. Cf. Lynda Sharp Paine, "Children As Consumers," *Business and Professional Ethics Journal* 3 (Spring/Summer 1984): 119–145. Paine argues persuasively that children ought not be viewed as capable of making responsible consumer choices. She does not emphasize the effects of advertising on the habits of thought and perception of children.

22. Jules Henry, *Culture Against Man* (New York: Random House, 1963), p. 49.

23. Ibid., p. 48.

24. Ibid., p. 75.

25. John Waide, "The Making of Self and World in Advertising," *Journal of Business Ethics* 6 (1987): 73–39.

26. Also, if most persons can be induced to fear the judgment of others and adopt the consumer lifestyle, the result will be a remarkably homogenous collection of otherwise isolated individuals. Advertising superficially promotes individuality by telling persons they can only truly find themselves with this or that product. Of course, it tells every individual the same thing. Ethnic or individual diversity is worn away.

27. Waide, "The Making of Self and World in Advertising," p. 73.

28. Beauchamp, "Manipulative Advertising," p. 3.

29. Joseph R. DesJardins and John J. McCall, "Advertising and Free Speech," in DesJardins and McCall, *Contemporary Issues in Business Ethics*, p. 105.

30. Also, Burton Leiser argues that the United States Supreme Court has seen fit to extend constitutional protection to commercial speech. See his "Professional Advertising: Price Fixing and Professional Dignity versus the Public's Right to a Free Market," *Business and Professional Ethics Journal* 3 (Spring/Summer 1984): 93–107.

31. Frederick Schauer, *Free Speech: A Philosophical Inquiry* (Cambridge: Cambridge University Press, 1982). Schauer notes problems with each of these arguments that I will ignore here.

32. Ibid., pp. 24–25.

33. Thomas Scanlon, "A Theory of Freedom of Expression," *Philosophy and Public Affairs* 6 (Winter 1972): 204–226.

34. Schauer, *Freedom of Speech*, p. 68. See also p. 53.

35. Virginia Held, "Advertising and Program Content," *Business and Professional Ethics Journal* 3 (Spring/Summer 1984): 61–76, p. 73.

36. On this, see G. David Garson, *Worker Self-Management in Industry: The West European Experience* (New York: Praeger Publishers, 1977).

37. See her "Advertising and Program Content," pp. 66–74. Also, see *Rights and Goods*, Chapter 12.

CHILDREN AS CONSUMERS: AN ETHICAL EVALUATION OF CHILDREN'S TELEVISION ADVERTISING

Lynn Sharp Paine

Television sponsors and broadcasters began to identify children as a special target audience for commercial messages in the mid-1960s.[1] Within only a few years, children's television advertising emerged as a controversial issue. Concerned parents began to speak out and to urge the networks to adopt codes of ethics governing children's advertising. By 1970, the issue had attracted the attention of the Federal Trade Commission (FTC) and the Federal Communications Commission (FCC). The FCC received some 80,000 letters in support of a proposed rule "looking toward the elimination of sponsorship and commercial content in children's program-

From *Business & Professional Ethics Journal*, vol. 3, no. 3/4 (1983): 119–125, 135–145. © Lynda Sharp Paine. Reprinted by permission of the author.

ming."[2] Public attention to the controversy over children's television advertising peaked between 1978 and 1980, when the FTC, under its authority to regulate unfair and deceptive advertising, held public hearings on its proposal to ban televised advertising directed to or seen by large numbers of young children. More recently parents have complained to the FCC about so-called program-length commercials, children's programs designed around licensed characters.[3]

As this brief chronology indicates, children's television advertising has had a history of arousing people's ethical sensibilities. In this paper I want to propose some explanations for why this is so and to argue that there are good ethical reasons that advertisers should refrain from directing commercials to young children. However, because so much of the public debate over children's advertising has focused on the FTC's actions rather than explicitly on the ethical aspects of children's advertising, a few preliminary remarks are called for.

First, it is important to bear in mind that the ethical propriety of directing television advertising to young children is distinct from its legality. Even if advertisers have a constitutional right to advertise lawful products to young children in a nondeceptive way, it is not necessarily the right thing to do.[4] Our system of government guarantees us rights that it may be unethical to exercise on certain occasions. Terminology may make it easy to lose sight of the distinction between "having a right" and the "right thing to do," but the distinction is critical to constitutional governance.[5] In this paper I will take no position on the scope of advertisers' First Amendment rights to freedom of speech. I am primarily interested in the moral status of advertising to young children.

A second preliminary point worth noting is that evaluating the ethical status of a practice, such as advertising to young children, is a different exercise from evaluating the propriety of governmental regulation of that practice. Even if a practice is unethical, there may be legal, social, economic, political, or administrative reasons that the government cannot or should not forbid or even regulate the practice. The public policy issues faced by the FTC or any other branch of government involved in regulating children's advertising are distinct from the ethical issues facing advertisers. The fact that it may be impossible or unwise for the government to restrict children's advertising does not shield advertisers from ethical responsibility for the practice.

Finally, I want to point out that public opinion regarding children's advertising is a measure neither of its ethical value nor of the propriety of the FTC's actions. Two critics of the FTC declared that it had attempted to impose its conception of what is good on an unwilling American public.[6] There is reason to doubt the writers' assumption about the opinions of the American public regarding children's advertising,[7] but the more critical point is the implication of their argument: that the FTC's actions would have been appropriate had there been a social consensus opposing child-oriented advertising. Majority opinion, however, is neither the final arbiter of justified public policy, nor the standard for assaying the ethical value of a practice like children's advertising. As pointed out earlier, constitutional limits may override majority opinion in the public policy arena. And although publicly expressed opinion may signal ethical concerns (as I suggested in mentioning the letters opposing commercial sponsorship of children's television received by the FCC), social consensus is not the test of ethical quality. We cannot simply say that children's advertising is ethically all right because many people do not object to it or because people's objections to it are relatively weak. An ethical evaluation requires that we probe our ethical principles and test their relation to children's advertising. Publicly expressed opposition may signal that such probing is necessary, but it does not establish an ethical judgment one way or the other.

…For purposes of this discussion, I will set aside the legal and public policy questions involved in government restrictions on children's advertising. Instead, as promised, I will explore the ethical issues raised by the practice of directing television advertising to young children. In the process of this investigation, I will necessarily turn my attention to the role of consumers in a free market economy, to the capacities of children as they relate to consumer activities, and to the relationships between adults and children within the family.

By *young children* I mean children who lack the conceptual abilities required for making consumer decisions, certainly children under eight. Many researchers have investigated the age at which children can comprehend the persuasive intent of advertising.[8] Depending on the questions employed to test comprehension of persuasive intent, the critical age has been set as low as kindergarten age or as high as nine or ten.[9] Even if this research were conclusive, however, it would not identify the age at which children become capable of making consumer decisions. Comprehending persuasive intent is intellectually less complex than consumer decisionmaking. Even if children appreciate the selling intent behind advertising, they may lack other conceptual abilities necessary for responsible consumer decisions. Child psychologists could perhaps identify the age at which these additional abilities develop. For purposes of this discussion, however, the precise age is not crucial. When I use the term *child* or *children* I am referring to "young children"—those who lack the requisite abilities.

Children's advertising is advertising targeted or directed to young children. Through children's advertising, advertisers attempt to persuade young children to want and, consequently, to request the advertised product.[10] Although current voluntary guidelines for children's advertising prohibit advertisers from explicitly instructing children to request that their parents buy the advertised product, child-oriented advertising is designed to induce favorable attitudes that result in such requests.[11] Frequently child-oriented ads utilize themes and techniques that appeal particularly to children: animation, clowns, magic, fantasy effects, superheroes, and special musical themes.[12] They may also involve simply the presentation of products, such as cereals, sweets, and toys, that appeal to young children with announcements directed to them.[13] The critical point in understanding child-directed advertising, however, is not simply the product, the particular themes and techniques employed, or the composition of the audience viewing the ad, but whether the advertiser intends to sell to or through children. Advertisers routinely segment their markets and target their advertising.[14] The question at issue is whether children are appropriate targets.

Advertising directed to young children is a subcategory of advertising seen by them, since children who watch television obviously see a great deal of advertising that is not directed toward them—ads for adult consumer products, investment services, insurance, and so on. Occasionally children's products are advertised by means of commercials directed to adults. The toy manufacturer Fisher-Price, for example, at one time advertised its

children's toys and games primarily by means of ads directed to mothers.[15] Some ads are designed to appeal to the whole family. Insofar as these ads address young children they fall within the scope of my attention.

My interest in television advertising directed to young children, as distinct from magazine or radio advertising directed to them, is dictated by the nature of the medium. Television ads portray vivid and lively images that engage young children as the printed words and pictures of magazines, or even the spoken words of radio, could never do. Because of their immediacy television ads can attract the attention of young children who have not yet learned to read. Research has shown that young children develop affection for and even personal relationships with heavily promoted product characters appearing on television.[16] At the same time, because of their immaturity, these children are unable to assess the status of these characters as fictional or real, let alone assess whatever minimal product information they may disclose.[17] Technical limitations make magazine advertising and radio advertising inherently less likely to attract young children's attention. Consequently, they are less susceptible to ethical criticisms of the sort generated by television advertising.

CHILDREN AS CONSUMERS

The introduction of the practice of targeting children for televised commercial messages challenged existing mores. At the obvious level, the practice was novel. But at a deeper level, it called into question traditional assumptions about children and their proper role in the marketplace. The argument advanced on behalf of advertising to children by the Association of National Advertisers (ANA), the American Association of Advertising Agencies (AAAA), and the American Advertising Federation (AAF) reflects the rejection of some of these traditional assumptions:

> Perhaps the single most important benefit of advertising to children is that it provides information to the child himself, information which advertisers try to gear to the child's interests and on an appropriate level of understanding. This allows the child to learn what products are

available, to know their differences, and to begin to make decisions about them based on his own personal wants and preferences.... Product diversity responds to these product preferences and ensures that it is the consumer himself who dictates the ultimate success or failure of a given product offering.[18]

The most significant aspect of this argument supporting children's advertising is its vision of children as autonomous consumers. Children are represented as a class of consumers possessing the relevant decision-making capacities and differing from adult consumers primarily in their product preferences. Children are interested in toys and candy, while adults are interested in laundry detergent and investment services. That children may require messages tailored to their level of understanding is acknowledged, but children's conceptual abilities are not regarded as having any other special significance. Advocates of children's advertising argue that it gives children "the same access to the marketplace which adults have, but keyed to their specific areas of interest."[19]

When children are viewed in this way—as miniature adults with a distinctive set of product preferences—the problematic nature of advertising to them is not apparent. Indeed, it appears almost unfair not to provide children with televised information about products available to satisfy their special interests. Why should they be treated differently from any other class of consumers?

There are, however, significant differences between adults and young children that make it inappropriate to regard children as autonomous consumers. These differences, which go far beyond different product preferences, affect children's capacities to function as responsible consumers and suggest several arguments for regarding advertising to them as unethical. For purposes of this discussion, the most critical differences reflect children's understanding of self, time, and money.

Child-development literature generally acknowledges that the emergence of a sense of one's self as an independent human being is a central experience of childhood and adolescence.[20] This vague notion, "having a sense of one's self as an independent human being," encompasses a broad range of capacities—from recognition of one's physical self as distinct from one's mother to accep-

tance of responsibility for one's actions and choices. Normally children acquire these capacities gradually in the course of maturation. While this mastery manifests itself as self-confidence and self-control in an ever-widening range of activities and relationships, it depends more fundamentally upon the emergence of an ability to see oneself as oneself. The reflexive nature of consciousness—the peculiar ability to monitor, study, assess, and reflect upon oneself and even upon one's reflections—underlies the ability to make rational choices. It permits people to reflect upon their desires, to evaluate them, and to have desires about what they shall desire. It permits them to see themselves as one among others and as engaging in relationships with others. Young children lack—or have only in nascent form—this ability to take a higher-order perspective on themselves and to see themselves as having desires or preferences they may wish to cultivate, suppress, or modify. They also lack the self-control that would make it possible to act on these higher-order desires if they had them.

Closely related to the sense of self, if not implicit in self-reflection, is the sense of time. Children's understanding of time—both as it relates to their own existence and to the events around then—is another area where their perspectives are special. Preschoolers are intrigued with "time" questions: "When is an hour up?" "Will you be alive when I grow up?" "When did the world begin and when will it end?" "Will I be alive for all the time after I die?" Young children's efforts to understand time are accompanied by a limited ability to project themselves into the future and to imagine themselves having different preferences in the future. It is generally true that children have extremely short time horizons. But children are also struggling with time in a more fundamental sense: they are testing conceptions of time as well as learning to gauge its passage by conventional markers.[21] Young children's developing sense of time goes hand in hand with their developing sense of self. Their capacity for self-reflection, for evaluating their desires, and for making rational choices is intimately related to their understanding of their own continuity in time.

Young children are in many ways philosophers: they are exploring and questioning the very fundamentals of existence.[22] Since they have not accepted many of the conventions and assumptions that guide ordinary commercial life, they frequently pose rather profound questions and make insightful observations. But although young children are very good at speculation, they are remarkably unskilled in the sorts of calculations required for making consumer judgments. In my experience, many young children are stymied by the fundamentals of arithmetic and do not understand ordinal relations among even relatively small amounts—let alone the more esoteric notions of selling in exchange for money. Research seems to support the observation that selling is a difficult concept for children. One study found that only 48 percent of six-and-a-half- to seven-and-a-half-year-olds could develop an understanding of the exocentric (as distinct from egocentric) verb *to sell*.[23] A five-year-old may know from experience in making requests that a $5.00 trinket is too expensive, but when she concludes that $5.00 is also too much to pay for a piano, it is obvious that she knows neither the exchange value of $5.00, the worth of a piano, nor the meaning of *too expensive*.[24]

What is the significance of the differences between adults and young children I have chosen to highlight—their differing conceptions of self, time, and money? In the argument for advertising quoted earlier, it was stated that advertising to children enables them "to learn what products are available, to know their differences, and to begin to make decisions about them based on [their] own personal wants and preferences." Ignore, for the moment, the fact that existing children's advertising, which concentrates so heavily on sugared foods and toys, does little either to let children know the range of products available or differences among them and assume that children's advertising could be more informative.[25] Apart from this fact, the critical difficulty with the argument is that because of children's, shall we say, "naive" or "unconventional" conceptions of self, time, and money, they know very little about their own personal wants and preferences—how they are related or how quickly they will change—or about how their economic resources might be mobilized to satisfy those wants. They experience wants and preferences but do not seem to engage in critical reflection, which would lead them to assess, modify, or perhaps even curtail their felt desires for the sake of other more important or enduring desires they may have or may expect to have in the future. Young

children also lack the conceptual wherewithal to engage in research or deliberative processes that would assist them in knowing which of the available consumer goods would most thoroughly satisfy their preferences, given their economic resources. The fact that children want so many of the products they see advertised is another indication that they do not evaluate advertised products on the basis of their preferences and economic resources.[26]

There is thus a serious question whether advertising really has or can have much at all to do with children's beginning "to make decisions about [products] based on [their] own personal wants and preferences" until they develop the conceptual maturity to understand their own wants and preferences and to assess the value of products available to satisfy them.[27] If children's conceptions of self, time, and money are not suited to making consumer decisions, one must have reservations about ignoring this fact and treating them as if they were capable of making reasonable consumer judgments anyway....

CHILDREN'S ADVERTISING AND BASIC ETHICAL PRINCIPLES

My evaluation of children's advertising has proceeded from the principle of consumer sovereignty, a principle of rather narrow application. Unlike more general ethical principles, like the principle of veracity, the principle of consumer sovereignty applies in the specialized area of business. Addressing the issue of children's advertising from the perspective of special business norms rather than more general ethical principles avoids the problem of deciding whether the specialized or more general principles should have priority in the moral reasoning of business people.[28] Nevertheless, children's advertising could also be evaluated from the standpoint of the more general ethical principles requiring veracity and fairness and prohibiting harmful conduct.

Veracity

The principle of veracity, understood as devotion to truth, is much broader than a principle prohibiting deception. Deception, the primary basis of the FTC's complaint against children's advertising, is only one way of infringing the principle of veracity.

Both critics and defenders of children's advertising agree that advertisers should not intentionally deceive children and that they should engage in research to determine whether children are misled by their ads. The central issue regarding veracity and children's advertising, however, does not relate to deception so much as to the strength of advertisers' devotion to truth. Advertisers generally do not make false statements intended to mislead children. Nevertheless, the particular nature of children's conceptual worlds makes it exceedingly likely that child-oriented advertising will generate false beliefs or highly improbable product expectations.

Research shows that young children have difficulty differentiating fantasy and reality[29] and frequently place indiscriminate trust in commercial characters who present products to them.[30] They also develop false beliefs about the selling characters in ads[31] and in some cases have unreasonably optimistic beliefs about the satisfactions advertised products will bring them.[32]

This research indicates that concern about the misleading nature of children's advertising is legitimate. Any parent knows—even one who has not examined the research—that young children are easily persuaded of the existence of fantasy characters. They develop (what seem to their parents) irrational fears and hopes from stories they hear and experiences they misinterpret. The stories and fantasies children see enacted in television commercials receive the same generous and idiosyncratic treatment as other information. Children's interpretations of advertising claims are as resistant to parental correction as their other fantasies are. One can only speculate on the nature and validity of the beliefs children adopt as a result of watching, for example, a cartoon depicting a pirate captain's magical discovery of breakfast cereal. Certainly, many ads are designed to create expectations that fun, friendship, and popularity will accompany possession of the advertised product. The likelihood that such expectations will be fulfilled is something young children cannot assess.

To the extent that children develop false beliefs and unreasonable expectations as a result of viewing commercials, moral reservations about children's advertising are justified. To the extent advertisers know that children develop false beliefs and unreasonable expectations, advertisers' devotion to truth and to responsible consumerism are suspect.

Fairness and Respect for Children

The fact that children's advertising benefits advertisers while at the same time nourishing false beliefs, unreasonable expectations, and irresponsible consumer desires among children calls into play principles of fairness and respect. Critics have said that child-oriented advertising takes advantage of children's limited capacities and their suggestibility for the benefit of the advertisers. As expressed by Michael Pertschuk, former chairman of the FTC, advertisers "seize on the child's trust and exploit it as weakness for their gain."[33] To employ as the unwitting means to the parent's pocketbook children who do not understand commercial exchange, who are unable to evaluate their own consumer preferences, and who consequently cannot make consumer decisions based on those preferences does indeed reflect a lack of respect for children. Such a practice fails to respect children's limitations as consumers, and instead capitalizes on them. In the language of Kant, advertisers are not treating children as "ends in themselves": they are treating children solely as instruments for their own gain.

In response to the charge of unfairness, supporters of children's advertising sometimes point out that the children are protected because their parents exercise control over the purse strings.[34] This response demonstrates failure to appreciate the basis of the unfairness charge. It is not potential economic harm that concerns critics: it is the attitude toward children reflected in the use of children's advertising that is central. As explained earlier, the attitude is inappropriate or unfitting.

Another frequent response to the charge of unfairness is that children actually do understand advertising.[35] A great deal of research has focused on whether children distinguish programs from commercials, whether they remember product identities, whether they distinguish program characters from commercial characters, and whether they recognize the persuasive intent of commercials.[36] But even showing that children "understand" advertising in all these ways would not demonstrate that children have the consumer capacities that would make it fair to advertise to them. The critical questions are not whether children can distinguish commercial characters from program characters,[37] or even whether they recognize persuasive intent, but whether they have the concepts of self, time, and money that would make it possible for them to make considered consumer decisions about the products they see advertised. Indeed, if children recognize that commercials are trying to sell things but lack the concepts to assess and deliberate about the products advertised, the charge that advertisers are "using" children or attempting to use them to sell their wares is strengthened. Intuitively, it seems that if children were sophisticated enough to realize that the goods advertised on television are for sale, they would be more likely than their younger counterparts to request the products.[38]

Harm to Children

Another principle to which appeal has been made by critics of television advertising is the principle against causing harm. The harmful effects of children's advertising are thought to include the parent-child conflicts generated by parental refusals to buy requested products, the unhappiness and anger suffered by children whose parents deny their product requests, the unhappiness children suffer when advertising-induced expectations of product performance are disappointed, and unhappiness experienced by children exposed to commercials portraying life-styles more affluent than their own.[39]

Replies to the charge that children's advertising is harmful to children have pinpointed weaknesses in the claim. One supporter of children's advertising says that the "harm" to children whose parents refuse their requests has not been adequately documented.[40] Another, claiming that some experts believe conflicts over purchases are instructive in educating children to make choices, denies that parent-child conflict is harmful.[41] As these replies suggest, demonstrating that children's advertising is harmful to children, as distinct from being misleading or unfair to them, involves much more than showing that it has the effects enumerated. Agreement about the application of the principle against causing harm depends on conceptual as well as factual agreement. A conception of harm must first be elaborated, and it must be shown to include these or other effects of advertising. It is not obvious, for example, that unhappiness resulting from exposure to more different life-styles is in the long run harmful.

Research indicates that children's advertising does contribute to the outcomes noted.[42] Certainly,

child-oriented television advertising is not the sole cause of these effects, but it does appear to increase their frequency and even perhaps their intensity.[43] I believe that a conception of harm including some of these effects could be developed, but I will not attempt to do so here. I mention this argument rather to illustrate another general ethical principle on which an argument against children's advertising might be based....

CONCLUSION

How might advertisers implement their responsibilities to promote consumer satisfaction and consumer responsibility and satisfy the principles of veracity, fairness, and nonmaleficence? There are degrees of compliance with these principles: some marketing strategies will do more than others to enhance consumer satisfaction, for example. One way compliance can be improved is by eliminating child-oriented television advertising for children's products and substituting advertising geared to mature consumers. Rather than employing the techniques found in advertising messages targeted to children under eleven,[44] advertisers could include product information that would interest adult viewers and devise ways to let child viewers know that consumer decisions require responsible decision-making skills. If much of the information presented is incomprehensible to the five-year-olds in the audience, so much the better.[45] When they reach the age at which they begin to understand consumer decision-making, they will perhaps have greater respect for the actual complexity of their responsibilities as consumers.

The problems of child-oriented advertising can best be dealt with if advertisers themselves recognize the inappropriateness of targeting children for commercial messages. I have tried to show why, within the context of a free market economy, the responsibilities of advertisers to promote consumer satisfaction and not to discourage responsible consumer decisions should lead advertisers away from child-oriented advertising. The problem of what types of ads are appropriate given these constraints provides a challenging design problem for the many creative people in the advertising industry. With appropriate inspiration and incentives, I do not doubt that they can meet the challenge.

Whether appropriate inspiration and incentives will be forthcoming is more doubtful. Children's advertising seems well entrenched and is backed by powerful economic forces,[46] and it is clear that some advertisers do not recognize, or are unwilling to acknowledge, the ethical problems of child-focused advertising.[47] The trend toward programming designed around selling characters is especially discouraging.

Even advertisers who recognize that eliminating child-oriented advertising will promote consumer satisfaction and consumer responsibility may be reluctant to reorient their advertising campaigns because of the costs and risks of doing so. Theoretically, only advertisers whose products would not withstand the scrutiny of adult consumers should lose sales from such a reorientation. It is clear that in the short run a general retreat from children's advertising would result in some lost revenues for makers, advertisers, and retail sellers of products that do not sell as well when advertised to adults. It is also possible that television networks, stations, and entrenched producers of children's shows would lose revenues and that children's programming might be jeopardized by the lack of advertisers' interest in commercial time during children's programs.

On the other hand, a shift away from children's advertising to adult advertising could result in even more pressure on existing adult commercial time slots, driving up their prices to a level adequate to subsidize children's programming without loss to the networks. And there are alternative means of financing children's television that could be explored.[48] The extent to which lost revenues and diminished profits would result from recognizing the ethical ideals I have described is largely a question of the ability of all the beneficiaries of children's television advertising to respond creatively. The longer-term effect of relinquishing child-focused advertising would be to move manufacturers, advertisers, and retailers in the direction of products that would not depend for their success on the suggestibility and immaturity of children. In the longer run, the result would be greater market efficiency.

NOTES*

An earlier version of this paper was delivered at a workshop on advertising ethics at the University of Florida in April 1984. I want to thank Robert Baum for organizing the workshop and to express my appreciation to all the workshop participants who commented on my paper, but especially to Katherine Clancy, Susan Elliott, Kathleen Henderson, Betsy Hilbert, Craig Shulstad, and Rita Weisskoff. I also want to acknowledge the helpful criticisms of Eric Douglas, Paul Farris, and Anita Niemi.

1. Richard P. Adler, "Children's Television Advertising: History of the Issue," in *Children and the Faces of Television*, ed. Edward L. Palmer and Aimee Dorr (New York: Academic Press, 1980), p. 241; hereafter cited as Palmer and Dorr.

2. Adler, p. 243.

3. Daniel Seligman, "The Commercial Crisis," *Fortune* 108 (November 14, 1983): 39.

4. For discussion of the constitutionality of banning children's advertising, see C. Edwin Baker, "Commercial Speech: A Problem in the Theory of Freedom," *Iowa Law Review* 62 (October 1976): 1; Martin H. Redish, "The First Amendment in the Marketplace: Commercial Speech and the Values of Free Expression," *George Washington Law Review* 39 (1970–1971): 429; Gerald J. Thain, "The 'Seven Dirty Words' Decision: A Potential Scrubbrush for Commercials on Children's Television?" *Kentucky Law Journal* 67 (1978–79): 947.

5. This point has been made by others. See, e.g., Ronald Dworkin, "Taking Rights Seriously," in *Taking Rights Seriously* (Cambridge, MA: Harvard University Press, 1977), pp. 188ff.

6. Susan Bartlett Foote and Robert H. Mnookin, "The 'Kid Vid' Crusade," *Public Interest* 61 (Fall 1980): 91.

7. One survey of adults found the following attitudes to children's commercials: strongly negative (23%); negative (50%); neutral (23%); positive (4%). These negative attitudes are most pronounced among parents of kindergarten-age children. The survey is cited in Thomas S. Robertson, "Television Advertising and Parent-Child Relations," in *The Effects of Television Advertising on Children*, ed. Richard P. Adler, Gerald S. Lesser, Laurene Krasny Meringoff, et al. (Lexington, MA: Lexington Books, 1980), p. 197; hereafter cited as Adler et al.

---

*Some notes have been deleted and the remaining ones renumbered.

8. E.g., M. Carole Macklin, "Do Children Understand TV Ads?" *Journal of Advertising Research* 23 (February–March 1983): 63–70; Thomas Robertson and John Rossiter, "Children and Commercial Persuasion: An Attribution Theory Analysis," *Journal of Consumer Research* 1 (June 1974): 13–20. See also summaries of research in David Pillemer and Scott Ward, "Investigating the Effects of Television Advertising on Children: An Evaluation of the Empirical Studies," Draft read to American Psychological Assn., Div. 23, San Francisco, California, August 1977; John R. Rossiter, "The Effects of Volume and Repetition of Television Commercials," in Adler et al., pp. 160–62; Ellen Wartella, "Individual Differences in Children's Responses to Television Advertising," in Palmer and Dorr, pp. 312–14.

9. Wartella, p. 313.

10. Compare the definition of "child-oriented television advertising" adopted by the FTC in its Final Staff Report and Recommendation: "advertising which is in or adjacent to programs either directed to children or programs where children constitute a substantial portion of the audience." See "FTC Final Staff Report and Recommendation," *In the Matter of Children's Advertising*, 43 *Federal Register* 17967, March 31, 1981, p. 2.

11. *Self-Regulatory Guidelines for Children's Advertising*, by Children's Advertising Review Unit, Council of Better Business Bureau, Inc., 3d ed. (New York, 1983), p. 6.

12. F. Earle Barcus, "The Nature of Television Advertising to Children," in Palmer and Dorr, pp. 276–77.

13. Barcus, p. 275.

14. Research has been developed to support advertisers targeting child audiences. See, e.g., Gene Reilly Group, Inc., *The Child* (Darien, CT: The Child, Inc., 1973), cited in Robert B. Choate, "The Politics of Change," in Palmer and Dorr, p. 329.

15. Thomas Donaldson and Patricia H. Werhane, *Ethical Issues in Business* (Englewood Cliffs, NJ: Prentice-Hall, Inc., 1979), p. 294. In a telephone interview a representative of Fisher-Price's advertising agency told me that Fisher-Price continues to focus its advertising on parents because most Fisher-Price toys appeal to the very young.

16. See "FTC Final Staff Report and Recommendation," pp. 21–22, n. 51, for a description of studies by Atkin and White. Atkin found that 90% of the three-year-olds studied and 73% of the seven-year-olds thought that selling characters like them. White found that 82% of a group of four- to seven-year-olds thought that the selling figures ate the products they advertised and wanted the children to do likewise.

17. Studies indicate that there is very limited use of product information in children's television advertising. Predominant are "appeals to psychological states, associations with established values, and unsupported assertions about the qualities of the products"; Barcus, p. 279.

18. Submission before the FTC, 1978, quoted in Emilie Griffin, "The Future Is Inevitable: But Can It Be Shaped in the Interest of Children?" in Palmer and Dorr, p. 347.

19. Griffin, p. 344.

20. E.g., Frances L. Ilg, Louise Bates Ames, and Sidney M. Baker, *Child Behavior*, rev. ed. (New York: Harper & Row, 1981).

21. On the child's conception of time, see Jean Piaget, *The Child's Conception of Time* (New York: Basic Books, 1970).

22. Some intriguing illustrations of children's philosophical questions and observations are recounted in Gareth B. Matthews, *Philosophy and the Young Child* (Cambridge, MA: Harvard University Press, 1980).

23. "FTC Final Staff Report and Recommendation," pp. 27–28, citing the work of Geis.

24. My five-year-old son reasoned thus to explain why a five-dollar piano would be too expensive.

25. Toys, cereals, and candies are the products most heavily promoted to children; Barcus, pp. 275–76.

26. The FTC concluded on the basis of relevant literature that children tend to want whatever products are advertised on television; "FTC Final Staff Report and Recommendation," p. 8. For data on the extent to which children want what they see advertised on television, see Charles K. Atkin, "Effects of Television Advertising on Children," in Palmer and Dorr, pp. 289–90.

27. The results of one study of children's understanding of television advertising messages suggested that although "parents cannot 'force' early sophistication in children's reactions to television advertising, their attention and instruction can enhance the process." Focusing on children's capacities to understand advertising rather than on their capacities to make decisions, the article supports the general proposition that the child's conceptual world differs in many ways from that of the adult. The critical question is, of course: even if we can promote earlier understanding of advertising and consumer decisions, should we do so? See John R. Rossiter and Thomas S. Robertson, "Canonical Analysis of Developmental, Social, and Experimental Factors in Children's Comprehension of Television Advertising," *Journal of Genetic Psychology* 129 (1976): 326.

28. For general discussion of this issue see Alan H. Goldman, *The Moral Foundations of Professional Ethics*, chap. 5 (Totowa, N.J.: Rowman and Littlefield, 1980).

29. See T. G. Bever, M. L. Smith, B. Bengen, and T. G. Johnson, "Young Viewers' Troubling Response to TV Ads," *Harvard Business Review*, November–December 1975, pp. 109–20.

30. "FTC Final Staff Report and Recommendation," pp. 21–22, n. 51, describes the work of Atkin supporting the

conclusion that children trust selling characters. Atkin found in a group of three- to seven-year-olds that 70% of the three-year-olds and 60% of the seven-year-olds trusted the characters about as much as they trusted their mothers.

31. "FTC Final Staff Report and Recommendation," at pp. 21–22, no. 51, describes the work of White, who found that many children in a group of four- to seven-year-olds she studied believe that the selling figures eat the advertised products and want the children to do likewise and that the selling figures want the children to eat things that are good for them.

32. Atkin, p. 300.

33. Quoted in Foote and Mnookin, p. 92.

34. June Esserman of Child Research Services, Inc., quoted in *Comments of M & M/Mars, Children's Television Advertising Trade Regulation Rule-Making Proceeding,* Federal Trade Commission (November 1978) p. 4.

35. *Comments of M & M/Mars,* p. 5. See also Macklin, n. 8, *supra.*

36. See n. 8, *supra.*

37. For a similar view of the relevance of children's ability to distinguish commercial characters from program characters, see Scott Ward, "Compromise in Commercials for Children," *Harvard Business Review,* November–December 1978, p. 133.

38. Recent research indicates that as children become more aware of advertising's persuasive intent, the frequency of their requests does not decline. This finding is contrary to earlier research purportedly showing that awareness of persuasive intent leads to a decline in number of requests; Rossiter, pp. 163–65.

39. Atkin, pp. 298–301.

40. Foote and Mnookin, p. 95.

41. *Comments of M & M/Mars,* p. 64. Cf. n. 27, *supra.*

42. Atkin, pp. 298–301. See also Scott Ward and Daniel B. Wackman, "Children's Purchase Influence Attempts and Parental Yielding," *Journal of Marketing Research,* August 1972, p. 318.

43. For example, one study found that heavy viewers of Saturday morning television got into more arguments with their parents over toy and cereal denials than did light viewers; Atkin, pp. 298–301. See also Ward and Wackman, p. 318.

44. The majority of advertising directed to children is targeted to children two-to-eleven or six-to-eleven years of age; "FTC Final Staff Report and Recommendation," p. 46.

45. For the view that children's special capacities and limitations should be respected but that children should not be "contained" in a special children's world isolated from that of adults, see Valerie Polakow Suransky, *The Erosion of Childhood* (Chicago: University of Chicago Press, 1982).

46. It was estimated that the coalition established to fight the FTC proceedings in 1978 put together a "war chest" of $15–30 million. According to news reports the coalition included several huge law firms, the national advertising association, broadcasters and their associations, the U.S. Chamber of Commerce, the Grocery Manufacturers of America, the sugar association, the chocolate and candy manufacturers, cereal companies and their associations, and more; Choate, p. 334. It is interesting to note that supporters of children's advertising tend not to be people who spend a great deal of time with children.

47. "In the area of children's products, the U.S. is an advertiser's paradise compared with many countries"; Christopher Campbell, International Marketing Director at the Parker Brothers subsidiary of General Mills, quoted in Ronald Alsop, "Countries' Different Ad Rules Are Problem for Global Firms," *Wall Street Journal,* September 27, 1984, p. 33. According to Alsop, "The other countries' aim is to protect kids from exploitation."

48. It is interesting to note that in 1949 42% of the children's programs broadcast were presented without advertiser sponsorship; Melody, p. 36.

Decision Scenario 1
SEVEN MARKETING PITCHES

Consider the following seven marketing techniques:

1. An ad claiming that the Honda Accord has high satisfaction ratings among first-year owners.

2. A TV commercial in which James Garner exhibits the sporty, fun experience of driving the Mazda RX-7.

3. An ad for the Chevrolet Camaro presenting it as enhancing sex appeal by displaying the car among a group of attractive young men/women (your pick) in bathing suits.

4. An ad for Allstate life insurance that pictures two houses, one of which is fully involved in a fire, with a voice-over informing us that the real tragedy has just happened in the other house:

The breadwinner died without sufficient life insurance to cover the mortgage.

5. An ad for a device that can summon medical assistance in an emergency; the ad shows an elderly woman falling down a flight of steps. Unfortunately, she is not wearing the device, and help arrives too late.

6. A Saturday morning TV ad for Smurf dolls; it is broadcast during a cartoon show starring the cute little creatures.

7. A subliminal message "Buy Coke" shown before intermission in a movie theater.

Which of these ads do you intuitively feel is a violation of the consumer's autonomy? If you feel as most people do, you will find the first ad unproblematic and the last ad to be a violation. If this is your response, you must identify the features of the subliminal technique that make it objectionable from the point of view of autonomy. You must also be consistent and willing to accept the conse-

quences of your analysis. For instance, if the feature that makes the subliminal technique unacceptable is also present in the ad aimed at children, you must make the same judgment about both ads.

The most common explanation of the usual reaction to the seventh case relates the consumer's being unaware of the appeal. The subliminal technique is intended to manipulate consumers by making them less likely to resist the desire the ad may generate. (Note that this explanation makes the technique objectionable even if the consumer ultimately decides *not* to buy the product.)

■ Some child psychologists contend that young children are unable to distinguish between commercials and normal programming. Does that make the sixth example as troublesome as the seventh?

■ Does the same analysis apply to the use of sexual suggestion? To appeals to fear among the elderly?

Decision Scenario 2

ADVERTISING'S IMAGE OF WOMEN

It has been estimated that U.S. children between the ages of two and five watch an average of thirty hours of television each week. At this rate, the average young person will watch some 350,000 television commercials by the end of high school. Given all forms of advertising (magazines, newspapers, packaging, radio, television) the average American will have seen some fifty million commercials by age sixty. Thus advertising is inescapable in our culture, and its socializing impact cannot be ignored. Ads not only describe products but also present images, values, and goals; they portray certain concepts of normalcy and sexuality, and they promote certain types of self-images. Advertising not only aims to provide information to consumers but also aims to motivate them. What images of women does it present, and what motivations does it appeal to?

Many ads seek to motivate women by suggesting that they are inadequate without a particular product. Cosmetic ads purvey an ideal form of female beauty—a form that is unattainable. Women are portrayed as having no facial wrinkles, no lines,

no blemishes—indeed, no pores. If you do not look like this, the ads suggest, you are not beautiful, and since no one (including the model) really looks like this, women need cosmetics to look beautiful. Beauty thus results from products and not from the woman herself. Advertising tells women that they should change their age (the "little-girl look"), weight, bust size, hair color, eye color, complexion—and even their smell. In many ads a woman's worth is measured not by her intelligence or her character or even her natural appearance. A woman's worth is measured by how closely she approaches an ideal created by an advertising agency.

Many ads also portray women as inferior to other women and to men. Women are seen as engaged in a constant competition with other women for the attention of men. When they are pictured with men, women are often shown as clinging to the male, as passive, as submissive. Men are seen in control, active, and dominant.

Besides feelings of inadequacy, many ads also use guilt to motivate women. The "housewife" is constantly being chided because the laundry is not as white nor does it smell as clean as the neighbor's. Her dishes have spots, her meals are unappealing, her floors and furniture have "wax buildup," and her clothes are out of style. Even when women are shown in the role of worker rather than home-maker, feelings of guilt and inadequacy are still reinforced. The working woman is portrayed as a superwoman who harmonizes perfectly the roles of career woman, mother, wife, and homemaker. Despite all of these demands, the woman still looks like a model. In those few cases where the harmony breaks down, the woman is shown as being respon-

sible for the breakdown or in need of drugs to cope with the stress. On the other hand, men are seldom seen as responsible for cooking, cleaning, and child care, or in need of drugs in order to cope.

- What kind of influence has advertising had on your own views of beauty, attractiveness, and sexuality?
- How does advertising influence our understanding of social role based on gender?
- To what degree have your family, friends, and classmates been socialized by advertising?

Decision Scenario 3
LISTERINE AND CORRECTIVE ADVERTISING

The Federal Trade Commission (FTC) has a legal mandate to prevent "unfair or deceptive acts or practices" and "unfair methods of competition." At one level this establishes a clear responsibility. The FTC should regulate false and deceptive advertising by investigating complaints and prohibiting those ads that are found to be unfair or deceptive. The most common method used by the FTC involves issuing a "cease and desist" order against the deceptive ad.

However, upon analysis it becomes clear that a "cease and desist" order can be a very ineffective remedy: A firm could deceptively advertise a product and reap the benefits of that deceptive ad until the FTC orders it to stop. A cease and desist order does nothing to correct the harms already done to consumers or competitors and does little about the effect that the ad might continue to have upon consumers. Thus, the FTC uses two other methods for remedying deceptive advertisements: (1) affirmative disclosure orders and (2) corrective advertising orders.

If an ad has been found to be deceptive because it contains incomplete, misleading, or partially true statements, as opposed to simple false claims, the FTC can require future versions of that ad to include an additional disclosure. For example, when advertisements for Geritol, a product that remedies iron-deficiency anemia, claimed that Geritol relieved tiredness, the FTC required future ads to

disclose that the product "will be of no benefit to the great majority of persons" who suffer from tiredness. However, since affirmative disclosure orders apply only to future versions of the ad that contain the particular deceptive claim, other remedies are needed.

Listerine is an antiseptic mouthwash that has been on the market with no change in formula since 1879. Direct advertising of Listerine began in 1921 and has always included claims that Listerine prevents, cures, or alleviates symptoms of colds and sore throats. In 1975, after almost three years of investigation, the FTC concluded that all of the claims regarding Listerine's effectiveness in fighting colds and sore throats were false. In addition to a cease and desist order, the FTC issued a corrective advertising order that required the following disclosure in the next $10 million of advertising for Listerine:

> Contrary to prior advertising, Listerine will not prevent colds or sore throats or lessen their severity.

Warner-Lambert, the makers of Listerine, challenged the FTC decision in court. In the first corrective advertising case to be reviewed by the courts, the Court of Appeals cited two factors in supporting the FTC. First, the claims regarding colds were demonstrably false. (Listerine claims to kill "germs" on contact, but [1] these bacteria do not cause colds, viruses do; [2] while Listerine does "kill millions of bacteria in the mouth," it also leaves millions.) Second, since these claims had been made since 1921, there was good reason to assume that consumers believed and would continue to believe these claims. However, the Court ruled that the opening statement "Contrary to prior advertising" could serve only to humiliate Warner-Lambert and therefore should be deleted.

- Was the FTC justified in issuing the corrective advertising order for Listerine? Are different First Amendment issues raised by "cease and desist," "affirmative disclosure," and "corrective advertising" orders?

- Might Warner-Lambert cite the fact that consumers continued to purchase Listerine as evidence that consumers did not believe the false claims? Might they claim that a cease and desist order and market forces alone would end the mistaken beliefs by consumers?

- The Court ruled that the phrase "contrary to prior advertising" would "humiliate" Warner-Lambert and could be required only if the FTC could show that there was an "egregious case of deliberate deception." Do you agree with this decision?

Decision Scenario 4
ADVERTISING HEADACHES

The nonprescription pain reliever market in the United States has sales of over $2 billion annually. The market essentially involves just three drugs (all called analgesics): aspirin, acetaminophen, and ibuprofen. This market is dominated by four major pharmaceutical companies. Sterling Drug controls a major share of the aspirin market with its product Bayer Aspirin. Johnson & Johnson produces an acetaminophen (Tylenol) and an ibuprofen product (Mediprin). American Home Products makes an aspirin (Anacin), an acetaminophen (Anacin-3), and an ibuprofen (Advil). Bristol-Meyers also produces aspirin (Bufferin and Excedrin), an acetaminophen (Datril), and an ibuprofen (Nuprin).

Since there is no chemical and therefore no medicinal difference between brands of acetaminophen and ibuprofen, and no significant difference between aspirins (some differ by having caffeine added to the aspirin; others have a coating), these companies have two basic choices for succeeding in the marketplace: They can compete over price, or they can rely on advertising. Evidence suggests that all have followed the advertising route. The regulation history of advertising for these products shows that this route has been controversial.

As long ago as 1944 the Federal Trade Commission (FTC) investigated Anacin for the claim that its "combination of highly proven and active ingredients" were superior to and different from aspirin (no evidence exists to support that the caffeine in Anacin improves its analgesic effect). Through the 1960s television ads claimed that Anacin offered "fast, fast relief." Bufferin was "twice as fast as aspirin," St. Joseph's aspirin was "faster than other leading pain relief tablets," and Bayer offered the "fastest relief of pain." Anacin also employed ads citing surveys that showed "three out of four doctors recommend the ingredients in Anacin" and calling Anacin's ingredients the "greatest pain fighter ever discovered." These ads did not disclose that this "ingredient" was plain aspirin.

The increasing popularity of acetaminophen throughout the 1970s brought with it similar advertising claims. "Last year hospitals dispensed ten times as much Tylenol as the next four brands combined" did not disclose that Johnson & Johnson supplied hospitals with Tylenol at costs well below what consumers pay. American Home Products sued Johnson & Johnson on the grounds that these ads implied that hospitals dispensed Tylenol because it was more effective than competing products. At the same time, American Home Products was advertising its acetaminophen, Anacin-3, by claiming that "hospitals recommend acetaminophen, the aspirin-free pain reliever in Anacin-3, more than any other pain reliever." The acetaminophen recommended by hospitals, of course, was Tylenol.

- If you applied both the "reasonable consumer" and the "ignorant consumer" standards, would these ads be deceptive? Are they unfair business practices?
- How might a defender of the free market like Milton Friedman analyze this scenario? Is this a

case of market failure or the result of businesses ignoring market principles?

- Should there be more regulation of advertising of medicines? Would such regulation involve undue government paternalism?

Decision Scenario 5
"BAIT AND SWITCH"

"Bait advertising" occurs when a seller makes an attractive but insincere offer to sell a product or service. Once the ad has attracted a customer, a salesperson tries to persuade the customer to "switch" to a more expensive product or a product with a higher profit margin. The Federal Trade Commission (FTC) has ruled that "bait and switch" is an unfair and deceptive marketing technique.

Bait and switch can involve a variety of sales tactics. After advertising a product, a store may purposely stock insufficient inventory to meet the increased demand; thus, when the first product is sold out, the second, more profitable item is substituted. Sometimes sales staff simply refuse to show the advertised product to customers. Another common technique involves criticizing or disparaging the advertised product, perhaps by reminding the customer that one "gets what one pays for" or by pointing out limitations of warranty or service. Other bait and switch techniques involve delaying delivery dates for the advertised product, knowingly demonstrating a defective sample, and using employee compensation methods that encourage salespeople to convince customers to purchase other products.

Of course, it is possible to employ bait and switch techniques without using untruths. A re-

tailer could advertise only the least expensive products, with salespeople pointing out quite truthfully that these products lack the features and quality of a more profitable alternative. It appears that the deception involved in bait and switch lies in the intention of the seller. On the other hand, bait and switch methods might be unfair not only to consumers but also to competing retailers and manufacturers. Consumers could be deceived (even by truthful statements) and thereby coerced into alternative purchases. Competitors can be hurt when their products lose in the marketplace. In some cases, manufacturers can lose doubly through bait and switch: Retailers may use money provided by a manufacturer to advertise their national brands, only to criticize these items when customers inquire, switching them to more profitable private brands. Thus manufacturers lose their advertising budget and have their products disparaged as well.

- How can truthful advertising claims be deceptive? How can the FTC determine an advertiser's intention? Are government agencies capable of regulating intentions? Is this even appropriate?
- How, exactly, are such techniques coercive? Can a reasonable consumer be coerced by truthful claims? Isn't this more a case of persuasion than coercion?

Decision Scenario 6
NEW, IMPROVED, . . . AND SMALLER

Consumer product companies often face a competitive marketplace where profit margins are slim and manufacturing cost increases frequent. Some companies have adopted a new technique called "downsizing" to respond to these pressures. They decrease product weight or quantity while holding package size and price constant. Consumer research suggests that consumers are less likely to process the label information that discloses the downsizing and the implicit price increase. Consumers, then, are less likely to respond as they would to a more obvious per package price increase. Downsizing can come in a variety of forms, some more creative than others. Perhaps the most common technique is to keep the exact same package but include less product. Some coffee manufacturers have a new twist on that strategy. They decreased the quantity of coffee in the can, but they claimed that a new "flaking" process allowed the consumer to get more brewed coffee per scoop. Other manufacturers reduce the package size and quantity, and lower the package price but increase the unit price. (New low price!) Another approach is to increase package size, quantity, and price but also increase unit price. (A variant of the old "economy size" package that had a higher unit price.)

This case was prepared from the following sources: Irwin Landau, "Why a Pound of Coffee Weighs 13 Ounces," *New York Times*, May 23, 1993 Section 3, p. 13; Steven Sakson (AP), "Will People Cough Up $50 for a $5 Drug?" *Philadelphia Inquirer*, October 14, 1994.

One drug manufacturer, barred from the continued use of an active ingredient in a prescription asthma drug, changed the formulation so that the new drug was similar in ingredients to an over-the-counter medication that cost one tenth the price. Another drug company halved the quantity of active ingredients while doubling the suggested dosage for an over-the-counter cold medication.

Some report that a manufacturer of laundry detergent launched a new brand with very high initial levels of the active cleaning agent, the detergent's most costly ingredient. Then it gradually reduced the levels of the cleaning agent while carefully tracking consumer response. When noticeable decreases in cleaning effectiveness began to cause decreased sales, the manufacturer increased the proportion of the cleaning agent again.

- Are companies that downsize intentionally deceiving because they are relying on market research that shows consumers are less likely to notice such price increases?
- Are there ethically relevant differences between the preceding examples?
- What responsibility does the consumer have to protect him- or herself in the marketplace? What effect does that responsibility have on the obligations of manufacturers and advertisers? Are any of the techniques described ones that consumers cannot protect against?

Decision Scenario 7
POLITICAL ADVOCACY MEETS HIGH-TECH AD AGENCIES

In its 1978 *Bellotti* decision, the United States Supreme Court struck down a Massachusetts

This case was prepared from the following sources: *First National Bank of Boston v. Bellotti* 435 U.S. 765; Elizabeth Kolbert, "Special Interests Special Weapon," *New York Times*, March 26, 1995; Katherine Seelye, "Agendas Clash in Bid to Alter Law on Product Liability," *New York Times*, March 8, 1995; Eric Schine and Catherine Young, "From the Folks Who Brought You Harry and Louise...," *Business Week*, April 17, 1995; Cyndee Miller, "Ads Are Huge Weapon in Battle Over Health Care Reform," *Marketing News*, September 12, 1994; Margaret Carlson, "Public Eye," *Time*, March 7, 1994.

statute that prohibited corporations from engaging in advocacy advertising on political issues. The Court, by a 5 to 4 majority, held that corporations are legal persons and, as such, are entitled to engage in debate over matters that come before the body politic. Of course, ads have often had political content to varying degrees. Even before the *Bellotti* decision, for example, oil companies were advertising devotion to national security in the expensive search for new and reliable sources of domestic crude oil. Congress was at the same time debating a windfall profits tax because oil companies were perceived to have profited handsomely from the effects of the Arab oil embargo. The *Bellotti* decision merely allowed more explicit expressions of political opinions.

Recently, corporate-sponsored political advocacy advertising has reached new levels of sophistication and directness. During the 1994 debate over health care reform in the United States, advertising expenditures by groups both opposing and supporting the Clinton plan topped $75 million. One ad, in particular, was seen as highly effective in generating opposition to the Clinton plan. The "Harry and Louise" ads featured a couple who expressed concern over the state of health care but who were fearful of the impact of Clinton's reform proposals. The Health Insurance Association of America, the sponsor of the ads, spent over $17 million trying to protect the private health insurance market from controls suggested in the Clinton reforms. The ads were widely regarded as one of the most successful tools used by those opposed to the reform proposal.

In 1995, advocacy ads urging reform of product liability law began to appear in media markets represented by legislators regarded as uncertain supporters of reform. They were paid for by a lobbying group, Citizens for a Sound Economy, that was funded by large corporate donations. Two important donors were CIGNA (an insurance company) and R. J. Reynolds (the tobacco giant). Both companies have huge stakes in the direction taken by product liability law.

The ads were created by the same team that produced the "Harry and Louise" spots. The agency produced a number of memorable liability reform ads. One features a volunteer emergency medical technician who plaintively wishes that the threat of lawsuits not be allowed to keep her from doing her job—saving lives. Another shows a team of Little Leaguers who disappear from the screen, representing the threat from lawsuits that, the commercial says, costs teams "more than bats, balls, and uniforms." When asked for statistics on that, a spokesperson for Little League Baseball, Inc., said,

"It's not incumbent on us to provide those numbers." These advocacy ads, and those from the health care debate, are notable both because of their emotional impact and because they represent the newest chapter in corporate political advocacy, where corporations sponsor apparently independent advocacy lobbies. (One commentator, likening these lobbies to artificial grassroots movements, called them "Astroturf campaigns.")

The usually conservative Justice Rehnquist, now Chief Justice, in his dissent from the *Bellotti* decision suggested the following:

> A State grants a business corporation the blessings of potentially perpetual life and limited liability to enhance its efficiency as an economic entity. It might reasonably be concluded that those properties, so beneficial in the economic sphere, pose special dangers in the political sphere....Indeed, the States might reasonably fear that the corporation would use its economic power to obtain further benefits than those already bestowed.

Despite Justice Rehnquist's reservations, corporate political advocacy activities appear to pass muster with the Supreme Court. They also appear to be a permanent and increasingly frequent part of political debate in the United States.

- Does the ability of a corporation to use its resources in advocacy ads threaten corporate domination of political debate?

- Does the fact that groups such as labor unions (the AFL-CIO spent $3 million on the health care debate) and the American Association for Retired Persons (AARP) also advertise guarantee a balanced debate on the public airwaves?

- Are advocacy ads effective at influencing opinion? Are they a good way to debate public policy issues? Do they contribute to informing the electorate?

- Even if you agree with Rehnquist's fears, what regulatory cures are there that would not be worse than the disease?

PART IV

Business and Society

12

Business and the
Environment

Does business, or anyone else for that matter, have *direct* ethical responsibilities to natural objects like animals, plants, and ecosystems? Or are all environmental responsibilities indirect, derived from more primary responsibilities to other people? Are the limits of business's environmental responsibilities best left to the market and the legal system?

The relation between business and the environment is far-ranging and complex. Indeed, environmental issues can raise some fundamental philosophical questions about both ethics (who and what should count, ethically?) and economics (is growth always good?). Business and the environment can intersect at many levels.

First, business activities cause many environmental problems. Acid rain, air and water pollution, toxic waste disposal, soil erosion, resource depletion, and the destruction of ecosystems are just some of these problems. Many observers believe that business is responsible for environmental cleanup because business is responsible for causing many of the problems in the first place.

Second, on a more general level, many believe that environmental problems are essentially economic problems. Environmentalists are, after all, concerned with the allocation of scarce resources, with risks and benefits, with the costs of cleanup, with the "production" of a cleaner and healthier environment. Many believe that these concepts—allocation of resources, risks and benefits, costs, production—are economic concepts and therefore we should turn to economics for advice and guidance. Not surprisingly, economists have addressed environmental issues in greater detail than have other social scientists. In this view, because environmental issues are economic issues and because what affects the economy affects business, the business community has reason to be concerned with environmental issues.

These debates are, in many ways, debates about *means* and not about *ends*. At first glance, concern for the environment is uncontroversial: No one wants to breath polluted air, no one wishes to drink contaminated water, no one wants to live atop a toxic waste dump. Thus, debates tend to focus on finding appropriate means to these ends. Of course, "appropriate" involves means that are efficient, cost-effective, and that balance out the trade-offs that must be made between competing goals. And this, according to many observers, is exactly what economics does. Economics seeks the most efficient distribution of costs (what are we giving up?) and benefits (what are we getting?).

Environmental and business interests intersect at a third level: What concepts and methods should we use in thinking about the environment? For many environmentalists, examining environmental issues in economic terms is part of the problem, not the solution. The problem lies in the very fundamental values, attitudes, and beliefs of our modern consumer culture.

This point is sometimes explained in terms of "shallow" and "deep" ecology. The concerns of many mainstream environmentalists—pollution, recycling, resource depletion—are characterized as "shallow" in that they are truly no more than symptoms of a "deeper" underlying problem. Just as a sneeze can be a nuisance and disrupt our daily routine, pollution or resource scarcity can be a nuisance and disrupt the routine of contemporary business. However, according to deep ecology, just as it is a mistake for a doctor to treat the sneeze without investigating the underlying cause, it is a mistake for environmentalists to be concerned with the merely symptomatic ills of pollution and recycling.

What are the deeper underlying causes? For many observers, they rest in the values and attitudes of our consumer and materialistic culture. Ours is a culture in which people are predominantly judged by what they possess: by their house, car, and clothes. In our culture, "more" is better; economic growth is an unquestioned goal. We judge entire societies—"developed," "undeveloped," "developing"—in terms of their ability to produce more and more "things." In such a culture, when people are fortunate enough to satisfy their basic wants—food, clothing, shelter—continued economic growth demands that new wants be created. If happiness is satisfying our wants, people can never be happy in such a growth-dependent culture.

Unfortunately, the primary way to fuel continued economic growth is to continue to develop and exploit the natural resources of the earth. Thus, we cannot hope to adequately address environmental destruction until we fundamentally change some very common and powerful attitudes and values. And this will require some very fundamental restructuring of the economy and of business.

ENVIRONMENT AND ECONOMICS

Perhaps the most influential perspective on business's environmental responsibility flows from the familiar free market approach to economics. This perspective, represented in our reading from William Baxter's classic book, *People or Penguins: The Case for Optimal Pollution,* argues that markets are best suited for determining environmental policy. Issues like pollution, conservation, and preservation are fundamentally issues of resource use and allocation. As such, we need to find ways to balance the competing views over the appropriate use of these resources. This balance is exactly the equilibrium between competing preferences that is attained by an efficient market; hence, markets are the best means for reaching this goal. There is, according to Baxter, an "optimal level" of pollution, as there would be an optimal level of resource use, an optimal level of preservation, and an optimal level of development.

There are a number of familiar challenges to this free market view. A variety of market failures, like the "externalities" of pollution, the lack of markets for such goods as endangered species and scenic vistas, the lack of property rights for such things as the oceans and the atmosphere, and the inability of future generations to represent their interests in contemporary markets, seem to raise insurmountable challenges for the pure free market view. In response to such challenges, some economists (often called "environmental economists") have developed models for reforming the market in ways that overcome these failures. Thus, these economists will seek to establish a "price" for such goods as endangered species, or have the interests of future generations "discounted" to capture their present value, or recommend issuing "pollution permits" that can be bought and sold on the open market. These reforms mimic the workings of the market and help us decide what the market would determine were it not for these market failures.

In our second reading, Mark Sagoff will have none of this. Reliance on economics, whether classical free market economics or contemporary environmental economics, to resolve environmental disputes is a fundamental mistake in reasoning. Environmental issues revolve around matters of value, conviction, and belief, not a matter of mere subjective preferences. As such, environmental issues properly belong in the domain of politics and public policy, not in the domain of economics.

The well-known Mineral King Valley case that follows this introduction provides an opportunity for evaluating these competing views. This case involved plans by the Disney Corporation to purchase public land and develop it into a ski resort. Defenders of this development argued that Disney's ability to earn greater profit from this land than could, say, the Sierra Club, proves that the public values ski resorts more than they value undeveloped wilderness. Critics argue that it would be a mistake to try to put a price on undeveloped wilderness and perform a cost–benefit analysis to decide between competing uses. In recent years, a similar Disney plan to develop a historical area in Virginia into a Civil War theme park provides yet another example of these issues.

LEGAL AND MORAL STANDING

The Mineral King Valley case raised fundamental ethical and philosophical questions as well. On behalf of the Sierra Club's attempt to block development of Mineral King Valley, law professor Christopher Stone argued that the natural objects in Mineral King Valley—the trees, animals, streams—should themselves be considered as having legal standing. Stone proposed that natural objects be given legal rights to sue to prevent development. In our third reading, Stone continues this line of argument that natural objects can be given legal, and perhaps moral, standing. Arguing by analogy with the legal standing for corporations, Stone claims that natural objects like trees meet all of the relevant criteria for having legal standing.

Moral standing is a fundamental question for philosophical ethics. Who or what deserves to be considered in ethical deliberation? Do only humans count? Do future generations of humans count? Do animals deserve to be considered in our ethical decisions? Do trees? Ecosystems? Christopher Stone's essay represents one of the first challenges to what is called "anthropocentric," or human-centered, ethics. Anthropocentric ethics would hold that only humans have moral standing. Therefore, any responsibility that business might have regarding the natural environment is indirect: Business has responsibilities only to human beings, but some responsibilities concerning the environment, for example, not to pollute, can be derived from other direct responsibilities to humans. Baxter's essay is clearly anthropocentric in this sense.

Nonanthropocentric ethics would hold that humans have direct ethical responsibilities to nonhumans. The philosophical strategy involved in these attempts is clear: Begin with an uncontroversial example of something with moral standing, for example, human beings. Identify those characteristics in virtue of which humans do have moral standing. Logic then commits us to saying that anything else possessing these characteristics also deserves moral considerability. Some utilitarians, for example, argue that the ability to feel pain, or "sentience," is a sufficient condition for moral standing. Since animals surely possess this characteristic, animals must be considered in any utilitarian calculation of maximum happiness. Thus, business practices that inflict pain on animals would, in this view, be ethically wrong. Other philosophers argue that the ability to make reasoned choices is the crucial characteristic for possessing rights. Some animals seem capable of doing this; thus, some animals should be granted moral rights.

The implications that these views have for business are enormous. If animals have moral standing, we would need to reform agriculture significantly. The way we raise and slaughter poultry, cattle, and pigs would need to change. Indeed, eating animals for food is morally suspect. Using animals as research specimens in the development of drugs, medical procedures, food, cosmetics, and countless other consumer products would need to be curtailed. The destruction of habitat for economic development would also come under close ethical scrutiny. The question of moral standing for nonhumans raises widespread, serious ethical concerns.

GROWTH AND SUSTAINABILITY

There is perhaps no more fundamental assumption of market economics and modern business practice than the belief that economic growth is good and economic stagnation or recession is bad. Yet many writers are now arguing that a growth-based, market economy must be replaced by one that takes economic sustainability as its goal. According to a common definition, an economic activity is sustainable if it is able to meet present needs without decreasing the ability of future people to meet their needs. The goal of economic activity, according to the sustainability model, is economic "development" rather than economic "growth." In this view, the responsibility of business is to improve the quality of life of presently living human beings without denying to our children and grandchildren an equal opportunity to live a similarly healthy and happy life.

In the fourth reading in this chapter, Norman Bowie argues that business has no special environmental responsibility. Once minimal moral constraints are met, constraints that essentially involve only the rights of human beings, business is free to pursue profits within the limits established by law. In Bowie's view, environmental responsibility rests with all of us: as citizens, to convince our political institutions to enact environmental legislation; and as consumers, to demand environmentally responsible products and services. Thus, the law and the market establish the nature of business's environmental responsibility.

In contrast, Joseph DesJardins argues that more dramatic steps are necessary to ensure an ethically responsible environmental policy. Present economic activities that use natural resources at unsustainable rates violate fundamental ethical responsibilities that we have to our children and grandchildren. We are putting them at risk of grave harm simply to meet our own consumerist demands. According to DesJardins, responsible business activity must be both economically and ecologically sustainable. Business needs to view natural resources as capital: We may use the capital to generate an income that we can live off of, but we have a responsibility not to deplete the store of capital and thereby deny future people an equal opportunity for a similar life.

CASE STUDY Walt Disney vs. The Sierra Club

Mineral King Valley is an area of great natural beauty in the Sierra Nevada Mountains in California, adjacent to Sequoia National Park. It had been a part of that park since 1926 and had been left undeveloped as a wilderness area. Beginning in the late 1940s, the U.S. Forest Service began to consider plans for developing Mineral King as a recreational site. During the 1960s the Forest Service accepted bids from private developers, including Walt Disney Enterprises, to create a complex of motels, restaurants, swimming pools, ski slopes, and other facilities that would accommodate up to fourteen thousand visitors daily.

Representatives of the Sierra Club objected to the plans. They favored maintaining Mineral King as an undeveloped wilderness area. Failing in its earlier efforts to convince the Forest Service to stop development, the Sierra Club filed suit in federal court seeking an injunction to prevent the commercial development of Mineral King Valley.

This case raises many of the most significant ethical issues concerning business, economics, and the environment. Consider first the thinking of the Forest Service. As public servants in a democratic society, the Forest Service sought a decision that would do the most good for society. But how to decide this? How does one measure what the public most wants when representatives of various public interests (the Sierra Club, Walt Disney) make conflicting demands? One very common answer, the answer suggested by market economics and the one presumably adopted by the Forest Service, is to determine what the public wants by looking to see what the public is willing to pay for. In effect, this is what the Forest Service did when it began accepting bids from private developers.

Walt Disney Enterprises was able to bid most for the right to develop this land because they believed (as did the financial institutions who would be loaning them the money) that they would be able to pay this price and still earn enough from this project to repay their loans and make a profit. They would be capable of doing all this, of course, because many people would be willing to pay large sums of money to visit a Disney ski resort high up in the picturesque Sierra Nevadas.

The Sierra Club was unable to compete with Disney in the bidding (they did not take part in the bidding but, presumably, could have). Although the Sierra Club does represent the interests of many citizens, apparently these people are unwilling to

pay as much as Disney, either because they value wilderness less or because there are so few of them. Nor could the Sierra Club raise financing for their purchase as did Disney since there is little reason to believe that they could earn enough from their use of Mineral King to repay the loan. Again, the American people seem willing to pay significantly more for a ski resort than for the opportunity to explore an undeveloped mountain valley.

Over time, the demand for undeveloped wilderness areas will increase as they are turned into ski resorts to meet this demand. As the supply of wilderness areas decrease, the demand increases and the price that people are willing to pay rises. As the supply of ski resorts increases, the demand will decrease and the price will come down. Eventually, the market will reach a point of equilibrium between ski resorts and wilderness areas, and the American people will get exactly as much of each as they demand. Thus, in one view, the Forest Service fulfilled its responsibilities when it awarded Mineral King Valley to the highest bidder. In effect, the Forest Service let the American people decide for themselves what they most wanted to do with their own land.

A second major issue arising out of this case concerns legal "standing." "Standing to sue" is the first legal requirement that an individual must meet in order to be recognized by a court. Standing establishes the right of the individual to seek legal relief by demonstrating that this person has some actual interest at stake. In many environmental cases, standing can be established straightforwardly. A person who lives downstream from a factory that is discharging toxic wastes into a waterway can establish standing by showing that she is being harmed by that discharge. However, in cases involving conservation of natural resources, standing is less clear.

In the Mineral King Valley case, the Sierra Club had to establish two facts to demonstrate standing: (a) that some legally recognized injury would occur unless the injunction was issued; (b) that the Sierra Club would be the victim of that injury. In this case, the majority of the Supreme Court agreed that destruction of the aesthetic and ecological well-being of the valley was, like an economic harm, deserving of legal recognition as an "injury" requiring redress. Thus, the Court seemed to place aesthetic and ecological harms on a par with economic harms. However, the majority concluded that the

Sierra Club failed to prove that its members were the victims of that harm.

In a dissenting opinion, Justice William O. Douglas argued that the legal concept of "standing" was too narrow. Douglas believed that the courts should allow natural objects themselves to have legal standing. On this view, the Sierra Club would be acting, not on behalf of its members, but on behalf of the valleys, meadows, rivers, trees, and even the clean air that would be harmed by development. In speaking of the valley, Douglas claimed that "those who hike it, fish it, hunt it, camp in it, frequent it, or visit it merely to sit in solitude and wonderment are legitimate spokesmen for it."

This case inspired law professor Christopher Stone to develop these ideas in his book *Should Trees Have Standing?* In this book, Stone offers a reasoned defense of the view that natural things such as trees, mountains, and ecosystems should be granted legal standing. Excerpts from that book are reprinted in this chapter.

In light of increasing public pressure and increasing costs, Disney Enterprises withdrew their plan to develop Mineral King Valley.

- Did the Forest Service reasonably represent the interests of the American people by looking to the market to determine the appropriate use of Mineral King Valley?
- If aesthetic and ecological values are to be given standing, how are they to be measured or objectively determined?
- Should trees and other natural objects have legal standing? Should they have moral standing? If a corporation is a legal person, why not rivers?
- If Disney succeeded in developing Mineral King into a ski resort, would you be inclined to visit? If the property remained undeveloped, would you visit? Which would you be willing to pay more for? Is willingness to pay an accurate measure of your values?
- Why assume that environmental groups like the Sierra Club should represent the interests of natural objects? Might not a lumber company or a carpenters' union claim that their interest in managing the forests and harvesting trees should give them standing? Who speaks for the trees?

PEOPLE OR PENGUINS: THE CASE FOR OPTIMAL POLLUTION
William F. Baxter

I start with the modest proposition that, in dealing with pollution, or indeed with any problem, it is helpful to know what one is attempting to accomplish. Agreement on how and whether to pursue a particular objective, such as pollution control, is not possible unless some more general objective has been identified and stated with reasonable precision. We talk loosely of having clean air and clean water, of preserving our wilderness areas, and so forth. But none of these is a sufficiently general objective: each is more accurately viewed as a means rather than as an end.

With regard to clean air, for example, one may ask, "how clean?" and "what does clean mean?" It is even reasonable to ask, "why have clean air?" Each of these questions is an implicit demand that a more general community goal be stated—a goal

From William F. Baxter, *People or Penguins: The Case for Optimal Pollution* © 1974 Columbia University Press. Reprinted with permission of the publisher.

sufficiently general in its scope and enjoying sufficiently general assent among the community of actors that such "why" questions no longer seem admissible with respect to that goal.

If, for example, one states as a goal the proposition that "every person should be free to do whatever he wishes in contexts where his actions do not interfere with the interests of other human beings," the speaker is unlikely to be met with a response of "why." The goal may be criticized as uncertain in its implications or difficult to implement, but it is so basic a tenet of our civilization—it reflects a cultural value so broadly shared, at least in the abstract—that the question "why" is seen as impertinent or imponderable or both.

I do not mean to suggest that everyone would agree with the "spheres of freedom" objective just stated. Still less do I mean to suggest that a society could subscribe to four or five such general objectives that would be adequate in their coverage to serve as testing criteria by which all other disagreements might be measured. One difficulty in the attempt to construct such a list is that each new goal added will conflict, in certain applications, with each prior goal listed; and thus each goal serves as a limited qualification on prior goals.

Without any expectation of obtaining unanimous consent to them, let me set forth four goals that I generally use as ultimate testing criteria in attempting to frame solutions to problems of human organization. My position regarding pollution stems from these four criteria. If the criteria appeal to you and any part of what appears hereafter does not, our disagreement will have a helpful focus: which of us is correct, analytically, in supposing that his position on pollution would better serve these general goals. If the criteria do not seem acceptable to you, then it is to be expected that our more particular judgments will differ, and the task will then be yours to identify the basic set of criteria upon which your particular judgments rest.

My criteria are as follows:

1. The spheres of freedom criterion stated above.

2. Waste is a bad thing. The dominant feature of human existence is scarcity—our available resources, our aggregate labors, and our skill in employing both have always been, and will continue for some time to be, inadequate to yield to every man all the tangible and intangible satisfactions he would like to have. Hence, none of those resources, or labors, or skills, should be wasted—that is, employed so as to yield less than they might yield in human satisfactions.

3. Every human being should be regarded as an end rather than as a means to be used for the betterment of another. Each should be afforded dignity and regarded as having an absolute claim to an evenhanded application of such rules as the community may adopt for its governance.

4. Both the incentive and the opportunity to improve his share of satisfactions should be preserved to every individual. Preservation of incentive is dictated by the "no-waste" criterion and enjoins against the continuous, totally egalitarian redistribution of satisfactions, or wealth; but subject to that constraint, everyone should receive, by continuous redistribution if necessary, some minimal share of aggregate wealth so as to avoid a level of privation from which the opportunity to improve his situation becomes illusory.

The relationship of these highly general goals to the more specific environmental issues at hand may not be readily apparent, and I am not yet ready to demonstrate their pervasive implications. But let me give one indication of their implications. Recently scientists have informed us that use of DDT in food production is causing damage to the penguin population. For the present purposes let us accept that assertion as an indisputable scientific fact. The scientific fact is often asserted as if the correct implication—that we must stop agricultural use of DDT—followed from the mere statement of the fact of penguin damage. But plainly it does not follow if my criteria are employed.

My criteria are oriented to people, not penguins. Damage to penguins, or sugar pines, or geological marvels is, without more, simply irrelevant. One must go further, by my criteria, and say: Penguins are important because people enjoy seeing them walk about rocks; and furthermore, the well-being of people would be less impaired by halting use of DDT than by giving up penguins. In short, my observations about environmental problems will be people-oriented, as are my criteria. I have no interest in preserving penguins for their own sake.

It may be said by way of objection to this position, that it is very selfish of people to act as if each person represented one unit or importance and nothing else was of any importance. It is undeniably selfish. Nevertheless I think it is the only tenable starting place for analysis for several reasons. First, no other position corresponds to the way most people really think and act—i.e., corresponds to reality.

Second, this attitude does not portend any massive destruction of nonhuman flora and fauna, for people depend on them in many obvious ways, and they will be preserved because and to the degree that humans do depend on them.

Third, what is good for humans is, in many respects, good for penguins and pine trees—clean air for example. So that humans are, in these respects, surrogates for plant and animal life.

Fourth, I do not know how we could administer any other system. Our decisions are either private or collective. Insofar as Mr. Jones is free to act privately, he may give such preferences as he wishes to other forms of life: he may feed birds in winter and do with less himself, and he may even decline to resist an advancing polar bear on the ground that the bear's appetite is more important than those portions of himself that the bear may choose to eat. In short my basic premise does not rule out private altruism to competing life-forms. It does rule out, however, Mr. Jones' inclination to feed Mr. Smith to the bear, however hungry the bear, however despicable Mr. Smith.

Insofar as we act collectively on the other hand, only humans can be afforded an opportunity to participate in the collective decisions. Penguins cannot vote now and are unlikely subjects for the franchise—pine trees more unlikely still. Again each individual is free to cast his vote so as to bene-fit sugar pines if that is his inclination. But many of the more extreme assertions that one hears from some conservationists amount to tacit assertions that they are specially appointed representatives of sugar pines, and hence that their preferences should be weighted more heavily than the preferences of other humans who do not enjoy equal rapport with "nature." The simplistic assertion that agricultural use of DDT must stop at once because it is harmful to penguins is of that type.

Fifth, if polar bears or pine trees or penguins, like men, are to be regarded as ends rather than means, if they are to count in our calculus of social organization, someone must tell me how much each one counts, and someone must tell me how these life-forms are to be permitted to express their preferences, for I do not know either answer. If the answer is that certain people are to hold their prox-ies, then I want to know how those proxy-holders are to be selected: self-appointment does not seem workable to me.

Sixth, and by way of summary of all the fore-going, let me point out that the set of environmen-tal issues under discussion—although they raise very complex technical questions of how to achieve any objective—ultimately raise a normative question: what *ought* we to do. Questions of *ought* are unique to the human mind and world—they are meaningless as applied to a nonhuman situation.

I reject the proposition that we *ought* to respect the "balance of nature" or to "preserve the envi-ronment" unless the reason for doing so, express or implied, is the benefit of man.

I reject the idea that there is a "right" or "morally correct" state of nature to which we should return. The word "nature" has no norma-tive connotation. Was it "right" or "wrong" for the earth's crust to heave in contortion and create mountains and seas? Was it "right" for the first amphibian to crawl up out of the primordial ooze? Was it "wrong" for plants to reproduce themselves and alter the atmospheric composition in favor of oxygen? For animals to alter the atmosphere in favor of carbon dioxide both by breathing oxygen and eating plants? No answers can be given to these questions because they are meaningless questions.

All this may seem obvious to the point of being tedious, but much of the present controversy over environment and pollution rests on tacit normative assumptions about just such nonnormative phe-nomena: that it is "wrong" to impair penguins with DDT, but not to slaughter cattle for prime rib roasts. That it is wrong to kill stands of sugar pines with industrial fumes, but not to cut sugar pines and build housing for the poor. Every man is enti-tled to his own preferred definition of Walden Pond, but there is no definition that has any moral superiority over another, except by reference to the selfish needs of the human race.

From the fact that there is no normative defini-tion of the natural state, it follows that there is no normative definition of clean air or pure water— hence no definition of polluted air—or of pollu-tion—except by reference to the needs of man. The "right" composition of the atmosphere is one which has some dust in it and some lead in it and some hydrogen sulfide in it—just those amounts that attend a sensibly organized society thoughtfully and knowledgeably pursuing the greatest possible satisfaction for its human members.

The first and most fundamental step toward solution of our environmental problems is a clear recognition that our objective is not pure air or water but rather some optimal state of pollution. That step immediately suggests the question: How do we define and attain the level of pollution that will yield the maximum possible amount of human satisfaction?

Low levels of pollution contribute to human satisfaction but so do food and shelter and education and music. To attain ever lower levels of pollution, we must pay the cost of having less of these other things. I contrast that view of the cost of pollution control with the more popular statement that pollution control will "cost" very large numbers of dollars. The popular statement is true in some senses, false in others; sorting out the true and false senses is of some importance. The first step in that sorting process is to achieve a clear understanding of the difference between dollars and resources. Resources are the wealth of our nation; dollars are merely claim checks upon those resources. Resources are of vital importance; dollars are comparatively trivial.

Four categories of resources are sufficient for our purposes: At any given time a nation, or a planet if you prefer, has a stock of labor, of technological skill, of capital goods, and of natural resources (such as mineral deposits, timber, water, land, etc.). These resources can be used in various combinations to yield goods and services of all kinds—in some limited quantity. The quantity will be larger if they are combined efficiently, smaller if combined inefficiently. But in either event the resource stock is limited, the goods and services that they can be made to yield are limited; even the most efficient use of them will yield less than our population, in the aggregate, would like to have.

If one considers building a new dam, it is appropriate to say that it will be costly in the sense that it will require x hours of labor, y tons of steel and concrete, and z amount of capital goods. If these resources are devoted to the dam, then they cannot be used to build hospitals, fishing rods, schools, or electric can openers. That is the meaningful sense in which the dam is costly.

Quite apart from the very important question of how wisely we can combine our resources to produce goods and services, is the very different question of how they get distributed—who gets how many goods? Dollars constitute the claim checks which are distributed among people and which control their share of national output. Dollars are nearly valueless pieces of paper except to the extent that they do represent claim checks to some fraction of the output of goods and services. Viewed as claim checks, all the dollars outstanding during any period of time are worth, in the aggregate, the goods and services that are available to be

claimed with them during that period—neither more nor less.

It is far easier to increase the supply of dollars than to increase the production of goods and services—printing dollars is easy. But printing more dollars doesn't help because each dollar then simply becomes a claim to fewer goods, i.e., becomes worth less.

The point is this: many people fall into error upon hearing the statement that the decision to build a dam, or to clean up a river, will cost $X million. It is regrettably easy to say: "It's only money. This is a wealthy country, and we have lots of money." But you cannot build a dam or clean a river with $X million—unless you also have a match, you can't even make a fire. One builds a dam or cleans a river by diverting labor and steel and trucks and factories from making one kind of goods to making another. The cost in dollars is merely a shorthand way of describing the extent of the diversion necessary. If we build a dam for $X million, then we must recognize that we will have $X million less housing and food and medical care and electric can openers as a result.

Similarly, the costs of controlling pollution are best expressed in terms of the other goods we will have to give up to do the job. This is not to say the job should not be done. Badly as we need more housing, more medical care, and more can openers, and more symphony orchestras, we could do with somewhat less of them, in my judgment at least, in exchange for somewhat cleaner air and rivers. But that is the nature of the trade-off, and analysis of the problem is advanced if that unpleasant reality is kept in mind. Once the trade-off relationship is clearly perceived, it is possible to state in a very general way what the optimal level of pollution is. I would state it as follows:

People enjoy watching penguins. They enjoy relatively clean air and smog-free vistas. Their health is improved by relatively clean water and air. Each of these benefits is a type of good or service. As a society we would be well advised to give up one washing machine if the resources that would have gone into that washing machine can yield greater human satisfaction when diverted into pollution control. We should give up one hospital if the resources thereby freed would yield more human satisfaction when devoted to elimination of noise in our cities. And so on, trade-off by trade-off, we should divert our productive capacities from the production of existing goods and services to the production of a cleaner, quieter, more pastoral nation up to—and no further than—the point at which we value more highly the next washing machine or hospital that we would have to do without than we value the next unit of environmental improvement that the diverted resources would create.

Now this proposition seems to me unassailable but so general and abstract as to be unhelpful—at least unadministerable in the form stated. It assumes

we can measure in some way the incremental units of human satisfaction yielded by very different types of goods. The proposition must remain a pious abstraction until I can explain how this measurement process can occur. In subsequent chapters I will attempt to show that we can do this—in some contexts with great precision and in other contexts only by rough approximation. But I insist that the proposition stated describes the result for which we should be striving—and again, that it is always useful to know what your target is even if your weapons are too crude to score a bull's eye.

AT THE SHRINE OF OUR LADY OF FATIMA *OR* WHY POLITICAL QUESTIONS ARE NOT ALL ECONOMIC
Mark Sagoff

Lewiston, New York, a well-to-do community near Buffalo, is the site of the Lake Ontario Ordinance Works, where years ago the federal government disposed of the residues of the Manhattan Project. These radioactive wastes are buried but are not forgotten by the residents who say that when the wind is southerly, radon gas blows through the town. Several parents at a recent Lewiston conference I attended described their terror on learning that cases of leukemia had been found among area children. They feared for their own lives as well. On the other side of the table, officials from New York State and from local corporations replied that these fears were ungrounded. People who smoke, they said, take greater risks than people who live close to waste disposal sites. One speaker talked in terms of "rational methodologies of decision making." This aggravated the parents' rage and frustration.

The speaker suggested that the townspeople, were they to make their decision in a free market and if they knew the scientific facts, would choose to live near the hazardous waste facility. He told me later they were irrational—"neurotic"—because they refused to recognize or to act upon their own

interests. The residents of Lewiston were unimpressed with his analysis of their "willingness to pay" to avoid this risk or that. They did not see what risk-benefit analysis had to do with the issues they raised.

If you take the Military Highway (as I did) from Buffalo to Lewiston, you will pass through a formidable wasteland. Landfills stretch in all directions and enormous trucks—tiny in that landscape—incessantly deposit sludge which great bulldozers then push into the ground. These machines are the only signs of life, for in the miasma that hangs in the air, no birds, not even scavengers, are seen. Along colossal power lines which crisscross this dismal land, the dynamos at Niagara send electric power south, where factories have fled, leaving their remains to decay. To drive along this road is to feel, oddly, the mystery and awe one experiences in the presence of so much power and decadence.

Henry Adams had a similar response to the dynamos on display at the Paris Exposition of 1900. To him, "the dynamo became a symbol of infinity."[1] To Adams, the dynamo functioned as the modern equivalent of the Virgin, that is, the center and focus of power. "Before the end, one began to pray to it; inherited instinct taught the natural expression of men before silent and infinite force."[2]

From *Arizona Law Review* 23 (1981): 1283–1298. Reprinted by permission of the author and the *Arizona Law Review*.

Adams asks in his essay "The Dynamo and the Virgin" how the products of modern industrial civilization will compare with those of the religious culture of the Middle Ages. If he could see the landfills and hazardous waste facilities bordering the power stations and honeymoon hotels of Niagara Falls he would know the answer. He would understand what happens when efficiency replaces infinity as the central conception of value. The dynamos at Niagara will not produce another Mont-Saint-Michel. "All the steam in the world," Adams wrote, "could not, like the Virgin, build Chartres."[3]

At the Shrine of Our Lady of Fatima, on a plateau north of the Military Highway, a larger than life sculpture of Mary looks into the chemical air. The original of this shrine stands in central Portugal where in May 1917, three children said they saw a Lady, brighter than the sun, raised on a cloud in an evergreen tree.[4] Five months later, on a wet and chilly October day, the Lady again appeared, this time before a large crowd. Some who were skeptical did not see the miracle. Others in the crowd reported, however, that "the sun appeared and seemed to tremble, rotate violently and fall, dancing over the heads of the throng."[5]

The Shrine was empty when I visited it. The cult of Our Lady of Fatima, I imagine, has only a few devotees. The cult of Pareto optimality, however, has many. Where some people see only environmental devastation, its devotees perceive efficiency, utility, and the maximization of wealth. They see the satisfaction of wants. They envision the good life. As I looked over the smudged and ruined terrain I tried to share that vision. I hoped that Our Lady of Fatima, worker of miracles, might serve, at least for the moment, as the Patroness of cost-benefit analysis. I thought of all the wants and needs that are satisfied in a landscape of honeymoon cottages, commercial strips, and dumps for hazardous waste. I saw the miracle of efficiency. The prospect, however, looked only darker in that light.

POLITICAL AND ECONOMIC DECISION MAKING

This essay concerns the economic decisions we make about the environment. It also concerns our political decisions about the environment. Some

people have suggested that ideally these should be the same, that all environmental problems are problems in distribution. According to this view, there is an environmental problem only when some resource is not allocated in equitable and efficient ways.[6]

This approach to environmental policy is pitched entirely at the level of the consumer. It is his or her values that count, and the measure of these values is the individual's willingness to pay. The problem of justice or fairness in society becomes, then, the problem of distributing goods and services so that more people get more of what they want to buy: a condo on the beach, a snowmobile for the mountains, a tank full of gas, a day of labor. The only values we have, according to this view, are those that a market can price.[7]

How much do you value open space, a stand of trees, an "unspoiled" landscape? Fifty dollars? A hundred? A thousand? This is one way to measure value. You could compare the amount consumers would pay for a townhouse or coal or a landfill to the amount they would pay to preserve an area in its "natural" state. If users would pay more for the land with the house, the coal mine, or the landfill, than without—less construction and other costs of development—then the efficient thing to do is to improve the land and thus increase its value. That is why we have so many tract developments, pizza stands, and gas stations. How much did you spend last year to preserve open space? How much for pizza and gas? "In principle, the ultimate measure of environmental quality," as one basic text assures us, "is the value people place on these…services or their *willingness to pay*."[8]

Willingness to pay: what is wrong with that? The rub is this: not all of us think of ourselves simply as *consumers*. Many of us regard ourselves *as citizens* as well. We act as consumers to get what we want *for ourselves*. We act as citizens to achieve what we think is right or best *for the community*. The question arises, then, whether what we want for ourselves individually as consumers is consistent with the goals we would set for ourselves collectively as citizens. Would I vote for the sort of things I shop for? Are my preferences as a consumer consistent with my judgments as a citizen?

They are not. I am schizophrenic. Last year, I fixed a couple of tickets and was happy to do so since I saved $50. Yet, at election time, I helped to vote the corrupt judge out of office. I speed on the highway; yet I want the police to enforce laws against speeding. I used to buy mixers in returnable bottles—but who can bother to return them? I buy only disposables now, but to soothe my conscience, I urge my state senator to outlaw one-way containers. I love my car; I hate the bus. Yet I vote for candidates who promise to tax gasoline to pay for public transportation. And of course I applaud the Endangered Species Act, although I have no earthly use for the Colorado squawfish or the Indiana bat. I support almost any political cause that I think will defeat my consumer interests. This is because I have contempt for—although I act upon—those interests. I have an "Ecology Now" sticker on a car that leaks oil everywhere it's parked.

The distinction between consumer and citizen preferences has long vexed the theory of public finance. Should the public economy serve the same goals as the household economy? May it serve, instead, goals emerging from our association as citizens? The question asks if we may collectively strive for and achieve only those items we individually compete for and consume. Should we aspire, instead, to public goals we may legislate as a nation?

The problem, insofar as it concerns public finance, is stated as follows by R. A. Musgrave, who reports a conversation he had with Gerhard Colm:

> He [Colm] holds that the individual voter dealing with political issues has a frame of reference quite distinct from that which underlies his allocation of income as a consumer. In the latter situation the voter acts as a private individual determined by self-interest and deals with his personal wants; in the former, he acts as a political being guided by his image of a good society. The two, Colm holds, are different things.[9]

Are these two different things? Stephen Marglin suggests that they are. He writes:

> The preferences that govern one's unilateral market actions no longer govern his actions when the form of reference is shifted from the market to the political arena. The Economic Man and the Citizen are for all intents and purposes two different individuals. It is not a question, therefore, of rejecting individual...

preference maps; it is, rather, that market and political preference maps are inconsistent.[10]

Marglin observes that if this were true, social choices optimal under one set of preferences would not be optimal under another. What, then, is the meaning of "optimality"? He notices that if we take a person's true preferences to be those expressed in the market, we may neglect or reject the preferences that person reveals in advocating a political cause or position. "One might argue on welfare grounds," Marglin speculates, "for authoritarian rejection of individuals' politically revealed preferences in favor of their market revealed preferences!"[11]

COST-BENEFIT ANALYSIS VS. REGULATION

On February 19, 1981, President Reagan published Executive Order 12,291[12] requiring all administrative agencies and departments to support every new major regulation with a cost-benefit analysis establishing that the benefits of the regulation to society outweigh its costs. The order directs the Office of Management and Budget (OMB) to review every such regulation on the basis of the adequacy of the cost-benefit analysis supporting it. This is a departure from tradition. Historically, regulations have been reviewed not by OMB but by the courts on the basis of the relation of the regulation to authorizing legislation, not to cost-benefit analysis.

A month earlier, in January 1981, the Supreme Court heard lawyers for the American Textile Manufacturers Institute argue against a proposed Occupational Safety and Health Administration (OSHA) regulation which would have severely restricted the acceptable levels of cotton dust in textile plants.[13] The lawyers for industry argued that the benefits of the regulation would not equal the costs.[14] The lawyers for the government contended that the law required the tough standard.[15] OSHA. acting consistently with Executive Order 12,291, asked the Court not to decide the cotton dust case in order to give the agency time to complete the cost-benefit analysis required by the textile industry.[16] The Court declined to accept OSHA's request and handed down its opinion in *American Textile Manufacturers v. Donovan* on June 17, 1981.[17]

The Supreme Court, in a 5–3 decision, found that the actions of regulatory agencies which conform to the OSHA law need not be supported by cost-benefit analysis.[18] In addition, the Court asserted that Congress, in writing a statute, rather than the agencies in applying it, has the primary responsibility for balancing benefits and costs.[19] The Court said:

> When Congress passed the Occupational Health and Safety Act in 1970, it chose to place pre-eminent value on assuring employees a safe and healthful working environment, limited only by the feasibility of achieving such an environment. We must measure the validity of the Secretary's actions against the requirements of that Act.[20]

The opinion upheld the finding of the District of Columbia Court of Appeals that "Congress itself struck the balance between costs and benefits in the mandate to the agency."[21]

The Appeals Court opinion in *American Textile Manufacturers v. Donovan* supports the principle that legislatures are not necessarily bound to a particular conception of regulatory policy. Agencies that apply the law therefore may not need to justify on cost-benefit grounds the standards they set. These standards may conflict with the goal of efficiency and still express our political will as a nation. That is, they may reflect not the personal choices of self-interested individuals, but the collective judgments we make on historical, cultural, aesthetic, moral, and ideological grounds.[22]

The appeal of the Reagan Administration to cost-benefit analysis, however, may arise more from political than economic considerations. The intention, seen in the most favorable light, may not be to replace political or ideological goals with economic ones, but to make economic goals more apparent in regulation. This is not to say that Congress should function to reveal a collective willingness-to-pay just as markets reveal an individual willingness-to-pay. It is to suggest that Congress should do more to balance economic with ideological, aesthetic, and moral goals. To think that environmental or worker safety policy can be based exclusively on aspiration for a "natural" and "safe" world is as foolish as to hold that environmental law can be reduced to cost-benefit accounting. The more we move to one extreme, as I found in Lewiston, the more likely we are to hear from the other.

SUBSTITUTING EFFICIENCY FOR SAFETY

The labor unions won an important political victory when Congress passed the Occupational Safety and Health Act of 1970.[23] That Act, among other things, severely restricts worker exposure to toxic substances. It instructs the Secretary of Labor to set "the standard which most adequately assures, to the extent feasible...that no employee will suffer material impairment of health or functional capacity even if such employee has regular exposure to the hazard...for the period of his working life."[24]

Pursuant to this law, the Secretary of Labor in 1977 reduced from ten to one part per million (ppm) the permissible ambient exposure level for benzene, a carcinogen for which no safe threshold is known. The American Petroleum Institute thereupon challenged the new standard in court.[25] It argued, with much evidence in its favor, that the benefits (to workers) of the one ppm standard did not equal the costs (to industry).[26] The standard therefore did not appear to be a rational response to a market failure in that it did not strike an efficient balance between the interests of workers in safety and the interests of industry and consumers in keeping prices down.

The Secretary of Labor defended the tough safety standard on the ground that the law demanded it.[27] An efficient standard might have required safety until it cost industry more to prevent a risk than it cost workers to accept it. Had Congress adopted this vision of public policy—one which can be found in many economics texts[28]—it would have treated workers not as ends-in-themselves but as means for the production of overall utility. This, as the Secretary saw it, was what Congress refused to do.[29]

The United States Court of Appeals for the Fifth Circuit agreed with the American Petroleum Institute and invalidated the one ppm benzene standard.[30] On July 2, 1980, the Supreme Court affirmed the decision in *American Petroleum Institute v. Marshal*[31] and remanded the benzene standard back to OSHA for revision. The narrowly based Supreme Court decision was divided over the role economic considerations should play in judicial review. Justice Marshall, joined in dissent by three other justices, argued that the Court had undone on the basis of its own theory of regulatory policy an act of Congress inconsistent with that theory.[32] He concluded that the plurality decision of the Court "requires the American worker to return to the political arena to win a victory that he won before in 1970."[33]

The decision of the Supreme Court is important not because of its consequences, which are likely to be minimal, but because of the fascinating questions it raises. Shall the courts uphold only those political decisions that can be defended on economic grounds? Shall we allow democracy only to the extent that it can be construed either as a rational response to a market failure or as an attempt to redistribute wealth? Should the courts say that a regulation is not "feasible" or "reasonable"— terms that occur in the OSHA law[34]—unless it is supported by a cost-benefit analysis?

The problem is this: An efficiency criterion, as it is used to evaluate public policy, assumes that the goals of our society are contained in the preferences individuals reveal or would reveal in markets. Such an approach may appear attractive, even just, because it treats everyone as equal, at least theoretically, by according to each person's preferences the same respect and concern. To treat a person with respect, however, is also to listen and to respond intelligently to his or her views and opinions. This is not the same thing as to ask how much he or she is willing to pay for them. The cost-benefit analyst does not ask economists how much they are willing to pay for what they believe, that is, that the workplace and the environment should be made efficient. Why, then, does the analyst ask workers, environmentalists, and others how much they are willing to pay for what they believe is right? Are economists the only ones who can back their ideas with reasons while the rest of us can only pay a price? The cost-benefit approach treats people as of equal worth because it treats them as of no worth, but only as places or channels at which willingness to pay is found.[35]

LIBERTY: ANCIENT AND MODERN

When efficiency is the criterion of public safety and health, one tends to conceive of social relations on the model of a market, ignoring competing visions of what we as a society should be like. Yet it is obvious that there are competing conceptions of what we should be as a society. There are some who believe on principle that worker safety and environmental quality ought to be protected only insofar as the benefits of protection balance the costs. On the other hand, people argue—also on principle—that neither worker safety nor environmental quality should be treated merely as a commodity to be traded at the margin for other commodities, but rather each should be valued for its own sake. The conflict between these two principles is logical or moral, to be resolved by argument or debate. The question whether cost-benefit analysis should play a decisive role in policy making is not to be decided by cost-benefit analysis. A contradiction between principles—between contending visions of the good society—cannot be settled by asking how much partisans are willing to pay for their beliefs.

The role of the *legislator,* the political role, may be more important to the individual than the role of *consumer.* The person, in other words, is not to be treated merely as a bundle of preferences to be juggled in cost-benefit analyses. The individual is to be respected as an advocate of ideas which are to be judged according to the reasons for them. If health and environmental statutes reflect a vision of society as something other than a market by requiring protections beyond what are efficient, then this may express not legislative ineptitude but legislative responsiveness to public values. To deny this vision because it is economically inefficient is simply to replace it with another vision. It is to insist that the ideas of the citizen be sacrificed to the psychology of the consumer.

We hear on all sides that government is routinized, mechanical, entrenched, and bureaucratized; the jargon alone is enough to dissuade the most mettlesome meddler. Who can make a difference? It is plain that for many of us the idea of a national political community has an abstract and suppositious quality. We have only our private conceptions of the good, if no way exists to arrive at a public one. This is only to note the continuation, in our time, of the trend Benjamin Constant described in the essay *De la liberté des anciens comparée à celle des modernes.*[36] Constant observes that the modern world, as opposed to the ancient, emphasizes civil over political liberties, the rights of privacy and property over those of community and participation. "Lost in the multitude," Constant writes, "'the individual rarely perceives the influence that he exercises," and, therefore, must be content with "the peaceful enjoyment of private independence."[37] The individual asks only to be protected by laws common to all in his pursuit of his own self-interest. The citizen has been replaced by the consumer; the tradition of Rousseau has been supplanted by that of Locke and Mill.

Nowhere are the rights of the moderns, particularly the rights of privacy and property, less helpful than in the area of the natural environment. Here the values we wish to protect—cultural, historical, aesthetic, and moral—are public values. They depend not so much upon what each person wants individually as upon what he or she thinks is right for the community. We refuse to regard worker health and safety as commodities; we regulate hazards as a matter of right. Likewise, we refuse to treat environmental resources simply as public goods in the economist's sense. Instead, we prevent significant deterioration of air quality not only as a matter of individual self-interest but also as a matter of collective self-respect. How shall we balance efficiency against moral, cultural, and aesthetic values in policy for the workplace and the environment? No better way has been devised to do this than by legislative debate ending in a vote. This is very different from a cost-benefit analysis terminating in a bottom line.

VALUES ARE NOT SUBJECTIVE

It is the characteristic of cost-benefit analysis that it treats all value judgments other than those made on its behalf as nothing but statements of preference, attitude, or emotion, insofar as they are value judgments. The cost-benefit analyst regards as true the judgment that we should maximize efficiency or wealth. The analyst believes that this view can be backed by reasons,[38] but does not regard it as a preference or want for which he or she must be willing to pay. The cost-benefit analyst tends to treat all other normative views and recommendations as if they were nothing but subjective reports of mental states. The analyst supposes in all such cases that "this is right" and "this is what we ought to do" are equivalent to "I want this" and "this is what I prefer." Value judgments are beyond criti-

cism if, indeed, they are nothing but expressions of personal preference; they are incorrigible since every person is in the best position to know what he or she wants. All valuation, according to this approach, happens *in foro interno;* debate *in foro publico* has no point. With this approach, the reasons that people give for their views do not count; what does count is how much they are willing to pay to satisfy their wants. Those who are willing to pay the most, for all intents and purposes, have the right view; theirs is the more informed opinion, the better aesthetic judgment, and the deeper moral insight.

The assumption that valuation is subjective, that judgments of good and evil are nothing but expressions of desire and aversion, is not unique to economic theory.[39] There are psychotherapists— Carl Rogers is an example—who likewise deny the objectivity or cognitivity of valuation.[40] For Rogers, there is only one criterion of worth: it lies in "the subjective world of the individual. Only he knows it fully."[41] The therapist shows his or her client that a "value system is not necessarily something imposed from without, but is something experienced."[42] Therapy succeeds when the client "perceives himself in such a way that no self-experience can be discriminated as more or less worthy of positive self-regard than any other...."[43] The client then "tends to place the basis of standards within himself, recognizing that the 'goodness' or 'badness' of any experience or perceptual object is not something inherent in that object, but is a value placed in it by himself."[44]

Rogers points out that "some clients make strenuous efforts to have the therapist exercise the valuing function, so as to provide them with guides for action."[45] The therapist, however, "consistently keeps the locus of evaluation with the client."[46] As long as the therapist refuses to "exercise the valuing function" and as long as he or she practices an "unconditional positive regard"[47] for all the affective states of the client, then the therapist remains neutral among the client's values or "sensory and visceral experiences."[48] The role of the therapist is legitimate, Rogers suggests, because of this value neutrality. The therapist accepts all felt preferences as valid and imposes none on the client.

Economists likewise argue that their role as policy makers is legitimate because they are neutral among competing values in the client society. The political economist, according to James Buchanan, "is or should be ethically neutral: the indicated results are influenced by his own value scale only insofar as this reflects his membership in a larger group."[49] The economist might be most confident of the impartiality of his or her policy recommendations if he or she could derive them formally or mathematically from individual preferences. If theoretical difficulties make such a social welfare function impossible,[50] however, the next best thing, to preserve neutrality, is to let markets function to transform individual preference orderings into a collective ordering of social states. The analyst is able then to base policy on preferences that exist in society and are not necessarily his own.

Economists have used this impartial approach to offer solutions to many significant social problems, for example, the controversy over abortion. An economist argues that "there is an optimal number of abortions, just as there is an optimal level of pollution, or purity....Those who oppose abortion could eliminate it entirely, if their intensity of feeling were so strong as to lead to payments that were greater at the margin than the price anyone would pay to have an abortion."[51] Likewise, economists, in order to determine whether the war in Vietnam was justified, have estimated the willingness to pay of those who demonstrated against it.[52] Following the same line of reasoning, it should be possible to decide whether creationism should be taught in the public schools, whether black and white people should be segregated, whether the death penalty should be enforced, and whether the square root of six is three. All of these questions arguably depend upon how much people are willing to pay for their subjective preferences or wants. This is the beauty of cost-benefit analysis: no matter how relevant or irrelevant, wise or stupid, informed or uninformed, responsible or silly, defensible or indefensible wants may be, the analyst is able to derive a policy from them—a policy which is legitimate because, in theory, it treats all of these preferences as equally valid and good.

PREFERENCE OR PRINCIPLE?

In contrast, consider a Kantian conception of value.[53] The individual, for Kant, is a judge of values, not a mere haver of wants, and the individual judges not for himself or herself merely, but as a member of a relevant community or group. The central idea in a Kantian approach to ethics is that some values are more reasonable than others and therefore have a better claim upon the assent of members of the community as such.[54] The world of obligation, like the world of mathematics or the world of empirical fact, is public not private, and objective standards of argument and criticism apply. Kant recognized that values, like beliefs, are subjective states of mind which have an objective content as well. Therefore, both values and beliefs are either correct or mistaken. A value judgment is like an empirical or theoretical judgment in that it claims to be *true* not merely to be *felt*.

We have, then, two approaches to public policy before us. The first, the approach associated with normative versions of welfare economics, asserts that the only policy recommendation that can or need be defended on objective grounds is efficiency or wealth maximization. The Kantian approach, on the other hand, assumes that many policy recommendations may be justified or refuted on objective grounds. It would concede that the approach of welfare economics applies adequately to some questions, for example, those which ordinary consumer markets typically settle. How many yo-yos should be produced as compared to how many frisbees? Shall pens have black ink or blue? Matters such as these are so trivial it is plain that markets should handle them. It does not follow, however, that we should adopt a market or quasi-market approach to every public question.

A market or quasi-market approach to arithmetic, for example, is plainly inadequate. No matter how much people are willing to pay, three will never be the square root of six. Similarly, segregation is a national curse and the fact that we are willing to pay for it does not make it better, but only us worse. The case for abortion must stand on the merits; it cannot be priced at the margin. Our failures to make the right decisions in these matters are failures in arithmetic, failures in wisdom, failures in taste, failures in morality—but not market failures. There are no relevant markets which have failed.

What separates these questions from those for which markets are appropriate is that they involve matters of knowledge, wisdom, morality, and taste that admit of better or worse, right or wrong, true or false, and not mere economic optimality. Surely environmental questions—the protection of wilderness, habitats, water, land, and air as well as policy toward environmental safety and health—involve moral and aesthetic principles and not just economic ones. This is consistent, of course, with cost-effectiveness and with a sensible recognition of economic constraints.

The neutrality of the economist is legitimate if private preferences or subjective wants are the only values in question. A person should be left free to choose the color of his or her necktie or necklace, but we cannot justify a theory of public policy or private therapy on that basis. If the patient seeks moral advice or tries to find reasons to justify a choice, the therapist, according to Rogers' model, would remind him or her to trust his visceral and sensory experiences. The result of this is to deny the individual status as a cognitive being capable of responding intelligently to reasons; it reduces him or her to a bundle of affective states. What Rogers' therapist does to the patient the cost-benefit analyst, does to society as a whole. The analyst is neutral among our "values"—having first imposed a theory of what value is. This is a theory that is impartial among values and for that reason fails to treat the persons who have them with respect or concern. It does not treat them even as persons but only as locations at which wants may be found. The neutrality of economics is not a basis for its legitimacy. We recognize it as an indifference toward value—an indifference so deep, so studied, and so assured that at first one hesitates to call it by its right name.

THE CITIZEN AS JOSEPH K.

The residents of Lewiston at the conference I attended demanded to know the truth about the dangers that confronted them and the reasons for those dangers. They wanted to be convinced that the sacrifice asked of them was legitimate even if it served interests other than their own. One official from a large chemical company dumping wastes in the area told them in reply that corporations were people and that people could talk to people about their feelings, interests, and needs. This sent a shiver through the audience. Like Joseph K. in *The Trial*,[55] the residents of Lewiston asked for an ex-

planation, justice, and truth, and they were told that their wants would be taken care of. They demanded to know the reasons for what was continually happening to them. They were given a personalized response instead.

This response, that corporations are "just people serving people," is consistent with a particular view of power. This is the view that identifies power with the ability to get what one wants as an individual, that is, to satisfy one's personal preferences. When people in official positions in corporations or in the government put aside their personal interests, it would follow that they put aside their power as well. Their neutrality then justifies them in directing the resources of society in ways they determine to be best. This managerial role serves not their own interests but those of their clients. Cost-benefit analysis may be seen as a pervasive form of this paternalism. Behind this paternalism, as William Simon observes of the lawyer-client relationship, lies a theory of value that tends to personalize power. "It resists understanding power as a product of class, property, or institutions and collapses power into the personal needs and dispositions of the individuals who command and obey."[56] Once the economist, the therapist, the lawyer, or the manager abjures his own interests and acts wholly on behalf of client individuals, he appears to have no power of his own and thus justifiably manipulates and controls everything. "From this perspective it becomes difficult to distinguish the powerful from the powerless. In every case, both the exercise of power and submission to it are portrayed as a matter of personal accommodation and adjustment."[57]

The key to the personal interest or emotive theory of value, as one commentator has rightly said, "is the fact that emotivism entails the obliteration of any genuine distinction between manipulative and nonmanipulative social relations."[58] The reason is that once the affective self is made the source of all value, the public self cannot participate in the exercise of power. As Philip Reiff remarks, "the public world is constituted as one vast stranger who appears at inconvenient times and makes demands viewed as purely external and therefore with no power to elicit a moral response."[59] There is no way to distinguish the legitimate authority that public values and public law create from tyranny.[60]

"At the rate of progress since 1900," Henry Adams speculates in his *Education,* "every American who lived into the year 2000 would know how to control unlimited power."[61] Adams thought that the Dynamo would organize and release as much energy as the Virgin. Yet in the 1980s, the citizens of Lewiston, surrounded by dynamos, high tension lines, and nuclear wastes, are powerless. They do not know how to criticize power, resist power, or justify power—for to do so depends on making distinctions between good and evil, right and wrong, innocence and guilt, justice and injustice, truth and lies. These distinctions cannot be made out and have no significance within an emotive or psychological theory of value. To adopt this theory is to imagine society as a market in which individuals trade voluntarily and without coercion. No individual, no belief, no faith has authority over them. To have power to act as a nation we must be able to act, at least at times, on a public philosophy, conviction, or faith. We cannot abandon the moral function of public law. The antinomianism of cost-benefit analysis is not enough.

NOTES

The author is Director and Research Scholar, Center for Philosophy and Public Policy and Center for Environmental and Estuarine Studies (Horn Point Laboratories), University of Maryland. A.B. 1963, Harvard College; Ph.D. 1970, University of Rochester. Work on this article was supported by the National Science Foundation and National Endowment for the Humanities, Grant No. OSS 8018096. Views expressed are the author's, not necessarily those of the NSF or NEH. The author is grateful for criticism received from colleagues, especially David Luban.

1. H Adams, *The Education of Henry Adams* 380 (2d ed. 1970).

2. Id.

3. Id. at 388.

4. For an account, see generally J. Pelletier, *The Sun Danced at Fatima* (1951).

5. 5 *New Catholic Encyclopedia* 856 (1967).

6. See, e.g., W. Baxter, *People or Penguins: The Case for Optimal Pollution* ch. 1: (1974). See generally A. Freeman, R. Haveman, A. Kneese, *The Economics of Environmental Policy* (1973) [Hereinafter A. Freeman].

7. Posner makes this point well in discussing wealth maximization as an ethical concept. "The only kind of preference that counts in a system of wealth-maximization," he writes, "is...one that is backed up by money—in other words, that is registered in a market." Posner, "Utilitarianism, Economics, and Legal Theory," 8 *J. Legal Stud.* 103, 119 (1979).

8. A. Freeman, note 6 above, at 23.

9. R. Musgrave, *The Theory of Public Finance* 87–88 (1959).

10. Marglin, "The Social Rate of Discount and the Optimal Rate of Investment," 77 *Q. J. Econ.* 95, 98 (1963).

11. Id.

12. 46 Fed. Reg. 13,193 (1981). The order specifies that the cost-benefit requirement shall apply "to the extent permitted by law."

13. *American Fed'n of Labor, etc. v. Marshall,* 617 F.2d 636 (D.C. Cir. 1979), cert. granted sub nom. *American Textile Mfrs. Inst., Inc. v. Marshall,* 49 U.S.L.W. 3208 (1981).

14. 49 U.S.L.W. 3523–24.

15. Id.

16. Id.

17. *American Textile Mfrs. Inst., Inc. v. Donovan,* 49 U.S.L.W. 4720 (1981).

18. Id. at 4724–29.

19. Id. at 4726–29.

20. Id. at 4733–34.

21. Id. at 4726–29.

22. To reject cost-benefit analysis as a basis for policy making is not necessarily to reject cost-effectiveness analysis which is an altogether different thing. For this difference, see Baram, "Cost-Benefit Analysis: An Inadequate Basis for Health, Safety, and Environmental Regulatory Decisionmaking," 8 *Ecology L. Q.* 473 (1980). *"Cost-benefit analysis...* is used by the decisionmaker to establish societal goals as well as the means for achieving these goals, whereas *cost-effectiveness analysis* only compares alternative means for achieving 'given' goals." Id. at 478 (footnote omitted). In practice, regulatory uses of cost-benefit analysis stifle and obstruct the achievement of legislated health, safety, and environmental goals. Id. at 473. Further, to the extent that economic factors are permissible considerations under enabling statutes, agencies should engage in cost-effectiveness analysis, which aids in determining the least costly means to designated goals, rather than cost-benefit analysis, which improperly determines regulatory ends as well as means. Id. at 474.

23. Pub. L. No. 91–596, 84 Stat. 1596 (1970) (codified at 29 U.S.C. § § 651–678 [1970]).

24. 29 U.S.C. § 655(b)(5) (1970).

25. *American Petroleum Inst. v. Marshal.* 581 F.2d 493 (5th Cir. 1978), aff'd, 448 U.S. 607 (1980).

26. 581 F.2d at 501–05.

27. Id. at 501.

28. See, e.g., R. Posner, *Economic Analysis of Law I & II* (1973). In G. Calabresi, *The Costs of Accidents* passim (1970), the author argues that accident law balances two goals, "efficiency" and "equality" or "justice."

29. *American Petroleum Inst. v. Marshall,* 581 F.2d 493, 503–05 (5th Cir. 1978).

30. Id. at 505.

31. 448 U.S. 607 (1980).

32. Id. at 719.

33. Id.

34. 29 U.S.C. §§ 655(b)(5) & 652(8) (1975).

35. For a similar argument against utilitarianism, see Hart, "Between Utility and Rights," 79 *Colum. L. Rev.* 828, 829–31 (1979).

36. B. Constant, *de la Liberté des Anciens Comparée à Celle des Modernes* (1819).

37. "Oeuvres politiques de Benjamin Constant," 269 (C. Louandre, ed. 1874), quoted in S. Wolin, *Politics and Vision* 281 (1960).

38. There are arguments that whatever reasons may be given are not good. See generally Dworkin, "Why Efficiency?" 8 *Hofstra L. Rev.* 563 (1980); Dworkin, "Is Wealth a Value?" 9 *J. Legal Stud.* 191 (1980); Kennedy, "Cost-Benefit Analysis of Entitlement Problems: A Critique," 33 *Stan. L. Rev.* 387 (1980); Rizzo, "The Mirage of Efficiency," 8 *Hofstra L. Rev.* 641 (1980); Sagoff, "Economic Theory and Environmental Law," 79 *Mich. L. Rev.* 1393 (1981).

39. This is the emotive theory of value. For the classic statement, see C. Stevenson, *Ethics and Language* chs. 1 & 2 (144). For criticism, see Blanshard, "The New Subjectivism in Ethics," 9 *Philosophy & Phenomenological Research* 504 (1949). For a statement of the related interest theory of value, see generally R. Perry, *General Theory of Value* (1926); E. Westermarck, *Ethical Relativity* chs. 3–5 (1932). For criticisms of subjectivism in ethics and a case for the objective theory presupposed here, see generally P. Edwards, *The Logic of Moral Discourse* (1955) and W. Ross, *The Right and the Good* (1930).

40. My account is based on C. Rogers, *On Becoming a Person* (1961); C. Rogers, *Client Centered Therapy* (1965); and Rogers, "A Theory of Therapy, Personality, and Interper-

sonal Relationships, as Developed in the Client Centered Framework," 3 *Psychology: A Study of a Science* 184 (1959). For a similar account used as a critique of the lawyer-client relation, see Simon, "Homo Psychologicus: Notes on a New Legal Formalism," 32 *Stan. L. Rev.* 487 (1980).

41. Rogers, note 40 above, at 210.

42. C. Rogers, *Client Centered Therapy* 150 (1965).

43. Rogers, note 40 above, at 208.

44. C. Rogers, note 42 above, at 139.

45. Id. at 150.

46. Id.

47. Rogers, note 40 above, at 208.

48. Id. at 523–24.

49. Buchanan, "Positive Economics, Welfare Economics, and Political Economy" 2 *J. L. & Econ.* 124, 127 (1959).

50. K. Arrow, *Social Choice and Individual Values I–V* (2d ed. 1963).

51. H. Macaulay & B. Yandle, *Environmental Use and the Market* 120–21 (1978).

52. See generally Cicchetti, Freeman, Haveman, & Knetsch, "On the Economics of Mass Demonstrations: A Case Study of the November 1969 March on Washington," 61 *Am. Econ. Rev.* 719 (1971).

53. I. Kant, *Foundations of the Metaphysics of Morals* (1969). I follow the interpretation of Kantian ethics of W. Sellars, *Science and Metaphysics* ch. vii (1968) and Sellars, "On Reasoning About Values," 17 *Am. Phil. Q.* 81 (1980).

54. See A. MacIntyre, *After Virtue* 22 (1981).

55. F. Kafka, *The Trial* (rev. ed. trans. 1957). Simon applies this analogy to the lawyer-client relationship. Simon, note 40 above, at 524.

56. Simon, note 40 above, at 495.

57. Id.

58. A. MacIntyre, note 54 above, at 22.

59. P. Reiff, *The Triumph of the Therapeutic: Uses of Faith After Freud* 52 (1966).

60. That public law regimes inevitably lead to tyranny seems to be the conclusion of H. Arendt, *The Human Condition* (1958); K. Popper, *The Open Society and Its Enemies* (1966); L. Strauss, *Natural Right and History* (1953). For an important criticism of this conclusion in these authors, see generally Holmes, "Aristippus In and Out of Athens," 73 *Am. Pol. Sci. Rev.* 113 (1979).

61. H. Adams, note 1 above, at 476.

SHOULD TREES HAVE STANDING?
TOWARD LEGAL RIGHTS FOR NATURAL OBJECTS

Christopher D. Stone

INTRODUCTION: THE UNTHINKABLE

In *Descent of Man,* Darwin observes that the history of man's moral development has been a continual extension in the objects of his "social instincts and sympathies." Originally each man had regard only for himself and those of a very narrow circle about him; later, he came to regard more and more "not only the welfare, but the happiness of all his fellowmen"; then "his sympathies became more tender and widely diffused, extending to men of all races, to the imbecile, maimed, and other useless members of society, and finally to the lower animals...."[1]

The history of the law suggests a parallel development. Perhaps there never was a pure Hobbesian state of nature, in which no "rights" existed except in the vacant sense of each man's "right to self-defense." But it is not unlikely that so far as the earliest "families" (including extended kinship groups and clans) were concerned, everyone outside the family was suspect, alien, rightless.[2] And even within the family, persons we presently regard as the natural holders of at least some rights had none. Take, for example, children. We know something of the early rights-status of children from the widespread practice of infanticide—especially of the deformed and female.[3] (Senicide,[4] as among the North American Indians, was the corresponding rightlessness of the aged.)[5] Maine tells us that as late as the Patria Potestas of the Romans, the father had *jus vitae necisque*—the power of life and death—over his children. A fortiori, Maine writes, he had power of "uncontrolled corporal chastisement; he can modify their personal condition at pleasure; he can give a wife to his son; he can give his daughter in marriage; he can divorce his children of either sex; he can transfer them to another family by adoption; and he can sell them." The child was less than a person: an object, a thing.[6]

The legal rights of children have long since been recognized in principle, and are still expanding in practice. Witness, just within recent time, *In re Gault,*[7] guaranteeing basic constitutional protections to juvenile defendants, and the Voting Rights Act of 1970.[8] We have been making persons of children although they were not, in law, always so. And we have done the same, albeit imperfectly some would say, with prisoners,[9] aliens, women (especially of the married variety), the insane,[10] Blacks, foetuses,[11] and Indians.

Nor is it only matter in human form that has come to be recognized as the possessor of rights. The world of the lawyer is peopled with inanimate right-holders: trusts, corporations, joint ventures, municipalities, Subchapter R partnerships,[12] and nation-states, to mention just a few. Ships, still referred to by courts in the feminine gender, have long had an independent jural life, often with striking consequences.[13] We have become so accustomed to the idea of a corporation having "its" own rights, and being a "person" and "citizen" for so many statutory and constitutional purposes, that we forget how jarring the notion was to early jurists. "That invisible, intangible and artificial being, that mere legal entity" Chief Justice Marshall wrote of the corporation in *Bank of the United States v. Deveaux*[14]—could a suit be brought in *its* name? Ten years later, in the *Dartmouth College* case,[15] he was still refusing to let pass unnoticed the wonder of an entity "existing only in contemplation of law."[16] Yet, long before Marshall worried over the personifying of the modern corporation, the best medieval legal scholars had spent hundreds of years struggling with the notion of the legal nature of those great public "corporate bodies," the Church and the State. How could they exist in law, as entities transcending the living Pope and King? It was clear how a king could bind *himself*—on his honor—by a treaty. But when the king died, what was it that was burdened with the obligations of, and claimed the rights under, the treaty *his* tangible hand had signed? The medieval mind saw (what we have lost our capacity to see)[17] how *unthinkable* it was, and worked out the most elaborate conceits and fallacies to serve as anthropomorphic flesh for the Universal Church and the Universal Empire.[18]

From Christopher D. Stone, *Should Trees Have Standing? Toward Legal Rights for Natural Objects* (Portola Valley, CA: Tioga Publishing Company, 1974), 3–18, 24, 27–33, 45–46, 48–54. Reprinted by permission.

It is this note of the *unthinkable* that I want to dwell upon for a moment. Throughout legal history, each successive extension of rights to some new entity has been, theretofore, a bit unthinkable. We are inclined to suppose the rightlessness of rightless "things" to be a decree of Nature, not a legal convention acting in support of some status quo. It is thus that we defer considering the choices involved in all their moral, social, and economic dimensions. And so the United States Supreme Court could straight-facedly tell us in *Dred Scott* that Blacks had been denied the rights of citizenship "as a subordinate and inferior class of beings, who had been subjugated by the dominant race...."[19] In the nineteenth century, the highest court in California explained that Chinese had not the right to testify against white men in criminal matters because they were "a race of people whom nature has marked as inferior, and who are incapable of progress or intellectual development beyond a certain point...between whom and ourselves nature has placed an impassable difference."[20] The popular conception of the Jew in the 13th Century contributed to a law which treated them as "men *ferae naturae,* protected by a quasi-forest law. Like the roe and the deer, they form an order apart."[21] Recall, too, that it was not so long ago that the foetus was "like the roe and the deer." In an early suit attempting to establish a wrongful death action on behalf of a negligently killed foetus (now widely accepted practice), Holmes, then on the Massachusetts Supreme Court, seems to have thought it simply inconceivable "that a man might owe a civil duty and incur a conditional prospective liability in tort to one not yet in being."[22] The first woman in Wisconsin who thought she might have a right to practice law was told that she did not, in the following terms:

> The law of nature destines and qualifies the female sex for the bearing and nurture of the children of our race and for the custody of the homes of the world....[A]ll life-long callings of women, inconsistent with these radical and sacred duties of their sex, as is the profession of the law, are departures from the order of nature; and when voluntary, treason against it....The peculiar qualities of womanhood, its gentle graces, its quick sensibility, its tender susceptibility, its purity, its delicacy, its emotional impulses, its subordination of hard reason to sympathetic feeling, are surely not qualifications for forensic strife. Nature has tempered woman as little for the juridical conflicts of the court room, as for the physical conflicts of the battle field....[23]

The fact is, that each time there is a movement to confer rights onto some new "entity," the proposal is bound to sound odd or frightening or laughable. This is partly because until the rightless thing receives its rights, we cannot see it as anything but a *thing* for the use of "us"—those who are holding rights at the time.[24] In this vein, what is striking about the Wisconsin case above is that the court, for all its talk about women, so clearly was never able to see women as they are (and might become). All it could see was the popular "idealized" version of *an object it needed.* Such is the way the slave South looked upon the Black.[25] There is something of a seamless web involved: there will be resistance to giving the thing "rights" until it can be seen and valued for itself; yet, it is hard to see it and value it for itself until we can bring ourselves to give it "rights"—which is almost inevitably going to sound inconceivable to a large group of people.

The reason for this little discourse on the unthinkable, the reader must know by now, if only from the title of the paper. I am quite seriously proposing that we give legal rights to forests, oceans, rivers and other so-called "natural objects" in the environment—indeed, to the natural environment as a whole.

As strange as such a notion may sound, it is neither fanciful nor devoid of operational content. In fact, I do not think it would be a misdescription of recent developments in the law to say that we are already on the verge of assigning some such rights, although we have not faced up to what we are doing in those particular terms.[26] We should do so now, and begin to explore the implications such a notion would hold.

TOWARD RIGHTS FOR THE ENVIRONMENT

Now, to say that the natural environment should have rights is not to say anything as silly as that no one should be allowed to cut down a tree. We say human beings have rights, but—at least as of the time of this writing—they can be executed. Corporations have rights, but they cannot plead the fifth amendment; *In re Gault* gave 15-year-olds certain rights in juvenile proceedings, but it did not give them the right to vote. Thus, to say that the environment should have rights is not to say that it should have every right we can imagine, or even the same body of rights as human beings have. Nor is it to say that everything in the environment should have the same rights as every other thing in the environment.

What the granting of rights does involve has two sides to it. The first involves what might be called the legal-operational aspects; the second, the psychic and socio-psychic aspects. I shall deal with these aspects in turn.

THE LEGAL-OPERATIONAL ASPECTS

What It Means to Be a Holder of Legal Rights

There is, so far as I know, no generally accepted standard for how one ought to use the term "legal rights." Let me indicate how I shall be using it in this piece.

First and most obviously, if the term is to have any content at all, an entity cannot be said to hold a legal right unless and until *some public authoritative body* is prepared to give *some amount of review* to actions that are colorably inconsistent with that "right." For example, if a student can be expelled from a university and cannot get any public official, even a judge or administrative agent at the lowest level, either (i) to require the university to justify its actions (if only to the extent of filling out an affidavit alleging that the expulsion "was not wholly arbitrary and capricious") or (ii) to compel the university to accord the student some procedural safeguards (a hearing, right to counsel, right to have notice of charges), then the minimum requirements for saying that the student has a legal right to his education do not exist.[27]

But for a thing to be *a holder of legal rights,* something more is needed than that some authoritative body will review the actions and processes of those who threaten it. As I shall use the term, "holder of legal rights," each of three additional criteria must be satisfied. All three, one will observe, go towards making a thing *count* jurally—to have a legally recognized worth and dignity in its own right, and not merely to serve as a means to benefit "us" (whoever the contemporary group of rights-holders may be). They are, first, that the

thing can institute legal actions *at its behest;* second, that in determining the granting of legal relief, the court must take *injury to it* into account; and, third, that relief must run to the *benefit of it....*

The Rightlessness of Natural Objects at Common Law

Consider, for example, the common law's posture toward the pollution of a stream. True, courts have always been able, in some circumstances, to issue orders that will stop the pollution....But the stream itself is fundamentally rightless, with implications that deserve careful reconsideration.

The first sense in which the stream is not a rights-holder has to do with standing. The stream itself has none. So far as the common law is concerned, there is in general no way to challenge the polluter's actions save at the behest of a lower riparian—another human being—able to show an invasion of *his* rights. This conception of the riparian as the holder of the right to bring suit has more than theoretical interest. The lower riparians may simply not care about the pollution. They themselves may be polluting, and not wish to stir up legal waters. They may be economically dependent on their polluting neighbor. And, of course, when they discount the value of winning by the costs of bringing suit and the chances of success, the action may not seem worth undertaking. Consider, for example, that while the polluter might be injuring 100 downstream riparians $10,000 a year *in the aggregate,* each riparian separately might be suffering injury only to the extent of $100—possibly not enough for any one of them to want to press suit by himself, or even to go to the trouble and cost of securing co-plaintiffs to make it worth everyone's while. This hesitance will be especially likely when the potential plaintiffs consider the burdens the law puts in their way:[28] proving, *e.g.,* specific damages, the "unreasonableness" of defendant's use of the water, the fact that practicable means of abatement exist, and overcoming difficulties raised by issues such as joint casuality, right to pollute by prescription, and so forth. Even in states which, like California, sought to overcome these difficulties by empowering the attorney-general to sue for abatement of pollution in limited instances, the power has been sparingly invoked and, when invoked, narrowly construed by the courts.[29]

The second sense in which the common law denies "rights" to natural objects has to do with the way in which the merits are decided in those cases in which someone is competent and willing to establish standing. At its more primitive levels, the system protected the "rights" of the property owning human with minimal weighing of any values: *"Cujus est solum, ejus est usque ad coelum et ad infernos."*[30] Today we have come more and more to make balances—but only such as will adjust the economic best interests of identifiable humans. For example, continuing with the case of streams, there are commentators who speak of a "general rule" that "a riparian owner is legally entitled to have the stream flow by his land with its quality unimpaired" and observe that "an upper owner has prima facie, no right to pollute the water."[31] Such a doctrine, if strictly invoked, would protect the stream absolutely whenever a suit was brought; but obviously, to look around us, the law does not work that way. Almost everywhere there are doctrinal qualifications on riparian "rights" to an unpolluted stream.[32] Although these rules vary from jurisdiction to jurisdiction, and upon whether one is suing for an equitable injunction or for damages, what they all have in common is some sort of balancing. Whether under language of "reasonable use," "reasonable methods of use," "balance of convenience" or "the public interest doctrine," what the courts are balancing, with varying degrees of directness, are the economic hardships on the upper riparian (or dependent community) of abating the pollution vis-à-vis the economic hardships of continued pollution on the lower riparians. What does not weigh in the balance is the damage to the stream, its fish and turtles and "lower" life. So long as the natural environment itself is rightless, these are not matters for judicial cognizance. Thus, we find the highest court of Pennsylvania refusing to stop a coal company from discharging polluted mine water into a tributary of the Lackawana River because a plaintiff's "grievance is for a mere personal inconvenience; and…mere private personal inconveniences…must yield to the necessities of a great public industry, which although in the hands of a private corporation, subserves a great public interest."[33] The stream itself is lost sight of in "a quantitative compromise between *two* conflicting interests."[34]

The third way in which the common law makes natural objects rightless has to do with who is regarded as the beneficiary of a favorable judgment. Here, too, it makes a considerable difference that it is not the natural object that counts in its own right. To illustrate this point, let me begin by observing that it makes perfectly good sense to speak of, and ascertain, the legal damage to a natural object, if only in the sense of "making it whole" with respect to the most obvious factors. The costs of making a forest whole, for example, would include the costs of reseeding, repairing watersheds, restocking wildlife—the sorts of costs the Forest Service undergoes after a fire. Making a polluted stream whole would include the costs of restocking with fish, water-fowl, and other animal and vegetable life, dredging, washing out impurities, establishing natural and/or artificial aerating agents, and so forth. Now, what is important to note is that, under our present system, even if a plaintiff riparian wins a water pollution suit for damages, no money goes to the benefit of the stream itself to repair *its* damages. This omission has the further effect that, at most, the law confronts a polluter with what it takes to make the plaintiff riparians whole; this may be far less than the damages to the stream, but not so much as to force the polluter to desist. For example, it is easy to imagine a polluter whose activities damage a stream to the extent of $10,000 annually, although the aggregate damage to all the riparian plaintiffs who come into the suit is only $3000. If $3000 is less than the cost to the polluter of shutting down, or making the requisite technological changes, he might prefer to pay off the damages (*i.e.,* the legally cognizable damages) and continue to pollute the stream. Similarly, even if the jurisdiction issues an injunction at the plaintiffs' behest (rather than to order payment of damages), there is nothing to stop the plaintiffs from "selling out" the stream, *i.e.,* agreeing to dissolve or not enforce the injunction at some price (in the example above, somewhere between plaintiffs' damages—$3000—and defendant's next best economic alternative). Indeed, I take it this is exactly what Learned Hand had in mind in an opinion in which, after issuing an anti-pollution injunction, he suggests that the defendant "make its peace with the plaintiff as best it can."[35] What is meant is a peace between *them,* and not amongst them and the river.

I ought to make clear at this point that the common law as it affects streams and rivers, which I have been using as an example so far, is not exactly the same as the law affecting other environmental objects. Indeed, one would be hard pressed to say that there was a "typical" environmental object, so far as its treatment at the hands of the law is concerned. There are some differences in the law applicable to all the various resources that are held in common: rivers, lakes, oceans, dunes, air, streams (surface and subterranean), beaches, and so forth. And there is an even greater difference as between these traditional communal resources on the one hand, and natural objects on traditionally private land, *e.g.,* the pond on the farmer's field, or the stand of trees on the suburbanite's lawn.

On the other hand, although there be these differences which would make it fatuous to generalize about a law of the natural environment, most of these differences simply underscore the points made in the instance of rivers and streams. None of the natural objects, whether held in common or situated on private land, has any of the three criteria of a rights-holder. They have no standing in their own right; their unique damages do not count in determining outcome; and they are not the beneficiaries of awards. In such fashion, these objects have traditionally been regarded by the common law, and even by all but the most recent legislation, as objects for man to conquer and master and use—in such a way as the law once looked upon "man's" relationships to African Negroes. Even where special measures have been taken to conserve them, as by seasons on game and limits on timber cutting, the dominant motive has been to conserve them *for us*—for the greatest good of the greatest number of human beings. Conservationists, so far as I am aware, are generally reluctant to maintain otherwise.[36] As the name implies, they want to conserve and guarantee *our* consumption and *our* enjoyment of these other living things. In their own right, natural objects have counted for little, in law as in popular movements.

As I mentioned at the outset, however, the rightlessness of the natural environment can and should change; it already shows some signs of doing so.

TOWARD HAVING STANDING IN ITS OWN RIGHT

It is not inevitable, nor is it wise, that natural objects should have no rights to seek redress in their own behalf. It is no answer to say that streams and forests cannot have standing because streams and forest cannot speak. Corporations cannot speak either; nor can states, estates; infants, incompetents, municipalities or universities. Lawyers speak for them, as they customarily do for the ordinary citizen with legal problems. One ought, I think, to handle the legal problems of natural objects as one does the problems of legal incompetents—human beings who have become vegetables. If a human being shows signs of becoming senile and has affairs that he is de jure incompetent to manage, those concerned with his well being make such a showing to the court, and someone is designated by the court with the authority to manage the incompetent's affairs. The guardian (or "conservator" or "committee"—the terminology varies) then represents the incompetent in his legal affairs. Courts make similar appointments when a corporation has become "incompetent"—they appoint a trustee in bankruptcy or reorganization to oversee its affairs and speak for it in court when that becomes necessary.

On a parity of reasoning, we should have a system in which, when a friend of a natural object perceives it to be endangered, he can apply to a court for the creation of a guardianship. Perhaps we already have the machinery to do so. California law, for example, defines an incompetent as "any person, whether insane or not, who by reason of old age, disease, weakness of mind, or other cause, is unable, unassisted, properly to manage and take care of himself or his property, and by reason thereof is likely to be deceived or imposed upon by artful or designing persons."[37] Of course, to urge a court that an endangered river is "a person" under this provision will call for lawyers as bold and imaginative as those who convinced the Supreme Court that a railroad corporation was a "person" under the fourteenth amendment, a constitutional provision theretofore generally thought of as designed to secure the rights of freedmen.[38]...

The guardianship approach, however, is apt to raise...[the following objection]: a committee or guardian could not judge the needs of the river or forest in its charge; indeed, the very concept of "needs," it might be said, could be used here only in the most metaphorical way....

...Natural objects *can* communicate their wants (needs) to us, and in ways that are not terribly ambiguous. I am sure I can judge with more certainty and meaningfulness whether and when my lawn wants (needs) water, than the Attorney General can judge whether and when the United States wants (needs) to take an appeal from an adverse judgment by a lower court. The lawn tells me that it wants water by a certain dryness of the blades and soil—immediately obvious to the touch—the appearance of bald spots, yellowing, and a lack of springiness after being walked on; how does "the United States" communicate to the Attorney General? For similar reasons, the guardian-attorney for a smog-endangered stand of pines could venture with more confidence that his client wants the smog stopped, than the directors of a corporation can assert that "the corporation" wants dividends declared. We make decisions on behalf of, and in the purported interests of, others every day; these "others" are often creatures whose wants are far less verifiable, and even far more metaphysical in conception, than the wants of rivers, trees, and land....

The argument for "personifying" the environment, from the point of damage calculations, can best be demonstrated from the welfare economics position. Every well-working legal-economic system should be so structured as to confront each of us with the full costs that our activities are imposing on society. Ideally, a paper-mill, in deciding what to produce—and where, and by what methods—ought to be forced to take into account not only the lumber, acid and labor that its production "takes" from other uses in the society, but also what costs alternative production plans will impose on society through pollution. The legal system, through the law of contracts and the criminal law, for example, makes the mill confront the costs of the first group of demands. When, for example, the company's purchasing agent orders 1000 drums of acid from the Z Company, the Z Company can bind the mill to pay for them, and thereby reimburse the society for what the mill is removing from alternative uses.

Unfortunately, so far as the pollution costs are concerned, the allocative ideal begins to break down, because the traditional legal institutions have a more difficult time "catching" and confronting us with the full social costs of our activities. In the lakeside mill example, major riparian interests might bring an action, forcing a court to weigh *their* aggregate losses against the costs to the mill of installing the anti-pollution device. But many other interests—and I am speaking for the moment of recognized homocentric interests—are too fragmented and perhaps "too remote" causally to warrant securing representation and pressing for recovery: the people who own summer homes and motels, the man who sells fishing tackle and bait, the man who rents rowboats. There is no reason not to allow the lake to prove damages to them as the prima facie measure of damages to it. *By doing so, we in effect make the natural object, through its guardian, a jural entity competent to gather up these fragmented and otherwise unrepresented damage claims, and press them before the court even where, for legal or practical reasons, they are not going to be pressed by traditional class action plaintiffs.* Indeed, one way—the homocentric way—to view what I am proposing so far, is to view the guardian of the natural object as the guardian of unborn generations, as well as of the otherwise unrepresented, but distantly injured, contemporary humans.[39] By making the lake itself the focus of these damages, and "incorporating" it so to speak, the legal system can effectively take proof upon, and confront the mill with, a larger and more representative measure of the damages its pollution causes.

So far, I do not suppose that my economist friends (unremittent human chauvinists, every one of them!) will have any large quarrel in principle with the concept. Many will view it as a *trompe l'oeil* that comes down, at best, to effectuate the goals of the paragon class action, or the paragon water pollution control district. Where we are apt to part company is here—I propose going beyond gathering up the loose ends of what most people would presently recognize as economically valid damages. The guardian would urge before the court injuries not presently cognizable—the death of eagles and inedible crabs, the suffering of sea lions, the loss from the face of the earth of species of commercially valueless birds, the disappearance of a wilderness area. One might, of course, speak of the damages involved as "damages" to us humans, and indeed, the widespread growth of environmental groups shows that human beings do feel these losses. But they are not, at present, economically measurable losses: how can they have a monetary value for the guardian to prove in court?

The answer for me is simple. Wherever it carves out "property" rights, the legal system is engaged in the process of *creating* monetary worth. One's literary works would have minimal monetary value if anyone could copy them at will. Their economic value to the author is a product of the law of copyright; the person who copies a copyrighted book has to bear a cost to the copyrightholder because the law says he must. Similarly, it is through the law of torts that we have made a "right" of—and guaranteed an economically meaningful value to—privacy. (The value we place on gold—a yellow inanimate dirt—is not simply a function of supply and demand—wilderness areas are scarce and pretty too—, but results from the actions of the legal systems of the world, which have institutionalized that value; they have even done a remarkable job of stabilizing the price.) I am proposing we do the same with eagles and wilderness areas as we do with copyrighted works, patented inventions, and privacy: *make* the violation of rights in them to be a cost by declaring the "pirating" of them to be the invasion of a property interest.[40] If we do so, the net social costs the polluter would be confronted with would include not only the extended homocentric costs of his pollution (explained above) but also costs to the environment *per se*.

How, though, would these costs be calculated? When we protect an invention, we can at least speak of a fair market value for it, by reference to which damages can be computed. But the lost environmental "values" of which we are now speaking are by definition over and above those that the market is prepared to bid for: they are priceless.

One possible measure of damages, suggested earlier, would be the cost of making the environment whole, just as, when a man is injured in an automobile accident, we impose upon the responsible party the injured man's medical expenses. Comparable expenses to a polluted river would be the costs of dredging, restocking with fish, and so forth. It is on the basis of such costs as these, I assume, that we get the figure of $1 billion as the cost of saving Lake Erie.[41] As an ideal, I think this is a good guide applicable in many environmental situations. It is by no means free from difficulties, however.

One problem with computing damages on the basis of making the environment whole is that, if understood most literally, it is tantamount to asking for a "freeze" on environmental quality, even at the costs (and there will be costs) of preserving "useless" objects. Such a "freeze" is not inconceivable to me as a general goal, especially considering that, even by the most immediately discernible homocentric interests, in so many areas we ought to be cleaning up and not merely preserving the environmental status quo. In fact, there is presently strong sentiment in the Congress for a total elimination of all river pollutants by 1985,[42] notwithstanding that such a decision would impose quite large direct and indirect costs on us all. Here one is inclined to recall the instructions of Judge Hays, in remanding Consolidated Edison's Storm King application to the Federal Power Commission in *Scenic Hudson:*

> The Commission's renewed proceedings must include as a basic concern the preservation of natural beauty and of natural historic shrines, keeping in mind that, in our affluent society, the cost of a project is only one of several factors to be considered.[43]

Nevertheless, whatever the merits of such a goal in principle, there are many cases in which the social price tag of putting it into effect are going to seem too high to accept. Consider, for example, an oceanside nuclear generator that could produce low cost electricity for a million homes at a savings of $1 a year per home, spare us the air pollution that comes of burning fossil fuels, but which through a slight heating effect threatened to kill off a rare species of temperature-sensitive sea urchins; suppose further that technological improvements adequate to reduce the temperature to present environmental quality would expend the entire one million dollars in anticipated fuel savings. Are we prepared to tax ourselves $1,000,000 a year on behalf of the sea urchins? In comparable problems under the present law of damages, we work out practicable compromises by abandoning restoration costs and calling upon fair market value. For example, if an automobile is so severely damaged that the cost of bringing the car to its original state by repair is greater than the fair market value, we would allow the responsible tortfeasor to pay the fair market value only. Or if a human being suffers the loss of an arm (as we might conceive of the ocean having irreparably lost the sea urchins), we can fall back on the capitalization of reduced earning power (and pain and suffering) to measure the damages. But what is the fair market value of sea urchins? How can we capitalize their loss to the ocean, independent of any commercial value they may have to someone else?

One answer is that the problem can sometimes be sidestepped quite satisfactorily. In the sea urchin example, one compromise solution would be to impose on the nuclear generator the costs of making the ocean whole somewhere else, in some other way, *e.g.*, reestablishing a sea urchin colony elsewhere, or making a somehow comparable contribution.[44] In the debate over the laying of the trans-Alaskan pipeline, the builders are apparently prepared to meet conservationists' objections halfway by re-establishing wildlife away from the pipeline, so far as is feasible.[45]

But even if damage calculations have to be made, one ought to recognize that the measurement of damages is rarely a simple report of economic facts about "the market," whether we are valuing the loss of a foot, a foetus, or a work of fine art. Decisions of this sort are always hard, but not impossible. We have increasingly taken (human) pain and suffering into account in reckoning damages, not because we think we can ascertain them as objective "facts" about the universe, but because, even in view of all the room for disagreement, we come up with a better society by making rude estimates of them than by ignoring them.[46] We can make such estimates in regard to environmental losses fully aware that what we are really doing is making implicit normative judgments (as with pain and suffering)—laying down rules as to what the society is going to "value" rather than reporting market evaluations. In making such normative estimates decision-makers would not go wrong if they estimated on the "high side," putting the burden of trimming the figure down on the immediate human interests present. All burdens of proof should reflect common experience; our experience in environmental matters has been a continual discovery that our acts have caused more long-range damage than we were able to appreciate at the outset.

To what extent the decision-maker should factor in costs such as the pain and suffering of animals and other sentient natural objects, I cannot say; although I am prepared to do so in principle.[47] Given the conjectural nature of the "estimates" in all events, and the roughness of the "balance of conveniences" procedure where that is involved,

the practice would be of more interest from the socio-psychic point of view, discussed below, than from the legal-operational....

THE PSYCHIC AND SOCIO-PSYCHIC ASPECTS

The strongest case can be made from the perspective of human advantage for conferring rights on the environment. Scientists have been warning of the crises the earth and all humans on its face if we do not change our ways—radically—and these crises make the lost "recreational use" of rivers seem absolutely trivial. The earth's very atmosphere is threatened with frightening possibilities: absorption of sunlight, upon which the entire life cycle depends, may be diminished; the oceans may warm (increasing the "greenhouse effect" of the atmosphere), melting the polar ice caps, and destroying our great coastal cities; the portion of the atmosphere that shields us from dangerous radiation may be destroyed. Testifying before Congress, sea explorer Jacques Cousteau predicted that the oceans (to which we dreamily look to feed our booming populations) are headed toward their own death: "The cycle of life is intricately tied up with the cycle of water...the water system has to remain alive if we are to remain alive on earth."[48] We are depleting our energy and our food sources at a rate that takes little account of the needs even of humans now living.

These problems will not be solved easily; they very likely can be solved, if at all, only through a willingness to suspend the rate of increase in the standard of living (by present values) of the earth's "advanced" nations, and by stabilizing the total human population. For some of us this will involve forfeiting material comforts; for others it will involve abandoning the hope someday to obtain comforts long envied. For all of us it will involve giving up the right to have as many offspring as we might wish. Such a program is not impossible of realization, however. Many of our so-called "material comforts" are not only in excess of, but are probably in opposition to, basic biological needs. Further, the "costs" to the advanced nations is not as large as would appear from Gross National Product figures. G.N.P. reflects social gain (of a sort) without discounting for the social *cost* of that gain, *e.g.,* the losses through depletion of resources, pollution, and so forth. As has well been shown, as societies become more and more "advanced," their real marginal gains become less and less for each additional dollar of G.N.P.[49] Thus, to give up "human progress" would not be as costly as might appear on first blush.

Nonetheless, such far-reaching social changes are going to involve us in a serious reconsideration of our consciousness towards the environment....

A radical new conception of man's relationship to the rest of nature would not only be a step towards solving the material planetary problems; there are strong reasons for such a changed consciousness from the point of making us far better humans. If we only stop for a moment and look at the underlying human qualities that our present attitudes toward property and nature draw upon and reinforce, we have to be struck by how stultifying of our own personal growth and satisfaction they can become when they take rein of us. Hegel, in "justifying" private property, unwittingly reflects the tone and quality of some of the needs that are played upon:

> A person has as his substantive end the right of putting his will into any and every thing and thereby making it his, because it has no such end in itself and derives its destiny and soul from his will. This is the absolute right of appropriation which man has over all "things."[50]

What is it within us that gives us this need not just to satisfy basic biological wants, but to extend our wills over things, to object-ify them, to make them ours, to manipulate them, to keep them at a psychic distance? Can it all be explained on "rational" bases? Should we not be suspect of such needs within us, cautious as to why we wish to gratify them? When I first read that passage of Hegel, I immediately thought not only of the emotional contrast with Spinoza, but of the passage in Carson McCullers' *A Tree, A Rock, A Cloud,* in which an old derelict has collared a twelve year old boy in a streetcar cafe. The old man asks whether the boy knows "how love should be begun?"

The old man leaned closer and whispered:

"A tree. A rock. A cloud."

...

"The weather was like this in Portland," he said. "At the time my science was begun. I meditated and I started very cautious. I would pick up something from the street and take it home with me. I bought a goldfish and I concentrated on the goldfish and I loved it. I graduated from one thing to another. Day by day I was getting this technique...."

...

..."For six years now I have gone around by myself and built up my science. And now I am a master, Son. I can love anything. No longer do I have to think about it even. I see a street full of people and a beautiful light comes in me. I watch a bird in the sky. Or I meet a traveler on the road. Everything, Son. And anybody. All stranger and all loved! Do you realize what a science like mine can mean?"[51]

To be able to get away from the view that Nature is a collection of useful senseless objects is, as McCullers' "madman" suggests, deeply involved in the development of our abilities to love—or, if that is putting it too strongly, to be able to reach a heightened awareness of our own, and others' capacities in their mutual interplay. To do so, we have to give up some psychic investment in our sense of separateness and specialness in the universe. And this, in turn, is hard giving indeed, because it involves us in a flight backwards, into earlier stages of civilization and childhood in which we had to trust (and perhaps fear) our environment, for we had not then the power to master it. Yet, in doing so, we—as persons—gradually free ourselves of needs for supportive illusions. Is not this one of the triumphs for "us" of our giving legal rights to (or acknowledging the legal rights of) the Blacks and women?...

...A few years ago the pollution of streams was thought of only as a problem of smelly, unsightly, unpotable water, *i.e.,* to us. Now we are beginning to discover that pollution is a process that destroys wondrously subtle balances of life within the water, and as between the water and its banks. This heightened awareness enlarges our sense of the dangers to us. But it also enlarges our empathy. We are not only developing the scientific capacity, but we are cultivating the personal capacities *within us* to recognize more and more the ways in which nature—like the woman, the Black, the Indian and the Alien—is like us (and we will also become more able realistically to define, confront, live with and admire the ways in which we are all different).

The time may be on hand when these sentiments, and the early stirrings of the law, can be coalesced into a radical new theory or myth—felt as well as intellectualized—of man's relationships to the rest of nature. I do not mean "myth" in a demeaning sense of the term, but in the sense in which, at different times in history, our social "facts" and relationships have been comprehended and integrated by reference to the "myths" that we are co-signers of a social contract, that the Pope is God's agent, and that all men are created equal. Pantheism, Shinto and Tao all have myths to offer. But they are all, each in its own fashion, quaint, primitive and archaic. What is needed is a myth that can fit our growing body of knowledge of geophysics, biology and the cosmos. In this vein, I do not think it too remote that we may come to regard the Earth, as some have suggested, as one organism, of which Mankind is a functional part— the mind, perhaps: different from the rest of nature, but different as a man's brain is from his lungs....

...As I see it, the Earth is only one organized "field" of activities—and so is the *human person*—but these activities take place at various levels, in different "spheres" of being and realms of consciousness. The lithosphere is not the biosphere, and the latter not the...ionosphere. The Earth is not *only* a material mass. Consciousness is not only "human"; it exists at animal and vegetable levels, and most likely must be latent, or operating in some form, in the molecule and the atom; and all these diverse and in a sense hierarchical modes of activity and consciousness should be seen integrated in and perhaps transcended by an all-encompassing and "eonic" planetary Consciousness.

...

Mankind's function within the Earth-organism is to extract from the activities of all other operative systems within this organism the type of consciousness which we call "reflective" or "self"-consciousness—or, we may also say to *mentalize* and give meaning, value, and "name" to all that takes place anywhere within the Earth-field....[52]

As radical as such a consciousness may sound today, all the dominant changes we see about us point in its direction. Consider just the impact of space travel, of world-wide mass media, of increasing scientific discoveries about the interrelatedness of all life processes. Is it any wonder that the term "spaceship earth" has so captured the popular imagination? The problems we have to confront are increasingly the world-wide crises of a global organism: not pollution of a stream, but pollution of the atmosphere and of the ocean. Increasingly, the death that occupies each human's imagination is not his own, but that of the entire life cycle of the planet earth, to which each of us is as but a cell to a body.

To shift from such a lofty fancy as the planetarization of consciousness to the operation of our municipal legal system is to come down to earth hard. Before the forces that are at work, our highest court is but a frail and feeble—a distinctly human—institution. Yet, the Court may be at its best not in its work of handing down decrees, but at the very task that is called for: of summoning up from the human spirit the kindest and most generous and worthy ideas that abound there, giving them shape and reality and legitimacy. Witness the School Desegregation Cases which, more importantly than to integrate the schools (assuming they did), awakened us to moral needs which, when made visible, could not be denied. And so here, too, in the case of the environment, the Supreme Court may find itself in a position to award "rights" in a way that will contribute to a change in popular consciousness. It would be a modest move, to be sure, but one in furtherance of a large goal: the future of the planet as we know it.

How far we are from such a state of affairs, where the law treats "environmental objects" as holders of legal rights, I cannot say. But there is certainly intriguing language in one of Justice Black's last dissents, regarding the Texas Highway Department's plan to run a six-lane expressway through a San Antonio Park.[53] Complaining of the Court's refusal to stay the plan, Black observed that "after today's decision, the people of San Antonio and the birds and animals that make their home in the park will share their quiet retreat with an ugly, smelly stream of traffic....Trees, shrubs, and flowers will be mowed down."[54] Elsewhere he speaks of the "burial of public parks," of segments of a highway which "devour parkland," and of the park's heartland.[55] Was he, at the end of his great career, on the verge of saying—just saying—that "nature has 'rights' on its own account"? Would it be so hard to do?

NOTES

1. C. Darwin, Descent of Man 119, 120–211 (2d ed. 1874). *See also* R. Waelder, Progress and Revolution 39 *et seq.* (1967).

2. *See* Darwin, *supra* note 1, at 113–14....

3. *See* Darwin, *supra* note 1, at 113. *See also* E. Westermarck, 1 The Origin and Development of the Moral Ideas 406–12 (1912)....

4. There does not appear to be a word "gericide" or "geronticide" to designate the killing of the aged. "Senicide" is as close as the Oxford English Dictionary comes, although, as it indicates, the word is rare. 9 Oxford English Dictionary 454 (1933).

5. *See* Darwin, *supra* note 1, at 386–93. Westermarck, *supra* note 3, at 387–89, observes that where the killing of the aged and infirm is practiced, it is often supported by humanitarian justification; this, however, is a far cry from saying that the killing is *requested* by the victim as his right.

6. H. Maine, Ancient Law 153 (Pollock ed. 1930).

7. 387 U.S. 1 (1967).

8. 42 U.S.C. §§ 1973 *et seq.* (1970).

9. *See* Landman v. Royster, 40 U.S.L.W 2256 (E.D. Va., Oct. 30, 1971)....

10. *But see* T. Szasz, Law, Liberty and Psychiatry (1963).

11. *See* note 22. The trend toward liberalized abortion can be seen either as a legislative tendency back in the direction of rightlessness for the foetus—or toward increasing rights of women. This inconsistency is not unique in the law of course; it is simply support for Hohfeld's scheme that the "jural opposite" of someone's right is someone else's "no-right." W. Hohfeld, Fundamental Legal Conceptions (1923)....

12. Int. Rev. Code of 1954, § 1361 (repealed by Pub. L. No. 89-389, effective Jan. 1, 1969).

13. For example, *see* United States v. Cargo of the Brig Melek Adhel, 43 U.S. (2 How.) 210 (1844). There, a ship had been seized and used by pirates. All this was done without the knowledge or consent of the owners of the ship. After the ship had been captured, the United States condemned and sold the "offending vessel." The owners objected. In denying release to the owners, Justice Story cited Chief Justice Marshall from an earlier case: "This is not a proceeding against the owner; it is a proceeding against the vessel for an offense committed by the vessel; which is not the less an offense...because it was committed without the authority and against the will of the owner." 43 U.S. at 234, quoting from United States v. Schooner Little Charles, 26 F Cas. 979 (No. 15,612) (C.C.D. Va. 1818).

14. 9 U.S. (5 Cranch) 61, 86 (1809).

15. Trustees of Darmouth College v. Woodward, 17 U.S. (4 Wheat.) 518 (1819).

16. *Id.* at 636.

17. Consider, for example, that the claim of the United States to the naval station at Guantanamo Bay, at $2000-a-year rental, is based upon a treaty signed in 1903 by José Montes for the President of Cuba and a minister representing Theodore Roosevelt; it was subsequently ratified by two thirds of a Senate no member of which is living today. Lease [from Cuba] of Certain Areas for Naval or Coaling Stations, July 2, 1903, T.S. No. 426; C. Bevans, 6 Treaties and Other International Agreements of the United States 1776–1949, at 1120 (U.S. Dep't of State Pub. 8549, 1971).

18. O. Gierke, Political Theories of the Middle Age (Maitland transl. 1927), especially at 22–30....

19. Dred Scott v. Sandford, 60 U.S (19 How.) 396, 404–05 (1856)....

20. People v. Hall, 4 Cal. 399, 405 (1854)....

21. Schechter, *The Rightlessness* of *Mediaeval English Jewry,* 45 Jewish Q. Rev. 121. 135 (1954) quoting from M. Bateson, *Medieval England* 139 (1904)....

22. Dietrich v. Inhabitants of Northampton, 138 Mass. 14, 16 (1884).

23. *In re* Goddell, 39 Wisc. 232, 245 (1875). The court continued with the following "clincher":

> And when counsel was arguing for this lady that the word, person, in sec. 32, ch. 119 [respecting those qualified to practice law], necessarily includes females, her presence made it impossible to suggest to him as *reductio ad absurdum* of his position, that the same construction of the same word...would subject woman to prosecution for the paternity of a bastard, and...prosecution for rape. *Id.* at 246.

> The relationship between our attitudes toward woman, on the one hand, and, on the other, the more central concern of this article—land—is captured in an unguarded aside of our colleague, Curt Berger: "...after all, land, like woman, was meant to be possessed...." Land Ownership and Use 139 (1968).

24. Thus it was that the Founding Fathers could speak of the inalienable rights of all men, and yet maintain a society that was, by modern standards, without the most basic rights for Blacks, Indians, children and women. There was no hypocrisy; emotionally, no one *felt* that these other things were men.

25. The second thought streaming from...the older South [is] the sincere and passionate belief that somewhere between men and cattle, God created a *tertium quid,* and called it a Negro—a clownish, simple creature, at times even lovable within its limitations, but straitly foreordained to walk within the Veil. W. E. B. DuBois, The Souls of Black Folk 89 (1924).

26. The statement in text is not quite true; *cf.* Murphy, *Has Nature Any Right to Life?,* 22 Hast. L. J. 467 (1971). An Irish

court, passing upon the validity of a testamentary trust to the benefit of someone's dogs, observed in dictum that "'lives' means lives of human beings, not of animals or trees in California." Kelly v. Dillon, 1932 Ir. R. 255, 261. (The intended gift over on the death of the last surviving dog was held void for remoteness, the court refusing "to enter into the question of a dog's expectation of life," although prepared to observe that "in point of fact neighbor's [sic] dogs and cats are unpleasantly long-lived...." *Id.* at 260–61).

27. *See* Dixon v. Alabama State Bd. of Educ., 294 F.2d 150 (5th Cir.), *cert. denied*, 368 U.S. 930 (1961).

28. The law in a suit for injunctive relief is commonly easier on the plaintiff than in a suit for damages. *See* J. Gould, Law of Waters § 206 (1883).

29. However, in 1970 California amended its Water Quality Act to make it easier for the Attorney General to obtain relief, *e.g.*, one must no longer allege irreparable injury in a suit for an injunction. Cal. Water Code § 13350(b) (West 1971).

30. To whomsoever the soil belongs, he owns also to the sky and to the depths. *See* W. Blackstone, 2 Commentaries *18.

31. *See* Note, *Statutory Treatment of Industrial Stream Pollution,* 24 Geo. Wash. L. Rev. 302, 306 (1955); H. Farnham, 2 Law of Waters and Water Rights § 461 (1904); Gould, *supra* note 32, at § 204.

32. For example, courts have upheld a right to pollute by prescription, Mississippi Mills Co. v. Smith, 69 Miss. 299, 11 So. 26 (1882), and by easement, Luama v. Bunker Hill & Sullivan Mining & Concentrating Co., 41 F.2d 358 (9th Cir. 1930).

33. Pennsylvania Coal Co. v. Sanderson, 113 Pa. 126, 149, 6 A. 453, 459 (1886).

34. Hand, J. in Smith v. Staso Milling Co., 18 F.2d 736, 738 (2d Cir. 1927) (emphasis added). *See also* Harrisonville v. Dickey Clay Co., 289 U.S. 334 (1933) (Brandeis, J.).

35. Smith v. Staso, 18 F.2d 736, 738 (2d Cir. 1927).

36. By contrast, for example, with humane societies.

37. Cal. Prob. Code § 1460 (West Supp. 1971)....

38. Santa Clara County v. Southern Pac. R.R., 118 U.S. 394 (1886)....

39. *Cf.* Golding, *Ethical Issues in Biological Engineering,* 15 U.C.L.A L. Rev. 143, 451–63 (1968).

40. Of course, in the instance of copyright and patent protection, the creation of the "property right" can be more directly justified on homocentric grounds.

41. *See* Schrag, *Life on a Dying Lake,* in The Politics of Neglect 167, at 173 (R. Meek & J. Straayer eds. 1971).

42. On November 2, 1971, the Senate, by a vote of 86–0, passed and sent to the House the proposed Federal Water Pollution Control Act Amendments of 1971, 117 Cong. Rec. S17464 (daily ed. Nov. 2, 1971). Sections 101(a) and (a)(1) of the bill declare it to be "national policy that, consistent with the provisions of this Act—(1) the discharge of pollutants into the navigable waters be eliminated by 1985." S.2770, 92d Cong., 1st Sess., 117 Cong. Rec. S17464 (daily ed. Nov. 2, 1971).

43. 334 F.2d 608, 624 (2d Cir. 1965).

44. Again, there is a problem involving what we conceive to be the injured entity.

45. N.Y. Times, Jan. 14, 1971, § 1, col. 2, and at 74, col. 7.

46. Courts have not been reluctant to award damages for the destruction of heirlooms, literary manuscripts or other property having no ascertainable market value. In Willard v. Valley Gas Fuel Co., 171 Cal. 9, 151 Pac. 286 (1915), it was held that the measure of damages for the negligent destruction of a rare old book written by one of plaintiff's ancestors was the amount which would compensate the owner for all detriment including sentimental loss proximately caused by such destruction....

47. It is not easy to dismiss the idea of "lower" life having consciousness and feeling pain, especially since it is so difficult to know what these terms mean even as applied to humans. *See* Austin, *Other Minds,* in *Logic and Language* 342 (S. Flew ed. 1965); Schopenhauer, *On the Will in Nature,* in Two Essays by Arthur Schopenhauer 193, 281–304 (1889). Some experiments on plant sensitivity—of varying degrees of extravagance in their claims—include Lawrence, *Plants Have Feelings, Too...,* Organic Gardening & Farming 64 (April 1971); Woodlief, Royster & Huang, *Effect of Random Noise on Plant Growth,* 46 J. Acoustical Soc. Am. 481 (1969); Backster, *Evidence of a Primary Perception in Plant Life, 10* Int'l J. Parapsychology 250 (1968).

48. Cousteau, *The Oceans: No Time to Lose,* L.A. Times, Oct. 24, 1971, § (opinion), at 1, col. 4.

49. *See* J. Harte & R. Socolow, Patient Earth (1971).

50. G. Hegel, Hegel's Philosophy of Right 41 (T. Knox transl. 1945).

51. C. McCullers, The Ballad of the Sad Cafe and Other Stories 150–51 (1958).

52. D. Rudhyar, Directives for New Life 21–23 (1971).

53. 136. San Antonio Conservation Soc'y v. Texas Highway Dep't, *cert. denied,* 400 U.S. 968 (1970) (Black, J. dissenting to denial of certiorari).

54. *Id.* at 969.

55. *Id.* at 971.

MORALITY, MONEY, AND MOTOR CARS
Norman Bowie

Environmentalists frequently argue that business has special obligations to protect the environment. Although I agree with the environmentalists on this point, I do not agree with them as to where the obligations lie. Business does not have an obligation to protect the environment over and above what is required by law; however, it does have a moral obligation to avoid intervening in the political arena in order to defeat or weaken environmental legislation. In developing this thesis, several points are in order. First, many businesses have violated important moral obligations, and the violation has had a severe negative impact on the environment. For example, toxic waste haulers have illegally dumped hazardous material, and the environment has been harmed as a result. One might argue that those toxic waste haulers who have illegally dumped have violated a special obligation to the environment. Isn't it more accurate to say that these toxic waste haulers have violated their obligation to obey the law and that in this case the law that has been broken is one pertaining to the environment? Businesses have an obligation to obey the law—environmental laws and all others. Since there are many well-publicized cases of business having broken environmental laws, it is easy to think that business has violated some special obligations to the environment. In fact, what business has done is to disobey the law. Environmentalists do not need a special obligation to the environment to protect the environment against illegal business activity; they need only insist that business obey the laws.

Business has broken other obligations beside the obligation to obey the law and has harmed the environment as a result. Consider the grounding of the Exxon oil tanker *Valdez* in Alaska. That grounding was allegedly caused by the fact that an inadequately trained crewman was piloting the tanker while the captain was below deck and had been drinking. What needs to be determined is whether Exxon's policies and procedures were

sufficiently lax so that it could be said Exxon was morally at fault. It might be that Exxon is legally responsible for the accident under the doctrine of respondent superior, but Exxon is not thereby morally responsible. Suppose, however, that Exxon's policies were so lax that the company could be characterized as morally negligent. In such a case, the company would violate its moral obligation to use due care and avoid negligence. Although its negligence was disastrous to the environment, Exxon would have violated no special obligation to the environment. It would have been morally negligent.

A similar analysis could be given to the environmentalists' charges that Exxon's cleanup procedures were inadequate. If the charge is true, either Exxon was morally at fault or not. If the procedures had not been implemented properly by Exxon employees, then Exxon is legally culpable, but not morally culpable. On the other hand, if Exxon lied to government officials by saying that its policies were in accord with regulations and/or were ready for emergencies of this type, then Exxon violated its moral obligation to tell the truth. Exxon's immoral conduct would have harmed the environment, but it violated no special obligation to the environment. More important, none is needed. Environmentalists, like government officials, employees, and stockholders, expect that business firms and officials have moral obligations to obey the law, avoid negligent behavior, and tell the truth. In sum, although many business decisions have harmed the environment, these decisions violated no environmental moral obligations. If a corporation is negligent in providing for worker safety, we do not say the corporation violated a special obligation to employees; we say that it violated its obligation to avoid negligent behavior.

The crucial issues concerning business obligations to the environment focus on the excess use of natural resources (the dwindling supply of oil and gas, for instance) and the externalities of production (pollution, for instance). The critics of business want to claim that business has some special obligation to mitigate or solve these problems. I believe

From *Business, Ethics, and the Environment: The Public Policy Debate*, eds. W. Michael Hoffman, Robert Frederick, and Edward Petry, Jr. (New York: Quorum Books, 1990), 89–97. ©1990 by The Center for Business Ethics at Bentley College. Reprinted by permission of the author and the publisher.

this claim is largely mistaken. If business does have a special obligation to help solve the environmental crisis, that obligation results from the special knowledge that business firms have. If they have greater expertise than other constituent groups in society, then it can be argued that, other things being equal, business's responsibilities to mitigate the environmental crisis are somewhat greater. Absent this condition, business's responsibility is no greater than and may be less than that of other social groups. What leads me to think that the critics of business are mistaken?

William Frankena distinguished obligations in an ascending order of the difficulty in carrying them out: avoiding harm, preventing harm, and doing good. The most stringent requirement, to avoid harm, insists no one has a right to render harm on another unless there is a compelling, overriding moral reason to do so. Some writers have referred to this obligation as the moral minimum. A corporation's behavior is consistent with the moral minimum if it causes no avoidable harm to others.

Preventing harm is a less stringent obligation, but sometimes the obligation to prevent harm may be nearly as strict as the obligation to avoid harm. Suppose you are the only person passing a 2-foot-deep [wading] pool where a young child is drowning. There is no one else in the vicinity. Don't you have a strong moral obligation to prevent the child's death? Our obligation to prevent harm is not unlimited, however. Under what conditions must we be good samaritans? Some have argued that four conditions must exist before one is obligated to prevent harm: capability, need, proximity, and last resort. These conditions are all met with the case of the drowning child. There is obviously a need that you can meet since you are both in the vicinity and have the resources to prevent the drowning with little effort; you are also the last resort.

The least strict moral obligation is to do good—to make contributions to society or to help solve problems (inadequate primary schooling in the inner cities, for example). Although corporations may have some minimum obligation in this regard based on an argument from corporate citizenship, the obligations of the corporation to do good cannot be expanded without limit. An injunction to assist in solving societal problems makes impossible demands on a corporation because at

the practical level, it ignores the impact that such activities have on profit.

It might seem that even if this descending order of strictness of obligations were accepted, obligations toward the environment would fall into the moral minimum category. After all, the depletion of natural resources and pollution surely harm the environment. If so, wouldn't the obligations business has to the environment be among the strictest obligations a business can have?

Suppose, however, that a businessperson argues that the phrase "avoid harm" usually applies to human beings. Polluting a lake is not like injuring a human with a faulty product. Those who coined the phrase *moral minimum* for use in the business context defined harm as "particularly including activities which violate or frustrate the enforcement of rules of domestic or institutional law intended to protect individuals against prevention of health, safety or basic freedom." Even if we do not insist that the violations be violations of a rule of law, polluting a lake would not count as a harm under this definition. The environmentalists would respond that it would. Polluting the lake may be injuring people who might swim in or eat fish from it. Certainly it would be depriving people of the freedom to enjoy the lake. Although the environmentalist is correct, especially if we grant the legitimacy of a human right to a clean environment, the success of this reply is not enough to establish the general argument.

Consider the harm that results from the production of automobiles. We know statistically that about 50,000 persons per year will die and that nearly 250,000 others will be seriously injured in automobile accidents in the United States alone. Such death and injury, which is harmful, is avoidable. If that is the case, doesn't the avoid-harm criterion require that the production of automobiles for profit cease? Not really. What such arguments point out is that some refinement of the moral minimum standard needs to take place. Take the automobile example. The automobile is itself a good-producing instrument. Because of the advantages of automobiles, society accepts the possible risks that go in using them. Society also accepts many other types of avoidable harm. We take certain risks—ride in planes, build bridges, and mine coal—to pursue advantageous goals. It seems that the high benefits of some activities justify the resulting harms. As long as the risks are known, it is not wrong that some avoidable harm be permitted so that other social and individual goals can be achieved. The avoidable-harm criterion needs some sharpening.

Using the automobile as a paradigm, let us consider the necessary refinements for the avoid-harm criterion. It is a fundamental principle of ethics that "ought" implies "can." That expression means that you can be held morally responsible only for events within your power. In the ought-implies-can principle, the overwhelming majority of highway deaths and injuries is not the responsibility of the automaker. Only those deaths and injuries attributable to unsafe automobile design can be attributed to the automaker. The ought-implies-can principle can also be used to absolve the auto companies of responsibility for death and injury from safety defects that the automakers could not reasonably know existed. The company could not be expected to do anything about them.

Does this mean that a company has an obligation to build a car as safe as it knows how? No. The standards for safety must leave the product's cost within the price range of the consumer ("ought implies can" again). Comments about engineering and equipment capability are obvious enough. But for a business, capability is also a function of profitability. A company that builds a maximally safe car at a cost that puts it at a competitive disadvantage and hence threatens its survival is building a safe car that lies beyond the capability of the company.

Critics of the automobile industry will express horror at these remarks, for by making capability a function of profitability, society will continue to have avoidable deaths and injuries; however, the situation is not as dire as the critics imagine. Certainly capability should not be sacrificed completely so that profits can be maximized. The decision to build products that are cheaper in cost but are not maximally safe is a social decision that has widespread support. The arguments occur over the line between safety and cost. What we have is a classical trade-off situation. What is desired is some appropriate mix between engineering safety and consumer demand. To say there must be some mix between engineering safety and consumer demand

is not to justify all the decisions made by the automobile companies. Ford Motor Company made a morally incorrect choice in placing Pinto gas tanks where it did. Consumers were uninformed, the record of the Pinto in rear-end collisions was worse than that of competitors, and Ford fought government regulations.

Let us apply the analysis of the automobile industry to the issue before us. That analysis shows that an automobile company does not violate its obligation to avoid harm and hence is not in violation of the moral minimum if the trade-off between potential harm and the utility of the products rests on social consensus and competitive realities.

As long as business obeys the environmental laws and honors other standard moral obligations, most harm done to the environment by business has been accepted by society. Through their decisions in the marketplace, we can see that most consumers are unwilling to pay extra for products that are more environmentally friendly than less friendly competitive products. Nor is there much evidence that consumers are willing to conserve resources, recycle, or tax themselves for environmental causes.

Consider the following instances reported in the *Wall Street Journal*. The restaurant chain Wendy's tried to replace foam plates and cups with paper, but customers in the test markets balked. Procter and Gamble offered Downey fabric softener in concentrated form that requires less packaging than ready-to-use products; however the concentrate version is less convenient because it has to be mixed with water. Sales have been poor. Procter and Gamble manufactures Vizir and Lenor brands of detergents in concentrate form, which the customer mixes at home in reusable bottles. Europeans will take the trouble; Americans will not. Kodak tried to eliminate its yellow film boxes but met customer resistance. McDonald's has been testing mini-incinerators that convert trash into energy but often meets opposition from community groups that fear the incinerators will pollute the air. A McDonald's spokesperson points out that the emissions are mostly carbon dioxide and water vapor and are "less offensive than a barbecue." Exxon spent approximately \$9,200,000 to "save" 230 otters (\$40,000 for each otter). Otters in captivity cost \$800. Fishermen in Alaska are permitted to shoot otters as pests. Given these facts, doesn't business have every right to assume that public tolerance for environmental damage is quite high, and hence current legal activities by corporations that harm the environment do not violate the avoid-harm criterion?

Recently environmentalists have pointed out the environmental damage caused by the widespread use of disposable diapers. Are Americans ready to give them up and go back to cloth diapers and the diaper pail? Most observers think not. Procter and Gamble is not violating the avoid-harm criterion by manufacturing Pampers. Moreover, if the public wants cloth diapers, business certainly will produce them. If environmentalists want business to produce products that are friendlier to the environment, they must convince Americans to purchase them. Business will respond to the market. It is the consuming public that has the obligation to make the trade-off between cost and environmental integrity.

Data and arguments of the sort described should give environmental critics of business pause. Nonetheless, these critics are not without counterresponses. For example, they might respond that public attitudes are changing. Indeed, they point out, during the Reagan deregulation era, the one area where the public supported government regulations was in the area of environmental law. In addition, *Fortune* predicts environmental integrity as the primary demand of society on business in the 1990s.

More important, they might argue that environmentally friendly products are at a disadvantage in the marketplace because they have public good characteristics. After all, the best situation for the individual is one where most other people use environmentally friendly products but he or she does not, hence reaping the benefit of lower cost and convenience. Since everyone reasons this way, the real demand for environmentally friendly products cannot be registered in the market. Everyone is understating the value of his or her preference for environmentally friendly products. Hence, companies cannot conclude from market behavior that the environmentally unfriendly products are preferred.

Suppose the environmental critics are right that the public goods characteristic of environmentally friendly products creates a market failure. Does that mean the companies are obligated to stop producing these environmentally unfriendly products? I

think not, and I propose that we use the four conditions attached to the prevent-harm obligation to show why not. There is a need, and certainly corporations that cause environmental problems are in proximity. However, environmentally clean firms, if there are any, are not in proximity at all, and most business firms are not in proximity with respect to most environmental problems. In other words, the environmental critic must limit his or her argument to the environmental damage a business actually causes. The environmentalist might argue that Procter and Gamble ought to do something about Pampers; I do not see how an environmentalist can use the avoid-harm criterion to argue that Procter and Gamble should do something about acid rain. But even narrowing the obligation to damage actually caused will not be sufficient to establish an obligation to pull a product from the market because it damages the environment or even to go beyond what is legally required to protect the environment. Even for damage actually done, both the high cost of protecting the environment and the competitive pressures of business make further action to protect the environment beyond the capability of business. This conclusion would be more serious if business were the last resort, but it is not.

Traditionally it is the function of the government to correct for market failure. If the market cannot register the true desires of consumers, let them register their preferences in the political arena. Even fairly conservative economic thinkers allow government a legitimate role in correcting market failure. Perhaps the responsibility for energy conservation and pollution control belongs with the government.

Although I think consumers bear a far greater responsibility for preserving and protecting the environment than they have actually exercised, let us assume that the basic responsibility rests with the government. Does that let business off the hook? No. Most of business's unethical conduct regarding the environment occurs in the political arena.

Far too many corporations try to have their cake and eat it too. They argue that it is the job of government to correct for market failure and then use their influence and money to defeat or water down regulations designed to conserve and protect the environment. They argue that consumers should decide how much conservation and protection the environment should have, and then they try to interfere with the exercise of that choice in the political arena. Such behavior is inconsistent and ethically inappropriate. Business has an obligation to avoid intervention in the political process for the purpose of defeating and weakening environmental regulations. Moreover, this is a special obligation to the environment since business does not have a general obligation to avoid pursuing its own parochial interests in the political arena. Business need do nothing wrong when it seeks to influence tariffs, labor policy, or monetary policy. Business does do something wrong when it interferes with the passage of environmental legislation. Why?

First, such a noninterventionist policy is dictated by the logic of the business's argument to avoid a special obligation to protect the environment. Put more formally:

1. Business argues that it escapes special obligations to the environment because it is willing to respond to consumer preferences in this matter.

2. Because of externalities and public goods considerations, consumers cannot express their preferences in the market.

3. The only other viable forum for consumers to express their preferences is in the political arena.

4. Business intervention interferes with the expression of these preferences.

5. Since point 4 is inconsistent with point 1, business should not intervene in the political process.

The importance of this obligation in business is even more important when we see that environmental legislation has special disadvantages in the political arena. Public choice reminds us that the primary interest of politicians is being reelected. Government policy will be skewed in favor of policies that provide benefits to an influential minority as long as the greater costs are widely dispersed. Politicians will also favor projects where benefits are immediate and where costs can be postponed to the future. Such strategies increase the likelihood that a politician will be reelected.

What is frightening about the environmental crisis is that both the conservation of scarce resources and pollution abatement require policies that go contrary to a politician's self-interest. The costs of cleaning up the environment are immediate and huge, yet the benefits are relatively long range (many of them exceedingly long range). Moreover, a situation where the benefits are widely dispersed and the costs are large presents a twofold problem. The costs are large enough so that all voters will likely notice them and in certain cases are catastrophic for individuals (e.g., for those who lose their jobs in a plant shutdown).

Given these facts and the political realities they entail, business opposition to environmental legislation makes a very bad situation much worse. Even if consumers could be persuaded to take environmental issues more seriously, the externalities, opportunities to free ride, and public goods characteristics of the environment make it difficult for even enlightened consumers to express their true preference for the environment in the market. The fact that most environmental legislation trades immediate costs for future benefits makes it difficult for politicians concerned about reelection to support it. Hence it is also difficult for enlightened consumers to have their preferences for a better environment honored in the political arena. Since lack of business intervention seems necessary, and might even be sufficient, for adequate environmental legislation, it seems business has an obligation not to intervene. Nonintervention would prevent the harm of not having the true preferences of consumers for a clean environment revealed. Given business's commitment to satisfying preferences, opposition to having these preferences expressed seems inconsistent as well.

The extent of this obligation to avoid intervening in the political process needs considerable discussion by ethicists and other interested parties. Businesspeople will surely object that if they are not permitted to play a role, Congress and state legislators will make decisions that will put them at a severe competitive disadvantage. For example, if the United States develops stricter environmental controls than other countries do, foreign imports will have a competitive advantage over domestic products. Shouldn't business be permitted to point that out? Moreover, any legislation that places costs on one industry rather than another confers advantages on other industries. The cost to the electric utilities from regulations designed to reduce the pollution that causes acid rain will give advantages to natural gas and perhaps even solar energy.

Shouldn't the electric utility industry be permitted to point that out?

These questions pose difficult questions, and my answer to them should be considered highly tentative. I believe the answer to the first question is "yes" and the answer to the second is "no." Business does have a right to insist that the regulations apply to all those in the industry. Anything else would seem to violate norms of fairness. Such issues of fairness do not arise in the second case. Since natural gas and solar do not contribute to acid rain and since the costs of acid rain cannot be fully captured in the market, government intervention through regulation is simply correcting a market failure. With respect to acid rain, the electric utilities do have an advantage they do not deserve. Hence they have no right to try to protect it.

Legislative bodies and regulatory agencies need to expand their staffs to include technical experts, economists, and engineers so that the political process can be both neutral and highly informed about environmental matters. To gain the respect of business and the public, its performance needs to improve. Much more needs to be said to make any contention that business ought to stay out of the political debate theoretically and practically possible. Perhaps these suggestions point the way for future discussion.

Ironically business might best improve its situation in the political arena by taking on an additional obligation to the environment. Businesspersons often have more knowledge about environmental harms and the costs of cleaning them up. They may often have special knowledge about how to prevent environmental harm in the first place. Perhaps business has a special duty to educate the public and to promote environmentally responsible behavior.

SUSTAINABLE DEVELOPMENT AND CORPORATE SOCIAL RESPONSIBILITY
Joseph R. DesJardins

What are the environmental responsibilities of business? According to both classical and neoclassical models of corporate social responsibility, business fulfills its environmental responsibility within the workings of a free market economic system, a system in which economic growth is an unquestioned value. I will argue that unless growth is constrained in ethically and ecologically significant ways, business activities will be ethically and ecologically deficient.

THE CLASSICAL MODEL

The classical model of corporate social responsibility is succinctly captured in this short quotation from Milton Friedman, perhaps its best-known defender:

> There is one and only one social responsibility of business—to use its resources and engage in activities to increase its profits so long as it stays within the rules of the game, which is to say,

engages in open and free competition, without deception or fraud.[1]

The rationale for this view clearly follows from the role of corporations within a free market economic system. Corporations are organized to provide the most efficient means for producing goods and services and thus for satisfying consumer demand. In an open and competitive market, the prices of goods and services are established by the willingness of consumers to pay for them. Willingness to pay, in turn, is a measure of how much value a consumer places on the particular product. Thus, increasing profits is evidence that goods and services are going to those consumers who most value them. Profits, therefore, are the measure of how efficiently a manager is using resources to meet consumer demand; maximum profit coincides with the most efficient use of resources in satisfying consumer demand.

What are the environmental implications of this view? Ultimately, the classical model of social responsibility denies that business has any direct environmental responsibility. Business need only pursue profits within the law. Environmental con-

Reprinted by permission of the author.

cerns will be adequately served by the workings of a competitive market. The responsibility of the rest of us, which presumably includes business leaders and lobbyists, is to ensure that the legal system protects and promotes the workings of the market.

Accordingly, the classical model sees business as cooperating with society in attaining the environmental goals freely chosen by consumers in the marketplace. But business serves these environmental goals not by taking on any special environmental responsibility, but by fulfilling its function within a free market economic system.

Philosophical challenges to the classical model are well known. I would mention only three that are particularly relevant for environmental concerns.

First, a variety of phenomena classified as *market failures* demonstrate that markets offer no guarantees of successfully meeting society's demands. Externalities like pollution and resource depletion, and goods for which no pricing mechanism exists, like the survival of an endangered species or the scenic beauty or historical significance of a landscape, provide examples of market failures that lead to environmental destruction.

A second philosophical challenge points out that business interests are not always identical to market goals. One way in which a corporate manager can maximize profits is to lobby government to protect the particular firm or the particular industry from market forces. The savings and loan bailout, import tariffs, farm price supports, the Chrysler bailout, and countless other examples amply demonstrate the divergence of business and market interests. In all of these examples the corporate goal of profit maximization (or, more to the point, survival) is incompatible with the market goal of optimal satisfaction of consumer preferences.

The final challenge raises a more general and familiar problem with the ethical goal of free market economics. Ultimately, the most fundamental ethical goal of the classical model is the maximum satisfaction of those individual preferences that get expressed in markets. The "good of society" that Friedman identifies as the goal of Smith's invisible hand is simply the satisfaction of consumer preferences. But given that human preferences can include those that are both silly and immoral, we have little reason to assume that the maximum satisfaction of preferences is an ethical goal. As Mark Sagoff has convincingly argued, there are only question-begging answers to this question.[2]

Depending on what people prefer, maximally satisfying preferences could turn out to produce results that are vacuous, trivial, immoral, unjust, or just plain foolish.

The environmental implications of this challenge are enormous. For the entire range of issues in which economic growth competes with environmental or ecological ends, the classical model will necessarily locate corporate responsibility on the side of economic growth. In this respect, "economic growth" is simply another phrase for increased satisfaction of consumer preferences. Whatever one thinks about any particular issue that clashes with economic growth—issues ranging from wilderness protection to conserving biodiversity, and from energy conservation to pollution control—it is surely wrong to assume that economic growth is always the morally preferable goal.

NEOCLASSICAL MODELS

Neoclassical models of corporate social responsibility attempt to reform the classical model in light of such philosophical challenges. According to Norman Bowie, "Something of a consensus has emerged in the past ten years regarding the social responsibility of business." Bowie refers to this "neoclassical" model of corporate social responsibility as holding that corporations ought to seek profits while nevertheless obeying a "moral minimum."[3]

Bowie's views are representative of the neoclassical revisions of the classical model. His views on business's environmental responsibilities, for example, offer answers to the three challenges just discussed. Bowie suggests that government regulation has a legitimate role in correcting market failure. Thus, the law steps in to impose obligations on business where markets fail. To counter the possibility that business might use its political influence to set the environmental agenda, Bowie argues that business has a special obligation "to avoid intervention in the political process for the purpose of defeating or weakening environmental legislation." Finally, to guarantee that the workings of the market have at least a minimal moral content, Bowie interprets the moral minimum as including protection of individual health, safety, and basic freedom.[4]

Two strategies for dealing with environmental concerns within the neoclassical model suggest themselves: One might argue to incorporate direct ethical responsibility to natural objects into the moral minimum, or one can leave it to the market to decide the environmental limits of business activities. Bowie's own views are straightforwardly anthropocentric, and he would argue against the first strategy. Given the requirement that any reasonable account of business's environmental responsibilities must be capable of influencing business's behavior, he may well be correct in foregoing this option. It seems unlikely that, at least in the short term, the business community would be motivated by attempts to grant moral standing to natural objects.

Bowie himself adopts the second strategy. He is willing to leave the extent of business's environmental responsibilities to the "social consensus" that emerges from the market and from the law. Once the moral minimum is met, business is responsible only to follow the demands of society, both those expressed in law and in the demands that consumers express in the market.

CHALLENGES TO THE NEOCLASSICAL MODEL

A brief consideration of the present economic, ecological, and population realities reveals the ethical difficulties with the neoclassical model. Consider three relevant facts. First, a significant percentage of the world's population lives at or below a minimal level of subsistence. One quarter of the world's population lives in industrialized countries, and these people consume 80 percent of the world's goods. To meet the simple needs and minimum demands of the other 75 percent of the world's population, significant economic growth is necessary over the next few decades. One estimate suggests that a fivefold increase in energy use and a five-to-tenfold increase in general economic activity would be required over the next fifty years to bring the standard of living for the *present* population of developing countries into line with that of people in the industrialized world.[5]

Second, even conservative estimates suggest that during these fifty years world population will double, bringing the total population to over eleven billion people.[6] Thus, economic activity would need to increase by ten-to-twentyfold to bring the standard of living of the *actual* world population in fifty years into line with that enjoyed by people in the industrialized present.

Third, we must recognize that the natural resources of the planet are ultimately the only source for this economic activity. The three standard factors of production—natural resources, capital, and labor—all derive from the productive capacity of the earth. In simple terms, raw material, energy, and food are the essential elements of all economic activity. One estimate suggests that if the world's population in forty years consumed nonrenewable mineral and petroleum resources at current U.S. rates, these resources would last fewer than ten years.[7]

The conclusion from these factors should be obvious. Any model of corporate social responsibility that does not address the capacity of economic activity to meet the basic needs of human beings in the near future will be morally inadequate. Continued business activity that ignores economic, ecological, and population realities will be socially irresponsible. As typically defended, neither classical nor neoclassical models succeed on these grounds because both presuppose a growth-based market economy.

THE "SUSTAINABILITY ALTERNATIVE"

The alternative that I will defend holds that business has a moral responsibility to ensure that its activities be ecologically sustainable. The "moral minimum" that constrains economic activity should be identified with ecological sustainability. Business remains free to pursue profits within the rules of the game, but the rules must be changed to include the obligation to leave natural ecosystems no worse off in the process.

Economists have long recognized that all markets operate within constraints, the physical limits imposed by scientific laws being the most obvious. The classical model of corporate social responsibility incorporates legal constraints as part of these limits, and the neoclassical model expands this to include moral constraints as well. The sustainable development model seeks to combine the natural constraints established by ecological laws with minimal moral constraints.

One simple statement of the concept of sustainability comes from the World Commission on Environment and Development. Sustainable development "meets the needs of the present without compromising the ability of future generations to meet their own needs."[8] Thus, business has an obligation to avoid harming the ecosphere, understood as the interdependent community of living organisms and their nonliving physical environment.

To say that business has an obligation to avoid harming the ecosphere is to say that business has an obligation to avoid any activities that decrease an ecosystem's long-term ability to sustain life. We might adopt "no harm to the entire ecosphere" as our *general* standard for the moral minimum, and regard the application of this standard to local ecosystems as what needs to be worked out in detail in specific cases.

In general, the implication of this is that business may continue to develop natural resources and convert them to meet the demands of the marketplace. Economic development is assumed on this model. However, business has the obligation to compensate ecosystems for the loss of productive capacity caused by its activity. A helpful image for understanding these responsibilities perceives natural resources as capital. Our goal should be maximum sustainable yield in which we live off of the income generated by that capital without depleting the investment itself.

More specifically, as we move from the "macrolevel" economic models towards the "microlevel" responsibilities of firms and industries, we should adopt three normative principles:

1. *Businesses should not use renewable resources at rates that exceed their ability to replenish themselves.* Agriculture and forestry are two industries that would have clear responsibilities in this respect. But any business that uses plant, animal, air, and water resources (in other words, most businesses) must ensure that these resources are being used at sustainable rates. Failure to do so would require reparation for these harms.

2. *Businesses should use nonrenewable resources only at the rate at which alternatives are developed or loss of opportunities compensated.* Industries that rely on nonrenewable resources, ranging from wilderness areas to fossil fuels, would be obligated to guarantee future generations the opportunity to obtain the benefits of these resources.[9] Humans value such resources not in themselves, but for the uses to which they are put. Once they are

used, we cannot recover these resources; we can, however, compensate future people for the loss of these resources by guaranteeing them equal opportunities for using (but not using up) these or similar resources.

3. *Businesses cannot produce wastes and emissions that exceed the capacity of the ecosystem to assimilate them.* Waste and inefficiency are more than just economic wrongs; they are moral and environmental wrongs as well. Using recycled materials in production, producing goods that can be recycled, and recycling by-products of production would be clear responsibilities. Indeed, the responsibility to take back a product after its consumer use, for example, recycling used cars, should also be a part of business's responsibilities.

We can sketch a wide range of more specific duties that comply with these general obligations. Obviously, we have the duty to conserve resources. Restoration of an ecosystem to its former productive capacity should be part of this moral minimum. Research and development aimed at finding ecologically benign products and production techniques is another ethical duty. Research and development aimed at providing present and future people with an equal opportunity for attaining a decent life should accompany any use of nonrenewable resources.

In summary, industries ought to be modeled on ecosystems:

> In such a system the consumption of energy and materials is optimized, waste generation is minimized and the effluents of one process— whether they are spent catalysts from petroleum refining, fly and bottom ash from electric power generation or discarded plastic containers from consumer products—serve as the raw material for another process.[10]

DEFENSE OF THE SUSTAINABILITY MODEL

The alternative model that I suggest allows business to continue pursuing profit within the "rules of the game," but argues that the rules of the economic game must change. Economic growth can no longer be the goal of economic activity. Sustainable development should establish the new ethical parameters for economics and business.

How might this alternative be defended? Briefly, it seems to me that the very same values that justify free markets and economic growth will, in light of present environmental and population realities, provide ample justification of the sustainability alternative. What are these values?

Utilitarians justify market economies by claiming that they maximize overall happiness. But surely economic activity that is not ecologically sustainable cannot maximize the overall good unless we artificially restrict our calculations to the present generation living in the developed world. At present, economic growth jeopardizes the future happiness of countless billions of people. The point of sustainable development is that economic development is not a zero-sum game. Used appropriately, natural resources can satisfy both present and future interests. No doubt we would have to change some of our present practices and recognize that we need not satisfy every desire (such as all the conveniences of a "throw-away" society), but we would not be "reduced" to subsistence living either. Thus, on a sustainable economic model (living off of the interest rather than the capital), we can ensure reasonably high levels of happiness into the indefinite future. Of any version of utilitarianism, this surely is the most justified alternative.

Market economies are also justified by appeal to individual rights of freedom and equality. Here, too, a plausible case can be made for thinking that sustainable economics better serves these values than growth-based free markets. Economic activity that uses natural resources at an unsustainable rate implicitly denies to our descendants an equal opportunity to use these resources. To justify unsustainable growth, we need to show why our freedoms and interests take precedence over the freedoms and interests of our children and grandchildren. At first glance, at least, I see no reason for believing that our freedoms and interests do take precedence.

More needs to be done, of course, to develop an ethical justification for the alternative of sustainable development. Much more needs to be done to specify the details of business's responsibility within this model. Nevertheless, the risks of uncritically accepting the status quo seem too high. Unrestricted economic growth cannot go on indefinitely, and the longer we go without acknowledging this fact, the greater the risk we create for future generations.

NOTES

1. Milton Friedman, *Capitalism and Freedom* (Chicago: University of Chicago Press, 1962), 133.

2. Mark Sagoff, *Economy of the Earth* (New York: Cambridge University Press, 1990).

3. Norman Bowie, "New Directions in Corporate Social Responsibility," in *Business Horizons* (July–August 1991): 56. Bowie's own views are developed in *Business Ethics* (Englewood Cliffs, N.J.: Prentice Hall, 1982) as well as in the second edition of that book, written with Ronald Duska (1990). Bowie applies this thinking to environmental matters in "Morality, Money, and Motor Cars," in *Business, Ethics, and the Environment: The Public Policy Debate*, eds. W. Michael Hoffman, Robert Frederick, and Edward Petry, Jr. (New York: Quorum Books, 1990), 89–97.

4. Norman Bowie, "Morality, Money, and Motor Cars," 91–95.

5. Jim MacNeill, "Strategies for Sustainable Development," in *Managing Planet Earth* (New York: Scientific American, 1990), 109–123.

6. Present estimates suggest that the rate of population increase is one billion people every nine to ten years. The doubling to eleven billion in fifty years is "conservative" in the sense that it assumes, contrary to trends, that the rate of increase will remain constant.

7. Robert Frosch and Nicholas Gallopoulos, "Strategies for Manufacturing," in *Managing Planet Earth* (New York: Scientific American, 1990), 98.

8. World Commission on Environment and Development, *Our Common Future* (New York: Oxford University Press, 1987).

9. An early version of this argument was offered by Brian Barry, "Intergenerational Justice in Energy Policy," in *Energy and the Future*, eds. Douglas MacLean and Peter Brown (Totowa, N.J.: Rowman and Littlefield, 1983).

10. Frosch and Gallopoulos, "Strategies," 98.

Decision Scenario 1
OZONE DEPLETION AND CONSUMER PRODUCTS

The summer of 1988 was one of the warmest on record, and parts of the Midwest suffered severe drought conditions. To some observers, this was evidence of the "greenhouse effect." The greenhouse effect theory claims the release of certain gases into the atmosphere leads to destruction of the high-altitude layer of ozone that surrounds the earth. When this protective layer is diminished, larger amounts of ultraviolet radiation enter Earth's atmosphere. This could lead to increased levels of cancer, cataracts, and damage to the human immune system. In addition, increased levels of certain gases trap the sun's heat within the atmosphere, causing temperatures to rise.

Many scientists believe that chlorofluorocarbons (CFCs) are most responsible for the damage to the ozone layer. These artificial chemicals are used in many consumer products and packages. In 1985, 150 million pounds of CFCs were used in the manufacture of polystyrene foam packages and food containers, and home insulation. Another 150 million pounds were used in solvents for dry cleaning, and in the production of airplanes, computers, and spacecraft. Approximately 100 million pounds were used in stationary air conditioning and refrigeration (homes, offices, and businesses), and 120 million pounds were used in car and truck air conditioning.

Consumers could help slow pollution of the atmosphere with wide-ranging changes in their behavior, such as going without air conditioning in cars. Consumers could buy spring mattresses, non-foam furniture, and paper products, and boycott foam coffee cups, foam insulation, and foam food packaging. Of course, individual consumers may not have a great incentive to change their behavior if other consumers do not do likewise.

- What would be a reasonable public policy regarding CFCs?
- Should the government step in?
- Should private firms take it upon themselves to do away with air conditioning?
- What if there is evidence that such decisions would put the firm at a competitive disadvantage?

Decision Scenario 2
BOOMER V. ATLANTIC CEMENT CO.

In 1962 the Atlantic Cement Company began operating a cement plant outside of Albany, New York. Over 300 residents of the area were employed at the plant, and by 1970 Atlantic had invested over $45 million in it. People living near the plant, including the Boomer family, filed suit against the company, claiming that the dust and vibrations caused by the plant were damaging both their health and property. These neighbors sought an injunction to require the plant to stop the dust and vibrations. Unfortunately, there was no technology that would allow the plant to continue operating without the dust and vibrations.

The courts decided that the Boomers and their neighbors were indeed suffering harms caused by the cement plant. It is normal in such cases for a court to issue an injunction. However, in this case the court reasoned that the costs that would be involved in closing down the plant far outweighed the costs of the harms being done to the neighbors. Accordingly, the court decided that Atlantic should pay the neighbors $185,000 for damages already done, and ongoing monthly payments to compensate them for the harms that they would continue to suffer. This amount, $535 per month, was calculated to be a fair market value for what they could receive if they were to rent their property. In calculating this amount, the court presumably figured that the neighbors would thus be free to leave the area and therefore the nuisance without suffering the economic loss of their property.

The case was appealed to New York State's highest court. This court agreed that the neighbors had established the existence of a nuisance and that it was normal in such cases to issue an injunction. The majority also agreed with the lower court that the disparity between the costs of closing the plant and the costs of the nuisances was too great to justify granting the injunction. However, instead of accepting the ongoing payment plan, this high court decided that Atlantic should pay only permanent damages for the total present and future economic loss to the neighbors' property.

In a dissenting opinion, one judge argued that the potential harms to the Boomers' health should have been factored into the calculation of costs involved. Further, he also argued that harms to the general public were being ignored in these decisions. In effect, the court was allowing a company to harm its neighbors as long as it paid a fee to do so.

- Is this a case in which individual rights were overridden by utilitarian calculation of costs and benefits?

- Should the courts have treated this case as a simple dispute between private parties, or was there a larger public concern at stake?

- How much harm (economic and otherwise) would have to be done to the Boomers to justify closing the plant?

Decision Scenario 3
THE EPA'S MANAGEMENT OF SUPERFUND

In 1980 Congress passed the Comprehensive Environmental Response, Compensation and Liability Act (CERCLA), better known as Superfund. This law created a $1.6 billion federal fund over a five-year period to be used in assisting the cleanup of hazardous wastes. The Superfund legislation also made corporate polluters jointly and severally liable for their waste disposal practices. The doctrine of joint and several liability allows the government to hold a corporation liable for all the cleanup costs at a toxic waste site even though that particular corporation might be responsible only for part of the waste dumped there. The Environmental Protection Agency (EPA) was given responsibility for administering the Superfund program.

In 1986 Congress passed the Superfund Amendments and Reauthorization Act (SARA). The new law enlarged the federal contribution to toxic cleanups to $8.5 billion over five additional years. Perhaps more significantly, SARA was an attempt to respond to difficulties that had become apparent in the EPA's management of Superfund.

This case was prepared from information in the following sources: Patricia Bradley, "The State Role in the New Superfund Program," a research monograph prepared for the Pennsylvania State Legislative Committee on Air and Water Pollution Control; *The Environmental Reporter*, Vol. 19, No. 5, pp. 174 and 179, No. 7, pp. 219–220, No. 8, pp. 260 and 267; and Kenneth Cohen, "Allocation of Superfund Costs Among Potentially Responsible Parties," *The Environmental Law Reporter*, vol. 18, no. 5: 10158–10164.

The EPA had pursued a policy of transferring toxic wastes from Superfund sites to specially approved landfills. Environmentalists criticized the policy as creating more problems because the landfill disposal tended only to create new hazardous waste sites. SARA directed the EPA to pursue permanent treatment and disposal methods rather than merely moving the wastes from one site to another.

Other aspects of the 1986 SARA included direction to the EPA (a) to use the most cost-effective remedy for cleanup, (b) to pursue negotiations with whose responsible for toxic wastes in order to reach a financial agreement about cleanup costs, and (c) to seek state involvement in approving the cleanup settlement.

Corporate critics of the Superfund program contend that it is unfair to those companies who are forced to pay more than would be required to clean up their own share of a toxic waste site. Further, they argue that the threat of joint and several liability in a litigated settlement blackmails companies into agreeing to pay more than a fair share of the cleanup costs.

Environmentalists, on the other hand, continue to criticize EPA's management of Superfund, citing a continued use of temporary and partial cleanups of toxic waste sites. They find that these continuing problems have their source in SARA's standards for negotiations over cleanup costs. Those standards require the EPA to seek private-party participation in proposing cleanup methods and in executing the cleanup itself. SARA also retained the requirement from CERCLA that the states pay 10 percent of cleanup costs. Politically, these two requirements put pressure on the EPA to come to consensual agreements with the states and the polluters, both of whom have vested interests in limiting the cost of cleanup. Thus, SARA's negotiation standards may militate against agreements that are capable of funding the more costly full and permanent disposal methods. Current congressional moves to reduce the federal contribution to Superfund will exacerbate the problem.

Now that Congress has banned ocean dumping and has placed stricter requirements on land disposal of wastes, permanent cleanup will become

even more urgent. With limited disposal capacity and with the high cost of full cleanups, one must wonder whether the economic lifestyle that generates so much toxic waste is ultimately sustainable in the long run.

- What justification is there for holding polluters jointly and severally liable? Are the same reasons offered to justify joint and several liability for injurious products applicable to pollution? (See Chapter Nine.)
- Should EPA be allowed to specify alternatives to full and permanent cleanup of toxic waste sites?
- Are toxic waste sites and their expensive cleanups an unpleasant but acceptable fact of contemporary life, or are they unacceptable costs that demand radical changes in lifestyle?

Decision Scenario 4
PACIFIC LUMBER

The 1980s witnessed a tremendous number of corporate takeovers financed largely by debt in the form of "junk bonds." Such "leveraged buy-outs" were driven by the possibility of enormous profits over short periods of time. Takeover specialists believed that they could either run the business more efficiently than present managers or, more commonly, that they could break up the existing company and sell it for large profits. "Junk bonds" refers to the risky loans that investors made to finance these takeovers. To balance the risk, these bonds promised high rates of return on investment. Since most of the purchase price for a takeover was financed by such high-interest loans, the new management (typically financial specialists with no experience in the particular industry involved) was under immediate pressure to generate substantial income to begin paying off the debt.

One such takeover target was Pacific Lumber Company, based in Humboldt County in northern California. Pacific Lumber was a publicly traded company run by the same family for almost one hundred years. The management philosophy of Pacific Lumber seemed to epitomize ethically responsible management. The company had a long

record of satisfactorily meeting or exceeding the needs of many stakeholders: workers, shareholders, the local community, and the forests that it harvested. Pacific Lumber paid its employees well in good times, supported them financially in bad times, guaranteed jobs for family members, and generously supported scholarships for employee children and employee pension funds. Despite all of this, Pacific Lumber provided a steady profit picture and steady rate of return for investors and was debt-free. Throughout its history, the company harvested little more than 2 percent of its trees annually, about equal to the annual growth rate of the trees. Unfortunately, perhaps Pacific Lumber managed its assets too responsibly.

Since the company was debt-free and possessed so many resources that it was not using to the maximum (for example, the other 98 percent of its forests), it made an inviting takeover target to outside financiers. In 1986, Charles Hurwitz and his company Maxxam, Inc., orchestrated a leveraged buyout of Pacific Lumber. Almost $800 million of the nearly $900 million purchase price was financed by high-interest junk bonds managed by Drexel Burnham Lambert, the home of the infamous junk-bond specialist and corporate raider Michael Milken.

The results of the takeover were predictable. The new owners increased the rate of timber harvest to help pay off their huge debt. Pacific Lumber was split into three separate concerns, and much of its debt was transferred to these new companies and refinanced with lower-interest loans, secured with the forest lands as collateral. Among these lands were thousands of acres of one hundred-year-old virgin redwood trees. The formerly overfunded pension plan was terminated. Some of this money was used to repay debt, and the rest was used to replace the pension fund with annuities purchased from an insurance company that Hurwitz owned. Employment in the area increased slightly as a result of the increased logging. From all appearances, the takeover was successful on economic grounds because virtually all resources were being used more efficiently after the takeover.

Hurwitz had been involved in numerous other controversial business deals. At one time he owned 24 percent of United Savings Association of Texas, a savings and loan company that was among the many that failed in recent years. This failure was traced to purchases of Drexel junk bonds that were also connected with Michael Milken. As a result of this collapse, taxpayers lost $1.6 billion and the Federal Deposit Insurance Corporation had a claim

for over $500 million against United Savings' parent company, the United Financial Group. In light of this, some defenders of the old-growth forests now threatened by Pacific Lumber's increased logging have proposed a "debt-for-nature" swap. This proposal, supported by some in Congress and in the California state legislature, would forgive some of the debt owed to the government in exchange for thousands of acres of old-growth Pacific forests.

- Is the efficient and short-term use of resources always the ethically most responsible use? Were Pacific Lumber's previous owners fulfilling their responsibility to shareholders when they did not maximize profits?

- Do two thousand-year-old sequoia trees possess a value beyond the economic value that they could bring as timber? How would you explain and defend your answer?

- Assuming that increased harvesting of timber proves economically beneficial to an entire region, do people outside the region deserve "standing" in debates about resource use?

- Should the government pursue the debt-for-nature swap? Is the company holding nature hostage to pay for its own financial mismanagement?

Decision Scenario 5
INDUSTRY AS ECOSYSTEM

Perhaps the most common image used in the science of ecology is that of the circle. Natural processes are often described as "cyclical." The water cycle involves evaporation, which leads to cloud formation, which leads to rain, which supports rivers, lakes, and oceans, which evaporate to form clouds, and so on. Likewise for other natural, life-supporting elements such as nitrogen, oxygen, and carbon. Indeed, ecology seems to suggest that life itself is cyclical: Simple molecules are converted to plants and animals that die and then decompose back into simple molecules, and the cycle begins again.

Some observers believe that industry should mimic ecosystems. Use of resources and energy

should be optimized with minimal waste, and products should be recycled back into the productive process with minimal loss. Recycling, of course, is not new. In recent decades the amount of paper, aluminum, and glass recycled has increased tremendously. Industrial uses of former waste products have also increased, from the use of sawdust in the manufacture of paperboard products to the use of waste steam in heating systems. (You might remember Film Recovery Inc. from Chapter Nine as an example of a firm that specialized, although irresponsibly, in silver recycling.)

This model can be extended well beyond simple recycling, however. One suggestion is to hold industry responsible for the full life of its products. After a product has been used for its normal life, the company that brought it to the market would be responsible for taking back the product and safely recycling it into usable resources. Thus, for example, automobile manufacturers would be responsible for taking back the used vehicle formerly thought of as "junk." Whatever parts of a product that are not used by the consumer, what is thought of as waste and typically thrown away, would be brought back into the system. Not only would this model reduce waste (one estimate is that the world population currently generates almost 200 billion tons of solid waste each year), but it would provide an incentive for industry to treat natural resources in ways that would be sustainable over the long term. This model is particularly relevant when thinking about the challenges faced by disposal of hazardous wastes. Companies marketing products that produce hazardous wastes would be required to take back the waste and recycle it into nonhazardous forms.

Of course, such a model would require major changes in the way we do business. Consumers would be more like renters, paying a price for the use of some product but not free to dispose of that product in just any way that they choose. Initially,

prices may rise as manufacturers must assume new costs, but this would provide opportunities and incentives for products that can be recycled inexpensively and with little waste. Further, waste disposal costs at present are not factored into the price of most products (they are "externalities," in the language of economists); thus, both consumers and producers are enjoying a free benefit at the expense of the rest of society. A market defender might argue that such costs should be internalized into the price of the product anyway.

- Should manufacturers be responsible for the final disposal of their products? Should industries that are unable to recycle their products be penalized for wasting resources?

- If we modeled industry on ecosystems, what might happen to the nuclear power industry, whose wastes remain dangerous for millions of years?

- Has the ability of manufacturers to pass on the costs of waste disposal created our throw-away society? Would a requirement that these costs be internalized into the price of the product encourage innovation or hurt the economy?

13

Discrimination in the Workplace

Race, Gender, Disabilities

U ntil the 1970s, white males made up the majority of the U.S. work force. By 1980, women made up 43 percent of the work force, African-American males 10 percent, and Hispanic males under 10 percent. It is estimated that during the 1990s 85 percent of the net growth in the U.S. work force will come from people of color, women, and immigrants.* There can be no denial that the U.S. workplace is undergoing significant cultural change. Workers in the 1990s are different from workers in the 1960s; they look different, they think differently, and they have different interests, needs, and values.

Yet, when looking at positions of power, prestige, and wealth today, we continue to see a population that is overwhelmingly white and male. Many explanations are possible for this fact. The choices that women made concerning work and family, the social expectations placed on women, and the size of the nonwhite population can go a long way toward explaining the demographics of the work force of earlier decades. But these explanations only go so far. Unjust, although sometimes legally sanctioned, discrimination against women and African Americans explains much of their absence from the workplace. It must surely also explain their continued absence from positions of power, prestige, and wealth.

"Discrimination" has several meanings. In one sense it refers to attitudes of hatred of, superiority to, and prejudice against people who are seen as different.

---

*These statistics are from *Handbook of Labor Statistics*, Bulletin 2340 (Washington, D.C.: U.S. Dept. of Labor, Aug. 1989), and William Johnston and Arnold Packer, *Workforce 2000* (Indianapolis: Hudson Institute, 1987).

Thus, identifying someone as a sexist suggests that he dislikes women, believes that they are inferior to men, and so on. We might call this *attitudinal* discrimination. In another sense, discrimination refers to how people are treated, or how society is arranged. What we might call *behavioral* discrimination refers to the fact that people are treated as inferior because they are different. Thus, we might speak of sexist hiring policies that deny women equal treatment in job opportunities.

It is important to see that these two types of discrimination are independent. One could have sexist attitudes, but not allow these attitudes to affect one's behavior toward women. One could also be a part of a system that treats women as inferior without oneself having conscious sexist beliefs.

While ethics would condemn both versions of discrimination, public policy and the law are ill-suited to counter attitudinal discrimination. Even if it were possible to change people's attitudes and beliefs, this would be undesirable in a democratic society that values freedom of thought and expression. But public policy can, and should, address discrimination in how people are treated. Here, both justice and the law are committed to equal treatment.

PUBLIC POLICY TO COUNTER DISCRIMINATION

We can see public policy aimed at countering discrimination as developing through three stages: equal treatment, affirmative action, and preferential treatment. As the first and perhaps most obvious step to counter discrimination, *equal treatment* policies guarantee legal access to social goods like jobs, promotions, and admissions to schools. Thus, it was in the name of equal treatment that the United States ended slavery and segregation, and granted women the right to vote. In effect, equal treatment amounts to a policy of passive nondiscrimination.

But typically the promise not to discriminate does little to change the imbalance in the workplace. People who have historically been disenfranchised might lack the experience, knowledge, or even the personal contacts that are often necessary in finding jobs. Both women and minorities might find the work environment unsupportive or even hostile once they get a job. We will reserve the term *affirmative action* for those programs that go beyond a passive acceptance of equal opportunity for all those who just happen to apply. Thus, affirmative action policies might actively recruit applicants from previously disadvantaged groups. Or they might establish programs or minority affairs offices to help support new hires. Such programs are affirmative action in the sense that they provide active, positive support for members of previously disadvantaged groups.

Preferential treatment policies, in contrast, extend to members of disadvantaged groups a different sort of consideration than that extended to others. Typically, preferential policies will actively prefer women or members of minority groups in hiring or promotion decisions.

In general, affirmative action policies do not raise serious ethical questions. Few object to a company policy aimed at recruiting women or African Americans, for example. The added "benefit" does not come at the expense of anyone else. When actual preference is given in hiring or promotion decisions, however, more significant ethical issues are raised. In particular, such issues are raised when an identifiable individual—the person who would have been hired or promoted were it not for the preference—is harmed by preferential decisions. Before considering the arguments for and against preferential treatment, it will be helpful to review different types of preferential treatment.

When a policy actually "prefers" members of disadvantaged groups over, typically, young white males, that policy effectively treats the characteristic of sex, race, or ethnic background as a qualification for the job. Thus, we can envision three types of preferential policies:

- Two equally qualified people apply for a job; person A is a member of a disadvantaged group and person B is not, so prefer A.

- Person A is a member of a disadvantaged group and is qualified for the job, so hire A (even if person B, who is not a member of that group, is more qualified).

- Person A is a member of a disadvantaged group, so hire A (regardless of other qualifications).

It is worth noting that the first policy is not significantly different from affirmative action. In the case of affirmative action, there is still some person, B, who is qualified and would have been hired had not the company actively gone out and recruited person A. But B has little room for complaint if person A is more qualified. This would typically be the goal under affirmative action policies. But suppose person A is not more qualified than B, but simply equally qualified. At this point the company has only three options: make the hiring decision on some random basis (flip a coin?); hire person B and help perpetuate discriminatory hiring practices (once again, the member of the disadvantaged group receives an undeserved disadvantage in the workplace); or hire person A and at least take one step towards ending discriminatory practices. Of course, person B is likely to complain at this point. But what legitimate claim can he make? He cannot claim some "right" to the job because any claim he can make can be made with equal strength by person A. At best he can claim that he was denied an equal opportunity to the job; the company should have flipped a coin.

However, since A and B are otherwise equally qualified, and since A has, but B lacks, a characteristic that can be seen as relevant for helping the employer accomplish some goal (namely, being a woman, or being a member of another disadvantaged group), A can be judged as more qualified in virtue of this very characteristic. Thus, it can be argued that being a woman, or being an African American, in a society that has systematically denied benefits like jobs and income to women and African Americans, is an additional qualification for a position.

Of course, hiring decisions are seldom this clear. It is difficult to imagine a situation in which we would say that two people are exactly "equal" in qualifications. In actual cases the situation will more likely resemble mere affirmative action (if person A is more qualified than B), or the second or third type of preferential policy described earlier. Unfortunately, these two policies do raise serious ethical questions. If person B is more qualified than person A, yet A is hired instead of B, then it would appear that B is being denied something he otherwise would have deserved. Whether B did suffer some ethically relevant harm, and if so whether this harm was overridden by some greater good, is at the center of the ethical controversy over preferential treatment.

Arguments For and Against

The arguments for and against preferential treatment fall into four broad types: critical arguments based on considerations of justice, critical arguments based on utilitarian calculation, supporting arguments based on justice, or supporting arguments based on utilitarian calculations.

To many observers the crucial questions focus on considerations of justice. All agree that there are some utilitarian considerations against preferential treatment: Some efficiency may be lost when the most qualified is not hired, anger and resentment can be created among white males, self-doubt can be created among women and minorities. There are also utilitarian considerations in support of preferential policies: successful role models are provided for younger women and minorities, diverse work forces can bring new and beneficial perspectives to the firm, and so forth. However, if it turns out that preferential policies are unjust, then these beneficial consequences must yield to the demands of justice. If preferential policies turn out to be a requirement of justice, then likewise the detrimental consequences must yield.

Objections to preferential policies based on considerations of justice often claim that they violate the rights of those who are not preferred (typically, a young white male). Some argue that preferential treatment violates the right of equal treatment and amounts to nothing other than "reverse discrimination." Others argue that preferential policies violate the rights of the most qualified candidates by giving jobs and promotions based on something other than desert. This position argues that a just society is a meritocracy in which benefits are distributed according to merit and qualifications.

Justice arguments in support of preferential treatment are often grouped as either forward-looking justifications or backward-looking justifications. Forward-looking justifications claim that preferential policies are necessary to bring us to a just society, where income, jobs, power, and prestige are no longer unjustly distributed along racial or sexual lines. Backward-looking justifications see preferential treatment as needed to compensate victims of past injustice.

This compensatory argument is presented and critiqued in our first reading by Robert Fullinwider. Fullinwider claims that compensation fails to provide an ethical justification of preferential treatment because it violates the rights of white males. Fullinwider appeals to the right of equal consideration for his ultimate defense.

In our second reading Richard Wasserstrom offers a critique of the merit objection to preferential treatment. Wasserstrom claims that our society is not a meritocracy and that there are good reasons for not being one. He goes on to offer a forward-looking defense of preferential treatment.

SEXUAL HARASSMENT

Besides the more blatant forms of discrimination in which they are denied jobs and promotions, working women face other unfair barriers as well. Sexual harassment in the workplace (which also may affect men) is one of the more serious of these barriers to equal and fair employment.

The Civil Rights Act of 1964 was a landmark piece of legislation that prohibited all forms of employment discrimination on the basis of race, color, religion, national origin, and sex. This was the primary federal law that enforced equal treatment in the workplace. In part, this law states:

> It shall be an unlawful employment practice for an employer: (1) to fail or refuse to hire or to discharge any individual, or otherwise to discriminate against any individual with respect to compensation, terms, conditions or privileges of employment because of such individual's race, color, religion, sex, or national origin or (2) to limit, segregate, or classify his employees or applicants for employment in any way which would deprive or tend to deprive any individual of employment opportunities or otherwise adversely affect his status as an employee, because of such individual's race, color, religion, sex, or national origin.

It took almost a decade after the passage of this act for courts to begin recognizing sexual harassment as a form of employment discrimination. Beginning in the mid-1970s, federal courts acknowledged that sexual harassment was an illegal form of sexual discrimination. In 1980, the Equal Employment Opportunity Commission issued clear guidelines that defined illegal sexual harassment:

> Unwelcome sexual advances, requests for sexual favors, and other verbal or physical conduct of a sexual nature constitute sexual harassment when (1) submission to such conduct is made either explicitly or implicitly a term or condition of an individual's employment, (2) submission to or rejection of such conduct by an individual is used as a basis for employment decisions affecting such individual, or (3) such conduct has the purpose or effect of unreasonably interfering with an individual's work performance or creating an intimidating, hostile, or offensive work environment.[*]

Based on the commission's ruling, two types of sexual harassment have been recognized: *quid pro quo* harassment and hostile work environment harassment. *Quid pro quo* (from the Latin for "this for that") harassment occurs when submission to sexual favors is made a condition for some job benefit. Such harassment can take the form of threats—"sleep with me or lose your promotion"—or sexual offers—"I can be a big help to your career if you'll go out with me." In both cases, a person exploits his or her position of authority in the workplace to obtain sexual favors from a co-worker. In both cases, workers face unjust and discriminatory obstacles in the workplace. The second type of sexual harassment has its roots in the Civil Rights Act's prohibition against acts that would tend to

---

[*]Equal Employment Opportunity Commission, 299 C.F.R. par. 1604.11(a).

deprive individuals employment opportunities or that adversely affect their work because of sex. Hostile work environment harassment occurs when the general sexual environment of a workplace is such that it interferes with a person's ability to do his or her job. Common examples would include repeated off-color jokes, lewd comments or suggestions, the display of sexually explicit or offensive material, touching, patting, or other physical contact. This conduct becomes sexual harassment when it is so distressing to a person that she or he finds it impossible to complete job duties.

In one sense, *quid pro quo* harassment raises familiar ethical and legal issues: Threats, intimidation, and coercion are common ethical and legal wrongs. In such cases, a worker would need only to prove that, in fact, the wrongful behavior occurred to prove the harassment claim. There are reasonably clear standards for what constitutes a threat or intimidating or coercive behavior. However, the issues are very different with hostile environment harassment. Here, one must show a continued pattern of activity and establish that this prevented the person's ability to do his or her job. But, how do we decide what behavior is "offensive" enough to prevent people from doing their job? How do we distinguish between flirting and harassment, between an innocent comment and a lewd remark? It seems that what one person finds to be offensive, another takes to be a mild joke. Whether a workplace is a "hostile" environment would seem to depend on individual points of view. Doesn't "offensiveness" lie in the eye of the beholder?

In cases where such disputes have arisen, courts have traditionally relied on what is called the "reasonable man" standard. (We saw this standard come into play in discussion of deceptive advertising: What one person finds deceptive, another finds mere puffery. Courts decide if an ad is deceptive by asking if it would deceive a "reasonable man.") With sexual harassment, however, an interesting philosophical question is raised: Is what is "reasonable" for men the same as what is "reasonable" for women? Might the reasonable "man" standard be biased against women? Should harassment be judged by a reasonable man standard or a reasonable woman standard? In the early 1990s, federal courts considered these questions, and in a 1991 case a Florida court concluded that the reasonable man standard was biased against women. Since this decision, courts have begun using a "reasonable woman" standard to interpret a hostile environment as one that a reasonable woman would find sufficiently offensive to prevent her from doing her job. Kathryn Abrams reviews some of these issues in "The Reasonable Woman," reprinted in this chapter.

DISABLED WORKERS

In 1990, the U.S. Congress passed, and President Bush signed into law, the Americans with Disabilities Act (ADA). Among other things, this law extends to people with disabilities the same rights to equal employment opportunities that the Civil Rights Act of 1964 granted to women and minorities. This law prohibits discrimination against people with disabilities and requires business to make reasonable accommodations to both employees and applicants with disabilities. In essence, then, the law both grants equal treatment to people with disabilities and requires affirmative action to be taken to accommodate their special needs. If a disabled person is otherwise qualified for a job, business has a responsibility to provide that person with an equal and fair opportunity to get and keep that job.

This law defines a disabled person as "one who has a physical or mental impairment that substantially limits a major life activity, has a record of an impairment, or is regarded as having an impairment." The ADA gives examples of disabilities such as mental retardation, cancer, muscular dystrophy, AIDS, emotional illness, visual impairments, alcoholism (but not active alcohol abuse), and physical handicaps. Drug abuse, weight, homosexuality, and poverty are conditions explicitly excluded from this law. It is estimated that there are forty-three million Americans who would be classified as disabled under these guidelines, 60 percent of whom are unemployed.* This law and these figures suggest that the American workplace will be changing even more in future years.

But is the ADA a good law? Is it merely the latest in a long line of government entitlements that create a new class of disadvantaged citizens with new rights? Or does the ADA appropriately reflect a more general moral obligation to people who face undeserved disadvantages? Does society have a responsibility to provide disabled people with jobs, or would our social obligation be exhausted by welfare and charity? These questions are examined by philosopher Gregory Kavka in his essay "Disability and the Right to Work." Kavka argues that disabled people have a strong right to employment that society in general and private employers in some cases have a duty to meet.

---

*See, for example, Jeffrey Allen, *Complying with the ADA* (New York: John Wiley & Sons, 1993), and Monroe Berkiowitz and M. Anne Hill, eds., *Disability and the Labor Market* (Ithaca, N.Y.: ILP Press, 1986).

CASE STUDY Gays Need Not Apply

Cracker Barrel Old Country Store Inc. is a restaurant and gift-shop chain with over one hundred stores throughout the American Southeast. The company, headquartered in Lebanon, Tennessee, has been rapidly expanding in recent years and has enjoyed strong and stable economic growth. Most of its stores are located off of interstate highways and serve "family-style" meals in the restaurants and inexpensive gifts in the adjacent "country store." In 1991 the company employed almost ten thousand people and had total sales of $200 million.

In early 1991 the company announced a new policy. Citing the "traditional American values" upon which the company was founded, the announcement declared that homosexual employees would be fired and that the company would no longer hire homosexuals in the future. The company targeted those "whose sexual preference fails to demonstrate normal heterosexual values which have been the foundation of families in our society." Homosexuality was inconsistent with those values and with "the perceived values of our customer base." As many as ten employees were dismissed shortly thereafter. One manager was quoted as telling a dismissed employee that "the policy was really aimed at effeminate men and women who have masculine traits who might be working as waiters and waitresses."

While the policy produced strong criticism and protests outside many stores, there was nothing illegal in the policy. At the time, only two states (and a few dozen cities) had laws that prohibit discrimination against gay and lesbian workers. Since then, several other states have passed similar laws, but none in which Cracker Barrel operates have such laws.

Later in 1991, Cracker Barrel announced that it was rescinding this policy. Although the company claimed that it would invite fired workers back, as late as a year later several who had been dismissed had not yet been rehired. The company strongly reiterated its commitment to equal opportunity and the "the letter and spirit of the law regarding nondiscrimination in the workplace." Of course, in the states in which they operate, and on the federal level, there is no law prohibiting discrimination against homosexuals.

In explaining the decision to implement the policy, company officials said: "In the past, we have always responded to the values and wishes of our customers. Our recent position on the employment of homosexuals in a limited number of stores may have been a well-intentioned overreaction to the perceived values of our customers and their comfort levels with these individuals."

This rationale calls to mind a similar defense used decades ago to exclude African Americans from jobs and professional schools. In one famous case, a Texas law school denied admission to African Americans because, in the opinion of the law school, few people in the segregated South would be likely to hire a black lawyer. Thus, it was not the school but the perceived prejudices of the local citizens that was responsible for the discrimination. Neither the law school nor Cracker Barrel indicated how they knew the attitudes and values of their customers.

In recent years, other companies have adopted very different policies concerning gays and lesbians in the workplace. Some firms, like IBM, Levi Strauss, General Motors, and AT&T, have adopted explicit antidiscrimination policies. Many others, like Lotus Software, permit same-sex partners to be covered under company health and insurance plans.

One major shareholder in Cracker Barrel Inc. was the pension funds of the City of New York, which owned over $6 million in stocks. New York City officials tried to use their influence to get Cracker Barrel to adopt an explicit antidiscrimination policy. Along with other minority stockholders, they tried to introduce an antidiscrimination resolution at the annual stockholders' meeting. Management excluded this resolution (and thereby denied all stockholders the opportunity even to vote on it) by claiming that this constituted interference with normal day-to-day operations. The Securities and Exchange Commission ruled in management's favor when this issue was appealed.

■ Should sexual orientation be included in the list of illegal grounds for employment discrimination? Why or why not? Could there be any cases in which sexual orientation is a job-relevant factor?

■ How far should a company go to satisfy the discriminatory demands of its customers? For example, if patients were uncomfortable with women doctors, would a hospital be justified in denying jobs to women physicians?

■ Some customers of Cracker Barrel were quoted as saying that the Bible prohibits accepting homosexuals. Could Cracker Barrel claim that their policy is a matter of religious freedom?

PREFERENTIAL HIRING AND COMPENSATION
Robert K. Fullinwider

If a man shall steal an ox, or a sheep, and kill it, or sell it; he shall restore five oxen for an ox, and four sheep for a sheep.

Exodus 22

Persons have rights; but sometimes a right may justifiably be overridden. Can we concede to all

job applicants a right to equal consideration, and yet support a policy of preferentially hiring female over white male applicants?

Judith Thomson, in her article "Preferential Hiring,"[1] appeals to the principle of compensation as a ground which justifies us in sometimes overriding a person's rights. She applies this principle to a case of preferential hiring of a woman in order to defend the claim that such preferential hiring is not unjust. Her defense rests upon the contention that

From *Social Theory and Practice*, vol. 3, no. 3 (Spring 1975): 307–320. Reprinted with the permission of the author and the publisher.

debt of compensation is owed to women, and that the existence of this debt provides us with a justification of preferential hiring of women in certain cases even though this involves setting aside or overriding certain rights of white male applicants.

Although she is correct in believing that the right to compensation sometimes allows us or requires us to override or limit other rights, I shall argue that Thomson has failed to show that the principle of compensation justifies preferential hiring in the case she constructs. Thus, by implication, I argue that she has failed to show that preferential hiring of women in such cases is not unjust. I proceed by setting out Thomson's argument, by identifying the crucial premise. I then show that Thomson fails to defend the premise, and that, given her statement of the principle of compensation, the premise is implausible.

THOMSON'S CASE

Thomson asks us to imagine the following case. Suppose for some academic job a white male applicant (WMA) and a female applicant (FA) are under final consideration.[2] Suppose further that we grant that WMA and FA each have a *right to equal consideration* by the university's hiring officer. This means that each has a right to be evaluated for the job solely in terms of his or her possession of job related qualifications. Suppose, finally, that the hiring officer hires FA because she is a woman. How can the hiring officer's choice avoid being unjust?

Since being a woman is, by hypothesis, not a job related qualification in this instance, the hiring officer's act of choosing FA because she is a woman seems to violate WMA's right to equal consideration. The hiring officer's act would not be unjust only if in this situation there is some sufficient moral ground for setting aside or overriding WMA's right.

Consider, Thomson asks us, "…those debts which are incurred by one who wrongs another. *It is here that we find what seems to me the most powerful argument for the conclusion that preferential hiring of women is not unjust" (emphasis added)*.[3] We are promised that the basis for justly overriding WMA's acknowledged right is to be found in the principle of compensation. But, at this crucial point in her paper, Thomson stops short of setting out

the actual derivation of her conclusion from the application of the principle of compensation to her imagined case. The reader is left to construct the various steps in the argument. From remarks Thomson makes in dealing with some objections to preferential hiring, I offer the following as a fair construction of the argument she intends.

Women, as a group, are owed a debt of compensation. Historically women, because they were women, have been subject to extensive and damaging discrimination, socially approved and legally supported. The discriminatory practices have served to limit the opportunities for fulfillment open to women and have disadvantaged them in the competition for many social benefits. Since women have been the victims of injustice, they have a moral right to be compensated for the wrongs done to them.

The compensation is owed by the community. The community as a whole is responsible, since the discriminatory practices against women have not been limited to isolated, private actions. These practices have been widespread, and public as well as private. Nowhere does Thomson argue that the case for preferring FA over WMA lies in a debt to FA directly incurred by WMA. In fact, Thomson never makes an effort to show any direct connection between FA and WMA. The moral relationship upon which Thomson's argument must rely exists between women and the community. The sacrifice on WMA's part is exacted from him by the community so it may pay its debt to women. This is a crucial feature of Thomson's case, and creates the need for the next premise: The right to compensation on the part of women justifies the community in overriding WMA's right to equal consideration. This premise is necessary to the argument. If the setting aside of WMA's right is to be justified by appeal to the principle of compensation, and the debt of compensation exists between the community and women, then something like the fourth premise is required to gain the application of the principle of compensation to WMA. This premise grounds the justness of WMA's sacrifice in the community's debt.

In short, Thomson's argument contains the following premises:

1. Women, as a group, are owed a debt of compensation.

2. The compensation is owed to women by the community.

3. The community exacts a sacrifice from WMA (i.e., sets aside his right to equal consideration) in order to pay its debt.[4]

4. The right to compensation on the part of women against the community justifies the community in setting aside WMA's right.

If we assume that the community may legitimately discharge its debt to women by making payments to *individual women,* then from premises 1–4 the conclusion may be drawn that WMA's right to equal consideration may be overridden in order to prefer FA, and, hence, that it is not unjust for the hiring officer to choose FA because she is a woman.

I shall not quarrel with the premises 1–3, nor with the assumption that *groups* can be wronged and have rights.[5] My quarrel here is with premise 4. I shall show that Thomson offers no support for 4, and that it does not involve a correct application of the principle of compensation as used by Thomson. I will examine the case for premise 4 [later]. In the next section I pause to look at Thomson's statement of the principle of compensation.

THE PRINCIPLE OF COMPENSATION

In the passage quoted earlier, Thomson speaks of those debts incurred by one who wrongs another. These are the debts of compensation. Using Thomson's own language, we may formulate the principle of compensation as the declaration that *he who wrongs another owes the other.*[6] The principle of compensation tells us that, for some person B, B's act of wronging some person A creates a special moral relationship between A and B. The relationship is a species of the relationship of *being indebted to.* In the case of compensation, the indebtedness arises as a result of wrongdoing, and involves the wrongdoer owing the wronged. To say that B owes something to A is to say that B's liberty of action with respect to what is owed is limited. B is under an obligation to yield to A what he owes him, and A has a right to it.[7] What B must yield will be a matter of the kind of wrong he has done A, and the optional means of compensation open to him. Thus, it is clearly the case that debts of compensation are grounds for limiting or overrid-

ing rights. But our being owed compensation by someone, though giving us some purchase on his liberty, does not give us carte blanche in limiting his rights. The debt is limited to what makes good our loss (restores our right), and is limited to us, his victims.

It might be that, for some reason, WMA directly owes FA compensation. If so, it would immediately follow that FA has a moral claim against WMA which limits WMA's liberty with respect to what he owes her. Furthermore, the nature of WMA's wrong may be such as to require a form of compensation interfering with the particular right we are focusing on—his right to equal consideration. Suppose the wrong done by WMA involved his depriving FA of fair opportunities for employment. Such a wrong may be the basis for requiring WMA, in compensation, to forego his right to equal consideration if he and FA were in direct competition for some job. This case would conform precisely to the model of Thomson's stated principle of compensation.

Thomsom makes no effort to show that WMA has interfered with FA's chances of employment, or done her any other harm. She claims that it is "wrongheaded" to dwell upon the question of whether WMA has wronged FA or any other woman.[8] As we have already seen, Thomson maintains that the relevant moral relationship exists between *women* and the *community.* Consequently, the full weight of her argument rests on premise 4, and I now turn to it.

APPLYING THE PRINCIPLE OF COMPENSATION TO GROUPS

Thomson asserts that there is a relationship of indebtedness between the community and women. Yet it is the overriding of WMA's right which is purportedly justified by this fact. The sacrifice imposed upon WMA is not due to his directly owing FA. The community owes FA (as a woman), and exacts the sacrifice from WMA in order that *it* may pay its debt. This is supposed to be justified by premise 4.

May the community take *any* act it sees fit in order to pay its debts?[9] This question goes to the heart of Thomson's case: what support is there for her premise 4? What is the connection between the community's liability to women (or FA), and

WMA's membership in the community? Can we find in the fact that the community owes something to women a moral justification for overriding WMA's right? In this section I explore two attempts to provide a positive answer to this last question. These are not Thomson's attempts; I consider her own words in the next section.

First, one might attempt to justify the imposition of a sacrifice on WMA by appeal to distributive liability. It might be urged that since the community owes FA, then every member of the community owes FA and thus WMA owes FA. This defense of premise 4 is unconvincing. While it is true that if the community owes FA then its members collectively owe FA, it does not follow that they distributively owe FA. It is not the case that, as a general rule, distributive liability holds between organized groups and their members.[10] What reason is there to suppose it does in this case?

Though this attempt to defend premise 4 is unsatisfactory, it is easy to see why it would be very appealing. Even though the indebtedness is established, in the first instance, between the community and FA, if distributive liability obtained we could derive a debt WMA owed to FA, a debt that arose as a result of the application of the principle of compensation to the community. In imposing a sacrifice on WMA, the community would be enforcing *his* (derived) obligation to FA.

Second, imagine a 36 hole, 2 round, golf tournament among FA, WMA, and a third party, sanctioned and governed by a tournament organizing committee. In previous years FA switched to a new model club, which improved her game. Before the match the third player surreptitiously substitutes for FA's clubs a set of the old type. This is discovered after 18 holes have been played. If we suppose that the match cannot be restarted or cancelled, then the committee is faced with the problem of compensating FA for the unfair disadvantage caused her by the substitution. By calculating her score averages over the years, the committee determines that the new clubs have yielded FA an average two-stroke improvement per 18 holes over the old clubs. The committee decides to compensate FA by penalizing the third player by two strokes in the final 18 holes.

But the committee must also penalize WMA two strokes. If FA has been put at a disadvantage by the wrongful substitution, she has been put at a disadvantage with respect to every player in the game. She is in competition with all the players;

what the third player's substitution has done is to deprive her of a fair opportunity to defeat all the other players. That opportunity is not restored by penalizing the third player alone. If the committee is to rectify in mid-match the wrong done to FA, it must penalize WMA as well, though WMA had no part in the wrong done to FA.

Now, if it is right for the committee to choose this course of action, then this example seems promising for Thomson's argument. Perhaps in it can be found a basis for defending premise 4. This example seems appropriately similar to Thomson's case: in it an organization penalizes WMA to compensate FA, though WMA is innocent of any wrong against FA. If the two situations are sufficiently alike and in the golfing example it is not unjust for the committee to penalize WMA, then by parity of reasoning it would seem that the community is not injust in setting aside WMA's right.

Are the committee's action and the community's action to be seen in the same light? Does the committee's action involve setting aside any player's rights? The committee constantly monitors the game, and intervenes to balance off losses or gains due to infractions or violations. Unfair gains are nullified by penalties; unfair losses are offset by awards. In the end no player has a complaint because the interventions ensure that the outcome has not been influenced by illegitimate moves or illegal actions. Whatever a player's position at the end of the game, it is solely the result of his own unhindered efforts. In penalizing WMA two strokes (along with the third player), the committee does him no injustice nor overrides any of his rights.

The community, or its government, is responsible for preserving fair employment practices for its members. It can penalize those who engage in unfair discrimination; it can vigorously enforce fair employment rules; and, if FA has suffered under unfair practices, it may consider some form of compensation for FA. However, compensating FA by imposing a burden on WMA, when he is not culpable, is *not* like penalizing WMA in the golf match. The loss imposed by the community upon WMA is not part of a game-like scheme, carefully regulated and continuously monitored by the community, wherein it intervenes continually to offset unfair losses and gains by distributing penalties and advantages, ensuring that over their lifetimes WMA's and FA's chances at employment have been truly equal. WMA's loss may endure; and there is no reason to believe that his employment position at the end of his career reflects only his unhindered effort. If the community exacts a sacrifice from WMA to pay FA, *it merely redistributes losses and gains without balancing them.*

Even though the golfing example looked promising as a source of clues for a defense of premise 4, on examination it seems not to offer any support for that premise. Indeed, in seeing how the golfing case is different from the hiring case, we may become even more dubious that Thomson's principle of compensation can justify the community in overriding WMA's right to equal consideration in the absence of his culpability.[11] Since Thomson never explicitly expresses premise 4 in her paper, she never directly addresses the problem of its defense. In the one place where she seems to take up the problem raised by premise 4, she says:

> Still, the community does impose a burden upon him (WMA): it is able to make amends for its wrongs only by taking something away from him, something which, after all, we are supposing he has a right to. And why should *he* pay the cost of the community's amends-making?
>
> If there were some appropriate way in which the community could make amends to its…women, some way which did not require depriving anyone of anything he has a right to, then that would be the best course of action to take. Or if there were anyway some way in which the costs could be shared by everyone, and not imposed entirely on the young white male applicants, then that would be, if not the best, then anyway better than opting for a policy of preferential hiring. But in fact *the nature of the wrongs done is such as to make jobs the best and most suitable form of compensation (emphasis added).*[12]

How does this provide an answer to our question? Is this passage to be read as suggesting, in support of premise 4, the principle that a group may override the rights of its (nonculpable) members in order to pay the "best" form of compensation?[13] If WMA's right to equal consideration stood in the way of the community's paying best compensation to FA, then this principle would entail premise 4. This principle, however, will not withstand scrutiny.

Consider an example: Suppose that you have stolen a rare and elaborately engraved hunting rifle from me. Before you can be made to return it, the gun is destroyed in a fire. By coincidence, however, your brother possesses one of the few other such rifles in existence; perhaps it is the only other model in existence apart from the one you stole from me and which was destroyed. From my point of view, having my gun back, or having one exactly like it, is the best form of compensation I can have from you. No other gun will be a suitable replacement, nor will money serve satisfactorily to compensate me for my loss. I prized the rifle for its rare and unique qualities, not for its monetary value. You can pay me the best form of compensation by giving me your brother's gun. However, this is clearly not a morally justifiable option. I have no moral title to your brother's gun, nor are you (solely in virtue of your debt to me) required or permitted to take your brother's gun to give to me. The gun is not yours to give; and nothing about the fact that you owe me justifies you in taking it.

In this example it is clear that establishing what is the best compensation (best makes up the wrongful loss) does not determine what is the morally appropriate form of compensation. Thus, as a defense of premise 4, telling us that preferential hiring is the best compensation begs the question.

The question of the best form of compensation may properly arise only after we have determined who owes whom, and what are the morally permissible means of payment open to the debtor. The question of the best form of compensation arises, in other words, only after we have settled the moral justifiability of exacting something from someone, and settled the issue of what it is that the debtor has that he can pay.

The case of preferential hiring seems to me more like the case of the stolen rifle than like the case of the golfing match. If WMA has a right to equal consideration, then he, not the community, owns the right. In abridging his right in order to pay FA, the community is paying in stolen coin, just as you would be were you to expropriate your brother's rifle to compensate me. The community is paying with something that does not belong to it. WMA has not been shown by Thomson to owe anybody anything. Nor has Thomson defended or made plausible premise 4, which on its face ill fits her own expression of the principle of compensation. If we reject the premise, then Thomson has not shown what she claimed—that it is not unjust to engage in preferential hiring of women. I fully agree with her that it would be appropriate, if not obligatory, for the community to adopt measures of compensation to women.[14] I cannot agree, on the basis of her argument, that it may do so by adopting a policy of preferential hiring.

BENEFIT AND INNOCENCE

Thomson seems vaguely to recognize that her case is unconvincing without a demonstration of culpability on the part of WMA. At the end of her paper, after having made her argument without assuming WMA's guilt, she assures us that after all WMA is not so innocent, and it is not unfitting that he should bear the sacrifice required in preferring FA.

> …it is not entirely inappropriate that those applicants (like WMA) should pay the cost. No doubt few, if any, have themselves, individually, done any wrongs to…women. But they have profited from the wrongs the community did. Many may actually have been direct beneficiaries of policies which excluded or downgraded…women—perhaps in school admissions, perhaps in access to financial aid, perhaps elsewhere; and even those who did not directly benefit in this way had, at any rate, the advantage in the competition which comes of confidence in one's full membership, and of one's rights being recognized as a matter of course.[15]

Does this passage make a plausible case for WMA's diminished "innocence," and the appropriateness of imposing the costs of compensation on him? The principle implied in the passage is, "He who benefits from a wrong shall pay for the wrong." Perhaps Thomson confuses this principle with the principle of compensation itself ("He who wrongs another shall pay for the wrong"). At any rate, the principle, "He who benefits from a wrong shall pay for the wrong," is surely suspect as an acceptable moral principle.

Consider the following example. While I am away on vacation, my neighbor contracts with a construction company to repave his driveway. He instructs the workers to come to his address, where they will find a note describing the driveway to be repaired. An enemy of my neighbor, aware some-

how of this arrangement, substitutes for my neighbor's instructions a note describing *my* driveway. The construction crew, having been paid in advance, shows up on the appointed day while my neighbor is at work, finds the letter, and faithfully following its instructions paves my driveway. In this example my neighbor has been wronged and damaged. He is out a sum of money, and his driveway is unimproved. I benefited from the wrong, for my driveway is considerably improved. Yet, am I morally required to compensate my neighbor for the wrong done him? Is it appropriate that the costs of compensating my neighbor fall on me? I cannot see why. My paying the neighbor the cost he incurred in hiring the construction company would be an act of supererogation on my part, not a discharge of an obligation to him. If I could afford it, it would be a decent thing to do; but it is not something I *owe* my neighbor. I am not less than innocent in this affair because I benefited from my neighbor's misfortune; and no one is justified in exacting compensation from me.

The very obvious feature of the situation just described which bears on the fittingness of compensation is the fact of *involuntariness*. Indeed I benefited from the wrong done my neighbor, but the benefit was involuntary and undesired. If I knowingly and voluntarily benefit from wrongs done to others, though I do not commit the wrongs myself, then perhaps it is true to say that I am less than innocent of these wrongs, and perhaps it is morally fitting that I bear some of the costs of compensation. But it is not like this with involuntary benefits.

Though young white males like WMA have undeniably benefited in many ways from the sexist social arrangements under which they were reared, to a large extent, if not entirely, these benefits are involuntary. From an early age the male's training and education inculcate in him the attitudes and dispositions, the knowledge and skills, which give him an advantage over women in later life. Such benefits are unavoidable (by him) and ineradicable. Most especially is this true of "that advantage… which comes of confidence in one's full membership [in the community] and of one's rights being recognized as a matter of course."

The principle, "He who *willingly* benefits from wrong must pay for the wrong," may have merit as a moral principle. To show a person's uncoerced and knowledgeable complicity in wrongdoing is to show him less than innocent, even if his role amounts to no more than ready acceptance of the fruits of wrong. Thomson makes no effort to show such complicity on WMA's part. The principle that she relies upon, "He who benefits from a wrong must pay for the wrong," is without merit. So, too, is her belief that "it is not entirely inappropriate" that WMA (and those like him) should bear the burden of a program of compensation to women. What Thomson ignores is the moral implication of the fact that the benefits of sexism received by WMA may be involuntary and unavoidable. This implication cannot be blinked, and it ruins Thomson's final pitch to gain our approval of a program which violates the rights of some persons.[16]

NOTES

1. Judith Thomson, "Preferential Hiring," *Philosophy and Public Affairs,* 2 (Summer 1973): 364–84.

2. Thomson asks us to imagine two such applicants *tied* in their qualifications. Presumably, preferring a less qualified teacher would violate students' rights to the best available instruction. If the applicants are equally qualified, then the students' rights are satisfied whichever one is picked. In cases where third party rights are not involved, there would seem to be no need to include the tie stipulation, for if the principle of compensation is strong enough to justify preferring a woman over a man, it is strong enough whether the woman is equally qualified or not, so long as she is minimally qualified. (Imagine hiring a librarian instead of a teacher.) Thus, I leave out the requirement that the applicants be tied in their qualifications. Nothing in my argument turns on whether the applicants are equally qualified. The reader may, if he wishes, mentally reinstate this feature of Thomson's example.

3. Thomson, 380.

4. The comments from which propositions 1–3 are distilled occur on pages 381–82.

5. For a discussion of these issues, see Robert Simon, "Preferential Hiring: A Reply to Judith Jarvis Thomson," *Philosophy and Public Affairs,* 3 (Spring 1974): 312–20.

6. There are broader notions of compensation, where it means making up for any deficiency or distortion, and where it means recompense for work. Neither of these notions plays a role in Thomson's argument.

7. On page 378, Thomson says: "Now it is, I think, widely believed that we may, without injustice, refuse to grant a man what he has a right to only if *either* someone else has a conflicting and more stringent right, *or* there is some very great benefit to be obtained by doing so—perhaps that a disaster of some kind is thereby averted…But in fact there are other ways in which a right may be overridden." The "other way" which Thomson mentions derives from the force of debts. A debt consists of rights and obligations, and the force of debts can perhaps be accounted for in terms of superior rights. Then, debts would not be a third ground, independent of the first listed by Thomson, for overriding a right.

8. Thomson, 380–81.

9. The U.S. Government owes Japanese companies compensation for losses they incurred when the President imposed an illegal import surtax. May the Government justly discharge its debt by taxing only Japanese-Americans in order to pay the Japanese companies?

10. See Joel Feinberg, "Collective Responsibility," *Journal of Philosophy,* 65 (7 November 1968); and Virginia Held, "Can a Random Collection of Individuals Be Morally Responsible?" *Journal of Philosophy,* 67 (13 July 1970).

11. George Sher, in "Justifying Reverse Discrimination in Employment," *Philosophy and Public Affairs,* 4 (Winter 1975), defends reverse discriminations to "neutralize competitive disadvantages caused by past privations" (165). He seems to view the matter along the lines of my golfing example. Thus, my comments here against the sufficiency of that model apply to Sher's argument. Also, see below…for arguments that bear on Sher's contention that the justification for discriminating against white male applicants is not that they are most responsible for injustice, but benefit the most from it.

12. Thompson, 383.

13. In the passage quoted, Thomson is attempting to morally justify the community's imposing a sacrifice on WMA. Thus, her reference to "best" compensation cannot be construed to mean "morally best," since morally best means morally justified. By best compensation Thomson means that compensation which will best make up the loss suffered by the victim. This is how I understand the idea of best compensation in the succeeding example and argument.

14. And there are many possible modes of compensation open to the community which are free from any moral taint. At the worst, monetary compensation is always an alternative. This may be second- or third-best compensation for the wrongs done, but when the best is not available, second-best has to do. For the loss of my gun, I am going to have to accept cash from you (assuming you have it), and use it to buy a less satisfactory substitute.

15. Thomson, 383–84.

16. But, if FA is not given preferential treatment in hiring (the best compensation), are *her* rights violated? In having a right to compensation, FA does not have a right to anything at all that will compensate her. She has a right to the best of the morally available options open to her debtor. Only if the community refuses to pay her this is her right violated. We have seen no reason to believe that setting aside the right of white male applicants to equal consideration is an option morally available to the community.

A DEFENSE OF PROGRAMS OF PREFERENTIAL TREATMENT
Richard Wasserstrom

Many justifications of programs of preferential treatment depend upon the claim that in one respect or another such programs have good consequences or that they are effective means by which to bring about some desirable end, e.g., an integrated, equalitarian society. I mean by "programs of preferential treatment" to refer to programs such as those at issue in the *Bakke* case—programs which set aside a certain number of places (for example, in a law school) as to which members of minority groups (for example, persons who are nonwhite or female) who possess certain minimum qualifications (in terms of grades and test scores) may be preferred for admission to those places over some members of the majority group who possess higher qualifications (in terms of grades and test scores).

Many criticisms of programs of preferential treatment claim that such programs, even if effective, are unjustifiable because they are in some important sense unfair or unjust. In this paper I present a limited defense of such programs by showing that two of the chief arguments offered for the unfairness or injustice of these programs do not work in the way or to the degree supposed by critics of these programs.

The first argument is this. Opponents of preferential treatment programs sometimes assert that proponents of these programs are guilty of intellectual inconsistency, if not racism or sexism. For, as is now readily acknowledged, at times past employers, universities, and many other social institutions did have racial or sexual quotas (when they did not practice overt racial or sexual exclusion), and many of those who were most concerned to bring about the eradication of those racial quotas are now untroubled by the new programs which reinstitute them. And this, it is claimed, is inconsistent. If it was wrong to take race or sex into account when blacks and women were the objects of racial and sexual policies and practices of exclusion, then it is wrong to take race or sex into account when the objects of the policies have their race or sex reversed. Simple considerations of intellectual consistency—of what it means to give racism or sexism as a reason for condemning these social policies and practices—require that what was a good reason then is still a good reason now.

The problem with this argument is that despite appearances, there is no inconsistency involved in holding both views. Even if contemporary preferential treatment programs which contain quotas are wrong, they are not wrong for the reasons that made quotas against blacks and women pernicious. The reason why is that the social realities do make an enormous difference. The fundamental evil of programs that discriminated against blacks or women was that these programs were a part of a larger social universe which systematically maintained a network of institutions which unjustifiably concentrated power, authority, and goods in the hands of white male individuals, and which systematically consigned blacks and women to subordinate positions in the society.

Whatever may be wrong with today's affirmative action programs and quota systems, it should be clear that the evil, if any, is just not the same. Racial and sexual minorities do not constitute the dominant social group. Nor is the conception of who is a fully developed member of the moral and social community one of an individual who is either female or black. Quotas which prefer women or blacks do not add to an already relatively overabundant supply of resources and opportunities at the disposal of members of these groups in the way in which the quotas of the past did maintain and augment the overabundant supply of resources and opportunities already available to white males.

The same point can be made in a somewhat different way. Sometimes people say that what was wrong, for example, with the system of racial discrimination in the South was that it took an irrelevant characteristic, namely race, and used it systematically to allocate social benefits and burdens of various sorts. The defect was the irrelevance of the characteristic used—race—for that meant that individuals ended up being treated in a manner that was arbitrary and capricious.

From *National Forum (The Phi Kappa Phi Journal)*, vol. LVIII, no. 1 (Winter 1978): pp. 15–18. Reprinted with permission of the author.

I do not think that was the central flaw at all. Take, for instance, the most hideous of the practices, human slavery. The primary thing that was wrong with the institution was not that the particular individuals who were assigned the place of slaves were assigned there arbitrarily because the assignment was made in virtue of an irrelevant characteristic, their race. Rather, it seems to me that the primary thing that was and is wrong with slavery is the practice itself—the fact of some individuals being able to own other individuals and all that goes with that practice. It would not matter by what criterion individuals were assigned; human slavery would still be wrong. And the same can be said for most if not all of the other discrete practices and institutions which comprised the system of racial discrimination even after human slavery was abolished. The practices were unjustifiable—they were oppressive—and they would have been so no matter how the assignment of victims had been made. What made it worse, still, was that the institutions and the supporting ideology all interlocked to create a system of human oppression whose effects on those living under it were as devastating as they were unjustifiable.

Again, if there is anything wrong with the programs of preferential treatment that have begun to flourish within the past ten years, it should be evident that the social realities in respect to the distribution of resources and opportunities make the difference. Apart from everything else, there is simply no way in which all of these programs taken together could plausibly be viewed as capable of relegating white males to the kind of genuinely oppressive status characteristically bestowed upon women and blacks by the dominant social institutions and ideology.

The second objection is that preferential treatment programs are wrong because they take race or sex into account rather than the only thing that does matter—that is, an individual's qualifications. What all such programs have in common and what makes them all objectionable, so this argument goes, is that they ignore the persons who are more qualified by bestowing a preference on those who are less qualified in virtue of their being either black or female.

There are, I think, a number of things wrong with this objection based on qualifications, and not the least of them is that we do not live in a society

in which there is even the serious pretense of a qualification requirement for many jobs of substantial power and authority. Would anyone claim, for example, that the persons who comprise the judiciary are there because they are the most qualified lawyers or the most qualified persons to be judges? Would anyone claim that Henry Ford II is the head of the Ford Motor Company because he is the most qualified person for the job? Part of what is wrong with even talking about qualifications and merit is that the argument derives some of its force from the erroneous notion that we would have a meritocracy were it not for programs of preferential treatment. In fact, the higher one goes in terms of prestige, power and the like, the less qualifications seem ever to be decisive. It is only for certain jobs and certain places that qualifications are used to do more than establish the possession of certain minimum competencies.

But difficulties such as these to one side, there are theoretical difficulties as well which cut much more deeply into the argument about qualifications. To begin with, it is important to see that there is a serious inconsistency present if the person who favors "pure qualifications" does so on the ground that the most qualified ought to be selected because this promotes maximum efficiency. Let us suppose that the argument is that if we have the most qualified performing the relevant tasks we will get those tasks done in the most economical and efficient manner. There is nothing wrong in principle with arguments based upon the good consequences that will flow from maintaining a social practice in a certain way. But it is inconsistent for the opponent of preferential treatment to attach much weight to qualifications on this ground, because it was an analogous appeal to the good consequences that the opponent of preferential treatment thought was wrong in the first place. That is to say, if the chief thing to be said in favor of strict qualifications and preferring the most qualified is that it is the most efficient way of getting things done, then we are right back to an assessment of the different consequences that will flow from different programs, and we are far removed from the considerations of justice or fairness that were thought to weigh so heavily against these programs.

It is important to note, too, that qualifications— at least in the educational context—are often not

connected at all closely with any plausible conception of social effectiveness. To admit the most qualified students to law school, for example—given the
way qualifications are now determined—is primarily
to admit those who have the greatest chance of
scoring the highest grades at law school. This says
little about efficiency except perhaps that these
students are the easiest for the faculty to teach.
However, since we know so little about what constitutes being a good, or even successful lawyer, and
even less about the correlation between being a very
good law student and being a very good lawyer, we
can hardly claim very confidently that the legal
system will operate most effectively if we admit only
the most qualified students to law school.

To be at all decisive, the argument for qualifications must be that those who are the most qualified deserve to receive the benefits (the job, the
place in law school, etc.) because they are the most
qualified. The introduction of the concept of desert
now makes it an objection as to justice or fairness
of the sort promised by the original criticism of the
programs. But now the problem is that there is no
reason to think that there is any strong sense of
"desert" in which it is correct that the most qualified deserve anything.

Let us consider more closely one case, that of
preferential treatment in respect to admission to
college or graduate school. There is a logical gap in
the inference from the claim that a person is most
qualified to perform a task, e.g., to be a good student, to the conclusion that he or she deserves to
be admitted as a student. Of course, those who
deserve to be admitted should be admitted. But
why do the most qualified deserve anything? There
is simply no necessary connection between academic merit (in the sense of being the most qualified)
and deserving to be a member of a student body.
Suppose, for instance, that there is only one tennis
court in the community. Is it clear that the two
best tennis players ought to be the ones permitted
to use it? Why not those who were there first? Or
those who will enjoy playing the most? Or those
who are the worst and, therefore, need the greatest
opportunity to practice? Or those who have the
chance to play least frequently?

We might, of course, have a rule that says that
the best tennis players get to use the court before
the others. Under such a rule the best players
would deserve the court more than the poorer

ones. But that is just to push the inquiry back one
stage. Is there any reason to think that we ought to
have a rule giving good tennis players such a preference? Indeed, the arguments that might be given
for or against such a rule are many and varied. And
few if any of the arguments that might support the
rule would depend upon a connection between
ability and desert.

Someone might reply, however, that the most
able students deserve to be admitted to the university because all of their earlier schooling was a kind
of competition, with university admission being the
prize awarded to the winners. They deserve to be
admitted because that is what the rule of the competition provides. In addition, it might be argued,
it would be unfair now to exclude them in favor of
others, given the reasonable expectations they
developed about the way which their industry and
performance would be rewarded. Minority-admis-
sion programs, which inevitably prefer some who
are less qualified over some who are more qualified, all possess this flaw.

There are several problems with this argument.
The most substantial of them is that it is an empirically implausible picture of our social world. Most
of what are regarded as the decisive characteristics
for higher education have a great deal to do with
things over which the individual has neither control nor responsibility: such things as home environment, socioeconomic class of parents, and, of
course, the quality of the primary and secondary
schools attended. Since individuals do not deserve
having had any of these things vis-à-vis other individuals, they do not, for the most part, deserve
their qualifications. And since they do not deserve
their abilities they do not in any strong sense deserve to be admitted because of their abilities.

To be sure, if there has been a rule which
connects, say, performance at high school with
admission to college, then there is a weak sense in
which those who do well at high school deserve,
for that reason alone, to be admitted to college. In
addition, if persons have built up or relied upon
their reasonable expectations concerning performance and admission, they have a claim to be
admitted on this ground as well. But it is certainly
not obvious that these claims of desert are any
stronger or more compelling than the competing
claims based upon the needs or advantages to
women or blacks from programs of preferential

treatment. And as I have indicated, all rule-based claims of desert are very weak unless and until the rule which creates the claim is itself shown to be a justified one. Unless one has a strong preference for the status quo, and unless one can defend that preference, the practice within a system of allocating places in a certain way does not go very far at all in showing that that is the right or the just way to allocate those places in the future.

A proponent of programs of preferential treatment is not at all committed to the view that qualifications ought to be wholly irrelevant. He or she can agree that, given the existing structure of any institution, there is probably some minimal set of qualifications without which one cannot participate meaningfully within the institution. In addition, it can be granted that the qualifications of those involved will affect the way the institution works and the way it affects others in the society. And the consequences will vary depending upon the particular institution. But all of this only establishes that qualifications, in this sense, are relevant, not that they are decisive. This is wholly consistent with the claim that race or sex should today also be relevant when it comes to matters such as admission to college or law school. And that is all that any preferential treatment program—even one with the kind of quota used in the *Bakke* case—has ever tried to do.

I have not attempted to establish that programs of preferential treatment are right and desirable. There are empirical issues concerning the conse-

quences of these programs that I have not discussed, and certainly not settled. Nor, for that matter, have I considered the argument that justice may permit, if not require, these programs as a way to provide compensation or reparation for injuries suffered in the recent as well as distant past, or as a way to remove benefits that are undeservedly enjoyed by those of the dominant group. What I have tried to do is show that it is wrong to think that programs of preferential treatment are objectionable in the centrally important sense in which many past and present discriminatory features of our society have been and are racist and sexist. The social realities as to power and opportunity do make a fundamental difference. It is also wrong to think that programs of preferential treatment are in any strong sense either unjust or unprincipled. The case for programs of preferential treatment could, therefore, plausibly rest both on the view that such programs are not unfair to white males (except in the weak, rule-dependent sense described above) and on the view that it is unfair to continue the present set of unjust—often racist and sexist—institutions that comprise the social reality. And the case for these programs could rest as well on the proposition that, given the distribution of power and influence in the United States today, such programs may reasonably be viewed as potentially valuable, effective means by which to achieve admirable and significant social ideals of equality and integration.

THE REASONABLE WOMAN:
SENSE AND SENSIBILITY IN SEXUAL HARASSMENT LAW
Kathryn Abrams

Is sexual harassment understood differently by men and women? If so (as seems likely), whose understanding should set the standard for court decisions? These questions, which lawyers have argued about for almost a decade, reached the general public with the Senate testimony of Anita Hill. But the ensuing debate—between partisans of a universal common sense and those who see perceptions of sexual harassment as gender-differentiated—has

thus far produced more heat than light. Although the debate has offered a fascinating window on movements within feminist theory, it has rarely yielded sufficient guidance for the judgment of actual cases.

The central challenge of sexual harassment litigation has been to define when harassment becomes sufficiently pervasive to create a "hostile environment." The Supreme Court accepted the idea of hostile-environment sexual harassment in 1986, but its pronouncements on the question of

From *Dissent* (Winter 1995): 48–55. Reprinted by permission.

pervasiveness have been frustratingly vague. Sexual harassment violates the law when it is "severe or pervasive [enough] to alter the conditions of plaintiff's employment and create an abusive working environment," or when it "unreasonably interferes with [plaintiff's] work performance and creat[es] a hostile, intimidating or offensive" environment. This proliferation of adjectives has raised more questions than it has answered. Is an "intimidating" or "offensive" environment different from an "abusive" one? Do certain kinds of conduct contribute more to the creation of such environments than others? Compounding these difficulties has been a question of perspective or vantage point in assessing the alleged abuse. Courts are frequently confronted with a plaintiff who argues that certain conduct starkly interferes with her work performance, and a defendant who argues that the same conduct is trivial, episodic, jocular, or nonintrusive. How can judges find an independent ground on which to stand in assessing these allegations?

The first solution offered by the courts was to assess the claims of the plaintiff from the perspective of the "reasonable person." This approach offered several advantages. First, it had the legitimizing pedigree of a long history in the law: courts had assessed the conduct of torts defendants from the standpoint of the "reasonable man" and later the (gender-neutral) "reasonable person" to determine whether they had met the required duty of care toward plaintiffs. Second, the specification of a vantage point distinct from that of the actual plaintiff offered reassurance to employers; it protected them from liability arising from idiosyncratic claims. Finally, the resort to a vantage point ostensibly accessible to any observer held the promise of reducing the growing confusion over the "pervasiveness" standard. In the long tradition of jurists who have sought procedural answers to festering substantive disputes, proponents of the "reasonable person" test appealed to perspective—in this case, a kind of universal common sense—to mitigate controversy over "pervasiveness."

But as feminist advocates soon made clear, the "reasonable person" standard only complicated the controversy. Their challenge to this standard reflected the confluence of two intellectual movements within feminist theory. The first was a tendency toward gender differentiation, characteristic of both cultural and radical feminisms. These

movements resisted the gender-neutrality characteristic of equality theories, which had described women as substantially similar to men. Cultural feminists argued that this move understated and undervalued the biological and social ways in which women differed from men. Radical feminists charged that the focus on women's conformity to male norms diverted attention from a system of power relations through which male characteristics become normative. Both groups bridled at the possibility that women's perspectives would be described in terms simultaneously applicable to men.

The second influential movement was the challenge to objectivist accounts of knowledge. Feminist writers assailed the notion of "truth" as something "out there," external to the position of the observer, accessible by certain neutral observational methods. The status of legal norms or social understandings as "true" or "neutral," and the legitimation of certain methods for gaining access to them, are incidents of power, they argued. Resisting such power meant exposing the extent to which understandings of social relations are shaped by social location. And it meant exposing those viewpoints considered to be neutral or true as another example of a partial perspective, distinguished only by the ability of its adherents to make their vision normative.

Resistance also required a challenge to objectivist modes of knowledge production. One important strategy in this effort has been a re-valuation of nondominant ways of knowing about the world. Some scholars, influenced by cultural feminism, have valorized "ways of knowing" they describe as characteristic of women: reasoning from personal experience is one example; choosing contextual reasoning over abstract principle is another. Other scholars, retaining a focus on the power dimension, have claimed an "epistemic advantage" for those at the bottom of reigning hierarchies. The oppressed, in this view, enjoy a double source of knowledge: their experience in a society built around the understandings of the privileged familiarizes them with those perspectives, but gives them a view from a subordinated social location that the privileged lack.

These diverse insights combined to fuel a critique of the "reasonable person" standard. Feminist advocates pointed first to the gendered origins of the standard. The "reasonable person" had its beginnings in the "reasonable man," a fellow who "takes the magazines at home and in the evening pushes the lawn mower in his shirtsleeves." (*Hall v. Brooklands Auto Racing Club,* 1933, quoting "unnamed American author.") As this early twentieth century elaboration reveals, what was being presented as universal common sense was in fact the sense of a particular, socially located person: one whose perspective was shaped by his freedom to relax with his magazines at home, and to enjoy sovereignty over his physical—and familial—domain. Moreover, the assertion of a single valid perspective on sexual harassment belied the gender differentiation that many kinds of research were beginning to reveal. Social scientists like Barbara Gutek pointed to a sharp divergence in the way men and women view sexualized conduct in the workplace. Men were likely to see sexualized words or gestures as flattering, indicative of long-term interest, and not threatening to professional progress; women were likely to associate them with manipulation, exploitation, or threat, and to see them as imperiling their professional prospects. Analyses like that of Catharine MacKinnon offered an explanatory social context for these differences. Women workers' experience of marginality within the workplace, and sexual vulnerability in and outside it, caused them to view the sexual inflection of work relations with a fearfulness unlikely to be shared by their male counterparts. Finally, feminists worried that the "reasonable person" standard might confirm the (largely male) judiciary in its unreflective assurance that it understood the phenomenon of sexual harassment. Judges might view it as authorizing them to decide cases on the basis of their own intuition: the same "common sense" that had marked the administration of the "reasonable person" standard in tort law—and the same "common sense" that had normalized the practice of sexual harassment in the first place.

All of these factors suggested the preferability of a "reasonable woman" standard. This formulation would explicitly challenge notions of a universal perspective. It would characterize the evaluation of harassment, like the experience of harassment itself, as a phenomenon strongly differentiated on the basis of gender. The gender-specific language would place male judges on alert that they could no longer rely on their unexamined intuitions. The

"reasonable woman" standard would replace those intuitions with a perspective that promised a radical revision of workplace conditions. Yet beyond the notion that such a perspective would "take harassment seriously"—viewing it neither as a right of the employer, nor as a harmless, if vulgar, form of male amusement—there was little explicit discussion of what insights or sensibilities it entailed.

As the eighties closed, this approach began to be embraced by the federal courts. In a landmark case called *Ellison v. Brady,* the Ninth Circuit Court of Appeals held that sexual harassment should be evaluated from the perspective of the "reasonable woman." In *Ellison* a woman received a series of letters from a colleague she barely knew, describing his love for and continuous surveillance of her. The trial court had shrugged off the behavior as a "pathetic attempt at courtship," but the Court of Appeals disagreed. It stressed the importance of considering the conduct from the standpoint of a "reasonable woman": "a sex-blind reasonable person standard," the court noted, "tends to be male biased and tends to systematically ignore the experiences of women." It held that, viewed from the perspective of a "reasonable woman," receiving "long, passionate, disturbing" letters from a person one barely knew represented sufficiently pervasive and severe harassment to create a hostile environment.

The court recognized the need, in such a context, to elaborate the differences in perspective between men and women. And it took a few steps in that direction, noting that conduct considered unobjectionable by men might be offensive to women, and stating that women's vulnerability to sexual assault gave them a "stronger incentive" to be concerned about sexual behavior in the workplace. But the largely passive stance of the *Ellison* court toward the elaboration of perspectival differences is expressed in its "hope that over time men and women will learn what conduct offends reasonable members of the opposite sex."

Both the strengths and the drawbacks of the *Ellison* opinion were underscored in the revolution catalyzed by Anita Hill. Women's denunciation of senators who failed to "get it" stressed the gendered character of perceptions of sexual harassment, and the need for a gendered standard of evaluation. The "reasonable woman" standard was, in fact, adopted by several additional courts in the wake of the Senate hearings. But the growing concern of even well-intentioned men with the "new rules of engagement" pointed to the need for explicit discussion of the determinants of gender difference in this area. Both men and women sought greater clarity about the ways in which their perceptions of sexual harassment diverged, and the "hope" for mutual understanding expressed by *Ellison* failed to fill the bill.

As the call for a fuller elaboration of women's perspectives continued, the "reasonable woman" standard began to be challenged from an unexpected quarter: the feminist movement itself. There were several sources of this attitudinal sea change. Some feminists worried that unitary images of female difference could be manipulated by hostile forces. Images of women that emphasized care or connection could be used to explain the absence of women from more competitive jobs—a link that was made in the notorious *Sears* litigation. "Women's ways of knowing" could be used to reinforce stereotypes of the intuitive or irrational woman. Others challenged accounts of strong gender differentiation as essentialist and potentially oppressive. A range of "anti-essentialist" feminists, led by lesbians and women of color, argued that unitary depictions of women replicated the false and exclusory universalism of the gender-neutral approach. Some asked whether the divergent social circumstances of women could possibly yield the same knowledge: how could modes of reasoning shaped by the domestic context, for example, apply to women who did not remain in the home or live within conventional families? Others argued that the unity presented in depictions of "women's experience" derived not from homogeneity but from erasure. Comparatively privileged white middle class women—through solipsism or strategic exclusion—had eclipsed the experiences of less privileged subgroups.

These insights made many feminists wary of the gathering momentum behind the "reasonable woman" standard. They worried that the "reasonable woman," like other paradigmatic "women" of feminist theory, would turn out to be white, middle class, and heterosexual. Others asked whether simply living as a woman assured a particular perspective on sexual harassment. The disparagement of sexual harassment claims by female "mavericks"

like Judge Maryanne Trump Berry gave some advocates pause. The "reasonable woman" might simply free women judges to resort to *their* intuitions, in ways that were not uniformly promising to female claimants. Moreover, the standard might fail to prompt the desired response from male judges—permitting them to indulge their own, biologized visions of female difference. So there was a growing division among feminist advocates over the "reasonable woman" standard, with some calling for a further elaboration or differentiation of the standard, and others seeking a return to gender neutrality or a rejection of all "reasonableness" criteria.

These differences among feminists were brought to the fore by the Supreme Court's second case on hostile environment sexual harassment: *Harris v. Forklift Systems* (November 9, 1993). That case presented the question of whether plaintiffs must demonstrate "serious psychological injury" in order to win their cases. But the court also agreed to consider whether hostile environment claims should be reviewed under a gendered or gender-neutral standard. Those feminist advocates who filed amicus briefs with the court were frankly divided on the question of the standard: the Employment Law Center and Equal Rights Advocates endorsed a "reasonable woman" standard, while Catharine MacKinnon and the Women's Legal Defense and Education Fund argued that "reasonableness" standards, whether gender-specific or gender-neutral, reinforce stereotypes and distract the court from the primary issue—the conduct of the defendant. The decision, when it came, was anticlimactic. Although the court resoundingly rejected the psychological injury requirement, it resolved the question of standard in less than a sentence, stating that the court should review plaintiff's claim according to the perspective of the "reasonable person," with no elaboration and no explanation of its decision.

It is hard to know what conclusions to draw from this cryptic affirmation of gender-neutrality. It suggests that a court that has displayed studied disinterest in group-based distinctions is not prepared to embrace a standard that underscores—and perhaps risks instantiating—gender difference. Some subset of male judges will now, no doubt, resort to their own, unschooled intuitions in evaluating sexual harassment cases. But has the court scuttled the entire project of introducing a new, non-dominant sensibility about sexual harassment into adjudication? I see no reason to draw so negative a conclusion. The first goal of the "reasonable woman" standard was to emphasize the gendered character of sexual harassment and prevent resort to a "common sense" that was likely to preserve the status quo. The second goal was to permit access to a distinct set of perspectives that would open the way for a transformation of workplace norms. Though the courts have made only limited progress in fleshing out these perspectives, their elaboration is essential to reshaping the perceptions of judges, and ultimately of those who structure the workplace. This second, and arguably more important, task can still be performed under a "reasonable person" standard.

My own argument begins with the anti-essentialist insight that neither modes of knowing nor particular bodies of knowledge are inextricably linked to biological set or social gender. There are things that women are more likely to know by virtue of having lived as women, There are practices—such as those involving devaluation or sexualization—to which they are likely to have a heightened sensitivity by virtue of having experienced them, heard about them repeatedly, or seen them applied to other women. But this likelihood cannot be collapsed into inevitability: some women have had few of the experiences that produce such sensitivity; others respond with indifference or denial; women who are aware of discriminatory practices may perceive them in different ways. Just as being female does not guarantee transformative perceptions of sexual conduct in the workplace, being male does not exclude the possibility of having, or developing, them. If perceptions of sexual harassment do not depend solely on biology, life experience, or gender-specific modes of knowing, but rather on varied sources of information regarding women's inequality—if such perceptions, in other words, are a matter not of innate common sense but of informed sensibility—then they can be cultivated in a range of women and men. The "reasonable person" standard, properly elaborated, might be a vehicle for the courts to play a role in this educative process. The reasonableness term, as Martha Chamallas has suggested, could be interpreted to mean not the average person, but the

person enlightened concerning the barriers to women's equality in the workplace.

What remains is the uncompleted task of elaborating the determinants of this "reasonable" perspective. What should legal decision makers—and actors in the workplace—know about women, work, and sex that would help them assess claims of sexual harassment in ways that transform the present, often oppressive assumptions of the workplace? I would emphasize four kinds of information that could be offered by expert testimony or by counsel in framing their clients' claims. Some might be included in judges' instructions, when these cases are tried to juries. They reflect the experience not of any paradigmatic woman but of diverse groups of women, in and out of the workplace.

(1) The first kind of information concerns barriers that women have faced, and continue to face, in the workplace. Women are newcomers to many work settings; the work they have traditionally performed has been poorly paid, socially undervalued, and situated on the lower rungs of occupational hierarchies dominated by men. Women's entry into nontraditional jobs has been met with outright hostility, expressed through conduct verging on physical intimidation. Once inside the workplace, women have been met by glass ceilings, by ostensibly neutral criteria that (barely) conceal gender-based judgments, by biologized assumptions about their ability to perform particular jobs.

Even in settings where women have not faced overt barriers, they have been confronted with reminders that workplaces were not designed to meet their needs: persistent demographic disparities, machinery constructed to male needs, failures to accommodate women's disproportionate parental responsibilities. As a result, many women feel that they are marginal participants in the workplace, that their hold on their job or on the respect of their superiors is tenuous and subject to factors not within their control. Sexualized conduct in the workplace may interact with all of these factors, inducing a sense of precariousness or professional threat that it would not necessarily induce in a man.

(2) The second kind of information decision makers require concerns the role of sexualized treatment in thwarting women in the workplace. The meanings assigned to sex by women in this

culture are various, and include physical pleasure, emotional connection, and opportunities for self-discovery and self-expression. Yet among the most familiar meanings, themes of intimidation, objectification, and devaluation are readily discernible. High rates of sexual assault by strangers and acquaintances have led many women to feel that their sexuality makes them physically vulnerable. The "myth of the black rapist" has produced a complicated legacy for black women, in which fears about physical security vie with suspicions of racial exploitation. Even in their less overtly threatening guises, sexual depictions of women may be trivializing, suggesting that women find their primary purpose in male attention, titillation or satisfaction.

It is largely these negative cultural themes that echo in sexualized treatment in the workplace. Sexual aggression, including violent forms of sexual assault, has been repeatedly used by employers and fellow employees to resist women's entry into blue-collar and other nontraditional workplaces. A male employer who propositions a female subordinate may be expressing a genuine interest, but it is also possible that he is asserting a combination of sexual and economic power, which reminds the woman of her social inequality. Even where the motivation is more ambiguous, the threatening or devaluative resonance may persist. Sexual epithets and targeted sexual talk, whatever their ostensible purpose, remind women that, despite their advancement to roles not technically defined by sex, they can still be treated as sexual objects or addressed in primarily sexual ways. The broader cultural backdrop to these forms of conduct needs to be made explicit, so that professedly well-intentioned men who defend sexual talk as harmless humor can understand that it may have connotations they do not see.

These elaborations of women's circumstances in many workplaces can, and have, been used to assist in the evaluation of sexual harassment claims. In *Lehmann v. Toys 'R' Us* (July 14, 1993), a New Jersey Supreme Court case decided days before *Harris,* Justice Marie Garibaldi pointed to women's historical marginality in the workplace and their vulnerability to sexualized abuse, to give content to a "reasonable woman's" perspective. These same factors, and those articulated below, could be used to explain a "reasonable person" standard as well.

The second two factors that courts should consider concern not the backdrop to sexual harassment but its consequences.

(3) Sexual harassment can produce a range of effects on the work lives of women. Although *Harris* has ruled out a requirement of psychological harm, many legal fact-finders still believe that harassment does not create a hostile environment unless women are rendered professionally nonfunctional. If a woman is able to drag herself to work and perform some acceptable version of her assigned tasks, decision makers—and employers—assume that the behavior has not reached an actionable level. Yet a statute that promises women an environment "free from discriminatory intimidation, ridicule, and insult" requires that fact-finders look further: there are many ways that sexual harassment can create impediments, even for the woman who continues to do her job. Propositions or touching from an unexpected source can make a woman fear sexual assault; sexual epithets may make her feel that she is being objectified. Both can affect not only her self-esteem but the conditions of her employment: they may impair her concentration or productivity, or undermine her confidence in herself as a worker.

Though sexualized treatment can affect the performance of women workers directly, many of its most far-reaching effects derive from its impact on her colleagues and associates. When a woman is addressed by her supervisor as if her most salient attributes were sexual, this may prevent other workers from viewing her seriously. Such impressions may affect evaluations or considerations for promotion. They may compromise the provision of assistance, training, or staff support, or may prevent her from developing the kinds of collegial relationships that facilitate progress in any employment setting. These varied impediments to job performance may have been what Justice Ginsberg had in mind when she stated, in her *Harris* concurrence, that sexual harassment makes it "harder for women to do their jobs" than it is for men. Judges should be aware of the range of effects that even sexualized talk can produce, in assessing the pervasiveness of alleged harassment.

(4) The final type of information that legal decision makers require is information about the responses of women workers to harassment. Provision of this information is, in a sense, defensive:

demonstration of some particular response should not, after *Harris,* be necessary for a plaintiff; but information about the ways that many women respond to harassing behavior may prevent judges from relying on stereotyped expectations about victims' responses. Empirical studies of sexual harassment suggest that fewer than 20 percent of women who believe they have been harassed complain to authorities within the workplace, and even fewer leave their jobs. Most women handle the problem with some combination of levity (where the conduct assumes a jocular tone), conversational management, or avoidance. An individual victim's response to sexual harassment is described by psychologists as a function of many things besides the nature of the conduct. Even exposure to the same kinds of oppressive influences may produce different responses in different women. A woman's personality type and the particular coping mechanisms she uses to respond to adverse circumstances may have a major impact on her reaction. Women with strong support from family and friends may be able to weather harassment with less psychological strain than women who lack such resources. What is known about women workers, and workers

more generally, suggests that their visible response to harassing conduct will be an unreliable gauge of the severity or the practical impact of the treatment. Providing fact-finders with this information places the individual victim's response in context, so as to prevent judges from "trying the victim" or neglecting more accurate indications of pervasive harassment they may have before them.

The court's embrace of the "reasonable person" standard is not an unequivocal step forward. It avoids promulgating falsely unifying images of women. But it also fails to jolt judges into recognition that their intuitive perspectives are not the only, or the preferable, vantage point on the claims before them. The challenge confronting feminist advocates is to provide this jolt by other means: not through the jarring, but so far unelaborated, mechanism of a gendered referent, but through illumination of those factors that have shaped women's responses to sexual harassment. If viewed as an invitation to offer concrete information about women's lives, the "reasonable person" standard may yet help legal decision makers to create a less oppressive workplace.

DISABILITY AND THE RIGHT TO WORK
Gregory S. Kavka

DEFINING THE PROBLEM

Do disabled people in advanced modern societies (like those of North America, Western Europe, and the Pacific Rim) have a right to work? Before we can begin to answer this question, we must be clearer about what it means. And this requires some preliminary comments on each of the question's key constituent terms. Of these, the notion of a disability (or handicap) is easiest to deal with, for we may adopt the broad definition contained in the Americans with Disabilities Act which says a disability is a physical or mental impairment that "substantially limits one or more of the major life activities of an individual." One could easily raise

philosophical quibbles about this definition: the concepts of "substantial" limits and "major" life activities (even when the latter is illustrated by paradigm examples like walking and talking) are vague, and the inclusion of mental impairments along with these vague terms raises the possibility that too many of us would qualify under it as disabled (for example, the ordinary neurotic whose social life is substantially limited by irrational inhibitions). However, any concept of disability is going to admit of degrees and have vague borders: the vagueness will have to be resolved largely by implicit social conventions about what sort of impairments count as genuine handicaps. So, despite the potential problems with the Disabilities Act definition of disability, I will not pause over the task of improving it.

Characterizing the right to work, as I intend it, is a more complex matter. For present purposes, we may think of rights, in general, as potential claims by (or on behalf of) someone to some thing (an object or a liberty to act) against someone else. These rights are moral or legal, and *prima facie* or absolute, according to whether the underlying rules, principles, and standards which ground and justify the potential claims in question are themselves moral or legal, *prima facie* or absolute. (A *prima facie* right is overridable by competing considerations, while an absolute right is not. Among the rights thought to be absolute by some theorists are the right not to be tortured and the right not to be punished for a crime one did not commit.)

The right of handicapped people to work that I argue for is a moral right; it will be justified by appeals to moral considerations. However, since important moral rights concerning economic matters should be protected by and embodied in the law, my arguments will aim at showing that disabled people should be accorded a legal right to work. Disabled people's right to work is *prima facie,* not absolute: it can, in principle, be overridden by competing rights or other considerations (such as economic feasibility). But it is, I will contend, a *strong prima facie* right: the moral arguments in its favor are substantial enough it would take competing moral considerations of considerable weight to override it. In particular, I will argue that a small gain in social utility or economic efficiency is not enough to override this right.

If the disabled have a moral right to work, against whom is it a right? That is, who bears the moral obligation to offer them jobs or help them obtain employment? The most general answer is society as a whole. But the way this right must be vindicated in practice means that specific obligations generated by the right may fall especially upon governments, particular government officials, and certain private employers.

Why this is so becomes clear when we address the critical question of just what handicapped people's right to work is a right to. The "right to work," as I use the term, is the right to participate as an active member in the productive processes of one's society, insofar as such participation is reasonably feasible. A number of aspects of this characterization require comment.

Most importantly, the right to work is a right to *employment;* it is a right to *earn* income, not simply a right to receive a certain income stream or the resources necessary to attain a certain level of welfare....

My "right to work" thesis makes the more controversial claim that disabled people in advanced societies have a right not only to receive a basic income, but to *earn* incomes at—or above—the basic maintenance level. I will argue for employment as a right, not a duty. I avoid the vexed question of whether disabled people should be forced to work for their basic support income if they do not want to do so. I focus on whether those disabled persons who want to work should be afforded special sorts of opportunities to do so.

What specific sorts of treatment or "special opportunities" are entailed by handicapped people's right to work? First, a right of nondiscrimination in employment and promotion—that people not be denied jobs on the basis of disabilities that are not relevant to their capacities to carry out the tasks associated with those jobs. Second, a right to compensatory training and education, funded by society, that will allow disabled people the opportunity to overcome their handicaps and make themselves qualified for desirable employment. Third, a right to reasonable investments by society and employers to make jobs accessible to otherwise qualified people with disabilities. Fourth, and most controversially, a right to minimal (or tie-breaking) "affirmative action" or "preferential treatment": being admitted, hired, or promoted when in competition with other equally qualified candidates. Spelled out in this way, the right of handicapped persons to work is seen to be, in its various elements, a right against society, government, and private employers.

In arguing for the disableds' right to work, in this sense, I limit my discussion in two ways to take account of problems of feasibility. I consider only the case of advanced modern societies; for in other societies, the economic resources needed to vindicate this right to any substantial degree are either not present or are very likely to be needed for even more urgent social tasks. And I acknowledge that employment of many people with severe handicaps may not be "reasonably feasible"—that is, it may be impossible or excessively costly. To take a recent example from the literature, I will not be arguing that we should hire blind persons to be school bus drivers. Nor do I think large costs should be sustained to retrain workers that become disabled very close to retirement age. But I will contend that applying a strict economic cost/benefit standard of hiring and training feasibility may be unfair to the disabled....

EFFICIENCY, JUSTICE, AND THE RIGHT TO WORK

In presenting my arguments for a right to work of the disabled, it will be useful to have a foil. For this purpose, I choose a blunt form of objection to that right, derived from the notion that the economic rights of the disabled are strictly limited by considerations of economic efficiency that imply the desirability of a free market in labor in which employers are entitled to hire whomever they regard as best qualified for the jobs they offer. The objection runs as follows: "Society's obligations to the disabled extend no further than the previously assumed obligation to provide a basic welfare minimum. Because of their special medical and equipment needs, this may require a larger cash stipend to most disabled people than would be necessary to support able-bodied persons at the same basic welfare level. But society has a right to provide the necessary economic resources to the disabled in whatever way it deems to be most efficient. Perhaps for some classes of disabled persons, training and continued employment will allow them to achieve (or exceed) the basic welfare minimum at less net cost to society as a whole than receiving a public stipend. And perhaps private employers can profitably employ disabled workers by exploiting public sympathy for them and successfully charging higher prices for products they have produced. But if society (and private employers) find it cheaper just to pension off the handicapped, because it would cost more to provide handicapped people with special training and equipment, and to determine which handicapped people may be profitably employed, this is their prerogative. Disabled people therefore have no more right to work than anyone else does. If they can compete successfully for jobs, if private employers or government agencies want to hire them for specific jobs because of their qualifications, they will be hired. If not, they have a right to support payments, but no right to employment." For ease of reference, I will henceforth refer to the viewpoint expressed in this objection as the Crude Economic Efficiency Position, or CREEP.

What is wrong with CREEP? At least three things that I can think of: it employs an inappropriate notion of efficiency, it fails to attach sufficient importance to self-respect and the means to self-respect, and it ignores key issues involving distributive justice....

Social Efficiency

CREEP says that the disabled have no right to work, and that society should see to their employment only to the extent that society (or individual employers) regard this as economically cost-effective. Though this line of argument seems to be based on a morally respectable *utilitarian* appeal to social efficiency, this is not really the case. First, CREEP is ambiguous between appealing to efficiency for society as a whole (including the handicapped) and appealing to efficiency for those who are offering aid to the handicapped (employers, the government, and taxpayers). The latter position is not a genuinely utilitarian one at all, and is supportable only if one believes that because the disabled are generally in a dependent role in these transactions, their interests are not to be counted (or counted equally) in determining which policies are most socially efficient overall. Second, the notion of "society" deciding the most efficient policies in these areas is ambiguous in a similar way: if efficiency decisions are left entirely to the discretion of particular employers, government bureaucrats, and managers, rather than being circumscribed politically, then the disabled (who currently occupy very few of these influential positions) will be effectively prevented from having their interests adequately represented where the relevant decisions are made. Third, by focusing on a narrow economic notion of efficiency, rather than a broader utilitarian notion, CREEP ignores the importance of key noneconomic values, like self-respect, that may justify ascribing to disabled persons a right to work as well as a right to a basic welfare level....

Distributive Justice and Self-Respect

Arguments purely in terms of economic efficiency or social utility, like CREEP, do not directly address questions of distribution. Once we turn to matters of distributive justice, the moral case for the disabled having a right to work is substantially strengthened.

The basic reason for this is that the handicapped typically are, in virtue of their condition, among the most disadvantaged members of advanced modern societies with respect to well-being and opportunities for well-being. By definition, a disability is a substantial impairment of a major life activity like seeing, hearing, walking, or talking. Two features of such impairments make them especially devastating to the welfare and life prospects of those who have them: their permanence and their pervasiveness.

People are often disabled temporarily, by disease or injury. But sick or injured people are not treated or regarded as a separate class of persons by society, and their work problems are dealt with by policies designed for "normal" workers—for example, sick leaves and short-term disability insurance. When people speak of the disabled or handicapped, however, they normally have in mind those who are in such a condition *permanently* (or at least for a period of years). It is the economic rights of such people—that is, those suffering long-term disablement—that is the subject of my discussion.

Significant permanent handicaps are usually pervasive, in the sense that their effects are not confined to a single sphere of the affected person's life, but tend to have damaging (or limiting) effects on all major spheres—family, personal, social, and recreational life, as well as economic and professional life. There are three closely related reasons for this. First, disabling impairments interfere with major activities that figure in all life spheres—seeing and talking, for example, are as much (or more) prerequisites of a normal social life as they are prerequisites of normal careers. Second, public and private environments, customs, and institutional structures are designed for people with normally functioning bodies and minds, and may create barriers to participation by the disabled. (Problems of physical access for people in wheelchairs is the most familiar example of this.) Third, and finally, all major spheres of life involve significant interaction with other people, who for a variety of psychological reasons may find it difficult to interact with disabled persons in normal ways, even when the disability in question is essentially irrelevant to the particular mode of interaction in question. In other words, the disabled tend to be stigmatized, as well as directly disadvantaged, in the interpersonal aspects of their activities....

Special social provision for the welfare of the disabled thus follows from practically any account of social justice—Rawlsian, egalitarian, need-centered, or whatever—that pays attention to how social welfare or resources are distributed and correspondingly prescribes improving the lot of society's least advantaged members But how does a right to work rather than a right to disability pensions follow from such distributive considerations?

The key mediating concept here is self-respect. Suppose that we agree with Rawls that self-respect is a vital primary good, something of great importance that any rational person is presumed to want. Now given actual human psychology, self-respect, is—to a considerable degree—dependent upon other people's affirmation of one's own worth. And in modern advanced societies, employment, earnings, and professional success are, for better or worse, positively correlated with social assessments of an individual's value. Further, beyond the reactions of other people, work and career identifications form significant parts of some people's conceptions of themselves and their own worth; hence, these identifications may contribute directly to the creation and sustenance of self-respect, and their absence will frequently have the opposite effect.

To be sure, "economic" criteria are not the only standards of value used by oneself or others to assess one's worthiness. But, because of the *pervasiveness* of disability, as noted above, satisfaction of standards of value in other important spheres of life are also usually negatively affected by handicaps. Thus, on average, the handicapped are likely to be less convenient social companions, more limited in their sports and recreational activities, less able to fulfill nurturing and helping roles within the family, and so on. Thus, nonworkplace bases of self-respect will also be harder for the disabled to fulfill, making it even more important that the workplace bases of self-respect be made available to them. (In addition, employment may foster success—and self-respect based on success—in the other spheres of life, as when one's social life is better because of friends one has made at work.)

In the end, then, the concept of self-respect plays a dual role in my refutation of CREEP. First, it serves as an example of an important aspect of utility that is overlooked in the narrow economic interpretations of CREEP. Once this narrowness is avoided, and the "indirect" utilitarian advantages of a social policy of training and employing the disabled are noted, it is evident that there are substantial utilitarian reasons in support of the disabled having a right to work. Second, the handicapped are disadvantaged in obtaining the bases of self-respect, a critically important good. And because of the way the psychology of self-respect interacts with the work ethic present in modern advanced societies, this disadvantage *cannot be rectified by transfer payments,* but (sometimes) can be rectified by training and employment opportunities. Hence, considerations of distributive justice, which prescribe easing the plight of society's less fortunate members, provide further support for ascribing to disabled people a right to work.

AFFIRMATIVE ACTION

A meaningful right to work for the disabled must entail an obligation of employers (and admissions officers) not to discriminate against handicapped people (that is, not to count their handicaps against them, except when those handicaps render them less able to perform the job in question). But should such a right also include an affirmative action requirement giving disabled persons some form of preference over others in hiring, promotion, and admissions decisions? In this section, I address this difficult question obliquely by considering which of the main arguments for and against affirmative action in the case of women and minorities also apply to the disabled. This will, I think, lead to the *conditional* conclusion that if affirmative action is justified for women and minorities, it is also justified for the handicapped.

There are, as I see it, three major groups of arguments in favor of affirmative action programs in general. First, there are *forward-looking utilitarian arguments,* emphasizing various good effects of bringing more representatives of the disadvantaged group in question into responsible positions in society. These good effects include members of disadvantaged groups serving as effective role-models, bringing different and illuminating perspectives to their work, and being more likely to use their skills, expertise, and influence to help other members of the group (or disadvantaged people in general). Second, there are *error-correction arguments.* They emphasize that, because of past obstacles faced by disadvantaged candidates and current (conscious or unconscious) prejudices against them by most employers, employers' estimates of the qualifications of disadvantaged candidates are likely to systematically underrate their capabilities. Hence, requiring preference, in principle, for the disadvantaged is really an attempt to correct systematic errors in practice and enable the best qualified people to be hired more often. Third, there are various forms of arguments for *compensatory justice,* saying that members of disadvantaged groups should be given hiring preference to compensate for past hiring discrimination against them or members of their group, or other disadvantages they suffered at the hands of society.

Do these arguments for affirmative action apply as well to the disabled as they do to women and minorities? For the most part, it seems they do. Consider, first, forward-looking utilitarian considerations. Successful handicapped persons can serve as role models for the many people who are disabled, as well as for others who face serious obstacles of other sorts in life. Nor is there any reason to think they would bring a less distinct perspective to their jobs or be less inclined to help others in their situation than are women and minorities.

Application of the error-correction argument is less clear in the case of the disabled. Potential employers are perhaps even more likely to underestimate the relevant abilities of the disabled than to underestimate the abilities of women and minorities, simply because the issue of "potential special problems" is raised by the mere existence of their handicaps. On the other hand, some of the main obstacles that permanently disabled people faced in the past in obtaining their current skills and qualifications—namely, their disabilities—will remain with them through their period of employment and will continue to constitute barriers to peak performance. This is different from the case of a woman or minority group member whose main obstacle in the past may well have been lack of opportunity—an obstacle that will largely be removed simply by providing that opportunity. Further, some of the disabled obtained their main qualifications prior to the onset of their disability; hence their possession of them is no special sign of merit or determination. Different aspects of the error-correction argument, therefore, point in different directions on the question of whether this argument is stronger as regards the handicapped or minorities and women.

Compensatory-justice arguments are an odd lot, and are not easy to assess in the present context. Arguments for affirmative action as a form of group compensation are even less plausible for the disabled than for minority groups, because disabled people do not form an "identity-grounding" resource-sharing community in the way that specific racial or ethnic groups often do. But then, group-compensation arguments are widely regarded as philosophically problematic anyway.

When it comes to compensation for past disadvantages suffered by the very individuals to be helped by affirmative action programs, the handicapped are more deserving in some respects and less deserving in others. They are more deserving in the United States, at least, because they have not previously had legal protection against discrimination. This means that the current generation of handicapped people who might be advantaged by affirmative action programs contains many individuals who may have suffered unfair, but legal, discrimination. The disabled may also be viewed as more deserving of compensation because of the pervasiveness of their disadvantages, as noted [earlier].

The disabled may be less deserving of affirmative action, on the other hand, because their disadvantages are less purely the result of society's misconduct and more the result of simple bad luck. And despite earlier legal protection from discrimination, women and minorities have continued to face discrimination in practice that may equal what the disabled have faced. The force of this last consideration, in particular, depends upon complex empirical matters that I am in no position to sort out.

Turning to arguments *against* affirmative action, there are four main lines of argument to consider. First, any departures from a pure merit system of hiring will harm economic efficiency. Second, affirmative action programs tend to help the most advantaged members of disadvantaged groups—for example, the middle-class minority student who is well-educated enough to compete for law school admission. Third, such programs are counterproductive for the very disadvantaged groups they are designed to help, since they undermine confidence

and stigmatize even the successful members of those groups as having needed preference to succeed. Fourth, and most important, such programs are unfair to more qualified candidates from groups not singled out for preference, since they are denied positions they would have otherwise obtained.

Do these same objections to affirmative action apply in the case of the disabled as well as women and minorities? The first clearly does, for I have interpreted the disableds' right to work as requiring efforts to employ them beyond the point of maximum economic efficiency. Further, the average "extra" costs of employment per worker may be higher in the case of the disabled than other disadvantaged groups because of the modifications in equipment and facilities that may be necessary to make certain jobs accessible to handicapped workers.

Nonetheless, the aggregate economic costs of the sort of affirmative action for the disabled which I espouse are kept within reasonable limits by three factors. The pool of work-age disabled people who want to work, and are able to do so at all, is likely to be relatively small (compared to the pool of employable women and minorities). And, as noted …below, I limit my advocacy to "tie-breaking" affirmative action for the disabled, which further restricts the effects of the policy. Finally, the argument for the right to work defended here advocates sacrificing *some* economic efficiency to provide job opportunities to the disabled, but it does not require sacrifices without limits. Its standard of "reasonable feasibility" implies that society's obligation to provide job opportunities for the handicapped lessens (and at some point disappears) as the marginal social cost of doing so increases.

The second objection, about *which* individuals in the disadvantaged group would benefit, seems less serious in the case of the disabled. For while it is likely to be the less disabled who would benefit most from preferential hiring, there need be no worry that these people have not been disadvantaged at all, as there might conceivably be in the case of middle-class minorities or women.

Objection three—about the counterproductive psychological and social effects on the members of the disadvantaged group of the affirmative action policy—appears to apply equally to the disabled and other disadvantaged groups. But it is an especially worrisome objection in the context of my argument, which defends opportunities for employment primarily as means for the disabled to achieve self-respect. Can self-respect be enhanced by receiving a job through government subsidies or affirmative action programs rather than open competition? Can self-respect be retained in a social environment in which others believe you were hired for reasons other than your qualifications? Can income received for work that is profit-making only with government subsidies said to be "earned" in a sense that will promote the sense of self-worth of the worker? If the answer to these questions is an unequivocal "no," then the right to work advocated in this paper would be essentially pointless.

I believe, however, that there are good reasons for answering these questions, as they apply to complex modern societies such as ours, in the affirmative. The first point to notice is that the relevant comparison in many cases will be between a member of a disadvantaged group having an "affirmative action" job rather than no job at all, or a good "affirmative action" job rather than a worse job. While the former alternatives may do less to promote self-respect than a good job otherwise obtained, it may do more to promote self-respect, and respect from others, than being unemployed or employed in a poor job. This is especially so if unemployment or menial employment—together with membership in a disadvantaged group—is regarded by society as characterizing "low worth" individuals.

Further, in a world of incomplete information and moral complexity, people judge their own—and others'—vocational worth by more than the criteria on the basis of which one was hired. Actual performance on the job is probably the most important measure of all, and hiring under affirmative action programs will give many members of disad-

vantaged groups opportunities to prove themselves at work that they would not otherwise have had. If, as the error-correction argument suggests, such people will—on average—perform better than their hirers initially expect, they will be able to earn the respect of themselves and others by their performance.

There is a down side to all this. Some highly qualified members of groups helped by affirmative action programs may have to deal with suspicions (on the part of themselves or others) that they have succeeded only because of their group membership. But their skills and performance should help them overcome these suspicions. And, given their *relatively* advantaged position, the burdens of this sort that they may bear would seem to be outweighed by the advantages provided to their less fortunate fellow group members.

The final objection to affirmative action, which is based on unfairness to the losing, but better qualified, candidates, clearly applies to affirmative action programs for the disabled as well as for other groups. For if you are unemployed, or underemployed, it will hardly matter to your well-being whether the job opportunity you lost was to a disabled person or a member of a racial minority group. Further, the observations…about the significance of employment as a support of self-respect in advanced modern societies underscore the force of this objection to affirmative action.

This does not affect our main conclusion, however. For if we review the various lines of argument for and against affirmative action, it turns out that for *each* line of argument discussed, preferential hiring for the disabled fares *as well or better,* on balance, as preferential hiring for women and minorities. Thus, if the latter programs are justified, the former surely are.…

Decision Scenario 1
UNITED STEELWORKERS OF AMERICA V. WEBER

For generations, blacks in America were denied jobs, were denied equal pay and promotions when they did get jobs, and were generally relegated to unskilled and semiskilled positions. Even many of these jobs were lost to increasing automation. Black unemployment was much higher than white and steadily worsening.

Congress passed the Civil Rights Act of 1964 to change all this. Title VII of that act reads, in part, that "It shall be an unlawful employment practice for any employer, labor organization, or joint labor-management committee controlling apprenticeship or other training or re-training, including on-the-job training programs to discriminate against any individual because of his race...." The legislative history of the act indicates that Congress believed that this would "open employment opportunities for Negroes in occupations which have been traditionally closed to them." But did the act prohibit any and all discrimination "because of... race," or only the insidious discrimination that historically had plagued blacks?

In 1974 United Steelworkers of America and Kaiser Aluminum entered into a collective-bargaining agreement that contained a plan "to eliminate conspicuous racial imbalances" in Kaiser's skilled craftwork positions. Future selection of trainees for these positions would be on the basis of seniority, except that 50 percent of the positions would be reserved for blacks until the percentages of blacks in these jobs approximated the percentage of blacks in the local labor force. At one Kaiser plant in Gramercy, Louisiana, for example, only 5 out of 273 (1.83 percent) skilled craftsworkers were black, despite the fact that 39 percent of the work force in the Gramercy area was black.

During the first year of the Kaiser–USWA plan, seven black and six white trainees were selected at the Gramercy plant. Several white workers who were denied admission to the training

program had more seniority than the most senior black trainee. One of those rejected workers, Brian Weber, filed suit claiming that the Kaiser–USWA plan violated the section of Title VII quoted above. A district court and, later, a court of appeals decided in favor of Weber, concluding that the plan did violate Title VII's prohibition against discrimination "because of race." Upon appeal, the Supreme Court overruled these decisions and found in favor of the Kaiser–USWA plan.

The majority opinion reasoned that a literal interpretation of the law without examination of the legislative history was misplaced. They reasoned that Congress sought to overcome the inequalities that resulted from past discrimination against blacks and that, therefore, a voluntary plan between employers and unions that had the same goals was consistent with the act. The minority opinion argued that the law explicitly prohibited any discrimination on the basis of race. In the words of Justice William Rehnquist, "Were Congress to act today specifically to prohibit the type of racial discrimination suffered by Weber, it would be hard pressed to draft language better tailored to the task than that found" in the section from Title VII quoted earlier.

- What, if anything, is the difference between the type of discrimination suffered by blacks for generations and that suffered by Weber?

- How might plans like Kaiser–USWA harm young white males? Is seniority a fair standard to use in determining qualifications? How would your views change if the Kaiser–USWA plan had been required by Congress rather than voluntarily established?

- To avoid such plans ultimately resulting in insidious discrimination against young white males, must they be ended somewhere? Where?

Decision Scenario 2
PREFERENTIAL TREATMENT FOR MEN?

There are many factors that a college or university considers when evaluating applicants for admission. A number of factors testify to a student's past academic accomplishments. High school grades, quality of courses taken, and letters of recommendation are obvious examples. Other factors relate to the potential contribution that a student might make to the school. Extracurricular activities like school band or newspaper, athletic abilities, and even geographic origin might fit in this category. Still other factors consider responsibilities that the school might owe. Thus, children of alumni or faculty might be given preference, as might veterans or state citizens in a government-supported school, or members of a religious community in a school with a religious affiliation. Finally, the school's own resources place limitations on the number of students who can be admitted to a particular major or college or assigned to on-campus living arrangements.

This variety of factors can lead to some interesting results. One student with relatively high SAT scores and high school grades might be denied admission while another student with comparable or lower scores is admitted because his parents are alumni who contribute financially to the college. Or we might find that average SAT scores and grades for students admitted to the College of Liberal Arts are lower than those for students admitted to the Engineering College. Likewise, students who will commute to classes might face lower standards than those who require on-campus housing.

The dean of admissions for a college of business at a major university has discovered that women who are applying for admission have, on average, higher grades and College Board scores than men.

This is not particularly unusual given differing social and cultural influences on male and female high school students. This dean calculates that if he decided solely on the basis of high school grades and College Board scores, the incoming freshman class would be 60 percent women and 40 percent men.

The dean has to consider several issues. The dormitory space on campus is equally divided between men and women, so a 60/40 split would create housing problems. The dean also believes that a 50/50 split of men/women is a preferable classroom environment and is preferable socially as well. He also believes that the different scores and grades are more a matter of social conditioning than they are of innate differences. Evidence shows that males will do comparable work once admitted. Finally, the dean recognizes that both the business college and the workplace are traditionally male. He wonders whether job placement problems might arise if his college graduated a relatively large percentage of women.

The dean decides to admit an equal number of men and women, even if this requires, on average, slightly lower standards for men than women.

- Is this a case of preferential treatment? Is it unfair? What does the case say about merit? Would you have a different opinion if the roles were reversed?

- Schools often give preference to students with diverse geographical backgrounds. Can a similar argument be used for diversity of ethnic background?

- How well might this case parallel the job market situation?

Decision Scenario 3
WOMEN WAGE EARNERS: LESS IS BEST?

Even when adjusted for such factors as education, experience, age, and type of job, statistics show that women continue to earn much less than men. Census data also show that women begin comparable jobs at lower salaries and that the gap between men and women increases as time goes on. It has been suggested that some women themselves, and not simply discrimination, have been responsible for differences in starting salaries. Many women may actually have lower expectations and consequently request lower salaries than men.

Place yourself in the role of personnel manager of a large accounting firm. You have interviewed a number of college seniors for several openings. In most ways the students are similar. They are seniors at the same business school, have taken the same courses, and have comparable grade point averages and experience. After conducting the interviews, you have settled upon six students to whom you intend to make offers; three are men and three are women.

You have a range from which you can offer starting salaries, with a difference of $5000 a year from the top to the bottom salaries. Since these candidates are all very well qualified and may have other offers, you want to offer a competitive salary. At the same time you need to keep your own company's costs to a minimum. At a final interview, you have asked each candidate about salary expectations and you have discovered that, in fact, the three women have lower salary expectations than the men. You have every reason to believe that you can hire the women at an average of $3000 a year less than the men, even though all six will be entering the same training program and will be doing the same jobs.

On one hand, you recognize that by starting at lower salaries the women will forever be at a disadvantage. Assuming comparable work and comparable evaluations, these employees will receive pay increases and bonuses that are a percentage of their base salary. Since they begin with a lower base, over time the women will fall farther and farther behind the men. From another perspective, to keep pace with the men's salary, these women will need to do superior work.

On the other hand, you do have a responsibility to your company to minimize costs. There is also some evidence that, at least in part, women have tended to leave your firm earlier and more often than men. Higher salaries for men, therefore, might be justified as an investment in the long run.

- Should you offer the women less? Should you advise them of what is happening?

- If the women were offered lower salaries, would this be a case of sexual discrimination? If so, who is responsible? If not, is there any ethical problem with unequal pay for equal work?

- What factors might contribute to the tendency for women to expect lower salaries? Are these factors ethically relevant?

Decision Scenario 4
SEXUAL HARASSMENT IN THE WORKPLACE: MERITOR SAVINGS BANK

In 1974 Michelle Vinson met Sidney Taylor, a vice president and branch manager of Meritor Savings Bank, to ask about the possibility of a job. Taylor gave her an application, which she completed and returned the next day; later that same day Taylor called to say she had been hired. With Taylor as her supervisor, Vinson was promoted during the next four years to teller, head teller, and assistant branch manager. In September 1978, Vinson notified Taylor that she was taking sick leave for an indefinite period. On November 1, 1978, the bank discharged her for excessive use of that leave.

Vinson later sued both Taylor and Meritor Savings, charging that during her four years at the bank she had "constantly been subjected to sexual harassment" by Taylor and that this constituted sexual discrimination. Vinson testified that during her probationary period as trainee, Taylor treated her in a fatherly way and made no sexual advances. Shortly thereafter, however, he invited her to dinner and, during the course of the meal, suggested that they go to a motel to have sexual relations. At first she refused, but out of what she described as fear of losing her job, she eventually agreed. She further testified that Taylor thereafter made continual demands upon her for sexual favors, usually at the bank, during and after business hours. She estimated that over the next several years she had intercourse with him forty or fifty times. In addition, she claimed that Taylor fondled her in front of her co-workers and at times touched or fondled other women employees as well. Taylor denied all charges of sexual misconduct, denied that he ever had had sexual relations with Vinson, and claimed that she made these charges only in response to a business-related dispute that led to her dismissal. The bank also denied all allegations and asserted that it was ignorant of and therefore could not be held responsible for Taylor's actions.

Several issues were brought before the U.S. Supreme Court in this case. First, is sexual harassment a form of sexual discrimination? The Civil Rights Act makes it unlawful "to discriminate against any individual with respect to his compensation, terms, conditions, or privileges of employment because of such individual's race, color, religion, sex, or national origin." Since Vinson was not denied any benefits of employment, and indeed may even have received additional benefits, could her relation with Taylor be described as discrimination? Further, since she consented to the sexual relations, could Taylor's behavior even be considered harassment? Also, is it fair to hold the bank liable for the misconduct of its managerial employees?

Courts have recognized two types of sexual harassment: *quid pro quo* and *hostile work environment*. In *quid pro quo* harassment, job opportunity or security is exchanged, implicit or explicitly, for sexual favors. The question of voluntariness is particularly relevant in these cases. Harassment in the form of a hostile work environment occurs when the workplace contains unwanted sexual advances, comments, and suggestions. A woman might be pinched, fondled, touched, or subjected to off-color jokes or stories. The result is that the work environment becomes so full of sexual harassment that it becomes intolerable.

In 1986 the U.S. Supreme Court ruled in favor of Vinson by holding that sexual harassment is a form of illegal sexual discrimination. The Court also upheld a lower court's acceptance of the hostile work environment form of harassment and, while not ruling definitively, left the door open to holding employers liable for sexual harassment in the workplace. Finally, the Court rejected the claim that harassment was not involved because Vinson voluntarily entered into the relationship with Taylor. The Court ruled that the crucial issue was that the harassment was "unwelcome," not whether it was voluntary.

- How, if at all, is this case of harassment a form of sexual discrimination? In what ways is it not?

- Would you describe Vinson's behavior as fully voluntary? Why or why not?

- What reasons could you offer for holding the bank responsible for the behavior of its manager? When does a firm cease to be responsible for the unethical behavior of its managers?

Decision Scenario 5
FEDERAL SET-ASIDES: FROM FULLILOVE TO ADARAND[1]

Federal government affirmative action policies cover more than individual hiring and promotion decisions. They can also involve rules for setting aside portions of federal contract money for minority-owned subcontractors. Municipal, state, and federal contract rules of the last two decades often required such affirmative action set-asides.

However, in its 1989 *Richmond* v. *Croson* decision, the United States Supreme Court ruled by a vote of 6–3 that cities and states may engage in racially conscious set-aside programs only if those programs 1) serve a compelling government interest and 2) are narrowly tailored to accomplish the purpose of remedying past discrimination. It ruled that the city of Richmond's 30% minority set-aside satisfied neither of these requirements. In the *Croson* case, five members of the court agreed that "while States may take remedial action when they possess evidence that their own spending practices are exacerbating a pattern of prior discrimination, they must identify that discrimination, public or private, with some specificity before they may use race-conscious relief." A sixth justice from the voting majority, Justice Scalia, rejected the idea that a state may use race-conscious remedies to address the effects of past discrimination.

The *Croson* court ruled that city or state racial classifications aimed at helping minorities were as constitutionally suspect as racial classifications aimed at discriminating against minorities. Since Richmond had not established proof of discrimination before establishing the program and since it had not proved that other, less extreme policies could not accomplish its goals equally well, the Court found that the Richmond law violated white contractors' guarantee of equal protection of the law under the Fourteenth Amendment.

The Court, however, had previously ruled that a federal set-aside program *was* constitutionally permissible. In its 1980 decision in *Fullilove v. Klutznick,* the Court (by a vote of 6–3) accepted a congressionally mandated 10% set-aside of contract money for minority-owned business enterprises. The Court based its decision on a clause of the Reconstruction Era's Fourteenth Amendment,

which gave Congress powers to ensure that racial discrimination would not continue. A plurality decision in *Fullilove* held that Congress has the "power under Section Five…to enforce, by appropriate legislation, the equal protection guarantee…Congress had abundant historical basis from which it could conclude that traditional procurement practices, when applied to minority businesses, could perpetuate the effects of prior discrimination, and that the prospective elimination of such barriers to minority firm access to public contracting opportunities was appropriate to ensure that those businesses were not denied equal opportunity to participate in federal grants.…" It also held that Congress's use of racial and ethnic criteria as a condition of federal grants was a valid means to accomplish its constitutional objectives and that there was no requirement that Congress act in a wholly colorblind fashion. It said explicitly that when a program "narrowly tailored by Congress to achieve its objectives comes under judicial review, it should be upheld if the courts are satisfied that the legislative objectives and projected administration of the program give reasonable assurance that the program will function within constitutional limits." Apparently, in 1980, the Court felt that the federal set-aside met these conditions.

In 1995, however, another case, one involving a federal set-aside that provided financial incentives for contractors to hire "socially or economically disadvantaged" subcontractors, came before the Court. In *Adarand v. Pena,* the Court, by a vote of 5–4, reached a different conclusion. While it did not rule the federal set-aside was unconstitutional, the Court did send the case back to the lower court, which had accepted the program, for re-hearing. The Supreme Court directed the lower court explicitly to decide whether the program served a "compelling interest" and was "narrowly tailored." The dissenting justices wondered about the majority's motivation in ordering a re-hearing. In their eyes, the set-aside clearly satisfied the compelling interest/narrowly tailored test since the earlier set-aside from *Fullilove* passed that test and this more recent highway contract program made even less use of racial preferences.

As for the permissibility of racial classifications, two members of the *Adarand* majority joined in an opinion stating: "The unhappy persistence of both the practice and the lingering effects of racial discrimination against minority groups in this country is an unfortunate reality, and government is not disqualified from acting in response to it...When race-based action is necessary to further a compelling interest, such action is within constitutional constraints if it satisfies the 'narrow tailoring' test..." The four dissenting Justices, of course, were willing to accept the program's race-conscious attempt to remedy past discrimination.

However, two other members of the majority, Justices Scalia and Thomas, rejected any use of race, holding that government must be totally colorblind. Thomas said that "government-sponsored racial discrimination based on benign prejudice is just as noxious as discrimination inspired by malicious prejudice."

The *Adarand* case has not yet been retried. Its outcome will turn on how the phrases "compelling interest" and "narrowly tailored" are interpreted. But while the outcome of this case is unclear, the mix of opinions on the Court guarantees that affirmative action will continue to be the subject of legal debate for quite some time.

- Are contract set-asides different in any way from preferential treatment in individual hiring? What opportunities for abuse are there in each type of program?

- All Justices accept that race may be considered in directly remedying specific acts of discrimination. They disagree, however, on whether race can be used in programs aimed at eradicating the effects of past discrimination. What are the practical effects of precluding race-conscious programs aimed at the effects of discrimination?

- Why would the Fourteenth Amendment have given Congress, and not the States, special powers to deal with discrimination?

NOTE

1. This case was prepared from the decisions in the following cases: *Fullilove v. Klutznick,* 448 U.S. 448; *Richmond v. Croson,* 488 U.S. 469; *Adarand v. Pena,* 1995 U.S. Lexis 4037.

Decision Scenario 6
HIDE THE WEDDING RING

Equal employment opportunity has opened many doors for women. In recent decades women have entered the work force in increasing numbers and with increasing success. Unfortunately, many barriers remain.

While women are now legally free to make their own choices to pursue careers, many women still face social expectations (their own and others') that limit their choices. Traditional social roles still demand that women bear primary child-care responsibility as well as primary responsibility for maintaining the family's household. In the trite image portrayed by Madison Avenue, every working woman must be "supermom."

Of course, employers recognize the additional demands that women face. They also recognize that time and energy spent raising children and maintaining a household is time and energy not spent on the job. Employers are legally prohibited from holding women to unequal and unfair standards, but a combination of experience and prejudice can convince an employer that young married women make risky employees. This is perhaps especially true in entry-level management positions where new hires are expected to devote significant amounts of time and energy climbing the competitive corporate ladder.

Business writer and consultant Felice Schwartz has studied the many demands placed on working women in the modern corporate world. She wrote an influential (and controversial) article for the *Harvard Business Review* in 1989 titled "Management Women and the New Facts of Life." Although she did not use the phrase, this essay was seen (usually by critics) as calling for a "mommy track" for those women who did not wish to enter the "fast lane" of corporate management. Schwartz did argue that corporations would only benefit from removing barriers that working women faced when they tried to balance work and family. In a later book, Schwartz relates a story of how some young women cope with these barriers.[1]

While visiting with some women MBA students at the Wharton School of Business (one of the very best business schools in the world), Schwartz was dismayed when she was told of a standard interviewing strategy. Some married women told her that they routinely removed their wedding rings when they went to a job interview. Over time it had become clear to women in the MBA program (remember, these women were among the finest business students in the world) that recruiters would not offer the best jobs to married women. The discrimination was no doubt subtle (since it is illegal), but it was real enough to give rise to this widespread defensive strategy. Apparently, recruiters believed that married women would not devote as much time and en-ergy to their jobs as would unmarried women (to say nothing of men).

- Do you think that it is reasonable for women to remove their wedding rings when going to a job interview? Do you think that it is a good job-seeking strategy? Is it an honest one?

- Given that some employers likely do discriminate against married women, what is the best public policy approach to this problem? What is the best strategy for an individual job applicant?

- Do married men face similar barriers? Why or why not?

NOTE

1. Felice Schwartz, *Breaking with Tradition: Women and Work, the New Facts of Life* (New York: Warner Books, 1992).

14

Ethics and Multinational Corporations

Multinational corporations, by their nature, are largely independent of the social policies of the nation-states in which they operate. Although the national subsidiaries of multinationals must obey the regulations of the host country, the ability of multinationals to move resources on a global scale gives them great discretion about wages, workplace safety, taxes, environmental standards, and the costs of production. If a multinational believes that the legal or political climate of a given nation would allow more profit to be made elsewhere, the mobility of its capital allows it to shift operations more easily than would be possible for the ordinary company—although the multinational must consider such factors as the skill and educational level of local labor forces in such a relocation decision. Multinationals, then, have the ability to evade the attempt to use public policy to control corporate behavior that has been the focus of much in this book.

The independence of multinationals also allows them greater influence on the creation of local and national policy. Those of us who have lived in major "rust-belt" metropolitan areas know how hard state and local governments try to attract and retain business operations. Even moderately sized local corporations can threaten relocation to another community. For fear of losing part of their tax base, local officials often make concessions on tax or regulatory policies in response to such threats. Multinationals, with their enormously greater capital, their mobility, their far-flung operations, and their lack of deeply ingrained community ties, have a greatly magnified ability to influence public policy. This is especially true when subsidiaries operate in Third World nations desperate for investment and employment.

Multinationals have been known to use this influence in ways that strain both legality and credulity. One of the most extreme examples is the case of International Telephone and Telegraph (ITT) in Chile. ITT had a profitable subsidiary telephone company in Chile. It feared reduced profits in the expected nationalization of that company by the government if the Marxist candidate for president, Salvadore Allende, were elected.

ITT attempted to block Allende's election through a series of maneuvers: ITT bankrolled Allende's opposition, including conservative newspapers. It lobbied Chilean legislators who would play a role in confirming the next president. It sought the support of the U.S. Central Intelligence Agency in creating economic disruptions that would prevent Allende's assent to the presidency. Even after Allende assumed office in 1970, ITT continued to undermine him through economic disruption by limiting credit, by political propaganda, and even through a boycott of Chile's important copper export trade.

Allende was eventually overthrown by a right-wing military group in 1973. The role of ITT in the overthrow is unclear, but the activities of the company provide a striking example of how multinationals can exert influence in the developing world. (Such influence is not complete, of course. Nations can attempt to limit it, for example, by placing restrictions on how much profit can be channeled offshore. These attempts are themselves subject to multinational lobbying, however.) The article in this chapter by Pat Werhane makes some comments on the degree to which multinationals have an obligation to refrain from "meddling" in local affairs.

Since the public policy tools of nation-states are of diminished effectiveness in controlling multinationals, international business may be an area where the primary constraint on corporate behavior comes from the values and commitments of those who shape corporate policy and corporate culture. The opportunities for exercising those values are numerous in multinational dealings in the Third World. As the decision scenarios illustrate, specific issues of moral importance for corporate decisions include whether to trade with repressive governments, whether to market products that other nations have judged unacceptably dangerous, whether to influence the direction of local economies toward export trade, and so on. If you are interested in international business operations, try to apply the moral values expressed throughout this text in arriving at positions on these and other questions for multinational business.

THE ETHICAL RELATIVIST APPROACH

The attempt to apply moral values in an international context raises the question of ethical relativism. Some persons hold that ethical values differ across cultures and that there is no objective way to discern whether one culture's set of values is better than another's. Some also claim that as a result of this, we cannot legitimately impose our values on those who disagree with us. A common example often offered to justify and illustrate these claims is the practice of bribery. Those who argue against the imposition of our values often point to the "fact" that bribery, much as we condemn it, is simply a traditional way of doing business in other cultures.

A number of points need to be made in response to this reasoning. First, the social acceptance of bribery may not be as widespread as it seems. Witness the government-toppling scandals that have occurred when bribery and corruption were exposed in Japan and Italy, nations that are often offered as examples of countries where bribes are accepted practice. Perhaps the citizens and mores of those nations are not as tolerant of bribery as we were led to believe. Perhaps the citizens see that bribes must cost someone money, probably themselves as consumers. Perhaps they see the unfairness inherent in widespread bribery when some competitors gain an undeserved advantage over others.

Second, there is a difference between bribery (an offer initiated by one party to entice another party to violate his or her duties and/or extend special treatment) and extortion (a demand by a party to be paid for not disregarding another party's rights). Given this difference, bribing seems always problematic because the briber is the initiator of the harmful and unfair offer. Extortion makes the corporation seem more like a victim.

Finally, in any case, the 1977 Foreign Corrupt Practices Act settles much of the debate for United States–based multinationals and their affiliates. It makes it illegal to offer payment to foreign officials in order to obtain business or favorable treatment. (Excluded from the scope of the act, however, are payments necessary to get clerical workers to perform their duties. The act is also silent on payments to nongovernmental employees.)

Also in need of reconsideration is the more theoretical appeal to ethical relativism as a way of blocking the application of moral values to international business practices. We refer you back to the box, "Ethical Relativism," in Chapter One for a more detailed discussion of some difficulties with relativism. Here we will make only a few brief points.

First, the claim that we cannot impose our values on others because values are relative has a name. It is known as normative ethical relativism, and it is widely regarded as an incoherent position. It claims, on one hand, that it is objectively wrong for us to impose our values on those who disagree and, on the other hand, that no moral values are objective. If the latter is true, there can be no justification for believing the former. We might choose to be tolerant of some differences, but that choice is itself a moral choice. Tolerance cannot be argued as the objectively correct approach once one adopts a relativist attitude.

Second, the fact that people disagree about particular moral matters does not establish that any moral opinion is as good as another. It may be that, in morality as in math, there are better and worse answers as well as procedures for arriving at them. The jump to relativism from the mere fact of disagreement is much too quick. Third, even if there is disagreement about specific ethical issues, that disagreement may mask agreement about more fundamental moral principles. The disagreement about specifics may be due to differences in the relevant circumstances or in the estimation of the relevant facts.

Finally, as philosopher Richard DeGeorge has argued, even if there is fundamental disagreement about basic moral principles, a person who is willing to surrender his or her principles in the face of disagreement is a person who lacks
integrity. Acting with integrity might mean that there are occasions when you
have to forgo doing business if the cost of that business is that you abandon your
values. For example, if you are really committed to the ideal of equal moral rights
for all persons, it will be impossible for you to pursue business as usual with enterprises that systematically discriminate or that use bonded labor. The only remaining choices in such circumstances are to "wash your hands" and terminate
all transactions with the offending enterprise, or to continue business in a way
that exerts a strong influence for change on that other enterprise. These were,
incidentally, the choices pressed on American businesses in South Africa in the
1980s. Neither liberals nor conservatives were willing to accept business as usual
with the apartheid regime in Pretoria. Liberals often urged full divestiture; conservatives, "constructive engagement" and adherence to the Sullivan Principles.
(See the article by Werhane for details about those principles.)

The consequence of having real moral commitments, then, is that there are
choices that are foreclosed. Integrity makes the "easy" rationalization of the ethical relativist much less easy. (Consider, in addition, the self-interested reason for
rejecting the radical relativist approach. There are costs to a business's identity,
culture, and morale if its policies do not reflect consistency and commitment.)

THE NONRELATIVIST APPROACH

An alternative approach to international business ethics is taken by those who
hold that not all moral values are relative. Instead, they would suggest that there
are objective, universally valid norms that apply to all human action. This nonrelativist approach argues that while there can be international differences in business practices that are acceptable, there are also other practices that are unethical
wherever they appear.

The difficulty of such a nonrelativist approach is determining when moral
beliefs are so significant that they ought to be maintained cross-culturally. Can
there be any core moral beliefs that have universal authority? The article by Tom
Donaldson argues that there is a moral minimum that is required of all international businesses. He tries to identify the content of that minimum with some
specificity, and he claims that there are at least ten fundamental international
rights that multinationals must respect.

Manuel Velasquez argues against a claim that multinationals have obligations
to promote the global "common good," defined as "the set of conditions that are
necessary for citizens...to achieve their individual fulfillment, and...in which all
the peoples of the world have an interest." While not condoning disregard for
the welfare of persons in the Third World, Velasquez says that there are conditions which make impossible the ascription of a responsibility to promote this
global common good. He explicitly applies his analysis to environmental responsibilities. You should compare Velasquez's and Donaldson's positions carefully.

What, exactly, would they disagree on? Are there any multinational obligations that they might both accept? You should also bring your understandings of environmental responsibility from Chapter Twelve to bear on this debate.

The reading by Werhane, and the case study by DeGeorge, discuss the specific issue of multinationals' responsibilities to workers. You should ask to what extent corporate moral obligations to employees might differ between nations. You should also compare Werhane's treatment of the Sullivan Principles, especially the revised, stronger version, to your beliefs about when continued transactions with immoral enterprises or regimes jeopardizes one's integrity.

Finally, most of this chapter's readings discuss the negative duty of corporations not to cause unjustifiable harm. You should consider the question of whether there are any positive corporate duties to remedy the plight of impoverished peoples in the Third World. Donaldson, for example, argues that duties to assist the deprived do not generally fall upon for-profit corporations. Do you agree that corporations can never have a positive duty to assist, an *obligation* to act charitably towards the impoverished? In answering that question, you should return to the discussions of positive and negative rights in Chapter Three and the box, "Positive and Negative Duties," in Chapter Four. Use those passages to help in your determination of whether there are ever any such corporate obligations, and if there are, specifically when and where they might arise.

CASE STUDY The Transfer of Dangerous Industries to Underdeveloped Countries
Richard T. DeGeorge

Consider the following case: Asbestos USA (a fictitious name) produces asbestos products for the U.S. market. It competes with asbestos products made in Mexico. It is able to compete, despite the fact that Mexican labor is so much cheaper than labor in the United States, because it operates more efficiently and with more advanced equipment than do the Mexican companies. We now know that asbestos causes cancer. Those exposed to it for long periods had a significantly higher rate of cancer than others. The rate was especially high for people who worked in asbestos plants. The United States therefore passed legislation requiring the introduction of a series of safeguards for people working in asbestos plants. Asbestos USA calculated the cost of implementing the safeguards and decided it could not implement them and still stay in business. Rather than close down completely, however, it moved its plant to Mexico, which has not passed comparable safety legislation. Asbestos USA contin-

ues to market its products in the United States, even though it manufactures its products in Mexico. There, it operates its equipment in the same way (i.e., without safeguards) as it did in the United States; however, it has to pay its workers only the going wage for the industry in Mexico.

By moving its plant to Mexico, is Asbestos USA acting immorally?

Exposure to asbestos tends to produce cancer in a significant number of people. This is the overriding consideration to which the American government reacted when it passed legislation requiring safeguards. No company, it has ruled, has the right to expose its workers to cancer if this can be prevented. The ruling is a defensible one. It applies to all industries and to all asbestos manufacturers. But obviously the U.S. rule applies only in the United States; it does not apply to asbestos factories in other countries. If Asbestos USA's imports were subject to an import duty, it would have little incentive to move to Mexico. But because this is not the case, it moved its plant. This move is better for its shareholders than if the company had gone out of

From Richard T. DeGeorge, *Business Ethics*, 4th ed. (Englewood Cliffs, N.J.: Prentice Hall, 1995), 495–500. © 1995. Reprinted by permission of Prentice Hall.

business. The asbestos products would be bought from Mexican firms anyway, so why not have an American company selling asbestos products to the United States, as well as Mexican companies? These considerations, however, fail to respond to the major issue: is it moral to expose employees to the danger of cancer when this can be prevented? If the answer is no, then it is not moral to so expose Mexican workers.

Which second-order principle is applicable to this case? Here is one possible principle: It is immoral to hire anyone to do work that is in some way dangerous to his or her life or health. But the principle, as stated, is too strong. Any job might be dangerous in some way; therefore, if it were immoral to hire someone to do work that was in any way dangerous, no one could be hired to do many jobs that seem perfectly acceptable. But we must also acknowledge that some jobs are more dangerous than others. Firefighters are paid to put out fires, but they know they risk their lives in doing so. Police are also paid to risk their lives. Yet most people would be reluctant to say that hiring people to do these jobs is immoral. The immorality, therefore, does not come from hiring people to do work that involves risk to life or health. But we can defend the principle that it is immoral to hire someone to do work that is known to the employer to involve significant risk without informing the prospective employee of that risk. This application of the principle of informed consent is defensible, as guaranteeing a fair exchange between consenting adults.

If we adopt this principle, then Asbestos USA could be morally right in hiring workers in Mexico, with working conditions that would not be allowed in the United States, if the potential workers were warned of the dangers. We can assume that once warned of the dangers, the workers would agree to work in the plant only if they received more pay than they would for comparable work in a factory in which they were not exposed to the danger of cancer. If this were not the case, it would be an indication that the people who were hired were in some way being forced into the jobs—were not free agents, contracting freely and knowingly to do dangerous work at pay they considered appropriate to make up for the increased risk. A contract between employer and employee is fair if both parties enter into the contract with adequate appropriate knowledge and if both freely agree to the terms of the contract.

The critics of Asbestos USA contend that the Mexican workers, even if they are informed of the dangers and are paid somewhat higher wages than

other workers are paid (Brazil requires triple pay for dangerous work), are forced because of the lack of work in Mexico to accept employment in asbestos plants, at less than adequate pay. Hence, the critics contend, despite protestations regarding informed consent, the workers are forced to take such jobs and are exploited in them.

Informed consent is *necessary* if the action is to be moral, but it is not *sufficient.* There are some things (e.g., selling oneself into slavery) to which no one can morally consent. There are also some conditions that are immoral for an employer to impose on his or her workers, even if the latter agree to work under those conditions. Consent is not enough because people who desperately need money may agree to work under almost any conditions. Built into capitalism is the tendency of employers to pay workers as little as possible and to spend as little as possible on a safe work environment. In the United States, this tendency has been offset by unionization and government legislation. In countries where it is not offset, employers can take unfair advantage of workers and engage in immoral practices. If Asbestos USA wishes to operate its plant in Mexico, it can morally do so only if it informs the workers of the risk, in terms they can understand; if it pays them more for undertaking the risk; and if it lowers the risk to some acceptable level. It need not be at the same level demanded by the Occupational Safety and Health Act (OSHA) in the United States, but morally, it cannot be at a level so high that risk is maximized rather than minimized. It would also be immoral not to eliminate risks that could be removed without extravagant cost. If, in Mexican plants, asbestos particles float freely through the air, collecting like cobwebs and if workers are not even given paper masks, it is clear that minimum safety standards are not being observed.

Why does the Mexican government not pass laws similar to those in the United States concerning safeguards for workers? Why do not all nations pass such laws, so as to preclude such moves as that made by Asbestos USA because it would be unprofitable? The answer is that not all countries are as affluent as the United States. A wealthy country can afford to spend more to protect the health of its people than can a much poorer country. The standards of cleanliness and safety that the United States can enforce by law are much higher than those that businesses in many countries could afford. Traditions also vary from country to country. There is no reason to think that the traditions of the United States are the only right ones and that all the world must become like us. This attitude is itself condemned by many because it is considered a form of U.S. imperialism. We are a democratic country, and our people enjoy a large measure of freedom. Some other countries are not democratic or are much less so. The literacy rate and the level of education of the average person are much higher in the United States than in many other countries. We must be careful not to set our standards as the model of what every nation should do if it wishes to be moral. Our standards do not constitute the moral norm. Although morality is universal and does not differ from country to country, conditions do differ from country to country, and therefore, what morality demands in different countries may well vary. What may be required by the principle of utility in one country may not be required by the same principle in another country, because the consequences of adopting the practice in each of the two countries may differ significantly. What may be prima facie right in both countries may be the proper thing to do in one country but not in the other because of conflicts with other duties or rights, owing to differing circumstances.

We return to our example of Asbestos USA. The Mexican government sometimes passes laws concerning health and safety, which are different from those passed in the United States. We cannot conclude that the Mexican government cares less for the welfare of its people than does the American government for its citizens. U.S. industry is more technologically developed than Mexican industry. Mexican industry is more labor-intensive, on the whole, than U.S. industry. Mexico seeks to attract foreign industry to help develop its potential, to train its people in work skills, and to bring in tax and other revenue. Imported industry also provides work for Mexicans who would otherwise be unemployed. Suppose that for these and similar reasons the Mexican government decides that it gains more by allowing somewhat unsafe factory conditions than by setting standards that would preclude the development of industry in the country. Suppose that the workers prefer working in Asbestos USA to not working at all. We can complain that it is unfair for people not to have work or that the contract of employment with such people is not free and hence morally marred. But granting all of this, it might still be true that Mexico and the Mexican people benefit more by Asbestos USA locating its plant in Mexico than by its not being there. If this were the case, then the move of Asbestos USA would not be immoral, providing it fulfilled the foregoing conditions.

Does this mean that it is moral to export cancer-producing industries to Mexico and other countries, where the regulations are more lenient than in the United States? The argument so far has considered Asbestos USA an isolated case. What will be the effect on Mexico and its people twenty years hence if such industries move there in significant numbers? Are the country and the people better off without such industries? How will the cancer cases be treated? What will happen to families of workers who get cancer? Are health provisions and pension plans provided for the workers?

Companies that wish to act morally must consider and attempt to answer these questions.

Ideally, there should be international agreements on minimally acceptable standards of safety in industry. In the absence of such standards moral sense and pressure must function until law can equalize the position of the worker vis-à-vis the employer. But moral sense and pressure seem to play little role in the policies of many international corporations. Paradoxically, some underdeveloped countries see the conditions for moral action, which have been discussed here, as impediments to the development of their countries, as requirements that keep them underdeveloped, and as the moralizing of Americans who are basically well off and do not understand other situations, including the aspirations of other people. The difficulty of knowing what will benefit the people in such countries most and of knowing what the people truly want— as opposed to what some governmental leaders say—is enormous. The difficulty forces us to be careful not to confuse what is morally right with what is proper for Americans. But American companies that are operating abroad and wish to be moral should not ignore the moral dimension of their actions; they should not simply follow the letter of the law in the countries in which they operate.

Is Asbestos USA immoral if it does not pay its Mexican employees the same wages that it paid its U.S. employees? The claim that it is immoral if it does not is a difficult one to sustain. Justice requires that people who do the same work should receive the same pay. A Mexican could rightly complain of injustice if he were paid less than an American for doing similar work in the same factory. But the principle applies only within the same factory, plant, or office.

The desirability of international minimal wage standards is obvious. But there is no visible movement in this direction, and multinational corporations on the whole have not attempted to promote such standards.

Finally, is it immoral for Asbestos USA to produce products in Mexico for sale in the United

States? Suppose a German company made cars in the United States exclusively for export to Germany. Would we claim that the German company was exploiting the United States? It is difficult to develop a principle under which we would make such a determination. Earlier, we suggested the principle that unless a foreign company benefits the country in which it operates, it exploits that country for its own advantage and so acts immorally. This rules out as immoral exploitation of one country, *A,* by another, *B,* that dominates *A* in such a way that *B* can force *A* to act contrary to *A's* own best interests. But if we consider the building of plants in sovereign states by firms from other countries, the host countries are able to prevent and prohibit such exploitation. If Asbestos USA were to force the demise of Mexican asbestos companies, it is difficult to see why it should be tolerated. But if it does not, there are many ways Asbestos USA might help the economy other than by producing its products for the Mexican market. It supplies work for its Mexican employees, teaches skills to the people it employs, pays taxes to the government, provides work for those who must build the plant in the first place, and purchases materials it needs locally to the advantage of the local economy. The workers in turn use their wages to buy goods, food, and shelter and so help support others in the economy. The Mexican government might well consider the trade-off to be to its advantage.

This analysis does not exonerate Asbestos USA on all counts. It has argued that Asbestos USA is not automatically guilty of the immoral practices attributed to it by typical critics.

We have not touched on the question of what the moral obligations of a multinational are in a country in which the government is repressive and in which the leaders care more for their own good and benefit than for the good of their people. If a government itself exploits its people and encourages foreign exploitation of its people by foreign firms that pay taxes to the government, or pay government officials directly, the government acts immorally. If a firm knowingly and willingly exploits its workers, even if it is legal to do so, it also acts immorally. But whether a particular firm is exploiting its workers often requires detailed investigation.

The critics of multinationals will have little patience with the analysis we have given of Asbestos USA. Even if multinationals *can* operate morally, they would assert that multinationals typically do not act morally. By outlining the conditions under which multinationals might act morally, the critics would maintain, we have given the impression that multinationals do act morally and that attacks on them are unwarranted. Such was not the intent. The temptations to act immorally are great in the international arena, and it would be surprising if many companies did not succumb. If moral restraints are ineffective, then the restraints on such activity must be international restraints. The abuses of multinationals underscore the need for effective international controls—controls, however, that the present international climate has not strongly fostered.

RIGHTS IN THE GLOBAL MARKET

Thomas J. Donaldson

Rights we take for granted are sometimes trampled abroad. Child labor plagues Central America, and dozens of interviews with workers in Central America conducted in the fall of 1987 reveal that most respondents started working between the ages of 12 and 14.[1] In other countries the rights to minimal education, free speech, basic nutrition, and freedom from torture are little more than dreams. What obligations do multinational corporations have in such contexts? Are they obliged not only to honor but to encourage the protection of such rights? Consider the claim that persons everywhere have a right to adequate food. What are we to say when a multinational corporation, working in a country where malnutrition is rampant, buys a parcel of land and converts it from the production of a staple food source to one for cash export? If the land is purchased from a wealthy landowner and converted from growing black beans to coffee, has the company indirectly violated a right to adequate food if it turns out that the purchase lowers the food supply?

These questions exist in a class of questions concerned with establishing minimal conditions upon the behavior of multinational corporations.

They are ones that have been largely neglected by academic researchers. Business academics have contributed significantly to understanding the problems of international business; they have offered a bounty of empirical analysis relevant to multinational corporations, and have conducted detailed inquiries into the structure of global markets and the strategies of multinational corporations.[2] Yet few of their efforts highlight the moral element. The notable exceptions are academics working out of the so-called social issues and business environment perspectives,[3] yet even here only a fraction of such normative work from academic business researchers has found application to multinational corporations, and when it has, the context has tended to be issue-specific, for example, Bhopal, or South African divestment.[4]

This paper will attempt to develop a list of fundamental human rights serviceable for international business. Ten specific rights are advanced to establish bottom-line moral considerations for multinational corporations. The paper concludes that corporations, individuals, and governments must respect these 10 rights, although it argues that the correlative duties that corporations must shoulder in honoring those rights are different from those of nation states and individuals. Much of the analysis is drawn from a more extensive treatment offered in my recent book, *The Ethics of International Business.*[5]

RIGHTS ESTABLISH MINIMAL CORPORATE RESPONSIBILITIES

We should first distinguish those corporate responsibilities that hold as minimal conditions from those that exceed the minimum. "Minimal" duties for multinational corporations are similar to Kant's "perfect" duties; that is, they are mandatory and allow no discretion as to when or how they are performed. A "maximal" duty, on the other hand, is one whose fulfillment would be praiseworthy but not absolutely mandatory. Our concern, in turn, is with "minimal," rather than "maximal" duties. Our aim is to inquire, for example, whether a foreign corporation's minimal duties include refusing to hire children in a Honduran assembly plant, even if doing so harms the company's competitive position. It is not to establish guidelines for exemplary or "model" multinational behavior.

Our strategy will be to assume that most if not all minimal responsibilities can be framed through the language of rights, a language recognized for establishing minimal moral obligations. Rights may be seen to lie at the rock bottom of modern moral deliberation. Maurice Cranston writes that the litmus test for whether or not something is a right is whether it protects something of "paramount importance."[6] If I have a right not to be tortured, then in violating that right you threaten something of paramount value to me. It would he splendid if you did even more—if, for example, you treated me with love and charity; but *at a minimum* you must respect my rights.

The flip side of a right typically is a duty,[7] a fact that gives aptness to Joel Feinberg's well-known definition of a right as a "justified entitlement *to* something *from* someone."[8] It is the "from someone" part of the definition that reflects the assumption of a duty, for without a correlative duty that attaches to some moral agent or group of agents, a right is weakened—if not beyond the status of a right entirely, then significantly. If we cannot say that a multinational corporation has a duty to keep the levels of arsenic low in the workplace, then the worker's right not to be poisoned means little.

Often, duties fall upon more than one class of moral agent. Consider, for example, the furor over the dumping of toxic waste in West Africa by multinational corporations. During 1988, virtually every country from Morocco to Zaire on Africa's west coast received offers from companies seeking cheap sites for dumping waste.[9] In the years prior, toxic waste dumping had become enormously expensive in the United States and Europe, in large part because of the costly safety measures mandated by U.S. and European governments. In February 1988 officials in Guinea Bissau, one of the world's poorest nations, agreed to bury 15 million tons of toxic wastes from European tanneries and pharmaceutical companies. The companies agreed to pay about $120 million, which is only slightly less than the country's entire gross national product. And in Nigeria, in 1987, five European ships unload toxic waste containing dangerous poisons such as polychlorinated biphenyls, or PCBs. Workers wearing thongs and shorts unloaded the barrels for $2.50 a day, and placed them in a dirt lot in a residential area in the town of Kiko.[10] They were not told about the contents of the barrels.[11] Who bears responsibility for protecting the workers' and inhabitants' rights to safety in such instances? It would be wrong to place it entirely upon a single group of agents such as the governments of West African nations. As it happens, the toxic waste dumped in Nigeria entered under an import permit for "non-explosive, non-radioactive and non-self-combusting chemicals." But the permit turned out to be a loophole; Nigeria had not meant to accept the waste and demanded its removal once word about its presence filtered into official channels. The example reveals the difficulty many developing countries have in generating the sophisticated language and regulatory procedures necessary to control high-technology hazards. It seems reasonable in such instances, then, to place the responsibility not upon a single class of agents but upon a broad collection of them, including governments, corporate executives, host country companies and officials, and international organizations. The responsibility for not violating the rights of people living in West Africa from the dangers of toxic waste then potentially falls upon every agent whose actions might harm, or contribute to harming, West African inhabitants. Nor is one agent's responsibility always mitigated when another "accepts" responsibility. To take a specific instance, corporate responsibility may not be eliminated if a West African government explicitly agrees to accept toxic waste. There is always the possibility—said to be a reality by some critics—that corrupt government officials will agree to accept and handle waste that threatens safety in order to fatten their own Swiss bank accounts.

Rights with international relevance should be viewed as occupying an intermediary zone between abstract moral principles such as liberty or fairness on the one hand, and national specifications of rights on the other.[12] International rights must be more specific than abstract principles if they are to facilitate practical implication, but be less specific than the entries on lists of rights whose duties fall on national governments if they are to preserve cosmopolitan relevance. One nation's particular social capacities or social traditions may favor the recognition of certain rights that are inappropriate to other nations. Citizens of a rich, technologically advanced nation, for example, but not of a poor, developing one, may be viewed as possessing a right to a certain technological level of health care.

You, as a citizen of the United States, may have the right to kidney dialysis; but a citizen of Bangladesh may not.

As a first approximation, then, let us interpret a multinational's obligations by asking which international rights it should respect, where we understand *international rights* to be sort of moral precepts that lie in a zone between abstract moral principles and national rights specifications. Multinationals, we shall assume, should respect the international rights of those whom they affect, especially when those rights are of the most fundamental sort.

But whose list of international rights shall we choose? Libertarians tend to endorse well-pruned lists of liberty-centered rights, ones that look like the first 10 amendments to the U.S. Constitution (tile Bill of Rights) without the subsequent constitutional amendments, while welfare liberals frequently endorse lush, well-tangled structures that include entitlements as well as freedoms. Who is to say that a given person's list, or a given country's list, for that matter, is preferable to another's?

One list receiving significant international attention, a list bearing the signatures of most of the world's nations, is the "Universal Declaration of Human Rights."[13] However, it and the subsequent "International Covenant on Social, Economic and Cultural Rights," have spawned controversy despite the fact that the Universal Declaration was endorsed by virtually all of the important post–World War II nations in 1948 as part of the affirmation of the U.N. Charter. What distinguishes these lists from their predecessors, and what serves also as the focus of controversy, is their inclusion of rights that have come to be called alternatively "social," "economic," "positive," or "welfare" rights. Nuances separate these four concepts, but they need not detain us; all formulations share the feature of demanding more than forbearance from those upon whom the right's correlative duties fall. All four refer to rights that entail claims by rights holders to specific goods, where such goods must at least sometimes be provided by other persons (although sometimes by unspecified others). The goods at issue are typically such things as food, education, and shelter. For convenience, we shall use the term "welfare rights" to refer to all claims of this kind. Some international rights documents even specify *as* welfare rights claims to goods that are now regarded as standard benefits of the modern welfare state. For example, Articles 22 through 27 of the Universal Declaration assert rights to social security insurance, employment, protection against unemployment, health care, education, and limits on working hours.[14]

Many have balked when confronted with such lists, arguing that no one can have a right to a specific supply of an economic good. Can anyone be said to have a "right," for example, to 128 hours of sleep and leisure each week? And, in the same spirit, some international documents have simply refused to adopt the welfare-affirming blueprint established in the Universal Declaration.[15] The issue is critical for establishing the minimal responsibilities of multinational corporations, for it is only to the extent that, say, the right to adequate food exists, that multinationals can be chided for violating it.

Henry Shue advances a compelling notion of welfare rights—one with special relevance to our task—in his book, *Basic Rights.*[16] Shue's guiding concept of a "basic right" entails the existence of welfare rights. The essence of a basic right, says Shue, is "something the deprivation of which is one standard threat to rights generally."[17] Basic rights include the right to subsistence, or "minimal economic security," to freedom of physical movement, security, and political participation. By way of explanation, the right to *subsistence* entails a claim to, e.g., "unpolluted air, unpolluted water, adequate food, adequate clothing, adequate shelter, and minimal preventative public health care."[18] The right to *freedom of physical movement* is a right to not have "arbitrary constraints upon parts of one's body, such as ropes, chains,…and the absence of arbitrary constraints upon the movement from place to place of one's whole body, such as…pass laws (as in South Africa)."[19] The right to *security* is a right not to be subjected to "murder, torture, mayhem, rape, or assault"; and the right to *political participation* is the right to have "genuine influence upon the fundamental choices among the societal institutions and the societal policies that control security and subsistence and, where the person is directly affected, genuine influence upon the operation of institutions and the implementation of policy."[20] The key to understanding a basic right for Shue is recognizing that it is a prerequisite for the enjoyment of other rights. Thus being secure from beatings is a prerequisite for the enjoyment of, e.g., the right to freedom of assembly, since one's freedom

to hold political meetings is dependent upon one's freedom from the fear of beatings in the event one chooses to assemble. Shue insists correctly that benevolent despotism cannot ensure basic rights. One's rights are not protected even by the most enlightened despot in the absence of social institutions that guarantee that basic rights will be preserved in the event such benevolence turns to malevolence.[21] Illusions, as the saying goes, are not liberties.

Shue's analysis, moreover, provides a formidable argument on behalf of such rights. The argument is successful because it unpacks the sense in which it is contradictory to support any list of rights without at the same time supporting those specific rights upon whose preservation the list can be shown to depend. It is a strategy with direct application to the controversy between defenders and critics of welfare rights, for if Shue is correct, even a list of *non*-welfare rights ultimately depends upon certain basic rights, some of which are welfare rights. His argument utilizes the following, simple propositions:

1. Everyone has a right to something.

2. Some other things are necessary for enjoying the first thing as a right, whatever the first right is.

3. Therefore, everyone also has rights to the other things that are necessary for enjoying the first thing as a right.[22]

We shall grasp Shue's point even better by considering, on the one hand, a standard objection to welfare rights, and on the other, a response afforded by Shue's theory. Now many who criticize welfare rights utilize a traditional philosophical distinction between so-called negative and positive rights. A "positive" right is said to be one that requires persons to act positively to *do* something, and a "negative" right requires only that people not deprive directly. Hence, the right to liberty is said to be a negative right, whereas the right to enough food is said to be a positive one. With this distinction in hand, it is common to conclude that no one can be bound to improve the welfare of another (unless, say, that person has entered into an agreement to do so); rather, at most they can be bound to *refrain* from damaging the welfare of another.

Shue's argument, however, reveals the implausibility of the very distinction between negative and positive rights. Perhaps the most celebrated and best accepted example of a negative right is the right to freedom. Yet the meaningful preservation of freedom requires a variety of positive actions: for example, on the part of the government it requires the establishment and maintenance of a police force, courts, and the military, and on the part of the citizenry it requires ongoing cooperation and diligent (not merely passive) forbearance. And the protection of another so-called negative right, the right to physical security, necessitates "police forces; criminal rights; penitentiaries; schools for training police, lawyers, and guards; and taxes to support an enormous system for the prevention, detention, and punishment of violations of personal security."[23]

This is compelling. The maintenance and preservation of many non-welfare rights (where, again, such maintenance and preservation is the key to a right's status as "basic") requires the support of certain basic welfare rights. For example, certain liberties depend upon the enjoyment of subsistence, just as subsistence sometimes depends upon the enjoyment of some liberties. One's freedom to speak freely is meaningless if one is weakened by hunger to the point of silence.

THE PROBLEM WITH "BASIC" RIGHTS

But while establishing the legitimacy of some welfare rights, Shue's argument is nonetheless flawed. To begin with, from the standpoint of moral logic, his methodology appears to justify the more important in terms of the less important. That is to say, insofar as a basic right is defined as one whose preservation is necessary for the preservation of all rights generally, the determination of what counts as "basic" will occur by a process that takes as fundamental all rights, including non-basic ones, and then asks which among those rights are rights such that their absence would constitute a threat to the others. Not only does this fail to say anything about the moral grounding or rights in general, it also hinges the status of the basic rights on their ability to support all rights, including non-basic rights, and this appears to place the hierarchical cart before the horse.[24] This problem enlarges when we notice that many of the so-called non-basic rights such as freedom of speech appear to be of equal impor-

tance to some so-called basic rights. One wonders why a few of the world's most important rights, such as the rights to property, free speech, religious freedom, and education, are regarded as non-basic. One can see why, given Shue's concept of a basic right, they are non-basic, but then one wonders whether they might be basic in an even more important sense.

Shue himself acknowledges that status as a basic right does not guarantee that the right in question is more important. At one point, while contrasting a non-basic right, such as the right to education, to a basic right, such as the right to security, he states, "I do not mean by this to deny that the enjoyment of the right to education is much greater and richer—more distinctively human, perhaps—than merely going through life without ever being assaulted." But he next asserts the practical priority of basic rights by saying, "I mean only that, if the choice must be made, the prevention of assault ought to supersede the provision of education."[25] So while denying that basic rights are necessarily more important than non-basic ones in all respects, he grants that they are more important in the sense that probably matters most: they are give priority in decisions where a choice must be made between defending one right and defending another. He concludes, "therefore, if a right is basic, other, non-basic rights may be sacrificed, if necessary, in order to secure the basic right."[26]

But what Shue leaves obscure is the matter of which rights *other* than basic rights are deserving of emphasis. For Shue, every right must occupy one of two positions on the rights hierarchy: it is either basic or not. But if so, then how are individuals, governments, and corporations to know which rights should be honored in a crunch? Shue clearly believes that individuals, governments, and corporations must honor *basic* rights, but how are the remaining non-basic rights to be treated? What of the right to freedom of speech, to property, or to a minimal education? Are these rights *always* to be given second-class status? And if they are to be given priority in some instances, then why? Then too, surely, Shue will agree that all *nation states* must honor the right to freedom of speech, but is the same true of all individuals and corporations? Does it follow that corporations must tolerate all speech affecting the workplace and never penalize offending workers, even when the speech is maliciously motivated and severely damages profitability? Similarly, are all states responsible for defending *all* other non-basic rights?

FUNDAMENTAL INTERNATIONAL RIGHTS

Let us adopt another method of approach. Let us attempt to determine which rights are most fundamental directly, i.e., by using criteria that ground fundamental rights. In other words, instead of employing an analytic argument that takes for granted a body of rights and then analyzes the logic of their interdependence (as Shue does), let us employ a normative argument that looks to the grounding of rights in general. Let us stipulate three conditions that will be independently necessary and jointly sufficient for considering a given prospective as (a) a right and (b) a right of fundamental importance. Such a right we shall label a "fundamental international right." These three conditions are that (1) the right protects something of extreme importance, that (2) it is subject to significant, recurring threats, and that (3) the obligations or burdens it imposes are economically affordable and fair with respect to the distribution of burdens generally. These three conditions resemble, although they are not identical to, three of the four conditions advanced by James Nickel, in his book, *Making Sense of Human Rights,*[27] for identifying rights imposing claims on nation-states. In the present context, however, they are advanced as having application to all three of the major classes of international actors, i.e., nation-states, individuals, and multinational corporations.

Consider each condition. The first recognizes that if claims are made to things that have little or only moderate importance, then even if those claims happen to be valid, they cannot aspire to the status of "rights." We are reminded of Maurice Cranston's "paramount importance" test cited earlier for bona fide rights. The second notes that rights also must be subject to what Shue calls "standard" threats or what Nickel has alternatively dubbed "recurrent" threats. A right must be subject to significant, recurring threats for the simple reason that the list of claims centering on interests of fundamental importance would otherwise expand indefinitely. And finally, as Nickel has shown convincingly, any right must satisfy what

could be called an "affordability-fairness" criterion in that it must impose obligations or other burdens that are in Nickel's words "affordable in relation to resources, other obligations, and fairness in the distribution of burdens." Part of the justification for this condition is as simple as the time-honored dictum in moral philosophy that "ought implies can," or, in other words, that no person or entity can be held responsible for doing something if it is not in their power to do it. We need only add the reasonable proviso that sometimes a duty may be of a kind that is discouraged for moral reasons, i.e., either because it conflicts with another bona fide obligation or because it constitutes an unfairness in the distribution of burdens.

Next, consider the following list of fundamental international rights:

1. The right to freedom of physical movement
2. The right to ownership of property
3. The right to freedom from torture
4. The right to a fair trial
5. The right to non-discriminatory treatment (i.e., freedom from discrimination on the basis of such characteristics as race or sex)
6. The right to physical security
7. The right to freedom of speech and association
8. The right to minimal education
9. The right to political participation
10. The right to subsistence

This seems a minimal list. Some will wish to add entries such as the right to employment, to social security, or to a certain standard of living (say, as might be prescribed by Rawls's well-known "difference" principle). Disputes also may arise about the wording or overlapping features of some rights: for example, is not the right to freedom from torture included in the right to physical security, at least when the latter is properly interpreted? We shall not attempt to resolve such controversies here. Rather, the list as presented aims to suggest, albeit incompletely, a description of a *minimal* set of rights and to serve as a point of beginning and consensus for evaluating international conduct. If I am correct, many would wish to add entries, but few would wish to subtract them.

The list has been generated by application of the three conditions and the compatibility proviso. Readers may satisfy for themselves whether the ten entries fulfill these conditions; in doing so, however, they should remember that in constructing the list one looks for *only* those rights that can be honored in some form by *all* international agents, including nation-states, corporations, and individuals. Hence, to consider only the issue of affordability, each candidate for a right must be tested for "affordability" by way of the lowest common denominator—by way, for example, of the poorest nation-state. If, even after receiving its fair share of charitable aid from wealthier nations, that state cannot "afford" dialysis for all citizens who need it, then the right to receive dialysis from one's nation state will not be a fundamental international right, although dialysis may contribute a bona fide right for those living within a specific nation-state, such as Japan.

Although the hope for a definitive interpretation of the list of rights is an illusion, we can add specificity by clarifying the correlative duties entailed for different kinds of international actors. Because by definition the list contains items that all three major classes of international actors must respect, the next task is to spell out the correlative duties that fall upon our targeted group of international actors, namely, multinational corporations.

Doing so requires putting the third condition from Nickel's revised list to a second, and different, use. This "affordability-fairness" condition—which, again, concerns the affordability of respecting a right from the perspective of an agent's resources, other obligations, and overall fairness in the distribution of burdens—was used first as one of the criteria for generating the original list of fundamental rights. There it demanded satisfaction of an affordability-fairness threshold for each potential respecter of a right. For example, were the burdens imposed by a given right not fair (in relation to other bona fide obligations and burdens) or affordable for nation-states, individuals, and corporations, then presumably the prospective right would not qualify as a fundamental international right. In its second use, to which it is about to be put, the condition goes beyond the judgment *that* a certain affordability-fairness threshold has been crossed to the determination of *what* the proper duties are for multinational corporations in relation

to a given right. In its second use, in other words, the condition's notions of fairness and affordability are invoked to help determine *which* obligations properly fall upon corporations, in contrast to individuals and nation-states. We shall use the condition to help determine the correlative duties that attach to multinational corporations in their honoring of fundamental international rights.

As we look over the list, it is noteworthy that except for a few isolated instances multinational corporations have probably succeeded in fulfilling their duty not to *actively deprive* persons of their enjoyment of the rights at issue. But correlative duties involve more than failing to actively deprive people of the enjoyment of their rights. Shue, for example, notes that three types of correlative duties are possible for any right, namely, duties to (1) avoid depriving, (2) help protect from deprivation, and (3) aid the deprived.[28]

While it is obvious that the honoring of rights clearly imposes duties of the first kind, i.e., to avoid depriving directly, it is less obvious, but frequently true, that honoring them involves acts or omissions that help prevent the deprivation of rights. If I receive a threat from Murder, Inc., and it looks like they mean business, my right to security is clearly at risk. If a third party has relevant information that if revealed to the police would help protect my right, it is no excuse for the third party to say that it is Murder, Inc., and not they (the third party), who wishes to kill me. Hence, honoring rights sometimes involves not only duties to *avoid depriving,* but to *help protect from deprivation* as well, and it is interesting that many critics of multinationals, have faulted them not for the failure to avoid depriving but for failing to take reasonable protective steps.

Similarly, the duties associated with rights can often include duties from the third category, i.e., that of *aiding the deprived,* as when a government is bound to honor the right of its citizens to adequate nutrition by distributing food in the wake of a famine or natural disaster, or when the same government in the defense of political liberty is required to demand that an employer reinstate or compensate an employee fired for voting for a particular candidate in a government election.

Nonetheless, the honoring by multinational corporations of at least *some* of the ten fundamental rights requires the adoption of only the first class of correlative duties, i.e., the duty to avoid depriving. Correlative duties do not extend either to protecting from deprivation or aiding the deprived, because of the relevance of the "fairness-affordability" condition discussed before. This condition requires, again, that the obligations or burdens imposed by a right must be affordable in relation to resources, other obligations, and fairness in the distribution of burdens. (Certain puzzles affecting the affordability-fairness condition are discussed later in the context of the "drug lord" problem.)

Corporations cannot be held to the same standards of charity and love as individuals. Nor can corporations be held to the same standards to which we hold civil governments for enhancing social welfare—since frequently governments are dedicated to enhancing the welfare of, and actively preserving the liberties of, their citizens. The profit-making corporation, in contrast, is designed to achieve an economic mission and as a moral actor possesses an exceedingly narrow personality. It is an undemocratic institution, furthermore, which is ill-suited to the broader task of distributing society's goods in accordance with a conception of general welfare. The corporation is an economic animal; although one may deny that its sole responsibility is to make a profit for its investors, one will surely wish to define its responsibilities differently than for civil governments.

Let us employ a "minimal/maximal" distinction to draw the inference that duties of the third class, i.e., to aid the deprived, do not fall upon for-profit multinational corporations, except, of course, in instances where the corporations themselves have done the depriving. For example, although it would be strikingly generous for multinationals to sacrifice some of their profits to buy milk, grain, and shelter for persons in poor countries, assisting the poor is not one of the corporations' minimal moral requirements; such minimal obligations belong more properly to the peoples' respective governments or, perhaps, to better-off individuals. If corporations possess duties to aid those deprived of the benefits of rights (except, again, in instances where they have done the depriving), then they possess them as "maximal" not "minimal" duties, which means that a given corporation's failure to observe them does not deprive that corporation of its moral right to exist. Furthermore, since rights impose minimal, not maximal duties, it follows that

whereas a corporation might have a maximal duty to aid the deprived in a given instance, their failure to honor that duty could not be claimed necessarily as a violation of someone's *rights*.

The same, however, is not true of the second class of duties, i.e., to protect from deprivation. These duties, like those in the third class, are also usually the province of government, but it sometimes happens that the rights to which they correlate are ones whose protection is a direct outcome of ordinary corporate activities. For example, the duties associated with protecting a worker from the physical threats of other workers may fall not only upon the local police but also to some extent upon the employer. These duties, in turn, are properly viewed as correlative duties of a person's right—in this instance, the worker's right—to personal security. This will become clearer in a moment when we discuss the correlative duties of specific rights.

The table of correlative duties (p. 516) reflects the application of the "affordability-fairness" condition to the earlier list of fundamental international rights, and indicates which rights do, and which do not, impose correlative duties upon multinational corporations of the three various kinds. A word of caution should be issued for interpreting the list: the first type of correlative obligation, i.e., of not depriving directly, is broader than might be supposed at first. It includes *cooperative* as well as exclusively individual actions. Thus, if a company has personnel policies that inhibit freedom of movement, or if a multinational corporation operating in South Africa cooperates with the government's restrictions on pass laws, then those companies actively deprive persons of their right to freedom of movement, despite the fact that actions of other agents (in particular, of the South African government) may be essential in effecting the deprivation. Similarly, in an instance where a corporation cooperates with political groups in fighting land reforms designed to take land from a tiny aristocratic minority (a minority that, say, owns virtually all of a country's usable land) for redistribution to peasants, those corporations may well—at least under certain circumstances—violate the right to private property.

Still, the list asserts that at least six of the ten fundamental rights impose correlative duties of the second kind upon corporations, that is, to protect from deprivation.[29] What follows is a brief set of commentaries discussing sample applications of

Minimal Correlative Duties of Multinational Corporations

Fundamental Rights	To Avoid Depriving	To Help Protect from Deprivation	To Aid the Deprived
Freedom of physical movement	X		
Ownership of property	X		
Freedom from torture	X		
Fair trial	X		
Non-discriminatory treatment	X	X	
Physical security	X	X	
Freedom of speech and association	X	X	
Minimal education	X	X	
Political participation	X	X	
Subsistence	X	X	

each of those six rights from the perspective of such correlative duties.

SAMPLE APPLICATIONS

Discrimination

The obligation to protect from deprivation a person's freedom from discrimination properly falls upon corporations as well as governments insofar as everyday corporate activities directly affect compliance with the right. Because employees and prospective employees possess the moral right not to be discriminated against on the basis of race, sex, caste, class, or family affiliation, it follows that multinational corporations have an obligation not only to refrain from discrimination but in some instances to protect the right to non-discriminatory treatment by establishing appropriate procedures. This may require, for example, offering notice to prospective employees of the company's policy of non-discriminatory hiring, or educating lower level managers about the need to reward or penalize on the basis of performance rather than irrelevant criteria.

Physical Security

The right to physical security similarly entails duties of protection: if a Japanese multinational corporation operating in Nigeria hires shop workers to run metal lathes in an assembly factory but fails to provide them with protective goggles, then the corporation has failed to honor the workers' moral

right to physical security (no matter what the local law might decree). Injuries from such a failure would be the moral responsibility of the Japanese multinational despite the fact that the company could not be said to have inflicted the injuries directly.

Free Speech and Association

In the same vein, the duty to protect the right of free speech and association from deprivation finds application in the ongoing corporate obligation not to bar the emergence of labor unions. Corporations are not obliged on the basis of human rights to encourage or welcome labor unions, but neither are they morally permitted to destroy them or prevent their emergence through coercive tactics; to do so would violate the workers' international right to association. Their duty to protect the right to association from deprivation, in turn, includes refraining from lobbying host governments for restrictions that would violate the right in question, and perhaps even to protesting host government measures that do violate it.[30]

Minimal Education

The correlative duty to protect the right of education may be illustrated through the very example used to open this paper: namely, the prevalence of child labor in developing countries. A multinational in Central America is not entitled to hire a 10-year-old child for full-time work because, among other reasons, doing so blocks the child's ability to receive a minimally sufficient education. While what counts as a "minimally sufficient" education may be debated, and while it seems likely, moreover, that the specification of the right to a certain level of education will depend, at least in part, upon the level of economic resources available in a given country, it is reasonable to assume that any action by a corporation that has the effect of blocking the development of a child's ability to read or write will be proscribed on the basis of rights.

Political Participation

In some instances corporations have failed to honor the correlative duty of protecting the right to political participation from deprivation. The most blatant examples of direct deprivation are fortunately becoming so rare as to be non-existent, namely, cases in which companies directly aid in overthrowing democratic regimes, as when United Fruit helped overthrow a democratically elected regime in Honduras during the 1950s. But a few corporations have continued indirectly to threaten this right by failing to protect it from deprivation. A few have persisted, for example, in supporting military dictatorships in countries with growing democratic sentiment, and others have blatantly bribed publicly elected officials with large sums of money. Perhaps the most celebrated example of the latter occurred when the prime minister of Japan was bribed with $7 million by the Lockheed Corporation to secure a lucrative Tri-Star Jet contract. Here, the complaint from the perspective of this right is not against bribes or "sensitive payments" in general, but to bribes in contexts where they serve to undermine a democratic system in which publicly elected officials are in a position of public trust.

Even the buying and owning of major segments of a foreign country's land and industry has been criticized in this regard. As Brian Barry has remarked, "the paranoia created in Britain and the United States by land purchases by foreigners (especially Arabs, it seems) should serve to make it understandable that the citizenry of a country might be unhappy with a state of affairs in which the most important natural resources are in foreign ownership."[31] At what point would Americans regard their democratic control threatened by foreign ownership of U.S. industry and resources? At 20 percent ownership? At 40 percent? At 60 percent? At 80 percent? The answer is debatable, yet there seems to be some point beyond which the right to

national self-determination, and in turn national democratic control, is violated by foreign ownership of property.[32]

Subsistence

Corporations also have duties to protect the right to subsistence from deprivation. Consider the following scenario: a number of square miles of land in an underdeveloped country has been used for years to grow black beans. Further, the bulk of the land is owned, as it has been for centuries, by two wealthy landowners. Poorer members of the community work the land and receive a portion of the crop, a portion barely sufficient to satisfy nutritional needs. Next, imagine that a multinational corporation offers the two wealthy owners a handsome sum for the land, and does so because it plans to grow coffee for export. Now *if*—and this, admittedly, is a crucial "if"—the corporation has reason to *know* that a significant number of people in the community will suffer malnutrition as a result; that is, if the company has convincing reasons to believe that those persons will not be hired by the company, or that if forced to migrate to the city they will earn less than subsistence wages, i.e., inadequate to provide proper food and shelter, then the multinational may be said to have failed in its correlative duty to protect persons from the deprivation of the right to subsistence. This despite the fact that the corporation would never have stopped to take food from workers' mouths, and despite the fact that the malnourished will, in Coleridge's words, "die so slowly that none call it murder."

Disagreements: The Relevance of Facts and Culture

The commentaries above are obviously not intended to complete the project of specifying the correlative duties associated with fundamental international rights; only to begin it. Furthermore, here—as in the matter of specifying specific correlative duties generally—disagreements are inevitable. Take the land acquisition case above. One may claim that multinationals are never capable of knowing the consequences of land purchases with sufficient certainty to predict malnutrition or starvation. The issue obviously requires debate. Furthermore, one may wish to argue for the moral relevance of predictions about the actions of other agents. If the corporation in question refrains from buying land, won't another corporation rush in with the same negative consequences? And might not such a prediction mitigate the former corporation's responsibility in buying land in the first place? Here both facts and meta-moral principles must be debated.

The same point arises in the context of an even more controversial issue, one related also to the right of persons to subsistence. Critics have asserted that by promoting high technology agriculture in developing countries where wealthier farmers are preferred risks for loans to buy imported seeds and fertilizer, multinationals encourage the syndrome of land concentration and dependence upon imported food and fertilizer, leading to the situation where proceeds from cash crops buy luxuries for the rich and where poor farmers are forced to sell their small plots of land and move to the city. Whether such practices do violate rights will obviously be a subject of controversy. But what is central to the resolution of such a controversy is the *empirical* question of whether such practices *do* lead to starvation and malnourishment. That is to say, the problem may be positioned for solution, but it is certainly not solved, by establishing the right to subsistence and its correlative duties: facts remain crucial.

More generally, the solution to most difficult international problems requires a detailed understanding not only of moral precepts but of particular facts. The answer does not appear, as if by magic, simply by referencing the relevant rights and correlative duties, any more than the issue of whether welfare recipients in the United States should be required to work disappears by appealing to the state's correlative duty to aid the disadvantaged. Elsewhere I propose an "ethical algorithm" to aid multinational managers in making difficult trade-offs between home and host country values,[33] but while that algorithm augments the appeal to fundamental international rights established in this paper, neither it nor any other theory can draw moral conclusions when key facts are in dispute. Put simply, when facts are in irreconcilable dispute, so too will be the moral outcome.[34]

It may be that some of the above rights would not be embraced, or at least not embraced as formulated here, by cultures far different from ours. Would, for example, the Fulanis, a nomadic cattle culture in Nigeria, subscribe to this list with the

same eagerness as the citizens of Brooklyn, New York? What list would they draw up if given the chance? And could we, or should we, try to convince them that our list is preferable? Would such a dialogue even make sense?[35]

I want to acknowledge that rights may vary in priority and style of expression from one culture to another. Yet in line with the conclusions of the earlier discussion of cultural relativism, I maintain that the list itself is applicable to all people even if they would fail to compose an identical list. Clearly the Fulanis do not have to accept the list of ten rights in question for it to constitute a valid means of judging the Fulani culture. If the Fulanis treat women unfairly and unequally, then at least one fundamental international right remains unfulfilled in their culture, and our discussion implies that their culture is poorer for that practice. Three of the rights are especially prone to varying cultural interpretation. These include that of non-discriminatory treatment (with special reference to women), to political participation, and to the ownership of property. The latter two raise tendentious political issues for cultures with traditions of communal property and non-democratic institutions. The list has no pretensions to solve these age-old political problems. While I may (as, in fact, I do) subscribe to a modified Lockean notion of property in which certain political systems incorporating social ownership violate individual rights, the right to property advanced in our list need not be so narrowly interpreted as to rule out any instance of public ownership. For example, even primitive societies with communal property practices might be said to recognize a modified version of the right to property if those practices entail mutually agreed-upon, and fairly applied, rules of use, benefit, and liability. I am not prepared to say that each and every such instance violates the right to own property.

Even so, there will be a point beyond which the public ownership of property violates individual rights. State ownership of all land and movable property violates the individual's right to own property. Is the point passed when a country nationalizes its phone systems? Its oil industry? Is it passed when a primitive culture refuses to subordinate family to individual property? Although it is clear that such questions are of decisive significance, it is equally clear that establishing such a point is a task that cannot be undertaken satisfactorily here.

The same holds true for interpreting the right to political participation. I affirm the merits of a democratic electoral system in which representatives are chosen on the basis of one-person-one-vote; yet the list should not be interpreted to demand a photocopy of U.S. or English style democracy. For example, it is possible to imagine a small, primitive culture utilizing other fair means for reflecting participation in the political process—other than a representative electoral system—and thereby satisfying the right to political participation.

The Drug Lord Problem

One of the most difficult aspects of the rights list proposed concerns the affordability-fairness condition. We can see it more clearly by reflecting on what might be called the "drug lord" problem.[36] Imagine that an unfortunate country has a weak government and is run by various drug lords (not, it appears, a hypothetical case). These drug lords threaten the physical security of various citizens and torture others. The government—the country—cannot afford to mount the required police or military actions that would bring these drug lords into moral line. Or, perhaps, this could be done but only by imposing terrible burdens on certain segments of the society that would be unfair to others. Does it follow that members of that society do not have the fundamental international right not to be tortured and to physical security? Surely they do, even if the country cannot afford to guarantee them. But if that is the case, what about the affordability-fairness criterion?

Let us begin by noting that the "affordability" part of the affordability-fairness condition does imply some upper limit for the use of resources in the securing of a fundamental international right (such that, for example, dialysis cannot be a fundamental international right). With this established, the crucial question becomes *how* to draw the upper limit. The preceding argument commits us to draw that limit through at least two criteria: first, compatibility with other, already recognized, international rights, and second, the level of importance of the interest (moral or otherwise) being protected by the right (the first of the three conditions). As for the former, we remember that the affordability-fairness principle already entails a "moral compatibility" condition requiring that the duties imposed be compatible with other moral duties. Hence, a

prima facie limit may be drawn on the certification of a prospective right corresponding to the point at which other bona fide international rights are violated. As for the latter, trade-offs among members of a class of prospective rights will be made by reference to the relative importance of the interest being protected by the right. The right not to be tortured protects a more fundamental interest than the right to an aesthetically pleasing environment.

This provides a two-tiered solution for the drug lord problem. At the first tier, we note that the right of people not to be tortured by the drug lords (despite the unaffordability of properly policing the drug lords) implies that people, and especially the drug lords, have a duty not to torture. Here the solution is simple. The argument of this chapter establishes a fundamental international right not to be tortured, and it is a right that binds all parties to the duty of forbearance in torturing others. For on the first pass of applying the affordability-fairness condition, that is, when we are considering simply the issue of which fundamental international rights exist, we are only concerned about affordability in relation to *any* of the three classes of correlative duties. That is, we look to determine only whether duties of *any* of the three classes of duties are fair and affordable. And with respect to the issue of affordability, clearly the drug lords along with every other moral agent can "afford" to refrain from actively depriving persons of their right not to be tortured. That is, they can afford to refrain from torturing. It follows that people clearly have the fundamental international right not to be tortured, which imposes at least one class of duties upon all international actors, namely, those of forbearance.

At the second tier, on the other hand, we are concerned with the issue of whether the right not to be tortured includes a duty of the government to mount an effective prevention system against torture. Here the affordability-fairness criterion is used in a second pass, one that helps establish the specific kinds of correlative duties associated with the right not to be tortured. Here surely all nation states can "afford" to shoulder duties of the second and third categories, i.e., of helping prevent deprivation, and of aiding the deprived, although the specific extent of those duties may be further affected by considerations of fairness and affordability. For example, given an instance like the country described in the drug-lord problem, it clearly seems questionable that all countries could "afford" to *succeed* completely in preventing torture, and hence the duty to help prevent torture presupposed by a fundamental international right to freedom from torture probably cannot be construed to demand complete success. Nonetheless, a fairly high level of success in preventing torture is probably demanded by virtue of international rights, because, as I have argued elsewhere,[37] the ordinary protection of civil and political rights, such as the right not to be tortured, carries a negative rather than positive economic cost. That is, the economic cost of allowing the erosion of rights to physical security and fair trial—as an empirical matter of fact—tends to exceed the cost of maintaining the rights.

CONCLUSION

What the list of rights and corollary corporate duties establishes is that multinational corporations frequently do have obligations derived from rights where such obligations extend beyond abstaining from depriving directly, to protecting from deprivation. It implies, in other words, that the relevant factors for analyzing a difficult issue like that of hunger and high technology agriculture include not only the degree of factual correlation existing between multinational policy and hunger but also the recognition of the existence of a right to subsistence along with a specification of the corporate correlative duties entailed.

Hence the paper has argued that the ten rights identified earlier constitute minimal and bedrock moral considerations for multinational corporations operating abroad. While the list may be incomplete, the human claims it honors, and the interests those claims represent, are globally relevant. They are, in turn, immune from the Hobbesian or relativistically inspired challenges offered by skeptics. The existence of fundamental international rights implies that no corporation can wholly neglect considerations of racism, hunger, political oppression, or freedom through appeal to its "commercial" mission. These rights are, rather, moral considerations for every international moral agent, although, as we have seen, different moral agents possess different correlative obligations. The specification of the precise correlative duties associated with such rights for corporations is an ongoing task

that the paper has left incomplete. Yet the existence of the rights themselves, including the imposition of duties upon corporations to protect—as well as to refrain from directly violating—such rights, seems beyond reasonable doubt.

NOTES

Portions of this essay are contained in Thomas Donaldson, *The Ethics of International Business* (New York: Oxford University Press, 1990), and are reprinted here with permission.

1. James LeMoyne, "In Central America, the Workers Suffer Most," *New York Times,* October 26, 1987, p. 1.

2. Some work explores the issue of political risk (for example, Thomas Poynter, *Multinational Enterprises and Government Intervention* (New York: St. Martin's Press, 1985); Thomas Moran, ed., *Multinational Corporations; The Political Economy of Foreign Direct Investment* (Lexington, MA: Lexington Books, 1985); and J. N. Behrman, *Decision Criteria for Foreign Direct Investment in Latin America* (New York: Council of the Americas, 1974); while other work explores the nature of international corporate strategy (See W. J. Keegan, "Multinational Scanning: A Study of Information Sources Utilized by Headquarters Executives in Multinational Companies," *Administrative Science Quarterly* (1974): 411–21; and D. Cray, "Control and Coordination in Multinational Corporations," *Journal of International Business Studies* 15, no. 2 (1984): 85–98); and still other work explores multinational public policy issues (See Lee Preston, "The Evolution of Multinational Public Policy Toward Business: Codes of Conduct," in Lee Preston, ed., *Research in Corporate Social Performance and Policy,* Vol. 10, Greenwich, CT: JAI Press, 1988).

3. This group has produced what is probably the best developed ethical literature from business schools. Their efforts evolve from the tradition of "business and society" research with roots in the sixties and early seventies. Contributors such as Buchholz, Cochran, Epstein, Frederick, Freeman, and Sethi have made significant advances, not only in developing descriptive studies with moral relevance, but in advancing normative hypotheses. See, for example, Rogene A. Buchholz, *Business Environment and Public Policy* (Englewood Cliffs, NJ: Prentice-Hall, 1982); Stephen L. Wartick and Philip L. Cochran, "The Evolution of the Corporate Social Performance Model," *Academy of Management Review* 10 (1985): 758–69; Edwin Epstein, "The Corporate Social Policy Process: Beyond Business Ethics, Corporate Social Responsibility, and Corporate Social Responsiveness," *California Management Review* 29 (Spring 1987); William C. Frederick, "Toward CSR3: Why Ethical Analysis is Indispensable and Unavoidable in Corporate Affairs," *California Management Review* 28 (1986): 126–41; R. Edward Freeman,

Strategic Management: A Stakeholder Approach (Boston: Pitman Press, 1984), and *Corporate Strategy and the Search for Ethics* (Englewood Cliffs, NJ: Prentice-Hall, 1988); and S. Prakash Sethi, "Corporate Law Violations and Executive Liability," in Lee Preston, ed., *Corporate Social Performance and Policy, Vol. 3* (Greenwich, CT: JAI Press, 1981), pp. 72–73, and S. Prakash Sethi et al., *Corporate Governance: Public Policy Social Responsibility Committee of Corporate Board* (Richardson, TX.: Center for Research in Business and Social Policy, 1979).

4. An exception is Duane Windsor's, "Defining the Ethical Obligations of the Multinational Enterprise," in W. M. Hoffman et al., eds., *Ethics and the Multinational Corporation* (Washington, DC: University Press of America, 1986).

5. Thomas Donaldson, *The Ethics of International Business* (New York: Oxford University Press, 1990). See especially Chapter 6.

6. Maurice Cranston, *What Are Human Rights?* (New York: Tamlinger, 1973), p. 67.

7. H. J. McCloskey, for example, understands a right as a positive entitlement that need not specify who bears the responsibility for satisfying that entitlement. H. J. McCloskey, "Rights—Some Conceptual Issues," *Australasian Journal of Philosophy* 54 (1976): 99.

8. Joel Feinberg, "Duties, Rights, and Claims," *American Philosophical Quarterly* 3 (1966): 137–44. See also Feinberg, "The Nature and Value of Rights," *Journal of Value Inquiry* 4 (1970): 243–57.

9. James Brooke, "Waste Dumpers Turning to West Africa," *New York Times,* July 17, 1988, p. 1.

10. Ibid.

11. Nigeria and other countries have struck back, often by imposing strict rules against the acceptance of toxic waste. For example, in Nigeria officials now warn that anyone caught importing toxic waste will face the firing squad. Brooke, "Waste Dumpers Turning to West Africa," p. 7.

12. James W. Nickel, *Making Sense of Human Rights: Philosophical Reflections on the Universal Declaration of Human Rights* (Berkeley: University of California Press, 1987), pp. 107–8.

13. See Ian Brownlie, *Basic Documents on Human Rights* (Oxford: Oxford University Press, 1975).

14. For a contemporary analysis of the Universal Declaration of Human Rights and companion international documents, see James W. Nickel, *Making Sense of Human Rights: Philosophical Reflections on the Universal Declaration of Human Rights* (Berkeley: University of California Press, 1987).

15. For example, the "European Convention of Human Rights" omits mention of welfare rights, preferring instead to create an auxiliary document ("The European Social Charter of 1961") which references many of what earlier had been treated as rights as "goals."

16. Henry Shue, *Basic Rights* (Princeton, NJ: Princeton University Press, 1982).

17. Ibid., p. 34.

18. Ibid., p. 20–23.

19. Ibid., p. 78.

20. Ibid., p. 71.

21. Ibid., p. 76.

22. Ibid., p. 31.

23. Ibid., pp. 37–38.

24. I am indebted to Alan Gewirth who made this point in a conversation about Shue's theory of basic rights.

25. Shue, *Basic Rights,* p. 20.

26. Ibid., p. 19.

27. James Nickel, *Making Sense of Human Rights* (Berkeley: University of California Press, 1987), pp. 108–19. The phrasing of the third condition is derived almost directly from Nickel's condition that "the obligations or burdens imposed by the right must be affordable in relation to resources, other obligations, and fairness in the distribution of burdens."

28. Shue, *Basic Rights,* p. 57.

29. It is possible to understand even the remaining four rights as imposing correlative duties to protect from deprivation by imagining unusual or hypothetical scenarios. For example, if it happened that the secret police or a host country dictatorship regularly used corporate personnel files in their efforts to kidnap and torture suspected political opponents, then the corporation would be morally obligated to object to the practice, and to refuse to make their files available any longer. Here the corporation would have a correlative duty to protect from deprivation the right not to be tortured. The list of rights identified as imposing correlative duties of protection was limited to six, however, on the basis of the fact that their protection is directly related to activities frequently undertaken by corporations in the real world.

30. The twin phenomena of commercial concentration and the globalization of business, both associated with the rise of the multinational, have tended to weaken the bargaining power of organized labor. It is doubtful that labor is sharing as fully as it once did in the cyclical gains of industrial productivity. This gives special significance to the right in question.

31. Brian Barry, "'The Case for a New International Economic Order," in J. Roland Pennock and John W. Chapman, eds., *Ethics, Economics, and the Law: Nomos Vol. XXIV* (New York: New York University Press, 1982).

32. Companies are also charged with undermining local governments, and hence infringing on basic rights, by sophisticated tax evasion schemes. Especially when companies buy from their own subsidiaries, they can establish prices that

have little connection to existing market values. This, in turn, means that profits can be shifted from high-tax to low-tax countries with the result that poor nations can be deprived of their rightful share.

33. See Donaldson, *The Ethics of International Business,* Chapter 5.

34. It is important to remember that it is "key" or "crucial" facts that are being discussed here. The 10 fundamental international rights are not to be eroded in every instance by the old argument that "we don't have enough facts." Such a defense clearly has its limits, and these limits are overstepped by the demand that evidence be definitive in every sense. An excellent example of excess in this vein is that of cigarette

companies denying that their products are dangerous because we do not yet understand the causal mechanism whereby cigarette smoking is correlated with cancer.

35. Both for raising these questions, and in helping me formulate answers, I am indebted to William Frederick.

36. I am indebted to George Brenkert for suggesting and formulating the "drug lord" problem.

37. Thomas Donaldson, "Trading Justice for Bread: A Reply to James W. Nickel," in Kenneth Kipnis and Diana T. Meyers, eds., *Economic Justice: Private Rights and Public Responsibilities* (Totowa, NJ: Rowman and Allenheld, 1985), pp. 226–29.

INTERNATIONAL BUSINESS, MORALITY, AND THE COMMON GOOD
Manuel Velasquez

During the last few years an increasing number of voices have urged that we pay more attention to ethics in international business, on the grounds that not only are all large corporations now internationally structured and thus engaging in international transactions, but that even the smallest domestic firm is increasingly buffeted by the pressures of international competition.[1] This call for increased attention to international business ethics has been answered by a slowly growing collection of ethicists who have begun to address issues in this field. The most comprehensive work on this subject to date is the recent book *The Ethics of International Business* by Thomas Donaldson.[2]

I want in this article to discuss certain realist objections to bringing ethics to bear on international transactions, an issue that, I believe, has not yet been either sufficiently acknowledged nor adequately addressed but that must be resolved if the topic of international business ethics is to proceed on solid foundations. Even so careful a writer as Thomas Donaldson fails to address this issue in its proper complexity. Oddly enough, in the first chapter where one would expect him to argue that, in spite of realist objections, *businesses* have international moral obligations, Donaldson argues only for the less pertinent claim that, in spite of

realist objections, *states* have international moral obligations.[3] But international business organizations, I will argue, have special features that render realist objections quite compelling. The question I want to address, here, then, is a particular aspect of the question Donaldson and others have ignored: Can we say that businesses operating in a competitive international environment have any moral obligations to contribute to the international common good, particularly in light of realist objections? Unfortunately, my answer to this question will be in the negative.

My subject, then, is international business and the common good. What I will do is the following. I will begin by explaining what I mean by the common good, and what I mean by international business. Then I will turn directly to the question whether the views of the realist allow us to claim that international businesses have a moral obligation to contribute to the common good. I will first lay out the traditional realist treatment of this question and then revise the traditional realist view so that it can deal with certain shortcomings embedded in the traditional version of realism. I will then bring these revisions to bear on the question of whether international businesses have any obligations toward the common good, a question that I will answer in the negative. My hope is that I have identified some extremely problematic issues that are both critical and disturbing and that, I believe, need to be more

From *Business Ethics Quarterly,* vol. 2, issue 1 (July 1992): 27–40. Reprinted by permission of the author.

widely discussed than they have been because they challenge our easy attribution of moral obligation to international business organizations.

I should note that what follows is quite tentative. I am attempting to work out the implications of certain arguments that have reappeared recently in the literature on morality in international affairs. I am not entirely convinced of the correctness of my conclusions, and offer them here as a way of trying to get clearer about their status. I should also note that although I have elsewhere argued that it is improper to attribute *moral responsibility* to corporate entities, I here set these arguments aside in order to show that even if we ignore the issue of moral responsibility, it is still questionable whether international businesses have obligations toward the common good.

I. THE COMMON GOOD

Let me begin by distinguishing a weak from a strong conception of the common good, so that I might clarify what I have in mind when I refer to the common good.

What I have in mind by a weak conception of the common good is essentially the utilitarian notion of the common good. It is a notion that is quite clearly stated by Jeremy Bentham:

> The interest of the community then is—what? The sum of the interests of the several members who compose it…It is vain to talk of the interest of the community, without understanding what is the interest of the individual. A thing is said to promote the interest or to be for the interest of an individual, when it tends to add to the sum total of his pleasure; or what comes to the same thing, to diminish the sum total of his pains.[4]

On the utilitarian notion of the common good, the common good is nothing more than the sum of the utilities of each individual. The reason why I call this the "weak" conception of the common good will become clear, I believe, once it is contrasted with another, quite different notion of the common good.

Let me describe, therefore, what I will call a strong conception of the common good, the conception on which I want to focus in this essay. It is

a conception that has been elaborated in the Catholic tradition, and so I will refer to it as the Catholic conception of the common good. Here is how one writer, William A. Wallace, O.P., characterizes the conception:

> A common good is clearly distinct from a *private* good, the latter being the good of one person only, to the exclusion of its being possessed by any other. A common good is distinct also from a *collective* good, which, though possessed by all of a group, is not really participated in by the members of the group; divided up, a collective good becomes respectively the private goods of the members. A true *common* good is universal, not singular or collective, and is distributive in character, being communicable to many without becoming anyone's private good. Moreover, each person participates in the whole common good, not merely in a part of it, nor can any one person possess it wholly.[5]

In the terms used by Wallace, the utilitarian conception of the common good is actually a "collective" good. That is, it is an aggregate of the private goods (the utilities) of the members of a society. The common good in the utilitarian conception is divisible in the sense that the aggregate consists of distinct parts and each part is enjoyable by only one individual. Moreover, the common good in the utilitarian conception is not universal in the sense that not all members of society can enjoy all of the aggregate; instead, each member enjoys only a portion of the aggregate.

By contrast, in the Catholic conception that Wallace is attempting to characterize, the common good consists of those goods that (1) benefit all the members of a society in the sense that all the members of the society have access to each of these goods, and (2) are not divisible in the sense that none of these goods can be divided up and allocated among individuals in such a way that others can be excluded from enjoying what another individual enjoys. The example that Wallace gives of one common good is the "good of peace and order."[6] Other examples are national security, a clean natural environment, public health and safety, a productive economic system to whose benefits all have access, a just legal and political system, and a system of natural and artificial associations in which persons can achieve their personal fulfillment.

It is this strong notion of the common good that the Catholic tradition has had in mind when it has defined the common good as "the sum total of those conditions of social living whereby men are enabled more fully and more readily to achieve their own perfection."[7] It is also the conception that John Rawls has in mind when he writes that "Government is assumed to aim at the common good, that is, at maintaining conditions and achieving objectives that are similarly to everyone's advantage," and "the common good I think of as certain general conditions that are in an appropriate sense equally to everyone's advantage."[8]

The Catholic conception of the common good is the conception that I have in mind in what follows. It is clear from the characterization of the common good laid out above that we can think of the common good on two different levels. We can think of the common good on a national and on an international level. On a national level, the common good is that set of conditions within a certain nation that are necessary for the citizens of that nation to achieve their individual fulfillment and so in which all of the citizens have an interest.

On an international level, we can speak of the global common good as that set of conditions that are necessary for the citizens of all or of most nations to achieve their individual fulfillment, and so those goods in which all the peoples of the world have an interest. In what follows, I will be speaking primarily about the global common good.

Now it is obvious that identifying the global common good is extremely difficult because cultures differ on their views of what conditions are necessary for humans to flourish. These differences are particularly acute between the cultures of the lesser developed third world nations who have demanded a "new economic order," and the cultures of the wealthier first world nations who have resisted this demand. Nevertheless, we can identify at least some elements of the global common good. Maintaining a congenial global climate, for example is certainly part of the global common good. Maintaining safe transportation routes for the international flow of goods is also part of the global common good. Maintaining clean oceans is another aspect of the global common good, as is the avoidance of a global nuclear war. In spite of the difficulties involved in trying to compile a list of the goods that qualify as part of the global common

good, then, it is nevertheless possible to identify at least some of the items that belong on the list.

II. INTERNATIONAL BUSINESS

Now let me turn to the other term in my title: international business. When speaking of international business, I have in mind a particular kind of organization: the multinational corporation. Multinational corporations have a number of well known features, but let me briefly summarize a few of them. First, multinational corporations are businesses and as such they are organized primarily to increase their profits within a competitive environment. Virtually all of the activities of a multinational corporation can be explained as more or less rational attempts to achieve this dominant end. Secondly, multinational corporations are bureaucratic organizations. The implication of this is that the identity, the fundamental structure, and the dominant objectives of the corporation endure while the many individual human beings who fill the various offices and positions within the corporation come and go. As a consequence, the particular values and aspirations of individual members of the corporation have a relatively minimal and transitory impact on the organization as a whole. Thirdly, and most characteristically, multinational corporations operate in several nations. This has several implications. First, because the multinational is not confined to a single nation, it can easily escape the reach of the laws of any particular nation by simply moving its resources or operations out of one nation and transferring them to another nation. Second, because the multinational is not confined to a single nation, its interests are not aligned with the interests of any single nation. The ability of the multinational to achieve its profit objectives does not depend upon the ability of any particular nation to achieve its own domestic objectives.

In saying that I want to discuss international business and the common good, I am saying that I want to discuss the relationship between the global common good and multinational corporations, that is, organizations that have the features I have just identified.

The general question I want to discuss is straightforward: I want to ask whether it is possible for us to say that multinational corporations with the features I have just described have an obligation to contribute toward the global common good. But I want to discuss only one particular aspect of this general question. I want to discuss this question in light of the realist objection.

III. THE TRADITIONAL REALIST OBJECTION IN HOBBES

The realist objection, of course, is the standard objection to the view that agents—whether corporations, governments, or individuals—have moral obligations on the international level. Generally, the realist holds that it is a mistake to apply moral concepts to international activities: morality has no place in international affairs. The classical statement of this view, which I am calling the "traditional" version of realism, is generally attributed to Thomas Hobbes. I will assume that this customary attribution is correct; my aim is to identify some of the implications of this traditional version of realism even if it is not quite historically accurate to attribute it to Hobbes.

In its Hobbsian form, as traditionally interpreted, the realist objection holds that moral concepts have no meaning in the absence of an agency powerful enough to guarantee that other agents generally adhere to the tenets of morality. Hobbes held, first, that in the absence of a sovereign power capable of forcing men to behave civilly with each other, men are in "the state of nature," a state he characterizes as a "war...of every man, against every man."[9] Secondly, Hobbes claimed, in such a state of war, moral concepts have no meaning:

> To this war of every man against every man, this also is consequent; that nothing can be unjust. The notions of right and wrong, justice and injustice have there no place. Where there is no common power, there is no law: where no law, no injustice.[10]

Moral concepts are meaningless, then, when applied to state of nature situations. And, Hobbes held, the international arena is a state of nature, since there is no international sovereign that can force agents to adhere to the tenets of morality.[11]

The Hobbsian objection to talking about morality in international affairs, then, is based on

two premises: (1) an ethical premise about the applicability of moral terms and (2) an apparently empirical premise about how agents behave under certain conditions. The ethical premise, at least in its Hobbsian form, holds that there is a connection between the meaningfulness of moral terms and the extent to which agents adhere to the tenets of morality: If in a given situation agents do not adhere to the tenets of morality, then in that situation moral terms have no meaning. The apparently empirical premise holds that in the absence of a sovereign, agents will not adhere to the tenets of morality: they will be in a state of war. This appears to be an empirical generalization about the extent to which agents adhere to the tenets of morality in the absence of a third-party enforcer. Taken together, the two premises imply that in situations that lack a sovereign authority, such as one finds in many international exchanges, moral terms have no meaning and so moral obligations are nonexistent.

However, there are a number of reasons for thinking that the two Hobbsian premises are deficient as they stand. I want next, therefore, to examine each of these premises more closely and to determine the extent to which they need revision.

IV. REVISING THE REALIST OBJECTION: THE FIRST PREMISE

The ethical premise concerning the meaning of moral terms, is, in its original Hobbsian form, extremely difficult to defend. If one is in a situation in which others do not adhere to any moral restraints, it simply does not logically follow that in that situation one's actions are no longer subject to moral evaluation. At most what follows is that since such an extreme situation is different from the more normal situations in which we usually act, the moral requirements placed on us in such extreme situations are different from the moral requirements that obtain in more normal circumstances. For example, morality requires that in normal circumstances I am not to attack or kill my fellow citizens. But when one of those citizens is attacking me in a dark alley, morality allows me to defend myself by counterattacking or even killing that citizen. It is a truism that what moral principles require in one set of circumstances is different from what they require in other circumstances. And in extreme circumstances, the requirements of morality may become correspondingly extreme. But there is no reason to think that they vanish altogether.

Nevertheless, the realist can relinquish the Hobbsian premise about the meaning of moral terms, replace it with a weaker and more plausible premise, and still retain much of Hobbes' conclusion. The realist or neo-Hobbsian can claim that although moral concepts can be meaningfully applied to situations in which agents do not adhere to the tenets of morality, nevertheless it is not morally wrong for agents in such situations to also fail to adhere to those tenets of morality, particularly when doing so puts one at a significant competitive disadvantage.

The neo-Hobbsian or realist, then, might want to propose this premise: When one is in a situation in which others do not adhere to certain tenets of morality, and when adhering to those tenets of morality will put one at a significant competitive disadvantage, then it is not immoral for one to likewise fail to adhere to them. The realist might want to argue for this claim, first, by pointing out that in a world in which all are competing to secure significant benefits and avoid significant costs, and in which others do not adhere to the ordinary tenets of morality, one risks significant harm to one's interests if one continues to adhere to those tenets of morality. But no one can be morally required to take on major risks of harm to oneself. Consequently, in a competitive world in which others disregard moral constraints and take any means to advance their self-interests, no one can be morally required to take on major risks of injury by adopting the restraints of ordinary morality.

A second argument the realist might want to advance would go as follows. When one is in a situation in which others do not adhere to the ordinary tenets of morality, one is under heavy competitive pressures to do the same. And, when one is under such pressures, one cannot be blamed—i.e., one is excused—for also failing to adhere to the ordinary tenets of morality. One is excused because heavy pressures take away one's ability to control oneself, and thereby diminish one's moral culpability.

Yet a third argument advanced by the realist might go as follows. When one is in a situation in which others do not adhere to the ordinary tenets of morality it is not fair to require one to continue to adhere to those tenets, especially if doing so puts one at a significant competitive disadvantage. It is not fair because then one is laying a burden on one party that the other parties refuse to carry.

Thus, there are a number of arguments that can be given in defense of the revised Hobbsian ethical premise that when others do not adhere to the tenets of morality, it is not immoral for one to do likewise. The ethical premise of the Hobbsian or realist argument, then, can be restated as follows:

> In situations in which other agents do not adhere to certain tenets of morality, it is not immoral for one to do likewise when one would otherwise be putting oneself at a significant competitive disadvantage.

In what follows, I will refer to this restatement as the ethical premise of the argument. I am not altogether convinced that this premise is correct. But it appears to me to have a great deal of plausibility, and it is, I believe, a premise that underlies the feelings of many that in a competitive international environment where others do not embrace the restraints of morality, one is under no obligation to be moral.

V. REVISING THE REALIST OBJECTION: THE SECOND PREMISE

Let us turn, then, to the other premise in the Hobbsian argument, the assertion that in the absence of a sovereign, agents will be in a state of war. As I mentioned, this is an apparently empirical claim about the extent to which agents will adhere to the tenets of morality in the absence of a third-party enforcer.

Hobbes gives a little bit of empirical evidence for this claim. He cites several examples of situations in which there is no third party to enforce civility and where, as a result, individuals are in a "state of war."[12] Generalizing from these few examples, he reaches the conclusion that in the absence of a third-party enforcer, agents will always be in a "condition of war." But the meager evidence Hobbes provides is surely too thin to support his rather large empirical generalization. Numerous empirical counterexamples can be cited of people living in peace in the absence of a third-party enforcer, so it is difficult to accept Hobbes' claim as an empirical generalization.

Recently, the Hobbsian claim, however, has been defended on the basis of some of the theoretical claims of game theory, particularly of the prisoner's dilemma. Hobbes' state of nature, the defense goes, is an instance of a prisoner's dilemma, and *rational* agents in a Prisoner's Dilemma necessarily would choose not to adhere to a set of moral norms. Rationality is here construed in the sense that is standard in social theory: having a coherent set of preferences among the objects of choice, and selecting the one(s) that has the greatest probability of satisfying more of one's preferences rather than fewer.[13] Or, more simply, always choosing so as to maximize one's interests.

A Prisoner's Dilemma is a situation involving at least two individuals. Each individual is faced with two choices: he can cooperate with the other individual or he can choose not to cooperate. If he cooperates and the other individual also cooperates, then he gets a certain payoff. If, however, he chooses not to cooperate, while the other individual trustingly cooperates, the noncooperator gets a larger payoff while the cooperator suffers a loss. And if both choose not to cooperate, then both get nothing.

It is a commonplace now that in a Prisoner's Dilemma situation, the most rational strategy for a participant is to choose not to cooperate. For the other party will either cooperate or not cooperate. If the other party cooperates, then it is better for one not to cooperate and thereby get the larger payoff. On the other hand, if the other party does not cooperate, then it is also better for one not to cooperate and thereby avoid a loss. In either case, it is better for one to not cooperate.

Now Hobbes' state of nature, the neo-Hobbsian realist can argue, is in fact a prisoner's dilemma situation. In Hobbes' state of nature each individual must choose either to cooperate with others by adhering to the rules of morality (like the rule against theft), or to not cooperate by disregarding the rules of morality and attempting to take advantage of those who are adhering to the rules (e.g., by stealing from them). In such a situation it is more rational (in the sense defined above) to choose not to cooperate. For the other party will either cooperate or not cooperate. If the other party does not cooperate, then one puts oneself at a competitive disadvantage if one adheres to morality while the other party does not. On the other hand, if the other party chooses to cooperate, then one can take advantage of the other party by breaking the rules of morality at his expense. In either case, it is more rational to not cooperate.

Thus, the realist can argue that in a state of nature, where there is no one to enforce compliance with the rules of morality, it is more rational from the individual's point of view to choose not to comply with morality than to choose to comply. Assuming—and this is obviously a critical assumption—that agents behave rationally, then we can conclude that agents in a state of nature will choose not to comply with the tenets of ordinary morality. The second premise of the realist argument, then, can, tentatively, be put as follows:

> In the absence of an international sovereign, all rational agents will choose not to comply with the tenets of ordinary morality, when doing so will put one at a serious competitive disadvantage.

This is a striking, and ultimately revealing, defense of the Hobbsian claim that in the absence of a third-party enforcer, individuals will choose not to adhere to the tenets of morality in their relations with each other. It is striking because it correctly identifies, I think, the underlying reason for the Hobbsian claim. The Hobbsian claim is not an empirical claim about how most humans actually behave when they are put at a competitive disadvantage. It is a claim about whether agents that are *rational* (in the sense defined earlier) will adopt certain behaviors when doing otherwise would put them at a serious competitive disadvantage. For our purposes, this is significant since, as I claimed above, all, most, or at least a significant number of multinationals are rational agents in the required sense: all or most of their activities are rational means for achieving the dominant end of increasing profits. Multinationals, therefore, are precisely the kind of rational agents envisaged by the realist.

But this reading of the realist claim is also significant, I think, because it reveals certain limits inherent in the Hobbsian claim, and requires revising the claim so as to take these limits into account.

As more than one person has pointed out, moral interactions among agents are often quite unlike Prisoner's Dilemmas situations.[14] The most important difference is that a Prisoner's Dilemma is a single meeting between agents who do not meet again, whereas human persons in the real world tend to have repeated dealings with each other. If two people meet each other in a Prisoner's Dilemma situation, and never have anything to do with each other again, then it is rational (in the sense under discussion) from each individual's point of view to choose not to cooperate. However, if individuals meet each other in repeated Prisoner's Dilemma situations, then they are able to punish each other for failures to cooperate, and the cumulative costs of noncooperation can make cooperation the more rational strategy.[15] One can therefore expect that when rational agents know they will have repeated interactions with each other for an indefinite future, they will start to cooperate with each other even in the absence of a third party enforcer. The two cooperating parties in effect are the mutual enforcers of their own cooperative agreements.

The implication is that the realist is wrong in believing that in the absence of a third-party enforcer, rational individuals will always fail to adhere to the tenets of morality, presumably even when doing so would result in serious competitive disadvantage. On the contrary, we can expect that if agents know that they will interact with each other repeatedly in the indefinite future, it is rational for them to behave morally toward each other. In the international arena, then, we can expect that when persons know that they will have repeated interactions with each other, they will tend to adhere to ordinary tenets of morality with each other, assuming that they tend to behave rationally, even when doing so threatens to put them at a competitive disadvantage.

There is a second important way in which the Prisoner's Dilemma is defective as a characterization of real world interactions. Not only do agents repeatedly interact with each other, but, as Robert Frank has recently pointed out, human agents signal to each other the extent to which they can be relied on to behave morally in future interactions.[16] We humans can determine more often than not whether another person can be relied on to be moral by observing the natural visual cues of facial expression and the auditory cues of tone of voice that tend to give us away; by relying on our experience of past dealings with the person; and by rely-

ing on the reports of others who have had past dealings with the person. Moreover, based on these appraisals of each other's reliability, we then choose to interact with those who are reliable and choose not to interact with those who are not reliable. That is, we choose to enter prisoner's dilemmas situations with those who are reliable, and choose to avoid entering such situations with those who are not reliable. As Robert Frank has shown, given such conditions it is, under quite ordinary circumstances, rational to habitually be reliable since reliable persons tend to have mutually beneficial interactions with other reliable persons, while unreliable persons will tend to have mutually destructive interactions with other unreliable persons.

The implication again is that since signaling makes it rational to habitually cooperate in the rules of morality, even in the absence of a third-party enforcer, we can expect that rational humans, who can send and receive fairly reliable signals between each other, will tend to behave morally even, presumably, when doing so raises the prospect of competitive disadvantage.

These considerations should lead the realist to revise the tentative statement of the second premise of his argument that we laid out above. In its revised form, the second premise would have to read as follows:

> In the absence of an international sovereign, all rational agents will choose not to comply with the tenets of ordinary morality, when doing so will put one at a serious competitive disadvantage, provided that interactions are not repeated and that agents are not able to signal their reliability to each other.

This, I believe, is a persuasive and defensible version of the second premise in the Hobbsian argument. It is the one I will exploit in what follows.

VI. REVISED REALISM, MULTINATIONALS, AND THE COMMON GOOD

Now how does this apply to multinationals and the common good? Can we claim that it is clear that multinationals have a moral obligation to pursue the global common good in spite of the objections of the realist?

I do not believe that this claim can be made. We can conclude from the discussion of the realist objection that the Hobbsian claim about the pervasiveness of amorality in the international sphere is false when (1) interactions among international agents are repetitive in such a way that agents can retaliate against those who fail to cooperate, and (2) agents can determine the trustworthiness of other international agents.

But unfortunately, multinational activities often take place in a highly competitive arena in which these two conditions do not obtain. Moreover, these conditions are noticeably absent in the arena of activities that concern the global common good.

First, as I have noted, the common good consists of goods that are indivisible and accessible to all. This means that such goods are susceptible to the free rider problem. Everyone has access to such goods whether or not they do their part in maintaining such goods, so everyone is tempted to free ride on the generosity of others. Now governments can force domestic companies to do their part to maintain the national common good. Indeed, it is one of the functions of government to solve the free rider problem by forcing all to contribute to the domestic common good to which all have access. Moreover, all companies have to interact repeatedly with their host governments, and this leads them to adopt a cooperative stance toward their host government's objective of achieving the domestic common good.

But it is not clear that governments can or will do anything effective to force multinationals to do their part to maintain the global common good. For the governments of individual nations can themselves be free riders, and can join forces with willing multinationals seeking competitive advantages over others. Let me suggest an example. It is clear that a livable global environment is part of the global common good, and it is clear that the manufacture and use of chloroflurocarbons is destroying that good. Some nations have responded by requiring their domestic companies to cease manufacturing or using chloroflurocarbons. But other nations have refused to do the same, since they will share in any benefits that accrue from the restraint others practice, and they can also reap the benefits of continuing to manufacture and use chloroflurocarbons. Less developed nations, in particular, have advanced the position that since their development

depends heavily on exploiting the industrial benefits of chloroflurocarbons, they cannot afford to curtail their use of these substances. Given this situation, it is open to multinationals to shift their operations to those countries that continue to allow the manufacture and use of chloroflurocarbons. For multinationals, too, will reason that they will share in any benefits that accrue from the restraint others practice, and that they can meanwhile reap the profits of continuing to manufacture and use chloroflurocarbons in a world where other companies are forced to use more expensive technologies. Moreover, those nations that practice restraint cannot force all such multinationals to discontinue the manufacture or use of chloroflurocarbons because many multinationals can escape the reach of their laws. An exactly parallel, but perhaps even more compelling, set of considerations can be advanced to show that at least some multinationals will join forces with some developing countries to circumvent any global efforts made to control the global warming trends (the so-called "greenhouse effect") caused by the heavy use of fossil fuels.

The realist will conclude, of course, that in such situations, at least some multinationals will seek to gain competitive advantages by failing to contribute to the global common good (such as the good of a hospitable global environment). For multinationals are rational agents, i.e., agents bureaucratically structured to take rational means toward achieving their dominant end of increasing their profits. And in a competitive environment, contributing to the common good while others do not, will fail to achieve this dominant end. Joining this conclusion to the ethical premise that when others do not adhere to the requirements of morality it is not immoral for one to do likewise, the realist can conclude that multinationals are not morally obligated to contribute to such global common goods (such as environmental goods).

Moreover, global common goods often create interactions that are not iterated. This is particularly the case where the global environment is concerned. As I have already noted, preservation of a favorable global climate is clearly part of the global common good. Now the failure of the global climate will be a one-time affair. The breakdown of the ozone layer, for example, will happen once, with catastrophic consequences for us all; and the heating up of the global climate as a result of the infusion of carbon dioxide will happen once, with catastrophic consequences for us all. Because these environmental disasters are a one-time affair, they represent a non-iterated prisoner's dilemma for multinationals. It is irrational from an individual point of view for a multinational to choose to refrain from polluting the environment in such cases. Either others will refrain, and then one can enjoy the benefits of their refraining; or others will not refrain, and then it will be better to have also not refrained since refraining would have made little difference and would have entailed heavy losses.

Finally, we must also note that although natural persons may signal their reliability to other natural persons, it is not at all obvious that multinationals can do the same. As noted above, multinationals are bureaucratic organizations whose members are continually changing and shifting. The natural persons who make up an organization can signal their reliability to others, but such persons are soon replaced by others, and they in turn are replaced by others. What endures is each organization's single-minded pursuit of increasing its profits in a competitive environment. And an enduring commitment to the pursuit of profit in a competitive environment is not a signal of an enduring commitment to morality.

VII. CONCLUSIONS

The upshot of these considerations is that it is not obvious that we can say that multinationals have an obligation to contribute to the global common good in a competitive environment in the absence of an international authority that can force all agents to contribute to the global common good. Where other rational agents can be expected to shirk the burden of contributing to the common good and where carrying such a burden will put one at a serious competitive disadvantage, the realist argument that it is not immoral for one to also fail to contribute is a powerful argument.

I have not argued, of course, nor do I find it persuasive to claim that competitive pressures automatically relieve agents of their moral obligations, although my arguments here may be wrongly misinterpreted as making that claim. All that I have tried to do is to lay out a justification for the very

narrow claim that *certain very special kinds of agents, under certain very limited and very special conditions, seem to have no obligations with respect to certain very special kinds of goods.*

This is not an argument, however, for complete despair. What the argument points to is the need to establish an effective international authority capable of forcing all agents to contribute their part toward the global common good. Perhaps several of the more powerful autonomous governments of the world, for example, will be prompted to establish such an international agency by relinquishing their autonomy and joining together into a coherently unified group that can exert consistent economic, political, or military pressures on any companies or smaller countries that do not contribute to the global common good. Such an international police group, of course, would transform the present world order, and would be much different from present world organizations such as the United Nations. Once such an international force exists, of course, then both Hobbes and the neorealist would say that moral obligations can legitimately be attributed to all affected international organizations.

Of course, it is remotely possible but highly unlikely that multinationals themselves will be the source of such promptings for a transformed world order. For whereas governments are concerned with the well being of their citizens, multinationals are bureaucratically structured for the rational pursuit of profit in a competitive environment, not the pursuit of citizen well-being. Here and there we occasionally may see one or even several multinationals whose current cadre of leadership is enlightened enough to regularly steer the organization toward the global common good. But given time, that cadre will be replaced and profit objectives will reassert themselves as the enduring end built into the ongoing structure of the multinational corporation.

NOTES

1. See, for example, the articles collected in W. Michael Hoffman, Ann E. Lange, and David A. Fedo, eds., *Ethics and the Multinational Enterprise* (New York: University Press of America, 1986).

2. Thomas Donaldson, *The Ethics of International Business* (New York: Oxford University Press, 1989).

3. Donaldson discusses the question whether *states* have moral obligations to each other in *op. cit.,* pp. 10–29. The critical question, however, is whether *multinationals,* i.e., profit-driven types of international organizations, have moral obligations. Although Donaldson is able to point out without a great deal of trouble that the realist arguments against morality among nations are mistaken (see pp. 20–23, where Donaldson points out that if the realist were correct, then there would be no cooperation among nations; but since there is cooperation, the realist must be wrong), his points leave untouched the arguments I discuss below which acknowledge that while much cooperation among nations is possible, nevertheless certain crucial forms of cooperation will not obtain among multinationals with respect to the global common good.

4. J. Bentham, *Principles of Morals and Legislation,* 1.4–5.

5. William A. Wallace, O.P., *The Elements of Philosophy, A Compendium for Philosophers and Theologians* (New York: Alba House, 1977), p. 166–67.

6. *Ibid,* p. 167.

7. "Common Good," *The New Catholic Encyclopedia.*

8. John Rawls, *A Theory of Justice* (Cambridge, MA: Harvard University Press, 1971), p. 233 and 246.

9. Thomas Hobbes, *Leviathan, Parts I and II,* [1651] (New York: The Bobbs-Merrill Company, Inc., 1958), p. 108.

10. *Ibid.* As noted earlier, I am simply assuming what I take to be the popular interpretation of Hobbes' view on the state of nature. As Professor Philip Kain has pointed out to me, there is some controversy among Hobbes scholars about whether or not Hobbes actually held that moral obligation exists in the state of nature. Among those who hold that moral obligation does not exist in Hobbes' state of nature is M. Oakeshott in "The Moral Life in the Writings of Thomas Hobbes" in his *Hobbes on Civil Association* (Berkeley-

Los Angeles: University of California Press, 1975), pp. 95–113; among those who hold that moral obligation does exist in Hobbes' state of nature is A. E. Taylor in "The Ethical Doctrine of Hobbes" in *Hobbes Studies,* ed. K. C. Brown (Cambridge: Harvard, 1965), pp. 41ff. Kain suggests that Hobbes simply contradicts himself—holding in some passages that moral obligation does exist in the state of nature and holding in others that it does not—because of his need to use the concept of the state of nature to achieve purposes that required incompatible conceptions of the state of nature; see his "Hobbes, Revolution and the Philosophy of History," in *"Hobbes's 'Science of Natural Justice,'"* ed. C. Walton and P.J. Johnson (Boston: Martinus Nijhoff Publishers, 1987), pp. 203–18. In the present essay I am simply assuming without argument the traditional view that Hobbes made the claim that moral obligation does not exist in the state of nature; my aim is to pursue certain implications of this claim even if I am wrong in assuming that is Hobbes'.

11. See *ibid.,* where Hobbes writes that "yet in all times kings and persons of sovereign authority, because of their independency" are in this state of war.

12. *Ibid,* pp. 107–8.

13. See Amartya K. Sen, *Collective Choice and Social Welfare* (San Francisco: Holden-Day, Inc., 1970), pp. 2–5.

14. See, for example, Gregory Kavka, "Hobbes' War of All Against All," *Ethics,* 93 (January, 1983), pp. 291–310; a somewhat different approach is that of David Gauthier, *Morals By Agreement* (Oxford: Clarendon Press, 1986) and Russell Hardin, *Morality Within the Limits of Reason* (Chicago: University of Chicago Press, 1988).

15. See Robert Axelrod, *The Evolution of Cooperation* (New York: Basic Books, Inc., 1984), pp. 27–69.

16. Robert Frank, *Passions Within Reason* (New York: W. W. Norton & Company, 1988).

THE MORAL RESPONSIBILITY OF MULTINATIONAL CORPORATIONS TO BE SOCIALLY RESPONSIBLE
Patricia H. Werhane

There is a truism that multinational corporations should act like good corporate citizens in the host countries and cities in which they operate. The grounds for this truism and the extent of these obligations have been variously spelled out by a

From W. Michael Hoffman et al., eds., *Emerging Global Business Ethics* (Westport, CT: Quorum Books, 1994), 136–142. From the Ninth Annual Conference on Business Ethics, Center for Business Ethics at Bentley College, Waltham, Mass. Reprinted with permission.

number of thinkers. These arguments include the idea that multinational corporations have a moral imperative to be socially responsible, which has sometimes been traced to a notion of a social contract.[1] The claim is that multinationals have at least implicit contracts to act in a morally decent manner in the countries and cities that allow them to do business. In return for the opportunity to exist and do business, corporations, like ordinary citizens, have obligations to contribute to the well-being of the community.

Alternately, one can develop an argument that as guests in a host country, corporations have special duties to their host—not merely to behave appropriately within the customs or mores of the host country, but, as guests, to contribute positively to the social well-being of that society.

One could also appeal to a rights theory or a sense of justice. As members of the universal community of human beings, and organizations created by human beings, multinationals have responsibilities to respect basic rights wherever they operate, including obligations not to cause harm, obligations to respect freedoms, and obligations to act in a fair manner in business dealings with all stakeholders. Such a position appears in at least two guises: (1) that a multinational has positive obligations to the community, or (2) that a multinational has merely negative obligations not to violate more rights nor to create more harm than the status quo.

Finally, one could take up a Friedmanesque argument that the social responsibility of managers of multinationals is to increase the return on investment for their shareholders within the restraints of law and custom. So, while a multinational's responsibility is to operate within the law and customs of the host country, it has no further commitments to social responsibility. Indeed, it would be a violation of fiduciary duties to extend such responsibilities.

All of these elaborations of the moral responsibility of multinationals to be socially responsible, are interesting and important, and they have been developed by a number of theoreticians. This chapter, however, deals with a more specific problem. If we assume that multinationals have some responsibilities to the communities in which they do business, what is the extent and limits of those responsibilities?

To begin, let's briefly discuss and eliminate from consideration the Friedmanesque position. This view has been labeled "Friedmanesque" because it is a caricature of Milton Friedman's much more carefully argued theses; but it is one that is often attributed to him. This position, in the exaggerated manner in which I have stated it, is problematic. If the primary responsibility of business is defined in terms of its fiduciary corporate-shareholder relationship, this conclusion allows corporations to do business under morally reprehensible

conditions if those conditions do not violate law or custom of the host country. So one would have been allowed to practice apartheid in South Africa, to discriminate against women in the workplace in Saudi Arabia, not to hire Palestinian PLO members in Israel, use dangerous pesticides, or market untested drugs in some Third World countries where such products are not illegal. Moreover, such a thesis does not take into account the consideration of customers, employees, or citizens of the host community as stakeholders, except when the well-being of those stakeholders directly affects the interests of the shareholders. So a multinational could pollute, export a country's natural resources, discriminate against some of its citizens, hire away its skilled laborers and professionals to work in the corporate home country, or produce or sell dangerous products, without impunity. This is not to argue that multinationals do this or that these activities are all always morally wrong. But each of these examples raises ethical issues which, if one takes a Friedmanesque position seriously, are not to be counted as important considerations in corporate decision making except as they affect fiduciary interests or violate law or custom.

A less offensive but restrained approach to the question of multinational social responsibilities emanates from a negative rights theory. In brief, if each of us has the right to be left alone and the right not to be interfered with, so too, nations have such rights. No institution, then, has a right to disturb that communal equilibrium or create harm to the citizens of that community. Therefore, as long as a company does not contribute to the further harm of a community (e.g., by adding to pollution, by creating more joblessness, interfering with local politics, not honoring contracts, or disobeying the law), and as long as that company does not contribute to further violations of human rights, a multinational would be fulfilling its social obligation to that host community.

Now there is nothing wrong with this point of view. But we tend to ask more of multinationals than that they merely mind their own business and do not create further harms. The question then becomes, what is the "more" we demand?

Let us look at the question of social responsibility from a more positive perspective. Let us consider the argument that corporations, like good citizens, have positive social responsibilities to the long-term viability and well-being of the community in which they operate, as well as ordinary moral obligations to other stakeholders (e.g., employees, customers, suppliers, and shareholders). It will turn out that while one is often worried that a Friedmanesque or a negative rights approach does not demand enough of multinational business, one must be equally cautious in spelling out the nature and extent of positive social responsibilities. For if one demands too much of business, and if a corporation accedes to our demands, a corporation could become overly paternalistic or politically embroiled in community affairs, an involvement that is neither desirable for the corporation nor the host community. In the case of multinationals, it shall be argued, its responsibility as a "guest" in another community is more restricted than that of a corporate citizen in its home country.

To attempt to answer the question, "What is the extent of moral responsibility of a multinational corporation to be socially responsible?," let us look at a concrete example—the famous Sullivan Principles and their adoption by American multinationals operating in South Africa. The original principles made six demands: (1) integrate workplace, washrooms, and eating facilities; (2) provide equal and fair employment practices for all employees; (3) provide equal pay for equal or comparable work; (4) expand training programs for non-whites; (5) increase non-whites in supervisory and managerial positions; and (6) improve housing and education opportunities for employees outside the workplace. These principles sound like motherhood and apple pie. But the sixth principle demands that companies be proactive in improving the quality of life outside the workplace. Generalized, this is the requirement that corporations contribute to the viability and long-term well-being of the community in which they operate.

The sixth Sullivan Principle appears to be a fairly straightforward, although sometimes costly, demand, but it could be quite complex indeed. For if a corporation, particularly a multinational, becomes involved in the social and educational affairs of a host community, a number of difficulties might crop up. For instance, while housing and education may be crucial for employee advancement (particularly in South Africa where, until recently there were restrictions on where non-whites could live and go to school), one must take care that the

extension of corporate obligations does not lead to the paternalism of nineteenth-century America where some companies, such as Pullman, provided housing, education, and a whole way of life for its employees, leading to a form of paternalism that affected the freedoms of these employees. In the past, this paternalism has been replicated by some multinationals such as the East India Company. So one would want to restrict the extent of multinational corporate social responsibility such that paternalistic outcomes would not reoccur.

Second, a corporation could find itself politically involved. In the 1978–1979 amplification of these principles, Reverend Sullivan asked corporations to "support the elimination of all…laws" that were discriminatory or prevented the free movement of non-whites. This was a demand that corporations not merely break South African law within the confines of their workplaces, but to become involved in revolutionary proactive schemes to change those laws. The requirement not only asked more of corporations than they are capable of executing, but it also threatened the value of national political sovereignty. This is not in any way an argument in favor of apartheid or a proposal that a corporation should accommodate that abhorrent phenomenon. Nor is it an argument that national sovereignty is an absolute value. But, as Michael Walzer has reminded us, interfering with that sovereignty should be undertaken only as a last resort, because it might be interpreted as suggesting that intervention should be the first instead of the last resort.[2] If nations are morally required to respect the sovereignty of each other, one should always question whether it is the role of corporations to conduct such interferences. It gives to a multinational, at least partially and temporarily, the status of nationhood, a status which is, at best, questionable.

Obviously, most corporations are not experts at political interference. This is neither their aim nor expertise and not their responsibility. Such demands not only ask too much of business—if corporations begin to engage in local politics of a host community they are overstepping their bounds as multinational visitors. If successful, a multinational company might succeed in interfering with the political balance of that community. One need only to be reminded of ITT's interactions with the Chilean government in the 1970s to worry about this possibility.

But, one might protest, if there are obvious social ills or political evils in a country in which one is doing business, if these violate rights of citizens of that country, and if a multinational has the power and resources to make improvements in these malaises, is it not its responsibility to do so? I would argue that even if totalitarianism, apartheid, human rights violations, lack of democratic procedures, etc. are evils, one surely questions the interference of one nation with another except on very stringent moral grounds. There is a presumption for national political sovereignty unless circumstances are most abhorrent. Nations are independent states. Because states are made up of individuals who have autonomous moral standing, they too have such standing. They are collectives made up of individuals whose autonomy is defined both by international law and by moral principle. Except in the most inhumane circumstances, a nation's right to self-determination ordinarily overrides most arguments for intervention.[3] If a nation seldom has justifiable moral grounds for intervening with the autonomy of another nation, a multinational corporation's positive moral responsibilities to become engaged in politics is an even more questionable conclusion. The fact that some multinationals have enormous capital resources, sometimes greater than the community in which they are conducting business, should give further strength to the arguments defending the presumption of sovereignty. The revised Sullivan Principles, then, ask too much of business, and its demands are antithetical both to the role of business and to political sovereignty.

Third, while one can make a viable argument that corporations have social responsibilities to their home communities, one must take care in transferring those same sorts of obligations to multinational settings. One is tempted to use a model such as the Lilly Corporation which has been very proactive in improving job opportunities and education in the Indiana community in which it is headquartered. Its aim has been to create a stable community, which is to its and the community's benefit.[4] But Lilly is a citizen of that community. There is a fine line, not merely between honoring one's obligations to a community and paternalism, but also between operating and interfering in a community where one is a guest rather than a citizen. To illustrate, the Minneapolis-based H. B. Fuller company

opened a glue manufacturing plant in Honduras, offering industrialization and a number of new jobs to that poor country. Unfortunately, the glue they manufactured became the "drug of choice" for street children who sniffed it and became addicted.[5] What is Fuller's social responsibility in this case? If Fuller stops manufacturing glue in Honduras, there is a loss of over a thousand jobs in a country with little industry and high unemployment. But if it engages in drug education and social reform in that country, it may overstep the bounds of being a "good guest," because these activities can entail interferences with the autonomy and politics of Honduras.

What, then, is the extent of the moral responsibility of multinationals to be socially responsible in a host community? How can we hold multinationals responsible for what they do without extending that requirement to duties that involve them in political and social activities in which they have no skills and which extend their power beyond that of corporate guest status in a host country? First, and most obviously, as a guest, a multinational has a social responsibility to obey the laws and respect the customs of the host country, except where exceptions are allowed and encouraged. The American corporations who practiced the Sullivan Principles within their company in South Africa are evidence of such an exception, because the South African government condoned the practice. Even so, a number of American companies did not have South African offices rather than either obey or disobey South African apartheid laws. Second, it is not the duty nor the privilege of multinationals to engage in political activities in another country or community where they are not citizens. The revised Sullivan Principles asked too much of corporations.

Third, if a corporation cannot uphold its own policies and code of ethics while operating in a foreign context, it should not engage in activities there. For example, if a corporation has an explicit affirmative action policy, it should think carefully before operating in Saudi Arabia.

Fourth, if what a company is engaged in, produces, or affects causes more harms to the citizens of a host country than the present status quo in that country, the multinational has a responsibility either to stop that activity or redress these harms. So H. B. Fuller, for example, must engage in some set of proactive activities that either prevents further uses of its glue as a drug or withdraw from Honduras. However, when those proactive activities involve interference with social or political life of a host country, one should only engage in such activities with utmost restraint.

How can one test whether a particular set of activities is required, desirable, or questionable as part of multinational social responsibility? One might ask the following types of questions:

1. Is this set of activities necessary? "Necessity" is often defined as: what is needed in order to do business in that community. But, in order to justify engaging in allegedly socially responsible activities in a host country a multinational must consider two other provisos: is the activity necessary to redress harms created by the company and/or necessary because of the laws and expectations of that community.[6] With these provisos one should ask:

2. Can this activity be carried out without interfering with the political sovereignty or social fabric of the host country?

3. If this activity requires social change, can it be carried out without violence to the acceptable practices of that society? Or, more simply put, would such a set of activities be acceptable to dispassionate rational persons in that society, even when performed by "foreigners"?

4. Does this set of activities pass a "publicity" test? That is, can these activities be made public in the community in which they are to occur? Can they be made public internationally?

5. Does this set of activities coincide with, or not contradict, common sense moral principles by which the corporation operates in its home country?

6. Can such activities be conducted in cooperation with the host country or are there conflicts?

The sixth question is very important, because often one can engage in socially responsible activities (or avoid morally questionable ones) by making agreements with the host country. In the case of H. B. Fuller, Fuller now works with the Honduras government in drug education; it assists but does not take the lead in such activities. It also packages the glue in larger, more expensive, containers not readily affordable by children.

In conclusion, one must be unduly cautious in ascribing social responsibilities to multinationals, particularly when they are guests in another community. Proactivism should be restrained. When there appear to be social ills that need redress, social ills caused by, or within the purview of, the multinational in question, social activism should be tempered by quiet cooperation with host country agencies. Problems of paternalism, political and social interference, threats to national sovereignty, and lack of expertise are such that the moral responsibility of a multinational corporation may be simply not to interfere or even not to do business in a particular milieu. This conclusion may seem too harsh both to those corporations wishing to expand economically and to those companies that take proactive social responsibility as part of doing business, but it is required of morally responsible corporations in transnational business environments.

NOTES

1. See, for example, Thomas Donaldson, *Corporations and Morality* (Englewood Cliffs, N.J.: Prentice-Hall, 1982). Donaldson uses the social contract argument to support the claim that corporations have moral responsibilities. He does not focus so much on the social obligations of such institutions.

2. See Michael Walzer, *Just and Unjust Wars* (New York: Basic Books, 1977), especially Chapters 4 and 6 for an expansion of this argument.

3. *Id.*

4. See "Eli Lilly Corporation," in Robert D. Hay, Edmund R. Gray, and Paul H. Smith, eds., *Business and Society* (Cincinnati: South-Western Publishing, 1976) 17–24.

5. See Norman Bowie and Stephanie Lenway, "H.B. Fuller in Honduras," in Thomas Donaldson and Patricia Werhane, eds., *Ethical Issues in Business,* 4th Ed. (Englewood Cliffs, N.J.: Simon and Schuster, 1993) forthcoming.

6. See Thomas Donaldson, *The Ethics of International Business* (New York: Oxford Univ. Press, 1989), especially Chapter Six.

Decision Scenario 1
BRAZIL: ECONOMIC DEVELOPMENT VERSUS ENVIRONMENTAL PROTECTION

Beginning in the early 1960s, Brazil's military government embarked upon a program of tremendous economic development. At least in theory, the goal of this program was to improve the quality of life for the citizens of this poor agrarian country. Almost thirty years later Brazil is one of the world's leading debtor nations; its citizens suffer from one of the world's lowest standards of living; it is the scene of some of the world's worst environmental destruction. These facts are closely connected.

The story of Brazil's "development" is a familiar one: A Third World country begins an aggressive plan to build factories, dams, highways, hydroelectric projects, and other necessities of a modern industrialized society. International banks and foreign lending institutions are anxious to finance these projects with large loans. But the environmental and cultural impact of these development projects is devastating.

In Brazil, millions of acres of tropical rain forests were destroyed, often by massive burnings during the dry seasons, but also by the harvesting of trees for lumber and fuel. Millions of people were forcibly relocated by these projects; millions more emigrated to the frontier in search of work, land, and wealth. Native tribes, some of whom had never before been in contact with the outside world, found their lands taken from them.

In the early 1970s drought and crop failures combined with a worldwide economic recession, bringing Brazil to the brink of economic collapse. To prevent this from happening, Brazil needed to raise large amounts of foreign money simply to pay the interest on the development loans from a decade earlier. A new, aggressive economic development program was launched, not to provide food and jobs for Brazilians but to raise cash. This difference is important, for an emphasis on internal economic development was supplanted by an emphasis on growing cash crops and producing goods for export.

This time development of the rain forests was explicitly targeted, and the environmental costs were willingly paid. At a 1972 United Nations conference on the environment, Brazil asserted its right to pay whatever environmental costs were necessary to achieve a level of economic development that is taken for granted in the industrialized world. Brazil accused the industrialized nations of hypocrisy in demanding that less developed countries refrain from the same kind of environmental exploitation that had fostered their own economic development.

Destruction of a tropical rain forest has frightening environmental effects. These forests are home to a large percentage of all biological species. Some scientists have estimated that 1.2 million species of plants and animals, nearly 25 percent of all species existing in the mid-1980s, will vanish by the end of the century as rain forests are decimated. The fertility of forest soil is surprisingly delicate. As trees are burned, their ashes provide nutrients for farming but only for a few years. When the soil's few nutrients are exhausted, farmers move on to burn new forest areas, leaving behind infertile land. Water pollution and many diseases like malaria and dysentery follow to plague areas where forests have been burned. Finally, rain forests serve a crucial role in the ecological cycle of carbon.

Scientists have come to recognize that large amounts of carbon dioxide in the atmosphere can produce a "greenhouse effect," with changes in climate associated with a global warming trend. In their normal growth cycle, plants absorb carbon dioxide from the atmosphere, releasing some of it slowly as they naturally die and decompose. Mass burnings of forests not only prevent these plants from removing carbon dioxide but significantly add to the amount present in the atmosphere because of the fast release. Deforestation is believed to account for almost half the carbon dioxide released into the atmosphere, and Brazil itself is responsible for 20 percent of that.

In recent years Brazil's civilian government has taken steps to control the destruction of these rain forests. The World Bank and other creditors have promised to work with the Brazilians to ensure that economic development does not entail environmental destruction. Nevertheless, Brazil continues to face major problems in paying its debts, going so far as to suspend interest payments in 1987. As this is written, it is difficult to see how Brazil can attain both environmental and economic health.

- International financial institutions like the World Bank have dual functions: the *banking* function of making loans and investments, and the *development* function of using these loans to further economic development. To what degree have these functions been compatible in Brazil?

- What responsibilities does the United States government have in this case?

- How would you respond to a Brazilian who claimed that environmental concerns are a luxury that only the economically developed countries can enjoy?

Decision Scenario 2
THE DALKON SHIELD AND SALES TO FOREIGN COUNTRIES

The A. H. Robins Company manufactured and sold the Dalkon Shield, an intrauterine birth control device (IUD). During the early 1970s, numerous complaints against the IUD were filed. Plaintiffs claimed that the Dalkon Shield caused infections and infertility, making hysterectomies necessary. In some cases the IUD perforated the uterus and entered the body, and in one case it attached itself to a woman's stomach, part of which required surgical removal.

Robins was slow to respond to these charges, and company physicians downplayed the complaints. In 1974 Robins stopped marketing the Dalkon Shield in the United States. The firm fought the product liability suits, often delving into the personal and sexual lives of the women who were injured. By the mid-1980s, however, Robins began losing major awards in court. They soon filed for bankruptcy protection as more and more suits neared settlement. Under court guidance, a

trust fund of some $2.5 billion was established for all present and future liability claims.

An estimated 100,000 users of the Dalkon Shield live outside the United States. Since Robins always maintained that the IUD was safe and effective when inserted and used properly, these foreign consumers were never advised to stop using the device.

- When marketing a product in a foreign country, should an American firm hold itself to the same standards as those established for domestic sales?

- What role should the U.S. government play in this case? Does the type of government (democracy, military dictatorship, for example) of the country importing the product matter?

- Do the additional facts presented here change your view of the case as presented in the decision scenario in Chapter Ten?

Decision Scenario 3
UNION CARBIDE'S POISON GAS DISASTER AT BHOPAL

On December 3, 1984, a pesticide plant owned by a national subsidiary of the Union Carbide Corporation in Bhopal, India, released a cloud of poisonous methyl isocyanate gas into the environment. People living in a densely populated slum across the street from the pesticide plant were exposed to the deadly

This case was prepared from material found in the following sources: *Barron's Financial Weekly*, February 20, 1989; *The Economist*, May 14 and July 23, 1988; *The Nation*, March 6, 1989; *Bhopal* by Paul Shrivastava (Ballinger, 1987).

gas cloud. Estimates are that three thousand persons were killed and that hundreds of thousands suffered nonlethal casualties in the largest industrial accident in history. Symptoms of the poisoning range from nausea to severe and permanent respiratory damage. By some estimates, victims of the disaster continue to die as a consequence of their exposure.

Union Carbide claimed that the release of gas was the result of sabotage by a disgruntled employee. The parent company also argued that any liability for the accident should fall upon its Indian subsidiary only. The total value of that subsidiary was estimated at $30 million. The Indian government, on the other hand, claimed that the accident was the fault of the corporation and that even if it was a case of sabotage, the sabotage was a forseeable occurrence and therefore was within the responsibility of the company to prevent. Moreover, the Indian government wanted to hold the parent company liable. (Interestingly, the subsidiary, Union Carbide of India, Ltd., was 51 percent owned by the parent company and 26 percent owned by official Indian government institutions.) An early ruling by an Indian district court ordered Carbide to pay interim compensation of $270 million before the trial began.

In other legal maneuvers before the main trial was to begin, the U.S. Supreme Court ruled that the trial should be held in the Indian jurisdiction. However, any judgment against the American parent company by the Indian Court would have to be enforced by U.S. courts.

In an out-of-court settlement with the Indian government that was approved by the Supreme Court of India, Union Carbide agreed to provide $470 million in compensation to be distributed to the victims by the Indian courts. Some observers are skeptical about the likelihood of the money's

reaching victims, because no distribution mechanism has been established and rampant government corruption is suspected.

The settlement is well below the initial $3.3 billion figure sought by the Indian government and close to the $450 million in insurance available to the company. As a result of the settlement, a loss of $.50 a share in 1988 profits was imposed, dropping the return per share to $1.09. After the settlement was announced, Union Carbide stock increased $2.00 a share in price. Share price had been in the high $20s before the accident and fell to a low of $18 after the accident. Estimates are that current share value in a takeover bid could reach $50.

■ If the Bhopal accident was truly the result of sabotage, should Union Carbide have any liability for damages caused by the release of the poison gas?

■ Was the Indian district judge's decision to order payment of interim compensation fair?

■ Assuming that Union Carbide was responsible for the accident, was the compensation fund reasonable in relation to the loss suffered by shareholders?

■ Would the fact that corruption was likely in the distribution of the damages be sufficient reason for Carbide to attempt to escape liability?

Decision Scenario 4

THE *KHIAN SEA:* INTERNATIONAL MARKET FOR TRASH

Like many large U.S. cities, Philadelphia is faced with a major trash problem: It simply is producing more garbage than it can dispose. In the past, most city trash went to landfills within Pennsylvania and in neighboring states, but these landfills are reaching capacity. The costs of shipping the trash to distant states is higher than citizens and public officials seem willing to pay.

A partial solution is to burn city trash in massive incinerators. Of course, incineration does not eliminate the disposal problem; it only reduces trash to ash, which still requires disposal. Philadelphia's two currently operating incinerators produce over fourteen hundred tons of ash per week. The city arranged for disposal of this trash through a private

contractor at a cost of $6 million per year. Although the ash was officially listed as "nontoxic, nonhazardous, and nonflammable," later analysis showed that the ash contained dioxins, arsenic, mercury, and other potentially dangerous substances.

In September 1986 some fourteen thousand tons of Philadelphia's incinerator ash was loaded aboard the ship *Khian Sea.* Initial plans were to dump the ash at an artificial island in the Bahamas. When the government of the Bahamas refused to accept the load of potentially hazardous ash, the *Khian Sea* began an odyssey that was to last years. From the Bahamas, the *Khian Sea* sailed to the Dominican Republic, where the ash was scheduled to be used as fill for a limestone quarry. When health concerns were again raised, the ship journeyed to Honduras, Chile, Costa Rica, Puerto Rico, St. Eustatius, the Dutch Antilles, and, in January 1988, to Haiti. Along the way, the ash was officially listed on ship's documents as "general cargo," "bulk construction material," and finally "soil fertilizer." When health concerns were raised about using the ash as fertilizer, the *Khian Sea* departed Haiti, leaving behind four tons that had already been off-loaded.

Since the contract with Philadelphia required proof of safe disposal before payment was made, the *Khian Sea* headed home to Philadelphia amid growing protests about the safety of its cargo and about the city's willingness to dump its trash in foreign countries.

For many countries with large foreign debts (often owed to the United States), the need for hard currency is judged more pressing than environmental concerns. A clean environment is seen as a luxury only the rich can afford; it can easily be a burden for countries seeking economic development. Thus allowing their lands to be used as a dumpsite can make economic sense to leaders of debt-ridden countries. Already Mexico, Morocco, South Africa, Taiwan, East Germany, Venezuela, and Spain have accepted large amounts of trash.

Upon returning to Philadelphia, the *Khian Sea* faced continuing controversy. The dumpsite along its dock was filled to capacity with ash, and the ship could not be unloaded. In the spring of 1988 the *Khian Sea* left Philadelphia illegally (the Coast Guard had judged the ship as unsafe because of mechanical troubles). It journeyed next to Senegal and then to Yugoslavia for repairs. The ship left Yugoslavia with a new name and passed through the Suez Canal. It arrived in Singapore late in November 1988 under yet another new name. The environmental group Greenpeace claimed that the ship still contained the ash as it left Suez but arrived in Singapore without the ash. Operators of the ship refused to disclose where the ash was dumped. Some speculate that it was dumped in the Indian Ocean.

- What responsibilities do U.S. cities have toward less developed countries who accept their trash? What responsibilities do private trash disposal firms have in all of this?

- If a foreign country accepts U.S. trash, should the U.S. disposer guarantee that the trash meets the same toxicity levels as those required for dumping trash within U.S. landfills? Does the type of government (such as democracy or military dictatorship) accepting the trash matter?

- What public policies concerning the dumping of trash in foreign countries would you recommend?

Decision Scenario 5
"WHEN IN ROME": INTERNATIONAL AFFIRMATIVE ACTION

In recent decades a number of questions have been raised concerning the conduct of U.S. business in foreign countries. American business executives have often been faced with a dilemma. When local customs and ethics conflict with one's own values, should an individual adapt to the local customs or insist on the enforcement of American values in a foreign land? The most publicized examples of this dilemma involve the payment of "gratuities" to foreign officials. In some countries, these payments are standard business practice and are considered to be little more than a thank-you. Americans would call such payments bribes or extortion and judge them to be seriously unethical.

Similar problems arise when foreign firms invest in the United States. To some foreign business executives, American ethics and social practices seem unfair or unreasonable. The hiring practices of some Japanese automobile firms operating in the United States are a case in point. There is some evidence to suggest that some Japanese auto manufacturers systematically exclude African Americans and other minorities when hiring.

Two issues are involved in this case; they must be kept distinct. First, discrimination on the basis of race is illegal within the United States. No one would suggest that the Japanese firms be allowed to violate the law. In a 1988 case, the Equal Employment Opportunity Commission announced that Honda of America had agreed to pay 370 African Americans and women some $6 million in back pay to resolve a discrimination complaint. There seems a clear ethical consensus: Violators of the law deserve punishment. Nevertheless, a number of more subtle issues remain. Before deciding on a plant location, some Japanese executives have been known to study the ethnic, religious, and racial makeup of the local community. Evidence shows that many Japanese firms choose to locate in rural, nonunion areas with a relatively small African American population.

A second issue concerns various customs and business practices that go beyond what is legally required. The United States auto industry has always employed a large number of African Americans. At one point 17 percent of all auto workers were African American, compared to an 11 percent African American population in the overall U.S. labor force. Typically unionized, these jobs provided many African Americans with decent pay and security at a time when they generally were suffering from widespread economic discrimination. The U.S. auto industry and its unions have always considered this factor one of their social responsibilities.

As U.S. auto manufacturers have lost their former market dominance, and as the Great Lakes region has suffered deindustrialization, many unionized African Americans living in the Midwest have been hard hit economically. The "Big Three"

U.S. automakers and the United Auto Workers have made an effort to offset these problems by seeking to employ many of these displaced workers at new plants and other locations. Japanese automakers seem to have no inclination to follow a similar pattern of recruiting displaced former auto workers.

One final point that deserves mention. Many local and state governments have developed plans for tax abatements and other economic incentives to attract Japanese investment in their community. In effect, these local communities compete in a bidding war to subsidize plant location.

- In deciding claims of racial discrimination, the Equal Employment Opportunity Commission will typically compare the racial composition of the local community with that of the work force. How might this fact influence a decision to locate a plant in an area with little or no African American population?

- Should a foreign firm conform to the social practices of U.S. firms when doing business in the United States? Should such practices be considered the price of doing business here? Would the competitive advantage gained by ignoring these practices be fair?

- What responsibilities do local communities have when developing an economic incentive package to attract foreign investment? If a city with a large African American population is at a competitive disadvantage when seeking foreign investment, are federal responsibilities created? What might they be?

Decision Scenario 6

CHILD AND BONDED LABOR: BUSINESS RESPONSIBILITY FOR SUPPLIER PRACTICES

The global economy has changed the relationship between manufacturers and workers. In the past, it

This case was prepared from the following sources: Farhan Bokhari, "Death Spotlights Plight of Child Laborers," *The Christian Science Monitor,* May 1, 1995; *New York Times,* April 19, 1995; "Eye to Eye with Connie Chung," April 6, 1995; "ABC World News Tonight," September 21, 1994; *United States Department of State 1993 Human Rights Report: Pakistani Human Rights Practices;* "The MacNeil-Lehrer Newshour," August 17, 1995.

was more likely that a manufacturer and its workers resided within the same national borders. Now, it is common for component parts to be made elsewhere and assembled in the manufacturer's plant. It is also common for entire products to be made elsewhere and to simply carry the manufacturer's label. These developments raise serious issues about workplace standards and about a manufacturer's responsibility for the practices of its suppliers. An actual story illustrates the difficulty.

Twelve-year-old Iqbal Masih gained international renown when he led a Pakistani children's movement to abolish the practice of bonded labor. For his campaign, Reebok gave him a $15,000 Youth in Action award. The bonded labor practice he campaigned against is a system where workers typically receive less than subsistence wages. To survive, workers take salary advances from their employers. This starts a cycle where workers work only to pay off those advances and where they find their debt escalating. It is, in essence, a form of slavery where people are forced to work without receiving wages.

When Iqbal was four, his family sold him into bonded labor in order to get money and food. He worked in a carpet factory where he was physically shackled to a loom. He earned one rupee (the equivalent of 3¢) while working fifteen hours a day. When he escaped from his employer, he owed 13,000 rupees in future work.

In Pakistan, it is estimated that 25 percent of the children between five and fifteen work in similar conditions in carpet weaving factories, brick kilns, and soccer ball workshops. Up to one third of the total labor force is composed of child labor. Pakistani law prohibits bonded labor, and it limits the workday for children to six hours of work. However, those laws are not frequently enforced.

Although some businesses that receive goods produced by child labor claim that it is an age-old practice of family work, the facts tell a different story. In villages, where crushing poverty is common and education unavailable, families often sell their children to factory owners to obtain money for the remaining family. Children, in reality, are not working in family businesses; they are serving as slave labor for owners of village workshops. The products of these village shops are then passed on to larger factories that have supply contracts with international firms.

In fact, some of the factories identified as receiving goods from workshops using children were supplying soccer balls to multinational sports equipment giants Adidas and, yes, even Reebok. Spokespersons expressed surprise that suppliers handled goods made with child labor. The reality of the countryside, though, is that there is great difficulty in preventing remote village workshops from using children. CBS's newsmagazine "Eye to Eye" even discovered one workshop that was supplying instruments for UNICEF, "the UN agency committed to abolishing child labor," as the network described.

Lest anyone think that such labor abuses are present only in the developing world, we should note that in August 1995 the United States Department of Labor raided a California garment-sewing sweatshop that used illegal Thai workers. Some of the workers were imported into the country under the guise of tourists; their airfare was paid for by their employers. The workers were paid less than $1.60 per hour, were detained in a guarded compound behind barbed wire, and were required to buy provisions from a "company store." The sweatshop owners deceived the retailers and manufacturers with whom they had contracts by also operating a legitimate garment-sewing plant through which they passed the goods made at the sweatshop. Montgomery Ward, Sears, Neiman Marcus, and the Gap were among the retailers and manufacturers whose labels were discovered at the sweatshop. Labor Department officials believe that this operation is not an isolated case.

- What responsibilities do multinational firms have for the practices employed by their suppliers? How far down the chain of supply do those responsibilities extend?

- What specific actions could Reebok or Unicef have taken to prevent, or at least make less likely, the use of child labor in their products?

- How would you define a fair wage in a country that suffers levels of poverty unimaginable to most Americans? What factors would you use to determine a wage's fairness: market forces of supply and demand; profit margins of factory owners and/or multinationals; income needed for subsistence?

- What responsibility do consumers have for perpetuating the use of such practices as child labor, bonded labor, and prison labor (as in China)?

Decision Scenario 7
DRUG SAFETY AND THE THIRD WORLD

The vast populations in the developing world represent a significant market for pharmaceutical manufacturers. Some critics have charged that the potential profits to be reaped there have led multinational drug firms to disregard the safety of Third World citizens. Two drugs have been the focus of particular complaints over the years.

Dipyrone is an analgesic (pain reliever) and antipyretic (fever reducer) that was sold widely throughout the world from the 1950s to the 1980s. By the late 1970s, however, it was disappearing from the market in industrialized nations. Medical authorities in many nations suspected that the drug caused agranulocytosis, a serious blood disorder marked by a sharp decrease in white blood cells and, therefore, in the body's ability to fight infection. Patients developing the disease have a high probability of death unless they receive prompt and modern medical treatment.

Medical authorities in the United States, Great Britain, and the European continent also found that dipyrone presented an unacceptable risk given that alternative treatments were available—namely aspirin, acetaminophen, and ibuprofen. Though the incidence of agranulocytosis in persons taking dipyrone was not firmly established, many still felt that the small but uncertain risk was too great. That judgment was made despite recognition that all the other products had risks as well. Aspirin can cause a serious disease, Reyes syndrome, if it is given to children. It and ibuprofen can cause stomach problems if taken in excess. Excess dosage of acetaminophen can cause liver damage. Nonetheless, dipyrone was judged to have an unacceptable risk/benefit profile. By the late 1970s in the United States, it was used only for terminal cancer patients.

In the Third World, however, multinationals continued through the 1980s to distribute the drug as a common remedy for pain and fever. In many cases, there were no warnings provided to the physicians, pharmacists, or patients on the label, package insert, or privately published physicians' reference books. Hoechst, a main supplier of the drug, claimed that given the risks and side effects of the other analgesics, it was as safe as aspirin.

In response to consumer pressures in the mid-1980s, many multinationals began to include warnings on the product label and package inserts, though the drug is still promoted widely. The private publishers of the physicians' references resisted changes but are now bowing to manufacturer demands for editorial approval of drug descriptions.

A second drug, depo-provera, also caused controversy for its use in the developing world. It is an injectable hormone that provides effective birth control for up to thirteen weeks. For years, the United States' FDA refused approval of the drug because there were concerns that it caused cancer in laboratory animals. Critics of its distribution in the Third World charged that drug firms were exposing women to unacceptable cancer risks. However, some physicians in the Third World argued that in their environment, death in childbirth was a greater risk than cancer and that depo-provera provided more effective birth control than condoms or the pill, which were often improperly used. The FDA recently approved the drug for use in the United States.

- A judgment of safety is a judgment that a level of risk is acceptable. Is it possible that the same drug is safe in one country but not in another? What differences could lead to that conclusion?

- Should drugs contain the same listing of indications and contraindications, the same warnings of side effects no matter where they are marketed?

- Dipyrone continues to be marketed in the Third World as a remedy for minor pain. Should drug companies cease that marketing? Does the list of available alternatives and their respective risks mean that dipyrone is an unnecessary and unacceptably harmful drug?

This case was prepared from the following sources: *For Export Only: Pharmaceuticals,* A Richter Productions Video, 1981; Milton Silverman et al., *Bad Medicine: The Prescription Drug Industry in the Third World* (Palo Alto, Calif.: Stanford University Press, 1992); John Quelch and Craig Smith, "Pharmaceutical Marketing Practices in the Third World," *Journal of Business Research,* vol. 23, 1991.

Index